The Gospel of Accordi W9-CRC-546

The Gospel of According to St. John

THE SUNDAY SERMONS OF THE GREAT FATHERS

VOLUME FOUR

Dr Toal's work contains what is in effect the spiritual inheritance of every Christian. The four volumes correspond with the main divisions of the Church's year and offer, in English and in relation to the gospel for each Sunday and greater festival or feast, an appropriate choice of sermons, given in person in the early centuries by the Great Fathers and Doctors of the Church to their faithful congregations—men and women who clearly faced many of the same problems as we do today.

The Fathers handed on and enriched a tradition which derives from the foundation of the Church. Their thoughts and teaching on the liturgical gospels cannot fail to add clarity and depth to any reader's understanding of these key passages from holy scripture; and this treasury of their commentaries will above all be of constant help to those whose work it is to preach and expound the gospel.

This fourth volume covers the period from the Eleventh Sunday after Pentecost to the Twenty-fourth and Last Sunday after Pentecost. The two formats (large and small) in which it is issued are identical with the previous volumes which cover Advent to Quinquagesima; Lent to the Sunday after the Ascension; and Pentecost to the Tenth Sunday after Pentecost.

Volume One: From the First Sunday of Advent to Quinquagesima

Volume Two: From the First Sunday in Lent to the Sunday after the Ascension

Volume Three: From Pentecost to the Tenth Sunday after Pentecost

Volume Four: From the Eleventh Sunday after Pentecost to the Twenty-fourth and Last Sunday after Pentecost

Theologis semper redeundum esse ad divinae revelationis fontes, . . . qui in Sacris Litteris et in Divina Traditione inveniantur.

"Those whose task it is to teach the word of God must ever have recourse to the sources of divine revelation; which are found in Sacred Scripture and in Divine Tradition."

Pope Pius XII, Encyclical, *Humani Generis*
12 August 1950

Nova sane rubricarum dispositione Brevarii, Officium Divinum paulisper contrahitur; intuitu praesertim multorum sacerdotum, qui in dies magis magisque pastoralibus sollicitudinibus onerantur.
Cum porro lectio quoque sanctorum Patrum aliquantisper quandoque minuatur, omnes enixe clericos hortamur, ut volumina Patrum, tanta sapientia ac pietate referta, assidue prae manibus legenda ac meditanda teneant.

"As a consequence of this new ordering of the rubrics of the Breviary, the Divine Office has now been slightly shortened; principally out of consideration for the many priests who more and more each day are burthened with pastoral cares.
"And since furthermore the Lessons taken from the holy Fathers are also, at times, somewhat shortened, We earnestly exhort all clerics to have by them the volumes of the Fathers, filled as they are with such wisdom and piety, for regular reading and meditation."

Pope John XXIII, Motu Proprio, *Rubricarum Instructum*
25 July 1960

THE
SUNDAY SERMONS
OF THE GREAT
FATHERS

A Manual of Preaching, Spiritual Reading
and Meditation

VOLUME FOUR

*From the Eleventh Sunday after Pentecost
to the Twenty-fourth and Last Sunday
after Pentecost*

TRANSLATED AND EDITED BY
M. F. TOAL, D.D.

Preservation Press

P.O. Box 612   Swedesboro, NJ 08085

Library of Congress Cataloging-in-Publication Data

Patristic homilies on the Gospels.
  The Sunday sermons of the great Fathers: a manual of preaching, spiritual reading, and meditation / translated and edited by M. F. Toal.
    p.   cm.
  Originally published Patristic homilies on the Gospels. Chicago: Regnery, 1955-1963.
  Contains Saint Thomas Aquinas' Catena aurea.
  Includes bibliographical references and indexes.
  Contents: v. 1. From the first Sunday of Advent to Quinquagesima—v. 2. From the first Sunday in Lent to the Sunday after the Ascension—v. 3. From Pentecost to the tenth Sunday after Pentecost—v. 4. From the eleventh Sunday after Pentecost to the twenty-fourth and last Sunday after Pentecost.
  ISBN 1-886412-14-6 (set: alk. paper). — ISBN 1-886412-15-4 (v. 1: alk. paper). — ISBN 1-886412-16-2 (v. 2: alk. paper). — ISBN 1-886412-17-0 (v. 3: alk. paper). — ISBN 1-886412-18-9 (v. 4: alk paper)
    1. Bible. N.T. Gospels—Sermons. 2. Sermons, English. 3. Church year sermons. 4. Bible. N.T. Gospels—Commentaries. 5. Fathers of the church. I. Toal, M. F. II. Thomas, Aquinas. Saint, 1225?-1274. Catena aurea. English. III. Title.
BS2555.A2T6 1997
252'.011 —dc21
                                                                                    96-44004
                                                                                        CIP

For information write Preservation Press:
P.O. Box 612, Swedesboro, NJ 08085

DANIELI · MANNIX

MELBOURNENSIUM · ARCHIEPISCOPO
VIRO · PRAECLARO · PASTORI · INDEFATIGATO
CHRISTI · CAUSA · PEREGRINO
ORDINARIO · SUO · VENERATISSIMO
HOC · OPUS · OLIM · INCHOATUM
IPSI · FAVENTI · ET · ADJUVANTI
NUNC · DEI · MUNERE · AD · FINEM · PERDUCTUM
AUCTOR
PIO · DEDITOQUE · ANIMO
DICAT

FOREWORD
TO THE FIRST VOLUME

THE author of the present work has had as his purpose to put into the hands of his fellow priests material of incomparable value, in a form easy of access, with a view to aiding them in the sacred ministry of preaching. This apostolic ministry is the one on which all else depends in the mission of the Church for the salvation of souls.

A large portion of it will always consist in homilies on the Gospels of the Sundays and Principal Feasts. Father Toal, in this first volume, has in view this sector of the preacher's work. For the Gospel of each Sunday and Feast he has brought together from the most reliable sources, and translated, all that he thought to be best and most useful in the homilies and expositions of the Fathers and of the Angel of the Schools.

Nothing more suited to his noble purpose could be conceived. The word of God contained in Scripture, and especially in the Gospels, has been given to the Church for the instruction of men. Sacred Tradition guided by the Spirit of God has expounded it in the writings of the Holy Fathers and Doctors.

Father Toal has placed in the easiest possible reach of the busy priest this treasure house of sacred lore, this quintessence of the doctrine of Tradition on each Gospel. What he supplies may, of course, not be all that may be usefully known in relation to it, but it is, and by long odds, the most important thing. A sermon well prepared on the matter here supplied cannot fail to be learned, solid, simple and effective.

What more can be said in praise of the utility of Father Toal's contribution? We shall all be grateful to him, and *his reward will indeed be great* (Mt. v. 12.)

MICHAEL BROWNE, O.P.
(Now Cardinal Michael Browne
Vatican   *Formerly Master of the Sacred*
24 November 1954   *Apostolic Palace)*

REFERENCE LIST OF
DOCTORS AND FATHERS IN THIS WORK

The Four Great Doctors of the East

1. St Basil the Great, Archbishop of Caesarea. A.D. 330–379.
2. St Cyril, Patriarch of Alexandria. † 444.
3. St Gregory Nazianzen, Patriarch of Constantinople. 329–390.
4. St John Chrysostom, Patriarch of Constantinople. 354–407.

The Four Great Doctors of the West

1. St Ambrose, Bishop of Milan. 339–397.
2. St Augustine, Bishop of Hippo. 354–430.
3. St Gregory the Great, Pope. 540–604.
4. St Jerome, Priest. 347–420.

Fathers, Doctors, Ecclesiastical Writers (Theologians and Scriptural Commentators)

1. Acacius, St, Bishop of Melitene. † 449.
2. Adelmus (Aldhelm), St, Abbot of Malmesbury, Bishop of Sherborne. † 709.
3. Aelred, Abbot of Rievaulx, homilist, historian. 1109–1166.
4. Alcuin Albin of York, Deacon; educator. 735–804.
5. Avitus (Alcimus), St, Bishop of Vienne. † c. 494.
6. Alexander, Monk, historian. Late fourth century.
7. Ambrosius Autpertus, Abbot of Volturnius. † c. 778.
8. Amedeus, Bishop of Lausanne. Early twelfth century.
9. Ammonius, Monk of Alexandria. Late fifth century.
10. Amphilochius, St, Bishop of Iconium. 339–400.
11. Anastasius Romanus, Abbot. Late ninth century.
12. Anastasius, St, Abbot of Mount Sinai. † 700.
13. Andreas, St, Archbishop, Crete. 660–740.
14. Anselm, Archbishop of Canterbury, Doctor. 1033–1109.
15. Antipater, Bishop of Bostra. † c. 460.
16. Antony, St, Abbot, monastic Founder, Egypt. 251–356.
17. Apolinaris the Elder, Priest. Late fourth century.
18. Arnoldus, Abbot, of Bonneval, Chartres. Mid twelfth century.
19. Asterius, St, Bishop of Amasea (Pontus). † c. 410.
20. Athanasius, St, Patriarch of Alexandria, Doctor. 296–373.

21. Basil, Bishop of Seleucia. † 459.
22. Bede, St, The Venerable, Priest and Doctor. 672–735.
23. Bernard, St, Abbot of Clairvaux, Doctor. 1090–1153.
24. Bruno, St, Bishop of Segni. 1048–1123.
25. Caesarius, St, Bishop of Arles; preacher. 470–543.
26. Choniates Michael, Metropolitan of Athens, chronicler. † 1215.
27. Chromatius, St, Bishop of Aquilea. Early fifth century.
28. Chrysippus, Priest of Jerusalem. † 479.
29. Clement, St, Pope and Martyr. † c. 90.
30. Clement of Alexandria. † c. 215.
31. Cyprian, St, Martyr, Bishop of Carthage. † 258.
32. Cyril, St, Patriarch of Jerusalem, Doctor. 318–386.
33. Didymus the Blind, of Alexandria, teacher. 310–395.
34. Dionysius, St, the Great, Patriarch of Alexandria. 190–264.
35. Dionysius, St, the Areopagite; companion of Paul. First Bishop of Athens
    (*Combefis*).
36. Eligius, St, Bishop of Noyon-Tournai. 590–660.
37. Ephraem the Syrian, St, Deacon and Doctor. † 373.
38. Ephraemius, St, Patriarch of Antioch. † 545.
39. Epiphanius, St, Bishop of Salamina. 415–403.
40. Eradius, succeeded St Augustine as Bishop of Hippo.
41. Eucherius, St, Bishop of Lyons. † 450.
42. Eulogius, St, Patriarch of Alexandria. † 608.
43. Eusebius, St, Bishop of Caesarea; historian. 260–341.
44. Eutychius, Patriarch of Constantinople. 512–582.
45. Euthymius Zigabonus, Greek Monk. † c. 1120.
46. Fulbertus, Bishop of Chartres. † 1028.
47. Fulgentius, St, Bishop of Ruspe (Africa). 468–533.
48. Gaudentius, St, Bishop of Brescia. † 410.
49. Germanus, St, Patriarch of Constantinople. † 730.
50. George, Metropolitan of Nicomedia. Late ninth century.
51. Gregory Thaumaturgus, St, Bishop of Neocaesareae. 213–270.
52. Gregory, St, Bishop of Nyssa, Doctor. † 394.
53. Haymo, Bishop of Halberstadt. † 858.
54. Hesychius, Priest of Jerusalem. † 472.
55. Hilary, St, Bishop of Poitiers, Doctor. † 315–367.
56. Hilary, St, Bishop of Arles. † 459.
57. Hildebertus, Archbishop of Tours. 1056–1133.
58. Hippolytus, St, Priest and Martyr. † 235.
59. Ignatius, St, Apostolic Father, Martyr and Bishop of Antioch. 50–117.
60. Ildefonsus, St, Bishop of Toledo. † 667.
61. Joannes (*Geometra*), Greek writer. c. 600–700.
62. John Damascene, Priest and Doctor. 676–754.
63. Josephius Flavius, St, Jewish historian. 37–101.
64. Josephus, Archbishop of Thessalonica. Early ninth century.
65. Irenaeus, St, Martyr, Bishop of Lyons. † 202.
66. Isidore, St, Abbot of Pelusium (Egypt). † 450.

67. Ivo, St, Bishop of Chartres. 1040–1116.
68. Justin, St, Martyr, Apostolic Father. 100–165.
69. Leontius of Byzantium; opposed Nestorians and Eutychians. 485–533.
70. Leo the Great, St, Pope and Doctor. † 461.
71. Macarius Senior, Disciple of St Antony, Abbot. † 390.
72. Maximus, St, Confessor. 580–662.
73. Maximus, St, Bishop of Turin. 380–465.
74. Melito, Bishop of Sardis (Asia Minor). † 190.
75. Methodius, St, Martyr, Bishop of Tyre. † *c.* 311.
76. Methodius, St, Patriarch of Constantinople. † 846.
77. Modestus, St, Archbishop of Jerusalem. † 634.
78. Nicetas, Bishop of Nemesiana (Serbia). † 335–411.
79. Nilus, St, of Ancyra, Abbot; Discp. of Chrysostom. † 430.
80. Odo of Morismond, Abbot, or, Odo of Battle (Cant.). *c.* 1200.
81. Origen, Priest and Confessor. 185–253.
82. Pacianus, St, Bishop of Barcelona. † 392.
83. Pantaleon, Priest; or, Pantaleon, Deacon; both of Constantinople and seventh century.
84. Patrick, St, Bishop and Apostle of Ireland. † 432.
85. Paulinus, St, Bishop of Nola. 353–431.
86. Peter Chrysologos, St, Bishop of Ravenna, Doctor. † 450.
87. Peter, the Venerable, Abbot of Cluny. † 1157.
88. Philo of Alexandria, Jewish teacher and philosopher. † *c.* 50.
89. Photius, Patriarch of Constantinople. 815–897.
90. Procopius of Gaza, Deacon. Composed *Catene* of S. Scrip. † *c.* 538.
91. Proclus, St, Patriarch of Constantinople. † 446.
92. Remigius of Auxerre. † 908.
93. Severianus, Bishop of Gabala. † 408.
94. Severus, Patriarch of Antioch (dep. 518). † 538.
95. Severus Sulpitius, Priest, Toulouse. † mid. fourth century.
96. Silvester, St, Pope. 314–355.
97. Sidonius Apollinaris, Bishop of Clermont. 430–480.
98. Sophronius, St, Patriarch of Jerusalem. 560–638.
99. Sozomenus, Church historian. † 447.
100. Simeon Metaphrastes, hagiogr. of Greek Church. Late tenth century.
101. Tertullian, ecclesiastical writer. 160–220.
102. Theoderet, Bishop of Cyprus. 393–457.
103. Theodore of Mopsuestia (also Antioch). 350–428.
104. Theodotus, St, Bishop of Ancyra. Martyred under Diocletian.
105. Theophanes, St, chronicler. 758–817.
106. Theophylactus, Patriarch of Bulgaria. 765–840.
107. Titus, Bishop of Bostra, Arabia Petrea. † 450.
108. Victor of Antioch, Priest. † 450.
109. Zeno, St, Bishop of Verona. † 372.

BIBLIOGRAPHY AND
ABBREVIATIONS

Bibliotheca Patrum Concionatoria, of P. Francois Combefis, O.P.
Edit. Paris 1681   BPC
Migne's *Patrologiae Cursus Completus.*
Series Graeca, Edition Paris 1886; Vols. 161   PG
Series Latina, Edition Paris 1844–66; Vols. 221   PL
Corpus Scriptorum Ecclesiasticorum Latinorum (current)   CSEL
Catena Aurea of St Thomas Aquinas, compiled 1261–7   CA
Catena Sexaginta-quinque Graecorum Patrum in Lucam, Quae
Quatuor simul Evangelistarum introduxit Explicationem.
Luce et Latinitate donata a Balthasare Corderio, Soc. Jesu.
Antwerp 1628   Catena GP
Catena Patrum Graecorum in S. Joannem, ex antiquissimo Graeco
codice MS nuncprimum in lucem edita, a Balthasare Corderio,
Soc. Jesus. Antwerp 1630   Catena GP
Patrologia Syriaca, Graffin   GPS
Sancti Ephraem Syri, Hymni et Sermones, Lamy. Malines 1882   Lamy
Sti Ephraem Syri Opera Omnia, Vossio. Cologne 1616   Vossio
Sermones Reperti, Miscellanea Agostiniana, Morin, O.S.B. Edit.
Rome 1930   MA
Enchiridion Symbolorum, Denzinger-Bannwart. Freiburg (Bris)
1928   Denz
Clavis Patrum Latinorum, Sacris Erudiri, 1951   Clavis
A Glossary of Later Latin, Souter. Oxford, 1949   GLL
Pour Revaloriser Migne, Tables Rectificatives, Glorieux. Lille 1952   PRM
Septuagint   Sept

NOTE ON THE ARRANGEMENT OF THIS BOOK

For each Sunday or Feast Day in the book there is given the Gospel of the Day,
and after that the parallel passages from other gospels where such passages exist.
In every case these are followed by an exposition of the Gospel taken from the
Catena Aurea of St Thomas Aquinas, which in turn is followed by a selection of
sermons on the Gospel.

NOTE ON PRELIMINARY MATERIAL

For General Preface to this work, and for Introduction to the *Catena Aurea,* see
Volume I.

CONTENTS

Together with an Exposition of the Gospel of each Sunday from the *Catena Aurea* of St Thomas Aquinas

xiii

ELEVENTH SUNDAY AFTER PENTECOST

I. ST ANTHONY ABBOT: WATCHFULNESS OF THE TONGUE

II. ST AMBROSE: ON BAPTISM, A CATECHETICAL INSTRUCTION

III. ST EPHRAIM THE SYRIAN: ON THE EVIL OF THE TONGUE AND
SIMILAR VICES

IV. ST GREGORY THE GREAT: HEARING THE WORD OF GOD

THE GOSPEL OF THE SUNDAY

MARK vii. 31–37

At that time: Jesus going out of the coasts of Tyre, he came by Sidon to the sea of Galilee, through the midst of the coasts of Decapolis. And they bring to him one deaf and dumb; and they besought him that he would lay his hand upon him. And, taking him from the multitude apart, he put his fingers into his ears: and spitting, he touched his tongue. And, looking up to heaven, he groaned and said to him: Ephpheta, which is, Be thou opened.

And immediately his ears were opened and the string of his tongue was loosed and he spoke right. And he charged them that they should tell no man. But the more he charged them, so much the more a great deal did they publish it. And so much the more did they wonder, saying: He hath done all things well: He hath made the deaf to hear, and the dumb to speak.

EXPOSITION FROM THE CATENA AUREA

V.31. *And going out of the coasts of Tyre he came . . .*

THEOPHYLACTUS: The Lord willed not to stay in the midst of Gentiles, so as to give no grounds to the Jews to point Him out as a transgressor of the Law, by seeking the company of the Gentiles; and so He immediately returns. Hence it is said that, *he came*

by Sidon to the sea of Galilee through the midst of the coasts of the Decapolis.

BEDE: The Decapolis was a region of ten cities to the east of the Jordan and opposite Galilee. That it is said that the Lord came *by Sidon to the sea of Galilee, through the coasts of the Deca-polis* does not mean He entered the territory of the Decapolis; nor is He said to cross the sea, but rather that He came as far as the sea coast, to a point opposite the centre of the Decapolis; which lay some distance eastwards from the sea. Then follows:

V.32. And they bring to him one deaf and dumb . . .

THEOPHYLACTUS: This is rightly introduced following the deliverance of one possessed by a demon; for this affliction was due to a devil.

V.33. And taking him from the multitude apart, he put . . .

PSEUDO-CHRYSOSTOM (*Victor of Antioch*): He takes the deaf and dumb person brought to Him, *apart from the multitude*, not to perform His divine wonders openly; teaching us to put away vain glory and pride: for there is nothing through which a man works wonders more than by giving himself to humility and observing modesty. *He put his fingers into his ears* Who could heal by a word; to show that the Body united to His Divinity, and to Its Operation, was endowed with the Divine power. Because of the sin of Adam, human nature had suffered much, and had been wounded in its senses and in its members. But Christ coming into the world revealed to us, in Himself, the perfection af human nature; and for this reason He opened the ears with His fingers, and gave speech by the moisture of His tongue. And so we read: *He put his fingers into his ears, and spitting, he touched his tongue.*

THEOPHYLACTUS: That He might show us that divine and holy are all the members of His sacred Body; and the saliva that undid *the string of his tongue.* For though saliva is but superfluous moisture, in the Lord all that is His is divine.

V.34. And, looking up to heaven, he groaned and said to him: Ephpheta, which is, Be thou opened.

BEDE: He looked up to heaven to teach us that it is from there the dumb must seek speech, the deaf hearing, and all who suffer healing. He groaned, not because He needed to seek with groaning anything from the Father (He Who together with the Father bestows all things on those who seek from Him), but that He might give us an example of groaning, when we must call upon the assistance of the heavenly mercy, in our own or in our neighbour's miseries.

PSEUDO-CHRYSOSTOM (*as above*): He also groaned as taking our cause upon Himself; and as having compassion on human nature: seeing the misery into which humanity had fallen.

BEDE: That He says, *Ephpheta*, which means: *Be thou opened*, refers strictly to the ears; for ears must be opened to hear, but the tongue, that it may speak, must be loosed from the bond of its own tardiness. Hence:

V.35. And immediately his ears were opened and the string of his tongue was loosed and he spoke right.

Wherein both natures of the one and the same Christ are clearly distinguished. Looking up to heaven He groans, as a man praying to God; then, as mighty with the power of

God, with a single word, He heals. Then follows:

V.36. *And he charged them that they should tell no man* . . .

JEROME: In which He teaches us not to glory in our strength, but in the Cross and in humiliation. PSEUDO-CHRYSOSTOM: He also told them to keep the miracle secret, lest the Jews through envy should put Him to death before due time.

JEROME: But a city set on a hill, and seen from all sides, cannot be hid; and humility ever precedes glory. So we read: *But the more he charged them, so much the more a great deal did they publish it.*

THEOPHYLACTUS: In this we are taught that when we give anything to another, we should not look for praise and recognition. But when we receive favours, we ought to praise and proclaim our benefactors, even though they may not wish it.

AUGUSTINE, HARMONY OF THE GOSPELS, IV, 4: But if He (as knowing the present and the future minds of men) was aware that the more He charged them not to publish it, so much the more would they publish it, why then did He forbid them, if not to make clear to the sluggish how much more joyfully, more fervently, they should proclaim Him whom He *commands* to make Him known, when they would not keep silent whom He forbade to speak? GLOSS: Because of the praise of those whom Christ healed, the wonder of the multitude and their making known of Christ's favours increased.

V.37. *And so much the more did they*

wonder, saying: *He hath done all things well;* that is: *He hath both made the deaf to hear and the dumb to speak.*

JEROME: *Tyre* is mystically interpreted as 'narrowness', and symbolizes Judea; to whom the Lord said: *For the bed is straitened* (Is. xxviii. 20), and from whom He turns away to other peoples. *Sidon* means 'hunting'. For an untamed beast is our generation; and *the sea* stands for our stormy inconstancy. The Saviour comes to save the Gentiles in *the midst of the Decapolis;* which is interpreted as signifying the commandments of the Decalogue. And the human race, throughout its many members, is reckoned as one man, devoured in the First Man by varying afflictions: it is blinded when it sees evil, deaf when it hears it, dumb when it speaks it. And they beseech Him, *to lay his hand upon him:* for many Patriarchs and just men hoped and longed for the coming of the Lord Incarnate.

BEDE: Or, he is deaf and dumb who has neither ears for the word of God, nor opens his mouth to speak it. It is necessary that those who have now learned both to hear and to speak the words of God, should offer such as these to the Lord, that He may heal them.

JEROME: He who is deserving of healing is ever led *apart* from restless thoughts, from unruly actions, from disordered speech. The fingers put in his ears are the words or the gifts of the Spirit; of Whom it is said: *He is the finger of God* (Exod. viii. 19). The spittle is the divine wisdom, which unties the bond on the lips of man, so that he may say: *I believe in God, the Father Almighty*, and all the rest. Looking up to heaven *He groaned*, that is, He taught us to groan, and to uplift to heaven the treasures of our heart: for by the groans of our compunction the empty joy of the flesh is purified, and our ears are opened to the sound of hymns, to canticles, to the psalms. He loosens our tongue, that it may bring forth the good word; which not even blows can silence.

I. St Anthony, Abbot
Watchfulness of the Tongue[1]

In His sacred Gospel Our Lord Jesus Christ says to us: *Enter ye in at the narrow gate* (Mt. vii. 13). Again He says: *That through many tribulations we must enter into the kingdom of God* (Acts xiv. 21). What this *narrow gate* is through which we must enter the wise Solomon makes clear to us where he says: *My son, give not thy mouth to cause thy flesh to sin* (Eccles. v. 5). And again: *The mouth of a fool is his destruction* (Prov. xviii. 7). Let us therefore strive to place a strong guard on our lips, that they may not utter anything evil: for evil speech is worse than all poisons.

All other wounds may be healed, but the wound of the tongue has no cure. The tongue of the dragon is less evil than that of the *whisperer*, which in turn comes from a most evil demon: for it provokes quarrelling and bitter strife between brethren, sows evil and discord among the peaceful, scatters many communities. If you permit the *whisperer* to approach you, he will strip you of every merit you possess. Whosoever becomes involved with him has already become a confederate in his bloodshed, in his murders, and in his slayings! for a *whisperer* and a murderer spawn the same whelp: if they do not slay you with the sword, they will bring the same disaster on you with the tongue.

The tongue of the *whisperer* differs little from the serpent's bite: rather, better to live with serpents and scorpions than dwell with a *whisperer*. A blasphemer or a tyrant is better than a *whisperer*. All sins are less grievous than those of the *whisperer*. The *whisperer* and those who give ear to him receive the same condemnation. Better for you to come close to fire and be burned, than come nigh to a *whisperer*. Should you tread on boiling pitch, and go carefully, you may escape hurt. But should you chance to pass by a *whisperer*, keep far from him, lest he lead you into irreparable disasters: for his mouth at all times is filled with treachery and death.

Because of these things I charge you severely, that you separate yourself from a *whisperer* as speedily as you can. Let him be a monk, let him be an anchorite, let him be a champion of virtue or but a novice, whoever he is, as long as he is a *whisperer*, fly from him. Though he should be your own father, or your brother, if he is a *whisperer*, keep far away from him. For it is better to dwell with a lion or a lioness than with one who is a *whisperer*. And do not be ashamed to fly from him: so that he shall not infect you with the poison of his sin

So then, my sons, have no part in murmuring; do your work earnestly and in silence: for he who is devoted to silence is close to God and His angels and dwells in heaven. For the Lord tells us that, *he that keepeth his mouth keepeth his soul* (Prov. xiii. 3). And then in the day of our visitation He shall say to us: *Blessed art thou, Israel,* because you kept watch on your tongue; *who is like to thee* (Deut. xxxiii. 29)? May the Lord preserve you in His grace and peace, Amen.

II. ST AMBROSE, BISHOP AND DOCTOR

On Baptism; A Catechetical Instruction[2]

I.1. *In which, treating of the sacraments, of which it was not fitting to speak to them before this* (being catechumens), *the Saint comes to the mystery of,* The Opening, *which, he teaches, was established by Christ in the healing of the man who was deaf and dumb.*

I shall now begin to instruct you on the sacrament you have received; of whose nature it was not fitting to speak to you before this: for in the Christian what comes first is faith. And at Rome for this reason those who have been baptized are called *the faithful* (*fideles*). And it was through faith that Abraham our father was justified, and not *by works* (Rom. iv. 2). Therefore, it was because you believed that you received baptism. It would be wrong for me to think otherwise: you would not have been called to grace unless Christ had deemed you worthy of it.

2. What then did we perform on Saturday last? The mystery of *The Opening.*[3] And the mystery of *The Opening* was commemorated when the priest touched your ears and nostrils. And this Our Lord Jesus Christ laid down for us in the Gospel, when they brought Him one who was deaf and dumb, and He touched his ears and his mouth: his ears because he was deaf; his mouth because he

was dumb. And He said: *Ephpheta.* This is a Hebrew word, and means: *Be thou opened.* The priest therefore touched your ears, that they might be opened to the words and to the exhortation of the priest.

3. But you will say to me: Why does he touch the nostrils? Christ touched the mouth, for it was there the man was dumb: so that he who could not speak of the heavenly mysteries might receive a voice from Christ. He touched him there because he was a man. Here however, since women also are to be baptized, and since the purity of the servant is not the same as that of the Master – what comparison can there be between them; for the one yields to sin, the Other forgives it, – so, out of reverence for the sacred rite, and because of the sanctity of his office, the bishop does not touch the mouth, but the nostrils: that you may receive the good odour of eternal charity, and that you may say: *We are the good odour of Christ unto God,* as the holy Apostle said (II Cor. ii. 15); and that you may be filled with the fragrance of faith and devotion.

II.4. *He explains the anointing of the Christian athlete, and, that he may animate them to keep their pledge of renunciation, he makes known to them the dignity of those in whose presence it was made, making this clear by examples.*

We came to the Baptistery. You entered it. You remember whom you saw there; and recall to mind what it was you said. Repeat it carefully! You met there a *Levite* (deacon); you met a priest. You were anointed, as a champion of Christ, about as it were to take part in the contest of this world. You freely offered yourself to fight in the battles of this contest. He who fights already possesses what he hopes for: for where the contest is, there also is the crown. You strive in this world and you are crowned by Christ; and it is for the battles of this world you are crowned. For though your reward is in heaven, that by which the reward is gained takes place here on earth.

5. When the priest asked you: *Do you renounce the devil and all his works,* what did you answer? *I do renounce him.* When he asked: *Do you renounce the world and all its delights,* what did you answer? *I do renounce them.* Be mindful then of the words you spoke, and let you never forget the seriousness of the pledge you have given. If you give a man a pledge you become indebted to him, so that you may receive his money. You hold yourself bound, and, if you do not pay, the lender presses you. If you refuse to pay you must go before a judge, and because of the pledge you gave, you will then be convicted.

6. Recall where you pledged yourself, and to Whom you pledged yourself. You saw there a Levite. He is a minister of Christ. You have seen him minister before the altar. There-fore through your pledge you are held bound, not on earth, but in heaven. Call to mind where you partook of the heavenly mysteries (*the Eucharist*). If we have here the Body of Christ, then here also His angels stand round about Him. You have read in the Gospel: *Wheresoever the body shall be, there also shall be the eagles* (Mt. xxiv. 28). Where Christ's Body is, there also are the eagles; who fly that they may leave earthly things and seek those of heaven. And why do I say this to you? Because those men, whosoever they are, who announce the Gospel are also angels; and they are seen by you to be received into the place of the angels.

7. How is this? Listen! Recall to mind the Baptist. John the Baptist was born of a man and of a woman. Yet hear how he also was an angel. *Behold, I send my angel before thy face, who shall prepare thy way before thee* (Mt. xi. 10). And listen also to the words of Malachy the prophet: *For the lips of the priest shall keep knowledge, and they shall seek the law at his mouth; because he is the angel of the Lord of hosts* (Mal. ii. 7). We tell you these things to make clear to you, publicly, the honour God has bestowed on the priesthood; and that it is not something conferred because of personal merits.

8. So you have renounced the world; you have renounced earthly things. Be careful therefore. A man who owes money has his liability always in mind. And you, you who owe Christ faith, be careful of your faith; which is more precious than money. For your faith is your eternal patrimony, money a temporal

one. Therefore, let you be always mindful of the pledge you gave, and then you will be very careful. If you keep before you what you promised, you will then fulfil your pledge.

III.9. *Although the neophytes see only the Font and the Ministers, greater are the things that are not seen.*

Then you came nearer. You saw the Font; and beside the Font stood the priest. And I cannot but think that there came to your mind also that which Naaman the Syrian thought; for though he was made clean, yet, before that, he doubted. Why was this? Let me tell you. Attend carefully.

10. You entered the Baptistery; you saw the water; you saw the priest, and you saw the minister. And lest perhaps one of you may have thought: Is this all? This is indeed all. It truly is all where there is all innocence, all kindness, all grace, all sanctification. You saw what was possible to the eyes of the body, to human sight. But you have not seen what was wrought; for these things are *not* seen. And the things that were not seen are greater far than those seen: *For the things which are seen are temporal; but the things which are not seen are eternal* (II Cor. iv. 18).

IV.11. *Our sacraments are prior in time, and more perfect, than those of the Jews; and herein is the significance of the word Pasch.*

So let me first say: pay attention to my words and weigh them well. We truly venerate the mysteries of the Jews, given to those who were our fathers; first, because of the antiquity of the mysteries, and then, because

of the sanctity of those who offered them. I shall show you that older and more perfect are the sacraments of the Christians than those of the Jews.

12. And as we are now speaking of baptism, what was earlier than the crossing over of the Jewish people through the midst of the sea? Yet the Jews who *crossed over* all died in the desert. But he who crosses over through this stream, that is, crosses over from earthly to heavenly things – and this is what Pasch means, *a crossing over*, a crossing over from sin to true life, from guilt to grace, from defilement to sanctification – he who crosses over through this stream does not die, but will rise again.

V.13. *In Naaman the leper it was prefigured that that water alone heals which possesses the grace of Christ. That Christ willed to be baptized for our sakes. For this reason the Holy Spirit, appearing in the form of a dove, did not descend upon Him before He entered the water of the Jordan; for it was only then the whole Trinity would be present.*

Now Naaman was a leper. And a certain serving maid said to his wife: 'If my master wishes to be made clean, let him go to the land of Israel, and he will find there one who can take away his leprosy.' She said this to his wife, and the wife repeated it to her husband, and Naaman told it to the King of Syria, and he, having a great esteem for Naaman, sent him to the King of Israel. And the King of Israel, when he heard that a man had been sent to him, to cleanse him of leprosy, *rent his garments*, the Scripture tells us (IV Kings v. 7). And on this Eliseus the prophet sent word to the King, saying: 'Why hast thou rent thy garments, as though God had not power to cleanse a leper? Send him to me.' The King sent Naaman to him, and when he came the prophet said to him: 'Go down to the Jordan and plunge in, and you will be healed.'

14. And Naaman began to think to himself and to say: 'Is this all? I come from Syria to the land of Judea and I am told: "Go down to the Jordan, and plunge in, and you will be healed." As if there were not finer rivers in my own land?' But his servant said to him: 'Master, why not do what the prophet says? Better to do it and see what comes of it.' And at this Naaman went down to the Jordan, and bathed in it, and came up healed.

15. What did this prefigure? With your eyes you have seen water. But all water does not heal: that water alone heals which has the blessing of Christ. The element itself is one thing; its consecration another. The action is one thing; its effect another. The action is wrought with water; its effect proceeds from the Holy Spirit. The water does not heal unless the Holy Spirit descends and blesses the water; as you read that when the Lord Jesus Christ was about to give us the form of baptism, He came to John, and John said to Him: *I ought to be baptized by thee, and comest thou to me? And Jesus answering, said to him: Suffer it to be so now. For so it becometh us to fulfil all justice* (Mt. iii. 14, 15). See how all u stice rests on baptism.

16. Why then did Christ descend

if not that this our flesh might be healed, the flesh He assumed from us? For Christ needed no washing away of His sins; He Who had committed no sin; but we needed it, we who are subject to sin. If then baptism is for us, its form was established for us: the form of our faith is made known to us.

17. Christ descended into the water, and John who baptized Him stood by him, and lo! the Holy Spirit descended, *as a dove*. He did not descend a dove, but descended *as a dove*. Recall to mind what I have told you: Christ took a body; He did not seem to take a body. Christ took upon Himself the reality of this flesh of ours, and a true body. The Holy Spirit however did not descend as a true dove, but in the form of a dove. Therefore John saw, and believed.

18. Christ descended, and the Holy Spirit descended. But why did Christ descend first, and afterwards the Holy Spirit: seeing that the form of baptism, and the manner of conferring it, require that first the Font shall be consecrated, and then that he descends into it who is to be baptized? For when the priest enters the baptistery, he first performs, by invocation, an exorcism of the element of water, and then prays that the Font may be sanctified, and that the power of the Eternal Trinity may become present. But Christ descended first, and afterwards the Holy Spirit. Why was this? So that we might see that the Lord Jesus did not stand in need of the mystery of sanctification, but that He was Himself to sanctify, and that the Spirit also would sanctify.

19. And so Christ descended into the water; and the Holy Spirit descended *as a dove*. Likewise the Father spoke *from heaven*. And so you have the presence of the Trinity.

V.20. *A figure of baptism is first seen in the Red Sea. The same, in fewer words, was shown from the Flood.*

The Apostle says that the Red Sea was a figure of this baptism, saying: *For our fathers were all baptized, in the cloud and in the sea* (I Cor. x. 2). And Paul adds: *Now these things were done in a figure of us* (v.6): to them in figure, to us in the reality. The Jewish people were hemmed in by the sea, and Moses *stretched forth his rod over the sea*. The Egyptian with his army was on one side, and on the other were the Hebrews, cut off by the sea. They could neither cross the sea, nor turn back towards the enemy. And they began to murmur.

21. Consider then; does it not encourage you that their prayers were heard? Although the Lord heard them, yet they were not without fault; because of their murmuring. It is your duty when you are in trouble to believe you will be delivered; not to murmur, but to call upon His name; to pray, not to utter complaints.

22. Moses stretched forth his rod, and he guided the people of the Hebrews; by night *in a pillar of fire*, by day *in a pillar of cloud* (Exod. xiv). And what is this light but the Truth; which pours forth a full clear light? And *the pillar of light*, what is it if not Christ the Lord, Who has scattered the darkness of unbelief, and poured forth the light of His truth and spiritual grace on human hearts? The Holy spirit is *the pillar of cloud*. The people were in the sea, and before them went *the pillar of light*. Then followed *the pillar of cloud*, as *the shadow* of the Holy Spirit. You see then how through water and the Holy Spirit a figure of baptism was revealed to us.

23. The Flood also was a figure of baptism; and the mysteries of the Jews most certainly did not then exist. If the *form* of baptism preceded them, you then see how the mysteries of the Christians are older than those of the Jews.

24. But for the present, because of the weakness of our voice, and for reasons of time, it will be enough for today to touch even lightly upon the mysteries of the Sacred Fount. Tomorrow, if the Lord gives me the strength and the opportunity to speak to you, I shall treat of it more fully. But your Charity needs to have your ears ready, and your hearts disposed, that we may share with you whatever we may find throughout the Scriptures, and that you may hold fast to it, and come to possess the grace of the Father, Son and Holy Ghost; the Trinity, to Whom belongs the everlasting kingdom, from all ages, and now and forever, world without end. Amen.

III. St Ephraim, Confessor and Doctor

On the Evil of the Tongue and Similar Vices[4]

The desires of this life vary in every man, so that each one may encounter *a strong conflict* (Wis. x. 12), in which he may constantly *exercise* his soul in virtue (I Tim. iv. 7). For there are those who are given to gluttony and excess, while they may abhor adultery. Others are swollen with pride, but will not commit theft. Others, despising the pleasures of the body, are devoured by avarice. There are those who are indifferent to personal adornment, but at the same time give themselves to dissipation. Others, who delight in wine, know nothing of pride. Some will have nothing to do with fornication, but in their heart deceit and hypocrisy flourish concealed. Then there are those who condemn extravagance, yet delight in speaking ill of others. And there are others who rise above one vice, and wallow wholeheartedly in another. Some are free from reproach in one direction, and most evilly disposed in another. Some escape one snare, and are buried alive in the filth of some other vice.

Many, and indeed endless, are the forms of vice, and they all deceive men gradually, From the smallest beginnings they slip heedlessly into greater sins. And when the devil seeks to overcome any man, he first considers what vice is it to which his nature is most inclined, so that, delighting in his bonds, he will not even wish to free himself. For our cunning and deceitful enemy well knows with what sort of bonds he can hold us; that should he force us unwilling into his snares, our soul, quickly breaking them, would soon regain its liberty. And so he embraces each one with bonds that to him are pleasant and agreeable, and to which he cheerfully consents.

Yet with God as our Leader the soul can deliver itself from all snares of the enemy. But now, though held fast by them, we are happy, and even proud of our servitude. For one who is held by the bonds of envy, since he is a stranger to lust, will believe himself wholly free. And one given to the vice of calumny believes, because he hates robbery and theft, that he is free of every bond. Each man's bonds are concealed from him; and like a drunkard he is unaware of the snares laid for him. Those filled with wine, because of their drunkenness, neither feel the bonds that hold them, nor see the snares laid for them. But the most kind God, at various times, lays as it were this sort of yoke on all men; and to each one according to his strength is allotted a burthen of trial.

At the time the Jews were building the Tabernacle all, both rich and poor, offered something, so as to share in its sanctification. Each offered a gift according to his means: one gold, one pearls, another precious stones, the poor gave carpets, and dressed skins. Rich women brought silks; poor widows brought dyed wool. And in this way the entire adornment of the Tabernacle was made up from the gifts of rich and poor alike; and Moses blessed them all (Ex. xxv, xxxix).

And the Lord received the vows of each one, of rich and poor: just as He had accepted what each one had offered, according to his means, for the building of the Tabernacle, so likewise did He receive, without regard for persons, the prayers and vows of each. For just as our enemy endeavours from time to time to destroy us, so the Lord at various times seeks to lead us to salvation. And just as the Good Thief by his single act of confession became a citizen of paradise, so by one word of blasphemy one man may become guilty of the fire of Gehenna. For if Mary, the sister of Moses, because of one evil speech, and though she was also a prophetess, was condemned and afflicted with leprosy, what punishment do they not deserve who, without any restraint, revile and speak ill of others?

And in what Mary said truth was put aside, because she spoke from a perverse and abusive mind.[5] If a just man reviles another, his own justice is filled with injustice. Correct a man with justice, and do not speak evil of him in secret, nor rebuke him publicly; and neither should you rail at him offensively in secret. Your justice is in vain if it is mingled with deceit or cruelty; just as that sanctity is rejected which is tainted with impurity. Useless likewise is that chastity which is mingled with unchaste desires. Vain the faith that is entangled with deceptions and predictions. Idle is that tranquillity that is but a pretence. Without value the beneficence that has pride as its associate. Fasting is of no avail where it is joined to detraction. Turn away from that charity that is disturbed by jealousy or envy.

And when we turn our minds to natural things, let us learn from what is written in the Scriptures. The beauty of truth is lost when it is stretched to cover wickedness. And even food will kill when poison is mingled in it. Because it is tainted by sacrifices and immolations, flesh that is clean is held unclean for common use. And so from things which are plain to us we come to see what is hidden and concealed. We have an example of this in the story of Mary the prophetess. Outwardly leprosy took possession of her body, because inwardly the leprosy of sin had already taken possession of her soul. Through the evil that was evident to all the sin within was revealed. By this most loathsome evil of leprosy we were taught how evil and detestable is this vice of envious ill-speaking of others. The body that is seen to be infected with leprosy is as it were a mirror of the unseen soul, whose blemish is thus revealed to us. From the corruption of the flesh we are shown how corrupt is the soul of the man who is evil-spoken and a detractor. Through her outward body she came to understand her own inward disposition. For as she had rebelled against her brother, so her own body rebelled against her; that from what had come upon herself, she might learn charity to others.

Let us also learn from this example to cherish true harmony and good will towards one another. For just as she grieved for what had happened to her body, God was grieved with her; because she had become worse than a stranger to her own brother. And so it is that because of his manifold sins, we oftentimes see a man's body afflicted and deformed by a variety of ills. Because he has allowed himself to become an enemy of God and of his neighbour, the members of his own body have become his enemies, so that he may learn from the disorder of his body to seek peace and harmony with others.

And it was noised throughout the whole camp that Mary had been of a sudden stricken with leprosy, because she had sharpened her tongue against her brother, *a man exceeding meek above all men* (Num. xii. 3); who then besought the Lord to heal her. And so, because of her unbridled tongue, the Just Avenger took away the merits of the prophetess. For the whispering and evil speaking in which foolish men delight is abominable to Him. And though He had glorified Moses by many signs and wonders, yet for having sinned by a slight fault of the tongue He shut him out from the Land of Promise. The great and fearful sea could not bar his way, but one word impatiently spoken stood like a wall in his path, and beyond it he could not pass.

If Moses, who was a God to Pharaoh (Ex. vii. 1), was shut out from the Land of Promise because of one word, how much more will not the evil speech of our tongue, by which we offend and hurt both God and man, shut us out from heaven? A holy fire destroyed the just priests, who, since they were to handle holy things, were holy in all their acts and offices, but defiled in their words (Lev. x). If these men suffered such punishments, shall our tongues regard this vice as of little importance? So let us make an end of reviling our neighbour with abuse and evil speaking. And then after this event the earth opened its mouth and swallowed those who had spoken evil; though it left the impure and the impious untouched

(Num. xvi. 30). The sea swallowed the Egyptians, but the earth swallowed the authors of discord, the evil-tongued, the whisperers. The leader of the army, in a time of famine, spoke in mockery against God (IV Kings vii), and because of this suffered the punishment he had earned: for he was trodden to death under the feet of the people at the gate of the city. And in this swift and sudden judgement the future is laid bare to you, according to the word of the Saviour, when he said that for every idle word we speak we shall render an account on the day of judgement.

The enemy therefore attacks the unhappy race of men with the manifold snares of occasions of sin. For some are held fast by an enemy spirit, as though oppressed. Others are led away like bondslaves. By nature and daily experience we are taught that some are lost because of or on account of others; and that they who owe nothing to anyone are nevertheless caught as debtors. And so in one way or another the debts of the just and unjust alike are brought to light. For in what relates to his own actions a man may be without fault; but in what concerns others he is found guilty. For if in his presence some one should belittle the truth, or attack some just man with unjust accusations, and he keeps silent; shall not his very silence be imputed to him as a crime? For listening to such a man, and not rebuking him, will he not appear to confirm as true the evil words of the speaker? The same can be said with regard to the authority of princes and rulers. For should someone, and even with good reason, attack a king who is doing wrong, those who are present will refuse to listen to what is said against the king. But should anyone continue to remain and give ear to what is being said, he is liable to a twofold punishment: because of the offensive words spoken against the king, and also for listening to them.

A detractor makes known something to you, and you give ear to him, and the harm he is eager to inflict with his tongue, you receive in secret into your ears; you mingle his bitter leaven with your own soul. From where did death arise if not from the ears of Eve, who when the serpent began to speak gave ready ear to him? For the evil demon is able, by the mouth of someone speaking, to slay even the one who keeps silent; and he whom he cannot destroy through his own words, he slays through his hearing. Those he sees innocent in their words, he slays in their thoughts. Our Saviour commanded the demons, who were confessing to the Truth, to keep silent. For He Who was Truth Itself desired no testimony from their eager words; but willed the things that are true to be made known by His own true preachers. And why did the Apostles refuse to listen to the demons who praised them (Acts xvi)? Was it not lest their own clean and just ears should be defiled by those unclean voices? If these just men shunned the praise of demons, as wholly tainted, who can give ear to those who speak evil of others? The subtle enemy is wont, by the appearance of truth, to deceive whoever permits him. And because of this the Saviour did not wish to hear from the demons even what was true.

The same rain moistens the sweet grass and the baneful, for the nature of the water is good in either case; and yet the good water contributes to the evil effect of the poisonous grass. The serpent as it feeds is mild and gentle, and yet of a sudden it changes to swift fury and then woe to the one it strikes. And so a lie, like deadly poison, is fashioned out of truth: for under the sweetness of the words lies hidden a deadly bitterness. To deceive the simple, the ancient serpent made use of a sweet tongue. You have an instance in Judas Iscariot, who hid his treachery under the friend's kiss of greeting, pretending peace while he wrought the betrayal of the Lord Who is the Searcher of the hearts of men. And if such deceit was used against the Creator Himself, what will the devil not use against you? O foolish of heart, who is more accursed than a liar than he who without cause gives ear to words? Of His own will the Saviour offered Himself to death, and gave no ear to those who received false testimony. Opening his mouth He tasted the vinegar mingled with gall. He Who had closed his ears to the words of the wicked one. He offered His mouth to the kiss of the traitor, but gave no answer to the deceiver. So may you offer your mouth to the kiss of those who speak evil, but never your ears. For if you offer your mouth to them, their kiss will condemn them. If you offer your ears, the taste of their words will slay you. It would be better to avoid both the taste and the smell of their poison. Why do you turn away from smoke, from steam, yet listen to a liar with eagerness and delight? You turn with aversion from an evil odour, yet you will sit in company with one speaking evil of others! Rightly should you guard

each member of your body from
what is harmful to it. If your body is
a stranger to lust, shield your tongue
from slandering. He who will not
give his body to lust, will yet with
his mouth lie and calumniate and
revile. One of your members is
weak, the others strong; but when
one member is troubled, the whole
body is troubled. Consider the soldier. Is not the soldier's whole body
protected by armour? Yet it will
happen that he is wounded through
an incautious disposition; for the
least chink in his armour may open
the way for a thrust, and bring swift
death to the soldier. How much
readier do we give death entry to
the soul through the openings of our
ears? Wide open are the windows of
the ears; through them death entered the world, and devoured all
nations, and still it remains unsated.
Close up your ears with bolts and
bars, that detraction and evil speaking may not enter through them.
Never look upon the sin of detraction as a venial one, or think it has
not power to kill the soul. Learn
from the birdtraps. They seem to be
trifling things, but they are not to be
despised. For it happens that a bird,
falling into a trap, will not be rent by
claws, nor its wings broken and
weakened by some cruel talon; yet,
though its body is untouched by the
trap, it remains wholly a captive.

The divine Apostle has declared
to us that one and the same is the
judgement that is decreed for murderers, for slanderers, for the wanton, and for adulterers. *None of these,
he says, shall possess the kingdom of
heaven* (I Cor. vi. 10). And equally
shall all these in the time of judgement be deprived of their eternal
inheritance. But that you may

understand that the punishment remains the same for all, ask yourself,
for what reason did Chanaan suffer
an eternal curse? Was it not because
he made a mockery of a just man?
It was not for some crime he was
condemned; it was because of his
mockery he incurred this fearful sentence, it was because of the wantonness of his tongue he suffered this
bitter chastisement. His thoughts
were harmless, but his tongue destroyed him. If he for a little mockery
suffered such punishment, who
should not be fearful, and shun the
mockery and derision from which
such execration and cursing has
come? For that just man Noah,
shutting Chanaan out from his blessing, delivered him to malediction,
and made known in him the judgement they were to suffer who delight
in mockery and derision. Just as the
man who, on the pretext of friendship, puts on an appearance of good
will brands himself as a liar and a
deceiver, so Chanaan, while pretending merriment, and amusing
others, prepares a curse for himself.

Listen to the most wise Solomon
explaining the evil, the punishments
that lie concealed in mockery and
derision. *He that mocks at man, reproaches his Maker* (Prov. xiv. 31;
xvii. 5 Sept.). For the mockery of a
man redounds against his Creator.
You observe someone who seems to
laugh openly. But what deceit, what
guile is hidden there you know not.
But the just Noah saw through the
deceit and, leaving the ignorant
Chanaan in his deceit, shut him out
from blessing; that from this, learning the evil of his laughter, he might
cease from laughing at his brother.

Semei taught us the evil of speaking against the innocent king (II

Kings xvi. 5 *et seq*.). And the Apostle has also uttered a fearful sentence against those who speak abusively to others (I Cor. v. 11). Let us consider what those who are given to evil speaking bring upon themselves. Semei brought destruction upon himself (III Kings ii, 8), not because of adultery, or for the sin of theft, but because he made use of evil words that contained false accusations; by means of which things done were made known and things not done were fabricated. For a mind that is goaded by affliction will pour out every kind of evil speech, and because of this the troubled mind of Semei wickedly abused the blameless David, accusing him of the death of Saul, when in fact he had frequently delivered Saul from death. And because he had unjustly accused the King of a grave crime, he was himself condemned by a just judge. Afterwards Solomon imposed certain bounds upon him, which he was not to cross, and which he promised to observe. But later the calumniator crossed them, so that his promise became a lie. And through a lie the calumniator, who had branded a just man with an unjust accusation, suffered the just punishment of his crime: the one who had turned the sharp edge of his tongue against an innocent man. and had sought to slay him as with a sword, in due time suffered the sharp edge of the sword and brought death upon himself in this world and put himself in danger of eternal punishment in the next.

Who will not turn in dread from evil speaking, for fear of bringing upon himself this twofold chastisement? And the Apostle condemns to the same punishment the effemin-

ate, adulterers, and those who speak evil. Esau forfeited his birthright through want of moderation. You also have a birthright. Beware lest you lose it, either through wantonness or through lack of moderation. That great man lost his; not because of great evils, but robbed himself for a trifle. Should you lose the Truth you yield to folly as Esau did. Take note of something truly significant: how words have superseded facts, and faith has been placed above the order and nature of generation. The gift of primogeniture, which it would seem could not be set aside, was taken away at a word; and what Esau held as a right of nature, Jacob won by the striving of faith. Faith and an oath together reveal they have the power of generation; and birthrights that were given up through the flesh are inherited through the spirit; and what an oath cast away, faith receives. O wondrous happening! that came to pass between the seller of his birthright and the buyer of the same. For he who deprived himself of it seems to have been destitute of understanding, and he who clothed himself in it continued blameless.

But how did Esau put off his birthright, which cannot be put aside? How did Jacob clothe himself with that which cannot be put on? And if this bartering between these young men is so above the order of nature that it cannot be adequately explained, who will dare to begin upon that question wherein is the ineffable mystery of the generation of the Son of God? But tell me: Why did Jacob, taking from Manasses the right of the firstborn, bestow it on Ephraim? (Gen. xlviii). Was it not that great dignity and honour might be given to Ephraim? For the right of the firstborn is full of wondrous portents, and of many and extraordinary offices. Baptism is prefigured there. And faith is signed and sealed within it. In it our source of strength is indicated. In it the glorious figure of virginity is brought before the mind. This honour Jacob bought for a price; and gave it freely to Ephraim (Gen. xxv; xlviii). And in this Manasses is not to be blamed, nor Ephraim praised; we must acknowledge rather the authority of the Giver, Who remains blameless.

Who then shall presume to criticize the birthright of the Gentiles? And should the Jews attempt this, let them remember that it had been taken away from Manasses. For He Who, to show His authority, took it away from him did not sin. God took it from them, because they had sinned; that by this He might make known His Judgement is just. And if Jacob is without blame, although he took away the rights of the firstborn from Manasses who had not sinned, who will dare to reproach Him Who as Just Judge has taken it away from the Jews who have slain the Lord? If such was the power of an oath that it could take away his birthright from Esau – when he simply swore an oath, and had no thought of perjury – to what punishment will they not be given who not alone bind themselves by oath, but violate their oath by perjury? If Esau did not will to withdraw from the pledges he had made, to his own great loss, how can you dare to break the pledges you have given for your own salvation? If Herod fulfilled the promise he had made to his own destruction (Mk. vi), will you not hold to the pledges you have made

for the sake of life eternal? And as insinuating speech took away the gift of the firstborn, so *reviling*, entering stealthily into the course of your life, can stain it with blood. For the tongue can wound no less than the sword. And the shameless word and thought can stain as adultery will. The veiled deceit lays a snare as surely as a trap. And evil counsel is as dangerous as poison to those who take it. For if Esau by his word alone stripped himself of his birthright, and lost it, how much more easily and more abundantly will not an unprofitable servant lose his soul? Even by delighting in deception, or by seeking things by deceitful means? He who disregards the reality of what he has promised, denying credibility to his own words, clothes himself with darkness, and deprives himself of the things that are for his salvation; while, on the contrary, by keeping faith with his own words, a man clothes himself with honour.

Speech when put to use has of itself the effect of a deed; and wicked deliberation is condemned no less than an evil deed. An unlawful look convicts as will an evil deed. Anger slays equally with the sword. Savage envy wounds as cruelly as a spear. And a false accusation will prepare a pit of destruction. Let us fly evil thoughts. For things dwelt on in thought are judged in the same way as deeds. Let us give our minds to worthy thoughts, for which as for good works a reward is laid up with Him Who searcheth *the counsels of the heart* (Is. lxvi. 18; I Cor. iv. 5). For a thought is as it were the likeness of a deed, and from it, as from the effective cause of all our deeds, depends the character of our deliberate act. Each thing has its contrary.

Light is contrary to darkness, sweetness to bitterness, waking to sleep. He Who made all things made nothing to which He did not join a contrary. And if man by his own devising reconciles contraries: after toil he takes rest, and where he can seeks remedies and medicines from both sea and land, to have at hand for every bodily sickness as need arises; how much more shall He, the Immortal Creator of all things, not dispose all things in order, so that there shall be at hand for all men that by which each may defend himself from our common enemy?

You have then been taught the use of these arms, O man, against whatever enemy or adversary opposes you. Should you neglect the things that are given you for your salvation, and you are overcome, for you in the Day of Judgement there shall be no excuse. Against the artifices of the enemy you have at hand a variety of arms. Should the enemy throw his fiery darts against us, have we not the impregnable shield of prayer? Should he wage within us a war of lustful desires, let us join to us against him, as comrade in arms, the love of our soul. Should he seek to lead us captive through iniquity, let us seek salvation by flying towards justice. Should he strive to wound through hate and malice, let you run towards fraternal charity. Should he attack you through arrogance and pride, oppose him with humility. Should he incite against you the concupiscences of the flesh, arm yourself swiftly with the breastplate of continence. If he shoots against you the darts of wantonness, put on against him the helmet of chastity. Should he seek to mislead us through the desire of riches, let us keep before

us the blessedness of poverty. Should he assail us with the vice of gluttony, let us take to ourselves the wings of fasting. And since envy is a source of ruin, there is charity at hand, if we wish it, which can correct and strengthen us.

As the enemy has arms to attack us, so have we arms for our defence. And should he like Pharaoh pursue us, we have a sea in which he shall drown (Ps. cxxxv. 15). If there is one who weaves snares for us on earth, in heaven there is One Who will deliver us. If he mocks at us as Goliath mocked, there is One Who like David will humble him (I Kings xvii). Should he be as swollen and uplifted as Sisara, he shall by the Church be utterly destroyed (Jgs. iv). Should he war against us like Sennacherib (the tyrant of Babylon) he can be overcome by sackcloth and ashes. Should he imitate the tyrant of Babylon, there shall not be wanting holy and just men such as was Daniel. Should he be as proud as Naaman, there shall be those who through fasting shall cast him down. Should he enkindle the flames of lust, there shall be those who will imitate the chaste Joseph. Which of his artifices is there we cannot defeat? What are the sicknesses, the ills, for which remedies are not prepared? What is there that is falsified and spurious for which we have not a furnace ready to prove it false? What snares has he ever laid for us, that have not been uncovered? What artifice has he ever set up which even foolish men cannot upset? What forces can he employ, that even a woman cannot defeat? What flames can he provoke that steadfast children cannot extinguish? He dug a pit, but Daniel despised it (Dan.

iii). The enemy sowed pride, but the humility of Moses trod it down. Naaman flattered Eliseus with gold, but the prophet despised and rejected it. Simon Magus offered the Apostles money, but Peter pro-

nounced upon him the sentence he deserved: *Keep thy money, to perish with thee* (Acts viii). In Christ Jesus our Lord, to Whom be glory and honour, now and for ever, world without end. Amen.

IV. St Gregory, Pope and Doctor
Hearing the Word of God[6]

Son of man, receive in thy heart and hear with thy ears all the words that I speak to thee (Ezechiel iii. 10).

1. There are those who when they read the sacred pages of the Divine Word, and have reached into its sublimer meanings, are disposed through a certain presumption of mind to disregard its simpler messages, as though given for those of simpler understanding, and are even inclined to change their meaning into something wholly different. Such men, if they rightly understood the sublimer things contained in the divine pages, would be far from neglecting its simpler messages; for the divine teaching speaks of certain great truths in a manner suited even to the minds of some children, who by steps of the mind as it were, grow in discernment, and come to an understanding of the loftier truths. For this reason the Lord here said to the holy prophet (regarding the divine book): *Son of man, eat all that thou shalt find.*

2. For whatever is found in Sacred Scripture is to be eaten; even its least words bring calm and order to simple men, and its higher teachings instruct the minds of the more discerning. Then the Lord goes on: *Eat this book and go speak to the children of Israel. And I opened my mouth, and he caused me to eat that book* (Ez. lii. 1, 2).

3. For the Sacred Scripture is our food and drink. And, because it is, the Lord warned us again through another prophet, saying: *I will send forth a famine into the land: not a famine of bread, nor a thirst of water, but of hearing the word of the Lord* (Amos viii. 11). We therefore, who have been deprived of His sacred word, have, He says, become weak from hunger and thirst, because, as He shows us, His words are our food and drink. Note how at times His words are called our food and at times our drink. For in the deeper truths, those that cannot be grasped unless they are explained to us, the Sacred Scripture is our food. For whatever needs to be explained that we may assimilate it, must be as it were masticated before we can swallow it. In truths that are clearer to us, His words are our drink. For we swallow a drink without need to chew it. . . . And so we drink in the more evident truths: for even when they are not explained to us, we are able to understand them. And since Ezechiel was to hear many divine truths that were obscure and difficult to grasp, the Lord did not say to him concerning the first volume: Drink; but, *Eat*. As though the Lord were to say in simple terms: First masticate this, and then swallow it; that is, study it well, and then understand it. And this is the way we should study

the divine words, so that we may know them, in that repenting of our iniquity, and knowing now the evil of the sins we have committed, we shall avoid committing them again.

4. And when after many tears we have come to have confidence in the forgiveness of our sins, let us draw others also towards the true life by means of these words we now have come to understand. For it is for this reason we must understand them: that they may be a means of help to ourselves, and that they may, by our spiritual effort, be also bestowed on others. So rightly does He here say: *Eat this book and go speak to the children of Israel.* As though He said to him concerning this sacred food: Eat, and be fed: be filled, and give forth; receive my word, and spread it among others; be strengthened, and labour:

5. And let us note what the prophet goes on to say: *And I opened my mouth, and he caused me to eat that book.* Another prophet testifies that the mouth means the heart, saying: *With deceitful lips and with a double heart have they spoken* (Ps. xi. 3). We therefore open our mouths when we prepare our minds to understand His Sacred Word. And so at the voice of the Lord the prophet opens his mouth; for the heart longs for the bread of the Lord's Teaching, that we may taste something of the food of Life. But even this is not within our power, unless He feeds us Who has commanded us to eat. For he is given food, who of himself is unable to eat. And since our human infirmity is unable to grasp heavenly words, He feeds us Who *in due season gives us our measure of wheat*

(Lk. xii. 42), in that while today we understand in the Sacred Word what yesterday we could not, and when tomorrow likewise we understand what today we cannot grasp, we are through the grace of divine providence being nourished with daily bread. For as often as Almighty God opens our understanding and places in our minds the food of His sacred words, so often does He stretch forth His hand to the mouth of our heart. He therefore gives us to eat of the *book*, when He opens our understanding by giving us to understand the meaning of Sacred Scripture, and when He fills our thoughts with its sweetness. And so He goes on:

V.3. And he said to me: Son of man, thy belly shall eat, and thy bowels shall be filled with this book which I give thee. And I did eat it: and it was as sweet as honey in my mouth.

Hear the Words of the Lord.

V.10. And he said to me: Son of man, receive in thy heart and hear with thy ears all the words that I speak to thee.

Let us carefully note that the prophet is told by the voice of the Lord, first to listen to His words, and afterwards speak them. For we shall hear God's words when we do this. And when we have first done this, then shall we safely speak them to our neighbours. And this the Evangelist Mark rightly confirms, telling us of a miracle the Lord wrought, saying: *And they bring to him one deaf and dumb; and they besought him that he would lay his hand upon him* (Mk. vii. 31). And he describes to us the order in which He cured him. *He put his fingers in his ears: and spit-*

*ting, he touched his tongue, And, look-
ing up to heaven, he groaned and said to
him: Ephpheta, which is, Be thou
opened. And immediately his ears were
opened, and the string of his tongue was
loosed and he spoke right.*

What does it mean that God the
Creator of all things, when He
willed to heal the man who was deaf
and dumb, put His fingers in the
man's ears, and, spitting, touched his
tongue? What is signified by the
Fingers of the Redeemer, if not the
gifts of the Holy Ghost? And this is
the reason why He said in another
place, when He had cast out a devil:
*If I by the finger of God cast out devils,
doubtless the kingdom of God is come
upon you* (Lk. xi. 20). And it is
recorded by another evangelist that
He said: *If I by the spirit of God cast
out devils, then is the kingdom of God
come upon you* (Mt. xii. 28). So from
either place we gather that the Spirit
is called the Finger of God. Therefore, to put His Fingers in the man's
ears, is to open the soul of the deaf
man to faith through the gifts of the
Holy Ghost.

And what does it mean that, spitting, He touched his tongue? For us
the saliva from the Redeemer's
mouth means the wisdom contained
in the divine word. For saliva flows
from the head into the mouth. So
when our tongue is touched by that
wisdom which He is, it is thereupon

made ready to preach His words.
And looking up to heaven, he groaned;
not that He had need to groan Who
Himself granted what (as man) He
prayed for, but to teach us to groan
to Him Who rules in heaven, that
our ears also may be opened by the
gifts of His Holy Spirit, and our
tongue loosed by the saliva of His
Mouth, that is, by the knowledge of
His divine words, so that we shall
proclaim them.

And then He said to the man:
*Ephpheta, which is, Be thou opened;
and immediately his ears were opened,
and the string of his tongue was loosed.*
And let us here note, that it was because of closed ears it was said: *Be
thou opened.* And to him the ears of
whose heart are opened to faith,
there will without doubt also follow
that the string of his tongue shall be
loosened; so that he may speak to
others, and encourage them so that
they also may do the good he himself has done. And here, fittingly,
was added: *And he spoke right.* For he
speaks right who first obeying God,
does what he tells others they must
do. Therefore, in all that our mind
dwells on, in all that we do, let us
pray that we shall at all times meditate according to His inspiration, and
act by His aid, Who lives and reigns
with the Father, in the Unity of the
Holy Ghost, world without end.
Amen.

NOTES

[1] PG 40, col. 965, *Sectio decima* of
'The Twenty Sermons of our Father
the Holy Anthony, Abbot, to his
sons who were monks': *That we
must be greatly on our guard against our
own tongue.*

[2] St Ambrose, on the Sacraments
Book 1, CSEL 73.

[3] In Western liturgies, before conferring the actual baptism, usually on
Saturdays, the priest, following the
example of the Lord (Mk. vii. 34),

moistens with saliva the ears and nostrils of the catechumen, saying, *Ephpheta, which is, be thou opened.* In the very first ages a simple sign (blessing) was made on these senses.

4 St Ephraim, Vossio, vol. 1, Sermon 43: *De Morbo Linguae, Aliisque Vitiis.*

5 Mary, the sister of Moses, and a prophetess, was stricken with leprosy because of her evil words, and her plotting against the authority of her brother, Numbers xii.

6 PL 76. Hom. 10 in Ezechiel 1, col. 886, pars. 1–5; Ezechiel iii. 10. Passages related to the Gospel extracted to elucidate some of its deeper meanings.

TWELFTH SUNDAY AFTER PENTECOST

THE GOSPEL OF THE SUNDAY

I

LUKE X. 23–37

At that time: Jesus said to his disciples: Blessed are the eyes that see the things which you see. For I say to you, that many prophets and kings have desired to see the things that you see, and have not seen them; and to hear the things that you hear, and have not heard them. And behold a certain lawyer stood up tempting him and saying; Master what must I do to possess eternal life? But he said to him: What is written in the Law? how readest thou? He answering said: *Thou shalt love the Lord thy God with thy whole heart and with thy whole soul and with all thy strength and with all thy mind; and thy neighbour as thy self.* And he said to him: Thou hast answered right. This do; and thou shalt live.

But he, willing to justify himself, said to Jesus: And who is my neighbour? And Jesus, answering said: A certain man went down from Jerusalem to Jericho and fell among robbers, who also stripped him and having wounded him went away, leaving him half dead. And it chanced that a certain priest went down the same way; and seeing him passed by. In like manner also a Levite when he was near the place and saw him, passed by. But a certain Samaritan, being on his journey, came near him; and seeing him was moved to pity. And, going up to him, bound up his wounds, pouring in oil and wine; and, setting him upon his own beast, brought him to an inn and took care of him. And the next day he took out two pence and gave to the host and said: Take care of him; and whatsoever thou shalt spend over and above, I, at my return, will repay thee. Which of these three, in thy opinion, was neighbour to him that fell among the robbers? But he said: He that showed mercy to him. And Jesus said to him: Go, and do thou in like manner.

22

EXPOSITION FROM THE CATENA AUREA

THEOPHYLACTUS: As a little before He had said: *No one knoweth who the Father is, but the Son, and to whom the Son will reveal him.* He calls His Disciples blessed, to whom, through Him, the Father was now being revealed. Hence we are told:

V.23. And turning to his disciples he said: *Blessed are the eyes that see the things which you see.*

CYRIL: He turns to them, for, rejecting the Jews as deaf and blind of mind, and unwilling to see, He offers Himself wholly to those who love Him; and declares that *blessed* are the eyes which were then seeing, before any others, the things they were beginning to see. This however we must know, that this seeing does not refer to the act of the eyes, but to the renewal of the soul through the favours bestowed; as if some one were to say: Such a man has seen good days, that is, he has rejoiced in good days, as in the psalm: *Mayest thou see the good things of Jerusalem* (Ps. cxxvii. 5). For many of the Jews had, with the eyes of the body, seen Christ performing divine works. Yet this did not bring blessedness to all of them: for they did not believe; and neither did they see the glory of God with the eyes of the soul. Our eyes therefore are declared *blessed* in this, that through faith we have seen the Word, for us made Man, signing us with the grace of His Godhead, that He may make us like to Himself through sanctity and justice.

THEOPHYLACTUS: He declares them *blessed*, and with them all who without guile look upon Him with eyes of faith; because the prophets and kings of old had longed for this: to see and hear God in the flesh; as follows:

V.24. *For I say to you, that many prophets and kings have desired to see the things that you see and have not seen them; and to hear the things that you hear and have not heard them.*

BEDE: Matthew, more explicitly, calls them *prophets and just men* (Mt. xiii. 17). For they are great kings; who knew how to rule, by dominating the impulses that tempted them, not consenting to them.

CHRYSOSTOM, *in John, hom.* 8: From this saying many think that the prophets were without knowledge of Christ. But if they longed to see what the Apostles saw, they knew He was to come among men, and that He would do what He did. For no one hungers for the things his mind is unaware of. They had therefore known of the Son of God. So He does not simply say: *They desired to see Me,* but, *the things which you see;* not, *to hear Me,* but, *to hear the things that you hear.* For they had seen Him, though not yet Incarnate, not living in this manner among men, nor speaking to them with such majesty.

BEDE: For they, looking from afar off, saw Him, *through a glass, in a dark manner.* But the Apostles, having the Lord in their midst, and learning, through questioning Him, whatever they wished to know, had no need to be taught through Angels or through any other kind of vision.

ORIGEN, *in Canticles, Catena GP*: But why does He say that *many* prophets desired this, and not all of them? Because it was said of Abraham, that *he saw* the day of Christ, *and was glad* (Jn. viii. 56); and this vision was given, not to many, but rather to a few. But there were other prophets and just men, not of such greatness as to attain to the vision of Abraham and to the immediate knowledge of the Apostles. And it is of these He says that they *have not seen* but that they *desired* to see.

2

V.25. *And behold, a certain lawyer stood up, tempting him.* . . .

BEDE: A little before this the Lord had said to them (v.20) that their names were *written in heaven*; and it was from this, as I think, the lawyer took occasion to tempt the Lord. *And, behold, a certain lawyer* . . . CYRIL: There were certain wordy persons going about through the whole country of the Jews, attacking Christ and saying, that He had said that the law of Moses was useless, and that He Himself had brought forward certain new teachings. The lawyer therefore, seeking to mislead Christ, so that he might say something against Moses, stood by Him, *tempting Him*, calling Him *Master*; yet not enduring to be taught by Him. And because the Lord was accustomed to speak of eternal life to those who came to Him, the lawyer makes use of this. And making this attempt with guile, he hears nothing in reply except what the commandments of Moses laid down. For there follows:

V.26. *But he said to him: What is written in the law? How readest thou?*

AMBROSE: He was one of those who believed themselves to be experts in the law; who knew its words, but ignored its obligations. And from this very chapter of the law He shows that they are ignorant of the law; proving to them that from the beginning the law proclaimed both the Father and the Son and made known the mystery of the Lord's Incarnation. For there follows:

V.27. *He answering said: Thou shalt love the Lord thy God with thy whole heart and with thy whole soul and with all thy strength and with all thy mind.*

BASIL, *in Catena GP*: That He says: *with all thy mind*, excludes sharing the love of the mind with other things. For whatever love you spend upon lower things, this you must necessarily take from the whole. For when some water is poured out from a full vessel, so much of necessity is taken from its fulness. So likewise in the soul, whatever love it gives to unlawful things, by so much must its love for God be lessened.

GREGORY NYSSA, *On Creation of Man*, 8: The power of the soul is seen in three certain things. One is the power of growth and of self nourishment; which is the sole power in plants. Another is that of sensitivity, by which the nature of irrational creatures is protected. But the perfect power of the soul is the rational power, manifested in human nature. Therefore, in saying the *heart*, He meant the bodily power, that is, the nutritive; in saying the *soul*, He refers to the middle or sensitive power; in saying the *mind*, He refers to the higher nature, that is, to the intellectual and reflective power.

THEOPHYLACTUS: Here then we are to understand, that every power of the soul is to be subjected to the divine love; and this strongly, not indifferently. On this account there is added: *and with all thy strength.*

MAXIMUS, *Catena GP*: With this in mind the law imposes on us a three-fold love of God, and for this end: To root out from us our threefold attachment to the world, which looks to possessions, to glory, and to pleasure; in which Christ also was tempted.

BASIL: Should some one ask: How can the divine love be obtained? we answer, that the divine love is not something that can be taught: neither did we learn from another how to enjoy the sunlight, or how to hold fast to life, or how to love our parents and those who rear us, nor, and how much more, to love God. But implanted within us is a certain as it were seed of the mind, which has within it the causes why man adheres to God. And the science of the divine commands receiving in trust this inward power of the soul, devotes itself to its loving cultiva-tion, carefully fostering it, to lead it to the perfection of divine grace.

For we love naturally what is good, and we love our own and those related to us, and we freely pour out our affection to those who do good to us. If therefore God is good, and if all things desire what is good, what is spontaneously done by us, is by nature present in us. And even though we are far from knowing Him through His Goodness, never-

theless, from this that we come from Him, we are bound to love Him beyond measure, that is, as our kin-dred. He is also a greater good to us than all whom we naturally love.

The first and chief commandment therefore is that of the love of God. The second completes the first, and is by it made perfect; that in which we are taught to love our neigh-bour. So we have: *And thy neighbour as thyself.* The aptitude to fulfil this commandment comes to us from God. Who does not know that man is a kind and social being, not wild and solitary? For nothing is so natural to us as to speak with one another, to seek each other's com-pany, to love our kindred. Since He in His Providence gives us the seeds of these things, He therefore re-quires of us the fruits of them.

CHRYSOSTOM, *hom.* 32 *in I Cor.*: Ob-serve how either precept requires of us the same overflowing fulfilment. For of God it says: *With thy whole heart*; of our neighbour: *As thy self.* And were this lovingly fulfilled, there would be neither slave nor free, victor nor vanquished, rich nor poor, nor would the devil have ever been known; for chaff would endure fire better, than the devil the flame of charity. So does the con-stancy of love overcome all things?

GREGORY, *Morals*, 19, 20: And since we are told: *Love thy neighbour as thyself,* how is anyone merciful, hav-ing compassion on another, who continuing to live wickedly has no compassion on himself? CYRIL, *Catena GP*: But when the lawyer had answered what was contained in the law, Christ, to whom all things are known, cuts through the net of his deceit. For there then follows:

V.28. *And he said to him: Thou hast answered right. This do; and thou shalt live.*

ORIGEN: From these things we may beyond doubt gather, that the *life* which is foretold by God the Creator of the World, and by the Scriptures handed down to us by Him of old, is life everlasting. For the Lord bears witness to this, taking these words from Deuteronomy, *Thou shalt love the Lord thy God* (vi. 5); and those from Leviticus, *Thou shalt love thy neighbour as thyself* (xix. 18). These words were also spoken against the followers of Valentine, of Basilides, and of Marcion.[1] For what else did He will that we should do in seeking eternal life, but what is contained in the law and the prophets.

3

V.29. *But he, willing to justify himself, said to Jesus: And who is my neighbour?*

CYRIL: The lawyer, praised by the Saviour for answering correctly, breaks out in pride; imagining that no one can be his neighbour, as though no one could be compared to him in virtue. And so we read: *He, willing to justify himself, said to Jesus: And who is my neighbour?* One sin after another encloses him as it were. For from the deceit by which he had tried to trip Christ, he falls into pride. Asking here, *who is my neighbour,* he is revealed to us as empty of the love of his neighbour, since he does not consider anyone as his neighbour; and consequently he is also empty of the love of God:

For he that loveth not his brother, whom he seeth, how can he love God whom he seeth not? (I Jn. iv. 20).

AMBROSE: He also said he did not know his neighbour, since he did not believe in Christ; and he who does not know Christ, does not know the law. Since he did not know the Truth, how could he know the law, which proclaims the Truth?

THEOPHYLACTUS: The Saviour however makes known to us who is our neighbour, not through his office or dignity, but through his nature; as though to say: Do not think that because you are just, no one is your neighbour. For all who share with you the same nature are your neighbours. Be you then a neighbour to them; not because of place, but from love, and out of concern for them. And to show us this He brings before us the example of the Samaritan. So there follows:

V.30. *And Jesus, answering, said: A certain man went down from Jerusalem to Jericho.*

GREEK (*or Severus Antioch in Catena GP*): Well did he use the name of our race. For He does not say: 'A certain one went down,' but, *A certain man.* For His words concerned all mankind. AUGUSTINE, *Questions on the Gospels,* II, 19: This man represents Adam, and stands for the human race. Jerusalem is that heavenly city of peace from whose happiness he has fallen. Jericho signifies the moon, and stands for our mortality; because it is born, increases, grows old and dies.

AUGUSTINE, *Against Pelagians,* III: Or we call Paradise Jerusalem; which is interpreted to mean, 'the vision of peace'. For man, before he sinned, dwelt in a vision of peace; that is, in Paradise, where, wherever he looked, there was peace and joy. From there, as it were humiliated, *he came down,* made wretched through sin, *to Jericho,* that is, to the world, in which, like the moon, all that rises dies.[2]

THEOPHYLACTUS. But He did not say *went down (descendit),* but that he *was going down (descendebat).* For human nature ever tends towards lower things; and during, not a part, but the whole of life seeks what is fleeting.

BASIL, *Catena GP.* This is also in keeping with the places, if you consider them. For Jericho lies in the deep valley of Palestine; while Jerusalem is seated on a height, occupying the summit of a mountain. Man therefore comes from the heights to the depths, so that he is caught by the robbers who are wont to dwell in the wilderness. Hence: *And fell among robbers.*

CHRYSOSTOM, *Catena GP:* First, we must feel pity for the misfortune of this man, who, alone and unarmed, fell among robbers, and who, unforeseeing and unwary, took the road on which he could not escape the hands of plunderers. For the unarmed cannot escape the armed, the unwary cannot escape the evil-disposed, the thoughtless those who plot injuries: for wickedness is ever armed with deceit, fortified with cruelty, and ready to attack with savagery.

AMBROSE: Who are these robbers but angels of the night, and of darkness, among whom he would not have fallen had he not, regardless of the divine commandment, exposed himself to them? CHRYSOSTOM, *as above*: The devil in the beginning of the world used treachery against man, to injure him; employing against him the poison of deceit, and devoting his malice to injuring him.

AUGUSTINE. *Against Pelagians,* as above: *He fell among robbers* therefore, that is, among the devil and his angels: who through the disobedience of the first man stripped human kind; that is, deprived them of the adornments of virtue, and wounded them, that is, injuring in them the power of free will. *Hence there follows: Who also stripped him and having wounded him went away.*

AUGUSTINE, *Questions on the Gospels,* II, 19: Or, they stripped man of immortality and, having wounded him, by persuading him to sin, left him half dead: for in the part of him which can know and understand God, man is alive; in the part however in which he has been weakened by sin, and overcome, he is dead. And this is the meaning of what follows: *Leaving him half dead.*

AUGUSTINE, *Against Pelagians,* as above: For one who is half dead is wounded in his vital activity, that is, in his free will; so that he is not able to return to the eternal life he has lost. And so he lay there; unable of his own powers to rise and seek a physician, God, to heal him.

THEOPHYLACTUS: Or, a man is said to be half dead after sin; for his soul is immortal, his body mortal; so that the half of man has succumbed to death. Or, because human nature hoped to obtain salvation in Christ; that it might not wholly succumb to death. In the measure that Adam sinned, *death entered the world* (Rom. v. 12). But in Christ's justice, death was to be destroyed.

AMBROSE: Or, they strip us of the garments of spiritual grace we received; and it is so they wound us. For if we preserve unspotted the garment of grace we put on, we cannot feel the blows of the robbers. BASIL: Or it may be understood that they first wounded him, and then stripped him. For the wounds precede the nakedness; that you may understand that sin precedes the loss of grace.

BEDE: Sins are called wounds, because by them the integrity of our nature is wounded. They *went away*; not ceasing however from their assaults, but concealing their snares by craft. CHRYSOSTOM, as above: This man therefore, that is, Adam, lay there destitute of the means of salvation, pierced by the wounds of his sins; whom neither Aaron the Priest, passing by, could help by his sacrifice; for we read:

V.31. *And it chanced that a certain priest . . . seeing him, passed by.*

Nor even his brother Moses, the Levite, could help by the law. So there follows:

V.32. *In like manner also a levite . . . saw him, and passed by.*

AUGUSTINE, *Against Pelagians*: Or, in the Priest and the Levite two different times are meant; namely, of the Law, and the Prophets. In the Priest,

the Law is signified; for which sacrifices and the priesthood were instituted. In the Levite, the voice of the Prophets; in whose times mankind could not be healed, because through the Law came the knowledge of sin, not its abolition (Rom. iii. 20).

THEOPHYLACTUS: But He says: *passed by*; for the Law came, and stood for its predestined time; then, unable to heal, went away. See also how by design the Law was not given to this end: to heal man. For man could not from the beginning receive the mystery of Christ; and so He says, *it chanced, that a certain priest*; a way we speak of things which happen without premeditation. AUGUSTINE, *Sermon 37*: Or, because the man going down from Jerusalem to Jericho is understood to have been an Israelite; it can be understood that the Priest passing by was his neighbour by race, yet *passed by*, leaving him lying there. And a Levite also *passed by*, likewise his neighbour by race to the man lying there, and he also ignored him.

THEOPHYLACTUS: They felt pity for him, I would say, when they became aware of him. But then, gripped by meanness, they went on their way. For this is indicated by the phrase, *passed by*.

AUGUSTINE, *as above*: A Samaritan passed by; remote from him by race, his neighbour by compassion. And he does what follows:

V.33. *But a certain Samaritan, being on his journey, came near him.*

Our Lord Jesus Christ willed that He Himself should be understood in this Samaritan. For Samaritan is interpreted to mean *guardian*; and is used of Himself: *Behold he shall neither slumber nor sleep that keepeth Israel*; for, *rising again from the dead, he dieth now no more* (Ps. cxx. 4; Rom. vi. 9). And to confirm this, when they said to Him: *Thou art a Samaritan, and hast a devil* (Jn. viii. 48), while denying He had a devil, for He knew Himself to be the banisher of devils, He did not deny He was the Guardian of the weak.

GREEK INTERPRETER (*or Severus of Antioch*) *in Catena GP*: Here Christ rightly speaks of Himself as a Samaritan. For when speaking to the lawyer who had prided himself in the Law, He willed to make clear that neither the Priest nor the Levite, in both of whom was presupposed a knowledge of the Law, had fulfilled the intention of the Law; whereas it was for this He had come: to fulfil the purpose of the Law.

AMBROSE: This Samaritan was also *going down.* For Who descends from heaven save only He Who ascends into heaven: The Son of man who is in heaven (Jn. iii. 13)? THEOPHYLAC-TUS: He says, *being on his journey*; as though inferring that he was making this journey on purpose: to cure us. AUGUSTINE, *Against Pelagians*, as above: He came in the likeness of sinful flesh, and so came as it were near him in appearance. GREEK, as above: Or, he was coming this road anyway; since he was a genuine traveller, not a wanderer, coming down to earth for our sake.

AMBROSE: And coming He became our closest neighbour, through compassion for us. And He came near us

by the gift of His mercy. So we have: *And seeing him was moved with compassion.* AUGUSTINE, as above: Seeing him lying there powerless, without movement, He was moved by compassion; for He found no merit in him which gave him the right to be healed. For the Lord himself, from (the likeness of) sin had *condemned sin in the flesh* (Rom. viii. 3); and accordingly we have:

V.34. *And, going up to him, bound up his wounds, pouring in oil and wine.*

AUGUSTINE, *Sermon* 37: What is there so distant, so remote, as God from man, the Immortal from mortals, the Just from sinners? Not remote in place, but remote in unlikeness. Since therefore He possessed in Himself two good things; namely, justice and immortality, and we two evil things: namely, iniquity and mortality, had He taken upon Him both our evils He would be as we are, and with us would have needed a redeemer. Therefore that He might not be what we were, but almost as we were, He was not a sinner like you, but became mortal like you; and taking upon Himself your punishment, but not assuming your guilt, He wiped out both guilt and punishment.

AUGUSTINE, *Questions on the Gospel,* II, 19: The binding up of the wounds is the correction of sin. *Oil* stands for the comfort of good hope, through the pardon given to restore us to peace. *Wine* stands for encouragement to work most fervently in the spirit.

AMBROSE: Or He binds up our wounds with His more austere commandments, and as He soothes us with the oil of forgiveness of sin, He rouses us as with wine by the threat of judgement.

GREGORY, *Morals* 20, 8 *in Job. xxix.* 25: Or, in the wine He suggests the sharpness of punishment; in the oil the mildness of love. With this wine let our corrupt parts be dressed; with the oil let the parts that are healing be soothed. Therefore let mildness be mingled with severity, and let there be a just measure of both the one and the other, so that those subject to us may neither be provoked by too great severity, nor weakened by too much mildness.

THEOPHYLACTUS: Or again: To speak with men is oil; with God, is wine, which signifies the Divinity: which no man can endure unless it is blended with oil, that is, with human association. So He has done some things as man, others as God. He therefore poured in oil and wine Who saved us both by His Humanity and His Divinity.

CHRYSOSTOM: Or, He poured in *wine,* that is, the Blood of His Passion, and the *oil* of His Anointing: that He might give us pardon through His Blood, and sanctify us through anointing with chrism. Our wounded parts are bound up by the heavenly Physician and, retaining His medicine within them, they are restored by its action to their former state of health. Then, having poured in both oil and wine, He sets him upon His own beast. So there follows: *And, setting him upon his own beast, brought him to an inn and took care of him.* AUGUSTINE, as above: His own *beast* is the Body in which He

deigned to come to us. To be placed upon His beast is to believe in the Incarnation of Christ.

AMBROSE: Or, He places us on His own beast when He bears our sins and suffers for us (Is. liii. 4). For man is become *like to a beast* (Ps. xlviii. 13). So He places us on His own beast, lest we *become like the horse and the mule* (Ps. xxxi. 9); so that by His assumption of our body He might take away the weakness of our flesh.

THEOPHYLACTUS: Or He placed him on His own beast, that is, upon His own Body: for He made us His own members, and the partakers of His Body. And the Law did not receive all: *The Ammonite and the Moabite shall not enter into the church of the Lord* (Deut. xxiii. 3). Now however he who in every nation fears the Lord is received by Him, if willing to believe, and to become a part of the Church. Because of this He says, that he *brought him to an inn.*

CHRYSOSTOM: The Church is the *inn* which in the journey of this world receives the weary and those that are overcome by the weight of their sins; where, casting aside the burthen of sin, the wearied traveller may rest, and rested is restored with healthful food. And this is what is meant by, *and took care of him.* Outside this inn is all that is evil and destructive; within is contained all peace and healthfulness.

BEDE: And well does He bring him to an inn whom He placed on His own beast: for no one shall enter the Church unless through baptism he is united to the Body of Christ.

AMBROSE: And because it served no purpose for this Samaritan to remain long on earth, He had to return whence He had descended. Hence there follows:

V.35. And the next day He took out two pence and gave to the host and said: Take care of him.

What is this *next day*, if not perhaps that of our Lord's Resurrection, of which it was said: *This is the day which the Lord hath made* (Ps. cvvii. 24)? The two pence are the two Testaments; upon which is impressed the Image of the Eternal King, by Whose price our wounds are healed. AUGUSTINE, as above: Or the two denarii are the two precepts of charity, which the Apostles received through the Holy Ghost to preach to others. Or the promise of life in the present and in the future.

ORIGEN: Or, the two denarii seem to me to be the knowledge of the mystery of how the Father is in the Son and the Son is in the Father, with which as payment the Angel endowed the Church, that she may lovingly care for the man entrusted to her, whom, as his suffering at the time demanded, He had also cared for. And he is promised that whatever of his own he shall spend on the healing of the half dead man, shall there be restored to him. So there follows: *And whatsoever thou shalt spend over and above, I, at my return, will repay thee.*

AUGUSTINE, as above: The innkeeper was the Apostle (Paul), who spent over and above, either the counsel that says: *Now concerning virgins I have no commandment of the Lord; but I give counsel,* or what he also earned

with his own hands, lest he be a burden on anyone of those who were still weak in the newness of the Gospel; though it was lawful to him to live by the Gospel (I Cor. vii. 25; I Thess. ii. 9). The Apostles also spent much *over and above*; as did in due time the Doctors also who spent *over and above* in the interpretation of the Old and the New Testament; for which they shall receive their reward.

AMBROSE: Blessed therefore is that innkeeper who can take care of the wounds of another; Blessed is he to whom Jesus says: *whatsoever thou shalt spend over and above, I, at my return, shall repay thee.* But when, Lord, will you return, save on the day of Judgement? For though Thou art everywhere always, and standing in the midst of us, we see Thee not. Yet there shall be a time when all flesh shall behold Thee coming again. Thou wilt pay then what Thou owest to the Blessed to whom Thou art a Debtor. Would that we were rich debtors, that we might pay back in full what we have received.

V.36. Which of these three, in thy opinion, was neighbour . . .

CYRIL, *Catena GP*: Then, having first said these things, the Lord fitly asks the lawyer: *Which of these three was neighbour to him that fell among the robbers?*

V.37. But he said: He that shewed mercy to him.

For neither Priest nor Levite had acted as neighbour to the sufferer, but he who had had compassion on him. Profitless the dignity of the

Priesthood and the learning of the Law unless it is confirmed by good works. Then follows: *And Jesus said to him: go, and do thou in like manner.*

CHRYSOSTOM: And though He says: Should you see someone afflicted, do not say: he no doubt is wicked; but rather, whether he be Jew or Gentile, but in need of help, do not hesitate to help him whatever the evils he may have yielded to.

AUGUSTINE, *Christian Doctrine*, I, 20: From this we are to understand that he is our neighbour to whom we should render the offices of compassion, should he be in need of them, or to whom we should have rendered them, had he needed them. From which it follows that he in turn must render the same to us, that he may be our neighbour. For the name neighbour has a relation to

something; and no one can be a neighbour except to a neighbour. Who does not see that no one is excepted from the offices of our compassion? For the Lord has said: *Do good to them that hate you* (Mt. v. 44). From which it is plain to us, that included in this commandment, by which we are bidden to love our neighbour, are the holy angels, who have served us in such great offices of mercy, and the Lord Himself, Who for this reason, willed also to be called our neighbour; making clear to us, that it was He Who had taken care of the man lying half-dead by the wayside.

AMBROSE: It is not kinship makes a neighbour, but compassion; and compassion accords with nature: for nothing is more in accord with nature than to help another who shares it.

I. ORIGEN, PRIEST AND CONFESSOR

What must I do for Eternal Life?[3]

While many were the precepts commanded under the Law, in the Gospel the Saviour has imposed on us only those, and in a summary form, which lead those who obey them to eternal life. And it is to this that this question of the lawyer here refers, when he says: *Master, what must I do, to possess eternal life?* And this is the lesson, from the Gospel according to Luke, that has been read to you to-day. And the Lord answered him in this way: *What is written in the Law? How readest thou? Thou shalt love the Lord thy God with thy whole heart and with thy whole soul and with all thy strength and with all thy mind; and thy neighbour as thyself.* And He said to

him: *Thou hast answered right. This do; and thou shalt live.*

There is no doubt that if you do this, concerning which the lawyer had questioned the Lord, you shall receive eternal life. At the same time we are clearly taught in this commandment of the Law that we are to love God. In the Book of Deuteronomy it is written: *Hear, O Israel, the Lord our God is one Lord, Thou shalt love the Lord thy God with thy u hole heart, and with thy whole soul,* and the rest; and *Thou shalt love thy neighbour as thyself* (Deut. vi. 4, 5; Lev. xix. 18). And the Saviour has given testimony concerning these commandments, saying: *On these two commandments dependeth the whole law and the prophets* (Mt. xxii. 40).

But the Doctor of the Law wishing to justify himself, and to show that no one was his neighbour, saying; *Who is my neighbour?* the Lord took occasion from this to speak a parable, which begins: *A certain man went down from Jerusalem to Jericho,* and so on. And He teaches us that no one was a neighbour to the man who was going down save he who had chosen to keep the commandments, and to prepare himself, that he might be a neighbour to any man who needed help. For this is what He laid down on concluding the parable: *Which of these three, in thy opinion, was neighbour to him that fell among robbers?* For neither the Priest nor the Levite were his neighbours; but, as the lawyer himself had answered, *only he that shewed mercy,* only he was a neighbour to him. And accordingly the Saviour says to him: *Go; and do thou in like manner.*

A certain one of the Elders, interpreting the parable, said that *the man who went down* is Adam; that *Jerusalem* means Paradise; *Jericho,* the world the *robbers,* the enemy powers; the *Priest* stood for the Law; the *Levite* for the Prophets; the *Samaritan* for Christ. The *wounds* stand for our disobedience. The *beast,* the Body of the Lord. The common house (*Pandochium*), that is, the *inn,* which receives all who wish to enter it, is interpreted as the Church. Furthermore, the two *denarii* are understood to mean the Father and the Son: the *innkeeper,* the Head of the Church, to whom the plan of the redemption and its means has been entrusted. And concerning that which the Samaritan promises at his

return, this was a figure of the Second Coming of the Saviour.

Though these things are reasonably and beautifully said, we must not however believe they relate to every man. For not every man has gone down from Jerusalem to Jericho, nor do all who dwell in this present world; save He Who was sent, Who came for the lost sheep of the house of Israel. The man therefore who came down from Jerusalem to Jericho, because He willed to come, fell therefore among robbers. And the robbers are none other than those of whom the Saviour says: *All others who came before me, were thieves and robbers* (Jn. x. 8). But it was not among thieves he fell, but among robbers, much worse than thieves, who, when the man on his way down from Jerusalem fell among them, stripped him and wounded him. What are those wounds? What are the injuries by which man was wounded? Vices and sins. Then because the robbers who had stripped and wounded him did nothing for the naked man, but wounding him again they left him, and so the Scripture says: *stripping him, and wounding him, they went away, leaving him,* not dead, *but half dead.*

And it chanced that first a priest, then a Levite, went down the same way, who perhaps had done some good to other men, but not however to this man, who had been on his way from Jerusalem to Jericho. For the priest who saw him, let us say, the Law saw him. The Levite, I would say, stood for prophecy. And seeing him they left him, and passed by. Providence was keeping the half dead man for One Who was stronger than the Law and the

Prophets; for the *Samaritan*, which means, a *guardian*. This is He Who guarding Israel neither slumbers nor sleeps (Ps. cxx. 4). This Samaritan set out on his journey because of the half-dead man; not from Jerusalem to Jericho, as the priest and the Levite descended; or if He did go down, He went down for the reason that he might save and guard the man who was about to die. To this Man the Jews had said: *Thou art a Samaritan and hast a devil* (Jn. viii. 48). And though He denied He had a devil, He did not deny He was a Samaritan. For He knew Himself to be a Guardian.

And so when He came nigh to the half-dead man, and saw him lying in his blood, moved by compassion He *came near* to him; to be a neighbour to him. He bound up his wounds; He poured oil into them, mixed with wine; nor did He say what we read in the Prophet: *There is no salve to apply to them, nor oil, nor binding* (Is. i. 6, Sept.). This is the Samaritan, Whose help and healing all need who are sick. And he above all needed this Samaritan's help, who going down from Jerusalem to Jericho had fallen among robbers, and, wounded by them, had been abandoned half dead. But that you may know that this Samaritan descended in accordance with God's Providence, to heal the one who had fallen among robbers, you shall be taught this clearly from the fact that He had brought with him bandages, that He had brought oil, that He had brought wine. And I believe that the Samaritan carried these things with him, not solely for this one half-dead man, but for others also who, for various reasons had been wounded, and would need to have their wounds bound up, and would need both oil and wine. He had with Him the oil of which it was written: *That he may make the face cheerful with oil* (Ps. ciii. 15). And there is no doubt that He Who had taken care of him, would also soothe with oil the swellings of his wounds.

And, adding something pungent, He cleans the wounds with wine, and places the man who had been wounded upon His own beast, that is, upon His own Body, Which as Man He had deigned to assume. This Samaritan bears our sins, and suffers for us, and lifts up the half-dead man, and brings him to an inn, that is into the Church, which receives all men, and denies its help to no one, and to which Jesus calls all men, saying: *Come to me, all you that labour and are burdened, and I will refresh you* (Mt. xi. 28). And after He brought him there, He did not at once disappear, but remains at the inn for a day with the half-dead man, and takes care of his wounds not only by day, but also by night; giving him every care and attention.

And when in the morning He was setting out, He takes from His own honest silver, from His own honest money, two *denarii*, and pays the innkeeper; no doubt the Angel of the Church; to whom He gives the command to care for him diligently, and bring back to health this man whom He also, because of the urgency of his need, had cared for. The two *denarii* seem to me to be the knowledge of the Father and the Son, and the knowledge of the mystery of how the Father is in the Son, and the Son is in the Father, which are given as a reward to the Angel, that he may take loving care of the man entrusted to him. And He promises him that whatever of his own he shall spend in healing of the half-slain man, shall there be repaid him.

Truly was this Guardian of souls, Who had shown compassion to him who fell among robbers, closer to him than the Law and the Prophets; showing Himself a neighbour not only in name but in deed. From the words of Christ that now follow it is possible therefore for us to imitate Christ, to have compassion on those who have fallen among robbers, to draw near them, to bind their wounds, pouring in oil and wine, to place them upon our own beast, and bear their burthens. And so the Son of God, exhorting us to like good works, says, not so much to the lawyer as to us also; *Go; and do thou in like manner.* And if we do *in like manner*, we shall come to the possession of eternal life in Christ Jesus, to Whom be glory and honour for ever and ever. Amen.

II. St Basil the Great, Bishop and Doctor

The First Commandment[4]

Luke x. 27

I. *The Order and Harmony of the Lord's Commandments . . .*

Since Scripture (Deut. xxxii. 7) has given us the right to ask questions, let us ask first of all whether there is any order or sequence in the Commandments of God, so that one is first, another second, and so on; or are they all so joined one to another that all are to be held in equal honour, each one having the character of being supreme, so that whoever desires to be secure may, as with a circle, make a beginning wherever he wishes?

The question is an old one, and was long ago put forward in the Gospels, when a certain lawyer coming to the Lord, said to Him: *Master, which is the great commandment in the law? And the Lord answered: Thou shalt love the Lord thy God with thy whole heart and with thy whole soul and with thy whole mind. This is the greatest and first commandment. And the second is like to this: Thou shalt love thy neighbour as thyself* (Mt. xxii. 36–39).

It is the Lord Himself therefore who has laid down the order of His Commandments; declaring that the first and greatest is the Commandment that speaks of the love of God. Second in order, and like to the first, or rather completing the first, and depending from it, He placed the Commandment to love our neighbour. So from these words, and from other similar sayings contained in Holy Scripture, the order and agreement of all the commandments of the Lord can be learned.

II. *On loving God, and that there is in man by nature a capacity and inclination to keep the commandments of God.*

Speak to us then first of loving God? For we have been taught that God is to be loved, and we long to learn how we shall succeed in doing this?

The love of God is not something we learn from another. Neither did we learn from another how to love the sunshine or how to defend our life. Nor has anyone taught us how to love our parents, or those who have reared us. And so, indeed much more, learning how to love God does not come to us from outside. But in the very commencement of the life of man, there is placed within us a certain seminal conception, having, from itself, the beginnings of a natural propensity towards this love.

And the School of the commandments of God, receiving this aptitude of the soul, begins to tend it with loving care, to nourish it with wisdom, to lead it by God's grace towards its perfect fulfilment. And so, approving of your zeal in this matter, as so necessary to attain this end, we shall with God's help and by the assistance of your prayers try, in the measure of the help given us by the Spirit, to awaken to life the spark of the divine love that is hidden within you.

But we must also keep in mind that this is but one virtue; yet such is its power that it inspires us and leads us towards the fulfilment of all the commandments. *If any one love me*, says the Lord. *he will keep my commandments* (Jn. xiv. 23). And again: *On these two commandments dependeth the whole law and the prophets* (Mt. xxii. 40). It is not our intention to give you a detailed account of each of the commandments, for dwelling in detail on each part we would lose our view of the whole; but, as best we can, and for our present purpose, we shall speak to you upon the love we owe to God; first however making this clear to you: That we have already received from God the power to obey and fulfil His commandments, so that we should not receive them reluctantly as though they were something new and beyond us; and neither should we be raised above ourselves, as though we were giving Him something more that we had received from Him.

And by means of this power, worthily and fittingly used, we shall adorn our lives with holiness and virtue. But should we misuse this, we are gradually and steadily carried downwards towards evil habit. And this is the true end and purpose of evil habit: The perverted use, also against God's command, of the power He has given us to do good; just as it is the essence of virtue to use these same powers in accordance with the command of the Lord, inspired by a pure conscience. And this being true, we can say the same of love. And so, receiving the command to love God, at once, from the first instant of our being, we possess the power to love. And we need no outward proof of this. Each can learn it from himself, and in himself. For by nature we long for what is beautiful, though we differ one from another as to what is beautiful. Yet, without teaching, we have a natural love for those near and dear to us, and prompt by nature with good will towards those who have done good to us. And what, I ask, is more to be desired, than the beauty of God? What thought more acceptable to the soul, than the splendour of God? What longing of the soul so piercing, so overwhelming as that arising in a soul now purified by God from every evil, and crying out from its true condition: *I am wounded with love* (Cant. ii. 5)? Ineffable and wholly indescribable are the lightnings of the divine beauty. Speech will not convey them, nor can our ear receive them. And though you may speak of the brightness of the morning star, of the moon's shining beauty, of the sun's light, compared with this true glory all other glories are poor and lowly, more distant from it than the thick moonless dark of night from the clearest noonday splendour. This beauty no eye of flesh may look on. Only by the mind and soul can we lay hold of it. And wherever it has shone upon the souls of the purified, ever unbearable is the urge of the longing that remains; and impatient now of this present life, they cry: *Woe is me, that my sojourning is prolonged!* (Ps. cxix. 5). *When shall I come and appear before the face of God?* (Ps. xli. 3). And again: *To be dissolved and to be with Christ, a thing by far the better* (Phil. i. 23). And: *My soul hath thirsteth after the strong living God* (Ps. xli. 3). And: *Now thou dost dismiss thy servant, O Lord* (Lk. ii. 29). And since they now held this present life a prison, they could scarce contain the force of the eager desire the divine love had awakened in them. And because of this inappeasable longing, to behold the divine Perfection, they prayed that the Vision of the joy of God might last throughout all ages. So is it that man of their own nature long for what is sublime and beautiful. And what is beautiful and lovable is also good. And God is good. And all things desire what is good. Therefore, all things desire God.

2. And so whatever is done freely of our own nature proceeds from our nature; provided evil has not perverted our judgement. To love God therefore is a debt we all must pay: to fail in this, is the most unendurable of evils. For, estrangement from God, and aversion from Him, are evils more intolerable than the torments of hell to come, more grievous to the one it happens to, than even the painless loss of the light of the eye, or for a living thing to cease from life. And if the love of our parents rises naturally in the young, and even the nature of dumb beasts bears witness to this, as well as the natural affection men bear from childhood towards their own mothers, let us not seem less rational than infants, more savage than wild beasts, revealing ourselves as without love, as estranged from our Creator? And even if we did not already know Him from His goodness, yet from the very fact that He made us we should love Him above all things, and be ever mindful of Him, and rest in His love as children rest in the arms of their parents.

Chief among those whom nature teaches us to love are those who do good to us. And this is a love not peculiar to man only; but is common to almost all creatures, leading them to love whoever has done good to them. *The ox knoweth his owner and the ass his master's crib.* May what then follows never be said of us: *But Israel hath not known me and my people hath not understood* (Is i. 3). As for the dog and other such creatures, what need is there to speak of how great is their good will towards those who care for them? If then we have a natural love for those who are good to us, and will suffer anything for them to repay their goodness to us, what words can rightly praise the gifts that God has given us? They are so many as to be beyond number; so great, so wondrous that for one alone (*creation*) we should give all thanks to the Giver. I shall not speak of the rest, which though of such surpassing greatness and beauty, are yet outshone in greatness by others still greater, as the sun outshines the stars, and seem in themselves lesser and more obscure. For I have not time, leaving aside the greater glories, to recount from these His lesser gifts the dimensions of the Divine Goodness.

3. We shall be silent of the sunrise, of the changes of the moon, of the changes of weather and season, of the rain that fills the clouds, of the springs that rise from the ground, of the sea, of the earth and of all that comes from it, of the creatures that dwell in the sea, of those that move in the air, the countless forms of living things, and of everything that is meant to serve our needs. But that which we cannot pass over, even if we could, which no man could pass over in silence, who is of sound mind, though to speak worthily of it is beyond our power, is this: that when God had made man to His own image and likeness, and honoured him with a knowledge of Himself, and endowed him above all living creatures of the earth with the gift of reason, and prepared for his delight the inconceivable joys of paradise, and then made him the first of earthly creatures, and even after he had been deceived by the devil and had fallen into sin and through sin into death and into things that deserved death, that even then He did not abandon him, but first gave him a law to help him, placed him under the protection of His angels, sent prophets to rebuke his wickedness and teach him justice, kept him from evil by threats, awakened in him by promises a desire to do good, and at times made known to special persons, that they

might warn others, the end of the good and of the wicked; that after these and every other favour He still has not abandoned us, though we continue in disobedience to Him.

The goodness of the Lord has not abandoned us. Nor have we deprived ourselves of His love for us through our own folly: treating lightly the One Who has done us so much honour. We have even been recalled from death and restored again to life through Jesus Christ our Lord Himself. And even the way in which this great goodness was shown to us is wondrous beyond measure: For, *being in the form of God, he thought it not robbery to be equal with God; but emptied himself, taking the form of a servant* (Phil. ii. 6, 7).

4. He has even taken our infirmities upon Him; he Has borne sufferings, He was wounded for us, and by His wounds we were healed (Is. liii. 4). He has redeemed us from the curse (*of the law*), *being made a curse for us* (Gal. iii. 13); endured for us a most shameful death, that He might bring us back to a glorious life. It was not enough to recall the dead to life, He gave us also the dignity of His own divinity; preparing for all mankind an everlasting rest that surpasses in the greatness of its joy every thought of man. *What then shall I render to the Lord for all the things He has rendered to me* (Ps. cxv. 12)? He is so good that He does not even look for a return; it is enough for Him that for the things He has given us, we but love Him in return.

When I recall these things to my mind, if I may speak of my own thoughts, I am filled with fear and terror, lest through failing in watchfulness of soul or through being absorbed in trifling things, I shall fall from the love of God, and become a reproach to Christ. For he who now assails us and strives by the allurements of this world to lead us by every deceit to forgetfulness of our Benefactor, attacking us, leaping at us that he may ruin our souls, will then, in the Presence of God, turn our neglect into a mockery of God, will gloat over our indifference, our apostasy; he who neither made us nor suffered death for us, shall then regard us as his servants, as his followers; because of our disobedience and contempt for the Commandments of God.

This offence to the Lord, this boasting of His enemy, seems to me more unendurable than the pains of hell: that we should become, to the enemy of Christ, a subject of boasting, a source of pride, to gloat over Him Who died for us and rose again; to Whom because of this we owe a greater thankfulness; as it is written (Rom. viii. 12). And so far we have but spoken to you of the love of God. For as we told you our intention was not to speak to you of all the Commandments of God, or of all that can be said of them; for that is impossible; but to place before you a certain summary of them, awakening in you, and ever reminding you of the love of God.

III. *On the love of our neighbour. We must then speak of the Commandment that is next in order and importance.*

1. We told you earlier that the Law was the cultivator, the nourisher of those powers which were implanted in us after the manner of a seed. Since we have been commanded in these words to love our neighbour as ourselves, let us consider whether we have also received from God the power to fulfil this commandment of God? Who does not know that man is a mild and sociable being, not a wild and solitary creature? For nothing is so congenial to our nature as to live together, to depend on one another, to love our kind. But the Lord giving us beforehand these seeds of loving, looks later for their fruit, saying: *A new commandment I give unto you: That you love one another* (Jn. xiii. 34). And since it was His will to uplift us to the fulfilment of this commandment, He laid it down that it was not by signs and wonders that His Disciples would be known; though He also gave them through the Holy Spirit the power to work these. What then does He say? *By this shall all men know that you are my disciples, if you have love one for another* (Jn. xiii. 35). And so He linked these two commandments together; so that the good we do our neighbour, He receives as done to Himself. For *I was hungry*, He said, *and you gave me to eat; I was thirsty, and you gave me to drink.* And then He goes on to add: *As long as you did it to one of these my least brethren, you did it to me* (Mt. xxv. 35, etc.).

2. And so through the first commandment we are able to fulfil the second; and through the second ascend again to the first. And whoever loves the Lord, it must follow that he also loves his neighbour. *For if any one love me*, He says, *he will keep my word* (Jn. xiv. 23). Then He says: *This is my commandment, that you love one another, as I have loved you* (Jn. xv. 12). And again, he who

loves his neighbour, fulfils the love he owes to God; for God accepts this love as an act of love offered to Himself. For this very reason Moses, a faithful servant of God, showed such love for his brethren that he desired that he himself should be blotted out of the book of life, if God would not pardon the sins of his people (Exod. xxxii. 32). Paul also dared to be an anathema from Christ for the sake of his *kinsmen according to the flesh* (Rom. ix. 3). For He wished, following Christ's example, to be-

come the price of them all; though he knew at the same time, that it could not happen that he would become a stranger to the love of God, who out of love for God, would put away from himself the favour of God in order to fulfil the greatest commandment; rather, that he would receive more than he gave. From what has been said it has been made abundantly plain to us, that the saints attained to this measure of the love of our neighbour that God demands of us. Amen.

III. St Basil the Great, Bishop and Doctor
Meditation On the Love of God and Our Neighbour[5]

1. They who have removed themselves from the cares of this world should watch over their own heart with all carefulness, so that they may not at any time deprive it of the thought of God, or defile the remembrance of His wonders with the images of earthly vanities. Rather, let the hallowed thought of God, impressed like a seal upon the soul, through the pure and continuous remembrance of Him, be ever borne about with us. For it is in this way that the love of God will come to us, urging us on to the daily task of keeping the Lord's commandments, and preserved in turn by them from failing or going astray. He who is strongly possessed by an ardent desire to follow Christ, is no longer able to turn his mind to anything related to this life, not even to the love of parents and kindred, should this be in any way opposed to the precepts of the Lord. That this is so, we know from the words: *If any man come to me, and hate not his father and mother, he cannot be my disciple* (Lk. xiv. 26).

And this the holy Disciples of the Lord also teach us; James and John, who with one mind left their father Zebedeus, and even the boat on which their whole livelihood depended. And Matthew also, leaving his booth, followed our Lord; and not only did he leave the profits of his calling, he also thought nothing of the dangers that threatened both him and his family, from the civil powers, for leaving without notice the task given him by the public authorities. To Paul also the whole world was crucified, and he to the world (Gal. vi. 14). For when the love of God fills the soul it makes nothing of every kind of contest; and even should all men shoot their darts at it because of Him it loves, they would delight rather than torment it. For if we have a natural affection and gratitude towards those who have been good to us, and will suffer any hardship to repay them the good they have done us, what words can fittingly describe the gifts of God? So great is their number, we cannot count them; so great, so wondrous that even for one of them we should never cease to give thanks to our Benefactor.

But He is so good, so kind, that He seeks nothing in return, content that we love Him for what He has given us. And at the thought of all His goodness, if I may reveal my own mind to you, I am full of dread and of fearful anxiety, lest through failing in watchfulness of soul, or because of absorption in vain things, I may fall away from the love of God and become a reproach to Christ. For in reproach to the Lord the devil will pride himself on our contempt for God, on our indifference, And he who neither created us nor suffered for us, will yet hold us up as partners in his own disobedience, in his own neglect to obey the commandments of God. Such an insult, offered to the Lord, and that we should give cause to the enemy of Christ to mock Him Who died for us and rose again, is to me more grievous than the pains of hell.

2. For we must love the Lord God with all the power to love that is in us. And we must also love our neighbour; and we must love even our enemies, that we may be perfect; imitating the kindness of our Father Who is in heaven, *Who maketh his sun to rise upon the good, and bad* (Mt. v. 45). And it is an evil thing to waste the power of love on other things. And if the good of charity is limited to the name of charity, it is a ridiculous thing to pick one here and one there, and give a share of charity to these only and exclude endless others from the favour of our common love. But if the friendship we make with evil men, who accept it, should lead to evil under the pre-text of friendship, we should then consider with whom we have joined ourselves. For if the Beloved Son of God is hated, what wonder if we too are hated by those in whom hate is supreme?

No building can stand if its joinings collapse; neither can the church grow and increase if it is not bound together by the bonds of peace and love. Nothing is so in accord with our nature as to live in peace with one another, to need one another, to love our kind. And we need each one of us the help of one another more than one hand needs the other. When I consider these bodily members of ours, that no one of them suffices of itself, how can I regard myself as sufficient for my own life? One foot cannot move in safety, unless supported by the other; nor will one eye see a thing well, without the company of the other, and applied with it to the thing we see. And we hear more accurately when the sound comes through the passages of both ears, and the grip of the hand is stronger when the fingers are joined together. In short, nothing done by nature, nothing that is done of our own free will is done outside the concord of those members which are of the same kind. Even our prayer is weaker than when we pray in common. Consider the natural common affection of the night-birds (bats), how they cling together like a garland, and do not regard a life that is single and solitary as more to be esteemed than a life united by peace and love. Nothing separates us from each other, unless we wish it ourselves. For we have one Lord, one faith, the same hope. If you think of yourselves as the head, the head cannot say to the feet: I have no need of you (I Cor. xii. 21). Or if you think of yourselves in another relationship, you cannot say to us who have been placed with you in the same body: We have no need of you. For one hand needs the other, and one foot steadies the other, the eyes see more clearly and distinctly through seeing together.

Do not let a thought such as this take hold of you: 'We are apart from the common miseries, and so what need have we to mingle with others?' For the Lord Who separated the islands from the continent by the sea has joined the island dwellers with those of the continent by charity. What divides the flatterer from the friend is principally this: the flatterer speaks only to please, the friend will not pass over in silence what is displeasing. Do you know what you should do for your neighbour? That which you wish others would do to you. Do you know what evil is? It is that which you do not choose to suffer from another. Since you heard from God the words: *By this shall all men know that you are my disciples, if you have love one for another* (Jn. xiii. 35), and since the Lord, about to complete the work of His Incarnation, left as a parting gift His peace to His Disciples; by saying: *Peace I leave with you, my peace I give unto you* (Jn. xiv. 27), I cannot say that, without love towards others, and without, as far as in me lies, peace towards all men, I am worthy to be called a disciple of Christ.

3. And so our charity should be the same to all men and common to all; as a man naturally will have a care for each of his members, de-

siring that all his body shall be equally healthy; since pain in one member afflicts the whole body. For he who loves one member of his company more than another reveals by this the imperfection of his own charity. Likewise, two things are unprofitable in company or in a family: Unseemly quarrelling and particular affections. For enmities arise from strife, and envy and suspicion because of particular friendships. For wherever there is a deprivation of equality, you have a cause and a beginning, among those deprived, of envy and hate. And just as the good God has bestowed His light equally on all, and makes His sun to rise on good and bad alike (Mt. v. 45), so those who imitate God, pour out on all alike the warm rays of their charity. For where charity fails and disappears, beyond any doubt hate will take its place. And if, as John says, *God is love* (I Jn. iv. 16), it then must follow that the devil is hate. He therefore who has charity within him, has God within him; so he who cherishes hate within him, cherishes the devil within him.

And because this is the nature of charity, we must show the same charity and equal charity to all men; and show likewise to all men the honour and respect that is due to each. And just as in our bodies the pain in one single member affects the whole body, and this too though some members are more important than others (for we are not equally injured by a hurt to the toes as by one to the eyes: though the pain be the same in both), in the same way we should show equal love and sympathy to all alike with whom we live together; while nevertheless showing, as is befitting, greater esteem to those who are the more deserving of it. And also among those joined to one another by the bond of a common spiritual life, let there be no greater affection between them because of bodily kinship; not even if one is the full brother of the other, or the son, or the daughter. For whoever in this follows the impulse of nature, such a person is not yet perfectly withdrawn from the natural affections, but rather is still ruled by the flesh. To God be glory for all ages and ages. Amen.

IV. St Gregory Nazianzen, Bishop and Doctor

On the Love of the Poor and Those Afflicted with Leprosy[6]

I. Men Brethren and fellow poor; for though measured by our small measures one may appear to be richer than another, yet are we all poor indeed and in need of God's grace; receive from me this sermon on the love of the poor, not in a meagre spirit, but lovingly, generously, so that you may receive the riches of a Kingdom. And at the same time pray that we may minister to you abundantly, and may nourish your souls by our words, and that we may break the Bread of the Spirit for those who hunger for it, as Moses long ago, raining food from heaven, and bestowing on man the bread of angels (Ex. xvi. 15; Ps. lxxvii. 25); or as feeding many thousands of men in the desert from a few loaves, so that all were filled, as Jesus later did (Mt. xiv. 15); He Who is the True Bread and the Author of True Life.

It is not at all easy, Brethren, to discover among the virtues the one which surpasses all the rest, and to give to it the primacy and the palm; just as it is not easy in a meadow filled with many and sweet-smelling flowers to find the fairest and most fragrant; each one in turn alluring our senses with its perfume and beauty, and inviting us to gather it first. As far as I am able to see, we must distinguish between them in this manner.

II. Faith is a beautiful thing, and so is hope and charity; these three. And Abraham is a witness to faith, being held just through faith (Gen. xv. 6), and Enos to hope, who, the first inspired by hope, *began to call upon the name of the Lord* (Gen. iv. 26), and together with him all the just who because of hope suffered much. Of charity, the divine Apostle is witness, who did not hesitate to speak fearfully against himself out of love of Israel (Rom. ix. 3); and also God Himself, Who is called *charity* (I Jn. iv. 8). And hospitality is a beautiful thing, and a witness to this among the just is Lot of Sodom (Gen. xix. 3), and among sinners, Rahab, a harlot (Jos. ii. 1), though not a harlot by inclination; who because of her zeal in hospitality, was held worthy of praise and of salvation.

A beautiful thing is brotherly love. And a witness to this is Jesus, Who willed not alone to be called our brother, but suffered Himself to be fastened to torment for our sake. And a beautiful thing is love of humanity; and of this a witness is the same Jesus, Who not alone created man that he might do *good works* (Eph. ii. 10), but also for us became man, uniting His image to this earthly clay, our Guide to all perfection, and our heavenly Protector.

Longanimity is a beautiful thing, as the same Person bears testimony, Who not only refused the help of legions of angels against those who laid hands on Him, and used violence against Him (Mt. xxvi. 53), Who not only rebuked Peter for taking the sword, but also restored his ear to the man from whom Peter had struck it (Lk. xxii. 50). And to this virtue Stephen the Disciple of Christ, later, also gave testimony, when he prayed for those who were stoning him (Acts vii. 59).

And beautiful again is mildness, as Moses and David bear witness, to whom above others holy Scripture gives testimony (Num. xii. 3; Ps. cxxxi. 1); and also their Teacher, Who did not strive, Who did not cry out, neither was His voice heard in the streets, Who opened not His mouth against those who led Him to the *slaughter* (Is. xlii, 2; liii. 7).

III. Beautiful is zeal, as Phineas testifies, who with the sword slew the Madianite woman and the Israelite together (Num. cxv. 7), that he might deliver the children of Israel from infamy; and for this was he renowned, and with him those who said: *With zeal have I been zealous for the Lord God of hosts*. And He Who said: *I am jealous of you with the jealousy of God;* and: *The zeal of thy house hath eaten me up* (III Kings xix. 14; II Cor. xi. 2; Ps. lxviii. 10). And they not alone said these things, but they were of this mind.

And good also is the discipline of the body, as the same Paul bears witness, who chastised his own body, bringing it into subjection (I Cor. ix. 27), and for the sake of Israel putting fear into those who, trusting in themselves, indulged their own bodies. And so does Jesus also, fasting, and submitting Himself to temptation, and defeating the tempter (Mt. iv. 1). And beautiful is watching and praying; and to this Jesus Himself testifies: watching before His Passion, and giving Himself to prayer. And beautiful is chastity, and beautiful is virginity; and let Paul convince you of this, laying down the law regarding both, and discerning with justice between marrying and not marrying (I Cor. vii). And Jesus also, by being born of a Virgin: that He might honour birth, and honour virginity still more. Beautiful is abstinence. And here we must believe David, who tasted only, but would not drink the water brought to him from the well of Bethlehem; pouring it upon the earth to God, and would not appease his great thirst at the price of another's blood.

IV. Beautiful is solitude and peace, and this Carmel of Elias teaches us (III Kings xviii. 42), and the desert of John (Lk. i. 80); and then that mountain to which Jesus often withdrew, that He might be alone with Himself in the silence (Mt. xiv. 23).

And good also is frugality; and to this Elias bears testimony, who was given food and refreshed by the poor widow (III Kings xvii. 19); and John, who was clothed in camel's hair (Mt. iii. 4); and Peter, who fed himself on a farthing's worth of lupins.[7] And beautiful is humility, and manifold the examples of it; above all that of the Lord and Saviour of all mankind, Who not alone humbled Himself, *taking the form of a servant* (Phil. ii. 6), but suffered Himself to be spat upon, and *was reputed with the wicked* (Is. i. 6; liii. 12): He Who had cleansed the world of sin, and, clothed as a servant, washed the feet of His Disciples (Jn. xiii. 5).

Beautiful is poverty, and indifference to wealth, as Zacheus testifies; and Christ also: Zacheus when Christ entered his house gave to God almost all that he had; the Lord when He told the rich young man that in this the perfection of life consisted. And, that I may shorten this, beautiful is contemplation, as likewise beautiful is activity; the one because rising from the earth and striving towards the Holy of Holies, it leads our soul back to its beginning, the other receiving Christ as a Guest and ministering to Him, and making known the power of His love *in good works*.

V. Each one of these virtues is a path to salvation, leading us safely to one of those blessed and eternal mansions; since many are the callings of our lives, and so many are the mansions in God's house, which are allotted to each one according to his merit (Jn. xiv. 2). So one steadfastly follows this virtue, another that. One many virtues, another, if he is able, all of them; striving only for this: that he may go forward, eager to make progress, that he may follow in His footsteps Who has pointed out the way, and Who guides our steps by the narrow way and gate that leads to the place of perfect happiness.

But if we are to believe Paul as well as Christ we must hold that charity, as the end of the Law and the prophets, is the first and greatest of the Commandments, and I find that the most perfect part of this virtue consists in love of the poor, in sympathy and compassion for our fellow man. By none of all these virtues is God better served than by mercy, for nothing is closer to Him than mercy; mercy and truth *go before His Face* (Ps. lxxxviii. 15); and we should offer Him mercy before justice. Nor shall He repay mercy by any other thing but mercy Who *sets judgement in weight, and justice in measure* (Is. xxviii. 17).

VI. And furthermore, in accord with the precept that bids us rejoice with the rejoicings and weep with those who weep, we should open our hearts to all who suffer affliction, whatever the cause. And since we are men, let us first give the offering of our compassion to men; to those in need through widowhood, to orphans, to the exile and the stranger, to those in need because of the cruelty of their own masters, or because of the harshness of judges, or through the inhumanity and rapacity of those who exact the tribute, or because of the cruel ferocity of robbers, or the greed of thieves or through the confiscation of their possessions, or through shipwreck. All these are equally unfortunate; and they look to our hands, as we in our need look to the hands of God. And of those again, they who have fallen from dignity and, unused to need, are more to be pitied than those long inured to want. But above all these must we be moved to pity for those who are being destroyed by the sacred disease[8] (leprosy), whose flesh is consumed even to the bones and marrow, betrayed by this weak, miserable and faithless body of ours to which, I know not how, I am yoked; nor how I am an image of God and at the same time commingled with this clay; which when healthy wars against me, yet grieves me when afflicted; which I love as a fellow servant, and hate as an enemy; which I fly from as a fellow-slave, and honour as a co-heir with myself. If I weaken it by self-denial, I have then no other fellow-worker to help me attain to the more perfect things: for which I know I was born, and through which I must ascend to God.

VII. I spare it as my helper, yet know not how I can be free of its unruliness, or how I shall not be cut off from God; weighed down as I am, my feet bound with fetters, and held fast to the earth. It is a beloved enemy, a treacherous friend. What harmony and what discord! What I fear, I must cherish; and what I love, I must fear. And before I attack it, I am reconciled to it; and before I can be at peace with it, I am again in conflict. What is this wisdom, this great mystery, that surrounds me? Is it that God, we being part of Him, and derived from above, wills that this should be (that we may not, becoming exultant and proud because of our dignity, despise our Creator), and that we should be held in continual warfare against our own body, so that we may never cease to look for help from Him, and that this conjoined weakness and discipline relates to the dignity of which we have been thought worthy, that we may know that we are at the same time the most abject and the highest of creatures, of earth and of heaven, fleeting yet immortal, heirs of light and fire or else of darkness, according to the way we incline? This is how we are commingled and, as it seems to me, for this reason: so that as often as we become exalted, because of this image, so often shall we be cast down again, because of this clay. Let him who will philosophize over these things, as we shall also, at a more suitable time.

VIII. Now to return again to what I had begun to speak of, turning aside to grieve over the infirmity of our bodies and over the sufferings that arise from its weakness, we must nevertheless, Brethren, have a care for this our natural body and fellow servant. For though I have called it an enemy, because of what I suffer, yet I cherish it as a friend, because of Him Who united me to it. And let us have a care for the bodies of others no less than the care each one has for his own body; whether it is sound and healthy, or consumed by this very disease.

For we are all one in the Lord, rich or poor, bond or free, sound or sick; and one is the Head of all, He from Whom are all things, namely, Christ. And what our members are to each other, this each one of us is to the other, and all to all. We must never neglect or fail those who have fallen into this public infirmity; nor should we rejoice more that our own bodies are healthy, than we should grieve because our brothers suffer. Rather we should fix in our minds the thought that the salvation of our own bodies and souls depend on this: that we should love and show humanity to these.

IX. There are those who are un-happy for this sole reason: because they are in want; which however time or labour or a friend or a neighbour or the change of the season will take away.[9] For such as these it is a grave thing, graver even than want, not only to be without the necessities of life, but also with-out the means to work to help themselves. And among these, greater always is the fear of illness than the hope of health. And because of this, hope, the one comfort of the unfortunate, is less kind to them than to others. To poverty is added sick-ness, another evil, the most grievous, the most dreaded of all, and by many the most readily invoked as a male-diction. The third is the evil that most men can neither approach nor en-dure to look upon, holding it rather as something to be abhorred and shunned; and this attitude of their fellow men is more terrible to the afflicted than the disease itself: know-ing that because of their affliction they have become an object of loathing to men. For my own part I cannot endure their affliction with-out tears; I am grief-stricken at the thought of it. May you too feel this; that you may wipe away their tears with your tears. And I do not doubt that of those who are assembled here, there are those who also feel this grief: lovers of Christ and of the poor, lovers of God, having within them God's own compassionating love. Of their suffering you are now witnesses.

X. Spread out before our eyes is a sight at once terrible and pitiful; un-believable to all save those who look upon it. Men dead yet living; muti-lated in many parts of their bodies; so afflicted they scarcely know who they are or who they were or where they came from. Rather are they the unhappy remains of men; crying out, so as to be recognized, the name of a father, of a mother, a brother, or some place. My father was so-and-so, one cries. So-and-so was my mother, says another. This is my name. You once knew me; you were my friend! And they cry out in this fashion because they can no longer be known by the faces they once possessed. They are men wholly cut off. They are stripped of all they once had; of money, of family, of friends, even of their own bodies. Alone among mortals, they both hate and pity themselves; not knowing which to grieve for most: the parts of their bodies they no longer possess or those that still re-main; those the disease has devoured, or those that remain to the disease: The one have perished miserably, the rest live on yet more miserably. The first have departed before burial; and as for the others, there is no one now to commit them to earth. Even the best and kindliest of men will show himself hard and in-human to these. Here only do we for-get we also are flesh; that we too bear about with us the body of our lowliness (Phil. iii. 21). And so far have we failed in the care of these our fellow men, that we think only of the safety of our own bodies by flying from them. And though there are those of us who will not fear to come near a body long dead, and smelling of decay, and who are in-different to the evil odours of living animals and who will put up with the presence of filth, but from such as these poor creatures we fly with all our might, scarcely enduring to breathe the same air with them.

XI. Who is closer to us than a father? Who has more feeling for us than a mother? Yet our very nature will separate us even from them. A father will grieve for the son he has begotten, whom he has reared, whom he regards as the sole light of his life, for whom times without number he has prayed to God; yet he will drive him from him, partly of his own will, in part compelled. A mother will remember the pangs of childbirth, her heart will be in anguish, she will call his name most pitifully; yet lamenting she will grieve for the living as for the dead, crying out: Unhappy son of an unhappy mother whom disease has so bitterly separated from me! My unhappy son, son now unknown to me, now seen only amid the crags, the mountains, the wilderness, living with wild beasts, a cave your shelter, and among men they alone will look at you who are filled of pity. And she will cry out in the sorrowful words of Job: Why were you made in the womb of your mother; why did you come forth from her, and not at once perish, that death might meet your birth! (Job. iii. 11). Why were you not cut off before due time, before you had tasted this bitterness, seeing you were to live out your life in sorrow; a life more bitter than death? And crying out like this, tears streaming from her eyes, the unhappy soul longs to embrace him, but she fears as an enemy the body of her own child. He is banished and driven forth; not as unworthy, but as unfortunate. A man may forgive a murderer, admit an adulterer to his house and even to

his table, receive a profaner of temples as a comrade, be a friend to those who injured him, but from the one who suffers this affliction he turns away as from some crime. Rather, wickedness is preferable to the disease. We accept inhumanity as worthy of the human spirit; but humanity and compassion as shameful.

XII. They are driven from the cities, shut out from the homes of men, from the market place, from the highways, from the gatherings of friends, from meetings. O the suffering! Even from water, from the streams which flow for the use of all men; even from the rivers, which are believed to be in some way tainted by them. And what is contrary to all belief, we drive them away as accursed, and so, since we do nothing for them, we recall them to us again. For we give them no shelter, no food, no remedies for their sores, no clothing to cover them. And so they wander through the days and the nights, impoverished, naked, shelterless, their wounds uncovered, recalling past times, calling upon their Creator, making use of one another's limbs in place of those they have lost. With their peculiar singing cry they invoke pity, pleading for a little bread, a morsel of some cooked food, a garment however ragged to clothe their nakedness; and for a little comfort. To them he is a kind person, not the one who helps them in their need, but he who simply does not drive them from him with bitterness. Not even shame can keep many of them from public gatherings, and they will come there, driven by total necessity. I am speaking rather of the sacred public assemblies which have been established for the welfare of souls, or for the celebration of the Mysteries, or in commemoration of those who died in witness to the truth; that we may imitate their virtues, whom we honour because of their sufferings. And these poor afflicted, because they are men, are shamed before men, and would rather that the mountains, the crags, the forests, even darkness and night might cover them. Yet they appear amongst us, laden with misery, moving us to tears; and this not in vain, for they remind us of our own infirmity, and convince us that nothing of things present, nothing that meets the eye is stable or enduring. They come among us; some longing to hear again the sound of a human voice, to see again the faces of men, others that they may receive some small help for their lives from those whose own lives are passed in luxury and comfort. But all come in the hope of receiving a little comfort; through speaking of their afflictions to those who have compassion for them.

XIII. Who is not touched to the heart by the groans, by the strange plaint of their singing? What ear can bear to hear it, what eye endure to see it? They huddle together, united by the common misery of their state; one with another adding to our pity. Each is to the other an added affliction: unhappy in their own suffering, yet more unhappy in their common suffering. Around them is a mingled assembly of people who grieve with them, but only for a while. They stumble about at the feet of men, in the dust and heat, struggling against the bit-

ter cold, against the rain, against the violence of the wind; they would be trodden on by men's feet did not men fear even to touch them. Their laments disturb the singing inside the sacred temples: their sad crying in conflict with the murmur from the sacred mysteries.

But what need is there to bring before you who are celebrating this solemn festival each single one of their misfortunes? Should I enlarge tragically and in detail upon all of them, I should, I know, move you also to tears, and you would feel more sorrow over them, than joy over the festival. But I am telling you these things, because I am not yet able to convince you, that at times grief is better than gladness, sorrow more than joy, and tears more becoming than laughter (Eccles. vii. 3).

XIV. These then, and much more besides, are the afflictions of those who are our brothers in God, whether you wish it or not; born with the same nature, formed of that same clay from which we in the beginning were formed, compounded of nerves and bones as we are, clothed in flesh and skin like our own; as holy Job says in a certain place (Job x. 11), reflecting on his own miseries, and despising that part of us which is seen. More than this; they also, if I may speak of the higher things, have received the same divine image as we have, and have perhaps guarded it better; even though their bodies have dissolved in corruption. They have put on the same Christ, *according to the inward man* (Rom. vii. 22), and to them the same *pledge of the Spirit* (II Cor. v. 5) has been given. They have been made sharers with us of the same laws, of the same doctrine, of the same Testaments, of the same assemblies, of the same Mysteries, of the same hope. Christ Who takes away the sins of the whole world, died for them as He died for us (Jn. i. 29). And even though they are now deprived of all earthly happiness, yet they are heirs with us to eternal life. They are buried with Christ, and with Him they return to life (Col. ii. 12). With Him they suffer, that *they may also be glorified with Him* (Rom. viii. 17).

XV. And what of us? We who are called by a great new name, who are named after Christ, we who are a holy people, a royal priesthood, a chosen people, a purchased people (I Pet. ii. 9), a pursuer of good works (Tit. ii. 14), followers of the gentle loving Christ (Mt. xi. 29), Who bore our infirmities (Is. liii. 4), Who humbled Himself to come among us, Who for our sake took upon Him the poverty of this earthly tabernacle of our body and became acquainted with sorrow, that through His poverty you might be made rich (II Cor. viii. 9). What, I say, of us, who have received so great an example of pity and compassion? What are we to think of these things, and what shall we do? Shall we look the other way? Shall we *pass by*? Shall we abandon them as dead, as loathsome, worse than serpents, as wild beasts? No, Brethren! Such a thing is unfitting for us, the flock of Christ, the flock of that Good Shepherd, Who went looking for the sheep that had strayed and restored the weak to strength (Ezech. xxxiv). Let such a thought be far from the human nature which

has made of compassion a law; taught mercy and compassion by our common weakness.

XVI. Are these unfortunate people to remain out under the sky, exposed, while we enjoy splendid homes and live in houses of choicest stone, adorned with gold and silver, covered with the finest mosaics, with pictures, with perspectives which hold and distract the eye? And of these dwellings, we live in some, and we are building others. For whom? Not always for our heirs; frequently for strangers, or for those who are perhaps not even our friends; they may even be for our enemies or, worst of all, for those who envy us. And these poor creatures, are they to remain covered with rags? Would that they were even covered, while we take our delight in soft flowing garments, woven from silk and linen, that shame us rather than adorn us (and I say the same of all that is idle and superfluous)! Others that we possess we store away, without use or gain, to be consumed by moths, or by time that consumes all things. And these have not enough to eat! Alas for my abundance, and for their most grievous misery! Are they to lie before our doors, weak and hungry, their bodies wanting in the very members by which they might plead; without voices to grieve, without hands to stretch forth, without feet to go to those who are rich, without breath to give tone to their lamentations; believing themselves to be favoured only in their eyes, believing that what is their most grievous affliction is their least: that they can no longer see their own deformity!

XVII. This is the state of these poor people. And we, strong and active, lie comfortably on our fine raised beds, soft and yielding, with more coverings than we need; and annoyed should we even hear the sound of a voice in pleading. And we must also have our floor covered with flowers, even out of season, our table smelling of the richest and sweetest perfumes, that we may be even more delicate, and around us pages standing in rank and order, their hair long and effeminate, the locks in clusters round their faces, adorned more than is becoming even for our greedy comfort. Others hold cups on their finger tips, in the most secure and delicate manner. Others with a fan of peacock feathers make a slight breeze above your heads, and with hand-made puffs of wind they keep the mass of your bodies cool; seeing to it also that the table is well supplied with meats (all the elements thus ministering to us: earth, sea, air and water). And we match the skills of cooks and pastry makers, to see which of them will most flatter our greedy and thankless stomach: a heavy burden, truly the beginning of every evil, an insatiable beast, and a most treacherous one, that comes to nothing as soon as food has ended.

These poor creatures think themselves fortunate if they receive their fill of water while we drink cup upon cup of wine, drink even to drunkenness and beyond it: those at least who are given to intemperance. And from many wines we reject some, others we approve, because of their special taste and fragrance, discoursing gravely upon this; and we consider it a serious lack if, besides our local wines, we have not at least some one of the rarer wines of other countries is not present; as though this wine were some lordly creature. And of course it is demanded of us that we should be, or appear to be, most delicate as to food, more lavish than need be, ashamed if we are not thought wicked, slaves of our stomach, and of the parts below the stomach.

XVIII. What have we to say to these things, O friends and brothers? What disease is it that afflicts our souls; a disease more grave than those that afflict the body? For these come against our will, the other remains with our consent. The one end with life, the other goes with us when we go from here. To those of sound mind the one is unfortunate, the other hateful. Why do we not while there is yet time, give help to our own nature? Why do we not while we are still in the flesh, have some concern for this humiliation of our flesh? Why do we live in pleasure in the presence of our brothers' affliction? Far be it from me that I should abound in riches, while they suffer in want; that I should be healthy, and not bring help to their wounds; that I should have food and clothing and rest beneath a roof, until, as far as my means permit, I bring food to them, clothe them, give them shelter!

In truth we must either leave all things for Christ, taking in all sincerity the Cross upon our shoulders, and light and as unburdened as possible and held back by no earthly tie follow Him, taking wing for that world above where, uplifted by humility, and enriched by poverty, we shall gain Christ in place of all things; or else we must share our possessions with Christ, so that our possession of them shall be sanctified by possessing them worthily and by sharing them with those who possess nothing. But if I shall sow for myself only, I shall sow indeed, but that others may eat; and, if I may use again the words of Job: *Thistles will grow up to me instead of wheat, and thorns instead of barley* (Job. xxxi. 40); and the burning south wind and the tempest carry away my labours, so that I labour in vain. And if I should also build barns, heaping up treasure from Mammon and for Mammon, perhaps in that very night I shall be asked for my soul and I must render an account of that which I have evilly gained.

XIX. Shall we not even now learn wisdom? Shall we not even now throw aside this want of feeling, that I may not call it meanness of soul? Shall we give no thought to human needs? Shall we not place the afflictions of others above our own needs? For in nature there is nothing fixed and stable in human affairs, nothing sufficient in itself, nothing that remains constant. The affairs of men revolve like a circle, bringing changes, now at one time, now at another; oftentimes in one and the same day, and even in the same hour. We should place greater trust in the stability of the inconstant winds, in the track of a ship passing across the sea (Wis. v. 10), in the vain dreams of the night that bring us a brief pleasure, in the sand castles of children playing by the sea, than in the happiness of men. Those who are wise will not place their trust in the things of this present life, but will lay up treasure for the time to come, and, because of the uncertainty, the

inequality of human destiny let them give their love to that Goodness which does not fade, so that they may gain one of three things: either that they shall never do what is evil (for oftentimes God heaps the secondary things that belong to this life on pious men, inviting them to show kindness to those in need); or that they may have confidence in themselves before God that they suffer affliction, not because of sin, but because of His will; or lastly, that they may rightly ask of others, as due to them, that humanity which they once used towards the needy, when they themselves had riches and did good works.

XX. *Let not the wise man*, says the Scripture, *glory in his wisdom, and let not the strong man glory in his strength, and let not the rich man glory in his riches* (Jer. ix. 23): even should he attain to the summit of wisdom, another to that of strength, another to that of riches. And to this I add: let not the famous glory in their fame, nor the healthy in their health, nor the beautiful in their beauty, nor the young in their youth, nor, in a word, in any of the things that men praise and esteem. And if a man must glory, let him glory in this, *that he understandeth and knoweth God* (Jer. ix. 24), that he grieved over the afflictions of others, and that he is laying up something good for himself for the life to come.

For all other things are fleeting and unstable and, as in a game of dice, pass from hand to hand, continually changing ownership, so that there is nothing a man holds as his own that will not pass from him with time, or that is not taken from him through man's ill will. But the higher things are real and enduring. They are never lost, never fade; neither is the hope of those that trust in them deceived: and to me this seems the reason why no good thing of this life is stable and enduring for men; and this also, that in any other thing, though beautifully wrought by the Designing Word or by that Wisdom which surpasses all understanding, we are always deluded by what the senses see, which changes and is changed, is carried here and there, up and down, which before we touch it escapes us, and this so that we, when we learn that there is nothing sure and enduring in earthly things, may turn steadfastly towards the gate of the life to come.

For what would we do were our prosperity to endure, seeing that fleeting and unstable though it is, it yet binds us to it by so many bonds, and makes of us such slaves to its pleasures and delusions, that we are unable to think of anything more perfect; and this though we hear and believe that we are made to the image of God's likeness; Which is above and Which is drawing us to Itself?

XXI. *Who is wise, and will understand these things* (Ps. cvi. 43)? Who will turn aside from the things that pass away? Who will give his soul to enduring things? Who will think of present things as though they were far away? Who will think of the things that rest on hope as certain and unchanging? Who will distinguish what is from what seems, and despising one pursue the other? Who will discern the figure from the reality, the earthly dwelling from the heavenly city, the place of sojourn from the true home, light

from darkness, the slime of the abyss from holy earth; who will discern body from spirit? Who will distinguish between God and the prince of this world, the shadow of death from life everlasting? Who will buy things to come with present things, riches that endure with those that are fleeting, with things visible things that are unseen?

Blessed therefore is he who understands these things and, separating them from inferior things by the sword of the Word (Heb. iv. 12), disposes his heart *to ascend by steps,* as David says in one place (Ps. lxxxiii. 6), and fleeing from this vale of tears, seeks for the things that are above (Col. iii. 1), and with Christ is crucified to the world, with Christ rises again, and with Christ ascends to heaven, heir to a life that shall be neither vain nor fleeting, where the serpent no longer bites *in the way* (Gen. xli. 17), nor lies *in wait for the heel* (Gen. iii. 15); since his head is now well guarded. And to us whom he has left behind, David, like a herald with a mighty voice, speaking from some lofty place, rightly cries out that we are *dull of heart* and that we seek *after lying* (Ps. iv. 3), and warning us not to attach our minds seriously to the things we see, that all delight we reap from this life is but as the fulness of corn and wine, which soon ends.

And the blessed Micheas, as I believe, observing this, and scorning the things we see upon this earth, which have only the appearance of good, exclaims: *Draw near to the eternal mountains; arise, and depart, for here there is no rest for you* (ii. 9, 10 Sept.); using almost the same words our Lord and Saviour used to exhort us when He said: *Arise, let us go hence*; meaning, not those only who were then His Disciples, nor as going simply from one place to another, as some are inclined to think, but that all of us and forever should turn from earth and the things of earth, and go hence to heaven and the things of heaven.

XXII. Let us therefore without delay give ear to the Word, and let us seek the peace of that other resting place, and throw away from us the abundance of this life, enriching ourselves only with that which is good in it; namely, let us through almsgiving become owners of our own souls; let us give of what is ours to the poor, that we may be rich in heaven. Do not give to the body only; give the soul its share. Do not give to the world only; give a portion also to God. Withhold something from the stomach, and dedicate it to the spirit. Snatch something from the fire, and hide it far from the devouring flame. Snatch it from the tyrant, and give it to God. *Give a portion to seven*, that is, to this life; *and also to eight* (Ecclus. xi. 2); that is, to Him Who after this life shall receive us. Give a little to Him, from Whom you have received much. Give even all to Him, Who has given all to you. You will never outdo God's generosity, even should you give your all, even should you add yourself to what you give. For to be given to God, this is also to receive Him. And however much you bring to Him, still more shall remain to you. Nor will you give anything that is your own; for all things flow from God. And as no man can outstrip his own shadow: for wherever we walk, it will always follow us or go before us;

nor can the body raise itself above the head, which ever remains above the body: so is it with our giving. We shall neither give God anything that is not His, nor surpass Him in giving.

XXIII. Consider from whence you have life, so that you breathe, so that you know and understand, and, greatest of all, so that you may know God, and may hope for the kingdom of heaven, and to be received among angels, and for the blessed vision of glory, now seen *through a glass in a dark manner*, but then in a purer, more perfect manner (I Cor. xiii. 12); also that you are a child of God, and an heir with Christ, and, I shall dare to say it, so that you may even become God Himself. From where has all this come to you; and from Whom? And that I may speak of the lesser things, which our eyes see: Who has given to you to see the beauty of the heavens, the course of the sun, the moon's orb, the multitude of the stars, the order and concord in all things as in a lyre, the unfolding of the seasons and their changes, the revolving of the years, the divisions of night and day, the growing things of the earth, the pouring forth of air, the depth and vastness of the sea, ever flowing, ever held in check, the deeps of rivers, the ceaseless flow of the winds?

Who gives you the rains, the tilling of the earth, the arts, homes, lands, government, our manner of life, and the love of our kindred? From where have you received the living creatures that serve you, and those given for your food? Who has made man the lord and ruler of all that is on the earth? And so that I need not speak of each single thing, who has bestowed all these things by which man is placed over all things? Is it not He Who now for all this, and in return for all this, asks you to love your fellow man? Let us not shame ourselves, receiving so much from Him, and hoping for more, by refusing God this one thing: kindness towards our fellow man.

And since He has set us apart from the beasts, and adorned us alone of all the creatures of the earth with reason, should we make beasts of ourselves, and allow ourselves to be corrupted by delicate living, either we are mad, or, I know not how to express it, we think that because of our barley and bran cakes, which we make so badly, we are of a nature superior to theirs. And as long ago, poets say there was a certain race of giants as well as other men: so we are above other creatures, as they were above men; as Nimrod was (Gen. x. 8), and *the race of Enach* (Num. xiii. 29), which long ago oppressed the Israelites, or those others because of whose sin the earth was purified by the flood. And since He Who is our God and Lord is not ashamed to be called our Father, shall we turn a deaf ear to the cry of our destitute kindred?

XXIV. Far from it, my friends and my brothers! Let us not become un-just stewards of the things entrusted to us, so that we shall not hear Peter rebuking us and saying: 'Let you be ashamed, you who hold back another's possessions. Resolve rather to imitate the justice of God, and then no one will be poor (Const. Ap. Clementis)'. Let us not weary our-selves heaping up treasure and keep-ing guard over it, while others faint

from want, lest the day come when we shall hear, first Amos, saying: *Hear this, you that crush the poor and make the needy of the land to fail, say-ing: When will the month be over, and we shall sell our wares; and the sabbath, and we shall open the corn: that we may lessen the measure and increase the sicle and may convey in deceitful balances* (viii. 5)? and so on in words that threaten the anger of God against those who use both a large and a small measure; or hear again Micheas censuring this same luxury for the reason that satiety begets lust, and those who lie *wanton on* ivory couches, *anointing themselves with the best ointments, eating the lambs of the flock and calves from the herd* (Amos vi. 4),[10] dancing and singing to the sound of music as though they be-lieved that such things would last forever and regarding them as harm-less, and given over to self-indul-gence, *they are not concerned for the affliction of Joseph* (Gen. x. 8), and this he adds to their sin of satiety. Let us take care this does not happen to us; that we too shall be so given over to pleasure, that we shall despise the mercy of God, Who permits these things, and does not immediately loose His anger against the hard hearts of sinners.

XXV. Let us then imitate the first and supreme law of God, Who sends down His rain on the just and unjust alike, and makes His sun to shine equally upon all (Mt. v. 45), Who spreads across the wide earth His rivers and streams, the woods for all living things, the air to the birds, waters to the things that live in the waters, and on all bestows the first helps to life. And His gifts are not under the dominion of anyone, not ruled by law, nor marked by boundaries, but all are owned in common, and abounding, and because of this they never fail; upholding the dignity of our nature by the worthiness of His gifts, bringing to light the riches of His goodness.

But men, if they have gold or silver and soft and precious garments and shining gems and such things beyond their need, things that are the cause of war and strife and of the very beginning of tyranny, they bury them in the ground and, above themselves with folly, close their hearts to pity for the needs of their fellow men. Not even from what is superfluous will they help those in total want. Oh the immense folly! the fearful madness of it! They never think, if nothing else, that riches and poverty, slavery and what we call freedom, and such terms, came among men with sin, as weaknesses that rushed in together with wickedness, and were its invention. *From the beginning,* says the Lord, *it was not so* (Mt. xix. 8). He Who created man at the beginning, created him free, endowed him with free will, ruled by the sole law of His commandment, and rich in the joy of paradise. And He willed the same for the rest of the race of men, bestowing it on them through that first seed. Freedom then, and wealth, lay simply in the observance of His single commandment: True slavery and poverty in its transgression.

XXVI. From this came hatred and strife and the deceits of the serpent tyrant, tempting us at all times with the bait of unlawful pleasures, setting the strong against the weak; and from then our race was divided, and greed defeated the nobility of our nature, making use even of law as an aid to its domination. But I would have you look back to our primary equality of right, not to the later division; not to the law of the strongest, but to the law of the Creator. Help nature with all your might. Reverence the ancient freedom. Reverence yourself. Cover the shame of your own kindred. Help the afflicted. Comfort those in sorrow. You who are strong, help the weak. You who are rich, help the poor. You who stand upright, help the fallen and the crushed. You who are joyful, comfort those in sadness. You who enjoy all good fortune, help those who have met with disaster. Give something to God in thanksgiving that you are of those who can give help, not of those who stand and wait for it; that you have no need to look to another's hands, but that others must look to yours. Grow rich, not only in substance, but also in piety; not only in gold, but also in virtue; or rather, only in virtue. Be more honoured than your neighbour, by showing more compassion. Be as God to the unfortunate, by imitating the mercy of God.

XXVII. For in nothing do we draw so close to God as in doing good to man. Though God does the greater things, and man the less; yet each, I believe, works according to his capacity. He made man; and when man is undone, He remakes him. Never despise fallen man. God has shown mercy to him in the highest degree; giving him, with other things, the Law and the Prophets, and before that, the natural unwritten law, the examiner of all our actions, which warns us, corrects us guides us. And lastly He gave us Himself, for our redemption, and for the life of the world, and with this, Apostles, Evangelists, Teachers, Pastors (Eph. iv. 11), healings, wonders, return to life, the undoing of death, victory over him who had defeated us, a Testament foreshadowing Him, the Testament of the True Reality, the gifts of the Holy Spirit, the mystery of the new salvation.

You however, if you also would do great things, and those by which your soul is helped (and in this also God has made you rich, if you so will), never refuse to do good to those who have need of you. First and before all things, give to him who asks of you, even before he asks; *showing mercy all the day, and lending all the day long* (Ps. xxxvi. 26), carefully seeking back both principal and interest; that is, increase (*of God*) in him you helped; for he always adds to his store of wisdom who prudently increases in himself the seeds of piety.

But if you cannot help in these greater things, then help in the second or lesser things, as far as you can. Give help. Help others to live. Give food, clothing, medicines, apply remedies to the afflicted, bind up their wounds, ask about their misfortunes, speak with them of patience and forbearance, come close to them, you will not be harmed, you will not contract their affliction; even though the timid believe this, misled by foolish talk. Or rather, with this pretext, they excuse their own timidity and lack of kindness, seeking safety in cowardice, as though it were something fine and prudent. And sound sense will tell you this, and physicians, and the

example of those who take care of these sick, of whom not one has fallen into danger through visiting them. And even should this action be not without danger, or the well-founded suspicion of it, you, O Servant of Christ, and lover of God and of men, do not because of this become mean and cowardly. Have confidence! Let compassion overcome your timidity; the fear of God your softness. Let the love of your fellow man rise above the promptings of self love. Do not despise your brother; do not pass him by! Do not turn away your face from him, as from something terrible, something fearful, to be shunned and disowned. He is your own member, though this calamity has deformed him. *The poor man has been left to thee* (Ps. x. 14, Sept.) as to God; though you should pass by over proud in spirit. Perhaps I have shamed you; saying these things to you. But I have set before you the rule of the love of your neighbour: even should those who are hostile turn you away from accepting it.

XXVIII. Whoever journeys on the sea is close to shipwreck; the nearer, the more boldly he navigates. Every man who has put on this body is brought close to the body's dangers, and the closer the more he goes about with his head in the air, not seeing who is in his path. While you sail with a fair wind, give a hand to the one who has suffered shipwreck. Do not wait to learn, in your own person, how great an evil is inhumanity, and how good it is to open your heart to those in need. Do not wish that the hand of God be stretched forth against those who walk with heads high, and pass by the poor. Learn of these things from the afflictions of others. Give something however small to the one in need; for it is not small to one who has nothing; neither is it small to God, if we have given what we could. Give promptly in the place of a large gift. And if you have nothing give of your tears. Great is the comfort to the afflicted of the sympathy that comes from the heart; and to suffer unfeigned for another's distress, will lighten the burden of their grief.

A man is not to be held in less honour than a beast, O Man; which, should it fall into a ditch or stray, the Law bids you lift out or lead back (Deut. xxii. 1; Ex. xxiii. 4). Whether there is something profound and more mysterious hidden here – for many of the things of the Law are deep and mysterious – is not for me to know, but for the Spirit, *Which searcheth all and knoweth all things* (I Cor. ii. 10). But as far as I can see, the Law laid this down, so that we might be led by the practise of humanity in lesser things, to a charity which is greater and more perfect. For if we are obliged to be kind and merciful towards dumb beasts, how much more is this due to our equals and to our kindred?

XXIX. And this our reason as well as law teaches us, and some of the wisest of men, among whom it has always been held, that it is more worthy to give than to receive, and that mercy is more desirable than riches. Why do I speak of our wise men? For to those outside we pay no heed: those who invent gods out of their own imaginations, as patrons of their vices, and give the first

place to Lucrius (Mercury); and what is worse, among some nations, offer human sacrifices to certain demons, and hold cruelty as part of their piety, and delight in such sacrifices; thinking by this to please their gods: the evil priests of evil and initiators of evil. And there are some even among our own people, a thing that makes one weep, who, far from helping or having compassion on these poor sick, will reproach them bitterly, insult them, make up empty, foolish speculations about them; and truly, *out of the ground they mutter speech, and their voices are heard in the air* (Is. xxix. 4); not in the ears that are used to and understand holy teaching. And they have the audacity to go further, and say: 'Their affliction is from God; and our good health comes from God. And who am I to undo the decree of God, and put myself forward as more kind than God? They are sick. Let them be sick! Let them be afflicted! Let them suffer misfortune! This is the will of God!'

And this is their sole manifestation of the love of God: You must take care of your money, and be insulting to the afflicted. From what such persons say it is very apparent that they are far from thinking that prosperity comes from God. For who would speak like this of the destitute, who confesses that God is the Giver of all blessings? For it is one and the same thing to receive something from God, and to possess it and use it as God wishes.

XXX. Whether it comes from God that these should be tormented is not yet manifest; just as it is not manifest whether this corruptible body of itself brings forth this irregularity, in its course as it were.[11] And who knows whether this man is being punished because of his wickedness, and this other uplifted as good and worthy of praise, and not the contrary: that this man is being uplifted because of his wickedness, and this other is being tested because of his virtue? The one uplifted, that he may fall the lower; and being first allowed his fill, all his wickedness bursts forth as some disease, so that he is the more fittingly punished in the end. The other, contrary to expectation, is tried hard so that, tested like gold in a furnace, he may be purified of even the least evil there may yet be in him. For no one, at least, no one born of human generation, is wholly free of stain, as we have heard (Job xxv. 4); even though one may appear more worthy than another. For I find a certain mystery of this kind in Sacred Scripture; but it would take too long to recount all the words of the Spirit on this subject. But who hath numbered the sand of the sea, and the drops of rain, and who hath measured the depth of the abyss? And who has searched out the deeps of the divine wisdom in all things (Ecclus. i. 2), through which He has made all things, and rules them as He wills and knows? It is enough for us to pass over with the Apostle the difficulty of understanding and contemplating this wisdom, and simply cry out in wonder: *O the depth of the riches of the wisdom and of the knowledge of God! How incomprehensible are his judgements, and how unsearchable his ways!* And, *Who hath known the mind of the Lord* (Rom. xi. 33, 34).? And, *who*, that I may speak with Job, *has come to the end of his wisdom*

(Job. xi. 7, Sept.)? *Who is wise, and he shall understand these things* (Os. xiv. 10); and will not measure what is above measure by that which cannot be perceived?

XXXI. Let another be rash and bold in these things; or rather, let no one be: I, for my part, shall not presume to say that someone's affliction is due wholly to wickedness, or their happiness to piety. For it will happen at times, and for our true profit, that the way of life of a wicked man is changed through affliction, and that a virtuous man is strengthened in his way by the comfort of the good things of this life. For it is not always and wholly the case that it is only at some future time that some receive the reward of their virtue, and others the punishment that is due to their misdeeds. *And they that have done good things shall come forth unto the resurrection of life; but they that have done evil, unto the resurrection of judgement* (Jn. v. 29).

But the outward appearance of the things of this life is one thing, their ruling another; though all concur in this: that what is just before God, may appear to us contradictory. Just as in a body, there are important members and others less so; some are large, some small; and again upon the earth the higher and the lower spheres balance one another, so that one thing taken with another, a creation of beauty and harmony is set before us, that we can see and admire. The same is seen in the work of an artist. The rough, crude form that first seemed without order or balance, is gradually seen to be wholly related to the method and purpose of his art, and has its place in the making of the work. And we perceive and confess this as soon as we have been allowed to see the perfected beauty of what he has made. And God is not ignorant of the rules of art, as we are; and neither are the things of this life ruled without order and design, merely because the reasons for what we see are yet unknown to us.

XXXII. To take an example from a certain natural infirmity from which men suffer: we are not very different from those who suffer from nausea and dizziness and who, when their head is spinning, see everything upside down. This is what happens to those we speak of. Such people cannot allow that God is wiser than themselves. As soon as something unexpected happens, they are taken with dizziness; when they ought rather to seek a reason for what they see and with a little care and diligence they might perhaps come to understand the reason. Or they could seek counsel with men who are wiser and more spiritual than themselves; for this is also among the gifts of the Spirit, and not at all possess this knowledge. Or lastly they should seek understanding by means of the purification of their lives, and pray for wisdom from Him Who is Wisdom.

But they prefer to turn (O the folly of man!), to the one nearest them, and maliciously declare that there is no order or purpose in any thing; for they themselves have discovered none; and so because of what they do not know, they are wise, or rather, if I may say so, in their excess of wisdom, they are ignorant and foolish. Then there are those who base their opinions on fortune and on chance; led astray

through accidental as well as through contrived happenings. Others base their convictions on the unaccountable and inexorable rule of the stars, arranging their affairs by their necessary and inalterable decree and this rule in turn is related to certain inevitable influences of both the fixed and the wandering stars; and of all this motion is master. Others again will, each according to his own notion, preying on the unfortunate race of men, divide up into various theories and terminologies what they themselves are neither able to perceive nor grasp of the workings of Divine Providence. And then there are those who blame Providence for great poverty, holding that It is concerned only with the things that are above and indifferent to what we most need: as though fearful, should many receive help, that God may be seen as a true Benefactor; or striving to show that He does not trouble Himself to help people.

XXXIII. But we may disregard such persons as these we have spoken of; for Holy Scripture has fittingly chastised them, where it says: *Their foolish heart was darkened. For, professing themselves to be wise, they became fools. And they changed the glory of the incorruptible God* (Rom. i. 21), and with their myths and shadows they blaspheme the Providence of God, that reaches from end to end of all things. We however, who follow reason, and are followers of Him Who is the Supreme Reason, have nothing to do with such imposters; nor should we listen to them, or have anything to do with them: even though they have plenty to say for themselves, and are able to delude men's minds with their novelties. We believe that God is the Maker and Author of all things; for in what other way could the universe exist, unless someone made it and gave it order? And we include with this the Providence which unites and holds all things together in harmony. For it must be that He Who is the Maker of all things has also the care of them; unless we are prepared to say that the universe is borne along by chance, as a ship driven by a storm, and that through the collapse of order in matter it will then dissolve and return again to its primeval confusion and chaos.

And we believe also that our Maker, or our Modeller, if you prefer to call Him this, has a special care of our lives; even though our lives are under the rule of things that are contrary one to the other, and perhaps it is because of this we are mistaken with regard to them, so that, because of the difficulty of understanding them, we look upwards in wonder to the Mind that is above them all. For what is readily taken in, is readily despised. But that which is above us, the harder it is to attain to it, the more do we value it; and that but awakens our longing, which evades our desire to know.

XXXIV. So let us then neither admire all healthfulness, nor condemn all sickness, nor give our heart to fleeting riches, that turn it from its true course, devouring as it were a part of our soul. Neither should we revolt against poverty, as wholly detestable and hateful. And let us discern when to have little esteem for that foolish healthfulness whose

fruit is sin, and to honour the sickness that is holy: holding in reverence those who have gained the victory through suffering, lest there may be some Job hidden among the sick, who, though he may scrape his festering body with a potsherd (Job ii. 8), is more to be revered than those that are sound in body; Lazarus gained salvation and found peace in Abraham's bosom.

XXXV. It seems to me we must show kindness and mercy to these poor afflicted for these reasons also: To curb the tongues of those so inhumanly disposed towards them, to give no justification for their foolish talk; justifying the same cruelty against ourselves; and also that we may show reverence to the greatest commandment of all, and towards its greatest Example. What a commandment this is? And how true and enduring? For not once or twice have the men who were filled with the Holy Spirit spoken of the poor and needy, nor have they spoken merely in words; nor have some spoken much, and others little, as though it were not something of great importance; but all without exception have spoken, and all with fervour. And they spoke of it as our first duty, or among the first; now exhorting us, now threatening us, now reproaching, at times praising those who did good, so that reminding us of it at all times they might lead us to the fulfilment of this commandment:

By reason of the misery of the needy and the groans of the poor, now will I arise saith the Lord (Ps. xi. 6). And who should not fear the Lord when He rises? *Arise, O Lord God, let thy hand be exalted: forget not the poor*

(Ps. ix. 33). Grant that He may not rise against us; and that we may not see His hand upraised against those who disobey Him; nor, what is worse, against the hard of heart. And again: *He hath not forgotten the cry of the poor* (Ps. ix. 13). And, *His eyes look upon the poor man* (His *eyes*, which are nobler than His *eyelids*, and more significant); *his eyelids examine the sons of men* (Ps. x. 5); that is, He bestows on them a briefer and secondary glance.

XXXVI. It may be that some one will say: 'But these words were said of the poor and needy who had suffered injustice.' It may be so. But let that also incite you to humanity. For if there is so much reason for humanity towards those who have suffered wrong, greater will be the reward for those who do good to them. For if *he that despiseth the poor, reproacheth his maker* (Prov. xvii. 5), he does honour to the Maker, who cares for what He has made. Again, when you hear the words of Scripture: *The rich and poor have met one another: the Lord is the maker of them both* (Prov. xxii. 2), do not then think He made this man poor, this other rich, that you may therefore war in safety against the poor. For it is not certain God made such a division. The psalmist tells us, He is equally the Maker of both, however unequal things may outwardly appear. But this should make you more loving and compassionate: so that where one thought may uplift you, the other will humble you and make you more modest. And what else does the Scripture say? *He that hath mercy on the poor, lendeth to the Lord* (Prov. xix. 17). Who would not have such

a Debtor, Who in due time will repay both loan and interest? And again it tells us: *By mercy and faith sins are purged away* (Prov. xv. 27).

XXXVII. Let us therefore purify ourselves through works of mercy. Let us by means of this beautiful herb remove from our souls all stains and all defilement; making them, some *white as wool*, some *white as snow* (Is. i. 18) according to the measure of the fervour and goodness of our heart. But let me add something you must rather fear. It is this. If there is in you no wound, no bruise, no swelling sores (Is. i. 6), no leprosy of the soul, no touch or a symptom, as of *something shining* (Lev. xiii. 2), which however small is still to be submitted to the Law, you still stand in need of the healing hand of Christ; and this at least out of reverence for Him Who was wounded for our iniquities, Who was bruised for our sins (Is. liii. 5). And you show reverence to Christ as often as you show yourself a kind and loving member of Christ.

And should the robber and oppressor of our soul find us on the way from Jerusalem to Jericho or elsewhere unarmed and unready, and wounds us, we may rightly say of ourselves: *My sores are putrified and corrupted, because of my foolishness* (Ps. xxxvii. 6). And if you are so stricken that you can neither seek help nor cure yourself, alas for the wound you have received, and how deep is your affliction. But if you are not wholly despairing, and are not wholly incurable, go to the Physician. Beg Him to cure your wounds by His wounds. Become like Him by being like Him; or rather, by small remedies heal yourself of great evils. *Say to thy soul: I am thy salvation* (Ps. xxxiv. 3); and also *Thy faith hath made thee whole* (Jn. v. 14). It is He has spoken all these words of compassion to you. Let you now be kind and merciful to those who suffer.

XXXVIII. *Blessed are the merciful*, says the Lord. *for they shall obtain mercy*. And not the least among the blessings is mercy. And *blessed is he that understandeth concerning the needy and the poor* (Ps. xl. 1). And again: *Acceptable is the man that sheweth mercy and lendeth* (Ps. cxi. 5). And in another place: *The just sheweth mercy, and lendeth all the day long* (Ps. xxxvi. 26). Let us grasp this blessing and, knowing we are called, let us be generous. Let not the night put an end to your pity. *Say not to thy friend: Go and come again, and to-morrow I will give to thee: when thou canst give now* (Prov. iii. 28). Let nothing come between your good will and the deed. This alone must suffer no delay: Kindness to another in need. *Deal thy bread to the hungry, and bring the needy and harbourless into thy house* (Is. lviii. 7); and do it with a joyful spirit. *He that showeth mercy*, says Paul, *let him show it with cheerfulness* (Rom. xii. 8). A kindness done promptly, is a kindness twice done. A favour done in a sour spirit, and because you must, is unlovely and without grace. We should be cheerful, not grieving, when we give mercy. If you break an evil bond or dissolve a contract that is oppressive (Is. lviii. 6), do it without pettiness and do it freely and without hesitation, and without muttering as to what will then happen?[12] What a great and wonderful thing to do! And deserving of such

a reward! *Then shall thy light break forth as the morning, and thy health shall speedily arise* (v. 8). Who now does not long for light and for healing?

XXXIX. I honour that purse of Christ (Jn. xii. 6) which encourages me to feed the poor, and also the agreement between Peter and Paul in which they divided between them the preaching of the Gospel, while sharing a common concern for the poor; and lastly that perfection in which it was laid down that he should give what he had to the poor (Mt. xix. 21). Is your kindness towards other freely given, or is it forced. Is it given because of the law or because of counsel? It is this latter I wholly desire and wish for you; for I am fearful of that *left hand side* and of *the goats*, and of the reproaches He shall make Who shall place them there (Mt. xxv. 33). Not because their hands have stolen what is another's, not because they have robbed and plundered, not because they have committed adultery or because they have done other forbidden things, but because they have not ministered to Christ in His poor.

XL. If therefore I have convinced you of anything, O Servants of Christ, who are my brothers and my fellow heirs, let us, while there is yet time, visit Christ in His sickness, let us have a care for Christ in His sickness, let us give to Christ to eat, let us clothe Christ in His nakedness, let us do honour to Christ, and not only at table, as some did (Lk. vii. 36), not only with precious ointments, as Mary did (Jn. xii. 3), not only in His tomb, as Joseph of Arimathea did, he who was a half-follower of Christ (Jn. xix. 38), not only doing him honour with gold, frankincense and myrrh, as the Magi did, and even before all these others we mention (Mt. ii. 11); but let us honour Him because the Lord of all will have mercy and not sacrifice (Mt. ix. 13), and goodness of heart above thousands of fat lambs (Dan.

iii. 40). Let us give Him this honour in His poor, in those who lie on the ground here before us this day, so that when we leave this world they may receive us into eternal tabernacles, in Jesus Christ our Lord, to Whom be there glory for all ages. Amen.

V. St Ambrose, Bishop and Doctor

The Good Samaritan[13]

A certain man went down from Jerusalem to Jericho, and fell among robbers (Lk. x. 23–37).

This is a simple account of a reality. And if we meditate deeply upon it, it will confirm for us certain wondrous mysteries. For Jericho is a figure of this world, to which Adam, cast forth from Paradise, the heavenly Jerusalem, because of sin, descended; that is, he descended from the things of eternal life to the things of this lower world: he who through, not change of place but change of will, had brought exile upon his posterity. For he was far changed from that Adam who had lived in untroubled blessedness, when he descended to earthly sinfulness and fell among robbers; and he would not have fallen among them, had he not exposed himself to them, through turning away from what God had laid down for him.

Who are these robbers, if not the angels of night and of darkness; who will at times change themselves into angels of light, but cannot remain so? These first of all strip us of the garments of spiritual grace we received, and this is how they are able to wound us. For had we preserved

the unstained garments we received, we could not feel the blows of the robbers. Watch therefore that they do not first strip you, as they stripped Adam in the beginning, as he was stripped of the protection of the divine commandment, as he was stripped of the garment of faith, and so received a deadly wound. In him all mankind would have been slain, had not this Samaritan, descending, taken care of his grievous wounds.

This was no ordinary Samaritan, who did not despise him whom the priest, whom the Levite had despised. And neither let you despise him because of the name of his people; the meaning of whose name will astonish you. For the word Samaritan means a defender. This is how it is interpreted. And who is a defender, if not He of Whom it was said: *The Lord is the defender of little ones* (Ps. cxiv. 6)? And as one man is a Jew in the letter, another in the spirit, so likewise one man is outwardly a Samaritan, another thing inwardly. Who then is this Samaritan who was going down? It is He *Who descended from heaven, and who had ascended into heaven, the Son of man who is in heaven* (Jn. iii. 13).

Seeing the man half dead, whom no one before Him had been able to cure; like that woman having an issue of blood *who had bestowed all her substance on physicians* (Lk. viii. 43); He *came near him*, that is, He came close to us by sharing our suffering, and a neighbour to us by showing us mercy.

And bound up his wounds, pouring in oil and wine.

Many are the remedies this Physician brings to heal us. His words are medicines. One word binds up our wounds, another soothes them with oil, another pours in wine. He binds our wounds by His more austere rule of life, He soothes us by the forgiveness of our sins, just as He urges us forward by the threat of His judgement.

And setting him upon his own beast.

Hear how He raises you up. *He bears our sins, and for us suffers* (Is. liii. 4, Sept.). And the Shepherd lays the weary sheep upon His own shoulders (Lk. xv. 5). For man had become like the beast (Ps. xlviii. 13). So He places us upon His own shoulders, lest we become like the horse and the mule (Ps. xxxi. 9); so that by taking upon Himself our body, He might do away with the weaknesses of our flesh.

And then He brought us to an inn; we who had become as beasts (Ps. lxxii. 23). It is to an inn they come who are weary from a long journey. And so the Lord takes us to an inn; He who *raises up the needy from the earth; lifting up the poor out of the dunghill* (Ps. cxii. 7). *And took care of him;* for fear the sick man might not be able to keep the precepts he had received.

But this Samaritan was not to stay long on earth. He must return whither He had come. *And accordingly the next day*, etc. What is this *next day*, if not the day of the Lord's Resurrection; of which it was said: *This is the day which the Lord hath made* (Ps. cxvii. 24)? *He took out two denarii, and gave to the host, and said: Take care of him.* What are these *two denarii*? Perhaps the two Testaments, upon which have been stamped the image of the Eternal King, by Whose price our wounds were healed? For we were redeemed by His Precious Blood, that we might escape the festering wounds of eternal death.

The innkeeper therefore receives the two *denarii* (and it would not be out of place to understand here, the four forms of these books; the Gospels). Who is he? He perhaps who says: *I count all things but as dung, that I may gain Christ* (Phil. iii. 8); from Whom he had received the care of the wounded man? An innkeeper therefore is he who said: *Christ sent me to preach the Gospel* (I Cor. i. 17). Innkeepers are they to whom it was said: *Go ye into the whole world and preach the Gospel to every creature. He that believeth and is baptized shall be saved* (Mk. xvi. 15, 16): saved from death, saved from the wound inflicted by the robbers. Blessed is that innkeeper who can cure another's wound.

Blessed is he to whom Jesus says: *Whatsoever thou shalt spend over and above, I, at my return, will repay thee.* He is a good steward who also spends over and above. Paul is a good steward, whose sermons and epistles are *over and above* the amount he had received. He had fulfilled the simple command of the Lord by toil of body and soul that was almost beyond measure; that he might relieve many of their grave sickness by the ministry of his spiritual comfort. Good therefore is the Innkeeper of his inn in which the ass knoweth the Lord's crib (Is. i. 3), and in which the lambs of the flock are gathered (Is. xl. 11); so that there shall be no easy assault upon the sheepfold by the wolves, howling and ravening without the fold.

He then promises payment when He returns. When will you return, O Lord, but on the Day of Judgement? For though Thou art everywhere at all times, and stand now in our midst, though we see Thee not, yet there shall be a time when *all flesh* shall behold Thee returning. Then Thou wilt repay what Thou owest. Blessed are they to whom Thou art Debtor! Would that we could repay what we have received, and that the office of Priest or of Levite (minister, *deacon*) might not

make us proud! How will you repay, O Lord Jesus? You promised the just that their *reward is very great in heaven* (Mt. v. 12). You will repay when You say: *Well done, good and faithful servant; because thou hast been faithful over a few things, I will place thee over many things. Enter thou into the joy of thy Lord* (Mt. xxv. 21).

And so since no one is more our neighbour than He Who has healed our wounds, let us love Him as our Lord, let us love Him as our neighbour; for nothing is closer than the Head to Its members. And let us also love him who is an imitator of Christ. Let us love him who in the unity of this Body has compassion on the need of another. For it is not kinship that makes a neighbour, but mercy. Because mercy accords with nature; for there is nothing so in accord with nature, than to help one who partakes of our nature. Amen.

VI. The Venerable Bede, Priest and Confessor

Blessed are the Eyes that See[14]

And turning to his disciples, he said: Blessed are the eyes that see and the things that you see (Lk. x. 23).

Not the eyes of the Scribes and Pharisees, which see only the Body of the Lord, but blessed those eyes that can see and know His divine secrets, of which He said to the Father: *Thou hast revealed them to little ones* (v. 21). Blessed are the eyes of the children to whom the Son has deigned to give the grace to know both Himself and the Father.

For I say to you, that many prophets and kings have desired to see the things that

you see, and have not seen them; and to hear the things that you hear, and have not heard them.

Abraham your father rejoiced that he might see my day: he saw it and rejoiced. Isaias also, and Micheas, and many other Prophets saw the glory of God; and because of this were called Seers. But all these saw Him through a glass in a dark manner, beholding Him and greeting Him from afar, while the Apostles had the Lord before their eyes, eating together with Him, and by questioning Him learning whatever they wished to know, and they had no need whatever to be taught by angels or by any kind of vision. Those whom Matthew more precisely calls *prophets and just men*, Luke speaks of as *many prophets and kings* (Mt. xiii. 17). For they are great kings; because they learned how to rule the impulses of temptations; by not yielding to them in surrender, but dominating and subjecting them.

And, behold, a certain lawyer stood up, tempting him, and saying: Master, what must I do to possess eternal life?

The lawyer who asked our Lord about eternal life, tempting Him, took occasion to tempt him from, I believe, the Lord's own earlier words, where He had said: *Rejoice in this, that your names are written in heaven.* But by this very temptation he makes clear to us, how true is the avowal of the Lord in which He says to the Father: *Thou hast hidden these things from the wise and prudent and hast revealed them to little ones.*

But he said to him: What is written in the law? How readest thou? He answering said: Thou shalt love the Lord thy God with thy whole heart and with thy whole soul and with all thy strength and with all thy mind; and thy neighbour as thyself.

In answering the lawyer, the Saviour sets before us the perfect road to the life of heaven. And to the man saying what is written in the law regarding the love of God and our neighbour, He says for the first time: *Thou hast answered right. This do, and thou shalt live.* And then when He had related the parable, and when the lawyer had replied that he was neighbour to the wounded man who had showed mercy to him, the Lord says to him

for the second time: *Go, and do thou in like manner;* that is: Remember that it is with such prompt mercy you must love and sustain your neighbour who is in need. And by this He has most clearly revealed to us, that it is charity alone, and not charity made known by word only, but that proved also by deed, which brings us to eternal life.

But he, willing to justify himself, said to Jesus: And who is my neighbour?

How empty the foolishness of vainglory! This lawyer, who according to the judgement of the Lord was wise and learned in the law, first pretends he does not know the command of the Law, not because he desires to humble himself among the little ones of Christ, but to justify himself, to capture the eyes of the crowd, by whom he would then be seen to answer wisely and well; He is not willing humbly to receive the *blessed eyes* that are *doves eyes, washed with the milk of innocence* (Cant. iv: 1; v, 12) with which he might have seen the hidden things of Christ. But the Lord answers him moderately, in order that He may teach us that every man becomes a neighbour to whomsoever he shows mercy, and at the same time this very parable describes in a special way the Son of God Himself, Who deigned by means of His humanity to become neighbour to us. But we must not so base our idea of the *neighbour* we are bidden to love as ourselves upon Christ, that we may determine the moral precepts of mutual fraternity by the rules of allegory.

And Jesus answering said: A certain man went down from Jerusalem to Jericho.

This man is interpreted as Adam, who stands for mankind. Jerusalem is that heavenly city of peace from whose blessedness he has fallen, and from which he has come down to this mortal and unhappy life. And well does Jericho, which is interpreted as the *moon*, stand for this ever-changing present life, since like the moon it is ever uncertain in its wanderings and in its changes.

And fell among robbers. Here for robbers understand the devil and his angels, among whom, as he came down, he fell. For had he not first through pride grown big within him, he would not have so easily fallen when tempted from without. True indeed are the words: *The spirit is uplifted before a fall* (Prov. xvi. 18).

Who also stripped him. They deprived him of the glory of the garment of immortality and innocence. For this is that *first robe* with which, according to another parable, the prodigal son, returning through repentance (Lk. xv. 22), was adorned, and, having lost it, our first parents saw themselves as naked, and put on the skin garments of a nature now mortal.

And having wounded him went away, leaving him half dead.

The wounds are sins, by means of which they implanted in his weakened body a sort of seedbed (if I may say so) of growing death, profaning the integrity of human nature. They went away, but not as ceasing from their assaults, but to conceal their attacks by craft. They left him half dead; for though they were able to strip him of the blessedness of im-

mortal life, they were not able to deprive him of the power of reason. For in that part of him in which he can taste and know God, man is alive. But in the part that is grown weak from sin and faints from wretchedness, he is dead; defiled by a mortal wound.

And it chanced that a certain priest went down the same way; and, seeing him, passed by. In like manner also a Levite, when he was near the place and saw him, passed by.

The Priest and the Levite, who seeing the wounded man passed by, signify the priesthood and ministry of the Old Testament, when the wounds of the clean sick could only be pointed out by the decrees of the Law, but could not be cured by them; for it was impossible (as the Apostle says) that by the blood of calves and lambs or by the blood of goats, *sin should* be taken away (Heb. x. 4).

But a certain Samaritan, being on his journey, came near him; and seeing him was moved with compassion.

The Samaritan, whose name means *Defender,* stands for the Lord, Whom the Prophet most fittingly implores to save him from falling among these robbers: *Keep me from the snare, which they have laid for me,* he cries; *and from the stumbling-blocks of them that work iniquity* (Ps. cxl. 9). He Who for us men and for our salvation, coming down from heaven, took the road of this present life and *came near him* who there lay perishing of the wounds inflicted on him; that is, *being made in the likeness of men, and in habit found as man* (Phil. ii. 7), came close to us in His compassion, and became our neighbour through the consolation of His mercy.

And, going up to him, bound up his wounds, pouring in oil and wine.

He binds up the sins, which He finds in men, by rebuking them; inspiring with the fear of punishment those who sin, and with hope those who repent. For He binds up our wounds when He commands us: *Do penance.* He pours in oil, when He adds: *For the kingdom of heaven is at hand* (Mt. iv. 17). He pours in wine also, when He says: *Every tree that doth not yield good fruit, shall be cut down and cast into the fire* (Mt. iii. 10).

And, setting him upon his own beast, brought him to an inn and took care of him.

The beast is His own Flesh, in which He deigned to come to us. On It He placed wounded man, *because He bore our sins in His Body upon the tree* (I. Pet. ii. 24); and according to another parable, *laid upon his shoulders* the lost sheep that was found, and brought it back to the flock (Lk. xv. 4). And so to be placed upon *His own beast*, is to believe in the Incarnation of Christ, and to be instructed in Its mysteries, and at the same time to be safeguarded from the assaults of the enemy. The inn is the present Church, where travellers, returning to their eternal home, are refreshed on their journey. And well does He bring to the inn the man He placed upon His own beast; for no one, unless he who is baptized, unless he is united to the Body of Christ, shall enter the Church.

And the next day he took out two pence and gave to the host and said: Take care of him.

The *next day* is, after the Resurrection of the Lord. For even before this He had, by the grace of His Gospel, enlightened those who sat in darkness and in the shadow of death (Lk. i. 79), but after His Resurrection there shone out the mightier splendour of His Perpetual Light. The *two pence* are the Two Testaments, in which are contained the Name and Image of the Eternal King. For the end of the Law is *Christ* (Rom. x. 4). These He took out next day, *and gave them to the host*: for it was then *He opened their understanding, that they might understand the Scriptures* (Lk. xxiv. 45). The next day the innkeeper received the *denarii*, as payment for taking care of the wounded man; for the Holy Spirit coming down, taught the Apostles *all truth* (Jn. xvi. 13), by means of which they would be able to preach the Gospel and to stand secure in instructing the Gentiles.

And whatsoever thou shalt spend over and above, I, at my return, will repay thee. The Innkeeper spends over and above the two pence he received when the Apostle says: *Now concerning virgins I have no commandment of the Lord; but I give counsel.* And again: *So also the Lord ordained that they who preach the Gospel should live by the Gospel* (I Cor. vii. 25; ix. 14). But we have not used this privilege, so as not to be a burden to any of you (I Thess. ii. 9). But at His return, the Debtor will repay what He promised; for the Lord, coming in judgement, shall say: *Because thou hast been faithful over a few things, I will place thee over many things. Enter thou into the joy of thy Lord* (Mt. xxv. 23).

Which of these three in thy opinion was neighbour to him that fell among robbers? But he said: He that showed mercy to him.

From these words Christ's mind has been made clear to us: That no one is more a neighbour to us than he who shows us mercy: even one who is not a priest of the city of Jerusalem, even one not a Levite from the same race, even if both were born and reared in the same city, but one was of another race; for it was rather he who was merciful, who became a neighbour. But, receiving this in its more sacred sense, since no one is more our neighbour than He who has healed our wounds let us love Him as *the Lord our God,* let us love Him as *our neighbour.* For nothing is so close as the head is to the members. Let us also love him who is an imitator of Christ. For this is what follows.

And Jesus said to him: Go, and do thou in like manner; that is, show that you truly love your neighbour as yourself, doing with love whatever you can do to help him, also in his spiritual necessities, to the praise and glory of God the Father, Son and Holy Ghost, Amen.

NOTES

[1] These denied that the God of the O.T. is the true God; nor do they, as Augustine notes, accept that the Judaic law was truly given by God.

[2] PG 45, col. 1609–64, *Hypomnesticon contra pelagianos et celestianos.* Inauthentic; possibly of Marius Mercator, about A.D. 435.

[3] PG 13, Hom. 34, col. 1886. From the Latin of St Jerome's translation.

[4] PG 31, col. 905, *Regulae Fusius Translatae.* A catechetical exposition of the First Commandment for his monastic brethren.

[5] PG 32, Sermon III, col. 1147. One of twenty-four sermons compiled from the works of St Basil by Simeon Logotheta; principally from the first exposition of the Longer Rules, letters, and the homilies of the Hexaemeron.

[6] PG 35, Oratio XIV, col. 857. *On the love of the poor.* (On the Lepers.) This sermon would have suited other Gospels, but is particularly suited to today's. The Saint here treats with power and beauty of that charity that is the highest flowering of the Christian soul, with a compassion and understanding of the working of charity, and its place in the Christian Dispensation, that scarcely any of the great Fathers has approached.

[7] The reference to St Peter's frugality is from some unknown source. Note, Combefis, l.c.

[8] *The sacred disease,* ἱερὰ νόσος; the sacred, therefore, great or mystical disease: Leprosy. This discourse was delivered (*circa* A.D. 373) probably at a hospice for the sick in Caesarea (built 370–1), and in the presence of his friend, St Basil M. of Caesarea.

[9] As such things are not lacking to our times, neither were they then. They were some of the earliest fruits of Christianity. The effective compassion of Basil is testified to by the many great institutes of mercy, forming a new town, with ample revenues for their upkeep, erected by him round outside the city of

Caesarea, of which now no trace remains.

¹⁰ The holy Preacher, or else some scribe, makes a slip in referring this (Amos vi. 4) to Micheas.

¹¹ By the use of the phrases, τὸ ἄτακτον, and καὶ παρ ἑαυτῆς, the *Theologos* anticipates the reality now established: that it is an 'irregularity' and that it is not produced by the body 'of itself', in its 'ordinary' course. This soundness of judgement was against the opinions of his day, and even of Aristotle, who favoured some form of 'spontaneous generation'. Men's instinct presupposed contagion, by some means.

¹² We have to admire the acumen with which the Saint interprets the passage from Isaias xlviii. 6. Just as in bestowing alms, as in receiving the needy, there is, often, much enquiry or suspicion as to whether they are deserving or not, etc. It is far better, for the sake of those who are deserving, to give alms even to the undeserving; lest we pass over the deserving, for fear of giving to the undeserving. Cf. PG 36, col. 909, note (35).

¹³ PL 15, *Evang. Sec. Lucam*, Lib. VIII, Incip. par 73, col. 1718.

¹⁴ PL 92, *In Lucae Evang. Expositio* Lib. III, Cap. X, col. 467. This luminous exposition is plainly drawn from the stream of Origen and Augustine.

THIRTEENTH SUNDAY AFTER PENTECOST

I. St Basil the Great: On Faith

II. St Augustine: Ingratitude

II. St Augustine: Thankfulness in Prosperity

IV. St Augustine: Bless the Lord and Honour His Bride

V. The Venerable Bede: Exposition of the Gospel

THE GOSPEL OF THE SUNDAY

Luke xvii. 11–19

At that time: As Jesus was going to Jerusalem, he passed through the midst of Samaria and Galilee. And as he entered into a certain town, there met him ten men that were lepers, who stood afar off and lifted up their voice, saying: Jesus, Master, have mercy on us. Whom when he saw, he said: Go, shew yourselves to the priests. And it came to pass, as they went, they were made clean. And one of them, when he saw that he was made clean, went back, with a loud voice glorifying God. And he fell on his face before his feet, giving thanks. And this was a Samaritan. And Jesus, answering, said: Were not ten made clean? And where are the nine? There is no one found to return and give glory to God, but this stranger. And he said to him: Arise, go thy way; for thy faith hath made thee whole.

EXPOSITION FROM THE CATENA AUREA

AMBROSE: After the parable that preceded, He then rebukes the ungrateful. For we are told that:

V.11. *And it came to pass, as he was going to Jerusalem . . .*

TITUS OF BOSTRA: That He might show that the Samaritans were people of good will, but the Jews ungrateful for the benefits He spoke of. For there was discord between the Jews and Samaritans, and as it were to reconcile them, He passes through the midst, to make both *into one new man.*

CYRIL: Then the Saviour manifests His glory, drawing Israel to faith. Hence follows:

V.12. *And as he entered into a certain town, there met him ten men that were lepers.*

Men driven from towns and cities, as unclean, under the Mosaic law.

72

TITUS: Because their common affliction had made them of one mind,
they were wont to live together; and
they waited about for Jesus' passing,
restless till they saw Christ approaching. Then follows: *who stood afar off*;
because Judaic law held leprosy unclean; but the law of the Gospel
holds that it is not outward leprosy,
but inward that is unclean.

THEOPHYLACTUS: They stood afar
off, as though ashamed of the uncleanness imputed to them. For they
thought that like others Christ also
would be repelled by them. So they
stood afar off from Him in place, but
they were brought close to Him by
their prayer. *For, the Lord is nigh unto
all that call upon him; to all that call
upon him in truth* (Ps. cxliv. 18).
Hence follows:

V.13. *And lifted up their voice, saying: Jesus, Master, have mercy on us.*
TITUS: They plead in the name of
Jesus, and gain the reality it stands
for: for Jesus means Saviour. They
say: *Have mercy on us*; knowing
through experience of His power.
They asked neither silver nor gold,
but that they might receive a body
that could be seen to be sound.

THEOPHYLACTUS: Nor did they
simply beg of Him, or ask of Him as
a mortal man. For they call Him,
Master, that is, Lord; by which they
seem almost to think He was God.
But He commands them to go show
themselves to the Priests. For they
were to learn whether they were
legally made clean of leprosy or not.

V.14. *Whom when he saw, he said:
Go, shew yourselves to the priests.*
CYRIL: For the law commanded that

those made clean from leprosy
should offer a sacrifice because of
being made clean. THEOPHYLACTUS:
To command them to go to the
Priests therefore meant nothing else
but that they were about to be
healed. So there follows: *And it came
pass, as they went, they were made
clean.*

CYRIL: From this the Chief Priests of
the Jews, who were envious of His
power, could see that they had been
suddenly and miraculously healed;
through Christ granting them health.

THEOPHYLACTUS: And though they
were ten, nine who were Israelites
were ungrateful; but the Samaritan
stranger, going back, gave thanks.
Hence we have:

V.15. *And one of them, when he saw
that he was made clean, went back, with
a loud voice glorifying God.*

TITUS: The purification he had received gave him confidence to draw
near to Jesus. So there follows:

V.16. *And he fell on his face before
his feet, giving thanks . . .*

His prostration and his prayer
making plain his faith and gratitude.
And there follows: *and this was a
Samaritan.*

THEOPHYLACTUS: From this one may
know that nothing prevents a man
from pleasing God, even though he
comes of a pagan people, so long as
his intention is good. Nor should
anyone born of holy people pride
himself on this: for the nine who
were Israelites, were ungrateful.
Hence follows:

VV.17, 18. *And Jesus, answering,*

said: Were not ten made clean? And where are the nine? There is no one found to return and give glory to God, but this stranger.

TITUS: By this we are shown that strangers were more ready for the faith: for Israel was slow to believe. Then follows:

V.19. *And he said to him: Arise, go thy way; for thy faith hath made thee whole.*

AUGUSTINE, *Questions on the Gospels,* II, 40: They may, mystically, be understood as lepers who, having no knowledge of the True Faith, *profess* various false doctrines. For these do not hide their ignorance, but proclaim it as the highest learning, and pride themselves on their discourses. Leprosy is a blemish of colour. True and false doctrines therefore mingled without order in a man's argument or discussion, and showing like colours on a human body, resemble leprosy which spots and blemishes human bodies with patches of true and false colour. The Church must shun such as these, so that they may, if possible, from afar off cry out with a loud voice to Christ. That they invoked Him as *Master,* does, I think, sufficiently indicate that false doctrine is a leprosy which a good teacher will wipe away.

We see that none of those upon whom the Lord bestowed corporal favours were sent to the Priests except lepers. For the Jewish Priesthood was a figure of the Priesthood of the Church. Other vices the Lord Himself heals and corrects, inwardly in the conscience; but teaching or the power to bestow the sacraments or to catechize by word, He gave to the Church.

Who, as they went, were made clean.

For the Gentiles, to whom Peter had come, and who had not yet received the sacrament of Baptism, by which we come spiritually to the Priests, are declared clean when *the grace of the Spirit was poured out on them* (Acts x. 44). Whosoever therefore in the society of the Church follows the true and perfect teaching, and by this shews himself free of the leprous patchwork of false doctrine, yet, still ungrateful, does not with devout humility, prostrate himself before God, Who made him clean, is like those of whom the Apostle says, *that, when they knew God, they have not glorified Him as God, or given thanks* (Rom. i. 21). And accordingly such as these will remain as imperfect; in the number of the nine. For nine need one that they may be joined together in a certain form of unity, and so become ten. He however who gave thanks is commended as a figure of the One Church. And because the others were Jews, they are declared to have lost through pride the kingdom of heaven, where unity is supremely guarded. But he who was a Samaritan, which is interpreted as *guardian,* attributing to Him from Whom he received it, what he had received, in accord with the words, *I will guard my strength for thee* (Ps. lviii. 10), guards with humble devotion the unity of the kingdom.

BEDE: He fell upon his face, because he was ashamed of the evils he remembers he had committed. He is bidden to rise, and *go his way;* because he who, knowing his own weakness, remains humble, is bidden through the consolation of the divine word, *To put forth his hand to strong things* (Prov. xxxi. 19). But if faith made him whole who had bowed down to give thanks; then want of faith ruined those who neglected to give glory to God for the favours they had received: for, as the previous parable shows, faith is increased through humility, so here the same is shown by these events.

I. St Basil the Great, Bishop and Doctor

Concerning Faith[1]

1. The continual remembrance of God is a holy thing, and of this pious remembrance there can never be enough for the soul that loves God. But to put into words the things of God is a bold undertaking. For our mind falls far below what is needed for this; while at the same time, words but feebly convey the thoughts of the mind. If therefore our understanding is left so far behind by the greatness of the things of God, and if our words are weaker than our understanding, how should we not be silent, for fear that the wonders of the things of God should be in danger through the feebleness of our words? Though the desire to give glory to God is implanted by nature in every rational creature, nevertheless we all alike are unable to praise Him fittingly. But though we differ one from another in our desire to praise and serve God, yet there is no one so blinds himself, so deceives himself, as to think that he has attained to the summit of human understanding. Rather, the further we advance in knowledge, the more clearly we perceive our own insignificance. So it was with Abraham. So it was with Moses. For when it was given to them to see God, as far as man can see God, then especially did they humble themselves: Abraham spoke of himself as, *dust and ashes* (Gen. xviii. 27), and

Moses said he was a stammerer and *slow of tongue* (Exod. iv. 10). For he knew the poverty of his tongue, and that it was unable to serve the greatness of the things he had grasped with his mind.

But since every ear is now open to hear me speak of the things of God, and since there is never enough in the Church of hearing of these things, confirming the words of Ecclesiastes about them: *The ear is not filled with hearing* (i. 8), we must therefore speak as best we can. But we shall speak, not of God as He is, but of God as far as it is possible for us to know Him. For though we cannot with mortal eyes see all that lies between heaven and earth, yet there is no reason why we should not look upon what we can see. So with our few words we shall now endeavour to fulfil what is required of us in the service of God; but in every word of ours we humbly bow before the majesty of His Divine Nature: for not even the tongue of Angels, whatever they may be, nor the tongues of Archangels, joined to those of every reasoning creature, would be able to describe its least part, much less attain to speak of the Whole.

But you, if you would speak of God, or hear of Him, go out from your body, put aside your bodily senses, leave this earth behind you, leave the sea behind you, set the skies beneath you, pass beyond the measuring of time, the procession of the seasons, the ordered perfection of the universe, rise above the heavens, pass beyond the stars, and the wonders that relate to them, their ordered movement, their magnitude, their service to all the universe, their harmony, their shining splendour, their ordered station, their motion, their rotation one in respect of another. Passing in mind beyond all these things, raised above them all, gaze in thought upon all the beauty there, upon the heavenly hosts, the Angelic Choirs, the Dignities of the Archangels, the Glory of the Dominations, the Seats of the Thrones, the Virtues, the Principalities, the Powers. Passing beyond all these, reaching upwards in thought beyond every created thing, uplifting the mind beyond them, now contemplate the Divine Nature: stable, immovable, unchangeable, impassable, simple, indivisible, *dwelling in light inaccessible* (I Tim. vi. 10), surpassing glory, goodness the most desired, beauty inconceivable; which fastens fiercely upon the soul, wounding it, yet cannot fittingly be spoken of in words.

2. There are the Father and the Son and the Holy Spirit: Nature Uncreated, Sovereign Majesty, Goodness Itself. The Father the beginning of all things, the Source of existence of all that is, the Root of all that lives. From Him comes forth the Fount of Life, Wisdom, Power, *the perfect Image of the invisible God* (Col. i. 15), the Son Begotten of the Father, the Living Word, Who is God, Who is with God (Jn. i. 2), not added to Him; Who is before all

ages, not afterwards acquired; a Son, not a possession; a Maker, not made; a Creator, not created; Who is whatever the Father is.

Son, I say, and Father. Note with me these particular terms. While remaining as Son, He is all the Father is; as the words of the Lord Himself bear witness, saying: *All things whatsoever the Father hath, are mine* (Jn. xvi. 15). All that belongs to the First Form, is found also in the Image. For, *we saw his glory*, says the Evangelist, *the glory as it were of the Only-Begotten of the Father* (Jn. i. 14); that is, He has not received all these wondrous things by gift or by grace, but by reason of their common Nature the Son shares with the Father the *glory* of the Godhead. For to receive, is common to everything created; to have by nature, belongs only to one who has been begotten. As Son therefore He possesses all that the Father possesses; and as the Only-Begotten, He holds this *all* within Himself as His; sharing no part of it with another. From this that He is called *Son*, we learn that He shares His Father's Nature, that He was not created by the Divine command, but that beaming forth unceasingly from His Substance, united timelessly to the Father, He is equal to Him in Goodness, equal in Power, equal in Majesty. For what is He but His Seal and Image, wholly manifesting the Father in Himself?

All that is said to you after this of His bodily state, of the Plan of man's redemption, that He showed Himself to us clothed in Flesh, His saying that He was *sent*, that of Himself He could do nothing, that He had received a command, and such things, let none of these give you grounds to lessen in any way the Godhead of the Only-Begotten. For the condescension of His coming down to you, does not lessen the power of His Majesty. Rather, think of His nature in a manner befitting the Godhead, but accept the lowlier things spoken of Him as relating to the task of our redemption. And were we now to speak, with exactness, of these things, we would without noticing it heap up a vast, an endless number of words upon the subject.

3. But to return to the subject we have set before us. The mind then that has been able to purify itself of all earthly affections, and to leave behind it every known creature, and, like some fish from the deep, swim upwards to the light, now attaining to the purity of the beginning, with the Father and Son, there shall look upon the Holy Spirit, Who by reason of His essential Unity of Nature with Them shares also in their Goodness, Their Justice, Their Holiness, Their Life. For *Thy Spirit*, it is written, *is good* (Ps. cxlii. 10). And again, He is *a right Spirit* (Ps. i. 12). And again, He is *Thy holy Spirit* (v. 13). And the Apostle also speaks of: *The law of the Spirit of life* (Rom. viii. 2). Of these things none has been received by Him, none afterwards added to Him; but as heat is inseparable from fire and radiance from light, so Sanctification cannot be separated from the Holy Spirit, nor the Giving of Life, nor Goodness, nor Justice.

There then is the Spirit, there in the Blessed Nature; not numbered with a multitude, but contemplated in the Trinity; singly made known to us, not included within the heavenly orders. For as the Father is one, and the Son one, so likewise is the Holy Ghost one. But the ministering spirits each in their single order, shine forth to us an innumerable host. Seek not then among creatures that Which is above creation. And lower not the Sanctifier among those He sanctifies. He fills the Angels, He fills the Archangels, He sanctifies the Powers He gives life to all. He is divided among all creatures, and though partaken of in different measure by each yet in nothing is He lessened by those who partake of Him. To all He gives of His grace, remaining unconsumed by those who partake of it. And while they who receive are filled, in nothing is He lessened. And just as the sun shines on our bodies and is enjoyed by them in varying degrees, while in no way is its heat diminished by those who share in it, so also the Spirit, while giving of His grace to all, remains Himself whole and undivided.

He enlightens all men, that they may know God. He breathes upon the Prophets, He gives wisdom to lawmakers, He consecrates priests, fills kings with strength, perfects the just, honours the wise and prudent, works in the gifts of healing, gives life to the dead, frees those who are in bonds, and of strangers makes children of adoption. And all this He accomplishes through *the new birth* (cf. Jn. iii. 4). He finds a publican who now believes, and makes him an Evangelist (Mt. ix. 9). He comes upon one who is a fisherman, and makes him a Teacher of divine things (Mt. iv. 19). He comes upon a persecutor who has repented, and makes him the Apostle of the Gentiles, a Preacher of the Faith, a Vessel of election (Acts ix. 15).

Through Him the weak become strong, the poor rich, the ignorant become wiser than the wise. Paul was weak, yet, through the Presence of the Spirit, the cloths that wiped the sweat of his body brought healing to those who touched them (Acts xix. 12). Peter too was clothed in a weak body, yet through the grace of the Spirit dwelling within him, the shadow of his body delivered the sick from their infirmities (Acts v. 15).

Peter and John were poor – for they had neither gold nor silver – yet they bestowed a healing more precious than much gold. The lame man that sat at the gate of the Temple received money from many people, yet remained a beggar. But receiving this grace from Peter he ceased to be a beggar, and leaping like a deer he began to praise God (Acts iii. 6). John knew not the wisdom of this world, but through the power of the Spirit he speaks of things that no human wisdom could come to know.

The Spirit dwells in heaven, yet fills the earth; and though present everywhere, is nowhere contained. He dwells Whole in each one, yet is wholly with God. He distributes His gifts, not as one who ministers, but of His own authority gives graces as He wills; for *He distributes*, says the Scriptures, *his gifts to each one as he wishes* (I Cor. xii. 11). He is *sent* in the Divine Plan of our Redemption, but acts of His own power. Let us beg of Him to help us by His Presence in our souls, and that He may never depart from us, through the grace of our Lord Jesus Christ, to Whom be glory and honour world without end. Amen.

II. St Augustine, Bishop and Doctor

Ingratitude [2]

The sinner shall borrow, and not pay again: but the just sheweth mercy, and shall give (Ps. xxxvi. 21).

The sinner receives, but he does not return. What does he not return? He does not return thanks. What does God wish of you, or what does God demand of you, save what is for your good? And how great the favours the sinner receives, for which he does not pay? He receives existence, that he is a man, and that‘ between him and the beast there is a great difference. He has received a bodily nature, and he has received with his body a variety of senses; eyes to see, ears to hear, nostrils to smell, a palate to taste, hands to touch, feet to walk, and also health of body. So far gifts such as these we have in common with the beasts. But man has received more; that is a mind that can understand, that can grasp truth, that can tell what is just from what is unjust, that has power to search for, to long for his Creator, to praise Him and to hold fast to Him. All this the sinner also receives, but not living justly he does not repay as he should. Therefore, *the sinner shall borrow*, and not pay again; he shall not repay Him, from Whom he received, nor give thanks; rather, for good he returns evil, and blasphemies, murmuring against God, contempt.

Therefore, he, *the sinner, shall borrow and not pay again; but the just sheweth mercy, and shall give.* The one because he has nothing; the other because he has. Here is poverty; here riches. The one receives, and will not repay. The other shows mercy, lends and is made rich. What if a man is poor? Even so he is rich. Look at His riches with eyes of faith only. For you look only at an empty purse; not at a conscience filled with God. Outwardly he has nothing, but within he has charity. How much can one give from charity, and not exhaust it! Even if a man is outwardly rich, it is still charity that gives, from what it possesses. And if outwardly it has nothing to give, it gives kindness, it offers counsel, if it can; it offers help, if it can. And if it can help neither by counsel nor with money, it helps in desire, or prays for the one in affliction, and perhaps for this it is heeded more than one who gives bread.

He has ever something to give whose breast is filled with charity. And that is charity which men also call good will. God asks no more of you, than He has placed within your heart. For a good will is never without something. And when you have no good will, you will give nothing to the poor of that of which you have no need. The poor help each other out of good will; and they are not without fruit, one from the other. You see a blind man led by one who sees; who since he has no money to give to the poor, lends his eyes to the man who has none. How could this happen, that he should lend his own members to one who was without them, unless he had that good will which is the treasure of the poor? That treasure in which there is most soothing peace, and true security. No thief is admitted, to the loss of this, no shipwreck feared. It preserves with itself what it holds within; bereft of all things, it is still full. The *just man,* therefore, *showeth mercy and shall give.*

Let us give thanks to our Lord and Saviour, Who without any previous merits of ours has healed our wounds, made us His friends who were His enemies, redeemed us from captivity, led us from darkness into light and recalled us from death to life; and humbly confessing our own infirmity, we implore His mercy, so that with mercy guiding us, He Who has deigned to give us His gifts and graces may also deign to safeguard and increase them, Who with the Father and the Holy Spirit liveth and reigneth world without end.[3] Amen.

III. St Augustine, Bishop and Doctor

Thankfulness in Prosperity[4]

For in his lifetime his soul will be blessed; and he will praise thee when thou shalt do well to him (Ps. xlviii. 19).

In his lifetime his soul will be blessed. Let your Charity reflect on these words: *In his lifetime his soul will be blessed.* As long as he lived he did well for himself. This all men say, but they speak falsely. It is blessing that comes from the desire of the one blessing, not from Truth Itself. For what is it you are saying? Because he ate and drank, because he did what he wished, and because he feasted splendidly every day, he therefore did well for himself. But I say he did badly for himself. It is not I who say this, but Christ. He did evil to himself. For Dives, when he *feasted sumptuously every day* (Lk. xvi. 19), thought he did well for himself. But when he began to burn in hell, then what he thought good was found to be evil. For what he had eaten among the living, he digested in hell. I speak here of evil-doing, brethren, on which he was wont to feast.

He ate rich banquets with the mouth of his body; with the mouth of his heart he ate injustice. What he ate among the living with the mouth of his heart; it was this he digested in hell amid torments. He had indeed eaten well in time; he digested unhappily in eternity. Do we then eat evil-doing? Someone will say: what is he saying? Do we eat evil? It is not I who say this; listen to the Scriptures: *As a sour grape is an affliction to the teeth, and smoke to the eyes, so is evil doing to . them that indulge in it* (Prov. x. 26, Sept.). For he who has eaten iniquity that is, he who has freely indulged in evil-doing, is unable to eat justice. For justice is bread. What bread? *I am the living bread which came down from heaven* (Jn. vi. 51). He is Himself the Bread of our heart. Just as he who eats sour grapes with the mouth of his body, has his teeth set on edge and is unable to eat bread; and must continue to praise what he sees, while unable to eat it; so he who indulges in iniquity, and eats sin in his heart, begins to be unable to eat bread; he praises the word of God, but does not do it.

Why is it he does not do it? Because when he begins to do it, he labours; just as we when we have

eaten sour grapes feel our teeth labouring when we try to eat bread. But what do they do whose teeth are on edge? They restrain themselves for a time from sour grapes, till their teeth become firm, and then apply themselves to the bread. So also do we praise justice. But if we would eat justice, let us restrain ourselves from evil doing; and there will be born in our heart, not alone the delight of praising justice, but also the power to eat it. For if the Christian says: 'God knows that my delight is in this, but I am unable to fulfil it'; his teeth are weakened, because he has long eaten of iniquity. Is justice therefore also eaten? If it were not eaten, the Lord would not have said: *Blessed are they that hunger and thirst after justice* (Mt. v. 6). Therefore since *in his lifetime his soul will be blessed:* in life it shall be blessed, but in death it shall be tormented.

He will praise thee, when thou shalt do well to him. Apply your minds to this and be fed. Keep it close within your hearts. Eat, reflect upon such persons; and be not such as they are. Beware of these words: *He will praise thee, when thou shalt do well to him.* How many are the Christians, brethren, who give thanks to God when they gain something! This is the meaning of: *he will praise thee, when thou shalt do well to him.* He will praise Thee, and he will say: Thou art truly my God. He has delivered me from prison; I will praise Him. Wealth comes his way; he praises God. He receives an inheritance; he praises God. He suffers loss; he curses Him. What kind of son are you, who when the Father corrects you, He then becomes hateful to you? Would he have corrected you, unless you had displeased Him? Or had you so displeased Him that He hated you, would He have corrected you? Then give thanks to your Corrector, that you may receive an inheritance from God Who corrects you. For when you are being corrected, you are being taught. And He corrects you often; for great is that which you are to receive. For if you weigh your correction against what you are to receive, you will find that being corrected is as nothing. The Apostle Paul says this: *For that which is at present momentary and light of our tribulation, worketh for us above measure exceedingly an eternal weight of glory.* But when? *While we look not,* he says, *at the things which are seen, but at the things which are not seen. For the things which are seen are temporal; but the things which are not seen are eternal* (II Cor. iv. 17, 18). And again: *The sufferings of this time, are not worthy to be compared with the glory to come, that shall be revealed in us* (Rom. viii. 18).

What therefore do you suffer? But, you say, you are suffering all the time. I agree. Suppose that from the moment of your birth, through all the years of your life till extreme age, and until you died, you suffered what Job suffered; what he suffered for a few days, another may suffer from infancy. What you suffer passes, comes to an end; what you are to receive, shall never end. I would not have you weigh your suffering against your reward. But weigh, if you can, the things of time against eternity.

He will praise thee, when thou shalt do well to him.

Brethren: Do not be like such persons. Understand that it is for this we are saying these things, it is for this we forewarn you, it is for this we treat of these things, it is for this we sweat and toil: Be not guilty of such things. Your daily tasks are a trial to you. Sometimes in your dealings you hear the Truth, and you blaspheme, you speak evil against the Church. Why? Because you are good Christians? If that be so, I'll join the Donatists. I'll become a pagan. Why then? Because you have bitten bread, and your teeth pain you. When you first saw this same bread, you used to praise it. You began to eat it, and your teeth hurt you: that is, when you began to hear the word of God, you were full of praise of it. But when you were told, do this, you speak evil of it.

You must not think or speak like this. Say this: This is good bread, but I am unable to eat it. Now, if you see it with your eyes, you praise it; but when you begin to put your teeth in it, you say: This is bad bread, and what sort of a man made it? And so it is you praise God, when God does well by you. And therefore you lie, when you sing: *I will bless the Lord at all times: his praise shall be always in my mouth* (Ps. xxxiii. 2). The song of your lips comes to an end in your heart. In the Church you sang: *I will bless the Lord at all times.* What do you mean by, *at all times?* If I make a profit at all times, He will be praised at all times. If now and then there is loss, He will not be blessed, He will be cursed. Certainly you bless the Lord at all times, and no doubt His praise is always in your mouth? But it will be the kind of blessing and praise just now described: *He will praise thee, when thou shalt do well to him.*

Turning then to the Lord God, the Father Almighty, let us, from a pure heart, and as far as our littleness can, offer Him fullest, overflowing thanks; with our whole soul beseeching His singular mildness, that in His good pleasure He will deign to hear our prayers, and by His power drive what is evil from our thoughts and actions, that He may increase our faith, guide our minds, grant us His holy inspirations and lead us to His own blessedness through Jesus Christ His Son.[5] Amen.

IV. St Augustine, Bishop and Doctor

Bless the Lord and Honour His Bride[6]

The mercies of the Lord I will sing for ever. Blessed be the Lord for evermore (Ps. lxxxviii. 1, 53).

Blessed be the Lord for evermore. Amen. Amen. Thanks be to His mercy. Thanks be to His grace. We but express our thanks; we do not give them, nor render them, nor make a return of them, nor repay them. We express our thankfulness in words; the reality we hold within us. He has freely saved us. He heeded not our iniquities; He sought us who did not seek Him. He found us, He redeemed us, He delivered us from the domination of the devil and from the power of demons. He bound us, to purify us by faith; by which He frees those enemies who do not believe, and cannot therefore be made clean. Let those who remain enemies say day after day what they will; day by day less and less will be left?[7] Let them resist Him, let them laugh; let them mock, not at the *destruction,* but at *the change of thy anointed.*[8] Do they not see that saying such things they come to nothing; either by not believing (Jn. iii. 18) or by dying?[9] For their cursing is only for a time; the blessing of the Lord is for evermore.

And to confirm the blessing, lest anyone be fearful, there is added: *Amen. Amen.* This is the signature of God's pledge to us. Secure therefore in His promises, let us believe in things past (Wis. viii. 8), let us learn of things present, and hope for the things to come. Let the enemy not turn us aside from the way; so that she may cherish us who gathers us as chickens under her wings. And neither let us stray from under her wings, lest the hawk in the sky bear off the still unfledged chickens. For the Christian ought not to hope in himself. If he wishes to be strong, let him be cared for in her maternal warmth. For she is that hen gathering her chickens under her wing the Lord spoke of when He reproached the unbelieving city of Jerusalem: *How often would I have gathered together thy children, as the hen doth gather her chickens under her wings, and thou wouldst not? Behold your house shall be left to you, desolate* (Mt. xxiii. 37, 38). For this was it written: *Thou hast made his strength a dread* (v. 41). And so since they would not be gathered under the wings of this hen, they have given us such a warning, that we should live in fear of the winged unclean spirits, daily seeking their prey. Let us enter in under the wings of this hen of the Divine Wisdom; since she because of her young was made weak unto death.

Let us love the Lord our God. Let us love His Church: Him as our Father, her as our Mother; Him as our Lord, her as His Handmaid; for we are the children of His Handmaid. And this marriage is joined together by a great love: let no one offend one partner, and seek to gain the favour of the other. Let no one say: 'I do go to idols; I also consult those who have familiar spirits, and the fortune tellers. All the same, I have not left the Church of God. I am still a Catholic.' While clinging to your Mother, you have offended your Father.

Again another will say: 'Far be it from me to do such things. I have nothing to do with soothsayers. I do not go looking for someone possessed by a spirit, nor seek advice through sacrilegious divinations; nor do I go to the worship of demons. And neither do I serve idols. But I am however a Donatist.' What does it avail you not to offend your Father, since He will punish your offences against your Mother?

What does it profit you to praise the Lord, to honour Him, to preach Him, believe in His Son and confess that He sits at the right hand of God the Father; while at the same time you blaspheme His Church? Does the example of human marriage not move you to correct your error? If you have some patron, to whom you pay respects each day, whose doorstep you wear out with your attentions, whom you, I will not say salute, but before whom you actually bow down and adore, paying him daily homage; supposing you were to make just one accusation against his wife, would you enter his house again?

Hold fast therefore, Dearly Beloved, let all of you with one mind hold fast to God our Father, and to the Church our Mother. Commemorate with sobriety the heavenly birthdays of the saints, that we may imitate those who have gone before us, and that they may rejoice over you who now pray for you, so that the blessing of the Lord may remain upon you for evermore. Amen and Amen.

V. The Venerable Bede, Priest and Doctor

Exposition of the Gospel[10]

And it came to pass that there met him ten men that were lepers (Lk. xvii. 12).

They may well be described as lepers who, while having no true knowledge of the faith, profess a variety of heretical teachings. For such people do not hide their ignorance, but proclaim it as the height of learning; priding themselves on what they have to say. There is no false doctrine in which some truth is not mingled. True doctrine therefore mixed without order with what is false, in a man's discussion or conversation, and showing like the colours in a body, resemble the leprosy that spots and blemishes the human body with patches of true and false colour. Such persons are to be excluded from the Church so that, if it is possible, placed afar off they may with a loud voice cry out to Jesus. And so aptly there follows:

Who stood afar off and lifted up their voice, saying: Jesus, Master, have mercy on us.

And rightly if they are to be saved do they call Jesus their Master. For when those that are to be healed humbly call Him Master (*Praeceptor*), they signify that they have gone astray from His teaching; and when they come back to the teaching of their Master, they soon return to the outward appearance of health. For there follows:

Whom when he saw, he said: Go, shew yourselves to the priests. And it came to pass, as they went, they were made clean.

We find that none of those to whom the Lord gave bodily favours were sent to the priests save lepers. For the priesthood of the Jews was a figure of the Royal Priesthood to come, which is in the Church, and in which all are consecrated who belong to the Body of Christ: the True and Supreme High Priest. And whosoever by the grace of God is without any trace of heretical falsity, or pagan superstition, or Jewish unfaith, or of even fraternal schism, let him, as free of diversity of colour, come to the Church, and let him show the true colour of the faith he has received. Other faults, such as those relating to the good health as it were of the members of the soul and of the senses, the Lord heals and corrects Himself, interiorly in the conscience and in the understanding. And even Paul, after the Lord had said to him: *Why persecutest thou me, and I am Jesus whom thou persecutest*, was nevertheless sent to Ananias, to receive the sacrament of the doctrine of the faith from the priesthood

which had been established in the Church, and so that his true colour might be approved; not because the Lord could not do all this by Himself (for who other than He does these things even in the Church?), but so that the fellowship of all the faithful by approving one another, and by making each other sharers in the teaching of the true Faith may, in all that is said, and in all the sacraments by which they are sealed, present as it were the appearance of one true colour.

Cornelius also, when told by an angel that his alms were accepted and his prayers heard, nevertheless, for the sake of unity both of doctrine and of sacraments, is bidden to send to Peter; as though to him and to his had been said: *Go, shew yourselves to the priests.* For as they went, they were made clean. For when Peter had come to them, and although they had not yet received the sacrament of baptism, and had not yet come spiritually to the priests, yet that they were made clean was made known both by the Holy Spirit descending upon them, and by the wonder of the gift of tongues (Acts x. 45, 46).

And one of them when he saw that he was made clean, went back, with a loud voice glorifying God.

This one who went back giving glory to God is a figure of the one Church, in devout humility before Christ. He falling down before the feet of the Lord, gives fitting thanks. For he truly gives thanks to God who repressing the thoughts of his own presumption, is humbly aware of how weak he is in himself; he who attributes no virtue to himself; who confesses that the good he does, is due to the mercy of his Creator. Hence, fittingly, He adds:

And this was a Samaritan. For Samaritan means *guardian.* And by this name that people is very aptly signified who, giving thanks, attribute all it has received to Him from whom it received it; as the singer in the psalm declares: *I will keep my strength for thee; for thou art my protector: my God, his mercy shall go before me* (Ps. lviii. 10). He falls on his face, ashamed because of the sins he remembers he has committed. For when a man is ashamed it is then he humbles himself. And for the same reason Paul said to certain persons who as it were lay face to the ground: *What fruit therefore had you then in those things of which you are now ashamed* (Rom. vi. 21)? On the other hand, of *the rider of the horse* (Amos ii. 15) that is, of the man lifted above himself by the glory of this world, is it said: *That his rider may fall backwards* (Gen. xlix. 17). And again, it was written of the persecutors of the Lord that, *They went backward and fell to the ground* (Jn. xviii. 6).

What does this mean, that the elect fall on their faces, and the reprobate falls backwards, if not that he who falls backwards does not, beyond doubt, see where he falls; while he who falls forward, sees where he is falling? The wicked therefore, since they do not see into what they are falling, are said to fall backwards; for they rush headlong where they cannot now see what will then happen to them. But the just fall as it were upon their faces; for moved by fear, they humble themselves: of their own will they throw themselves down amid things visible, that they may be raised up amid things invisible.

And Jesus, answering said: Were not ten made clean? And where are the nine?

One added to nine completes a symbol of unity. By it a certain whole is arrived at, so that number goes no further, except that it returns again to one, and this rule is observed in all numbering, to infinity. So nine need one that they may be joined together under a certain aspect of unity, and become ten. One has no need of the rest to keep its unity. For this reason as the one who gave thanks is approved and praised as a sign of the One Church, so the nine who did not give thanks, now rejected, are shut out from the communion of this oneness. And so shall others like them remain imperfect in the number of the nine. And rightly does the Saviour ask where are they; as though He knew them not. For, with God, to know is to choose; not to know, is to reject.

There is no one found to return and give glory to God, but this stranger.

As to the body, it is easy to see that a man may have no leprosy; and yet he may not be sound of soul. But in the light of this miracle, it troubles the mind to know how one who is thankless can be said to be *made clean?* But it is now easy to see, that this also can happen that someone within the society of the Church may know her true and pure doctrine, and may interpret it all in accord with the Catholic rule of faith; he may distinguish the creature from the Creator, and by this show that he is free as it were from leprosy, from the spots of lies, and nevertheless be ungrateful to

God and Lord Who made him clean, because uplifted in pride, he has not thrown himself down in loving humility to give thanks, and so has become like those of whom the Apostle said: *When they knew God, they have not glorified Him as God or given thanks* (Rom. i. 21). Saying, *they knew God*, Paul shows that they had been made clean of leprosy; yet he goes on to call them ungrateful.

And he said to him: Arise, go thy way; for thy faith hath made thee whole.

He who had fallen in humble devotion at the Lord's feet, is told to rise, and go on his way. For whoever is acutely aware of his own unworthiness, and humbles himself before God, is told by the comforting divine word, to rise, and to put his hand to *strong things* (Prov. xxxi.

19); and growing daily in merit, go on his way to *the more perfect things* (Heb. vi. 1). For if faith made him whole who had hurried back to give thanks to his Saviour and to the One Who had made him clean, unfaith has brought spiritual ruin to those who, receiving favours from God, fail to return and give Him glory.

And so this lesson is joined to the one preceding it in the gospel (that of the unprofitable servants) for this reason; that there we learn, through the parable, that faith must grow through humility, while here more clearly we are shown by actual happenings, that it is not only confession of faith, but also the doing of the works that follow faith, which makes *whole* those who believe, and give glory to the Father Who is in heaven. Amen.

NOTES

[1] PG 31, Homily XV.

[2] PL 36, col. 370, *Enarratio in Psalmum* xxxvi. Sermon 2, vers. xxi, par. 13.

[3] Prayer taken from the close of Sermon CCCXXXIII. PL 38.

[4] PL 36, col. 561, *Enarratio in Psalmum* xlviii. Sermon II, par. 9.

[5] Prayer from the close of Sermon LXVII. PL 38.

[6] PL 37, col. 1139, par. 14, *Enarratio in Psalmum* lxxxviii, vers. 53.

[7] A (prophetical) reference to the unceasing growth of the number of the faithful, and also a possible reference to Isaiah xxiv. 6 and 13.

[8] Ps. lxxxviii. 52. This mystical passage seems to include reference to

the *change the reproach of thy servants* (verse 51) wrought, not alone in Christ, the Anointed, through His death and glorification, but also that wrought in His Mystical Body. The *change* seems identical with the *renewal* of Isaiah xl. 31; the *renovation* of Titus iii. 5. Their reproach is against Christ and His members; glorified in and through Him. It may also refer to the satanic jealousy of the changes in a soul that is being perfected, variously, by Christ's grace.

[9] Referring evidently to the Judgement; cf. Is. xxiv. 17, 18.

[10] PL 92. *Expos. in Lucam*, col. 542. V.c. 17.

FOURTEENTH SUNDAY AFTER PENTECOST

I. Basil the Great: Christian Labour

II. St John Chrysostom: No Man Can Serve Two Masters

III. St John Chrysostom: The End of Labour

THE GOSPEL OF THE SUNDAY

Matthew vi. 24–33

At that time: Jesus said to his disciples: No man can serve two masters. For either he will hate the one and love the other; or he will sustain the one and despise the other. You cannot serve God and mammon. Therefore, I say to you, be not solicitous for your life, what you shall eat, nor for your body, what you shall put on. Is not the life more than the meat and the body more than the raiment? Behold the birds of the air, for they neither sow nor do they reap nor gather into barns; and your heavenly Father feedeth them. Are not you of much more value than they? And which of you by taking thought can add to his stature one cubit? And for raiment why are you solicitous? Consider the lilies of the field, how they grow; they labour not, neither do they spin. But I say to you that not even Solomon in all his glory was arrayed as one of these. And, if the grass of the field, which is today and to-morrow is cast into the oven, God doth so clothe; how much more you, O ye of little faith? Be not solicitous therefore, saying: What shall we eat; or, What shall we drink; or, Wherewith shall we be clothed? For after all these things do the heathens seek. For your Father knoweth that you have need of all these things. Seek ye therefore first the Kingdom of God and his justice; and all these things shall be added unto you.

EXPOSITION FROM THE CATENA AUREA

I

CHRYSOSTOM, *Opus Imperfectum*, *Homily* 16: In a preceding verse (22), the Lord had said that he who has a spiritual mind, he can keep his body without sin; but he who has not, cannot do this. Here He gives the reason, saying:

V.24. *No man can serve two masters.*

GLOSS: Or, because earlier it had been said that good actions become bad when done for a temporal motive; against this some could say, I do good works for earthly as well as for heavenly reasons. And against this the Lord says: *No man can serve two masters.*

CHRYSOSTOM, *Homily 22 in Matthew:* Or again: In the preceding verses He had rebuked the tyranny of avarice for many and grave reasons. Now He puts forward others still graver. Wealth injures us not only because it arms robbers against us, and because it darkens the mind, but also because it drives us away from God's service. And this He proves from common notions, saying: *No man can serve two masters.* He means two imposing contrary commands: for concord makes many one. And this is shown by what He adds: *For either he will hate the one.* He speaks of two, to show it is easy to change to what is better. For if one says: 'I have become the slave of money, because I love it,' He shows it is easy to return to a better state; that is, by not enduring its servitude, by despising it.

GLOSS: Or: He seems to speak here of two different kinds of servants. For some will serve freely out of love, others servilely from fear. If therefore anyone out of love serves one of two contrary masters, it must follow he will hate the other; but if he serves from fear, it must follow that while he bears with one, he will not have any regard for the other. Therefore, as God or earthly things rule a man's heart, in each case he will be drawn towards contrary things: for God draws His servants to the higher things; earthly things draw us to the lower. And so as it were concluding, He says: *You cannot serve God and mammon.*

JEROME: Mammon is a Syrian word for riches. Let the covetous, who calls himself a Christian, pay heed to this; that he cannot at the same time serve both Christ and riches. Yet He did not say: He who has riches, but: He who is the servant of riches. For he who is the servant of riches, guards money like a servant; but whoever has shaken off the yoke of servitude to money, bestows it as a master.

GLOSS: *Mammon* also means the devil, who has command over riches; not that he may dispose of them, unless when God permits; but because by means of them he deceives men.

AUGUSTINE, *Sermon on Mount,* II, 14, 47: For he who serves mammon, that is, riches, truly serves him who placed, because of his perversity, over these earthly things is referred to by the Lord as, *the prince of this world.* Or again: Who the two masters are is shown when He says: *You cannot serve God and mammon;* that is, you cannot serve both God and the devil at the same time. A man will therefore *either hate the one,* that is, the devil *and* love the other; that is, God; or *sustain the one and despise the other.* He who serves mammon must put up with a hard master. For when, caught by his own greed, he becomes the slave of the devil, he does not love him. As one wedded through great desire to the maidservant of another, must put up with harsh servitude, though having no love for the one whose maidservant he loves. He said: *He will despise the one*, not: He will hate the other. For no one can with a true conscience hate God. But he will despise Him; that is, he will not fear Him when he feels secure because of God's goodness.

2

AUGUSTINE, as above: Because the Lord teaches above that he who wishes to serve God and is careful not to offend Him must not think he can serve two masters, has need to be careful for fear that, though not seeking for superfluous things, his heart nevertheless should become divided in two about necessary things or become taken up with concern for them. And so He says:

V.25. *Therefore, I say to you, be not solicitous for your life (anima, soul), what you shall eat, nor for your body, what you shall put on.*

CHRYSOSTOM, as above: He does not say this, that the soul needs food; for it is incorporeal; but he is here speaking according to common usage: but it cannot remain in the body, unless the body be fed. AUGUSTINE, as above: Or, soul may here mean the animal life of man.

JEROME: In some codices is added: *Nor what you shall drink.* Therefore we are not wholly free of concern for what nature bestows on all, beasts of burthen, irrational and rational creatures alike. But we are bidden not to be *solicitous* as to what we shall eat; for it is in the sweat of our brow we shall eat bread: we must face toil, put away solicitude. The words: *Be not solicitous*, are to be taken as relating to corporal food and clothing:

for we must be ever solicitous for our spiritual food and clothing.

AUGUSTINE, *On Heresies*, c. 57: There are certain heretics called *Euchites*, who hold that a monk may not work even for his own sustenance; and who proclaim themselves monks in order to be free of all need to work. AUGUSTINE, *The Work of Monks*, c. 1: For they say that when the Apostle said: *If any man will not work, neither let him eat* (II Thess. iii. 10), he did not impose work of a bodily nature, such as that of tillers of the soil or artisans. For he could not be contrary to the Gospel, where the Lord Himself says: *Therefore, I say to you, be not solicitous etc.* We must therefore accept these words of the Apostle as referring to spiritual works, of which he says elsewhere: *I have planted, Apollo watered* (I Cor. iii. 6). And they accordingly think they are conforming to Apostolic and Evangelical teaching, when they believe that the Gospel lays down, that we are not to be concerned with the corporal needs of this life, and that the Apostle spoke only of spiritual food and labour when he said: *If any man will not work, neither let him eat.*

Let us then first show that the Apostle wished that the servants of God should also labour at corporal works. For he had begun by saying: *For yourselves know how you ought to imitate us; for we were not disorderly among you. Neither did we eat any man's bread for nothing; but in labour and in toil we worked night and day, lest we should be chargeable to any of you. Not as if we had not power; but that we might give ourselves a pattern unto you, to imitate us. For also, when we were with you, this we declared to you: that, if any man will not work, neither let him eat* (II Thess. iii. 7–10). What can be said to this, seeing that he confirmed what he taught by his own example, that is by labouring bodily? For that he laboured bodily is shown in the Acts of the Apostles, where it is said that he remained with Aquila and his wife Priscilla because he was of the same trade, *and laboured with them* (*now they were tentmakers by trade*, xviii. 3); and yet the Lord had laid it down, that as a Preacher of the Gospel, as a soldier of Christ, as a planter in the Vineyard, as a shepherd of the Flock, he should live by the Gospel. But he did not ask for the wage that was due to him: to give an example to those who began to demand what was not due to them.

Let those hear this who have not this power which he had: namely; that working only in the spirit, they should eat their bread without bodily labouring for it. But if they are Evangelists, if they are ministers of the altar, if they are dispensers of the Sacraments, they have this power. Or if in the world they had the means to sustain life without labouring, and, turning to God, had distributed this to the poor, then their weakness must be believed, and borne with. And it does not matter where they distributed their goods to the poor, since among Christians there is but one commonwealth. But they who come to the service of God from simple country living, or from following some craft or trade or from humble toil, if they do not work, there is no excuse for them. For it is in no way fitting that in a life where senators become labourers, labourers should become idlers; or that where the masters of great

lands renounce the comforts of life, rustic labourers should live in luxury. And when the Lord says: *Be not solicitous*, He does not say they should not procure these things, as they are needed, where they may do so honestly,[1] but that they should not have their mind on these things; nor do whatever they are bidden to do in the preaching of the Gospel for the sake of them. And a little earlier He had spoken of this intention of mind, as *thy eye*.[2]

CHRYSOSTOM, as above: Or, it can be comprehended in another way. For since the Lord had taught us to think little of money, lest someone should say: but how are we to live, if we throw everything away? He adds: *Therefore I say to you, be not solicitous for your life*. GLOSS (interl.): That is: do not be held back from eternal things, by earthly anxiety.

JEROME: We are therefore bidden, not to be solicitous as to what we shall eat, for it is already laid down that in the sweat of our brow shall we eat bread. So labour is laid upon us; anxiety is to be put aside.

CHRYSOSTOM, *Op. Imp. Hom.* 16: Bread is not to be acquired through solicitude of the spirit, but by the labour of the body. And to those who labour well it abounds, as a reward for their industry; but it is withheld from the idle, as a punishment from God. But the Lord confirms our hope; and first He descends from the greater to the less, He says: *Is not the life more than the food, and the body more than the raiment?*

JEROME: He Who has bestowed the

greater things, will also give us the less. CHRYSOSTOM, as above: For unless He had willed to preserve what is, He would not have willed to create it. To what He so made that it must live by food, He must give food as long as it is His will that it should live.

HILARY: Or again: Because the mind of the unbelieving is corrupted concerning the care of those who will live in the life after death, they are unnecessarily concerned about the future appearance of our bodies at the resurrection of the dead, and as to what their food shall be in eternity, so He goes on to say: *Is not the life more than the food?* He will not suffer our hope of resurrection to be troubled with anxiety over food and drink and clothing, lest through concern over trifling things, we should affront Him Who has given us more precious things; namely, soul as well as body.

3

CHRYSOSTOM, *Op. Imp. Hom.* 16: After He had confirmed our hope, coming down from what is greater to what is less, He again confirms it, by ascending from what is lesser to what is greater; when He says:

V.26. *Behold the birds of the air, for they neither sow, nor do they reap.*

AUGUSTINE, as above: c. 23: There are some who say that they therefore should not work, since the birds of the air neither sow nor reap. Why do they not note what follows: *nor gather into barns?* How can they wish to have both idle hands and full barns? Why do they grind corn, and bake it? For the birds do not do this. And if they do find people they can persuade to bring them prepared food each day, do they not at least draw water from the wells, and set it on the table for themselves; which birds do not? But if they are not compelled even to draw water for themselves, then they have gone one degree higher in justice than those who were in Jerusalem in the beginning, and who made bread for themselves out of the corn sent to them by the brethren from Greece, or at least had it made; which birds will not do! (Cf. Acts xi. 28–30).

They cannot keep to this, that they should put nothing by for the morrow; since for days on end they shut themselves off from the sight of men, and allow no one near them, to give themselves with greater fervour to prayer. Perhaps the holier men are, the less are they like the birds? Therefore, what He says of the birds of the air, He says for this reason: that no one may think that God has no care for His own servants, since His Providence reaches even to the care of these creatures. Neither is it anyone but He Who feeds those who labour with their hands. Nor even though God had said: *Call upon me in the day of trouble, and I will deliver thee* (Ps. xlix. 15), ought the Apostles not to have fled, but wait to be captured, that God might deliver them as He delivered the three children from the fiery furnace. For as anyone questioning the saints who fled in this way would be answered, that they should not tempt God, and that God, if He willed, would then do what was to be done to deliver them, as Daniel was delivered from the lions, and Peter from chains, when they were at the point where they could no longer help themselves. And since

He had given them power to fly, should they be saved through flight, it was He Who saved them.

So should anyone raise the question from the Gospel, about the birds of the air who neither sow nor reap, those servants of God who are able to find their food by the works of their hands will readily answer: if through some sickness or occupation we cannot work, He will feed us as He feeds the birds who labour not. But since we can, we should not tempt God, because what we can do, this we do through His gift. That we live on this earth is His gift, Who gives us what enables us to live. And He feeds us Who feeds the birds, as He has said: *Your heavenly Father feedeth them. Are not you of much more value than they?*

AUGUSTINE, *Sermon on the Mount*, II, 15, 51: That is, you are of more value: for a rational being, like man, has a higher place in the order of things than unreasoning creatures, such as birds. AUGUSTINE, *City of God*, XI, 16: Yet often a man will pay more for a horse than a slave, for a jewel than a maidservant; not for reasons based on value, but on need, or the desire of pleasure.

CHRYSOSTOM, as above: For God made all living things for man; but man for Himself. The more precious man is as a creature, the more will God care for him. If then the birds shall find their food without toil, shall man not find it, to whom God has given both the knowledge to labour, and the expectation of making it fruitful?

JEROME: There are some who seek to go beyond the bounds of our fathers,

and fly in the air, and are plunged into the deep. These will have it that *the birds of the air* signify the Angels and the other powers who serve God, who without any care of theirs are fed by God's providence. But if this is so, how then do they explain what follows: *Are you not of much more value than they?* Let us then take the words in their simple meaning, that if the birds, without thought or care, and which today are, and tomorrow are not, are fed by God's providence, how much more will He not feed men, to whom He has promised eternity?

HILARY, ch. V in *Matthew*: It could be said that under the name of birds, He is exhorting us by the example of the unclean spirits, for whom, without care to seek or collect it, food is provided by the power of the eternal Counsel, and that He is relating His words to the unclean spirits when He adds: *Are you not of much more value than they?* From the superiority implied in the comparison, He shows the distance between iniquity and sanctity. GLOSS: Not only by the example of the birds, but also by demonstration, He teaches us that to be and to live, our own care does not suffice, but that this is done by divine providence, saying:

V.27. *And which of you by taking thought, can add to his stature one cubit?*

CHRYSOSTOM, as above: For it is God Who each day makes the increases of your bodies, though you do not perceive it. If therefore the providence of God works daily in you, how shall it cease in respect of what you need? If you by taking thought cannot add the least part to your body, how can you by taking thought save the whole body?

AUGUSTINE, *Sermon on the Mount*, II, 15, 51: Or these words may relate to what follows, as though He said: It is not through us the body has reached its present stature: from which we may know that should we wish to add to our present stature one cubit, we could not. So leave the care of covering the body to Him Whose care has brought it to its present stature.

HILARY: Or again: As proved by the example of the spirits, He has secured our confidence as to our bodily needs, so He leaves the question of clothing to our common sense. For since He shall raise again into a perfect man the body of each one who has drawn breath, and since it is only He can add one or more cubits to each one's stature, we offend Him when we are anxious about our clothing; that is, about the appearance of our body; since it is He Who will add to each one to make each one's body equal.

AUGUSTINE, *City of God*, XXII, 15: If Christ rose again in the same Body in which He died, it is unbecoming to say that at the general resurrection, He will add to His own Body a size it had not when He appeared to His Disciples in the Body they knew, so that He may be equal to the tallest. But should we say that all bodies, of big and little alike, shall be remade to the measure of the Lord's Body, much would be lost to the bodies of many men; though He promised that, *not a hair of the head of any of you shall perish*

(Acts xxvii. 34). So each one will receive again his own stature, as he had it in youth, if he died an old man, or as he was to receive it, had he died before that age. And for this reason the Apostle does not say, *unto the measure of the* stature, but, *unto the measure of the age of the fulness of Christ* (Eph. iv. 12); because the bodies of the dead shall rise in that age of youth and strength to which, we know, Christ attained.

4

V.28. *And for raiment why are you solicitous? Consider the lilies of the field.*

CHRYSOSTOM, *Hom.* 22 *in Matthew*: After He had shown that we were not to be solicitous concerning our food, He passes on to what is less important; for clothing is of less importance than food. And so He says: *And for raiment why are you solicitous?* He does not here use the example of the birds, though He might have spoken of the peacock or the swan and similar examples. Instead He uses the example of the lilies, saying: *Consider the lilies of the field.* He wishes from two things to make known the divine superabundance; namely, from the magnificence of their beauty, and from the insignificance of the creatures that are sharers in such beauty.

AUGUSTINE, *Sermon on the Mount*, II, 15, 52: These examples are not to be considered allegorically; looking for the meaning of *the birds of the air*, or, *the lilies of the field*. They are put before us that we may, by means of lesser things, be instructed in what is greater.

CHRYSOSTOM, *Op. Imp.*, *Hom.* 16:

Lilies in due season grow into leafy fronds, clothed in beauty, and filled with fragrance. And what earth does not give to its root, God in His invisible care bestows. In all things the same fulness is to be seen; that they may not be held to be made by chance, but seen to be ordered by the providence of God. By saying, *they labour not*, He comforts men. By saying, *neither do they spin*, He comforts women.

CHRYSOSTOM, *Hom.* 22 in *Matthew*: Saying this, He forbids, not work, but solicitude, as earlier, where He speaks of sowing. CHRYSOSTOM, *Op. Imp.*: And that He may commend yet more the providence of God in these things, which surpasses all human diligence, He adds:

V.29. *But I say to you, that not even Solomon in all his glory was arrayed as one of these.*

JEROME: For in truth what silk, what royal purple, what precious tapestry can compare with the beauty of flowers? What so blushes as the rose? What so shines in beauty as the lily? That no dye surpasses the purple of the violet, is the judgement rather of the eye than of any tongue.

CHRYSOSTOM, *Hom.* 22 in *Matthew*: As what is false differs from what is true, so does our raiment differ from that of the flowers. If therefore Solomon, who was more adorned than all other kings, was surpassed in glory by the beauty of the flowers, how can you exceed their beauty? And Solomon was surpassed by the flowers' beauty, not once, nor twice, but all his reign. And this is what He means by: *In all his glory*. Not even for a day was he arrayed as the flowers.

CHRYSOSTOM, *Op. Imp.*: Or, He says this because Solomon, though he did not labour at what clothed him, yet he commanded. And where there is command, there also will be the resentment of those who serve, and frequently the wrath of the one commanding. But these, even unknowing, are so clothed.

HILARY: Or the lilies stand for the shining beauty of the heavenly Angels, whom God has clothed with the brightness of His glory. They toil not, neither do they spin; for at their beginning the Angelic Powers received what they shall always be. And since in the resurrection men shall be like to angels, He willed that they should hope for the beauty of a heavenly garment, like to the Angels in brightness.

CHRYSOSTOM, as above: If God so cares for earthly flowers, which are born for this only, that they may be seen, and then perish, will He neglect men, whom He has created, not that they may be seen for a time, but that they may be seen for ever? And this is what He means by the words:

V.30. *And if the grass of the field, which is today and tomorrow is cast into oven, God doth so clothe; how much more you, O ye of little faith?*

JEROME: *Tomorrow* in Sacred Scripture means the future; as Jacob makes clear: *And my justice shall answer for me tomorrow before thee* (Gen. xxx. 33). GLOSS (Ordin.) on *In clibanum mittitur*): Some codices have: *is cast into the fire*, or, *on to the heap*; which conveys the same idea as oven.

CHRYSOSTOM, *Hom.* 22 in *Matthew*:

He does not now call them lilies, but, the *grass of the field*, to show their small value; adding another note of insignificance: *which is today*. He did not say of it, *and tomorrow is not*, but what is still more fleeting: *and tomorrow is cast into the oven*. Saying: *How much more you?* He teaches implicitly the dignity of men; as though He said: You to whom He gave a soul, whose body He has formed, to whom He sent the prophets and to whom He gave His Only-Begotten Son. GLOSS: He says: *O ye of little faith;* for *little* is that *faith* which is not sure even in little things.

HILARY: Or again, by *grass* He refers to the Gentiles. If then but a corporal eternity (*aeternitas corporalis*) is given to the Gentiles, as they are then to be delivered to the fires of judgement, how unfitting that the saints should doubt of eternal glory, seeing that an eternity of punishment is laid up for the wicked?[3]

REMIGIUS: Spiritually, by *the birds of the air*, holy men are signified, who are born again of the water of sacred baptism, and who in their devotion reject earthly things and seek those of heaven; of these is it said that the Apostles are of more value: for they are the princes of all the saints. By the lilies we may understand the holy men who, without the forms of the ritual of the law, pleased God by faith alone; of whom it was said: *My beloved to me, who feedeth among the lilies* (Cant. ii. 16). Holy Church is also signified by the lilies; because of the purity of its faith and the good odour of its life; of which it was said: *As the lily among thorns.* By the *grass* unbelievers are signified; of

whom it was said: *The grass is withered and the flower is fallen* (Is. xl. 7). By *the oven*, eternal damnation; so that its meaning is: if God bestows the good things of this world on the unbelieving, how much more will He not give us those of eternity?

5

V.31. *Be not solicitous therefore, saying: What shall we eat; or, What shall we drink; or, Wherewith shall we be clothed?*
GLOSS: After He had thus, singly, excluded solicitude concerning food or clothing, by examples drawn from the lesser creation, He here fittingly excludes both anxieties, saying: *Be not solicitous therefore. . . .*

REMIGIUS: The Lord thus repeats this monition to show us how important it is; and the more deeply to impress it upon our hearts. RABANUS: Note that, He does not say: Do not seek for or be solicitous for your food or drink or clothing, but, *for what ye shall eat, or what ye shall drink, or wherewith ye shall be clothed.* In this He seems to me to rebuke those who spurning common food or dress, require for themselves either richer or more austere food or clothing than that of those with whom they live.

GLOSS: There is also another needless solicitude that arises from the folly of men: when they hoard both harvests and money more than is necessary and, neglecting spiritual things, become intent on these; as though they despaired of the goodness of God. And this is forbidden. Hence He adds:

V.32. For after all these things do the heathens seek.

CHRYSOSTOM, *Op. Imp.*: For they believe it is Fortune (*Fate*), and not Providence that rules human affairs. Nor do they hold that their lives are subject to the judgement of God, but rather ruled by chance. And so deservedly they live in fear and despair; as though there was no one directing their lives. He however who believes that he is ruled by God's judgement, trusts to the Hand of God for his food. Hence follows: *For your Father knoweth that you have need of all these things.*

CHRYSOSTOM, *Hom.* 22 in *Matthew*: He does not say; God knoweth, but: *Your Father knoweth,* to lead them to greater confidence. For if He is our Father, it cannot be that He will abandon His children, since not even human fathers could bear to do this. He says: *That you have need of all these things,* so that since such things are necessary, all the more should we put aside solicitude. For what kind of father is he who will not give his children even what is necessary? But for superfluous things, it is not reasonable to have the same assurance.

AUGUSTINE, *On the Trinity*, XV, 13: God did not learn these things at any given time. He foreknew before all time, and without beginning of knowing, all future temporal things; and, amongst them, what we would ask of Him and when.

AUGUSTINE, *City of God*, XII, 18: As to those who say that the knowledge of God cannot reach to this infinity of things, they should then say that God does not know all numbers, which are most certainly infinite. The infinity of numbers is not incomprehensible to Him Whose understanding is beyond numbering. Accordingly, if whatever is known is comprehended within the limits of the one knowing, then all infinity is contained in some ineffable manner in God's knowledge, because His knowledge is infinite.

ST GREGORY NYSSA (*or Nemesius*), *On Man*, 1, 4, 6, 7: His Providence is shown by signs such as these: The permanence of the universe, especially of the things that are born and die; the position and order of all things that are ever maintained in the same manner. How can this be without some ordering power? But some say, God has indeed the care of all that exists in the enduring universe, and that of this only His Providence takes care; but that individual things depend on chance. Now there are but three reasons for denying the Providence of God over single things. Either that God does not know that it is good that He should care for particular things; or, that He does not wish to; or, that He cannot. But ignorance is wholly alien to His blessed nature. How can that be hidden from God of which no wise man is ignorant: That if particular things collapse, the universe would collapse? But there is nothing to prevent all individual things from perishing, if no power has a care for them.

If however He does not wish this good, this will be for one of two reasons: either through indifference, or because this would be unworthy of Him. Indifference arises from one of two things: either we are indifferent because we are drawn away by some pleasure or because we leave off through fear; and either thought is an offence to God. If they say this concern is unworthy of God, that it is unworthy of such blessedness to stoop to little things, how, when a workman who has the care of all that concerns some thing will leave no least detail without his attention, knowing that each single part contributes to the good of the whole, is it not unfitting to assert that God the Creator is less provident than any craftsman.

If He cannot, then God is weak, and powerless to help us. But if the reason of His providence with regard to single things is incomprehensible to us, we should not therefore say that there is no Providence; for that would be the same as saying that, since we do not know how many men there are, there are therefore no men.

CHRYSOSTOM, *Op. Imp.*: And so he who believes he is ruled by the will of God, let him commit his food to the Hand of God. Let him think upon good and evil; for unless he is solicitous concerning these, he will neither avoid evil, nor put his hand to good. And so there is added:

V.33. *Seek ye therefore first the kingdom of God and his justice.*

The kingdom of heaven is the reward of good works. *His justice* is the way of service to God, by which we go to this kingdom. If therefore you think of what the glory of the saints shall be, you must then either keep from evil through fear of punishment, or hasten to do good through desire for glory. And if you have thought on the justice of God; that is, on what God hates and on what

God loves, justice itself will show you His ways; which those who love Him follow. Not as to whether we were rich or poor shall we render an account, but as to whether we have done well or ill; which is within our power. GLOSS (interlin.): Or that He says, *His justice*, is as though He says: It is through Him, not through yourselves, that you become just.

CHRYSOSTOM, as above: And even the earth is cursed because of man's sins, so that it does not bring forth; according to the words of Genesis: *Cursed is the earth in thy work* (iii. 17). But it is blessed when we do good. Therefore, seek His justice, and bread will not be wanting to you. And so there follows:

And all these things will be added unto you.

AUGUSTINE, *Sermon on the Mount*, II, 16, 53: Namely, temporal things; which He clearly shows are not the reasons because of which we should do good; but which are nevertheless necessary. The kingdom of God and His justice is our good; and the end we must set before us. But since in this life we are in battle to reach this kingdom, and since this life cannot go on without these necessities, *these things*, He says, *shall be added unto you.*

That He uses the word *first*, signifies that this (*the Kingdom of God*) is to be looked for later; that it is first, not in time, but in importance: the one is our true *good*; the rest are needed that we may attain to this. For example: we should not preach the Gospel that we may eat; for then we would hold the Gospel as less than food; but we eat that we may preach the Gospel. But if we who *seek first* the kingdom of God and His justice, that is, place this above all other things, so that we seek other things because of it, we should have no anxiety lest what we need will be wanting to us; and accordingly He says: *all these shall be added unto you;* that is, suitably and so that they shall be no hindrance to you: so that while you seek them, you shall not be turned aside from the other end; nor set two ends before you.

CHRYSOSTOM, *Hom.* 12 in *Matthew:* And He did not say: They shall be given to you, but, *they shall be added to you;* so that you may learn that things present are as nothing to the greatness of the things to come.

AUGUSTINE, *Sermon on the Mount,* II, 17, 58: When we read that the Apostle laboured in hunger and thirst, let us not think in our minds that God failed in His promises to him: for at times such things are a help. That Physician, to whom we have wholly entrusted ourselves, knows when to give and when to withhold; as He judges what is expedient for us. For if at times we lack things (which God will often permit, to exercise us), let this not weaken our purpose, but rather, now tested, let it confirm us.

I. ST BASIL, BISHOP AND DOCTOR

Christian Labour[4]

I. Work and Prayer

1. Since Our Lord Jesus Christ says that, *the workman,* not simply anyone or everyone, *is worthy of his food* (Mt. x. 10); and since the Apostle commands us to labour, *working with our hands the thing which is good,* that we may have something to give to *him who is in need* (Eph. iv. 28), it is very evident that we should all work earnestly and well. Nor is it fitting to presume that our desire of serving God gives us an excuse for being idle, or for avoiding labour, rather it is a greater reason for effort, for greater labours, and for patience in afflictions, so that we also may say: *In labour and painfulness, in much watchings, in hunger and thirst* (II Cor. xi. 27).

For this way of living is profitable to us, not only for the mortification of our bodies, but also because of charity towards our neighbour; that through us God may provide what is needed for our weaker brethren; in accord with the example handed down to us in the Acts by the Apostle, where he says: *I have shewed you all things, how that so labouring you ought to support the weak* (Acts xx. 35). And again: *That you may have something to give to him that suffereth need;* through which we shall be judged worthy to hear the words: *Come, ye blessed of my Father, possess you the kingdom prepared for you from the foundation of the world. For I was hungry, and you gave me to eat; I was thirsty, and you gave me to drink* (Mt. xxv. 34).

2. What need have we to dwell on the great evil of idleness, since the Apostle has laid it down clearly: *that if any man will not work, neither let him eat* (II Thess. iii. 10)? Just as

food is needed for the daily nourishment of the body, so also does the body need work, according to its powers. Not without reason did Solomon write in praise of her, that *hath not eaten her bread idle* (Prov. xxxi. 27). And again, of himself the Apostle says: *Neither did we eat any man's bread for nothing; but in labour and toil we worked night and day* (II Thess. iii. 8); though as a preacher of the Gospel he had the right to live by the Gospel. And the Lord has also linked idleness with wickedness, saying: *Wicked and slothful servant* (Mt. xxv. 26). And the wise Solomon not only praises the labourer in the words already cited, but also rebukes the sluggard by a comparison with the tiniest creatures saying: *Go to the ant, O sluggard; and consider her ways* (Prov. vi. 6).

We have reason therefore to be fearful, lest in the day of judgement He Who gave us the power to work shall also require of us works worthy of the power He has given us. For He says: *Unto whomsoever much is given, of him much shall be required* (Lk. xii. 48). And since there are those who use prayer and the recitation of the psalms as a means to escape work, we must know that in certain things each work has its due time; *All things have their season,* as Ecclesiastes tells us (iii. 1). But for prayer and psalmody, as for many other things, there is no time that is not fitting; so that while our hands are engaged in their various tasks, with our tongue (if this be possible and edifying, and, if not, then with our hearts), let us give praise to God, *in psalms and hymns and spiritual canticles,* as it is written (Col. iii. 16). And so let us perfect our work with prayer, giving thanks to Him Who

has given our hands the power to work, and our minds the power to gather knowledge; and Who has given us the material of our work, that in the tools we use, and that on which we use our skill; praying that the work of our hands may be directed to the end of pleasing God.

3. In this way we create within the soul a fitting disposition; for in every act of ours we are both asking God that He may bless our work, and giving thanks to Him Who has given us the power to work; and, as I said, keeping ever before our minds the end of pleasing Him. If this is not true, who can reconcile the two different sayings of the Apostle; namely: *Pray without ceasing,* and: *In labour and toil we worked night and day?* And since we are to give thanks at all times, and since this is seen to be necessary to our life both reason and nature have shown, we ought therefore never neglect the times of prayer that have been established in our brotherhoods, and which we have so arranged that each time in turn may serve to recall to mind, in a particular way, the blessings we receive from God.

The matutinal prayer (on rising), so that we may consecrate to God the first movements of the soul and of the mind, and take no other care upon us until we have been gladdened by the thought of God, as it is written: *I remembered God, and was delighted; and was exercised, and my spirit swooned away* (Ps. lxxvi. 4); nor apply our body to labour until we have done what is written: *To thee will I pray: O Lord, in the morning Thou shalt hear my voice. In the morning I will stand before thee, and will see* (Ps. v. 4, 5).

And again at the third hour let us rise to pray, and let the brethren be called together, even if they are dispersed each at his different task, and let them lift up their souls in prayer, recalling to mind that it was about the third hour that the gift of the Spirit was given to the Apostles, and let all with one mind adore Him, that they also may become worthy, so that the gift of holiness may be given to them, at the same time praying Him, that as the Guide of our Way He may teach us what is profitable to us; as he prayed who said: *Create a clean heart in me, O God: and renew a right spirit within my bowels. Cast me not away from thy face: and take not thy Holy Spirit from me. Restore unto me the joy of thy salvation: and strengthen me with a perfect Spirit* (Ps. i. 12–14). And in another place: *Thy good Spirit shall lead me into the right land* (Ps. cxlii. 10). And so let us resume our work.

4. Should any of you because of work or circumstance of place find themselves at a distance, let them without hesitation observe what has been laid down for all; *for*, says the Lord, *where there are two or three gathered together in my name, there am I in the midst of them* (Mt. xviii. 20). We decided that prayer is necessary at the sixth hour also, following the example of the saints, who say: *Evening and morning, and at noon, I will speak and declare: and he shall hear my voice* (Ps. liv. 18). And that we may be delivered from attack, and from *the noonday devil* (Ps. xc. 6), let us also at this time recite the ninetieth psalm. It was the Apostles who made known to us the need for prayer at the ninth hour, in the Acts, in which we are told that Peter and John went up into the temple at *the ninth hour of prayer* (iii. 1).

When day is done, let us give thanks both for what we have received throughout the day, and for what we have done rightly; and let us make confession of what we have not done, and of every sin, voluntary, or involuntary or even hidden from us, in word or in deed and even in our heart, that we may bring upon us God's mercy for all of them. For to examine ourselves upon what we have done is a great help against falling into the same sins again. Because of this Scripture says: *The things you say in your hearts, be sorry for them upon your beds* (Ps. iv. 5).

5. Again, as the night begins, let us ask that our rest be preserved from sin, and free from evil imaginings. And at this hour also we have need to say the ninetieth psalm. Paul and Silas have handed down to us the middle of the night as a time when we need to pray; as we read in the narrative of the Acts of the Apostles, in these words: *And at midnight, Paul and Silas, praying, praised God* (Acts xvi. 25). And the Psalmist likewise, where he says: *I rose at midnight to give praise to thee: for the judgements of thy justification* (Ps. cxviii. 62). And again before the dawn we must rise to pray, so that day may not find us upon our beds in sleep; in accord with the words: *My eyes to thee have anticipated the morning: that I might meditate on thy words* (v. 148).

None of these times must be neglected by those who have given themselves to live for the praise and glory of God and of His Christ. But I consider that it is useful to have diversity and variety in the prayers and psalms that are recited at fixed hours; for with sameness, the soul may become inattentive, and be distracted; but when the psalms and canticles vary at each hour, its love is refreshed and its attention renewed.

II. The Purpose of Work

And this also must be kept in mind, that he who labours ought to do so, not that he may serve his own needs but that he may be able to fulfil the command of the Lord Who said: *I was hungry, and you gave me to eat.* For to be solicitous for one's self was wholly forbidden by the Lord, when He said: *Be not solicitous for your life, what you shall eat, nor for your body, what you shall put on;* and again a second time, when He added: *For after all these things do the heathens seek.* Each one therefore, in undertaking any task, should have this purpose in mind: to serve the need of others, not his own ends. In this way he will escape the charge of self love, and will receive a blessing for his fraternal love from the Lord Who said: *As long as you did it to one of these my least brethren, you did it to me* (Mt. xxv. 40).

And let no one think that our words are contrary to those of the Apostle, who said: *We charge them that working they would eat their own bread* (II Thess. iii. 12). These words were meant for the lazy and disorderly; telling them that it was better for each one to earn his own bread, and not be a burthen to others, than to lead a life of idleness. *For,* he says, *we have heard there are some among you who walk disorderly; working not at all, but curiously meddling. Now,* he says, *we charge them that are such and beseech them by the Lord Jesus Christ that, working with silence, they would eat their own bread.* And this a little before also: *Neither did we eat any man's bread for nothing, but in labour and toil we worked night and day, lest we should be chargeable to any of you* (II Thess. iii. 11, 12, 8), relates to the same intention; since the Apostle out of fraternal charity had subjected himself to labour beyond what was required of him, to rebuke the disorderly. But he who strives after perfection, let him work day and night, *that he may have something to give to him that suffereth need.* And let us in all things have before our mind the desire to please God, to profit our soul, and to fufil the command of the Apostle, who said: *Therefore, whether you eat or drink, or whatsoever else you do, do all to the glory of God.* Amen.

II. St John Chrysostom, Bishop and Doctor

No Man Can Serve Two Masters[5]

1. *To be the slave of money is the greatest evil; to despise it the greatest good. Christ provides what is necessary for us; taking from us what is contrary to our need.*

See how the Lord detaches us gradually from the love of earthly things, and instructs us in various ways concerning contempt of riches, to drive out from us the tyranny of

the love of money. He was not content with the things He had spoken
earlier (in the Sermon on the
Mount), many and great though
they were; but goes on to add others
yet more terrible. For what can be
more fearful than what He now
teaches us: that through the love of
money we are in danger of being
banished from the service of Christ?
And what more desirable than that
through contempt of it, we shall
come to receive His love and good
will? I now say again to you, what
I am always saying: that Christ
urges His hearers to obedience to
His words, both by means of what
is profitable to them, and by what is
painful; like a good physician, pointing out the disease that comes
through neglect, and the good health
that will come through obedience to
His directions.

See here then how He again
points out what gain there is for us
in this life; how He prepares for us
things that are useful, and takes from
us what is a danger to us. It is not
for this only that wealth is harmful
to you, He says: because it arms
robbers against you, or because it
can wholly darken your mind; but
also because it drives you from the
service of God, and makes you slaves
of soulless riches; harming you as
much by making you slaves of what
you should rule, as by driving you
from the service of God, Whom
before all others you must serve.
For as in the preceding parable (*of
the treasure that rusts*), He shows us
that the harm is twofold; namely,
laying up treasure where rust consumes it, and not laying it up where
no thief can break in; so here also
He shows us that our loss is twofold:
To be turned away from serving

God, and to be made slaves of
mammon.

He does not state this at once, but
first prepares the way for it by a
general reasoning, saying: *No man
can serve two masters*; that is, two
masters who command us to do contrary things. For unless this were so,
there would not be two masters. For
the *multitude of the believers had but
one heart and one soul* (Acts iv. 32):
for though divided into many
bodies, yet, all being of one mind,
the many made one. Then enlarging
on this, He says: Not only will he
not serve, he will also hate and turn
from: *For either he will hate the one,
and love the other: or he will sustain the
one and despise the other.* And He
seems to say the same thing twice.
Yet not without a purpose, but to
show how simple it is to change to
what is better. So that you might
not say, 'I am enslaved once and for
all; I am dominated by riches', He
shows that you have the power to
change your way of life; and just as
you went from this life to that, so
you can go from that life to this.

After He had spoken in this
general way, so as to lead His hearers
to make a careful judgement on the
words He had spoken to them, and
not be led away from the true
nature of things, and when He had
secured their agreement with Him,
then He lets us see what He has in
mind. For He goes on to say: *You
cannot serve God and mammon.* We
shudder to think of what we have
compelled Christ to say; to place
God side by side with mammon.
And if this is a horrifying thing, it is
still more horrifying to do this by
our own acts: to prefer the tyranny
of gold, to the fear and love of God.

'But why not? Did not this happen among the ancients?' Far from it. 'How then,' you may say, 'was Abraham, was Job, so honoured?' I am not speaking of riches; I am speaking of those who are the slaves of riches. Job was indeed rich. But he was no slave of mammon. He possessed riches and ruled them, as a master, not as a slave. He held all he had as though he were the steward of another man's riches. And not only did he not rob others of what belonged to them, he gave what was his to those in need. And what was greater, he took no delight in present things, as he himself declares: *If I have rejoiced over my great riches, and because my hand had gotten much* (Job. xxxi. 25)? And so he did not grieve when he lost them. But the rich now are not like this, but rather in a state worse than any slave, and as though paying tribute to some tyrant. For the minds of such men become a sort of stronghold, held by money; and from there each day money sends out its commands, commands that are fulfilled by the violation of justice, and decency; and there is no one who does not obey. There is no need here to philosophize. For God once and for all has declared that it is not possible for the service of mammon to accord with the service of God. Therefore do not say it is possible. For when the one master commands you to plunder, the Other to give away what is yours; the One commands you to be chaste, the other to commit fornication; the one invites you to drunkenness and gluttony, the Other to restrain our appetites; again, when the One counsels you to think little of present things, the other to hold fast to them; the one tells you to adore rich marbles and

gilded walls and pannelled ceilings, the Other not to esteem them, but to honour virtue only; how can there be concord between them?

2. *Why Christ speaks of mammon as a master. The evils that arise from riches.*

Here the Lord speaks of mammon as a *master*, not that it is this of its own nature, but because of the misery of those who submit themselves to it. In the same way the belly is called a *god* (Phil. iii. 19), not because it has the dignity of a master, but because of the degradation of those who are its slaves; an affliction worse than any punishment and, apart from any punishment, fit retribution for whoever is led captive by it. For who are more wretched than those who, once having had God for their Master, forsake the mild rule of His Kingdom for this cruel tyranny; and this when they must suffer so much because of their sin even in this present life? For in this life their loss is beyond telling: litigation, abuse, struggles, persecutions, a maiming of the soul, and, worst of all, this service of mammon casts us down from the highest good we can ever enjoy; which is to serve God.

After He had taught us by all this the profit there is for us in contempt of riches, and this too with respect to the actual safety of our riches, and also the gain in peace of soul; then, so that we shall acquire true wisdom, and become steadfast in the service of God, He prepares us for the mastery of this counsel. For this is the perfection of law-giving; not alone to lay down what is right and just, but also to make it possible. For this reason He goes on to say: *Be not solicitous for your life, what you shall eat.* He says this lest any one should say: 'And what then? If we throw away everything, how are we to live?' To this He makes a fitting answer. For had He said at the beginning: *Be not solicitous,* His words might have seemed too severe. So, after He had pointed out the humiliation that arises from the love of money, He then makes His counsel acceptable. And for the same reason He does not simply say: *Be not solicitous,* but, adds the reason, and then imposes the precept. For after He had said: *You cannot serve God and mammon,* He then goes on to say: *Therefore I say to you, be not solicitous. Therefore!* Why *therefore?* Because of the dread severity of the penalty. For the injury you suffer is not in riches only; the wound avarice inflicts is a vital wound, and brings with it the loss of your salvation. It casts you forth from God, Who made you, Who loves you. *Therefore I say to you: Be not solicitous.*

After He has shown that the wound is beyond telling, he then enlarges on this teaching. For He commands us not only to cast away what is ours, but also forbids us take thought for the food we need, saying: *Be not solicitous for your life, what you shall eat.* Not that the soul needs food, for it is incorporeal. He spoke here in accord with common usage. For though the soul needs no food, it could not remain in the body unless the body is fed. And He did not simply say this, but here makes use of certain reflections; some based on our own life, some on other examples.

From the things of our own life He says: *Is not the life more than the food and the body more than the*

raiment? He Who has given us the greater, will He deny us what is less? He Who made the body that needs food, can He refuse it the food it needs? So He does not simply say: *Be not solicitous for what you shall eat, or for what you shall put on,* but adds: *Be not solicitous for your life, for your body;* because it was from them He was now about to draw examples, continuing His instruction by means of comparisons.

Now the soul (or life) He gave once for all; and it remains as it is; but the body increases each day. So pointing to both: to the immortality of the one, the fleeting nature of the other, He goes on to ask: *Which of you by taking thought can add to his stature one cubit?* Silent about the soul, which receives no increase, He speaks only of the body; showing us by this, that it is not the food increases it, but the providence of God. And this Paul also shows us, but in another way, where he says: *Therefore, neither he that planteth is anything, nor he that watereth; but God that giveth the increase* (I Cor. iii. 7).

From the things therefore that belong to our own life He exhorts us thus far. Now from other examples, He says: *Behold the birds of the air.* That no one may say that it is good for us to be solicitous, He disproves this by a proof from what is greater, and by an example from what is less. From what is greater, namely, from the soul and body; from what is less, namely, from the birds. For He says, if Providence has care for creatures that are so far below you, will it not also care for you? He spoke in this way because they were just a throng of simple people. But He did not speak like this to the devil. How did He speak? He said: *Not in bread alone doth man live, but in every word that proceedeth from the mouth of God* (Mt. iv. 4). Here He speaks of birds, and in a manner to bring them sharply to their senses: a method that has the greatest effect in giving counsel. Yet the impiety of some men has reached such folly as to attack the examples He uses. For it is not fitting, they say, for one who is training moral character to use as examples creatures which are taught by nature; for they have their capacity from nature.

3. What are we to say to this? That even if they have this power by nature, can we not attain to it by our own will? For the Lord did not say: 'Behold the birds of the air, how they fly'; something impossible to us; but, how they are fed, without taking thought; which is possible to us if we will it. And they have proved this who have done so by their works. We must therefore bow down before the supreme Mind of the Lawgiver, Who when He could have set before us an example from among men, and have spoken of Elias, of Moses, of John, and of other such men, who were not solicitous for their food; but, the better to hold them by His words, He puts before them an example taken from these unthinking creatures. For had He spoken of these just men, the people could have answered, that they had not yet become such men as these were. But now, silent about these holy men, and speaking only of the birds, He cuts them off from every excuse, and doing so imitates the Old Law. For the Old Testament sends us to

the bee (Ecclus. xi. 3), and to the ant (Prov. vi. 6), and to the turtle and the swallow (Jer. viii. 7). And it is no small proof of man's dignity, that we can of our own will acquire, what they have from nature.

If then God takes such care of the creatures He has made for our sake, how much more will He not provide for our own needs? If He cares for the servants, how much more will he not care for their masters? And so He says: *Behold the birds of the air.* And He did not add: 'For they neither buy nor sell'; for these were among things strictly forbidden,[6] but, *they neither sow, nor do they reap.* What does this mean, someone will say; Are we not to sow? He did not say we are not to sow, but that we are not to be *solicitous.* Neither did He say we were not to work, but that we must never be fainthearted, nor wear ourselves out with anxieties. He commanded us to eat; but not to be over-concerned about it. David of old laid the foundations of this discourse, speaking in this mysterious way: *Thou openest thy hand: and fillest with blessing every living creature* (Ps. cxliv. 16); and again: *Who giveth to beasts their food: and to the young ravens that call upon him* (Ps. cxlvi. 9).

And who are they, you will say, who are not solicitous? Have you not heard of those great men I spoke of? Have you not read of Jacob, departing with nothing from his father's house? Have you not heard his prayer, when he said: *If God shall give me bread to eat, and raiment to put on* (Gen. xxviii. 20), which was certainly not the prayer of one who was solicitous for his life, but rather of one who looked to God for all things. And this the Apostles also did; leaving all things, and being wholly without care, and the *five thousand* and the *three thousand* (Acts ii. 45; iv. 4).

But if you, when you hear these words, cannot yet free yourself from these strong bonds of solicitude, consider the futility of this state of mind, and make an end of your solicitude. *For which of you,* He says, *by taking thought can add to his stature one cubit?* See how from what is evident, He makes plain what is obscure. For by taking thought you cannot add one least part to your own body; so neither can you gather food for yourself, even though you think you can. From this it is clear, that it is not the pains we take that accomplishes all things, but the Providence of God, even in the things in which we seem to labour; so that should He abandon us, no care of ours, no thought, no labour, nor anything of this kind would ever succeed; and all our effort would end in nothing.

4. *The Commands of God can be fulfilled.*

Let no one therefore think that God's commands are impossible to us. For there are many who even now observe them. And though you do not know them, that is nothing to wonder at. For even Elias thought himself alone, yet heard the words: *And I will leave me seven thousand men in Israel* (III Kings xix. 18). So it is evident that even now there are many who follow the Apostolic way of life; like the *three thousand* and the *five thousand* long ago. But if we do not believe this, it is not because there are none who live holy lives, but because we are ourselves far

from doing this. Just as a drunkard will not readily believe there are persons who do not drink even water; though in these very days many monks practise this. Nor will he who has sinned with countless women, readily believe virginity is possible; nor will he who robs others, believe that any one of his own choice would give up what is his own; nor will they who are consumed all day by anxieties, readily accept this teaching. But that there are many who have come to this perfection we could show you, from the numbers who practise this discipline in our own days. For you now however, it is enough to learn not to be grasping, that almsgiving is a beautiful thing, to know also that you must give to others a share of what is yours. If you do this well, Beloved, you will soon go on to higher things.

Meanwhile therefore let us put away from us all excessive luxury, and be content with what is fitting and moderate; and let us learn to acquire by honest labour all we are to possess. For even the blessed John, when he was speaking to those who collected the tribute, and to the soldiers, told them simply, *to be content with their pay* (Lk. iii. 14). He desired to lead them to the practice of higher things, but since they were not yet ready for them, he spoke to them instead of these lesser things. For had he spoken to them of higher things, they would have paid no heed to him; and would likely have also given up the lesser things.

For this reason we want you to exercise yourselves in fulfilling these lesser Christian duties. Meanwhile, we well know that the burden of voluntary poverty is yet too heavy for you; heaven is not more distant from earth, than you are from such self-denial. Let us, therefore exercise ourselves in these least commandments; for this will be no small encouragement to you. For even if some among the Greeks have attained to what we are speaking of, and have given up all things, yet they have not done this from the right intention. But we shall be satisfied with you if you give alms plentifully; for if we do this we shall soon go on to higher things. But if we fail to do this, how shall we be worthy of forgiveness who, taught that we must surpass in good works the saints of the Old Law, show plainly that we are lower even than Greek philosophers? What are we to say, when we who should be like angels and children of God, do not even behave like men? For to rob others, to be rapacious, is not the conduct of civilized men, but of wild beasts. And they are even worse than wild beasts who attack each other. For wild beasts do this because of their nature. But we have been adorned with reason; and when we sink down to this baseness, so far below our nature, how can we deserve pardon?

Therefore keeping before our mind those degrees of self discipline which have been set before us, let us strive to attain at least to those midway on the road, so that we may be delivered from the wrath to come and, drawing ever nearer, may come at last to the very crown of all blessings; and may it be given to each one of us to attain to this, by the grace and love of Jesus Christ our Lord, to Whom be glory and honour for ever. Amen.

III. St John Chrysostom, Bishop and Doctor

The End of Labour[7]

Mildness and clemency are not everywhere profitable. There are times when a teacher has need of something sharper. When a pupil is dull, and slothful, there is need of a goad to pierce his dullness. And this the Son of God has used on this present occasion, and oftentimes elsewhere. For the multitude had again overtaken Jesus, and began to flatter Him, and to say to Him: *Rabbi, when camest thou hither?* Then, to make clear to them He esteemed honour or praise from no man, and looked to one thing only: their salvation, He replies by correcting them, and this not solely to correct them, but also to reveal, and make public, what was in their minds.

What does He say to them? *Amen, amen, I say to you,* speaking clearly and firmly, *that you seek me, not because you have seen miracles, but because you did eat of the loaves and were filled.* He rejects their praise and rebukes them with His words; not sharply or excessively, but doing this with moderation. He did not say: 'You gluttons; you slaves of your stomachs. I wrought great wonders and you did not follow me, nor marvel at them.' No. What He said was spoken mildly, and in this manner: *You seek me, not because you have seen miracles, but because you did eat of the loaves and were filled;* here referring not only to past signs but also to this present one; saying this only to arouse them. It was not, He said, the wonder of the loaves that struck you, but that you had been filled by them.

And they showed at once He was not speaking at random, guessing as it were; and that this *was* the reason they had followed him: To be filled again with bread. And it was to draw down the subject of bodily food that they went on to say a little later: *Our fathers did eat manna in the desert*; again speaking of food, and again inviting correction. However, He does not limit Himself to correcting them; He also instructs them. And so He begins to teach them in these words:

Labour not for the food which perisheth, but for that which endureth unto life everlasting, which the Son of man will give you. For him hath God, the Father, sealed; as though He had said: Do not be solicitous for this kind of food, but for spiritual food. But since there are some people who, wishing to live a life of idleness, have misinterpreted these words, as meaning that Christ was here putting an end to bodily toil, this is the place to answer them. For they are trying to deceive all Christianity; and because of their own sloth, they are prepared to bring ridicule on it.

Let us however first listen to Paul. What does Paul say? He says: *Remember the words of the Lord Jesus, how he said: It is a more blessed thing to give, rather than to receive* (Acts xx. 35). But how can he give who has nothing? And how then did Jesus say to Martha: *Martha, Martha, thou art careful and art troubled about many things; but one thing is necessary. Mary hath chosen the best part which shall not be taken away from her* (Lk. x. 41, 42).

And again: *Be not solicitous for tomorrow* (Mt. vi. 34).

We must now explain all these things, not only that we may make others give over their idleness, if they wish, but lest there should seem to be any contradiction in the words of God. For elsewhere the Apostle says: *We entreat you, brethren, that you abound more; and that you use your endeavour to be quiet; and that you do your own business and work with your own hands, as we commanded you; and that you walk honestly towards them that are without* (I Thess. iv. 10, 11). And again he says: *He that stole, let him now steal no more; but rather let him labour, working with his hands the thing which is good, that he may have something to give him that suffereth need* (Eph. iv. 28). Here Paul is not simply telling us to work, but to work so that we shall have something to give to the needy. And elsewhere he says again: *For such things as were needfull for me and them that are with me, these hands have furnished* (Acts xx. 34). And to the Corinthians he said: *What is my reward then? That preaching the Gospel I may deliver the Gospel without charge* (I Cor. ix. 18). And when he came into that city, *he remained with Aquila and Priscilla and worked with them; now they were tentmakers by trade* (Acts xviii, 3).

We must labour but without solicitude.

But all these sayings seem to be in strong conflict with what was said in the beginning (*Labour not for the food that perisheth, etc.*). So we must find an explanation. What therefore shall we say in reply? That we are *to take no thought* does not mean we are *not to work*. It means that we are not to be bound fast to the things of this life; that is, that we are not to be solicitous for the morrow's rest: to look upon that as something of secondary importance. For a man may work, yet lay up nothing for the morrow. A man may work, yet have no care for the morrow. For work and solicitude are not the same thing. Let a man work, not as trusting to himself in his work, but so that he may have something to give to another in need.

And the words the Lord spoke to Martha do not refer to work or to working, but to this: That we should know the fitting time of things. And that the time for listening is not to be consumed on purely carnal things. The Lord in speaking to Martha was not inclining her mind towards idleness, but rather towards listening to Him. 'I have come,' He says, 'to teach you what you need to know. And you are troubled about the midday meal! You have in mind to receive Me as a guest; to give me a good meal! But prepare another kind of meal for Me. Prepare for Me a zealous hearing; and let you rather be anxious for the things for which your sister longs.' He was not refusing her hospitality. No; far from it. How could He? But He wanted to make clear to her that she ought not, at a time meant for listening, be busy about other and lesser things.

And when He said: *Labour not for the food that perishes* (v. 27), He is not saying this that we may live in idleness (*for idleness hath taught much evil,* Ecclus. xxxiii. 29); but telling us that we must both work and work to give to others. For this is the food that does not perish. But if a man is an idler, or the slave of his stomach, or given to luxury, such a man

labours for the food that perishes. But if any man, from the fruits of his own toil, gives to Christ to eat and to drink and clothes Him, there is no one so senseless, so foolish as to say that this man labours for the food that perishes: for this is what we are promised a kingdom for, and with it all those other blessings. This is the food that endures, *unto life everlasting.*

But since at this time this people understood nothing of faith, and since neither had they any desire to learn Who He was Who had worked these wonders, or by what power, and had only one thing in mind: To fill their stomachs without having to work, Jesus rightly calls this, *the food which perishes.* 'I fed your bodies,' He says, 'that you might be led to seek this other Food, which endures unto life everlasting, which nourishes the soul; but you come running after Me for this earthly food. You do not therefore understand that I am not leading you to this ineffectual perishable food, but to Food which is enduring, which nourishes the soul, not the body, and gives it life eternal.'

When He had said these great words that concerned Himself, and said also that He is about to give them this Food, for fear His words might confuse them, and to make this gift credible, He says that this bounty is to come to them from the Father. For when He says: *Which the Son of Man will give you,* He added: *For him hath God the Father sealed;* that is, hath sent, to bring this Food to you. And this can be explained in another way. For elsewhere Christ also says: *He that received his testimony, hath set to his seal that God is true* (Jn. iii. 33); that is, 'has made it clearly manifest', as it seems to me. For to say that, *God the Father hath sealed,* can only mean that He has made known, has revealed by His testimony. For He also revealed Himself. Since however He was speaking to Jews, He also brings before them the testimony of the Father.

2. *We must ask of God that which is fitting. The vanity of present things. That which is to come is without end, whether punishment or reward.*

Let us learn therefore, beloved, to ask of God things which are worthy of being asked for. For such things, I mean the things of this life, in whatever way they touch us, will bring us no harm. For if we are rich, it is only here we enjoy the pleasures of riches; and if fall into poverty, we shall suffer nothing dreadful. For the bright things of this life or the dark have little power to give us either pleasure or pain. Both are of little account, and swiftly pass away. And so they are rightly called a *way*;[8] for they pass by, and do not long endure. But the things to come endure without end; punishment and Kingdom alike. For these let us have great concern: that we escape the one, and gain the other. What profit is there in present delight; here today, tomorrow fled? Today a shining flower; tomorrow scattered dust. Today a bright fire; tomorrow dead ashes.

But it is not so with spiritual things. They remain ever shining, ever flowering, each day a greater joy. These riches are never lost, never given up, never come to an end, never cause anxiety nor envy nor blame. They neither destroy the body nor corrupt the soul, nor awaken jealousy, nor provoke malice; as with earthly riches. This glory does not lead a man to senseless folly; does not inflame him, does not come to an end, does not fade. The rest and the delight of heaven remains, it goes on, ever unchanging and immortal. For it has no limit; it has no end.

Let us, I beseech you, long for this life. For if we long for this life, we shall place no value on the things of the present time; rather we shall despise them all and laugh at them. And even should we be invited as a guest of the king, and than this nothing seems more desirable, yet, having this hope within us, we should think nothing of it: for those held fast in the desire of heavenly things, must hold this of no importance. For whatever has an end, must not be too much sought after. All that ceases, and is but today, and tomorrow is not, even something very great, let it be to you as something very small and of little value.

Let us therefore not cling to things that even now are fleeing from us, but to the things that remain and endure, so that we may be blessed with them for ever, by the grace and loving kindness of Jesus Christ our Lord, through Whom and with Whom be there glory to the Father, together with the Holy Spirit, now and forever, and throughout all ages and ages. Amen.

NOTES

¹ The text of Nicolai adds, after the words: *unde honeste poterunt* (whence they honestly can), the verb *vivere* (*unde honeste poterunt vivere*). *Vivere* is not in the Migne text of St Augustine (PL 40, I, Ch. 26). Combefis and Guarenti have not *vivere*; a verb which substantially modifies both text and meaning. The quotations from this brief but trenchant work are, *sparsim*, from chapters 21–26. Its confutations will always find application, given human nature.

² Verse 22, preceding.

³ The severity of this interpretation rests on this: That the *Gentiles*, which here means those opposed to God, to Christianity, and to the People of God, are likened to *grass*; which yields no fruit. And though grass does not grow that it may be cast into the fire, nor does God use such care in clothing it, to the end that it may be burned; yet here, as a figure of the *Gentiles*, and like the barren fig tree, it too shall be cast into the fire. Cf. PL 9, V, 12, col. 918.

⁴ PG 31, *Regulae* (Monasticae) *Fusius Tractatae* (The Long Rules), *Responsiones* XXXVII *et* XLII; col. 1010 and col. 1023.

⁵ PG 57, Homilia XXI, col. 293.

⁶ Such dealings were forbidden to the early Christians, because at the time they could scarcely be engaged in without sin; since profit normally was possible only through cheating and stealing. They had been expressly forbidden as unbecoming to followers of Christ; though not intrinsically evil, but normal and necessary services. But since at this time the pagan world had yet to be convinced of sin in even the most ordinary but supreme moral questions; how much more was it not necessary and difficult to teach right and wrong in lesser matters?

⁷ PG 59, Hom. XLIV, in *Joannem*, col. 247.

⁸ Examples: *There is a way that seemeth to a man;* and again: *The wise servant shall prosper, and his way shall be made straight;* and, *every way of a man seemeth right to himself;* Prov. xiv. 12, 15; xxi. 2; etc. Mt. vii. 13, 14; Jn. xiv. 6, etc.

FIFTEENTH SUNDAY AFTER PENTECOST

I. St Augustine: The Three Whom Jesus Raised to Life

II. St Peter Chrysologos: The Raising of the Widow's Son and on the Resurrection of the Dead

III. St Gregory the Great: The Resurrection of the Body

IV. The Venerable Bede: The Gates of Death

THE GOSPEL OF THE SUNDAY

Luke vii. 11-16

At that time: Jesus went into a city that is called Naim; and there went with him his disciples and a great multitude. And when he came nigh to the gate of the city, behold, a dead man was carried out, the only son of his mother; and she was a widow. And a great multitude of the city was with her. Whom when the Lord had seen, being moved with mercy towards her, he said to her: Weep not. And he came near and touched the bier. And they that carried it stood still. And He said: Young man, I say to thee, arise. And he that was dead sat up and began to speak. And he gave him to his mother. And there came a fear upon them all; and they glorified God, saying: A great prophet is risen up amongst us: and God hath visited his people.

Exposition from the Catena Aurea

CYRIL, *Catena G.P.*: The Lord joins wonder to wonder. In the previous miracle, when *they besought him earnestly*, he went at once. Here He came unsummoned, as we are told:

V.11. *And it came to pass afterwards, that he went into a city.*

BEDE: Naim is a city of Galilee within two miles of Mount Thabor. By the divine will *a great multitude* went with the Lord; that there might be many witnesses to this great miracle. So we read: *And there went with him his disciples and a great multitude.*

GREGORY NYSSA, *On the Soul and Resurrection*: We come to a proof of the resurrection of the dead, not from the words of the Saviour but from His deeds, Who, beginning His miracles in lesser things, prepares our faith for what is greater. For first, in the desperate sickness of the centurion's servant, He as it were takes in hand His power to raise the dead. After this, when He restores to life the son of the widow, who was being carried to the grave; a miracle of higher power; He leads men's minds towards faith in the resurrection. Hence there follows:

112

V.12. *And when he came nigh to the gate of the city, behold, a dead man was carried out, the only son of his mother.*

TITUS OF BOSTRA: For if someone had said of the centurion's servant, that he was not going to die; to silence such a presumptuous tongue, it is here related that Christ meets a young man already dead, the only son of a widow. For there follows: *And she was a widow. And a great multitude of the city was with her.*

GREGORY NYSSA: The greatness of her affliction is set out in a few words. The mother was a widow, without hope of other sons; with no one to whom she might turn in place of the son now dead. He only had she nursed. He was the sole source of gladness in her house. All that is sweet and precious to a mother, this he alone had been to her. CYRIL: An affliction that awakens compassion, moving us to grief and to tears. Then follows:

V.13. *Whom when the Lord had seen, being moved with mercy towards her, he said to her: Weep not.*

BEDE: As though saying: Cease to weep for him as dead whom in a moment you shall see rise living. CHRYSOSTOM (or TITUS, in *Catena GP*): He Who comforts the afflicted, bidding her not to weep, teaches us that we are to be consoled in the presence of the dead by the hope of their resurrection. Life meeting death halts the bier. Then follows:

V.14. *And he came near and touched the bier. And they that carried it stood still.*

CYRIL, *Book 4, 14 in John*: He works the miracle, not only by word of mouth, but also touching the bier; that you may know that the sacred Body of Christ has power to save mankind. For it is the Body of Life, and the Flesh of the Omnipotent Word, Whose power it possesses. For as iron applied to fire will do the work of fire, so flesh, after it had been united to the Word, Which gives life to all things, also becomes life-giving, and a banisher of death.[1]

TITUS: The Saviour, however, is not like Elias, weeping over the son of Sarepta (III Kings xvii); nor like Eliseus, who laid his own body on the body of the dead (IV Kings iv); nor like Peter, who prayed over Tabitha. He it is Who calls forth the things that *are not, as though they were*; Who can speak to the dead as though they lived. So we read: *And he said: Young man, I say to thee, arise.*

GREGORY NYSSA: That He said, *young man*, signified that he was in the flower of his age, drawing near to manhood; who a little before was the light of his mother's eye, now drawing near to the time of marriage, the hope of her race, the young branch of her succession, the staff of her old age.

TITUS: He to whom this command was given, instantly rose up. For the divine power is irresistible. There is no delay; no urging through prayer. So there follows:

V.15. *And he that was dead sat up and began to speak. And he gave him to his mother.*

Here are the marks of a true resurrection. For the body that is dead cannot speak; nor would the woman have brought home a dead and lifeless son. BEDE: Fittingly does the Evangelist record that the Lord was first *moved with mercy* towards the mother, and in consequence raises her son to life; that in the one case He might give us an example of compassion, in the other increase our faith in His wondrous power. Then follows:

V.16. *And there came a fear on them all; and they glorified God, saying: A great prophet is risen up among us; and God hath visited his people.*

CYRIL: This was much for an unfeeling and an ungrateful people. For in a little while they would regard Him neither as a prophet, nor for the profit of the people. This miracle could not be hidden from any one living in Judea. So we read:

V.17. *And this rumour of him went forth throughout all Judea and throughout all the country round about.*
AMBROSE (*Maximus in Catena GP*): It is fitting to record that we have seven accounts of resurrection from the dead before that of the Lord. Of these the first is that of the son of the widow of Sarepta (III Kings xvii), the second of the son of the Sunamitess (IV Kings iv), third that caused by the remains of Eliseus (IV Kings xiii), the fourth this of Naim, the fifth that of the daughter of the ruler of the Synagogue, the sixth that of Lazarus, the seventh that which took place at the passion of Christ: for *many bodies of the saints that had slept arose* (Mt. xxvii. 52). The eighth was Christ's, Who, free of death, lived on as a sign that the general resurrection, which is to come in the eighth age, shall not be

annulled by death, but shall remain and shall not be undone.

BEDE: The dead man who was carried out through the gates of the city before the eyes of a multitude, signifies man struck senseless by the mortal disaster of sin, and not hiding his soul's death in the chamber of his heart, but making it known to men by the evidence of word and deed: bearing it through the gates of the city as it were. For I think the gates of the city stand for one or other of the bodily senses. He is fittingly spoken of as the only son of his mother; for one is our Mother, made up of many persons: the Church; and every soul that remembers it was redeemed by the death of Her Lord, knows that the Church is a widow.

AMBROSE: For I see this widow, surrounded by a multitude of people, as more than the woman who, through her tears, obtains the resurrection of the young man who was her only son; for the reason that it is Holy Church, seeing their tears, recalls to life from the way of death, and from death itself this younger people; and who is forbidden to weep for him, since he was to rise again.

BEDE: Or, the error of Novatius is confuted, who, striving to make void the cleansing of the repentant, denies that Mother Church, weeping because of the spiritual death of those that were born to her, should be consoled by the hope that life shall be restored to them.[2]

AMBROSE: This dead man was carried to the grave on a bier made from the four elements. But he had the hope of rising again, because he was borne on wood. For though it had before been a source of loss to us, yet, after Christ had touched it, it began to help us to Life; that it might be a sign that salvation was to overflow to the Church through the yoke of the Cross. For we lie lifeless upon a bier, when either the fire of unrestrained desires consumes us, or when coldness overflows in us, or the power of our soul is weakened by slothful habit of body.

BEDE: Or the bier on which the dead man is carried is the evilly secure conscience of the desperate sinner. And they who carry him to burial, are either unclean desires, or the seductions of evil company; who stood still when the Lord touches the bier. For the conscience that is touched by the fear of heavenly judgement, will often, restraining carnal desires, and those who unjustly praise it, return again to itself; answering the voice of the Saviour calling it back to life.

AMBROSE: If therefore there is a

grave sin which you cannot wipe away by the tears of your repentance, let the Church your Mother weep for you, while the multitude stands by. Soon you will rise from death, and begin to speak the words of life, and fear will come upon them all; for by the example of one, all are converted. They also shall glorify God, Who has given us such remedies to escape death.

BEDE: The Lord *hath visited his people*, not only once by the Incarnation of His Word, but by sending It at all times into our hearts. THEOPHYLACTUS: By the widow you may also understand a soul that has lost its husband, that is, the divine word. For the son is the understanding, borne without the city of the living; the casket is its body, which some indeed speak of as a tomb. The Lord touches it, and He raises it up; making him return to new life who, rising up from sin, begins to speak and to teach others; for before he would not have been believed.

I. ST AUGUSTINE, BISHOP AND DOCTOR

The Three Whom Jesus Raised to Life[3]

LUKE vii. 11–15

I. *Miracles of the Lord are wrought in bodies and in souls.*

The miracles of our Lord and Saviour Jesus Christ, move deeply all who hear of them and believe in them; some in one way, some in another. Some look with astonishment upon His corporal miracles, but have no eyes for the greater miracles. Some now look with

greater wonder at the miracles wrought in men's souls, which, they hear were formerly wrought in men's bodies. The Lord Himself says: *For as the Father raiseth up the dead and giveth life; so the Son also giveth life to whom he will* (Jn. v. 21). This does not mean the Son gives life to some, the Father to others; but that Father and Son give life to the same persons: for the Father does all things through the Son. Let no one therefore who is a Christian doubt, that even now the dead are raised. Every man has eyes to see the dead rise up, as the widow's son spoken of in the Gospel just read, rose up. But not all can see men who were dead in heart rise up, save those who are themselves risen in heart. It is a far greater miracle to raise to life one who will live for ever, than to raise someone who must die again.

II. *The Two Kinds of Death.*

The widowed mother rejoiced over the young man restored to life. Mother Church rejoices daily over men restored to life in the spirit. He was dead in his body; they in the soul. His visible death was mourned before all; their invisible death is neither seen nor thought of. He sought them Who had known they were dead. And He alone had known they were dead Who had power to make them live. For unless the Lord had come to raise the dead, the Apostle would not have said: *Rise, thou that sleepest, and arise again from the dead; and Christ shall enlighten thee* (Eph. v. 14). The words, *Rise, thou that sleepest,* you understand as addressed to one who sleeps. But when you hear, *and arise from the dead,* understand them of one dead. The visibly dead are often spoken of as *sleeping.* And certainly to Him Who has power to waken them, they are sleeping. A dead man is to you a dead man; shake him, prod him as you will, he will not waken. But to Christ he lay sleeping to whom He said, *Arise*; and immediately he arose. No one can so easily waken one who sleeps in his bed, as Christ wakens him from the grave.

III. *The Three Dead Restored by Christ. The Miracles of Christ worked for a sign. An appropriate similitude.*

We read that the Lord visibly restored three persons to life; thousands invisibly. How many dead He visibly restored, who knows? For all that He did is not written down. John tells us this. *But there are also many other things which Jesus did, which if they were written every one, the world itself, I think, would not be able to contain the books that should be written.* (Jn. xxi. 25). There were then no doubt many others raised to life; but it is not without purpose that three have been commemorated. For our Lord Jesus Christ wished that what He wrought corporally should also be understood spiritually. For He did not work miracles simply as miracles; but so that what He did might appear wondrous to those who saw them, and convey truth to those who would understand them.

Just as the man who sees the letters in a well written manuscript, but does not know how to read, will praise the hand of the writer, admire the beauty of the letters, but what they convey, the meaning of the characters, of this he knows nothing. He praises with his eyes; but his mind understands nothing. Another will both praise the skill of the writer and understand his meaning: that is, one who can not alone see what all can see, but can also read; which he cannot do who has not learned to read. So they who saw the miracles of Christ, and did not understand what they meant or what they as it were said to those who understood them, wondered only that the miracles had happened. Others however both wondered at the miracles, and understood their meaning.

In Christ's school we must be like these last. For he who says that Christ worked miracles for this only, that they should be nothing but miracles, can say with equal reason, that when Christ looked for figs on the fig tree, He did not know it was not the time for fruit (Mt. xxi). For it was not the season for figs, as the Evangelist tells us. Yet, being hungry, He looked for fruit on the tree. Did Christ not know that which every country person knew? Did the Creator of the tree know less than the minder of the tree? So when the Lord, being hungry, looked for fruit from the tree, He was also intimating that He was seeking something else. And He finds the tree covered only with leaves, and destitute of fruit, and curses it; and at once it withers away and dies (Mt. xxi. 19; Mk. xi. 13).

What had the tree done, not bearing fruit? Was its fruitlessness the fault of the tree? No. But there are people who are fruitless through their own fault. The Jews, knowing the teaching of the Law and not fulfilling it, are a tree covered with leaves, but yielding no fruit. I have said this to make clear to you that the Lord wrought miracles for this reason also, that through them He might also signify something else: that from them we should learn more than that they were wondrous, divine signs.

IV. *The Raising of the Three Dead.*

Let us see then what it is He wishes us to learn from these three dead He raised to life? He raised to life the dead daughter of the ruler of the synagogue, who *besought him*

much for his daughter who was sick: that He would deliver her from her sickness. And on His way to her, it was announced she was dead, and word was also brought to her father that it would now be useless to trouble the Master further, saying: *Thy daughter is dead: why dost thou trouble the master any further?* But the Master continued on His way, saying to the father of the girl: *Fear not, only believe.* He came to the house, and there finds the preparation for her burial now complete. And He says to them: *Why do you weep? The damsel is not dead, but sleepeth* (Mk. v. 22–43)? She was asleep: asleep to Him Who had power to waken her. And waking her, He gave her back living to her parents.

And He also wakened this young man, the son of a widow, because of whom we are now speaking to Your Charity; as the Lord shall give us to speak. You have heard how he was wakened to life. The Lord was coming towards the city, and just then a dead man was being carried through the gates. Moved by mercy towards the weeping mother, a widow, now bereft of her only son, He did as you heard when the Gospel was being read; saying: *Young man, I say to thee, arise.* And the young man who had been dead rose up, and began to speak. And the Lord restored him to his mother.

He also wakened Lazarus from the tomb. And on this occasion, since the Disciples knew the sick man, Jesus said: *Lazarus our friend sleepeth* (for Jesus loved Lazarus). And they thinking this sleep would do him good, answered: *Lord, if he sleep, he shall do well.* But Jesus, now speaking more openly, says to them: *I tell you, that Lazarus our friend is dead.*

In each case He spoke the truth; To Me he is sleeping, to you he is dead (Jn. xi. 11 *et seq.*).

V. *These three dead are figures of three kinds of sin. Evil habit.*

These three dead stand for three kinds of sinners; whom even now Christ continues to raise from the dead. The daughter of the ruler of the synagogue was dead within her house. She was not yet carried forth from the privacy of its walls for all to see. There within, she was raised to life, and restored living to her parents. The second dead was not now in his house; neither was he yet buried. Carried forth from his house, he was not yet committed to the earth. He Who raised to life the dead girl who was not yet borne forth, now raises to life the dead man being carried forth; but not yet buried. A third miracle remains: To raise to life one already buried. And this He does in the case of Lazarus.

There are those who have sin within their hearts; but have not yet sinned in deed. Someone is inwardly shaken by lust. The Lord Himself said: *Whosoever shall look on a woman to lust after her, hath already committed adultery with her in his heart* (Mt. v. 28). He has not yet drawn near her in body, but already he has consented in his heart. He has within him one now dead, but not yet carried forth. And as happens, as we know, and as men experience each day, should he at some moment hear the word of God, hear as it were the voice of the Lord saying to him: *Arise*, he will condemn his consent to sin, and his soul will breathe again in saving health and charity. The man dead in his own house rises again; the heart revives within

the secrecy of the soul. This resurrection of a dead soul has taken place within the secrecy of the conscience, as within the walls of a house.

Others, after inward consent to evil, proceed to the outward act; as though carrying forth the dead: so that was hidden in secrecy, now appears for all to see. These who have *come forth* in outward deed, are these now past hope? Far from it. Did not Jesus say also to the young man: *I say to thee, arise?* Did He not restore him to his mother? So also he who has sinned in deed shall be restored to life, should he be warned and wakened by the word of truth, and shall rise again at the voice of Christ. He could come forth on the way, but he could not perish for ever.

But they who doing evil, become also involved in evil habit, so that the very habit of evil will not let them see that it is evil; will in turn become defenders of their own evil deeds. They rage when they are rebuked, like the Sodomites long ago, who said to the just man who rebuked them for their most evil inclination: *You came here as a stranger, not as a judge* (Gen. xix. 9). So dominant among them became the practice of this abominable foulness, that wantonness now became justice; and one who opposed it, more to be censured than one who practised it. Persons like these, pressed down by malignant habit, are as though buried. What am I saying, brethren? They are in fact so buried, that we may say that of them which was said of Lazarus: *he now stinketh.* The hard power of this habit is like a great stone laid upon the tomb; pressing down upon the soul, not suffering it either to breathe or to rise again.

VI. *The Four Steps of Sin.*

Of Lazarus it was said: *He is now four days dead*. And it happens also that the soul arrives at this habit of which I am now speaking by a sort of fourfold progress. In the first step, there is a touch of delight within the heart. In the second, there is consent. In the third, there is deed. In the fourth, there is habit. There are those who so wholly reject things plainly unlawful from their thoughts, that they are not even tempted (cf. Wis. iv. 2). There are those who are tempted, yet do not consent. Death is not here; but it has in a measure begun. To the allure of temptation, consent is added: and this is already damnation. Following consent comes the act of sin. Act changes into habit; and then hope dies in the unhappy soul; so that we may say of him: *By this time, he stinketh; for he is now of four days*.

The Lord then comes; to Whom all things were of course easy. But here He reveals a certain difficulty. He groans in the spirit, and makes plain that we need to cry out with a loud voice in rebuke, to raise those who have grown hard in evil habit. Nevertheless, at the voice of the Lord, crying *with a loud voice*, the bonds that seemed inescapable are burst asunder. The dominion of hell trembled; and Lazarus is restored to the living. And the Lord also delivers from evil habit those who are four days dead. For even he who is four days dead, to Christ, Whose desire is to raise him from the dead, he is but sleeping.

What then did Christ say? Consider well this raising to life. Lazarus came forth living from the tomb; yet could not walk. To His Disciples the Lord says: *Loose him, and let him go*. He raises the dead; they loose those bound. Observe well that here there is something which belongs to the majesty of God alone; raising the dead to life. Someone buried in evil habit is rebuked, by the word of Truth. How many are rebuked, but pay no heed! Who is it Who then acts within him who does pay heed? Who breathes life into him? Who drives out the hidden death, and give back the hidden life? Left to themselves after rebukes and after corrections, is it not true that men will begin to think within themselves of how evil is the life they are leading, how evil the habit they are buried under? Then, grieved with themselves, they resolve to change their lives. Such as these have risen again; they who grieved over what they were, have returned to life. But, returning to life, they are unable to walk. The bonds of their former guilt remain. He who has returned to life has need to be loosed and let go. And this task the Lord has given to His Disciples, to whom He said: *Whatsoever, you shall loose upon earth shall be loosed also in heaven* (Mt. xviii. 18).

VII. *We must rise up speedily from sin.*

Let us, dearly beloved, so receive this teaching, that they who are alive, may live; and that they who are dead, may return to life. If a man's sin is but conceived in the heart, and not yet come forth in deed: let him repent of his thought; let him correct it; let the dead rise up within the house of his conscience. Or if he has already committed what he thought of; even he must not despair. The man dead within his house did not rise; let him arise when borne forth. Let him repent of what he has done, and let him return to life at once. Let him not go down to the dark of the grave; let him not become buried under the great weight of habit.

It may be that even now I am speaking to such a man; to one now buried under the unyielding stone of habit and who now dead four days, *stinketh*. Yet not even he must despair: he is dead, in the depths; but Christ is on high. He knows, by crying out *with a loud voice*, how to destroy these heavy loads; He knows how, through Himself, to raise the soul within to life; giving it to His Disciples to loose. But let such sinners also do penance. When Lazarus was raised to life, after four days in the grave, no evil odour remained in the living man. And so let those who are living, live; and those who are dead, in whichever of these three deaths they find themselves, let them act at once, to rise here and now from the dead.

Turning then to the Lord our God, let us give thanks to Him Who without any merit of ours has healed our wounds, made us friends who were His enemies, redeemed us from slavery, led us from darkness to light and from death to life. And humbly confessing our own weakness, let us implore His mercy, and that He may deign not only to defend us from evil, but also increase in us His gifts and graces, Who with the Father and the Holy Spirit liveth and reigneth God for ever and ever.[4] Amen.

II. St Peter Chrysologos, Bishop and Doctor

On the Raising of the Widow's Son and the Resurrection of the Dead.[5]

Today the blessed Evangelist as he tells us of the restoration to life through Christ of the only son of a widow who, lying clothed in funeral bands upon the bier of death, and with a multitude following, was on his way to the grave, touches our hearts, moves our souls, and fills our ears with fear and wonder. But let the unbelieving wonder, the Jews be astonished, and let the world fear. But as for us, why should we wonder: we who believe that the dead of every age shall at the voice of Christ rise again from their graves?

The dead, says Isaias, *shall rise, and they that are in the tombs shall rise again* (xxvi. 19; Sept.). And the words of the Lord are: *The hour will come when the dead shall hear the voice of the Son of God; and they that hear shall live* (Jn. v. 25). To this the Apostle adds: *In a moment, in the twinkling of an eye, at the last trumpet; for the trumpet shall sound and the dead shall rise again incorruptible* (I Cor. xv. 52).

What is this trumpet, which declares war against hell, rolls back the stone from the tomb, thunders forth life to the dead, and gives to all as they rise from their graves victory amid light everlasting? What is it? It is that to which the Lord referred above: *The dead shall hear the voice of the Son of God.* Not this the trumpet that from a horn of wood or brass gives forth a mournful bellow, calling to war, but the Voice that comes from the heart of the Father, from the mouth of the Son, the call to life to those that are in heaven and in hell.

And, at the last trumpet. The trumpet that in the beginning called the world from nothing, the same on the last day shall recall the world from death; and that which in the beginning raised man from the slime, the same at the end shall recall him from the dust. Brethren, we believe this: that the trumpet of the divine voice separated light from darkness, brought together this globe, purified the elements, divided the world, raised the firmament on high, made the earth appear, placed a boundary to the sea, submerged the deeps, set all things in order and harmony, and commanded their continuing obedience. And that this world might not be a horrid emptyness, He furnished it with inhabitants and established each in their various places. In the heavens He placed His Angels, who live by the spirit only; on earth the varying kinds of living beings. He set winged creatures to fly in the air, and in the waters creatures both great and small, so that a multitude might dwell there. And in a wondrous way He so united the whole mass of these separate elements that there should be no confusion; yet so that the separateness of each thing might not sunder this unity.

Hence is it that the sequence of day and night is so ordered that labour follows rest and rest comes after labour. Hence also the sun and moon each in turn encompasses the limits of the world, so that the sun with its recurring light may give a greater brightness to the day and the moon with its pale light may not leave the night in total darkness. Hence too the stars in their courses vary in their hour of rising, to mark the time by night and guide the traveller. Hence the seasons that come and go, and begin again to be as they are about to end. Hence seeds put forth, bud, mature, grow old, fade, die and are buried again in the life-giving furrow, and dissolving through corruption, from their salutary death return to life again; from corruption perpetually recurring, their natures are again renewed.

And if brethren, the Voice of God, the trumpet of Christ, through the days, the months, the seasons, the years, calls and recalls, leads forth and leads back, bids to be and bids not to be, gives to death and restores to life, why shall He not do once in us that which He does without ceasing in all other things? Or does the divine power fail only with us: with us for whom alone the Divine Majesty of God has done all that we have said?

Man, if for thee all that God has made, returns from death to life, why should you not live again from death through God? Or does God's Creation fail in thee alone: for whom every creature daily lives, moves, is changed, renewed? Brethren, this I say, not with any desire to make nothing of the power of the wonders of Christ, but that I may exhort you, that by the example of this one rising from the dead, we may be roused to faith in the resurrection of all men, and may believe that the Cross is the plough of our body, faith its seed, the grave its furrow, dissolution its bud, time its period of waiting; so that when the spring of the Lord's Coming shall smile on us, the full green of our bodies shall rise again in a life-giving harvest, that will know no end, no old age, that shall not be bound into bundles, nor suffer the winnowing flail. For leaving our former straw in death, the new fruit of our glorified body shall rise again in the harvest of eternal life.

If at the earthly tears of one widow Christ was so moved that He came to meet her on the way, to dry the tears of grief falling from her eyes, to strike again at death, to bring back a man, to raise a body, to bring back life, to change weeping into joy and change a sorrowful burial into a festival of birth, to give back living to his mother one already lying upon the bier of death, what will He not do, now glowing in His strength, in answer to the unceasing prayer of His Church, to the sweat of blood of His Spouse? For the Church pours forth her tears in unceasing supplication, and through her martyrs a sweat of blood, that Christ meeting her shall restore her only son, the Christian people, whom so many generations bear to death, from the bier of mortality to the everlasting joy of the Heavenly Mother.

But as the time of Christ's Birth has come, and the Heavenly Wonder a Virgin was to bring forth now shines forth, and now that, not a star, but the Risen Sun Itself announces the birth of the Divine King, let us hasten all to adore Him, and let us with sacred gifts confess that our God and King has come forth from the Virginal temple. Let us offer gifts; we must offer a public gift to the New Born King; let us offer gifts: for he who does not give, adores in vain. The Magi teach us this, who laden with gold, kindled with incense, sanctified with myrrh,

bow down before the cradle of Christ. But what if that which the Magi did, a Christian will not do? What if amid the joy of Christ Newborn, the poor weep, the captive groans, the stranger weeps and the exile laments? The Jewish people ever honoured the sacred festivals with a tenth of what they possessed. What must a Christian think of himself who honours them with not even a hundredth?

Brethren, let no one think I am saying this for the sake of rhetoric, and not with a mind that grieves. I do grieve. I grieve indeed when I read that the Magi filled the cradle of Christ with gold, and see Christians leave the altar of Christ's Body bare; and this at a time when the hunger of the poor, the sorrowing multitudes of captives spread far and wide.

Let no man say, 'I have nothing'; since God asks of you, not what you have not, but what you have. For the two brass mites of the widow were received as acceptable to God. Let us be generous to the Creator, that His creation may be generous to us. Let us help our neighbour in his need, that we may be delivered in our necessities. Let us heap high the altar of God, that He may fill our barns with a plentiful harvest. And if we do not give, let us not complain if we do not receive. May our God Himself give you in abundance His present and His future blessings, through Jesus Christ our Lord, to Whom be all honour and everlasting glory, together the Holy Spirit, now and forever, and throughout all ages and ages. Amen.

III. St Gregory the Great, Pope and Confessor

The Resurrection of the Body[6]

Job xix. 25–27

For I know that my Redeemer liveth, and in the last day I shall rise out of the earth. And I shall be clothed again with my skin: and in my flesh I shall see my God. Whom I myself shall see, and my eyes shall behold; and not another. This my hope is laid up in my bosom.

For I know that my Redeemer liveth.

1. *Job clearly foretells Christ the Redeemer.* Job speaking, not of, *my* Creator but of, *my Redeemer*, is clearly giving testimony to Him Who, after He had created all things, that He might deliver us from captivity, appeared Incarnate among us and freed us by His Passion from perpetual death. And note with what faith the holy man binds himself to the power of His Divinity of Whom it was said through Paul: *For, although he was crucified through weakness, yet he liveth by the power of God* (II Cor. xiii. 4). For he says: *I know that my Redeemer liveth*; as if openly declaring: Any unbeliever knows He was scourged, derided, slapped upon the face, crowned with a crown of thorns, defiled with spittle, crucified, put to death; but I, with sure faith believe, that after His death He lives, and I freely proclaim, that *my Redeemer liveth*; He Who died at the hands of the wicked. But tell us clearly I beg you, Blessed Job, what you believe, through His Resurrection, concerning the resurrection of your own flesh also? He answers: *And in the last day I shall rise out of the earth.*

2. *Christ died that we might not fear to die; He rose that we might hope to rise again*: Because the Resurrection He revealed to us in His own Person, He shall in time bring to pass in us. For He has promised us this Resurrection which He showed us in Himself; because the members must share the glory of their Head. Our Redeemer for this reason took death upon Him, that we might not be afraid to die; He showed us His own Resurrection, that we might hope that we too shall rise again. And He willed this same death might not continue longer than three days, lest, should resurrection be delayed in Him, we might wholly despair of it. And rightly does the Prophet say of Him: *He shall drink of the torrent in the way: therefore shall he lift up the head* (Ps. cix. 7). For He has deigned to drink of the torrent as it were of our suffering, and not in a place of rest, but *in the way*: for He tasted of death in passing, that is, for the space of three days; for in that death which touched Him, He did not as we do continue till the end of time.

And so when He rose on the third day, He showed us what is to come after, in His Body, which is the Church. By His own example He showed us what He has promised as our reward, so that the faithful, knowing He has risen, might themselves hope for the reward of resurrection at the end of the world. We now, in the death of the flesh, shall remain in dust till the end of time; but He on the third day blossomed forth from the dryness of death, that by this renewal of His own Flesh, He might make known to us the power of His Divinity.

And this was fittingly prefigured in the twelve rods Moses placed in the Tabernacle (Num. xvii. 2). For when the priesthood of Aaron, who was of the tribe of Levi, had become despised, and his tribe held unworthy to offer holocausts; it was commanded that twelve rods, for the twelve tribes, should be placed within the Tabernacle. And lo! the rod of Levi blossomed; showing the power of the priesthood of Aaron. What is conveyed by this sign, but that all we who lie in death till the end of the world, shall like the rest of the rods remain unflowering? But while the other rods remained sapless, the rod of Levi came forth in flower; as the Body of the Lord, that is, of our True Priest, placed in the dryness of death, has burst forth in the flower of the Resurrection. And as by this flowering Aaron was rightly known to be a Priest, so by the glory of His Resurrection our Redeemer, Who is of the tribe of Juda and of Levi, is revealed as our Intercessor.

Behold then how the rod of Aaron now blooms from its dryness, while the rods of the twelve tribes remain withered; as the Body of the Lord now lives after death, while our bodies are held back from the glory of the resurrection until the end of time. And here he makes careful reference to this same long delay; saying: *And in the last day I shall rise out of the earth.*

3. *The Resurrection of many of the dead strengthens our own faith.*

We possess therefore the hope of our own resurrection, when we think of the glory of our Head. But so that no one in his secret heart might say: 'Christ rose from the dead because He was at the same time both God and man, that the death He suffered in His humanity, He overcame in His Divinity; but we, who are but simple men, we cannot rise from this sentence of death,' at the time of Christ's Resurrection there arose, *many bodies of the saints that had slept* (Mt. xxvii. 52). And this took place, that He might give us in Himself a proof of our own resurrection, and confirm this by the resurrection of others who were in nature like us; so that where man might despair of attaining to what had taken place in God made man, he could expect this to happen in himself, when he knew it had happened in those whom he could not doubt were men like himself.

4. *Faith in the resurrection is built up.*

There are some who when they see the soul leave the body, and the body dissolve in corruption, and this corruption change to dust, and this dust so resolved into its final elements that it can no longer be seen by human eyes, despair of the resurrection of the body. And when they see dry bones they have no faith that they themselves shall ever again be reclothed in flesh and once more grow green with life. Should these not have faith in the resurrection from obedience, they should at least believe in it from reason. For what does the world in all its elements picture to our eyes each day but our own resurrection? At each moment of day this temporal light as it were dies, while, with night's shadows, that which we look upon slowly fades from sight, and daily as it wer rises again, when light, night once more pressed down, is restored anew to our eyes. As the seasons unfold we see the trees lose their green, and cease from bearing. Then lo! of a sudden the leaves appear, coming forth by a kind of resurrection almost from dry wood; we see it swell with fruit, and the whole tree living again, clothed once more in splendour. We see tiny seeds cast unendingly into the moist earth; from which a little later we see them rise again as great trees, bearing leaves and fruit.

Let us now consider the tiny seed of some tree, cast into the earth that a tree may come from it, and let us try to discover, if we can, where in the smallness of the seed lay hidden this so great tree that came from it; where the wood, where the bark, where the greenness of the leaves, where the richness of its fruits? Was anything of this seen in the seed cast upon the earth? Yet by the unseen power of its Maker, wondrously ordering all things, within that tender seed was hid the roughness of the bark, within its frailty lay the firmness of its strength. What wonder then if the finest dust, reduced in our eyes to its ultimate elements, should resume again the form of man when He wills it Who from these least seeds renews the mighty trees?

Since we have been created creatures of reason, we should gather hope of our resurrection from the sight and contemplation of all things that are. But because the power of reason had grown dull in us, by the grace of the Redeemer we were given a proof. For our Creator came to us, He suffered death, He made manifest His own Resurrection, that we who would not accept the hope of resurrection from reason, might cling to it by His help and example.

And so let the blessed Job declare: *I know that my Redeemer liveth, and in the last day I shall rise out of the earth.* And let him who has no hope that this can happen in himself, be shamed by the words of the man who believed in the midst of a pagan world; and let him think of the pain he shall suffer, who knowing that the resurrection of the Lord has already taken place, will yet not believe in his own; when he believed in his own resurrection, who still waited in hope for that which was to be accomplished in the Lord Jesus.

5. *The Nature of our bodies after the resurrection.*

Now that I know of the resurrection, I ask to learn the manner of this resurrection. For I believe that I shall rise again, but I desire to know of what nature shall I be? For I must know whether I shall rise again in some other subtle or perhaps ethereal body, or in this body in which I die? For if I rise again in another, ethereal body, it will no longer be I who shall rise. For how can that be a true resurrection, if there cannot be a true body? Plain reason tells me that if the body is not true, then beyond doubt there shall be no true resurrection. Nor can it be rightly called a resurrection, when that does not rise which died. O Blessed Job, take from us these clouds of doubt, and as you through the grace of the Holy Spirit have already begun to speak to us of our hope of resurrection, make clear to us if our flesh shall truly rise again. There follows: *And I shall be clothed again with my skin.*

6. *The error of Eutychius is refuted, who once said our future bodies would be impalpable and more ethereal than air.*[7]

As long as he speaks plainly of skin, all doubt of a true resurrection is taken away, for our body, as Eutychius, a bishop of the city of Constantinople wrote, will not in the glory of that resurrection be impalpable, or more refined than the winds and the air. For in the glory of that resurrection our bodies shall indeed be subtle, as a consequence of their spiritual power, yet palpable because of the reality of their nature. It was for this reason our Redeemer showed His Hands and His side to the Disciples who were doubting His Resurrection, offering them His bones and His flesh to touch, saying: *Handle, and see; for a spirit hath not flesh and bones, as you see me to have* (Lk. xxiv. 39).

When I was living in the city of Constantinople at the time of this Eutychius, I put this testimony from the Gospel to the truth of our resurrection before him. He replied: 'The Lord did this, to remove all doubt of His Resurrection from the hearts of His Disciples.' To this I said: 'This is a truly extraordinary thing you are here advancing: namely, that doubt should arise in us, from the same grounds which took away all doubts from the hearts of the Disciples?' For what could be more defectively stated than that we should be led to doubt of the reality of Christ's Body, through that same proof by which His Disciples were restored to faith and freed of every doubt? For if you assert He did not possess that which He showed them, and which confirmed the faith of His Disciples, then our faith is destroyed.

He then went on to say, that the Lord had the palpable Body He showed them. But after He had confirmed the hearts of those who touched Him, all that could be touched in the Lord was then reduced to a certain subtility. To this I answered: 'It is written that *Christ rising again from the dead, dieth now no more; Death shall no more have dominion over him* (Rom. vi. 9). If therefore after His Resurrection anything of His Body could suffer change, contrary to the truth of what Paul has said, then after His Resurrection the Lord returned to death. And what person however foolish would say this, except one who denies the true Resurrection of His Body?' To this he objected, saying to me: 'Since it is written, *that flesh and blood cannot possess the kingdom of God* (I Cor. xv. 50), on what ground can we believe that the body shall truly rise again?' To this I replied: 'In Sacred Writ flesh is spoken of in one way in regard to its nature, in another in regard to its guilt or corruption. Of flesh as nature was it written: *This now is bone of my bones, and flesh of my flesh* (Gen. ii. 23); and, *The Word was made flesh, and dwelt amongst us* (Jn. i. 14). Of flesh as guilt it was written: *My spirit shall not remain in man for ever, because he is flesh* (Gen. vi. 3). And the Psalmist says: *And he remembereth that they are flesh: a wind that goeth and returneth not* (Ps. lxxxvii. 39).' And it was in this sense Paul said to the disciples: *But you are not in the flesh, but in the spirit* (Rom. viii. 9). It was not that the persons to whom he was writing were no longer in the body, but that they had mastered the impulses of the body's desires; and being now free through the power of the Spirit, were no longer *in the flesh.*

Accordingly, Paul saying, *that flesh and blood cannot possess the kingdom of God,* means that flesh here stands for guilt, not for our nature. For in his next words he shows he was speaking of flesh as guilt, when he adds: 'Neither shall corruption possess incorruption. Therefore flesh shall be in the glory of that heavenly kingdom, in its nature, but *not in the passion of lust;* and, the sting of death overcome, it shall reign incorrupt for ever.'

7. *Eutychius' answers and evasions.*

To this Eutychius at once answered that he agreed to this; yet he continued to deny that the body could rise palpable from the dead. And in the treatise he had written on the resurrection, he had included also the testimony of the Apostle Paul, saying: *That which thou sowest is not quickened, except it die first. And that which thou sowest, thou sowest not the body that shall be; but bare grain* (I Cor. xv. 36); striving by this to show that our flesh shall either be impalpable, or else not the same flesh; seeing that the holy Apostle, speaking of the glory of the resurrection, has said that, *what is sown is not the body that shall be;* But this is speedily answered. For the Apostle Paul, when he says: *Not the body that shall be; but bare grain,* is telling us what we can see; namely, that grain is born with stalk and leaves, though sown without either stalk or leaves. He therefore, to increase the glory of the resurrection, did not say the grain shall not be there, but that what before it had not, it shall now also have. But Eutychius, while denying the true body shall rise

again, does not say that it shall have what it once had not, but that it shall not have what it once had.

8. *The Emperor decides the work of Eutychius shall be burned. Death of Eutychius; his error abjured.*

Going on with this question for a long time we began to feel a great resentment towards one another. Then the Emperor, Constantine Tiberius of pious memory, received us both in private to learn of the disagreement between us. After weighing the written presentation of the case by either side, he decided that the book Eutychius had written on the resurrection should be committed to the flames, destroying also his written presentation. Upon leaving I became very ill, and the same happened to Eutychius, who died a little later. At the time of his death, as there was almost no one who followed his teaching, I dropped the prosecution of it, lest I should appear to be shooting arrows at his ashes. But while he was still alive, and while I was ill with fever, to those I knew who went to visit him he would say, holding the skin of his hand before their eyes: 'I confess that in this flesh we shall all rise again.' And this, they would tell me, he used at one time wholly deny.

9. *The Resurrection of the Dead proved from Job's words.*

Putting aside these reflections, let us seek carefully whether in the light of the words of Job, there shall be a true resurrection and a true body in the resurrection. For we may now no longer doubt the hope of our resurrection, since he says: *And in the last day I shall rise out of the earth.* He has also taken away anxiety regarding the true restoration of our body, when he says: *And I shall be clothed again in my skin.* And to free our mind from any ambiguity, he continues: *And in my flesh I shall see my God.*

Job believed that the body is restored to its former state.

Behold his confession to the truth of the resurrection; here is the body, here is the skin. What is there left for men to doubt? If the holy man believed this, even before the Lord's Resurrection, that our bodies shall be renewed in their prime of life, how grievous will be our sin of doubt if we do not believe in the resurrection of the flesh after the proof our Redeemer has given us? For if our body is not palpable after the resurrection, then surely he who rises is not the same as he who dies; a wicked thing to believe: that I die, and another rises! And so I ask you, Blessed Job, tell us what you believe, and take from our minds all scruple on this question. Then follows: *Whom I myself shall see, and my eyes shall behold, and not another.*

10. *Our body after the resurrection shall be the same as to nature, but different in glory.*

For if after the resurrection, as the followers of certain errors believe, there shall be no palpable body, but that the ethereality of an invisible body shall be called flesh, though the substance of flesh is not there, then indeed one is the body that dies, and another that which rises. But the blessed Job destroys this opinion of theirs with the truth of his words, when he says: *Whom I myself shall see, and my eyes shall behold, and not*

another. And we, following the faith of Job, and believing that the Body of our Redeemer was truly palpable after the Resurrection, profess, that after our future resurrection our flesh shall be the same, and different: the same in nature, different through glory; the same in its reality, different in its power. It shall indeed be subtle, because it shall be incorruptible. It shall be palpable, because it shall not lose the essence of its true nature. And then the holy man goes on to declare with what hope he holds to his faith in the resurrection, and with what certainty he awaits it. He continues: *This my hope is laid up in my bosom.*

11. *Job most certain of his own resurrection.*

There is nothing we hold more firmly than what we have laid up in our bosom. In his bosom therefore he has laid up his hope, in that he has taken to himself with true certainty the hope of our resurrection. But just as he knew that the day of his resurrection would come, so now, in his own voice, or in that of the holy and universal Church, he rebukes the wickedness of evildoers, and foretells the judgement that will follow on the day of resurrection. For immediately he adds: *Why then do you say now: Let us persecute him, and let us find occasion of word against him? Flee then from the face of the sword; for the sword is the avenger of iniquities. And know ye that there is a judgement.*

12. *Because of the judgement that will follow the resurrection, he urges the wicked to do penance* (verses 28 and 29).

In the first verse he rebukes the deeds of the wicked; while in the next he warns them of the penalties of the divine judgement. For he says: *Why then do you say now: let us persecute him, and let us find occasion of word against him?* Because the wicked when they listen with evil design to what is being said, and look to find grounds for accusation in the mouth of the just, what else are they doing but *looking for an occasion against him,* to give them a pretext to accuse him, and in their accusation to spread out the branches of their evil loquacity? But the holy man, when he suffers such affliction from the wicked, does not grieve against them, but rather over them, and rebukes them for the things they have wickedly thought, and shows them the evils they may escape, saying to them: *Flee then from the face of the sword: for the sword is the avenger of iniquities. And know ye that there is a judgement.*

Everyone who does evil, even by despising fear, knows not the judgement of God. For if he knew that this was to be feared, he would not do what shall there be punished. For there are men who have heard of the words, Last Judgement, but by their evil way of life show they do not know what they mean. For when a man does not fear it as he ought, he does not yet know with what a mighty tempest of terror it will approach. Had he learned to think upon the fearful significance of this dread trial, he would prepare in fear against the day of wrath.

To fly from the face of the sword, is to propitiate the severity of this strict visitation before it happens. For the terror of the Judge can be only avoided before the judgement. Now unseen, He can be appeased by our prayers. But in judgement at that dread trial, He can be seen, but cannot be appeased; then in wrath shall He repay the evil deeds He has long suffered in silence. So it is now we must fear our Judge; now while He refrains from judgement, while He bears with us, a little longer, while He suffers the evil He sees, lest, when once His hand has struck in vengeance, He shall strike the more severely in judgement, the longer He has waited before judgement. Amen.

IV. The Venerable Bede, Priest and Confessor

The Gates of Death[8]

Luke vii. 11-16

And there went with him his disciples and a great multitude. And when he came nigh to the gate of the city, behold, a dead man was carried out, the only son of his mother.

This dead man, carried forth from the gates of the city, in the sight of many, is a figure of man struck senseless by the fatal wound of his sins. No longer concealing this death of the soul within the chamber of his heart, he brings it forth by the evidence of word and deed to the knowledge of all men; as though bearing it through the gates of his city. And rightly is he spoken of as *the only son of his mother*: for though assembled together from many persons one is the perfect, immaculate virgin, Mother Church, and each one of the faithful rightly professes himself a son of the Church. For whoever is called, and initiated in the faith, he is a son. When she teaches others, she is a mother. Was he not moved with a mother's love towards her little ones, who said: *My little children, of whom I am in labour again, until Christ be formed in you* (Gal. iv. 19)?

The gate of the city through which the dead man was carried out is, I think, any one of the bodily senses. For he who sows discord among brethren (Prov. vi. 19), and he who has *spoken iniquity on high* (Ps. lxxii. 8), is carried out from the gate of his mouth. And he who looks on a woman, *to lust after her* (Mt. v. 28) bears the tokens of his death through the gate of his eyes. He who listens to evil tales, to licentious songs, to calumny or detraction, freely opens his ears and makes them the gate of death of his soul. And whoever will not guard his other senses, leaves open a way for death to enter.

Lord Jesus, I beseech Thee, make all the gates of my city, gates of justice, that going in to them, I may give praise to Thy name (Ps. cxvii. 19), and praise to Thy majesty; that visiting it often with Thy heavenly ministers, Thou may meet no evil odour of a dead body carried forth, but that salvation shall possess its walls, and praise its gates (Is. lx. 18).

And she was a widow; and a great multitude of the city was with her.

Every soul which remembers that it has been redeemed by the death of her Lord and Spouse confesses that the Church is a widow. By the divine will a great multitude *went with Jesus*, and a great multitude *was with her*, so that at the appearance of this wonder there might be many witnesses; many who would glorify God.

Whom when the Lord had seen, being moved with mercy towards her, he said to her: Weep not.

Do not, He says, weep for him as dead whom in a moment you will see rise again living. Here, mystically, the teaching of Novatian is confuted, who in pride gloried in his own freedom from sin, and sought to make empty the purification from sin of the humbly repentant; denying that the Church, our true Mother, weeping over the spiritual death of the children born to her, should be consoled by the hope that life would again be restored to them.[9] And fittingly does the Evangelist remind us, that the Lord was first *moved with mercy towards the mother*, so that He raises her son to life; that in the one case, He might give us an example of compassion to imitate; in the other, build up our faith in His wondrous power.

And he came near and touched the bier. And they that carried it stood still.

The bier on which the dead man was carried signifies the evilly unconcerned conscience of the hopeless sinner. They who bear him to the grave, are the unclean desires which drag a man down to destruction, or the poisonous allurements of flattering associates, who add to his sins, while they enjoy his favours: despising those who sin, they bury them as under a mound of earth. Of these was it said in another place: *Let the dead bury their dead* (Mt. viii. 22):

for the dead do indeed bury their dead, when sinners caress others like themselves with evil favours, overwhelming them by the weight of evil flattery, so that they cannot hope to rise again.

And they that carried it stood still, when the Lord touched the bier; as the conscience, when touched by the fear of heavenly judgement, keeping back the pressing throng of carnal delights, and the multitude that wickedly praise it, returns to itself, and answers in haste the Voice of the Saviour calling it back to life. So fittingly there follows: *And he said: Young man, I say to thee, arise. And he that was dead sat up and began to speak. And he gave him to his mother.* He sits up who was dead, when the sinner returns to life through compunction of soul. He begins to speak, who shows signs of returning life to all who had encouraged him to sin. He is given back to his mother who, by the decision of the bishop, is returned to the communion of the Church.

And there came a fear upon them all; and they glorified God, saying: A great prophet is risen up among us. The more hopeless the death of a soul recalled to life, the more souls are reformed by its example. Consider the prophet David. Think of Peter the Apostle. The more exalted they were, the greater their fall. And the greater their fall, the greater their joy and gratitude for the mercy that raised them again. And the more loving the Lord's mercy appears in them, the more secure the hope of salvation for all who repent; so that rightly do all present declare, *that God hath visited his people.* He has visited them not once only, through the Incarnation of His Word; He visits them at all times, by sending His Word into our hearts, to awaken us to life in Christ Jesus our Lord. Amen.

NOTES

[1] St Cyril, speaking of the life-giving power of the Body of Christ, taken from the Virgin (PG 73, col. 578, In John, IV), says that even in raising the dead to life, the Saviour we learn, used not only the word and the will of God, but willed also to make His Body a Co-operator in the miracle; to show that It can vivify; and that with Him It has done this: His own, not another's body. So when He raised the daughter of Jairus to life He took her hand (Mk. v. 35); and at Naim He touched the bier. Through His Body we shall come to immortality.

[2] The heresy of Novatian consisted in denying that the Church had power to give absolution in certain cases: the idolatry of the lapsed in the persecutions was unforgiveable, he said. This, St Cyprian, on whom he pressed his errors, declared is opposed to the Creed and to the Interrogation at Baptism. Such severity was not new. Tertullian resisted St Callistus' forgiveness of adultery, as an innovation. There are no biographical details of Novatian available.

[3] PL 38, Sermo. XCVIII. The sermon is also concerned with the evil of sodomy; which the Saint treats of in restrained terms.

[4] Prayer taken from the close of Sermon 333, PL 38.

[5] PL 52, Sermo 103, Col. 487.

[6] From *Moralium in Job*; xix. 25 *et seq*. Cf. PL 75, Lib. XIV, Caput 54: 67–78, col. 1074.

[7] Eutychius I, Patriarch of Constantinople, 512–82. Not to be confused with Eutyches of the fifth century and the Monophysite heresy. Eutychius opposed this heresy, to the point of banishment and exile. Very late in life he formed certain defective notions regarding the Resurrection, which Gregory, then Apocrisarius (Legate) at Constantinople, confuted, as he here recounts, arguing from Luke xxiv. 39. At his death, Eutychius repeated the full confession of the Blessed Job (verses 25–27).

[8] PL 92, *In Lucae Evangelium Expositio*, Lib. II, 7, col. 417.

[9] See note 2.

SIXTEENTH SUNDAY AFTER PENTECOST

I. St Antony Abbot: On Humility and on Deceit

II. St Basil: On Modesty and Vainglory
III. St Basil: On Envy

IV. St John Chrysostom: Moral Exhortation to Humility

V. St Augustine: Meditation on the Humility of Christ

THE GOSPEL OF THE SUNDAY

Luke xiv. 1–11

At that time: When Jesus went into the house of one of the chief of the Pharisees, on the sabbath day, to eat bread, they watched him. And, behold, there was a certain man before him that had the dropsy. And Jesus answering, spoke to the lawyers and Pharisees, saying: Is it lawful to heal on the sabbath day? But they held their peace. But he, taking him, healed him and sent him away. And answering them he said: Which of you shall have an ass or an ox fall into a pit and will not immediately draw him out on the sabbath day? And they could not answer him to those things.

And he spoke a parable also to them that were invited, marking how they chose the first seats at the table, saying to them: When thou art invited to a wedding, sit not down in the first place, lest perhaps one more honourable than thou be invited by him; and he that inviteth thee and him come and say to thee: Give this man place. And then thou begin with shame to take the lowest place. But, when thou art invited, go, sit down in the lowest place; that, when he who inviteth thee cometh, he may say to thee: Friend, go up higher. Then shalt thou have glory before them that sit at table with thee. Because everyone that exalteth himself shall be humbled; and he that humbleth himself shall be exalted.

EXPOSITION FROM THE CATENA AUREA

I

CYRIL: Though the Lord knew the malice of the Pharisees, nevertheless He partook of their hospitality, so that by His words and miracles He might do some good among those present. For this reason we read:

V.1. *And it came to pass, when Jesus went into the house of one of the Pharisees, on the sabbath day, to eat bread, that they watched him:*

To see if He would ignore the Law, or do any of the things that were forbidden on the sabbath day.

And so when the dropsical man came among them, by a question Jesus checks the arrogance of the Pharisees, seeking to find fault with Him. Hence we read:

VV.2 and 3. *And, behold, there was a certain man before him that had the dropsy. And Jesus, answering, spoke to the lawyers and Pharisees, saying: Is it lawful to heal on the sabbath day?*

BEDE: That Jesus is said to have answered relates to the words: *And they watched him.* For the Lord knows the thoughts of men. THEOPHYLACTUS: By His question He makes public their foolishness: for while God blesses on the seventh day, they prevent good works on that day. A day that does not allow the doing of good works is accursed.

V.4. *But they held their peace.*

BEDE: And well did they, when questioned, hold their peace. For they see that whatever they say would be said against themselves. If it is lawful to heal on the sabbath why do they watch the Saviour to see if He will heal on that day? If it is not lawful, why do they care for their cattle on the sabbath? And so there follows: *But they held their peace.* CYRIL: Avoiding the snares of the Jews, He delivers the man from his dropsy; who, for fear of the Pharisees, does not ask to be healed, but simply stands by; so that, moved by compassion at his appearance, Jesus might heal him: The Lord knows this, and does not ask him if he wishes to be healed; but there and then heals him. Hence follows: *But He taking him, healed him and sent him away.*

THEOPHYLACTUS: In doing this the Lord was not concerned to see whether He gave scandal to the Pharisees or not, but looked only to do good to one in need of His help. For it is right, when what we are doing yields great good, to pay no heed to the scandal of the foolish. CYRIL: And as the Pharisees continued in their foolish silence, Christ reproves their unvarying forwardness, using in this certain reflections. Hence there follows:

V.5. *And answering them he said: Which of you shall have an ass or an ox fall into a pit and will not immediately draw him out, on the sabbath day?*

THEOPHYLACTUS: As though to say: If the law forbids you to have compassion on the sabbath, then neither should you have a care for your son, should he fall into danger on the sabbath. But why do I speak of your son, when you will not neglect even your ox, should you see it in danger?[1] BEDE: In which He makes clear to the Pharisees watching Him, that He is accusing them also of avarice, revealing greed in their concern for animals. How much more should Christ not help man, who is more precious than any beast?

AUGUSTINE, *Gospel Questions*, II, 29: He aptly compares the dropsical man to the beast that fell into a well, for he was encumbered with water; just as He compares the woman He had called *bound*, and whom He had *loosed*, to a beast that is loosed to be led to water. BEDE: By this apt example He solves the question: to show them that they are accusing Him of breaking the sabbath by a work of charity, who themselves break it by works of covetousness. Hence there follows:

V.6. *And they could not answer him to these things.*

Mystically, the dropsical man is a figure of one overwhelmed by the flow of carnal pleasures: for dropsy is a disease named from excess of watery humour. AUGUSTINE, as above: Or, we may rightly compare the dropsical man to a covetous rich man: For the more the one is swollen with excess of water, the more he thirsts; so also the other: The more he abounds in riches, which he does not use well, the more eagerly he desires them.

GREGORY, *Morals in Job*, xviii, 19: Rightly therefore is the dropsical man healed in the presence of the Pharisees: for by the bodily sickness of the one, is signified the weakness or the sickness of heart and soul of the others. BEDE: Well does He speak in this parable of the ass and the ox, as signifying either the wise and the foolish, or both peoples: namely, the Jews, laden with the yoke of the Law; and the Gentiles, unbroken by any law. It is the Lord draws all men out who have sunk into the pit of concupiscence.

2

V.7. *And he spoke a parable also to them that were invited, marking how they chose the first seats at table, saying to them:*

AMBROSE: He first heals the dropsical man, in whom excess of the body's fluid oppressed the activity of the soul, and extinguished the ardour of his spirit. Then we are taught humility, when we are forbidden to be eager for the higher place at a wedding feast.

V.8. *When thou art invited to a wedding, sit not down in the first place.*

CYRIL: Here He shows that we are rash and deserving of rebuke, should we rush eagerly towards the places of honour that do not belong to us. Then follows: *lest perhaps one more honourable than thou be invited by him.*

V.9. *And he that invited thee and him come and say to thee: Give this man place. And then thou begin with shame to take the lowest place.*

CHRYSOSTOM: And so he who was eager for prominence, does not obtain what he desired, but suffers a repulse; and striving to gain honour is not honoured. And as nothing is more to be desired than modesty, the Lord leads the minds of His listeners to the opposite of this conduct. He tells us not only must we not be eager for the first place, but bids us seek the lowest. Hence follows:

V.10. *But when thou art invited, go, sit down in the lowest place.*

CYRIL: For should someone not desire a place above others, he shall be given this; according to the divine sentence. For there follows: *That, when he who inviteth thee cometh, he may say to thee: Friend, go up higher.* In saying this, He is not harshly rebuking, but mildly advising them: for a word to the wise suffices. And so it is for humility a man is crowned with honour. For there follows: *Then shalt thou have glory before them that sit at table with thee.*

BASIL (*Regulae Disp.* 21): To take the lowest place at feasts, as the Lord advises, is a fitting thing to do; but again, to seize it forcibly is a thing to be condemned, as disturbing order and causing confusion. Contending for the last place, you will be no different from those who strive for the first. Accordingly, as the Lord here says, it is for him who gives the feast, to decide the order of place. We should have a patient concern for one another, doing all things becomingly and in order; and not for the sake of how we may appear before the crowd. Neither should we make a show of humility by resisting strongly: humility is practised rather by simple submission; refusal shows pride more decidedly than taking the first place when invited to do so.

THEOPHYLACTUS: Let no one think the teaching the Lord here gives is of little importance, or unworthy of the sublimity of the Word of God. For you do not call a physician kind who undertakes to heal gout, but refuses to treat a cut finger or an aching tooth. And how can the sickness of vanity be a little thing, when it throws into disorder those seeking the first places? It was therefore fitting that the Teacher of humility should cut off every branch of this evil root. And consider also, that, with the supper ready, and with the craving for the first place troubling the foolish, and in the presence of the Saviour, it was a suitable time for a word of advice.

CYRIL: Having shown by this simple example the humiliation of the vainglorious, and the exaltation of the humble, to this small incident He

joins something great; instructing all the faithful:

V.11. *Because everyone that exalteth himself shall be humbled; and he that humbleth himself shall be exalted.*

And this is the utterance of the Divine Judgement, not of human experience: for in this world, many who desire honour gain it; while those who humble themselves, remain unknown. THEOPHYLACTUS: But in the end, he who thrusts himself into honours is not honoured by all men: while honoured by some, others will speak ill of him, sometimes even while honouring him.

BEDE: But since the Evangelist calls this admonition a parable, let us consider briefly its mystical content. Whoever was invited and has come to the nuptials of Christ and His Church, let him not, glorying in his own merits, set himself above the other members of the Church to whom he is joined by faith. For he shall give place to one more honourable, invited after him, who has surpassed him in activity in following Christ, and with shame must fill the lowest place, when, learning of the greater things others have done, he lowers the exalted notions he had of his own works. But when a man sits in the lowest place, in accord with the words: *The greater thou art, the more humble thyself in all things: and thou shalt find grace before God* (Ecclus. iii. 20). the Lord, when He comes, finding him humble, shall bless him with the name, *friend,* and shall bid him go higher: For, *Whosoever shall humble himself as a child, he is the greater in the kingdom of heaven* (Mt. xviii. 4). And well does He say: *Thou shalt have glory*: That you may not begin to seek *now* the glory laid up for you at the end.

The parable may also be understood of this life, for the Lord comes daily in to His marriage feast, putting down the proud, and sometimes giving such gifts of His Spirit to the humble that the company sitting down, that is, the faithful, are astonished, and glorify them. From the general conclusion that follows, it is clearly manifest, that the preceding discourse of the Lord is to be understood mystically. For not every one who exalts himself before men is humbled; neither is everyone who humbles himself in the sight of men, exalted by them. But, he who prides himself on his merits, he shall be humbled by the Lord; and he who humbles himself because of the favours he has received, he shall be exalted by Him.

I. ST ANTONY, ABBOT AND EGYPTIAN FATHER OF THE CHURCH

On Humility; and on Deceit[2]

I. Humility

Brethren, the Prophet says: *But to whom shall I have respect, but to him that is poor and little and of a contrite spirit, and that trembleth at my words* (Is. lxii. 2)? And in the Gospel the Lord says the same: *Learn of me, because I am meek, and humble of heart; and you shall find rest to your souls* (Mt. xi. 29). He therefore who has gained humility, has already become a dwelling place of the Most High God; and has attained to sublimity of soul, to the love of innocence, to peace and to charity. Come then, dispose your heart towards humility, and do not walk in the company of devils in pride of heart. For God and His angels and saints turn away from the proud in heart. Whosoever therefore walks in the pride of his own heart, is an associate of demons.

Because of pride of heart the heavens were bowed down, the foundations of the earth were shaken, the deeps of the sea were troubled and angels were cast down from glory, and became demons because of their pride of heart. Because of this the Almighty was angered, and caused fire to come forth from the abyss, and waves to rise up as a sea of fire (Num. xvi). Because of pride of heart He made hell, and its torments. Because of pride of heart bonds were made and scourges, with which the devil is tormented because of the pride of his heart. Because of pride of heart the abyss of hell was made, and the worms that do not die or sleep (Mk. ix. 45). Because of pride of heart the fiery chariots were made, the torment of burning flames, the coals of living fire. Because of pride of heart all things are troubled and thrown into disorder, and men war against each other, and from this came tyranny.

All this has happened through pride of heart. The pride of heart of men is unclean before God: but hearts that are humble and contrite the Lord will not despise. The Mercy of God, my beloved brothers and sons, coming to us from on high, became humble to His last breath. And because of this we glory with the psalmist, saying: *See my* *abjection and my labour: and forgive me all my sins* (Ps. xxiv. 18).

II. Deceit

Let us lift up our hands and hearts to the Most High God Who is in heaven, and let us strive to keep far from that first sin of all, namely, the deceit that was in Cain; of which it was written: *Deliver me, O God, from the unjust and deceitful man* (Ps. xlii). The deceitful man deceives only his own soul; for his deceit returns upon his own head; as was written in the Psalm: *His sorrow shall be turned on his own head: and his iniquity shall come down upon his crown* (vii. 17). Be not familiar with an evil man, nor the companion of an unjust man, nor have anything whatsoever to do with him; but shun him as you would a garment that reeks of the corruption of the dead.

For the tongue of a deceitful man provokes strife among peoples, and the shedding of blood. He who enters into a friendship with a deceitful woman, enters into the same with a most wicked devil. He who enters into friendship with a deceitful man, joins company with spillers of blood, and becomes guilty of his own death. Far, far better to dwell in solitude, than in the company of a treacherous man. Make no friendship with a treacherous man; and go not into any house with him; for if you once enter, he will drag you down to his own foulness. You are safer in the company of wild beasts, than in the company of a deceitful man.

And should such a man approach you pleasantly, and speak mildly with you; nevertheless, should you once trouble his heart, of a sudden the hidden guile bursts forth and he will destroy you when you least expect it. Because of this let God be with you, as He was with our Fathers, with Abraham and Isaac and Jacob, that He may deliver you from him whose *strength is in his loins* (Job xl. 11); that is, the devil, who at all times looks with malice on men who serve God, and strives to catch them with his hook, that he may devour them.

But we have One Who makes intercession for us (Heb. vii. 25), Jesus Christ our Lord, Who has given us power to tread down his strength (Lk. x. 19). The eye that is not filled with seeing, and the ear that is not filled with hearing (Eccles. i. 8; a reference to St Paul), tells us that love is the fulfilling of the law (Rom. xiii. 10). The fulfilment of such things as these: That you be all of one heart in Christ Jesus; helping one another, loving one another as brothers, having compassion on one another, so that the Lord may prepare our hearts to fulfil His commandments, until the day of the manifestation of the fulness of His Glory in Jesus Christ, unto all generations that are without corruption: the brethren whom I love, through Christ Jesus; to Whom be Glory and Honour, now and for ever, throughout all ages and ages. Amen.

II. St Basil the Great, Bishop and Doctor

Meditation on Humility and on Vainglory[3]

1. It is not possible for a man to control his anger when abused, or to overcome trials with patience when afflicted, if he is not willing to take the last and the lowest place among other men. But a man who has attained to true humility will not be troubled by offensive or ignominious words, since he is already aware of his own great unworthiness even before he is insulted. And should he be called a beggar, he already knows he is poor, and in want of everything, and that he has need each day of God's help. If he is spoken of as insignificant and of no importance he is already aware of this in his own heart: that he was made from clay. In a word, let me say that he is *great* in heaven who humbly submits to his neighbour, and, without any cause for shame, bears patiently accusations made against him, even though they are false, if by this he may be at peace with his brother.

And it is not easy to keep one's soul humble in the midst of difficulties, just as it is not easy not to be proud in prosperity and honour. And the proud, the more they are flattered, the more disdainful they become. The manner of one who is humble of heart is modest and somewhat downcast. Such as these also dress simply and for use, not cultivating the hair, or particular about clothing; so that the appearance mourners put on is natural to them. And as to dress, let the outer garment (tunic) be held in place by a girdle, not fastened above the waist, like a woman's, nor yet loosely, so that the garment is slack, which

looks foolish. And as to your manner of walking, let it not be sluggish, which shows a dull relaxed soul. Neither should it be too quick, or strutting, lest your movements show a mind that is rash, or lacking in good sense. The purpose of clothing is to provide suitable covering for the body both winter and summer. Avoid what is striking in colour. And as to quality, it should not be too fine, or effeminate. For a man who indulges in bright colours is no different from a woman who paints her face and dyes her hair. Let your clothes be sufficiently thick, so that you have no need of another to keep you warm. Shoes should cost little; yet they should be such as we need. The practice of modesty consists in this; in being content with things that are cheap and simple, and in being watchful against the affectations of vainglory.

A man is vainglorious who will do or say anything for the sake of this world's miserable applause. As, for instance, a man who gives alms to be honoured by others. He receives his reward (Mt. vi. 2); though he is neither generous nor compassionate. Or a man who is temperate, so as to be praised for his moderation. He is not temperate; since he is not striving for this virtue, but for the credit that will come to him through this virtue. Ananias for example (Acts v.), in the beginning, was not compelled to consecrate his property to God by a vow. But thinking only of human glory, when he had consecrated it to God by his promise, so as to be honoured by others for his generosity, keeping back a part of the price, he so provoked against himself the anger of God, whose minister Peter was, that he was not even given time to repent. For the Lord Who resists the proud, and brings the wicked down even to the earth (Ps. cxlvi. 6), has Himself promised that He will bring down the folly of the proud. And He Who humbles the proud will therefore also free them from that resemblance they have to the devil, the father of all pride, and will Himself guide them so that they may become disciples of the One Who says: *Learn of me, because I am meek and humble of heart.*

And why do you esteem yourself so highly, as though you who had defeated nations, and brought down the might of kingdoms? May not the axe swell with pride for the same reason; for it has brought low many mighty trees? And likewise the saw, that has cut up the firm and solid wood? But the axe does not cut without hands, nor the saw cut up without the one who draws it through the wood.

2. Should you see your neighbour commit a sin, see that you think not only of his sin, but that you also think of what he does, and has done well, and doing this you will oftentimes find that he is better than you are; when you consider all he has done, and not a part. God does not judge a man on a part of his life only. He says: *I know their works and their thoughts; I come that I may gather them together* (Is. lxvi. 18). And when the Lord rebuked Josaphat for the sin he had just committed, He recalled the good he had also done, saying to him: *But good works are found in thee* (II Par. xix. 3). Humility therefore will often save a man who is guilty of many and grievous sins. Do not then justify yourself above some other man, for fear that though justified by your own sentence, you shall be condemned by the just sentence of God.

If you think you have done something good, then give thanks to God; do not place yourself above your neighbour. For how have you helped your neighbour by confessing the faith, or by suffering exile for the name of Christ, or by bearing hardships in patience? The profit is yours, not another's. Take care not to fall as the devil fell who, uplifted above men, was brought low by a Man, and delivered to men as a footstool to be trodden on. In a word, be mindful of that saying: *God resisteth the proud, and giveth grace to the humble* (Jas. iv. 6). Keep close to you the Lord's words: *Everyone that exalteth himself shall be humbled; and he that humbleth himself shall be exalted* (Lk. xiv. 11).

Neither let you be an unjust judge in your own case. Do not try it with favour towards yourself; taking note of whatever good you have done, forgetting the evil. Do not take pride in today's good actions, whilst giving yourself full pardon for past or recent wicked ones. Rather, should you be pleased and satisfied with some present action, bring before your mind another kind of action from the past, and then your foolish pride will cease. The most difficult of all things seems to be to know one's self. For not alone does our eye look outwardly, and not use its power to look at itself, but our mind also; so sharp to note the sins of others, it is slow to see its own sins. Neither should you be too severe, or too prompt, in rebuking others. Do not judge in anger; for this is a ruthless thing. Do not condemn for trifles; as though you were yourself faultless in the sight of the law. And those who have been overtaken by some fault, treat them with a spirit of mildness, as the Apostle warns us: *Considering thyself, lest thou also be tempted* (Gal. vi. 1). For should we offend in something, we are the better for a little rebuke. But where we have done no wrong, why should we be made to suffer?

For myself, Brethren, I have always striven more not to be noticed, than they strive to be seen who look for notice. Let you show as much zeal in seeking not to be praised by men, as others show in seeking praise. But if you have been raised to honour, and men surround you with respect and reverence, then be as those subject to you. For he who wishes to be first, the Lord commands that he shall be the servant of all (Mk. x. 44). The great Moses, who in all things was mild and gentle, when God sent him to rule His people, prayed: *I beseech thee, Lord, choose another whom thou wilt send* (Ex. iv. 13). Because of this the Lord urged him, as it were with persistence; as though by this confession of his own unsuitability, he showed that he was worthy of being placed over the people. It was in the light of this example that Scripture lays down the counsel: *Seek not to be made a judge unless thou have strength enough to extirpate iniquities* (Ecclus. vii. 6).

But the words of the prophet Isaias makes plain that the refusal of those who were called to rule rebel-lious peoples was not a rule for all. For Isaias did not simply say: *Make me not a ruler*, but *make me not a ruler of this people* (Is. iii. 7). And he gave the reason. *Because their tongue and their devices are against the Lord.* And so when Moses was called to this prominence, and to be leader of such a people, he pleads to be spared this honour. *Who am I*, he says, *that I should go to Pharao, and should bring forth the children of Israel out of Egypt?* (Ex. iii. 11). And again he says: *I beseech thee, Lord, I am not eloquent from yesterday and the day before; and since thou hast spoken to thy servant, I have more impediment and slowness of tongue* (iv. 10). And also: *I beseech thee, Lord, send another whom thou wilt send*. But the Lord said to him: *Go thou, and lead this people whither I have told thee. My angel shall go before thee* (Ex. xxxii. 34). And what does Moses answer? *If thou thyself dost not go before, bring us not out of this place* (xxxiii. 15). Isaias however, though he had heard nothing like this, but only of the people's need of an apostle among them, offers himself freely, and places himself in the midst of dangers.

What was in the minds of these two men? The thought of Moses was that: this is a sinful people. It has need of One Who can forgive its sins; and this is not possible to angels. Angels are the instruments of God's punishments on those who sin; their sins they are not able to pardon. Therefore let the True Lawgiver come: He Who has power to save, and Who alone has power to forgive sin. Isaias, however, in the fervour of his love, held as nothing what this people might do to him. Let us imitate the fervour and humility of these two men, that we may also be

sharers of their future joy and blessing in Christ Jesus our Lord, to
Whom with the Father and the
Holy Ghost, be there glory and
honour and majesty now and for
ever, world without end. Amen.

III. St Basil, Bishop and Doctor

On Envy[4]

1. God is good, and the Giver of good things to those who are worthy of them. The devil is evil, and the contriver of wickedness every-where. And just as freedom from envy is the consequence of good-ness, so malice obeys the devil. Let us therefore, Brethren, be on our guard against the passion of envy, so that we may not become partner in the works of our Adversary; and find ourselves condemned together with him. For if the man who is puffed up with pride *falls into the judgement of the devil* (I Tim. iii. 6), how shall the envious escape the punishment prepared for the devil? For nothing more destructive springs up in the souls of men than the passion of envy, which, while it does no harm to others, is the dominant and peculiar evil of the soul that harbours it. As rust consumes iron, so does envy wholly consume the soul it dwells in. More than this. As vipers are said to be born through devouring the maternal womb, so envy devours the soul that gives it birth.

Envy is the pain that arises from another's good fortune. And be-cause of this the envious man is never without pain, never without grief of mind. Is his neighbour's field fertile? Does his house abound in good things? Is its owner without care, and wanting for nothing? All this but feeds his affliction; an increase of pain to the envious; so much so that in

nothing does he differ from a man stripped naked and wounded by all men. Is someone brave and manly; in good health? Such things are like a wound to the envious. Is another more pleasing in appearance? This is like a blow to the envious. Is another endowed with many gifts of soul? Is he respected and admired, because of his wisdom, his elo-quence? Is another man rich, gener-ous of his wealth to the poor and needy, honoured for his benevo-lence? All these things are like so many wounds and blows that strike the envious to the heart.

And the worst of this sickness of soul is that the sufferer cannot make it known; but with bowed head and downcast eyes he suffers torment, he grieves, he perishes of his affliction. Asked of what he is suffering, he is ashamed to reveal his disease and confess, 'I am envious and bitter: the gifts of my friends are a torment to me. I grieve at my brother's happiness, I cannot endure the sight of another's good fortune.' For this is what he must say if he would tell the truth. But unwilling to speak out, he conceals in the depths of his mind the sickness that smoulders within, consuming him.

2. And so he neither seeks the help of a physician for his disease, nor finds a remedy to drive out his sickness; though the Scriptures are filled with such remedies. He looks

for but one remedy for his affliction: to see one of those he envies fall into misfortune. This is the goal of his hate: to see someone he envies miserable instead of happy, to see one who is admired pitied. Then he is at peace. And when he sees him weeping, when he sees him in affliction, he is his friend. He does not rejoice with them that rejoice, but he weeps with them that weep (Rom. x. 15). He pities him in his changed circumstances, not however from human tenderness, or from sympathy; with kind words for his former state, but so that he may make his present circumstances seem worse. He speaks well of his son, when he is dead; honouring his memory with a thousand praises: how fine he was, how beautiful to see, how gifted, how balanced in everything. But while he lived his tongue had not a good word for him. But should he see many others adding their praises to his, he changes again, and envies the dead. He admires riches, after they have been lost. He praises grace and vigour of body, when disease has laid it low. In a word, he is an enemy of things present, their friend when they have perished.

3. What could be more deadly than this disease, which is a corruption of life, a defilement of our nature, a hatred of the things God has given us, a contradiction of God? What urged the devil, the beginner of evil, to wage fierce war against man? Was it not envy? It was through envy he came to war openly against God; enraged against Him because of His great bountifulness to man, but avenging himself on man because he is powerless against God.

We see these very qualities revealed in Cain, the first disciple of the devil, who taught him envy and murder; kindred crimes, which Paul has joined together in the words: *full of envy, murder* (Rom. i. 29). What was it Cain did? He saw another honoured by God, and burned with envy. He killed the one who was honoured, that he might insult Him Who honoured him. Since he could not attack God, he turned his hatred to the murder of his own brother.

Let us fly, brethren, from this wickedness of soul that would teach us to war against God, this mother of murder that does violence to our nature, that knows no kinship; a most senseless evil. Why must you grieve, man, you who have suffered nothing? Why must you show enmity to those who enjoy good things, while taking nothing that is yours? Should you be enraged because someone does you a kindness, are you not then an enemy of your own profit? Saul was of such a nature, for whom the very greatness of the things David had done for him was the reason of his war against him. For first, cured of madness by the wondrous harmony of David's music, he attempts to transfix with a lance the giver of this favour. Then with his army he was delivered from the enemy, and delivered from the insults of Goliath; and when the women dancing at his victory proclaim that David's part in it is ten times that of Saul: *Saul slew his thousands, and David his ten thousands* (I Kings xviii. 7), because of this one sentence, and because of the truth of what they proclaimed, he tried to kill David with his own hand, and then attacked him by treachery.

And when David was forced to fly, he still did not cease from enmity, but prepared an army of three thousand chosen men and went out to search the desert for him (I Kings xxiv. 3). Had Saul been asked the reason for his persecution of David, clearly he would have to answer that it was because of the favours David had done to him.

At the very time Saul was pursuing him, David came upon him as he slept, and could readily have slain his persecutor, yet again was he spared by this just man, who would not lay a hand on him. But not even for this favour did Saul relent; but once more gathers his armies and pursues him, and is once again intercepted, in a cave, by David, where he even more clearly revealed his great virtue, and Saul his own manifest wickedness.

Envy is the most implacable form of hatred. For favours will make friends of those who would otherwise be enemies, but to show kindness to the envious only provokes him the more. And the more he receives, the more aggrieved and embittered he becomes. He is more angered by the worth of his benefactor, than thankful for his gifts. How the envious surpass even wild beasts in the savagery of their disposition! Could even savages surpass them in cruelty? Dogs will become gentle when you feed them, lions when their wounds are treated, but the envious become more savage, should you once do them a favour.

4. What caused the high-minded Joseph to be sold as a slave? What but the envy of his brethren? And here it is worth while to note the foolishness of envy. For being fearful that a dream should come true, they sell their brother into slavery (Gen. xxxvii. 28), as if, made a slave, he would never be adored by them. But if a dream is true, what arts can prevent its fulfilment? If it is false, why envy the one who is deluded? But the Providence of God made nothing of their foolish scheme. The means they believed would prevent the fulfilment of the prophecy, were those that prepared the way for it. For had Joseph not been sold as a slave, he would not have come to Egypt, and would not, because of his chastity, have been thrown by a woman's treachery into prison, nor have become a high servant of Pharaoh, nor an interpreter of his dream; through which he was made prince of Egypt, and was then adored by his brethren, who came to him when there was a wheat famine among them.

Turn now in your mind to the greatest envy, linked to the greatest of all happenings, which burst forth from the rage of the Jews against Christ. For what cause was He envied? Because of His miracles. And what were these miracles? The healing of those in need: the hungry were fed; and they attacked the One Who fed them. The dead were raised again to life; and they envied the One Who recalled them to life. Demons were cast out; and they made snares for the One Who had commanded them to go out. Lepers were made clean, the lame walked again, the deaf heard, the blind saw, and He Who had done all this they persecuted.

And lastly they delivered the Author of life to death, they scourged the Deliverer of men, and they condemned to death the Judge of the world. So do the evils of envy reach to all things. And so from the beginning of the foundations of the world until the end of time, the Devil, the Destroyer of life, by means of this sole weapon, wounds and strikes down all men. He who rejoices in our destruction, he who fell himself through envy, is preparing the same path for us by means of this same vice. Wise indeed is he who forbade us sit at the table with an envious man (Prov. xxiii. 6); and by sitting *at table*, he is warning us against all association with him. Just as we are careful to keep what is inflammable from the fire, so are we to avoid the company of the envious, and so should we keep from friendly association with the malicious, and from the darts of their envy.

For we cannot be caught by the snares of envy unless we approach to familiarity with it. In the words of Solomon: *Envy is from a man's neighbour* (Eccles. iv. 4, Sept.). For it is. A Scythian is not envious of an Egyptian, but each will envy one of the same nation. And among people of the same nation, those not known are not envied, but those with whom we are familiar; and among these again, it arises between persons of the same age, the same kinship, among brothers. As red blight is a pest in the growing wheat, so is envy a pest among friends.

In this evil there is one thing can be praised: that the more it is aroused, the more bitter it is to the one it masters. As a javelin shot with great force, should it strike a resisting object, will fly back at the thrower, so does the thrust of envy, leaving the one envied unwounded,

become the wound of the one envying. Who, by the torments he inflicts on himself, lessens what his neighbour possesses? But the envious consumes himself, pining away through grief. Nevertheless, those who labour under this affliction are looked upon as more deadly than venomous serpents: for they inflict poison through a wound, and then the part bitten begins to putrefy. But there are those who believe that envious persons can do harm by their eyes alone, so that persons in good health, and in the flower of their age, will wither away through their envy, and of a sudden lose their good health, as though it were washed away by some deadly stream, corrupting and destroying, flowing from their envying eyes. For my part, however, I dismiss this as popular credulity and old wives' tales. But I say this, that the demons, haters of whatever is good, where they find natures akin to their own, they use them in every kind of way for their own evil purposes. So they may even use the very eyes of the envious as instruments of their purpose. Do you not shrink in horror from being the tool of an evil demon? Yet you entertain within you, the wickedness through which you will become an enemy of those who have done no wrong; an enemy even of God, Who is good and free of all envy?

5. Let us fly from this insupportable vice. It is the teaching of the serpent, an invention of demons, seed sown by an enemy, a pledge of torment to come, a barrier to the love of God, the way to Gehenna, the loss of the kingdom of heaven. The envious can be known even by

their faces. With them the eye is dry and lustreless, the cheek withered, the brow furrowed, the mind perturbed by the violence of their feeling, their judgement upon things lacking the criterion of truth. For them no work of virtue is worthy of praise, no power of speech, though adorned with judiciousness and grace; nor any of the things that men seek and admire. Just as vultures in their flight will pass over fields and meadows, places sweet and pleasant, drawn by the odours of corruption, and flies pass over what is healthy, to swarm upon what is prurient, so the envious have no eyes for the splendours of life, for the grandeur of virtue, but only for what is decayed and rotten.

And should someone stumble, as will happen to men, they make it public. They will strive to make men known by their falls; just as bad painters will gain prominence for their pictures by a distorted nose or by some swelling or defect of nature or accident, so the envious are adept at distorting the appearance of what is good, at calumniating virtue through its opposing vice. A man who is courageous, they will say is reckless; a temperate man, unfeeling; a just man, harsh; a prudent man cunning. They speak of a man of great generosity as vulgar, of a liberal man as prodigal, while a careful man is mean, and in general what ever virtue a man may possess, they will give it a name taken from its opposite vice.

Well then! Is our sermon to be but a denunciation of this vice! That would be only half its cure. To point out to a sick man the seriousness of his disease, so that he may take due care of himself, is not an unprofitable thing to do. But to leave him to suffer, not to lead him as it were by the hand towards good health, is nothing other than to abandon a man lying in his sickness. What then are we to do? How are we, as a beginning, to avoid contracting his sickness; or should it attack us, how can we be cured? The first step is, that we should not look upon anything in the affairs of men as either great or impressive: neither their wealth nor their perishable glory nor their health of body. Let us not believe that our highest good consists of these so fleeting things, but rather remember that we are called to the enjoyment and possession of real and eternal blessings. And so, the one who possesses much is not to be envied because of his riches, nor the ruler because of his rank, nor the strong because of his health of body, nor the wise because of the wisdom of his speech. All these things are but instruments of virtue to those who use them well; they do not in themselves contain happiness. He however who uses them ill is to be pitied: he is like a man receiving a sword against the enemy, who instead turns it deliberately against himself. But when a man uses rightly the things of the present life, and in a manner that accords with right reason, and as a steward of the things of God, not using them for his sole pleasure, he is, because of his love of his brother, and because of the justice and humanity of his life, deserving of both love and praise.

Again a man may be noted for his prudence, and held in honour through the word of God, because he is a teacher of divine truth. Be not envious of such a man, and never wish that as a teacher of the Holy Scriptures he should be silent; because, through the grace of the Spirit, he is praised by those who hear him. For the good he does is yours also, sent to you by means of your brother's gift of teaching: provided you receive it. But then, no one blocks up a gushing fountain, nor will anyone close his eyes to the sunlight, or envy those who enjoy it; rather, all pray that they too may enjoy these things. And so when the spiritual word is welling forth in the Church, or when some pious heart gushes forth like a fountain from the gift of the Spirit, why not give ear with joy? Why not receive these graces with thankfulness? But the applause of those who listen pierces you, and you would that no one might receive profit, no one receive praise. What excuse can there be for such things in the presence of the Judge of our hearts?

We must therefore suppose that the gifts of nature serve the good of the soul. He however who abounds in wealth and dominion, and in great understanding, and in health of body, and uses these gifts rightly is to be loved and respected, as holding certain endowments that serve the common life; provided he uses them in accord with right reason, so that he is liberal with his abundance to those in need, and has care for the weak in body; and looks upon what is over and above his own needs as belonging as much to whoever is in want as to himself. He who is not of this mind is to be pitied rather than envied; in that he possesses greater opportunities for evil doing. For this is to perish from excess of planning and striving. For if wealth is a source of wrong, the rich man is to be pitied. If however it serves the ends of virtue, there is no ground for envy; since its common use is intended for the good of all; unless there is someone so engulfed in wickedness, that he envies himself even what is good. In a word, if in your mind you are uplifted above human things, and intent upon that good which is truly worthy of praise, you will be far from thinking that whoever possesses any perishable or earthly riches must be either happy or to be envied. It is impossible for a person who is of this mind, who does not look upon earthly things as precious, ever to feel envy.

And if you are eager for glory, and you wish to shine above others, and so cannot endure second place; for this also is an occasion of envy; then direct your ambition as though it were a stream of water towards the cultivation of virtue. Let the desire to enrich yourself be wholly absent from your mind, and the desire to be esteemed because of your worldly riches. For these things do not rest with you. But be just and temperate and prudent and courageous and patient in all that you suffer in serving God. For it is in this way you will save your soul; and the greater your virtues, the more you shall shine above others. For virtue does rest with us, and can be acquired by our loving efforts; while great riches, gifts of body, rank and dignity, are not in our power to acquire. If then virtue is a greater and more enduring possession, and held in greater honour by all men, it is this we should strive for. But it cannot be born in the soul, unless the soul is free of all violence of feeling; and free above all of envy.

6. You know how great an evil hypocrisy is? Well hypocrisy is the fruit of envy. For more than any other vice, envy begets duplicity. For while showing outwardly the appearance of friendship, it will cherish hate within the heart, and like rocks hidden in the sea, covered by shallow waters, of a sudden will bring disaster to the unwary. Therefore, if death comes to us from this source as from a spring, and brings with it the loss of every blessing, estrangement from God, the defeat of His laws, the undoing in a moment of all the good we have done throughout our life, then let us comply with the counsel of the Apostle, and let us not be made desirous of vainglory, *provoking one another, envying one another* (Gal. v. 26); but let us rather, *be kind one to one another;* let us be *merciful, forgiving one another, even as God hath forgiven you* (Eph. iv. 32), in Christ Jesus our Lord, with Whom be there glory to the Father and to the Holy Ghost, throughout all ages and ages. Amen.

IV. St John Chrysostom, Bishop and Doctor

Moral Exhortation to Humility[5]

ABRAHAM TO LOT: *Let there be no quarrel, I beseech thee, between me and thee; for we are brethren; if thou wilt go to the left hand, I will take the right: if thou choose the right hand, I will pass to the left* (Gen. xiii. 8).

You now know how evil it is to take the first places, and to pay no attention to what is right and becoming? You have seen how good it is to be mild and reasonable, to yield the first place, and to take the lowest. And see how in the course of our instruction we have come to understand, that he who chooses the first place for himself derives no profit from it; but that he who chooses the lowest place, becomes daily more regarded and respected by all, and esteemed in all things.

And not to prolong our instruction on this point, this I would exhort you, that you become imitators of the blessed Patriarch, Abraham, and that you should never be desirous of the first places, but rather be mindful of the counsel of the blessed Paul, who bids us yield to one another in honour (Rom. xii. 10), and that, rising above ourselves, we should be eager for the lowest place; as Christ in today's Gospel has said; concluding: *And he that humbleth himself shall be exalted.*

What then can compare with this, that yielding first place to others, we come to enjoy a higher place; that esteeming others above ourselves, we come to the highest honour. I exhort you therefore: let us be eager, let us strive to imitate the humility of the Patriarch, to follow in his footsteps who, even before the law, gave such an example of holy wisdom to us who live under the Dispensation of grace. For it was true humility of spirit this illustrious man showed to one who was not only inferior to him in virtue, but also in age and all other respects. Consider how this venerable man yields to the other, who was the younger, the uncle to the son of his brother; he who had received such graces from God, to one who had nothing to show in his favour, and how that which he as a young man should say to his elder and to his uncle, this the patriarch says to the young man.

Let us therefore show honour and respect, not alone to those that are older than us, but also to our equals. For it is no humility to do what you ought to do, or are compelled to do: that is not humility, but duty. It is true humility to give way to those who are seen to be less than us. And if we are truly wise, we shall consider no one as less than ourselves, but all men as our superiors.

And this I say to you, not because of what we are, immersed in so many sins, but even should anyone be conscious to himself of innumerable virtuous actions, he shall have no profit of his so many good works unless he looks upon himself as the lowest of men. For this is humility; when someone who has reason to be honoured, remains obscure and unknown, and holds himself modestly. For then he is uplifted to true honour, according to the promise of our Lord, Who said: *Everyone that humbleth himself shall be exalted.*

Let us therefore, I beseech you, let us all be earnest in striving through humility to come to the summit of true glory, that we may receive from the Lord the reward of the just, and be worthy of the same ineffable blessings, through the grace and mercy of our Lord Jesus Christ, to Whom with the Father and the Holy Ghost be there glory and honour, now and forever, throughout all ages. Amen.

V. St Augustine, Bishop and Doctor

Meditation on the Humility of Christ[6]

We commend to you, dearest brethren, the humility of Christ Jesus our Lord; rather, He commends it to us Himself. Reflect upon the wonder of His humility. The prophet Isaias cries out: *All flesh is grass, and all the glory thereof as the flower of the field. The grass is withered and the flower is fallen: but the word of our Lord endureth for ever* (xl. 6, 8). How he contemns and humbles the flesh! And how he exalts and praises the word of God!

Again I say, and again give ear: behold the lowliness of the flesh: *All flesh is grass, and all the glory thereof as the flower of the field.* And what does he say of the grass? What of the flower of the field? He goes on to tell us. Do you wish to hear what he says of the grass? *The grass is withered, and the flower is fallen.* And what of the word of God? *It endureth for ever.* Let us know the Word that endureth for ever.

Listen to the Evangelist as he praises the Word. *In the beginning was the Word, and the Word was with God, and the Word was God. The Same was in the beginning with God. All things were made by him; and without him was made nothing. What was made in him was life: And the life was the light of men* (Jn. i. 1–4). Great this praise of the Eternal Word. Sublime the praise of the Word of God enduring for ever. And after this what does the Evangelist say? And the Word was made flesh, and dwelt among us.

Had God the Word done only this; had He only become Flesh, His humility would be unbelievable. And blessed are they who believe this unbelievable thing: for it is from unbelievable things our faith is made up. That the Word of God became grass, that dead He rose again, that God was crucified, are unbelievable things. It was because your sickness had become great, it was healed through unbelievable things. For He came, the humble Physician, He finds man lying sick; He shares his sickness, inviting man to become a sharer in His Divinity. He was offered in suffering, destroying suffering; and hung dying upon a Cross, that He might destroy death. He became Food for us: that we might eat, and be healed.[7]

For whom is this Food; whom does it nourish. Those who imitate the Lord in His humility. If you will not imitate His humility, how much more shall you not imitate His divinity? Imitate His humility if you can. When? How? He Who is God became a man. You who are man, know that you are a man. Would that you might know clearly what He became for you! Know thyself, for His sake. Let you reflect on this, that you are a man, and yet of such value that because of you God became man. Do not attribute this happening to your own lofty spirit, but to His mercy. For God our Lord redeemed us by His Blood; willing that the price of our souls should be His Blood, His innocent Blood.

2. And since I began, brethren, by saying that had God only humbled Himself to this; that He became a man, who could have looked for more from Him? For you would not humble yourself to this; that from being a man you would become an animal: something not unlike man? And should you so humble yourself, that from being a man you became a beast, you would have not humbled yourself, as God has humbled Himself. For a man to become a beast, what was rational would become something irrational; yet what was mortal would be mortal: for man is mortal, and a beast is mortal; man is born, and a beast is born; man is conceived, as a beast is conceived; man eats corporal food, and increases as a beast increases. How many things has he not in common with the beast! In one thing only is he different: In his reasoning soul, upon which has been imprinted the image of the Creator. Yet God Who became man, the Eternal Who became mortal, took flesh from the substance of our race, without sin, became man, was born, taking upon Him that in which He would suffer for us.

But at this point He has not yet suffered. Contemplate Him now; what He has become for you, before He suffers. Is this lowliness a little thing? God has become man. O man! reflect that you are a man. It is because of you that God is man: And you do not acknowledge you are a man? Let us consider, brethren, who they are who do not wish to know they are men? Who are they; who are they who will not accept they are men? They are those who justify themselves, and blame God. Does one of them suffer something harsh or severe in this present life: From his tongue comes nothing but blame for God, praise of himself; and crying out in indignation at his affliction, he will admit no sin, rather he boasts of his merits, and exclaims: 'God, what have I done to Thee? Why must I suffer these things?'

'God, what have I done to thee?' says man to God. Let God answer him. 'Well indeed do you say: "What have I done to Thee?" For to me you have done nothing. All this have you done to yourself.' For had you done something to God, you would have done something that would please Him: for this is to serve Him. But now, whatever you have done, you have done to yourself: for you followed your own will, and ignored His authority. It is plain that if this is what you mean you are speaking the truth. For what *can* you do to God, that you should cry out: 'What have I done to Thee?' He who throws a stone at heaven, does it fall on heaven or on himself? What you have thrown has not remained there, but has fallen on you. So is it with all blasphemies, should you hurl them at God: so is it with all insults; so is it with whatever stirs up your sacrilegious, impious and insolent mind: whatever you hurl upwards, falls back with far greater weight upon yourself.

3. What was it you would have done to God? You would have done something to Him had you obeyed His word. Had you done what He commanded you, you might well cry out: 'What have I done to Thee?' But now instead, look well into this justice of yours, examine your conscience, enter in to your own heart, make no noise without, look inward, to the inner chambers of your heart. See whether it is true or not that you have done no wrong; see whether you are not suffering what you deserve, for something you have done, for which you now suffer some affliction; for all that is owing to the sinner is the scourge of burning and eternal fire. You abandoned your God; and you followed your own desires. What is it you suffer, when you feel the scourge? Correction: not damnation.

If God scourges you in this life, He is not angry with you. Do not offend Him because He chastises you; do not provoke Him, that He may spare you. Provoke Him by murmuring, and He will abandon you. Fly towards the scourge of the Chastiser, not from it; bow beneath it: where it falls, hasten thither. He knows where He strikes, and where to find thee; and in vain do you hide from His eyes Who is everywhere. Do you desire to escape from an angry God? Then fly to an appeased One: fly nowhere from Him, only to Him.

You thought to escape from Him when you lifted your heads in pride. Humble them, and fly to Him. *He scourgeth every son whom he receiveth* (Heb. xii. 6). You think it unworthy of yourself to suffer chastisement. And do you also disdain to receive from Him an inheritance? Your Good Father trained *thee for an inheritance* (Deut. viii. 5). He is Good, both when He spares thee, and when He chastises thee; and everywhere truly Merciful. (*Explicit De Humilitate Domini Nostri Jesu Christi.*)

Turning then to the Lord our God, we pray that the power of His mercy may strengthen our hearts in His holy truth, and confirm and give peace to our souls. May His grace abound in us, and may He have pity on us, and deliver us from all evil, and help us to please Him for ever, through Jesus Christ our Lord His Son, Who with Him and the Holy Ghost lives and reigns for ever and ever. Amen.

NOTES

[1] Many codices have *son*, for *ass*.

[2] PG 40, cols. 966, 976, *Sermones XX, S. Antonii Abbatis*. Serm. 5 and 20, col. 966.

[3] PG 32, *Sermones XXIV*, compiled by Symeon Logotheta, from the works of St Basil M. Sermo. XX, col. 1354.

[4] PG 31, col. 372, *Sermo XI*.

[5] PG 53, col. 311, *in fine*, Hom. 33 in *Genesis*, xiii, peroration.

[6] *Miscellania Agostiniana, Sermones Reperti*, Mai, XXII, p. 314. The Prologue of St John as in the text of the sermon. The punctuation of verses 4 and 5, as here given by the late Cardinal Mai, conflicts with tradition; especially with Chrysostom and Augustine. See vol. I of this work, pp. 134 *et seq.*, from the exposition of the Catena Aurea on the Prologue.

[7] Elsewhere also the holy Doctor teaches that the Eucharist relates to the humility of Christ; cf. First Discourse on Ps. xxxiii, par. 6: Christ willed that we should find healing in His Body and Blood. And how can it be that He gives us His Body and Blood? (Cf. Mt. xxvi.) Because of His humility. For unless He were humble, these would be neither eaten nor drunken. Here is His humility. For man ate the Bread of Angels; as it was written: *He gave them the Bread of heaven: man ate the Bread of Angels* (Ps. lxxxvii. 24, 25); that is, man ate the Word, on which the Angels are fed eternally, and which is equal to the Father.

SEVENTEENTH SUNDAY AFTER PENTECOST

I. ORIGEN: THE GREATEST AND FIRST COMMANDMENT

II. ST AUGUSTINE: MEDITATION ON THE MYSTERY OF THE WORD INCARNATE

III. ST GREGORY: THIS IS MY COMMANDMENT, A MEDITATIVE DISCOURSE

THE GOSPEL OF THE SUNDAY

MATTHEW xxii. 34–46

At that time: The Pharisees came to Jesus, and one of them, a doctor of the law, asked him, tempting him: Master, which is the great commandment in the law? Jesus said to him: *Thou shalt love the Lord thy God with thy whole heart and with thy whole soul and with thy whole mind.* This is the greatest and first commandment. And the second is like to this: *Thou shalt love thy neighbour as thyself.* On these two commandments dependeth the whole law and the prophets. And the Pharisees being gathered together, Jesus asked them, saying: What think you of Christ? Whose son is he? They say to him: David's. He then saith to them. How then doth David in spirit call him Lord, saying: *The Lord said to my Lord, Sit on my right hand, until I make thy enemies thy footstool?* If David then call him Lord, how is he his son? And no man was able to answer him a word; neither durst any man from that day forth ask him any more questions.

PARALLEL GOSPELS

MARK xii. 28–31

And there came one of the Scribes that had heard them reasoning together, and, seeing that he had answered them well, asked him which was the first commandment of all. And Jesus answered him: The first commandment of all is: *Hear, O Israel; the Lord thy God is one God. And thou shalt love the Lord thy God*

LUKE x. 25–28

And, behold, a certain lawyer stood up, tempting him; and saying: Master, what must I do to possess eternal life? But he said to him: What is written in the law? How readest thou? He answering said: *Thou shalt love the Lord thy God with thy whole heart, and with thy whole soul and with all thy strength and with thy whole heart and with thy whole soul and with thy whole mind and with thy whole strength.* This is the first commandment. And the second is like to it: *Thou shalt love thy neighbour as thyself.* There is no other commandment greater than these.

all thy mind; and thy neighbour as thyself. And he said to him: Thou has answered right. This do, and thou shalt live.

EXPOSITION FROM THE CATENA AUREA

MATTHEW xxii. 34–46

I

JEROME: After the Pharisees had been refuted in the matter of the coin of the tribute, and after they had seen the faction of their opponents also defeated (*the Sadducees*), they should have learned caution, and not laid further snares, but malice and spite drove them on unashamed. So there follows:

V.34. *The Pharisees, hearing he had silenced the Sadducees, came together.*

ORIGEN (*Tr. 23 in Matthew*): Jesus had silenced the Sadducees, showing us that the brightness of truth will impose silence on the voice of falsehood. As a just man will be silent when silence is called for, and will speak and not be silent when it is time to speak, so is it ever the way of all teachers of error to be silent concerning the truth, but not to cease from talking. JEROME: And therefore the Pharisees and the Sadducees, thought opposed to one another, are of one mind in tempting Christ.

CHRYSOSTOM (*Opus Imperfectum* 42): Or, the Pharisees came together to defeat Him by numbers Whom they could not defeat by reason: arming themselves with numbers, they confess themselves naked of truth. They say among themselves: Let one

speak for all, and all speak through this one. So if he triumphs, all shall appear to triumph; if he is defeated, then he alone shall appear confuted. So there follows:

V.35. *And one of them, a doctor of the law, asked him, tempting him.*

ORIGEN, as above: We should therefore look on all who question any teacher to trap him, not to learn from him, as brothers of this Pharisee; according to the words: *As long as you did it to one of these my least brethren, you did it to me.* AUGUSTINE, *Harmony of the Gospels,* II, 73: Let us not be concerned here because Matthew says the man who questioned the Lord was tempting Him, while Mark says nothing of this, and also that he concludes his account saying, that the Lord Jesus said to the man who had answered Him wisely: *Thou art not far from the kingdom of God* (Mk. xii. 34). For it could be that although he had approached to tempt Him, the Lord's answer may have changed him. Neither need we take this *tempting* in a bad sense, as though he were trying to trap an enemy, but rather as a careful approach to one unknown to him whom he wishes to test. Not without reason was it written: *He that is hasty to give credit is light of heart* (Ecclus. xix. 4). What he asks is then related:

V.36. *Master, which is the great commandment in the law?*

ORIGEN: He calls Him Master, tempting Him: since he did not utter the word as a Disciple of Christ. If therefore anyone does not learn something from the Word, nor give himself to Him with his whole heart, yet calls Him Master, he is a brother to the Pharisee who tempted Christ. Therefore, when the Law was being read, before the Coming of the Saviour, it may be that they disputed among themselves as to which was the great commandment in it. For unless this question had long been disputed among themselves, and not solved, until Jesus coming taught this, this Pharisee would not have put the question.

CHRYSOSTOM, as above: He asks concerning the great commandment, who had not begun to observe the least. Only a man who has fulfilled the lesser justice, ought to ask about the greater. JEROME: Or he asks, not about the commandments, but which is the first and great commandment: so that, since all the commandments God commanded are great, whatever He answers the Pharisees may have a pretext to attack Him. CHRYSOSTOM, as above: But the Lord so answers him, that with His first words He at once pierces the false conscience behind the question. Hence follows:

V.37. *Jesus saith to him: Thou shalt love the Lord thy God, etc.*

Thou shalt love, He says, not; Thou

shalt fear. For it is a greater thing to love than to fear. To fear is the character of slaves; to love, of children. Fear springs from coercion; love from liberty. He who serves God in fear will indeed escape punishment, but does not receive the reward of justice; because he did good, not freely, but because of fear. God therefore does not wish that men should fear Him, in a servile manner, as an owner, but love Him as a Father; since He gave men the Spirit of adoption.

To love God *with thy whole heart* means the heart is not inclined to the love of any one thing more than it is to the love of God. To love God *with thy whole soul* means to keep the soul steadfast in truth, and to be firm in faith. For one is the love of the heart, another the soul's love. The love of the heart is in a certain measure carnal; as we also love God with our bodily heart: which we cannot do unless we withdraw our hearts from the love of worldly things. The love of the heart therefore is felt in the heart. The love of the soul is not felt, but perceived; for it consists in a judgement of the soul. For he who believes that with God is all good, and that outside of Him there is nothing of good, he loves God with his whole heart. To love God *with thy whole mind* means that all the faculties are at the disposition of God: he whose understanding serves God, whose wisdom concerns God, whose thought dwells on the things of God, whose memory is mindful only of His blessings, loves God with his whole mind.

AUGUSTINE (*Doctrine of Christ*, I, 22): Or again. You are commanded to love God *with thy whole heart*, so that all your thoughts: *with thy whole soul*, so that your whole life: and *with all thy mind*, so that all your understanding may be devoted to Him from Whom you have that which you bestow. Thus He has left us no part of our lives that is not devoted to Him, nor wills that we should delight in any other thing. And whatever else has entered the soul, to be loved by it, let it be drawn into that channel in which the whole impetus of our love runs: for man is at his highest when, with his whole life, he goes forward towards the Unchangeable Good. GLOSS (interl.): Or *with thy whole heart*; namely, understanding; *with thy whole soul*, that is, will; *with thy whole mind*, that is, memory; so that you neither will, think or remember what is contrary to It.

ORIGEN: Or again: *With thy whole heart*, that is, in all thought, action and remembrance; *with thy whole soul*, that is, ready to lay it down in the service of God; *and with thy whole mind*, that is, bringing forth nothing but what is of God. And see if you cannot here take *heart* for intellect, by which we search into things intelligible to us, and *mind* for utterance; for it is by the mind we bring forth each single thing, and discourse and give utterance by means of each thing it makes known. If the Lord had not answered the Pharisee who came tempting Him, we would not be able to determine that one commandment was greater than another. But when the Lord, answering, says:

V.38. *This is the greatest and the first commandment.*

We here learn His decision concerning the commandments: That this is the chief commandment, and that there are lesser ones down to the least. And the Lord replies that it is not only the greatest, but also the first: not in the Scriptural order, but in the order of the dignity of its virtue. They alone take upon them the greatness and primacy of this commandment, who not only love the Lord their God, but also take upon them these three conditions: namely, that they shall love Him *with their whole heart*, etc. And He taught not only that this is the chief and first commandment, but also that the second is like the first. Hence follows:

V.39. *And the second is like to this: Thou shalt love thy neighbour as thyself.*

If he *who loves iniquity, hates his own soul* (Ps. x. 6), it is manifest he does not love his neighbour as himself; since neither does he love himself. AUGUSTINE (*Doctrina Christiana*, I, 30): It is clear that every man is to be regarded as our neighbour: because we must do evil to no man. And if everyone to whom we should show mercy, or who should show mercy to us, is rightly called our neighbour, it is manifest that in this commandment, in which we are bidden to love our neighbour, the holy angels are included; who bestow so many works of mercy on us, as we may easily learn from the Scriptures. And for the same reason our Lord also willed to be called our neighbour; for the Lord Jesus signifies to us that it is He Who helped the man lying half dead by the wayside.

AUGUSTINE, *The Trinity*, VIII. 6: He

who loves men should love them either because they are just, or that they may become just. And so should man love himself; either as just, or that he may become just; for so he will without danger love his neighbour as himself. AUGUSTINE, *Doct. Christ.*, I, 22: But if you should love yourself, not because of yourself, but because of Him Who is the most befitting end of all your love, let another not take it ill, that it is because of God you love him. Whoever therefore rightly loves his neighbour, should so act with him, that he too may love God with his whole heart.

CHRYSOSTOM, *Opus Imperfectum*: He who loves man is as he who loves God: for man is God's image, in which God is loved, as a king is honoured in his image. And it is for this reason the second commandment is said to be like the first. HILARY: Or again: That the commandment which follows is like the first, means that the obligation and the merit in each is the same. For no love of God that excludes Christ, and no love of Christ that excludes God can be a help to salvation. Then follows:

V.40. *On these two commandments dependeth the whole law and the prophets.*

AUGUSTINE, *Gospel Questions*, I, 33: *Dependeth*, He said; that is, they are referred to them as to their end. RABANUS: The whole decalogue leads to these two commandments as to their end: The precepts of the first table to the love of God, the precepts of the second table to the love of our neighbour. ORIGEN: Or, because he who has fulfilled all that

is written concerning the love of God and our neighbour, is worthy of receiving from God the great reward, of understanding all the law and the Prophets.

AUGUSTINE, *The Trinity*, VIII, 7: Since there are two precepts on which depend the whole law and the prophets: The love of God, and of our neighbour, not without reason does Scripture frequently put one in place of both. Either the love of God, as in the words: *And we know that to them that love God all things work together unto good;* or the love of our neighbour, as in the words: *All the law is fulfilled in one word, Thou shalt love thy neighbour as thyself* (Rom. viii. 28; Gal. v. 14). And the reason is that if a man loves his neighbour, then he will also love God: for it is from one and the same love that we love God and our neighbour; God however, for His own sake; ourselves and our neighbour, for God's sake.

AUGUSTINE, *Doctrine of Christ*, I. 30, 26: Since the divine nature is more perfect and above ours, the command to love God is separate from that to love our neighbour. And if by *yourself* you understand your whole being, that is, body and soul, and your neighbour in the same way, then in these two commandments there is nothing of all that we must love left out. For when the love of God precedes, the love of our neighbour follows; and the measure of this love is also laid down: That you love him as yourself. Nor, at the same time, is the love of yourself by yourself left out.

2

V.41. *And the Pharisees being*

gathered together, Jesus asked them . . .

CHRYSOSTOM, *Opus Imperfectum*: The Jews, thinking Christ was a mere man, tempted Him: they would not have tempted Him, had they believed He was the Son of God. Christ therefore wishing to show them that He knew the deceit of their hearts, and also that He was God, did not will to declare the truth openly, lest they should thereby find a pretext to accuse Him of blasphemy and rage against Him the more, yet not willing to remain wholly silent; for it was this He had come for: To make known the Truth; He then asks them such a question, that the question itself would show them Who He was. And so we are told that *The Pharisees being gathered, Jesus asked them:*

V.42. *Saying: What think you of Christ? Whose son is he?*

CHRYSOSTOM, *Homily in Matthew,* 72: He first asked His Disciples what others said of Christ, and then what they themselves said. But not so with these: for they would certainly have said that He was a deceiver and evil. They believed that the Christ was to be a mere man; and so they said that He is a son of David. And this is what follows: *They say to him: David's.* He however corrects them, and quotes the Prophet's testimony concerning His Rule, and the true nature of His Sonship, and the dignity He shares with His Father. Hence:

V.43. *He saith to them: How then doth David in spirit call him Lord, saying?*

JEROME: This testimony is from the hundredth and ninth psalm. The Lord therefore is called David's Lord, not because He was descended from him in the flesh, but because of His eternal generation from the Father, preceding the father of His flesh. And he calls Him his Lord, not by error, or of his own will, but through the Holy Spirit.

V.44. *The Lord said to my Lord: Sit on my right hand, until I make thy enemies thy footstool?*

REMIGIUS: That He says: *Sit on my right hand* is not to be understood as meaning that God has a body, and a right hand and a left. To sit at the right hand of God means to abide in equality of honour and dignity with the Father. CHRYSOSTOM, *Ex Opus Imperfectum*: I believe He propounded this question not only against the Pharisees, but also against heretics. For in respect of the flesh He was truly the son of David, but his Lord in respect of His Divinity. CHRYSOSTOM, *Homily 72 in Matthew*: He did not stop at this point, but goes on: *Until I make thy enemies thy footstool*; that by this He might make them fearful, or at least apprehensive, to gain them.

ORIGEN: God places the enemies of Christ as a footstool beneath His feet not only to their loss, but also for their salvation.

REMIGIUS: *Until* is used for indefinite time; so that the meaning is: Sit Thou for ever, and let Thy enemies be for ever beneath Thy feet. GLOSS: That it is the Father places His enemies beneath His Son's feet, does not signify want of power in the Son, but the Oneness of their nature: For the Son also subjects enemies to the Father, because He glorifies the Father on earth. From this authority He concludes:

V.45. *If David then call him Lord, how is he his son?*

JEROME: To this day this question helps us against the Jews. For they who believe the Christ is yet to come, say He is a mere man but a holy one and of the House of David. And so we who are taught by the Lord ask them: If he is a mere man, and but the son of David, how does David call him his Lord? To break down the force of this question, the Jews make up frivolous answers, and speak about Abraham's servant, whose son was Damascus Eliezer (Gen. xv. 2), and say that this psalm was written of this person; because after the overthrow of the Five Kings, the Lord said to *his* lord, Abraham, that is: *Sit on my right hand until I make thy enemies thy footstool.* Let us then ask how did Abraham say the things that follow; and let us make them tell us how Abraham was *begotten before the day star*, and

how he was a Priest of the order of Melchisedech, *for whom* Melchisedech *offered bread and wine*, and *from whom* he received tithes of the spoils of battle!

CHRYSOSTOM, *Ex Homily*, 72 *in Matthew*: He put this question only to make an end of their disputations, as though it were decisive, and sufficed to close their mouths. Hence follows:

V.46. *And no man was able to answer him a word; neither durst any man from that day forth ask him any more questions.*

From then on they held their peace, not willingly, but because they had no more to say. ORIGEN: Had they put their question from a desire to learn, He would never have put them this question, so that from then on they would not dare to question Him again. RABANUS: From this we understand that the poison of envy can be defeated, but that with difficulty will it remain quiet.

I. ORIGEN, PRIEST AND CONFESSOR

The Greatest and First Commandment[1]

MATTHEW xxii. 34–40

1. When our Lord answered the Sadducees, who would not hear of the resurrection, by proving it to them from the testimony of the Law, Matthew tells us that Jesus silenced the Sadducees, willing to show us by this that the brightness of truth will ever put to silence the bitter and injurious voice of falsehood. As our Saviour by His teaching reduced the Sadducees to silence, showing them with divine authority that their

belief was false, so will the followers of Christ ever do the same from the Scriptures, before which, in accord with all sound learning, every voice of Pharaoh must be dumb: that voice in which, glorying in himself, he said, *The river is mine, and I made it,* as is written in Ezechiel (Ezech. xxix. 9).

The Sadducees therefore, who said there was no resurrection, questioned the Saviour about things that were written; thinking to put Him to silence. But neither Jesus nor His Disciples are at any time ever obstructed by the impious. It was fitting therefore that the Sadducees should be put to silence by Christ. For a just man will be silent, knowing that there is *a time to keep silence and a time to speak* (Eccles. iii. 7); yet he is not dumb. And while a just man will keep silence, though he is not dumb, it is ever the way of Sadducees and of all who teach falsehood to be dumb, but not to keep silence: For though dumb with respect to the truth, they will nevertheless not be silent. So it was not to man, but to the sea, the Lord said: *Peace, be still*; rebuking it when it was stormy.

But now the Pharisees, who believed in the resurrection, hearing Jesus had silenced the Sadducees, come together; they come together when the truth of the resurrection has triumphed, who had not come together until the Sadducees were silenced. But though they came together because the proof of the resurrection had prevailed, nevertheless, one of them questioned Him, not as wishing to learn from Him what he was asking, but as tempting the Lord God. Everyone therefore who questions any bishop or teacher on any article of faith, and questions him, not with a mind to learn, but in order to trip him up, is to be regarded as a brother of this Pharisee who sought by his question to tempt the Saviour. For all that is done to the holy servants of Christ, whether by those who love them, or by those who are their enemies, He takes wholly to Himself: for we must consider what is not written in the Scriptures in the light of what

was written. For the sake of those who hunger and thirst it was written: *I was hungry*; and, *I was thirsty*. And, because of the naked and of those who are strangers, because of the sick, and those who are in prison: *I was naked*; and, *I was a stranger*; and, *I was sick*, and, *I was in prison*. And to this we may also add: I suffered afflictions, I was beaten, I was tempted, and all such things. And as, in the things which are written in the Scriptures, the words of the Lord truly apply, where He says: *As long as you did it to one of these my least brethren*, so when the just man suffers persecution, when evil is spoken of him, or when he suffers anything of this kind, set Christ in the midst of those who do this injury; saying to them: When you do an injury to one of the least of these, it is Me you have assailed, it is against Me you have spoken evil.

2. Let us now consider the proposition of the tempter. *Master*, he says, *which is the great commandment in the law?* He calls Him, *Master*, tempting Him; for it was not as a disciple of Christ he spoke these words. This will be clearer from an example we shall give you. Let us, for instance, say that a father is the father of his son, and no one can rightly call him father save his son. And a mother is the mother of her own daughter, and no one can call her mother except her own daughter. So a master is the master of his own pupil or disciple, and a disciple is the pupil of his own master. Therefore, no one can rightly say to him, Master, except his own disciple. So you see that it was because of this, that not all who call

Him Master, speak truthfully, but only those who are of a mind to learn from Him, that He said to His Disciples: *You call me Master, and Lord: and you say well; for so I am* (Jn. xiii. 13). Rightly therefore do the Disciples of Christ call Him Master; and when keeping His word rightly do they call Him Lord. And for this reason rightly also did the Apostle declare: *Yet to us there is but one Lord Jesus Christ, by whom are all things, and we by him* (I Cor. viii. 6). And remember that other saying of our Lord, in which He tells us: *It is enough for the disciple that he be*, not simply, as the master but: *as his master* (Mt. x. 25).

If there is anyone therefore who does not learn from the Word, and does not submit himself to Him with his whole soul, that he may become His loved plant (Mt. xv. 13), yet presumes to call Him: *Master*, he is brother to that Pharisee who came tempting Christ, and calling Him *Master*. And everyone who says: *Our Father who art in heaven*, should not possess *the spirit of bondage in fear, but the spirit of adoption of sons* (Rom. viii. 15). He however who has not the spirit of adoption of sons, and yet says: *Our Father who art in heaven*, lies; since he calls God his Father, when he is not a son of God.

But this is the question: *Which is the great commandment in the law?* And at this point it is fitting that we explain to you something of the difference between commandments. For some are *great*, and some are derived from them. So we must examine them as to their order, down to the least. For if the Lord had not answered the Pharisee who came tempting Him and saying: *Which is the great commandment in the law*, we would not then think that one commandment was greater than another. But now, since He has answered him, and has said: *Thou shalt love the Lord thy God with thy whole heart and with thy whole soul and with thy whole mind. This is the greatest and the first commandment*, we have learned the judgement we needed to know concerning the commandments: That there are chief commandments, and there are lesser ones, down to the least.

Consider again what it was the Pharisee asked: *Which is the great commandment in the law?* The Lord in answering him teaches us that not only is the commandment to love God *the greatest*, but that it is also *the first*: First, not in the Scriptural order, but in the excellence of its virtue. And here is a fitting place to note, that though it is made up as it were of many commandments, as it stands it is now, He said, the greatest and first commandment: *Thou shalt love the Lord thy God with thy whole heart and with thy whole soul and with thy whole mind.* The second is like the first and, because of its likeness, also great: *Thou shalt love thy neighbour as thyself*; so that following this we may understand that there is another which is third in order and greatness, and another which is fourth; and so numbering the precepts of the law in their order, and receiving wisdom from God, one may order each one down to the least: And this is the work of Christ alone, Who is *the power of God and the wisdom of God* (I Cor. i. 24).

And so from the time of Moses till the coming of the Saviour, it is probable that when the law was being read this question was asked: Which of these is the greatest commandment? For the Pharisee would not have asked it, had an answer not been sought, and not found, until Jesus coming taught not only which was the greatest and also the first; and that the second was like the first. It was the Pharisee's own task then to find out which was third, fourth and so on. Supposing you asked whether there was a commandment which had not both these attributes: greatest and first; but only one of them, I believe you will find that Paul speaks of such a commandment, to the Ephesians. *Honour thy father,* he says, *and thy mother, which is the first commandment with a promise; that it may be well with thee, and thou mayest be long-lived upon the earth* (vv. 2, 3). Here then is a *first* commandment; yet not a *great* one: *Honour thy father and thy mother.*

And if there is some commandment *great,* yet not a *first,* you will ask how they compare in greatness. Since in comparing them some will be least, it is useful to recall an example our Lord Himself gave. *He therefore,* He says, *that shall break one of these least commandments, and shall so teach men, shall be called the least in the kingdom of heaven* (Mt. v. 19). And the Saviour answering the Pharisee tempting Him, and laying down which was the first and great commandment, and adding that the second was like it, namely: *Thou shalt love thy neighbour as thyself,* added this saying: *On these two commandments dependeth the whole law and the prophets.*

The Apostle however says to the Romans: *Thou shalt not commit adultery. Thou shalt not kill. Thou shalt not steal. And, if there be any other commandment, it is comprised in this word: Thou shalt love thy neighbour as thyself* (xiii. 9). Let us see then if it is the same to say that the whole law and the prophets depend on the two commandments of the love of God and our neighbour, as to say that every commandment is summed up in the commandment: *Thou shalt love thy neighbour as thyself,* or that all the commandments both depend on and are summed up in either commandment.

Someone then says: The commandments depend one from the other, the second from the first and greatest; the third from the second, and so on; all after the second depending from the one preceding; and that the Apostle said, in view of its end, every commandment depends on this: *Thou shalt love thy neighbour as thyself;* but that the Saviour taught that these two commandments govern all the rest. Another will ask how it was said that: *Thou shalt not commit adultery. Thou shalt not kill. Thou shalt not steal. And, if there be any other commandment, it is comprised in this word: Thou shalt love thy neighbour as thyself.* Therefore, he will say, that first commandment: *Thou shalt love the Lord thy God with thy whole heart,* etc., is also comprised in this commandment: *Thou shalt love thy neighbour as thyself.* How can what the Apostle said be true: *And, if there be any other commandment,* etc., unless the first commandment regarding the love of God is comprised in the second, which is like the first?

And if the first is comprised in the second, then the second must be greater than the first. Every commandment then, even the first and greatest, is comprised in this second: *Thou shalt love thy neighbour as thyself*, for loving ourselves, we also love God the Author of our love, so that we are able to love one another and are loved by one another. For giving thanks that we are rational beings, and called to the knowledge of God, and that we receive His grace and blessings, we include the love of God in the second and like commandment.

The first therefore and greatest commandment of the law is: *Thou shalt love the Lord thy God with thy whole heart and with thy whole soul and with thy whole mind*. And he takes something from its primacy and greatness who subtracts anything from the entirety of this commandment; that is, either from that part which says: *With thy whole heart*, or from: *With thy whole soul*, or from: *With thy whole mind*. And it may well be that all they who love God and their Lord fulfil this commandment in part only, unless they fulfil it in all respects and love Him with their whole heart and with their soul and with their whole mind. They alone accept within themselves its greatness and primacy who not only love the Lord their God, but have also taken it upon themselves to fulfil these three conditions; namely, that with their whole heart they hold within themselves the fulness of this love, and its thoughts and actions; and with their whole soul, that is, ready to lay it down for the service of God Who created all things, whenever the profit of His Word demands it: for God is loved with thy whole soul, when no part of the soul is seized by anything that is out of keeping with the faith; and with their whole mind thinking and

speaking of nothing else but the things of God.

And see if you can put understanding for *heart*: the intellect which searches into intelligible things; showing their source and beginning, which is God: it being the mind's task to give them utterance. For it is by the mind we give utterance to each single thing, and by it we as it were consider within us by means of each thing made known to it, and give it utterance. And if anyone understands acutely this commandment of love in the light of these three conditions we have spoken of, and reflects upon the love of God as it exists in each one of the faithful, he will find the whole commandment fulfilled in one perhaps, or in two, or in a third. And should all be considered under this aspect, the love of God will be found wanting in them, or present among them but more or less, and this because the commandment says, with thy whole heart, or because it says, with thy whole soul, or, with thy whole mind.

3. The second commandment is like the first, since it commands the love of man, made in the image of God, and perhaps also in His likeness. In the exposition of the command to love our neighbour, these things must also be learned. Since in accord with what is said in the tenth psalm, *He that loveth iniquity, hateth his own soul*, and in accord with what is said in Proverbs, *He that rejecteth instruction, despiseth his own soul*, it is evident, that no one who loves iniquity loves his neighbour as himself, since neither does he love himself; and that no one who rejects instruction, loves his neighbour as

himself, since he does not even love his own self. And so it comes about that he who *loves iniquity*, both hates his own soul, and is unable to fulfil the second commandment. And in the same way whoever rejects instruction loves sin: and so he who rejects any word of the teaching of God, hates his own soul.

4. After this you will ask how the whole law and the prophets depend on these two commandments? For the text seems to indicate to us that everything that was written, either in the Book of Exodus, or Leviticus, or in Numbers or Deuteronomy, depend on these two commandments. But how does the law concerning leprosy, or those suffering an issue of blood, or menstruation, depend on these two commandments? How again does the prophecy concerning the fall of Jerusalem, or the vision of Egypt in Isaias and the other prophets, how does the vision of Tyre or whatever was prophesied of Tyre, or of the prince of Tyre, how does even the vision of the fourfooted beasts in the desert that we read of in Isaias depend on these two commandments?

This to me appears to be the meaning of the passage in question. He who fulfils all that is written concerning the love of God and his neighbour is worthy of receiving the highest of God's favours, of which the first is *the word of wisdom* through the Holy Spirit, through which comes *the word of knowledge* according to the same Spirit (I Cor. xii. 8). Made worthy of all these gifts he rejoices in the wisdom of God, his heart filled with the love of God, his whole soul illumined by the light of

knowledge, and his whole mind by the word of God. And receiving such gifts from God, he now truly understands that the whole law and the prophets are but part of all the wisdom and knowledge of God, and understands that the whole law and the prophets depend on, and have as their beginning the love of the Lord God and of our neighbour, and that the perfect fulfilment of our duty to God consists in love.

The things we have said here will suffice for you. Nevertheless, to show its greatness, it is fitting we should also place before you what follows: *Charity is patient, is kind; charity is not puffed up, dealeth not perversely; is not ambitious, is not provoked to anger, thinketh no evil; rejoiceth not in iniquity, but rejoiceth with the truth; beareth all things, believeth all things, hopeth all things. Charity never falleth away* (I Cor. xiii. 4–8). No one weak of soul possesses charity, nor he who does what is contrary to mildness, nor he who burns with the jealous fury of his brother against Joseph, or of Aaron and Mary against Moses. And no one who is puffed up with pride has charity, nor he who deals wrongly with another, nor whoever is inflamed with anger. Again, no one who soiled by evil thoughts can have charity in his heart.

He who has charity will never rejoice in any injustice, but will always share in rejoicing in the truth. He who has charity will bear all tribulations patiently, and does not in part believe, but *believeth all things*; he does not hope in part, but *hopeth all things*; There is nothing love will not endure, for it *endureth all things*. And since charity never fails, the Apostle, filled with confidence, cries out that he has wholly embraced it. *Who shall separate us from the love of Christ? Shall tribulation? Or distress? Or famine? Or nakedness? Or danger? Or the sword? As it is written: For thy sake, we are put to death all the day long; we are accounted as sheep for the slaughter* (Rom. viii. 35, 36). And because of charity he declares: *But in all these things we overcome, because of him that loved us.* And from that charity that never fails, come these words from this same voice: *For I am sure that neither death, nor life, nor angels, nor principalities, nor powers, nor things present, nor things to come, nor might, nor height, nor depth, nor any other creature, shall be able to separate us from the love of God which is in Christ Jesus our Lord.* Amen.

II. ST AUGUSTINE, BISHOP AND DOCTOR

Meditation on the Mystery of the Word Incarnate[2]

MATTHEW xxii. 41–46

I. *That Christ is the Messiah is proved against the Jews.*

When the Jews were asked, as we have just heard while the Gospel was being read, how our Lord Jesus Christ Whom David himself called his Lord, was the son of David, they could not answer. For of the Lord they knew only what they saw in Him. To them He appeared a son of man: that He is the Son of God was hidden from them. Because of this they believed He could be defeated, and because of this they mocked Him hanging upon the wood; exclaiming: *If he be the Son of God, let him come down from the cross; and we will believe him* (Mt. xxvii. 40, 42). They saw one form of Him; there was another they did not know. Had they known it, they would never have crucified the Lord of glory (I Cor. ii. 8).

They knew however that the Christ was the son of David. And even now they hope for His Coming. It is hidden from them that He has come. But it is hidden because they willed it so. For not acknowledging Him on the cross, the knowledge of Him reigning in glory should not be theirs. For in Whose name are all peoples called, and blessed (Gen. xxii. 18), if not in His Whom they thought was not the Christ? And this son of David, truly of the seed of David according to the flesh, is a son of Abraham. If it was said to Abraham: *In thy seed shall all the nations of the earth be blessed,* and they now see all nations blessed in our Christ; why are they hoping for what has already come, and why are they not fearful of what *is* to come?

For our Lord Jesus Christ, making use of prophetic testimony to assert His authority, referred to Himself as *the stone* (Mt. xxi. 42); such a *stone* that whoever stumbles upon it, shall be bruised; but upon it shall fall, it will grind to powder (Lk. xx. 17, 18). One stumbles on it when it lies upon the ground. Lying on the ground, it shakes whoever falls over it; coming from on high, it crushes the proud. Already the Jews have been shaken by their former stumble. What awaits them is to be crushed by His glorious Coming, unless that, while they still live, they confess Him so that they may not die. For

God is patient, and daily invites them to faith.

II. *The same argument.* And when the Jews could not answer the question put to them by the Lord, asking whose son they said Christ was; they answering, the Son of David, He adds and proposes another question: How then doth David call him Lord, saying: *The Lord said to my Lord: Sit on my right hand, until I make thy enemies thy footstool? If David then call him Lord, how is he his son?* He did not say, 'He is not his son,' but, *How is he his son? How,* as He uses it, is the word of one asking, not denying; as though He said: 'You say well that Christ is David's son, but David himself calls Him his Lord? How can He whom David calls his Lord be his son?' Had the Jews been instructed in the Christian faith, which we hold, had they not closed their hearts to the Gospel, had they wished to have within them the true life of the spirit; instructed in the faith of the Church, they would have answered His question, and would have said: Because in *the beginning was the Word, and the Word was with God, and the Word was God,* this is *how* He is David's Lord; and because, *the Word was made flesh, and dwelt among us,* this is *how* He is David's Son. But not knowing this, they are dumb; and with their mouths closed, they did not even keep their ears open, so that being instructed they might learn what they could not answer when asked.

III. *The Mystery of the Incarnation is made known to the worthy.*

And because it is a great thing to know this mystery, how He is David's Lord and David's Son, how the one Person is both man and God, how in the form of man He is less than the Father, in the form of God equal to the Father; again, how He says, *The Father is greater than I* (Jn. xiv. 28), and again that *I and the Father are one* (Jn. x. 30); because this is a great mystery, and that we may grasp it, you must be trained in virtue. For this mystery is sealed to the unworthy, revealed to those who are worthy. Nor is it with stones, nor iron bars, nor fists, nor feet that we come to the Lord's door and knock. It is our life knocks; it is to our life the door is opened. The heart seeks, the heart asks, the heart knocks; He opens to the heart. But the heart that seeks worthily, that knocks and asks worthily, must be virtuous. It must first love God for His own sake; for this is the true love of God: nor seek from Him for other reward than Himself. For than Him there is nothing more perfect. And what precious thing can he ask of God, for whom God Himself has no value? He gives us the earth, and you rejoice, lover of the earth, and made from earth. If you rejoice, when He gives us the earth; how much more should you not rejoice when He gives you Himself, Who made heaven and earth? God therefore is to be loved for Himself. The devil, not knowing what took place in the breast of the holy Job, reproached him as with a great crime, saying: *Does Job serve God for nothing?*

IV. *The devil a deceitful Adversary.* Therefore, if our adversary makes this accusation, we ought to be in fear lest this be said against us. For we have to deal with an adversary who is a great liar. If he seeks to invent what does not exist, how much more will he not accuse us of what is true? Yet we can rejoice that we have a Judge Whom our accuser cannot deceive. Had we a man as judge, our enemy could invent for him as he willed; for there is no one cleverer at inventing than the devil. Even now it is he who invents all the false accusations made against the saints. Since his accusations avail nothing with God, he scatters them among men. And what does this profit him, since the Apostle says: *For our glory is this: the testimony of our conscience* (II Cor. i. 12)?

But do not think he contrives these false accusations without cunning? Well he knows the evil he can work with them, unless the vigilance of faith resists him. And it is for this he circulates evil about the good: that the weak may then think they are not any good, and so let themselves be carried away by their own evil desires and become corrupted; saying to themselves: Who is there keeps a commandment of God? Or who observes chastity? And when a man believes that no one does, he himself becomes this 'no one'. It is in this way then the devil works. But Job was a man against whom he could invent nothing: for his life was known and open to all. But because he had much wealth, the devil made this accusation against him (*Does Job serve God gratis?*); which, if it were true, might be in his heart, but could not be seen in his conduct. He worshipped God, he gave alms; and with what mind he did this no one knew, not even the devil. But God knew. God gives testimony to His servant; the devil calumniates God's servant. God permits Job to be tried; he is proved just, the devil is confounded. Job is found to worship God for His own sake; to love Him for His own sake: not because He gave him anything, but because He has not taken away Himself. For he says: *The Lord gave, and the Lord taketh away. As it hath pleased the Lord so is it done. Blessed be the name of the Lord* (Job i. 21). The fire of trial came close to him; but it found him gold, not stubble. It took away the dross; but did not turn him to ashes.

V. *Why morals are spoken of, following the question concerning Christ. Ecclesiastical honours.*

To understand the mystery of God, how Christ is both God and man, the heart must be purified. It is purified by our manner of living, by a Christian life, by chastity, holiness, love, and by a *faith that worketh by charity* (Gal. v. 6). This that I here speak of may be likened to a tree that has its root in the heart. For the things we do proceed solely from the root of the heart; where, if you plant greed, thorns spring up; if you plant charity, good fruit come forth. Immediately after this question, proposed to the Jews, which they could not answer, the Lord goes on to speak of a worthy manner of life, in order to show why these men were unworthy to understand what He had asked them. For, wretched in their pride as they were, since they could not answer Him, they should at least have said: 'We do not know. Tell us, Master.' But they were struck dumb by the question; nor did not open their mouths to ask Him. And at once the Lord begins to speak of their pride.

Beware, He says, *of the Scribes, who love to sit in the first chairs in the synagogues, and they love the first places at feasts* (Mk. xii. 38, 39). Not because they receive them, but because they love them. For here he reproached their hearts; and He could not be a Reproacher of hearts unless He was a Searcher of hearts. For it is fitting that a servant of God who holds a certain dignity in the Church, should be offered the first place there: because if it is not offered to him, whoever denys it to him does wrong. At the same time it is not good for him to whom it is given. And so it is fitting that when Christians assemble, those who are placed over the congregation should be seated in a higher place, to be distinguished by their seat, and so that their office may be indicated; but it is not fitting that they should be inflated with pride because of where they sit; but rather, that they look upon this honour as a burthen they must account for.

But who knows whether they love this or not? This is a thing of the heart; and of the heart there can be no judge save God. And the Lord Himself warned His disciples not to fall into this source of danger. For in another place He says: *Beware of the leaven of the Pharisees and Sadducees* (Mt. xvi. 6). And when the disciples began to think He said this because they had brought no bread with them, He answered them by saying: *Have you forgotten how many thousands were fed from five loaves? Then they understood that he called their* (the Pharisees') *teaching leaven.* For they loved these earthly privileges; but of the things of eternity, they neither feared what was

evil nor loved what was good. And so their hearts being closed, they could not understand what the Lord had asked them.

VI. *How the mind becomes capable of grasping the mysteries.*

What must God's Church do to comprehend that which it was the first to be given to believe? Let it make its soul capable of receiving what shall be given it. That it may do this, that is, that the soul may become capable, the Lord our God as it were holds His promises out of our reach; He does not withdraw them. He so withholds them that we may stretch ourselves towards them. We strain, and therefore we grow. And so we grow, that we may reach what He promised us. Think of the Apostle *stretching forth* towards the withheld promises: *Not as though I had already attained, or were already perfect. Brethren, I do not count myself to have apprehended. But one thing I do: forgetting the things that are behind and stretching forth myself to those that are before, I press towards the mark, to the prize of the supernal vocation of God in Christ Jesus* (Phil. iii. 12–14). He ran his race on earth; but the palm of victory hung suspended from heaven. On earth therefore he ran his race: but it was in the spirit he ascended. Behold him then: *Stretching forth*, his gaze fastened on the suspended promises. I press towards the mark, he says, to the prize of the heavenly calling of God in Christ Jesus.

VII. *No one ascends into heaven save he who remains fast to Christ.*

Let us then journey forwards; nor need we anoint our feet, nor seek a beast of burthen, nor a vessel to carry us. Hasten in desire, walk in love, ascend by charity. What need to seek the way? Keep close to Christ, Who descending and ascending has made Himself the Way. Do you wish to ascend? Hold fast to Him ascending. For you cannot raise yourself. Because *no man hath ascended into heaven, but he that descended from heaven, the Son of man who is in heaven* (Jn. iii. 13). If no man ascends, but He Who descends, and He is the Son of man our Lord Jesus Christ; do you too wish to ascend? Then become a member of Him Who alone ascends. For He, the Head, is *one man* with the other members. And since no one can ascend, but He Who in His body, has become His member, the saying is fulfilled, that: *No man ascends, but he that descended*. If no one ascends, but He Who descends, can you not then say: How, for example, did Peter ascend, or how did Paul ascend, or how did the Apostles ascend? The answer is: What do Peter and Paul and the other Apostles, and all the faithful, hear from the Apostle? They hear: *You are the body of Christ, and members of member* (I Cor. xii. 27). If then the Body of Christ and its members belong to *one man*, let you not make two of them. For He left father and mother, and clave to His wife, they might be two in one flesh (Eph. v. 31). He left His Father, in that here below He did not show Himself as equal to the Father: but emptied Himself, taking the form of a servant (Phil. ii. 7). He left His Mother, the Synagogue, of whom He was born according to the flesh. He clave to His Spouse, that is, to His Church. And when He re-counted this testimony, He signified to us that it is not lawful to dissolve marriage.

Have ye not read, He said, *that he who made man from the beginning, made them male and female? And they two*, He said, *shall be in one flesh. What therefore God hath joined to-together, let no man put asunder* (Mt. xix. 4). And what does *two in one flesh* mean? He goes on to tell us: *Therefore, now they are not two, but one flesh.* No man ascended, but He that descended.

VIII. *Christ and the Church one man.* That you may know that, in the Body of Christ, not in His Divinity, the Bridegroom and the Bride are *one man*: For in regard to His Divinity, what He is, we cannot be. For He is the Creator; we the created; He the Maker, we the made; He is the Founder, we the founded. But that we might be one with Him in Him, He willed to become our Head; taking from us the Flesh in which He would die for us. That you may therefore know this whole is *One Christ*, He said by the mouth of Isaias: *As a bridegroom decked with a crown, and as a bride adorned with her jewels* (Is. lxi. 10). He is the Bride-groom; He is the Bride. He is the Bridegroom in the Head; the Bride in the Body. For, *they two*, He said, *shall be in one flesh*; and, *now they are not two, but one flesh*.

IX. *We come to the vision of God by faith and good works.* And so as members of His Body, let us, brethren, live a holy life, and love God for His own sake, that we may come to understand this mystery. He Who showed Himself to earthly pilgrims in the form of a servant, has laid up for those who reach Him the form of God. By means of the form of a servant, He prepared the way; in the form of God, He has made ready our eternal home. And since it is hard for us to grasp this mystery, yet not hard to believe it: For, says Isaias, *if you will not believe, you shall not continue* (vii. 9): let us walk by faith as long as we are are absent from the Lord (II Cor. v, 6, 7), till we come to that Vision where we shall see Him face to face.

And walking by faith, let us labour well. And in our good works, let there be a pure love of God, a generous love of our neighbour. We have nothing with which we can help God. But since we have what can help our neighbour; giving it those in need we shall be blessed by Him Who abounds in all things. So let everyone help another from what he has; giving to the poor what is over and above his own needs. One man has money: let him feed the poor, let him clothe the naked, let him build a church; whatever good money can do, let him do. Another has the gift of counsel: let him be a guide to his neighbour, let him scatter the darkness of doubt by the light of his own charity. Another has a store of doctrine: let him draw

forth from this cellar of the Lord, let him nourish his fellow-servants, let him bring back those who are following false teaching, let him seek after those who have strayed; let him do what he can. There are things which even the poor can give one another: one may lend his feet to the lame, another his eyes as guides to the blind, another visit the sick, another bury the dead. These are things all may do; so that it is scarce possible to find one who has not that which he can give to help another. And last of all, there is that great good of which the Apostle speaks: *Bear ye one another's burthens; and so ye shall fulfil the law of Christ* (Gal. vi. 2).

May then the power of God's mercy strengthen our heart in His truth. May He confirm and grant peace to our souls. May His grace abound in us; may He have pity on us, and remove scandals from our path and from the path of His Church and from before all who are dear to us; and may He by His power and in the abundance of His mercy enable us to please Him for ever through Jesus Christ His Son our Lord, Who with Him and the Holy Spirit liveth and reigneth world without end. Amen.

III. St Gregory, Pope and Doctor

This is My Commandment: That you love one another[3]

A Meditative Discourse: Given to the People in the Basilica of the holy martyr Pancratius on his natal day

John xv. 12–16

1. Since all the Sacred Writings are filled with the commandments of the Lord, why does He say of Charity, as if it were some singular

commandment: *This is my commandment, that you love one another?* if not for the reason that every commandment is a commandment solely of love, and that all of them are one single precept; because, whatever is commanded, is based solely on love. For as the many branches of a tree derive from one root, so the multitude of virtues derived from one charity. And a branch of good work has no freshness, unless it remains rooted in charity.

The commandments of the Lord therefore, are many, and one: many in the diversity of their works, one in their root of love. And He teaches us how we are to hold fast to this love, Who, in many places of Holy Scripture, commands us to love our friends in Him, and our enemies because of Him. For he truly possesses charity who loves his friends in God, and his enemy because of God. For there are those who love their neighbours, but because of the bond of kinship or blood; and the Sacred Scriptures do not forbid them this love. But one is the love to which nature spontaneously inclines us, and another the love to which we are obliged in obedience to the Lord's commands. The former truly love their neighbour; nevertheless they do not attain to the sublime rewards of love because the love they bestow is not spiritual but carnal. So when our Lord said: *This is my commandment, that you love one another,* He at once adds: *As I have loved you;* as though He were to say simply: Love one another as I have loved you.

2. And here, dearest brethren, we must keep carefully in mind, that our ancient enemy, whenever he draws our mind to the love of earthly things, will then stir up against us some neighbour, one weaker than ourselves, who will begin to strive to take away from us whatever it is we love. And he, our ancient enemy, will do this, not simply to take away from us our earthly possessions; but to kill charity within us. For of a sudden we burn with hate; and while all eager to be victors in this outward strife, we receive a grievous wound within. While outwardly we defend what are but trifles, inwardly we are losing what is precious: in giving our love to a temporal thing, we lose true love. No doubt he who seeks to rob us is an enemy. But once we begin to hate our enemy, we begin to lose what is good in us.

So therefore, when we outwardly suffer anything from a neighbour, let us rather be on our guard within, against the hidden robber, who is never more surely beaten, than when we love the robber without. For the supreme proof of our charity is, that we love even him who is against us. It was for this that Truth Itself endured the torments of the Cross, and in His love prayed even for His tormentors, saying: *Father, forgive them, for they know not what they do.* What wonder then that His Disciples while they lived loved their enemies, seeing their Master loved His enemies even as they put Him to death?

And in the next verse the Lord goes on to describe the perfection of this love, when He says: *Greater love than this no man hath, that a man lay down his life for his friends.* The Lord had come to die even for His enemies, and yet He said that He was about to lay down His life for His friends; to show us clearly that since we can draw profit from our enemies by loving them, even those who persecute us are also our friends.

3. But there is no one now who persecutes us unto death. How then can we prove we love our enemies? But there is that which we ought to do in the peace of Holy Church, by which we shall know whether in a time of persecution we would have laid down our lives for love. The same John firmly declares: *He that hath the substance of this world, and shall see his brother in need, and shall shut up his bowels from him; how doth the charity of God abide in him?* (I Jn. iii. 17). For the same reason John the Baptist also says: *He that hath two coats, let him give to him that hath none* (Lk. iii. 11). He therefore who in a time of peace will not give his cloak for the love of God, how would he lay down his life in a time of persecution? Therefore, that the power of charity may be invincible in a time of persecution, let it be nourished with compassion in times of peace: so that we may first learn to offer our possessions to Almighty God, then afterwards ourselves.

4. There follows: *You are my friends.* O how great the mercy of our Creator! We are not even worthy servants, and yet He calls us friends. How great the dignity of men, to become friends of God? You have heard of the glory of this dignity; learn also of the weariness of the contest. *If you do the things that I command you.* You are My friends, if you do the things I command you. As if He says simply: You rejoice in the summit, but think also of the weary toil to reach that summit.

We know that when the sons of Zebedee asked through their mother that one might sit at the right hand of God, the other at his left, they heard in reply: *Can you drink the chalice that I shall drink?* (Mt. xx. 22). Already they were striving for the places of honour; but Truth recalls them to the way by which they can come to glory. As though He says: Already the place of honour delights you; but before that let you *exercise* yourselves on the road of toil. It is by the chalice we attain to majesty. If your soul longs for what delights it, let it drink first of what afflicts it. So through the bitter cup of confession we come to the joy of true health.

I will not now call you servants; for the servant knoweth not what his lord doth. But I have called you friends; because all things, whatsoever I have heard of my Father, I have made known to you (v. 15). What are *all the things* He has heard from the Father, and which He has willed to make known to His servants, that He may make them His friends, if not the joys of inward charity, if not the feasts of our heavenly home, which He daily makes known to us through the inspirations of His love? For when we love the heavenly and celestial things we have heard of; loving them, we already know them: for to love is to know.

He has therefore made known *all things* to those who, changed from earthly desires, have now begun to burn with the flame of a higher love. The Prophet from afar saw these friends of God, when he said: *To me thy friends, O God, are made exceedingly honourable* (Ps. cxxxviii. 17) A friend we call the keeper as it were of our soul. So the psalmist, when he saw the elect of God separated from the love of this world, obedient to the will of God in His heavenly commandments, he marvels at these friends of God, exclaiming: *To my thy friends, O God, are made exceedingly honourable.* And as if asked at once to tell the reason of this so great honour, adds immediately: *Their dominion is exceedingly strengthened.*

See how the elect of God subdue the flesh, grow strong in spirit, command demons, shine with virtue, despise things present, and proclaim with their life and with their tongue their true home. They love it even in dying for it; and come to it by the way of torment. They can be slain; but not made to bow the knee: *strengthened exceedingly is their dominion.* In the very passion in which they died in the body, see how sublime of soul they were. Where did this come from, if not from the strengthening of the power of their dominion?

But you, you think to yourself, souls such as these are few? Hear then what follows: *I will number them, and they shall be multiplied above the sand.* Look, brethren, look at the whole world. It is filled with martyrs. We who see them are scarcely as many as we have witnesses to the Truth. Their number is known only to God. To us they are multiplied above the sands of the sea: for how many they are is beyond our power to know.

5. But whoever comes to this dignity, that he is called a friend of God, let him look within himself and note that the gifts he sees, have been added to him. Let him attribute nothing to his own merits; lest of a sudden he become an enemy of God. Because of this the Lord continues: *You have not chosen me; but I have chosen you; and have appointed you, that you should go and bring forth fruit* (v. 16). It is I have sown you in grace. I planted you, that of your own will you may go, and labouring bring forth fruit. I said, that of your own will you may go: for to will to do something, is already to go in the mind.

He goes on to say what kind of fruit they should bring forth: *And your fruit shall remain.* All that we toil for in this world lasts but till our death; and then death coming separates us from the fruits of our labour. But what we do for eternal life, the fruit is preserved for us even after death; and then begins to appear, when the fruits of bodily labour begin to be seen no more. Where these last end, there that other reward begins. He therefore who has already come to the knowledge of eternal things, in his soul the fruits of this world become valueless. Let us labour for the fruit that remains. Let us labour for the fruits, which, when death makes an end of all things, have their beginning from death. That the harvest of God has its beginning from death, the Prophet bears witness who says: *When he shall give sleep to his beloved: behold the inheritance of the Lord* (Ps. cxxvi. 2, 3). Every one who sleeps in death, loses his inheritance. But when God has given His beloved sleep, this is the inheritance of the Lord; for it is after they have come to death, that the elect of God shall obtain their inheritance.

6. Then follows: *That whatsoever you shall ask of the Father in my name he may give it to you.* See how He here says: *Whatsoever you shall ask the Father in my name he may give it to you.* And in another place, He again

says through the same Evangelist: *If you ask the Father anything in my name, he will give it to you. Hitherto, you have not asked anything in my name* (Jn. xvi. 23, 24). If the Father gives us all that we ask for in the name of His Son, how was it that Paul thrice besought the Lord, yet did not receive what he prayed for; but rather was told: *My grace is sufficient for thee; for power is made perfect in infirmity* (II Cor. xii. 9)? Did not this mighty preacher ask in the Name of the Son? Why then did he not receive what he asks for? How then can it be true that whatever we ask the Father in the Name of His Son, the Father will give us, if an Apostle asked in the name of the Son, to be delivered of an angel of Satan, and yet even his prayer was unheard?

Now since the name of the Son is Jesus, and since Jesus signifies Saviour, or also, Salvation, he therefore asks in the name of the Saviour, who asks for what relates to the true health of his soul. Should he ask for what is not expedient for salvation, he does not ask the Father in the name of Jesus. So the Lord says to these same still unconfirmed Apostles: *Hitherto you have not asked the Father anything in my name.* As though saying simply: You have not asked in the name of the Saviour, because you did not know to seek for eternal salvation. For the same reason Paul's prayer also was not heard: because it was not to the profit of his soul's salvation that he should be delivered from temptation (II Cor. xii. 9).

Dearest Brethren, we see in what numbers you have assembled for the solemnity of the martyr. You kneel down, you beat your breast, you raise your voices in praise and prayer to God, your faces wet with tears. But think within you, I beseech you, of the petitions you offer. Think whether you are asking in the name of Jesus; that is, if you are asking for the joys of eternal salvation? For in the House of Jesus you do not seek Jesus, if in the temple of eternity, you ask for the things of time. This one in his prayers seeks a wife, another a house, another begs for clothing, another to be given food. And in our need we should ask these things from Almighty God. But we must also be ever mindful of the commandment we received from this same Redeemer: *Seek ye first the kingdom of God and his justice, and all these things shall be added to you* (Mt. vi. 33).

But we do not err when we seek these things from Jesus: provided we do not seek them beyond due measure. But there is a certain thing that is far more serious, namely, that someone should ask for the death of an enemy; striving to obtain by prayer what he cannot secure by the sword! And though he lives on when someone has cursed him, nevertheless, he who uttered the curse is already guilty of his death. God commands us to love our enemies; and we dare to ask God to slay our enemy! Whosoever prays in this manner, even in his very prayers is at war with his Creator. For this it was said (in a figure of Judas): *And may his prayer be turned to sin* (Ps. cviii. 7). And in truth that prayer is turned to sin which prays for what God to Whom we pray has forbidden.

8. And so He Who is Truth tells us: *And when you shall stand to pray,*

forgive, if you have aught against any man (Mk. xi. 25). We shall show you this virtue of pardon more clearly if we put before you one example from the Old Testament. When Judea had sinned against the justice of her Maker by her deliberate offences, the Lord, forbidding His prophet to pray for them, says: *Do not thou pray for this people, nor take to thee praise and supplication for them* (Jer. vii. 16). *If Moses and Samuel shall stand before me, my soul is not towards this people* (ib. xv. 1). What does it mean that, passing over many of the fathers of old, Moses and Samuel only are brought before us, their wondrous power to intercede made known to us, while at the same time we are told that not even they can intercede for this people? As if the Lord said simply: I shall not listen even to these whom, because of their great merits, I cannot despise. Why then are Moses and Samuel more powerful in prayer than the other fathers, if not that in the whole of the Old Testament only these two are said to have also prayed for their enemies? One was stoned by the people (Ex. xvii. 4), yet he prayed to the Lord for those who stoned him. The other was removed from his leadership, yet when asked to pray for the people he declares: *Far from me be this sin against the Lord, that I should cease to pray for you* (I Kings xii. 23).

If Moses and Samuel shall stand before me, my soul is not towards this people. In other words: I shall not listen even to these men praying for their friends, whom I know, because of their great goodness, pray even for their enemies. The true power of prayer therefore depends on the depth of your charity. And so each one will receive what he rightly prays for so long as his soul is not darkened by hatred of an enemy. And often we triumph over a resisting spirit, if we pray also for our enemies. And when our lips move in prayer for them, God grant that love may also have its place in our heart. For often we pray for our enemies, but do so more from precept than from love. For we pray even for the life of our enemies, and yet fear lest our prayer be heard. But since our Eternal Judge looks rather to the mind than to our words, he asks nothing for his enemy, who does not pray for him from charity.

9. But say that an enemy has done us grave injury, has caused us loss, done harm to those who help us, persecuted those who love us? These things might be remembered, if our sins had not to be forgiven. For our need our Advocate has composed a prayer; and He Who is our Advocate is also Judge in the same case. And in the prayer He made, He inserted this condition: *Forgive us our trespasses as we forgive them who trespass against us.* And because He is our Judge, Who before was our Advocate, He listens to the prayer He made. Therefore, while not doing this, we either say: *Forgive us our trespasses as we forgive them that trespass against us*; and by saying this bind ourselves the more; or else we leave out this condition in prayer, and then our Advocate will not recognize the prayer He made, and will at once say within Himself: 'I know what I taught them; this is not the prayer I made.'

What must we do therefore, brethren, but bestow on our brothers the love of true charity? Let no malice remain in our heart. May Almighty God be mindful of our love of our neighbour, that He may have mercy on our sins. Remember what we have been commanded to do: *Forgive, and you shall be forgiven.* We too have debtors, and we also are debtors. Let us then forgive what is owed to us, that we may be forgiven what we owe. But the mind resists this: It desires to fulfil what it hears, yet struggles against doing this.

We stand by the tomb of a martyr, who by that death we know of gained a heavenly kingdom. And if we do not lay down our body for Christ, let us at least humble our spirit. This is a sacrifice that is pleasing to God; and in His compassionate judgement he will approve the victory of our peace. For He sees the struggle of our heart; and He Who gives rewards *to them that overcome* (Apoc. ii. 7, 17), will help those now striving in battle, through Jesus Christ His Son, Who with Him lives and reigns in the unity of the Holy Spirit, God for ever and ever. Amen.

NOTES

[1] PG XIII, col. 1599, Series Comment. *in Matthaeum,* xxii. 34–7. A searching study of the precept of the love of God; more suited to meditation than exposition. Indeed the three homilies selected for this Sunday, are all essentially meditative discourses. Natal day, i.e., the anniversary of his martyr's death.

[2] PL XXXVIII, col. 567, *Sermo* XCI. The truth of the Mystical Body very clearly explained while treating of the mystery of the Incarnation. The reality of the Mystical Body, the *One Christ,* composed of Head and Members (the Church), might be described as the operative truth, if one may say so, in the mind of St Augustine; and indeed of all the great Fathers, who form the stream of Divine Tradition. It would not be possible to set forth in one discourse, to a modern audience, the mass of divine truth contained, and expressed with such precision, in this discourse. It is a subject more for careful meditation: and for this there could be nothing more authoritative and fruitful; or for several short homilies.

[3] PL LXXVI, col. 1204, *Homilia* XXVII. Spoken to a simple congregation, but filled with mystical instruction.

[4] 'They became Apostles, they became the leaders of the Church, they became as rams leading their flocks; *strengthened exceedingly was their dominion.*' Augustine, *in Psalmos loc. cit.*

EIGHTEENTH SUNDAY AFTER PENTECOST

I. St Ambrose: The Healing of the Paralytic

II. St Gaudentius: 'One Work I Have Done; and You All Wonder'

III. St Peter Chrysologos: On the Healing of the Paralytic

IV. St Gregory the Great: God Man's House

V. St Gregory the Great: Man Delivered by Trials: Mystical Joy

THE GOSPEL OF THE SUNDAY
MATTHEW ix. 1-8

At that time: Jesus, entering into a boat, passed over the water and came into his own city. And, behold, they brought to him one sick of the palsy lying in a bed. And Jesus, seeing their faith, said to the man sick of the palsy: Be of good heart, son. Thy sins are forgiven thee. And, behold, some of the scribes said within themselves: He blasphemeth. And Jesus, seeing their thoughts, said: Why do you think evil in your hearts? Which is easier, to say, Thy sins are forgiven; or to say, Arise, and walk?

But that you may know that the son of man hath power on earth to forgive sins (then said he to the man sick of the palsy), Arise, take up thy bed and go into thy house. And he arose and went into his house. And the multitude, seeing it, feared, and glorified God that gave such power to men.

PARALLEL GOSPELS

MARK ii. 1-12

And again he entered into Capharnaum after some days. And it was heard that he was in the house. And many came together, so that there was no room; no, not even at the door. And he spoke to them the word. And they came to him, bringing one sick of the palsy, who was carried by four. And, when they

LUKE v. 17-26

And it came to pass, on a certain day, as he sat teaching, that there were also Pharisees and doctors of the law sitting by, that were come out of every town of Galilee and Judea and Jerusalem; and the power of the Lord was to heal them. And, behold, men brought in a bed a man who had the palsy; and they sought

177

could not offer him unto him for the multitude, they uncovered the roof, where he was; and opening it they let down the bed wherein the man sick of the palsy lay. And, when Jesus had seen their faith, he saith to the sick of the palsy: Son, thy sins are forgiven thee. And there were some of the Scribes sitting there and thinking in their hearts: Why doth this man speak thus? He blasphemeth. Who can forgive sins, but God only? Which Jesus presently knowing in his spirit that they so thought within themselves, saith to them: Why think you these things in your hearts? Which is easier, to say to the sick of the palsy: Thy sins are forgiven thee; or to say: Arise, take up thy bed, and walk? But that you may know that the son of man hath power on earth to forgive sins (he saith to the sick of the palsy), I say to thee: Arise, Take up thy bed and go into thy house. And immediately he arose and, taking up his bed, went his way in the sight of all; so that all wondered and glorified God saying: We never saw the like.

means to bring him in and to lay him before him. And when they could not find by what way they might bring him in, because of the multitude, they went up upon the roof and let him down through the tiles with his bed into the midst before Jesus. Whose faith when he saw, he said: Man, thy sins are forgiven thee. And the Scribes and Pharisees began to think, saying: Who is this who speaketh blasphemies? Who can forgive sins but God alone? And when Jesus knew their thoughts, answering, he said to them: What is it you think in your hearts? Which is easier to say: Thy sins are forgiven thee; or to say: Arise and walk? But, that you may know that the son of man hath power on earth to forgive sins (he saith to the sick of the palsy), I say to thee: Arise, take up thy bed and go into thy house. And immediately rising up before them he took up the bed on which he lay; and he went away to his own house, glorifying God. And all were astonished; and they glorified God. And they were filled with fear, saying: We have seen wonderful things today.

EXPOSITION FROM THE CATENA AUREA

CHRYSOSTOM, *Homily 29 in Matthew*: Prior to this Christ had shown His greatness through teaching, for He taught them *as one having* power (Mt. vii. 29); through the leper, when He said: *I will, be thou made clean*; through the Centurion, who had said: *But only say the word, and my servant shall be healed*; through the sea, which He had calmed with a word; through the demons, who had confessed Him. Here again, in

another and greater way, He compels His enemies to confess His equality of honour with the Father. And to show this, there follows:

V.1. *And, Jesus entering into a boat, passed over the water and came into his own city.*

Entering into a boat, He crosses over Who could cross the sea on foot: but it was not His will to work miracles at all times, lest He take from the purpose of the Incarnation. CHRYSOLOGOS: The Creator of all things, the Lord of the world, after He had for us straitened Himself within our flesh, began to have an earthly fatherland, began to be a citizen of a Jewish state, began to have parents: He Who is Himself the Parent of all parents; that love might draw those whom fear had driven away. CHRYSOSTOM: *His own city* here means Capharnaum. One city received Him at birth: Bethlehem; another reared Him: Nazareth; yet another received Him as an inhabitant: Capharnaum.

AUGUSTINE, *Harmony of the Gospels*, II, 25, 58: Or again: That Matthew here writes of the Lord's *own city*, and Mark of Capharnaum, would be more difficult to reconcile if Matthew had said Nazareth. Now since Galilee itself could be called Christ's city (*civitas=state*), since Nazareth was in Galilee; as the whole Roman Empire composed of many cities is called the *Civitas Romana* (Roman state); who will doubt that the Lord coming into Galilee, is rightly said to have come *into His own city*, to whatever town of Galilee He came: especially Capharnaum, since it had become important in Galilee, and was regarded as its metropolis? JEROME: Or we may understand as *His own city*, none other than Nazareth: from which He was also called a Nazarene.

AUGUSTINE, as above: And in accord with this, we may say that Matthew passed over all Jesus did after He had come into His own city, until He came to Capharnaum, and here added the account of the healing of the paralytic; just as the Evangelists

do in many places, omitting things that took place in between, as though what they then add had followed without any interval; and in this way here is added:

V.2. *And, behold, they brought to him one sick of the palsy lying in a bed.*

CHRYSOSTOM: This paralytic is not the one spoken of by John (v. 5). For he lay beside the pool; this was in Capharnaum. The first had no one to help him; this man had friends to care for him, who, carrying him, had brought him there. JEROME: They brought him lying on a bed; for he was unable to come in by himself.

CHRYSOSTOM: Not everywhere does He ask of the sick only that they should have faith; as for instance when they were mad, or for any reason out of their mind. So here is added: *And Jesus seeing their faith.* JEROME: Not his faith who was brought to him; but theirs who had brought him. CHRYSOSTOM: Because they reveal such faith, He reveals His Power; with full authority forgiving his sins. Hence follows: *Jesus said to the man sick of the palsy: Be of good heart, son. Thy sins are forgiven thee.*

CHRYSOLOGOS: How much will a man's own faith avail with God, with Whom the faith of others availed so much, that He healed the man both within and without. The paralytic hears the words of pardon, and is silent; giving no thanks: for he longed rather for the healing of his body than of his soul. Rightly therefore does Christ regard the faith of those who bring him, rather than the folly of the sick man.

CHRYSOSTOM: Or, great also was the faith of this sick man: For he would not have suffered himself to be let down through the roof, as another Evangelist relates, unless he believed. JEROME: O wondrous humility! Despised and weak, all his members enfeebled; yet He calls him son whom the priests would not deign to touch. Son also, because his sins are forgiven: by which we are given to understand, that many bodily infirmities befall us because of sin. And therefore perhaps his sins were first forgiven, that the cause of his infirmity removed, his health might then be restored.

CHRYSOSTOM: The Scribes in their eagerness to defame the Lord, unwittingly proclaim what happened. Christ uses their envy to make known this wonder: for in the superabundance of His wisdom, He proclaims what He has done by means of His enemies. Hence follows:

V.3. *And, behold, some of the Scribes said within themselves: He blasphemeth.*
JEROME: We read in the Prophet: *I am he that blot out thy iniquities* (Is. xliii. 25). And so the Scribes, because they believed Jesus was a man, and because they did not understand the words of God, accuse Him of the crime of blasphemy. Seeing their thoughts, He showed Himself God, Who knows the hidden things of the heart, and though silent as it were says: By the same power by which I see into your thoughts, I also forgive men their sins. See your-

selves what happened to the paralytic. So there follows:

V.4. *And Jesus seeing their thoughts, said: Why do ye think evil in your hearts?*
CHRYSOSTOM: He did not dissipate their suspicion regarding Himself; thinking He had said these words as God. For if He were not equal to God the Father, He should have said: 'I am far from having this power: To forgive sin.' Instead He confirms the contrary, by His words and by the sight of a miracle. So there follows:

V.5. *Which is easier, to say, Thy sins are forgiven thee; or to say, Arise, and walk?*
The more the soul is greater than the body, the greater is it to forgive sin than to heal the body. But because the former is not visible, and the latter is, He does what is the lesser but more evident, to prove something greater, but less evident.

JEROME: Whether the paralytic's sins were forgiven or not He alone knew Who forgave them. But both the man who arose, and those who saw him rise, were able to confirm the truth of the words: *Arise, and walk;* though one and the same is the power to heal the body and to forgive sins. But between saying and doing, there is a wide distance. Let there be therefore a visible sign, that the spiritual wonder may be proved. Hence follows:

V.6. *But that you may know that the son of man hath power on earth to forgive sins.*
CHRYSOSTOM: Above, He did not say to the paralytic: I forgive thee

thy sins; but, *Thy sins are forgiven thee.* But because the Scribes had begun to resist Him, He shows His higher power, saying: *That the son of man hath power on earth to forgive sins.* And to show He is Equal to the Father, He does not say: 'The Son of man needs power to forgive sin'; but: that He has it.

GLOSS (interlinear): These words, *that you may know,* may be either Christ's, or the Evangelist's. As though the Evangelist said: These doubted His power to forgive sin, but, *that you may know that the son of man has power,* He says to the paralytic. If, however, we say Christ spoke those words, we must understand them in this way: You doubt that I can forgive sin: but, *that you may know that the son of man hath power to forgive sin;* and here the sentence is imperfect, but action follows in place of a consequent. Then we read: *Then saith he to the man sick of the palsy, Arise, take up thy bed and go into thy house.*

CHRYSOLOGOS: So that that which had been the proof of his infirmity might become a witness to his healing. *And go into thy house:* lest healed by Christian faith you may die in the unbelief of the Jews. CHRYSOSTOM: He commanded this, so that what had been done might not be looked upon as a delusion. Accordingly, to show the reality of what had been done, there is added:

V.7. *And he arose, and went into his house.*

Nevertheless those standing about were still earth-minded in thought; hence there follows:

V.8. *And the multitude seeing it, feared, and glorified God that gave such power to men.*

For had they truly reflected within themselves, they would have acknowledged He was the Son of God. Meanwhile it was no small gain that they should esteem Him as greater than all men, and as come from God.

HILARY: Mystically; rejected by Judea, He returns to His own city. The City of God is the believing people. Into this He enters by a boat; the Church. CHRYSOLOGOS: Christ did not need the ship, but the ship had need of Christ: for without celestial guidance, the ship of the Church cannot cross the sea of this world. to gain the heavenly harbour.

HILARY: In the paralytic, all the Gentiles are brought to Him to be healed. He accordingly is brought by the ministry of angels; he is called *son,* because he is the work of God; the sins of his soul are forgiven, which the Law could not forgive. For faith only justifies. Then he manifests the power of the resurrection, when, by taking up his bed, he teaches that in heaven bodies shall be without infirmity.

JEROME: In figure, the soul lying sick in its body, its power enfeebled, is offered to the Lord, the Perfect Physician, to be cured. AMBROSE: For everyone who is ill should seek helpers (*monitores*) in prayer, to pray for his restoration to health; through whom the faltering feet of our actions may be reformed by the remedy of the heavenly word. They therefore are monitors of the mind, who raise the spirit of the hearer to the higher things; even though it now lies listless in the feebleness of the outward body.

CHRYSOLOGOS: In this world the Lord does not consider the inclinations of the foolish, but looks rather to the faith of another; neither does the physician consult the inclinations of the sick, when the infirm man asks for what is harmful. RABANUS: To *rise* means to withdraw the soul from carnal desires. To *take up thy bed*, is to raise the body above earthly desires to the delights of the spirit. To *go into his house* is to return to paradise, or, to internal watchfulness of one's self, lest it should sin again.

GREGORY, *Morals in Job*, xxxiii, 19: Or, by the bed bodily pleasure is

signified. He is therefore bidden that now restored to health he should bear that on which he had lain sick: for every man who still delights in sin, lies sick in his bodily lusts; but healed, he bears this: for after this he endures the afflictions of this same flesh, in whose desires he before found rest.

HILARY: *And the multitudes seeing it, feared.* It is a fearful thing to be dissolved in death with our sins unforgiven by Christ: for there is no return to the eternal home for those whose sins remain unforgiven. But this fear ended, glory is given to God, that by His Word power has been given to men and a way to the forgiveness of sin, to the resurrection of the body, to our return to heaven.

I. ST AMBROSE, BISHOP AND DOCTOR
The Healing of the Paralytic[1]
LUKE v. 18, 19

And, behold, men brought in a bed a man who had the palsy; and they sought means to bring him in and to lay him before him. And when they could not, they let him down through the tiles before Jesus.

The healing of this paralytic was not a casual happening; neither was it a simple healing, since the Lord prepares for it by prayer (v. 16); not indeed to obtain help, but as an example to us: He was giving us a pattern to imitate; for He had no need to pray. Here therefore, with the doctors of the law coming from all Galilee, from Judea and from Jerusalem, we have described for us, among the cures of other persons, the healing of this paralytic.

But first of all let us say again what we have said before: That anyone who is sick should seek the help in prayer of others, that they may be restored to health; that through their intercession, the enfeebled frame of our body, the wavering footsteps of our deeds, may be restored to health by the remedy of the heavenly word. Let there therefore be certain helpers of the soul (*monitores*), to raise the soul of man, even lying indifferent in the weakness of the outer body, so that by their assistance it may be easy for a man to raise himself and lower himself again, to be placed in the sight of Jesus; worthy to appear in the Lord's sight. For the Lord looks with affection on the humble: *Because he hath regarded the humility of his handmaid* (Lk. i. 48).

Whose faith when he saw, he said: Man, thy sins are for forgiven thee.

Great is the Lord, Who pardons some because of the merits of others; and while subjecting some to trials, He forgives others their sins. Why should not the prayer of your fellow-man avail with you, when a servant had both the merit of pleading for another before God and the privilege of obtaining what he prayed for? Learn you who judge, to forgive. Learn you who are sick, to gain health through prayer. Should you be diffident because of your grave sins, seek the prayers of others, call upon the Church to pray for you, and in His regard for her, the Lord will give what He could refuse to you.

And though we must not withhold faith from this account, in that we truly believe that the body of this paralytic was healed, take note nevertheless of the healing of the interior man, whose sins were forgiven, which fact, since the Jews assert only God can forgive, proclaims that He is truly God, while at the same time they, by asserting this, proclaim their own falseness. That they may praise the greatness of the work (i.e., to forgive sin), they deny His true greatness. And so, seeking no word of faith from them, the Son of God receives testimony both from them and from His works.

Unfaith cannot confess, cannot believe. So while testimony is not wanting to His Divinity, faith is wanting for their salvation. For the more strongly do they confess Him

who confess Him unwillingly, and the greater their guilt in denying what is proved by their own assertions. Great truly is the madness of this faithless people: That confessing God alone can forgive sin, they refuse to believe God as He forgives sins. But the Lord, wishing to save sinners, and to show that He is God, both by His knowledge of things hidden and by the wonders of His works, goes on to say:

Which is easier to say: Thy sins are forgiven thee; or to say: Arise and walk?

In this place He gives a complete likeness of the resurrection. Healing wounds of mind and body, He forgives the sins of souls and makes an end of the infirmity of the flesh: This is to cure the whole man. And though it is a great thing to forgive men their sins (for who can forgive sins but God alone, Who also forgives them through those to whom He has given the power of forgiving sin?[2]) nevertheless, it is a much more divine work to give resurrection to their bodies; because the Lord is Himself the Resurrection.

But, that you may know that the Son of man hath power on earth to forgive sins (he saith to the sick of the palsy), I say to thee: Arise, take up thy bed and go into thy house.

This bed he is told to take up, what does it mean but that he is told to raise up the human body? This is the bed that David washed each night as we read: *I will wash my bed: I will water my couch with my tears* (Ps. vi. 7). This is the bed of pain upon which our soul lies sick in the grievous torment of a burthened conscience. But if anyone bear this

bed according to the commandments of Christ, it is no longer a bed
of pain, but of rest. Because what
was death, begins now to be rest;
by the mercy of the Lord Who has
changed our sleep of death into the
grace of the delight of the Lord. He
is bidden not only to take up his
bed, but also to return to his house;
that is, he is told to return to Paradise; for that is man's true home and
the first to receive him: lost, not by
law, but by fraud. Rightly therefore
is his home restored to him; since
He has come Who destroyed the
deed of fraud, and restored his right.

*And immediately rising up before them
he took up the bed on which he lay; and
he went away to his own house, glorifying God.*

There is no delay in his return to
health: one is the moment of speaking and healing. Unbelieving they
see him rise up; astonished they see
him on his way. They are disposed
to fear rather than believe the wonders of divine mercy. Had they
believed, they would not have
feared, but loved: for perfect love
casts out fear (I Jn. iv. 18). And so
these men, since they did not love,
began to speak evil. To those who
were thinking evil, Jesus says: *Why
do you think evil in your hearts?* Who
says this? The High Priest. He saw

the leprosy in the hearts of the Jews,
and shows them they are worse than
lepers. The leper He made clean, He
bids show himself to the priest, and
offer a gift (Mt. viii. 4). The priest
turns lepers away; so that they shall
not contaminate others with their
leprosy.

Thee alone I follow, Lord Jesus,
Who heals my wounds. For what
shall separate me from the love of
God, which is in Thee? Shall tribulation, or distress, or famine? I am
held fast as though by nails, and
fettered by the bonds of charity.
Remove from me, O Lord Jesus,
with Thy potent sword, the corruption of my sins. Secure me in the
bonds of Thy love; cut away what is
corrupt in me. Come quickly and
make an end of my many, my hidden and secret afflictions. Open the
wound lest the evil humour spread.
With Thy new washing, cleanse in
me all that is stained. Hear me, you
earthly men, who in your sins bring
forth drunken thoughts. I have
found a Physician. He dwells in
heaven, and distributes His healing
on earth. He alone can heal my pains
Who Himself has none. He alone
Who knows what is hidden, can take
away the grief of my heart, the fear
of my soul: Jesus Christ. Christ is
grace, Christ is life, Christ is Resurrection.[3] Amen.

II. St Gaudentius, Bishop

One Work I have done; and you all wonder[4]

John vii. 21

You will recall that I promised Your
Charity that I would with God's
help explain more fully to you why
it was that the Lord declared that He

had *done one work*; at which this most
unenlightened Jewish people took
scandal, and, inflamed with evil
rage, assailed with blasphemous

abuse the Giver of blessing, saying: *Thou hast a devil; who seeketh to kill thee?* And together with this, they begin to plot how they shall deliver the Lord of Life to a death of torment.

We have seen from the testimony of this Evangelist that Christ had wrought, not one, but many, indeed innumerable works. For so he writes at the end of the book: *But there are also many other things which Jesus did; which if they were written every one, the world itself, I think, would not be able to contain the books that should be written* (xxi. 25). But some studious listener will perhaps say: In the first part of this Gospel, the Lord says: *One work I have done; and you all wonder.* In the parts that follow, He performed an amount of miracles, and for this reason there does not seem to be anything left for discussion.

But examining what is said in this book prior to these words, I find that Christ our God had performed very many wondrous works up to this point in the Gospel. For already He had seen Nathanael, before Philip had called him, when he was under a fig tree (Jn. i. 48). Already He had by His power changed the simple liquid of clear shining water into the taste and colour of wine. Already, when asked by him, He had with a word healed the son of the Ruler, before He visited him. Already He had disclosed the hidden sins of the Samaritan woman, and when she confessed God, He had cleansed her from the spiritual well (iv. 29). Already with a word He had cured or rather formed anew, the limbs of the paralytic, withered for eight and thirty years. Already He had full fed five thousand men from five

barley loaves and two fishes; ending their repast with a yet greater miracle: for the amount that remained after He had fed so many hungry people, was greater than the food placed before Him. Already He had walked upon the waters; so that as He walked the tossing waves had not touched the soles of His feet.

But in this catalogue of wonders He had done yet *one work* more, which, to the ignorant people who raged against Him, seemed to have given as it were likely grounds to attack Him: namely, that He had healed a paralytic on the sabbath (Jn. v. 10) when the Law commanded rest. And so Christ, Who had come *not to destroy* the Old Law *but to fulfil it*, as though guilty of the violation of the sabbath, suffers the insults and derision of the Jews.

At this point, dearest brethren, I am compelled, putting aside for a time this portion of the Gospel, to explain to you the significance of the sabbath: lest anyone should believe that the persecution of the Just by the wicked was justified. For this paralytic, of whom it is related that he was cured by Christ on the sabbath, suffered the calumny of the Jews for this; that on the day he was cured, he was seen carrying his bed. *It is the sabbath,* they say, *it is not lawful for thee to take up thy bed* (Jn. v. 10). And the man who was cured answered: *He that made me whole, he said to me: Take up thy bed and walk.* And a little later he says: *It was Jesus who made me whole* (v. 15).

Still untaught from his Jewish ignorance, but now grateful for the sound body he had received; since he was unable to give those who attacked him a reason for what had happened, he points out to them the

Author both of the command and of the miracle. *He that made me whole, he said to me: Take up thy bed, and walk;* and he added: *Jesus it is,* he says, *who made me whole*; or, It is the son of David Who made me whole; or, The son of Joseph it was who made me whole. For these were the names then used by the Jewish people in speaking of Christ the Lord our Saviour.

But what does this mean? *Jesus it is,* he says, *who made me whole?* For as a Hebrew he knew that the name *Jesus* derives from the power of healing. The Saviour is indeed called Jesus, as the angel declared, when he spoke to Joseph concerning Christ *in his sleep. Thou shalt call his name Jesus:* he says, *for he shall save his people from their sins* (Mt. i. 21). He therefore, he says, *made me whole;* and His Name is Salvation. And how could Salvation be forbidden by the Law from saving, or be changed in its nature by the creation of the sabbath, so that it is no longer Salvation? Let us see, dearest brethren, whether in fact the Law did exclude a work of healing on the sabbath rest? *Six days shalt thou labour,* it says, *and shalt do all thy works, But on the seventh day is the sabbath of the Lord thy God, thou shalt do no work on it* (Ex. xx. 9, 10): *unless what is done for any soul.*[5]

Human nature, especially that of the Jews, is prone by desire to do bodily rather than divine works. So one day of the week was set apart, the sabbath, on which they were compelled to cease from carnal works, and occupy themselves with divine works only. Nor was it permitted to cook food on the sabbath, nor to make a journey, lest under the pretext of human necessity,

earthly things might be placed before divine. Notwithstanding this, when the Jews later, neglecting the spiritual works the Lord commanded for their soul's salvation, devoted all that was lawful on the sabbath to luxury and ease, the Lord cries out to them without ceasing through the Prophet: *The new moons and the sabbaths and other festivals I will not abide. My soul hateth your new moons and your solemnities* (Is. i. 13, 14).

Your sabbaths, He says; not Mine. For the things you do are not Mine. *My* fasts and *My* sabbaths, which I imposed upon you to be observed, command you to fast from sin, to cease from evil works, and give yourselves to good works. But on the contrary, your sabbaths and your fasts are disturbed by quarrels, and filled with wantonness and excess. Coming therefore as man, the Giver of the Law, when He wrought works of healing for every soul, did not destroy the Law, but rather fulfilled it: for He taught on that sabbath which He in His Providence had decreed. For it was written: *Thou shalt do no work of thine on the sabbath* (Non facies in eo ullum opus tuum nisi quod fit pro omni anima). *Work of thine,* it says; that is, human. And there is added: *Save what is done for any soul,* that is, to save any soul. And so we read that the earlier just under the Law worked on the sabbath for the salvation of souls. For seven days Jesus the son of Nave, at the command of the Lord, went round the city of Jericho, with the Levites and Priests bearing the Ark of the Covenant; and at the divine command the hostile walls fell down, so that the souls of the Jews were delivered from the danger of war (Josue vi). You will note that the sabbath is also numbered by seven days, beginning the count from any day you will.[6]

And so when he said, *Jesus it is, who made me whole*, the Jews are warned, through the similarity of the name, not to condemn such works. Therefore Christ the Lord, when He healed a withered hand, or someone afflicted with dropsy, or cured paralysis on the sabbath, as the true Lord of the sabbath, safeguarded what He had done by the testimony of His own Law; saying to the Jews: It is lawful to help an animal on the sabbath; but a soul, do we save that, or lose it? Desiring by this to lead them to this understanding of the Law, I believe, as we explained above; at the same time reproaching them because they did not understand the significance of *thy work* (*opus tuum*), and the meaning of, *what is done for any soul*.

Christ therefore works on the sabbath for the salvation of the soul. And, He works on the sabbath, and fulfils the Law, while explaining the terms of the Law, while He makes clear the different kinds of works, while He does what the Law allows on the sabbath days, making this sabbath day, made holy by His blessing, holier by His favours. For the works due on the sabbath He gave back as divine blessings, bestowed on that day to every soul that believes. But that He might show the Jews that He worked always with the Father, Who would then also work in His Body, He says to them: *My Father worketh until now; and I work* (Jn. v. 17). And for this the Jews persecuted Him the more, *because he did not only break the sabbath, but also said God was his Father,*

making himself equal to God (v. 18).

The blessed Evangelist has clearly taught us that He is Equal to God the Father Who is by nature His true Son. And, though the testimony of the ancients had preceded Him, nevertheless the Lord did not desire to bring forward any such testimony; for fear, since these were scattered here and there, and ancient, they might be looked upon as uncertain, and due simply to chance; but chose rather to answer them by day to day instances and examples, so that when they were refuted, they could in no way say that it was not so.

One work I have done, He says, *and you all wonder* (Jn. vii. 21). What is this work? That I cured a paralytic on the sabbath. And He adds: *Therefore Moses gave you circumcision; not because it is of Moses* (Jn. vii. 22), *but of the Fathers;* that is, from Abraham, who was the first to be circumcised (Gen. xvii. 11), and from the other Patriarchs. *And on the sabbath day,* He says, *you circumcise a man. If a man*, He says, *receive circumcision on the sabbath day, that the Law of Moses may not be broken; are you angry at me, because I have healed the whole man on the sabbath day? Judge not according to the appearance; but judge just judgement,* as though He said: The Law commands that only a work which is for the soul may be done on the sabbath. And by the same Law it is commanded with regard to circumcision, that every male whatsoever that is not circumcised on the eighth day from its nativity, *that soul shall be destroyed out of his people* (Gen. xvii. 12–14). Therefore, it is for the soul you circumcise a man on the sabbath day. In the same way it is for the soul that

I on the sabbath healed *the whole man*. It is lawful therefore to do a good work for the soul on the sabbath day. And if you judge that I by this work have violated the sabbath, you condemn yourselves as guilty unceasingly of the violation of the sabbath. *Judge not according to appearance; but judge just judgement.*

With such reasonable patience did our Lord Jesus overcome His His enemies: He Who came down from the Father to this world, that He might overcome it by patience. But let us consider briefly the virtue of this last saying of His. *Judge not*, He says, *according to appearance; but judge just judgement*. This general rule is our true guide, I believe; it keeps within the bounds of what is just and fair, was laid down for all man, is known to many, but loved by few. It was laid down so that we shall not be flatterers of the rich of this world, that we may not favour the unbelieving by an unjust judgement, nor take the part of the impious, the cruel, the rapacious, the wanton, the dishonest, even by a timid silence; but also so that we shall not with unjust praise commend those who are rather deserving of every censure, or also, what is more odious than any foulness, that we may not allow ourselves to be enslaved by another man's money; lost to Christian freedom in our greed for evil gains. Or lest seduced by the beauty of some bodily form we should, by an unjust decision, be drawn away from the severity of truth, and from *just judgement*; for of despising riches is it written: *If riches abound, set not your heart upon them* (Ps. lxi. 11); and of disregarding beauty of body, God said to the Priest Samuel, who was about to choose a king from the sons of Jesse: *Look not on his countenance, nor on the height of his stature, or beauty of face, for man sees the face, but God beholds the heart* (I Kings xvi. 7). Because of this the blessed David, the youngest and the despised, was uplifted by the sacred oil to kingship, and grew by the grace of God from lowliness to the summit of dignity; and of this he glories in a special canticle, singing: *I was a little one among my brethren.*[7]

Profitably therefore for all circumstances does Christ tell us: *Judge not according to appearance; but judge just judgement*. And which of us, most dearly beloved, is now prepared to observe all that I have said to you? *Blessed are they that keep judgement and do justice at all times* (Ps. cv. 3). Therefore, though this counsel is, as I have said, for all men, it was directed in particular to the Jews, who had judged Christ, though working wonders, as being from his appearance only a man; not seeing from the wonders He wrought that He was God. And in this sentence He also includes, and in no small measure, the heretics who blaspheme the Son of God; because, seeing only the lowliness of the Body He took upon Himself, they presume to sit in judgement upon the substance of His immeasurable Divinity.

But we, brethren, who *by his grace are saved through faith* (Eph. ii. 8), let us judge with just judgement, preserving moderation of mind in every action of our daily life. For just judgement belongs to the nature of the reasoning soul; so that it chooses to serve God rather than serve the world; that it resolves to obey the commands of Christ, and not be corrupted by the deceits of the devil; so that it is steadfast in adhering to spiritual things, not becoming entangled in the vices of the flesh; so that it judges that the eternal blessedness of things to come, is to be placed before the fleeting pleasures of this world. Upright in heart, therefore, let us in all the commandments and justifications of the Lord, walk in this life with *just judgement*, that we may merit to be sharers of life everlasting with the eternal Son of God, Who in Omnipotence abides with the Father and the Holy Spirit, for ever and ever. Amen.

III. St Peter Chrysologos, Bishop and Doctor

On the Healing of the Paralytic[8]

Matthew ix. 1–8

Today's lesson makes clear to us that Christ in His human actions wrought divine mysteries, and that in His visible works He had in mind invisible ends. *Entering into a boat*, it says, *he passed over the water and came into his own city.* Is this not He Who thrusting aside the waves of the sea laid bare its deeps, that the people of Israel might pass *on dry ground* through the midst of fearful waves as between mountains (Exod. xiv)? Is this not He Who supported the feet of Peter upon the crests of the waves, so that his watery path upon the sea stayed firm beneath his step (Mt. xiv)? And why does He deny Himself the service of the sea, to make the brief crossing of the lake in a hired boat? *Entering into a boat*, it says, *he passed over the water.*

And why should we wonder, brethren? Christ came to take upon Him our infirmities, and confer on us His powers; to seek what is human, to give what is divine; to receive injuries, and return them with honours; to suffer affliction, and bring healing to others: for the physician who does not suffer infirmities, knows not how to cure infirmities; and he who is not weak with the weak, cannot bring health to the weak. Christ therefore, had He remained within His own powers, would have had nothing in common with men; and unless He conformed to the way of life of our body, His taking of flesh would have been in vain. He therefore shared our necessities, that by these human needs He might be proved a true man.

Entering into a boat, it says. Christ enters the ship of His Church, that He may calm at all times the waves of the world; that He may conduct those who believe in Him by a tranquil voyage to their heavenly country; and make fellow citizens of His own city, those He had made sharers of His humanity. It is not Christ therefore Who needs the ship, but the ship that needs Christ; for without its Heavenly Pilot the ship of the Church would be unable to pass through the sea of the world, amid so many and such great hazards, and reach the heavenly harbour.

These things, brethren, we have said with regard to the spiritual meaning of the Gospel. Let us now consider the order of what took place. *Entering into a boat, it says, he passed over the water and came into his own city.* The Creator of all things, the Lord of the whole world, after He had for our sake confined Himself within our body, began to have a human country, began to be a citizen of the country of Judea. He began to have parents, Who was the Parent of all men, that His love might draw, His Charity attract, His affection win, His humanity persuade those whom the devil had driven away, fear had scattered, divine law made exiles.

He came into his own city, And, behold, they brought to him one sick of the palsy lying in a bed. And Jesus, it says, *seeing their faith, said to the man sick of the palsy: Be of good heart, son, Thy sins are forgiven thee.*
The paralytic hears the words of pardon, and says nothing; neither does he offer thanks in return; for he longed more for the cure of his body than of his soul; he grieved over the temporal afflictions of his enfeebled body, but had no tears for the eternal penalty of the loss of his soul: judging that the present life was more agreeable than the future. Rightly did Christ look with favour on the faith of those who had brought him there, and ignore the foolishness of the man lying sick; so that by the merit of others' faith the soul of the paralytic was healed before his body.
Seeing their faith, it says. You perceive in this place, brethren, how God does not heed the inclinations of the foolish, nor does He regard the faith of those who are ignorant of Christian truth, nor trouble with the foolish desires of the weak, but that He will come to our aid because of another's faith, which He bestowed by grace alone: for whatever comes from the Divine Will, He will not deny. And when, brethren, does a physician ask for or pay heed to the inclinations of the sick: since a sick man will always crave for and ask for things that may be harmful. Instead, he will make use, now of the iron, now of fire, now of the bitter draught, and apply them even to the unwilling, so that when well they will understand what was done for them, which they could not when ill. And if a man will take no notice of insults, and be indifferent to abuse, that he may bring life and health to those affected by disease; how much the more will not Christ the Physician, in His divine goodness, draw to salvation those who are sick from the wounds of sin, or sinking in the delirium of some vice; even the reluctant and unwilling?
O if we but chose! Brethren, if we but chose to look into every paralysis of our mind, and see our soul as it lies abandoned upon its bed of sin; we would see it clearly as Christ sees us; each day looking with patience on our sinful desires, drawing us, urging us, even unwilling, towards His saving remedies!
Son, He says, *thy sins are forgiven thee.* Saying this, He intimates that it is His will that men should know He is God; though now as man still hidden to human eyes. Through His signs and wonders He was already compared with the prophets who, through Him, had also wrought signs and wonders. Now He began to implant in human breasts that He was God: for to forgive sin, since it is beyond the power of man, is the particular sign of divinity.

The envy of the Pharisees proves this: for when He said: *Thy sins are forgiven thee; the Pharisees answered: He blasphemeth. Who can forgive sins but God alone?* O Pharisee! who knowing, knows not; who confessing, denies; who bearing witness, attacks! If it is God Who forgives sins, why is Christ not God to you: He Who by one act of forgiveness is proved to have taken away the sins of the whole world? *Behold,* says Scripture, *the lamb of God who taketh away the sins of the world* (Jn. i. 29). But that you may have yet greater proofs of His Divinity: listen to Him who pierced the secret of your breast; look upon Him Who reached into the hidden places of your thoughts; understand Him Who lays bare the secret counsels of your heart!

And Jesus, it says, *seeing their thoughts, said: Why do you think evil in your hearts? Which is easier, to say, Thy sins are forgiven thee; or to say, Arise and walk? But that you may know that the Son of Man hath power to forgive sins (then said to the man sick of the palsy): Arise, take up thy bed and go into thy house. And he arose and went into his house.*

He Who searches into the souls of men had seen beforehand the evil counsels of their minds, and now proclaims the power of His Divinity by the witness of this miracle, as He brings together the members of this weakened body, draws firm the nerves, joins bone to bone, restores flesh and blood, strengthens the joints, and puts in motion the feet that just now lay buried in a living dead body. *Take up thy bed*; that is, take up that which bore thee, change places; so that what was the proof of thy sickness may now give testimony to thy soundness, that thy bed of pain may be the sign of My healing, that its weight may be the measure of the strength restored to thee. *Go,* He says, *into thy house*; so that cured by Christian faith, you may not die in the streets of Jewish unfaith, but may live for ever with Christ Jesus our Lord, Who is blessed for ever and ever. Amen.

IV. St Gregory the Great, Pope and Doctor

God Man's House[9]

As a cloud is consumed, and passeth away: so he that shall go down to hell shall not come up (Book of Job, vii. 9)
I. For the damned, *There is no return to pardon, or to what they loved.*

A cloud hangs in the upper air; but pressed by the wind it is driven on and floats away; in the sun's heat it will dissolve, and so it vanishes. And so is it with men's hearts, which through the gift of reason soar upwards to the heights, but pressed by the breath of an evil spirit, they are borne hither and thither by the evil impulses of their own desires. But, in the stern presence of the Heavenly judge, they dissolve as if by the heat of the sun, and then, once delivered to the place of suffering, return no more to this freedom to serve God. And so listen to the holy man Job, describing this upward soaring, the course and decline of man's life, telling us: *As a cloud is consumed, and passeth away: so he that shall go down to hell shall not come up.* As though he were to say simply: 'Soaring high, he fails who by exalting himself goes towards his own destruction; whom, if sin has once dragged down to punishment, mercy shall no more return to pardon.' And so he goes on:

V.10. *Nor shall he return any more into his own house.*

II. *The house of the soul is that in which it dwells by loving. The hearts of the despairing are like clouds. They are scattered.*

As a house is the corporal dwelling of the body, so to each mind that is a house where it is wont through desire to dwell. Once a man is given over to eternal punishment, he is recalled no more to that house to which he had clung fast from love; and thereafter he *shall return no more into his own house.* Even the name of hell can signify the sinner's despair; for of it the psalmist says: *In hell, who shall confess thee?* (Ps. vi. 6). For this reason was it also written: *The wicked man when he has come into the depths of sins, becomes contemptuous* (Prov. xviii. 3). For whosoever succumbs to wickedness, dying, leaves wholly behind him the life of justice. And he who after he has sinned, is also overwhelmed by the weight of despair, what is this but, after dying, to be buried in the torments of hell? Well therefore is it said: *As a cloud is consumed, and passeth away: so he that shall go down to hell shall not come up*; for it will often happen that despair goes in company with evil; and the way of return is thus cut off. Rightly therefore are the hearts of the despairing compared to clouds; because they grow dark in the mists of evil belief, and dark

from the multiplicity of their sins. But dissolved, they vanish; for in the splendour of the Last Judgement they come to nothing.

House is also used to mean the dwelling-place of the heart. So to a certain man who was cured was it said: *Go into thy house* (Mk. v. 19); for it is fitting that a sinner, after he is forgiven, should return to his own mind, lest he yield again to that for which he will justly be punished. But he who has *gone down to hell*, he shall come up no more to his own house: for he whom despair has overwhelmed, it sends forth from the dwelling place of his heart, and he is unable to return within again; for, once driven forth, urged on he falls daily to lower and lower things. For man was made to look upon his Creator, to dwell upon His beauty, to live in the joy of His love. But sent out of himself through disobedience, he has lost the *place* of his soul; for wandering in darkened ways, he has gone far from the dwelling place of the true light. So fittingly there is also added: *Neither shall his place know him any more.*

III. *God is the place (house) of man; abandoned through disobedience. At the judgement, God shall not know them who here despised him.*

The *place* of man, but not his place in space, is the Creator Himself, Who created man that he might dwell within Himself. This *place* man abandoned when, giving ear to the voice of the tempter, he abandoned the love of the Creator. But when Almighty God, redeeming us, showed Himself to us in a bodily manner, and, if I may say so, following in pursuit of man who had fled from Him, He came to us as a *place* wherein He might keep lost man. If the Creator may not be spoken of as a *place*, the psalmist praising God would not have said: *The children of thy servants shall dwell there* (Ps. ci. 29). For we do not say *there*, unless referring to some particular place.

But even after they have been helped by the Redeemer, many fall into the darkness of despair; and they fall the more terribly, the more they despise the remedies of salvation He now offers them. Rightly then is it said of the man who is damned: *Neither shall his place know him any more.* For the more he now despises God Whose gifts recall him to the grace of reparation, the more his Creator, then stern and terrible, shall not know him at the judgement. So let us carefully note, that he does not say: Neither shall he know his own place any more,' but says: *Neither shall his place know him any more.* For since knowing is here attributed not to a man, but to a *place*, the word *place* plainly refers to the Creator Himself, Who, coming as a stern Judge to Judgement, shall say of those who have continued in iniquity: *I know you not whence you are* (Lk. xiii. 25). But the Elect, seeing the reprobate so severely rejected, daily purify themselves the more earnestly from the stains of the evil they have committed. And when they see others who shall perish grow cold through the love of this life, they rouse themselves earnestly to tears of repentance. Hence of the Just the Psalmist says: *The saints shall rejoice in glory: they shall be joyful in their beds* (cxlix. 5). For when men turn away from the evils outside them, they begin to rejoice in glory, safe in the secret places of their souls, through Jesus Christ our Lord. Amen.

V. St Gregory the Great, Pope and Doctor

Man is Delivered by Trials: Mystical Joy[10]

Job xxxiii. 16–20

V.16. *Then he openeth the ears of men, and teaching instructeth them in what they are to learn.*

I. *They who cease from outward works, are led to compunction of heart.*

When men's minds are at rest from outward things, they hear with a ready ear the things that come before the inward judgement. And dwelling carefully on their secret trials as upon their outward scourges they grieve in tears without ceasing. So rightly is it said that God teaches men with discipline (*eos instruit disciplina*): for to a mind that meditates, wounding itself in repentance, the groans of its compunction are as the stripes of a beating. And of this Solomon, uniting this twofold chastisement, says: *The blueness of a wound shall wipe away evils: and stripes in the more inward parts of the belly* (Prov. xx. 30). By the blueness of a wound, discipline of bodily correction is meant; but by *stripes in the inward parts of the belly*, the inward wounds of compunction of soul. For as the stomach is distended by food, so is the mind when blown up with evil thoughts. The lividness of a wound therefore and the inward affliction of the heart, both wipe away our sins: for outward chastisements wash away our guilt, and compunction will pierce with the sting of repentance the soul that is puffed up. But they differ in this: that while the stripes of blows cause pain, the grieving of compunction has a good flavour. The one, afflicting us, cause pain; the other, while afflicting us, refreshes us. In the one, grief of mind is joined to pain of body; in the other, grief of mind and joy unite. Yet compunction, since it wounds the mind is, not unfittingly, also called discipline.

II. *How compunction afflicts the soul; as shown by Paul and David.*

There are four states in which the soul of the just man is strongly affected by compunction. When reminded of his sins, he considers where he was; when in fear of the judgement of God, and, reflecting upon himself, he thinks upon where he shall be; when dwelling carefully on the evils of the present life, grieving he thinks of where he is; when he contemplates the joys of his heavenly home, to which he has not yet come, and mourning beholds where he is not. Paul had recalled to mind his own sins and, because of them, was grieving over what he had been, when he said: *I am not worthy to be called an Apostle, because I persecuted the church of God* (I Cor. xv. 9). Again, dwelling minutely on the divine judgement, he was in fear of the evil to come when he said: *I chastise my body and bring it into subjection; lest perhaps, when I have preached to others, I, myself, should become a castaway* (I Cor. ix. 27). Again, he was reflecting on the

evils of this present life, when he said: *While we are in the body we are absent from the Lord* (II Cor. v. 6). And: *But I see another law in my members, fighting against the law of my mind and captivating me in the law of sin that is in my members. Unhappy man that I am, who shall deliver me from the body of this death?* (Rom. vii. 23).

And again, as he considered the joys of his heavenly home, he says: *We see now through a glass in a dark manner; but then face to face. Now I know in part; but then I shall know even as I am known* (I Cor. xiii. 12). And again: *We know, if our earthly house of this habitation be dissolved, that we have a building of God, a house not made with hands, eternal in heaven* (II Cor. v. 1). And again, contemplating the good things of this house, he says to the Ephesians: *That you may know what the hope is of his calling and what are the riches of the glory of his inheritance in the saints, and what is the exceeding greatness of his power towards us, who believe* (Eph. l. 19–19).

The blessed Job, reflecting on the evils of this present life, says: *The life of man upon earth is a warfare* (Job vii. 1). And David likewise says: *All things are vanity; every man living; and though man walks in the image of God, yet he is disquieted in vain* (Ps. xxxviii. 6–7). And again, contemplating his eternal home, and thinking of the evils in which he was then placed, and dwelling on the joys from which he was still far away, he cries out: *Woe is me, that my sojourning is prolonged* (Ps. cxix. 5)! And, *I said in the excess of my mind: I am cast away from before thy eyes* (Ps. xxx. 23). Uplifted in ecstasy (which our translators rightly call *fear*: *in pavore meo*), he saw himself cast forth from the face of God's sight. And after this vision of inward light, which had flashed in his soul like a beam of glory through the grace of contemplation, he returned to himself; knowing now, from what he had there seen, the joys he was still deprived of, and the evils amid which he still must live. For no man can see as they are the evils of this present life, unless enabled through some glimpse of contemplation to draw near and see the joys of our heavenly home. From this he knew he had been cast forth from the sight of God's eyes. For uplifted he saw that which, returned to himself, he mourned he could not of himself see here below.

III. *The effect of compunction in the perfect.*

Such compunction is wont to touch more intimately the soul that is perfect and drive from it all the bodily imaginings that insolently crowd upon it, and through it the soul strives to fasten the eye of its heart upon that beam of Boundless Light. It is through the body's infirmity it has drawn into itself these images of bodily forms. But when filled with compunction it is wholly watchful, and repulses all phantasies that come before it so that, while it is seeking the Truth, the image of some fleeting thing shall not delude it. For since it was through them it has fallen beneath itself, freed of them it strives to rise above itself. And when it has been unfittingly assailed by many of them, it strives to compose itself, so that, triumphing by the strong power of love, it

may contemplate Him Who is One and Incorporeal.

IV. *The taste of contemplation as only a swift touch upon the soul. Hence the grief of the pious bereft of its delight.*

And from this Source the soul at times is given an inward taste of some unexperienced sweetness, and of a sudden breathed on by the glowing Spirit is in some way made new; and it longs the more, the more it tastes of what it loves. And it craves within it for this which inwardly has tasted sweet to it: for through the love of this sweetness it has become vile in its own sight. And after it has, as it may, received this within it, it comes then to know what it was before without it. It strives to cling to it, but is still held back from its strength by its own weakness; and unable to look upon its purity, it weeps sweet tears, and sinking back upon itself makes of its tears the bed of its own weakness. For it cannot fasten the eye of its mind upon That which for a swift moment it beheld within itself; because by the force of long habit it is impelled downwards. And in the midst of this it sighs with longing, it burns with love, it struggles to go above itself, but overcome with weariness sinks back again to its own familiar darkness.

But because the soul so touched has to endure within it a grave struggle against itself, and because all this striving within us with ourselves, while it holds us, causes us no small pain, mingled however with delight, Eliu,[11] after he had said that God speaks to us, *by a dream in a vision by night* (v. 15), and that our ears are opened by His words (v. 16), rightly calls this opening of our ears *discipline*: for the more the sound of this inner enlightenment breaks upon us through the inspiration of His inward grace, the more does it touching us afflict us. For no one would outwardly grieve over what he is, if he could not inwardly perceive what he yet is not. When we look into ourselves and see that we were wonderfully created, but that we were cheated through our own fatal consent to the devil's persuasion, we note that what we were made is one thing, what we have made ourselves another: that in our creation we were without flaw, but that by sin we have become corrupt. And so when we are pierced by compunction we long to escape from what we have made ourselves, and to be made again into that which we were when first made.[12] So fittingly there then follows: V. 17. *That he may withdraw a man from the things he is doing, and may deliver him from pride.*

V. *Through compunction we are turned away from the sins we formerly committed, and delivered from pride.*

What has man done of himself except sin? And it is written: *Pride is the beginning of all sin* (Ecclus. x. 15). It is well said therefore, that when a man has turned away from the things that he has done, he is delivered from pride. To overstep the Creator's commands by sin is to rise in pride against Him: for when a man refuses obedience to God, he as it were casts off the yoke of His authority. But on the contrary, he who longs to turn away from what he has done, acknowledges that which God has done, and, flying from his own deeds, returns humbly to the state in which God created him, choosing to be that which God

made him. And because it is through this enlightenment that we are received in eternal glory and escape eternal punishment, he appropriately continues: V. 18. *Rescuing his soul from corruption: and his life from passing to the sword.*

VI. *In this way the soul is rescued from corruption and from the sword of divine justice.*

For every sinner is compelled to pass from the corruption of sin in this life to the sword of punishment in the next: that there he may justly be punished for the evil he delighted in here. We must therefore note that God, speaking to us in a dream, first delivers us from corruption, and then from the sword: For He rescues from torment there, the soul He here withdraws from the delight of sin. And there he need fear no more the sword of judgement, who after his healing here has not been defiled by the stain of sin. Rightly therefore does he say: *Rescuing his soul from corruption: and his life from passing to the sword.* For to pass from corruption to the sword is, after an evil life, to come to the punishment we must suffer. He continues: V. 19. *He rebuketh also by sorrow in the bed; and he maketh all his bones to wither.*

VII. *In the present life, every peace we prepare for ourselves is troubled by temptations. Whatever the retreat, we cannot live without temptations.*

In Sacred Scripture, bed or pallet, and also couch sometimes stand for pleasures of the body, sometimes for the refreshment of good works, sometimes for rest in the ordinary sense. For what is meant in the Gospel when the Lord says to a certain man who was healed: *Arise, take up thy bed and go into thy house* (Mk. ii. 11), but that by the bed pleasure of body is signified? And he is commanded to bear as a healthy man, that on which he had lain as a sick one: for every one who still delights in sin, lies sick in the pleasures of his flesh. But now healed he bears that upon which he had lain sick, because raised from his sins by divine assistance, he must afterwards bear with the assaults of that flesh in whose desires he had before found rest.

Again by *bed*, the refreshment of good works is also signified. It is in this sense the Apostle Peter says in the Acts of the Apostles: *Eneas, the Lord Jesus Christ healeth thee; arise, and make thy bed* (Acts ix. 34). For what is meant by *arise* if not: forsake the evil you have been committing? And what does *make thy bed* mean, if not: labour in those works of blessing in which you should find rest? So that by rising up, he may forsake the things he once did; and by making his bed, learn what he should have done.

And both these things the Prophet briefly sums up by saying: *Decline from evil and do good* (Ps. xxxvi. 27). For a man *to decline from evil* is to rise up from that on which he lay; *to do good* is to do the works in whose reward he must find rest. For he who declines from evil but still does not do good, has indeed risen up from the bed on which he lay, but has not yet prepared the bed on which he must find rest.

And again, *bed* or *couch* is also used to signify earthly rest; as it is written: *Thou hast turned all his couch in his sickness* (Ps. xl. 4). For when someone who is weary of earthly

cares is urged by divine grace to leave the toiling ways of this world, he will give thought to how he may escape the desires of this present life and rest from its labours. And then he will search for a way of life that will give him the desired peace, longing to find a place, a bed as it were, of rest from all his toils. But as long as a man is still in this life, however he may be placed, however secret his retreat, he can never be wholly free from temptations; and oftentimes he will find a greater anguish of temptation in the place he prepared for his peace. Rightly then does the Prophet say: *Thou hast turned all his couch in his sickness.* As though he said: All that a man prepares here for his rest, Thou in Thy hidden judgement doth alter to his disquiet. And this is done by the loving purpose of God, so that for the time of their earthly pilgrimage the life of His Elect may be *troubled*.

VIII. *We are afflicted in this life by the supremely good purpose of God, so that we may not love the way more than the end of our journey.*

For this present life is but a way by which we travel towards our heavenly home. And because of this we are, in the inscrutable wisdom of God, wearied by frequent disquiet, so that we may not come to love the way more than our home. For there are travellers who when on their way see some smiling field, while they delight in its beauty, they slow their steps and turn aside from the straight path they had begun. The Lord therefore has made the way of this world hard for His Elect in their journey to Him, so that none of them may take his rest in this life, enjoying the beauty of the way, but may hasten speedily towards Him rather than linger by the way; or lest, delighting in the way, they come to forget they once longed for their heavenly home.

And so because in this life all the peace we may perhaps have prepared for ourselves may be disturbed, rightly is it said that: *He rebuketh also by sorrow in the bed* (v. 19); that is, in our rest in this present life He troubles us, either by the darts of temptation, or by the scourge of some affliction. For often for a brief while a human soul will be left to its devotions untroubled by temptation. Presently, by reason of those efforts in which it is peacefully engaged, by reason of those very virtues in which it strives to advance, and while feeling it is making progress, it becomes elated. And so by the loving dispensation of our Ruler it is subjected to the shock of temptation, that by means of it this elation at its progress may be subdued. It is because of this that after he had said: *He rebuketh also by sorrow in the bed*, he appropriately adds: *And he maketh all his bones to wither*.

IX. *Through temptation we learn what we can do of our own power, and what by divine favour.*

By *bones* in Sacred Scripture we understand powers (*virtutes*); as it is written: *The Lord keepeth all their bones, not one of them shall be broken* (Ps. xxxiii. 21). And this is not said of the bones of the body, but of the powers of the mind. For we know with certainty that many of the bones of the martyrs were bodily broken, and that the Lord's executioners broke the legs of that thief to whom it was said: *This day thou shalt be with me in paradise* (Lk. xxiii.

43), as well as those of the other thief on his cross.

Therefore, when He rebukes us, *by sorrow in the bed*, He makes all our bones wither: for when in that peace we make for ourselves in this world we are tormented by the scourge of temptation, we who perhaps might have been elated at our virtues are humbled through loathing of the weakness we find within us. For when we are progressing towards God as we desire, we would begin to believe we were souls of great strength if some temptation did not assail our progress. But since the Divine Dispensation so deals with us that while making progress we shall not forget our weakness; and that tempted we recall it, so that in our progress we may understand what we are from divine favour, and in our temptation what we are of our own strength. And such temptation would indeed lead us wholly astray were we not protected from above. Yet it assails us, though it does not break us; it incites us, though it does not move us; it shakes us, but does not make us fall: that we may see that it is because of our own weakness we are shaken, because of divine grace we stand firm.

And because often a soul conscious of good within it, and recalling to mind its virtues, will feel a certain pleasure and grow fat as it were with contentment at the thought of its own completeness, it is well said that in time of temptation all the bones wither; for when our weakness is disclosed by the probings of temptation, of a sudden all that serene and green contentment with our own virtue is withered by the sharp anguish of fear, and we who weighing up our good works believed ourselves something, shaken a little are terrified that we are about to perish. Then all delight in our goodness turns to fear of punishment. Then we find we are wicked: we who a little before thought ourselves saints. Our mind grows weak; our eyes grow dull. All that before smiled on us now vanishes. Light itself is hateful; and only the dark of sadness pours into the soul. Nothing we see gives joy; all the eye meets is sorrow. And so he goes on: *Bread becomes abominable to him in his life, and to his soul the meat which before he desired* (v. 20).

And so it is, as we have said above, that in the hidden dispensations of Providence, it is permitted that we shall be tried in this way, so that we who through divine grace make progress in virtue, may also be mindful of our own weakness; and that we who by His grace advance in virtue, may through the remembrance of our own frailty offer to God a sacrifice of humility, through Jesus Christ our Lord.[13] Amen.

NOTES

[1] PL 15, col. 1638, *Expos. Evang. sec. Lucam.*, V, 10–15.

[2] Cf. PL 15, col. 1639, 13, *Quis enim potest peccata dimittere nisi solus Deus, qui per eos quoque dimittit, quibus dimittendi tribuit potestatem?* Ambrose could not have proclaimed in clearer words the power of forgiving sins given by Christ to the ministers of His Church.

[3] The last paragraph is taken from the prayer Ambrose puts in the mouth of Matthew on his conversion. Cf. par. 27; col. 1644; also par. 116, col. 1728.

[4] PL 20, col. 920.

[5] This final clause is an exception, allowed in the Law of the Sabbath, and is called by Rabbinical authorities: *periculum animae*; whence arose the proverb: *Periculum vitae pellit sabbatum.* Cf. note i, PL 20, col. 924.

[6] Some Jewish scholars hold that Jericho was taken on the sabbath day. Cf. *loc. cit.*, note j. In Hebrew Jesus and Josue are the same.

[7] This psalm is not found in the Vulgate. In the Septuagint it is found placed after Psalm 150, under the title: 'This psalm is a genuine one of David, though supernumary, composed after he had fought in single combat with Goliath.'

[8] PL 52, col. 339. *Sermo L.*

[9] PL 75, col. 820, *Morals in Job,* Book VIII, in Job vii. 9, 10, paragraphs 33–5. Job is declaring the miseries of man's life; addressing himself to God, beginning with the memorable: *The life of man upon earth is a warfare, and his days are like the days of a hireling.* These two selections from St Gregory the Great's work on the Book of Job are meditative rather than homilistic; but relate to and treat of the theme of the Gospel of this Sunday; on which material is scarce among the Fathers. It reveals the Saint's extraordinary spiritual discernment and wisdom, and the depth of his knowledge and understanding of Holy Scripture. The selections are included rather as material for spiritual guides. The work is one of great gravity; unlike the somewhat genial character of his public sermons which are filled with a tender sim-

plicity directed at simple congregations: though these latter, the Homilies on the Gospel, of which forty have come down to us, far excel in significance and authority the *Morals*. The latter are an earlier, private work. The homilies contain the teaching of the Church, spoken by the Supreme Pontiff, and constitute, as the *Foreword* to this work so authoritatively says 'the quintessence of the doctrine of Tradition on each Gospel.'

[10] PL 76, Book XXIII of *Morals in Job*, xxxiii, 16–20, col. 275.

[11] *Eliu the son of Barachel the Buzzite, of the kindred of Ram* (Chapter 32, verse 2) who took up the reproof of Job when his three friends *had ceased to answer Job*.

[12] 'In a dream the outward senses are at rest and inward things seen. If we wish to contemplate inward things, let us rest from outward things. The voice of God is truly heard as if in a dream, when, with souls at peace, we are at rest from the tumult of this world, and the divine precepts are dwelt on in a deep silence of the mind.' Book 23, par. 37.

[13] Concluding reflection (last paragraph) from 51, *loc. cit.*

NINETEENTH SUNDAY AFTER PENTECOST

I. Origen: Those Called to the Wedding

II. St Augustine: The Wedding Garment

III. St Gregory the Great: On the Gospel: Preparation

THE GOSPEL OF THE SUNDAY

Matthew xxii. 1–14

At that time: Jesus spoke to the chief priests and Pharisees in a parable, saying: The kingdom of heaven is likened to a man, a king, who made a marriage for his son. And he sent his servants to call them that were invited to the marriage; and they would not come. Again he sent other servants, saying: Tell them that were invited, Behold I have prepared my dinner; my beeves and fatlings are killed, and all things are ready: Come ye to the marriage.

But they neglected and went their ways, one to his farm and another to his merchandise. And the rest laid hands on his servants and, having treated them contumeliously, put them to death. But, when the king had heard of it, he was angry; and sending his armies, he destroyed those murderers, and burnt their city.

Then he saith to his servants: The marriage indeed is ready; but they that were invited were not worthy. Go ye therefore into the highways; and as many as you shall find, call to the marriage. And his servants, going forth into the ways, gathered together all that they found, both bad and good; and the marriage was filled with guests. And the king went in to see the guests; and he saw there a man who had not on a wedding garment. And he saith to him: Friend, how camest thou in hither not having on a wedding garment? But he was silent.

Then the king said to the waiters: Bind his hands and feet, and cast him into the exterior darkness. There shall be weeping and gnashing of teeth. For many are called, but few are chosen.

Exposition from the Catena Aurea

Chrysostom, *Homily 70 in Matthew*: Because he had just said that: *The kingdom of God shall be given to a nation yielding the fruits thereof* (xxi. 43), He here shows to what nation. Hence we are told:

V.1. *And Jesus, answering, spoke again in parables to them, saying:* Gloss (*interlinear*): He says, *answering*; that is, countering their evil thoughts concerning His own death. (Cf. Jn. xi. 47–54). Augustine,

Harmony of the Gospels, II, 71, 139: Matthew alone relates this parable. Luke relates one something similar; but it is not the same, as the narrative itself shows (cf. Lk. xiv. 16–24).

V.2. *The kingdom of heaven is likened to a man, a king, who made a marriage for his son.*

GREGORY, *Homily* 38 *in Gospel*: Here, *the marriage* signifies the present Church; there (*in Luke*), *the supper*, means the final and eternal banquet: for many enter the first who will leave it; while whosoever once enters the latter shall no more go forth from it. And should anyone hold that this is the same lesson, we may perhaps so understand it, that while Matthew relates the incident of the casting forth of the man who had entered without a wedding garment, Luke is silent concerning it. That the latter speaks of a *supper*, the former of a *dinner* is not a difficulty; for in former times the dinner took place daily at nones, and often dinner was also called supper.

ORIGEN, *in Matthew*, Tr. 20: The kingdom of heaven, in respect of its ruler, is likened to a man who is a king. In respect of Him Who co-reigns there, to the son of the king. And in respect of those who belong to the kingdom of the king, to the servants and those invited to the nuptials; and among these are the armies of the king. But he also says, a man who is a king, *a man, a king* (ἀνθρώπῳ βασιλεῖ: *homini regi*); that He may speak as a man to men; and may rule men not suffering themselves to be ruled by God. The kingdom of heaven shall then cease to be like to a man, when jealousy and discord and all other sins and passions have ended, and we shall have ceased to walk in the way of men, and shall see Him as He is. For now we see Him not as He is, but as He has become for our redemption.

GREGORY: God the Father made a marriage for God the Son when he joined Him to human nature in the womb of the Virgin. But because a marriage union is made between two persons, far be it from us to think that the Person of the Redeemer is made from a union of two persons. We say He has existence in and from two natures, but we shun as evil the belief that He is made from two persons. More accurately therefore may it be said that the Father King made a wedding for His Son King in this, that through the mystery of the Incarnation He united the Holy Church to Him. And the bridal chamber of This Spouse was the womb of the Virgin Mother.

PSEUDO-CHRYSOSTOM: Or again: When the resurrection of the saints is accomplished, then the Life, which is Christ, shall receive man, absorbing his mortality in His own immortality. Now we receive the Holy Spirit, as a pledge of the union to come; then we shall have Christ more fully in us (cf. I Cor. xv. 54).

ORIGEN: Or, for the marriage of the Bride and Bridegroom; that is, of Christ with the soul, understand, the reception of the Word; and for Its fruits, good works. HILARY: Justly has the Father already *made* this marriage; for this eternal association and promised union of the New Body is already perfect in Christ.

V.3. *And he sent his servants to call them that were invited to the marriage; and they would not come.*

PSEUDO-CHRYSOSTOM: Therefore, they had already been invited when he sent his servants. For men had been invited from the time of Abraham, to whom Christ's Incarnation had been promised. JEROME: *He sent his servant;* who beyond doubt was Moses, through whom He gave the Law to those invited. If however we read it as *servants,* as many copies have it, this must refer to the prophets. For those invited by them had refused to come. Then follows:

V.4. *Again he sent other servants, saying: Tell them that were invited,* etc.

By the servants sent the second time it is better to understand the Prophets, rather than the Apostles; and the same if the reading above was *servant.* But if you read it as *servants,* then the servants sent a second time are to be understood as the Apostles. PSEUDO-CHRYSOSTOM: Whom He sent when He said to them: *Go ye not into the way of the Gentiles, but rather to the lost sheep of the house of Israel* (Matt. x. 5). ORIGEN: Or, the servants first sent to call those invited to the wedding are the Prophets, converting the people by their prophecies to the joy and return of the Church to Christ. They who first invited refused to come, are they who refused to hear the words of the Prophets. The *other servants* again sent, stand for another group of Prophets. HILARY: Or, the servants first sent, to call the invited, are the Apostles. Those invited earlier who are exhorted that they should now come are the people of Israel: for they had

been called through the Law to eternal glory. It was therefore, the special task of the Apostles to admonish those whom the Prophets had invited. Those sent the second time with the task of teaching, are the Apostolic men, their successors.

GREGORY: But because those who were first invited refused to come to the marriage feast, in the second invitation He now says: *Behold, I have prepared my dinner.* JEROME: The prepared dinner, and the beeves and the slain fatlings, may be either a metaphorical description of the Royal riches; that through material things spiritual riches may be known; or we can understand here the greatness of His truths, and the fulness of God's teaching in the Law.

PSEUDO-CHRYSOSTOM: Therefore, when the Lord said to the Apostles: *Go preach, saying: The kingdom of heaven is at hand* (Mt. x. 7), by this He meant what is said here: *I have prepared my dinner;* that is, I have provided my tables with abundance from the Law and from the Prophets of the Scriptures. Hence follows: *My beeves and fatlings are killed.* GREGORY: By *my beeves (tauri mei)* are signified the Fathers of the Old Testament; who with the permission of the law gored their enemies, with the horn of physical power (cf. Deut. xxxiii. 17). *Fatlings* mean fatted animals. By these are symbolized the Fathers of the New Testament; who, receiving the sweet grace of inward enrichment, are uplifted on wings of contemplation from earthly desires to heavenly things. He therefore says: *My beeves and fatlings are killed;* as though to say: Reflect upon the deaths of the

Fathers who preceded you, and purpose some amendment of your lives.

PSEUDO-CHRYSOSTOM: Or again, He therefore says, *beeves and fatlings*, not as though the beeves were not also fat, but because not all the beeves were fattened. Therefore the *fatlings* symbolize only the Prophets, who were filled with the Holy Spirit; the *beeves* those who were priests as well as Prophets, such as Jeremias and Ezechiel: for as the beeves (*tauri*) are the leaders of the herd, so also are the Priests the leaders of the people.

HILARY: Or again, the beeves are a figure of the glorious martyrs, who confessing God were offered up as chosen victims. *The fatlings* are spiritual men, nourished on heavenly bread to soar like birds, who will fill others from the abundance they have eaten.

GREGORY: Note that in the earlier invitation nothing is said of beeves and fatlings, while in the second it is recorded that they are now killed: for the Omnipotent God, when we refuse to hear His words, will add examples: so that all we believe impossible, becomes easier to surmount, the more we hear that others have overcome.

ORIGEN: Or, *the dinner* prepared is the word of God; by *beeves* are meant certain great utterances of God; *fatlings*, the sweet and delectable. For if anyone utters words that are timid and not firm, and lacking any great power of reason, what they utter will seem thin and weak. But when with each proposition uttered examples are brought forward, replete with the proofs of reason, such discourses are fatlings. As for example, should anyone give a discourse on chastity, it might correctly be put before us as a dove. But if he utter the same holy discourse replete with solid proof from the Scriptures, so as to delight as well as strengthen the souls of his listeners, then what he has uttered is a *fatling*.

PSEUDO-CHRYSOSTOM: That He says, *and all things are ready*, is to be understood as meaning that the Scriptures are filled with what we wish to know for salvation. He who is ignorant, will find there what he needs to learn. Whoever is self-willed, what he will fear. He who is in danger, will find there what has been promised us; which will rouse him to work. GLOSS: Or, *all things are ready*, means: the entrance to the kingdom of heaven, before closed, is now open through faith in My Incarnation.

PSEUDO-CHRYSOSTOM: Or, He means, *all things are prepared*, which relate to the mystery of the Lord's Passion and our redemption. He says: *Come ye to the wedding*, not on foot, but by faith and morals. *But they neglected*. He makes clear how they neglected when He adds:

V.5. *But they neglected and went their ways, one to his farm and another to his merchandise.*

CHRYSOSTOM, *Homily 70 in Matthew:* Although these seem reasonable occupations, yet we learn from this that even if what detains us is necessary, we must place spiritual things before all others. But to me it seems that they put forward these tasks as an excuse for their own indifference. HILARY: For men are taken up with worldly ambition as with a farm; many however are held back by affairs simply through greed for money.

PSEUDO-CHRYSOSTOM: Or again: when we do something by the labour of our hands, as, for example, when we work in the fields or vineyards, or work in wood or iron, we as it were cultivate our farm. When we seek gain, but not through the labour of our hands, this may be called *merchandise*. O unhappy world! And unhappy those who pursue it! For it is ever the desires of the world that shut men out from the True Life.

GREGORY: He therefore who pretends to hold precious the Mystery of the Incarnation, and to live according to it, yet is intent on earthly labour, or given up to worldly activity, refuses to come to the royal nuptials, going as it were to his farm or to his merchandising. And often, which is more grievous, some who are called not only refuse the grace, but even act against it. So there follows:

V.6. *And the rest laid hands on his servants and, having treated them contumeliously, put them to death.*

PSEUDO-CHRYSOSTOM: Or, by the farm is signified the peoples of the Jews, whom the attraction of this world has separated from Christ. By *merchandise* is meant the Priest and other ministers of the Temple, whom, coming to the service of the Law and the Temple from the desire of gain, avarice separates from faith. Of these he did not say that they were

evilly disposed, but that *they neglected.* For they who from hate or envy crucified Christ, they were evilly disposed. But they who held back by their *merchandise* did not believe; of these it was not said that they were malignant, but that *they neglected.*

Yet the Lord is silent concerning His own death; for He had spoken of it in the preceding parable. But He makes plain to them the death of His Disciples, whom the Jews, after His Ascension, put to death; stoning Stephen and killing James the son of Alpheus; and because of these things Jerusalem was destroyed by the Romans. And let us note that anger is not attributed to God in its strict sense, but metaphorically. When He chastises, He is then said to be angry. So here we read:

V.7. *But, when the king had heard of it, he was angry.*

JEROME: When He invited to the wedding, and wrought works of mercy, the word *man* is used of Him. But now that He comes to punish, He is silent about the *man*, and speaks only of the *King*.

ORIGEN: Let them say who sin against the God of the Law and of the Prophets and of all Creation, if He (Who is here called *man* and put before us as *angry*) is the Father of Christ? If they say He is, they are compelled to confess that many things are said of Him that only apply to the passible nature of men: not that He is passible, but because He has acted in a manner that accords with the passible nature of men. And it is in this way that we are to take the anger of God, His repentance and other similar things which we find in the Prophets. Then there follows: *and sending his armies, he destroyed those murderers and burnt their city.*

JEROME: By these *armies* we understand the Romans under Titus and Vespasian who, having killed the people of Judaea, burned their traitorous city. PSEUDO-CHRYSOSTOM: The Roman army is called the army of God, because *the earth is the Lord's, and the fulness thereof* (Ps. xxii. 1). Nor would the Romans have come to Jerusalem unless the Lord had sent them.

GREGORY: Or, the Angelic Hosts are the armies of our King. Sending his armies therefore, He is said to have slain the murderers: for every judgement against man is executed by Angels. *He* therefore *destroyed those murderers,* because He slays persecutors. *He burnt their city*: for not only their souls, but also the body in which they dwelt, are tormented by the eternal fire of Gehenna.

ORIGEN: Or, *the city* of the wicked, is the assembly of those who, each according to his own dogma, concur in the wisdom of the rulers of this world. This the King burns and exterminates, as though made up of evil buildings.

GREGORY: But He Who sees Himself despised in His invitations, will not have the marriage feast of His Son empty: For at some time or other the word of God will find where it comes to rest. Hence He adds:

V.8. *Then he saith to his servants.*
ORIGEN: That is, to the Apostles; or to the Angels who have been placed over the calling of the Gentiles. *The marriage indeed is ready.* REMIGIUS: That is, the whole mystery of the Redemption of man is now prepared and perfected. *But they that were invited,* that is, the Jews, *were not worthy:* for *not knowing the justice of God, and seeking to establish their own, they have adjudged themselves unworthy of life eternal* (Rom. x. 3). The Jewish people are now rejected; the people of the Gentiles received at the marriage feast. So there follows:

V.9. *Go ye therefore into the highways; and as many as you shall find, call to the marriage.*
JEROME: For the people of the Gentiles were not in the ways, but in the *openings* of the ways (*exitibus viarum*—highways, squares?).

REMIGIUS: Which are the errors of the Gentiles. PSEUDO-CHRYSOSTOM: Or, *the ways* are all the callings of this world; as, philosophy, warfare, etc. He says therefore: *Go ye into the openings of the ways:* that they may call men of every kind to the faith. Just as chastity is a way that leads to God, so fornication is a way that leads to the devil; and so on for the other virtues and vices. He therefore commands them to invite men of every kind and condition of life to the faith.

HILARY: By *way* we must also understand the time of this world; and so they are told to go *to the exits of the ways:* for past sins are forgiven to all men. GREGORY: Or again. In sacred Scripture *ways* stand for actions. So by *the exits of the ways* we understand the failure of actions: for they whose earthly activities have failed, more readily come to God.

ORIGEN: Or again: I believe that this first call to the marriage was to certain more worthy souls. For God in the first place wishes those to come to the feast of the divine discourses who are more capable of understanding them. And since those who were of this kind would not come at this invitation, other servants are sent to urge them, and promising that, if they come, they will receive a dinner prepared by the King.

For as in corporal things, there is one who is the bride, others who invite, others who are invited to the wedding; so God knows the various orders of souls, their powers, and the reasons why some are called to the state of bride, others to the order of those servants who invite, others are numbered among the wedding guests. But they who were first invited neglected those first sent to invite them, as being poor in understanding, and went their separate ways: in which they delighted more than in the things the King had promised by His servants. Yet they are milder than those others who abused the servants sent to them, and put them to death; those, namely, who dared by means of astutely prepared arguments to hinder and gain over the servants sent to call them, and who were not prepared for answering their specious questions; and these they also insulted, or put to death. There follows:

V.10. *And his servants, going forth into the ways, gathered together all that they found, both bad and good; and the marriage was filled with guests.*

ORIGEN: The servants going forth: Christ's Apostles from Judea and Jerusalem, or the Holy Angels from their hidden dwellings, and coming to the diverse ways of diverse peoples, they gather together whomsoever they find. And they do not look to see if they had been bad or good before their calling. The *good* here means the more humble and upright of those who came to the worship of God and to whom the words of the Apostle apply: *When the gentiles, who have not the law, do the things that are of the law; these are a law unto themselves* (Rom. ii. 14). JEROME: For among the gentiles there is an infinite diversity: since we know that some are more disposed towards the vices; others because of probity of character, are devoted to the virtues. GREGORY: Or this means that in the present Church there can neither be bad without good, nor good without bad. But he is not good who refuses to put up with the bad. Then follows: *And the marriage was filled with guests.*

ORIGEN: The *marriage*, namely, of Christ and the Church, *was filled*, when those who were found by the Apostles, now restored to God, sat down at the wedding to feast. But since it was necessary that good and bad be called, not that the bad were to remain bad, but so that they should put off the garments that are unbecoming to a wedding, and put on nuptial garments (namely, the bowls of *mercy, mildness,* etc., Col. iii. 12), the King therefore comes *out to see the guests*, before the *dinner* is set before them: that He may keep with Him those wearing the nuptial garment in which He delights, and condemn those without it. Hence there follows:

V.11. *And the king went in to see the guests.*

PSEUDO-CHRYSOSTOM: Not because there is any place where He is not; but where He wills *to see*, for judgement, there He is said to be present; where He does not will, there He is as it were absent. The day of His seeing is the Day of Judgement, when He will visit the Christians; reclining at the table of the Scriptures. ORIGEN: Going in, He finds one who has not changed his manner of living. Hence there follows: *And he saw there a man who had not on a wedding garment.* He speaks of *one*: for they are all of one kind who, after faith, keep the evil disposition they had before believing.

GREGORY: What are we to understand by the nuptial garment, if not charity? Because it was in this the Lord clothed Himself, when He came to espouse the Church to Himself. He therefore goes in to the wedding feast without a wedding garment, who has faith in the Church, but not charity.

AUGUSTINE, *Against Faustus*, XXII, 19: Or, he enters the marriage feast without a nuptial garment who seeks there his own glory, not that of the Bridegroom. HILARY: Or, the nuptial garment is the grace of the Holy Spirit, and the shining lustre of that heavenly state which, received for a good confession of faith under questioning, is retained immaculate and without spot unto the assembly of the Kingdom of heaven.

JEROME: Or the nuptial garment is the commandments of the Lord, and the works which fulfil both the Law and the Gospel, and which become the garment of the *new man*, for he who bears the name of Christian on the day of judgement and is found not to possess it, shall forthwith be condemned. Hence there follows:

V.12. And he saith to him: *Friend, how camest thou in hither not having on a wedding garment?*

He calls him *friend*, because he had been invited to the wedding, as though he becomes a friend through faith. But He rebukes him for discourtesy, because he had dishonoured the nuptial perfection with his soiled garment. ORIGEN: And since he who sins, and does not put on the Lord Jesus Christ, has no excuse, there follows: *But he was silent.* JEROME: For in that hour there shall be no place for forwardness, nor opportunity for excuse; since all the angels and the world itself shall be witnesses of his sins.

ORIGEN: Not alone is he cast forth from the marriage who dishonoured the nuptials, but he is also, by the King's jailers, fettered in his power of walking, which he had not used to a good end; and in his power to lay hold of things, which he employed in no good work. He is condemned to a place that is a stranger to all light, called *exterior darkness.* So there follows:

V.13. *Then the king said to the waiters: Bind his hands and feet, and cast him into the exterior darkness. There shall be weeping and gnashing of teeth.*

GREGORY: Then by the severe sentence of Judgement, his feet and hands are bound who refused to be bound from evil works by the amendment of his life; or punishment will then bind those whom sin has now bound from good works. AUGUSTINE, *The Trinity*, XI, 6: The entanglement of evil and of distorted desires are the fetters which bind him who so acts that he is cast into exterior darkness. GREGORY: We call blindness of heart, interior darkness; exterior darkness, the eternal night of damnation.

PSEUDO-CHRYSOSTOM: Or, by this is meant the diversity of torments inflicted on sinners. For first there is exterior darkness, interior, which is lesser, then the *lowest hell* (Deut. xxxii. 22). *There shall be weeping and gnashing of teeth.* JEROME: The greatness of these torments is shown by a metaphor taken from our bodily members; in the weeping of the eyes, and the gnashing of the teeth. See also in the binding of hands and feet, in the weeping of the eyes, and in the gnashing of teeth, a proof of the truth of the resurrection of the body.

GREGORY: So that there teeth may gnash which here took delight in gluttony; there eyes shall weep which here turned hither and thither in unlawful desire: for each single member shall suffer punishment for the sins in which they served as instruments. JEROME: And since in the marriage feast it is not the beginning that concerns us, but the end: there is added:

V.14. *For many are called, but few are chosen.*

HILARY: To invite all without distinction is a refinement of public benevolence. To be *chosen* from among the invited, or *called*, will depend on the worth of our merits. GREGORY: For there are some who do not even begin to do good; and some do not continue in the good they begin. The less therefore each man knows what is to come, the more must he look with fear to himself.

PSEUDO-CHRYSOSTOM: Or again: As often as God tries His Church, He goes in to it, to see the guests. And should He find one not having on a wedding garment, He asks him: Why did you become a Christian, if you neglect these works? Christ then delivers such a one to His ministers; that is, to certain masters of seduction; and they bind *his hands*, that is, his good works, and *his feet*, that is, the movements of his soul; and they cast him into exterior darkness; that is, amid the errors of the Gentiles, or of the Jews, or into heresy. The nearer darkness is that of the Gentiles; for they have not heard the truth they reject. The exterior darkness is that of the Jews, who have heard but have not believed. But the outermost darkness is that of heretics, who have both heard and learned the truth.

I. ORIGEN, PRIEST AND CONFESSOR

On those called to the Wedding[1]

And Jesus answering, spoke again in parables to them, saying: The kingdom of heaven is likened to a man king, who made a marriage for his son. And he sent his servants to call them that were invited to the marriage, etc., to the words: *For many are called but few are chosen.*

This parable also appears clear and easy to understand. In it a man, indeed a king, is put before us as a figure of God and the Father of Christ; the nuptials of the king's son as the restoration of the Church, the Bride of Christ, to Christ her Spouse; the servants sent to call those invited to the wedding stand for the prophets who by their prophesies strove in due season to recall the people from the error of their ways, to lead them to the joy of the restoration of the Church to Christ.

But those first called would not come; and they are those who would not hear the prophets. The other servants sent are another group of prophets. The dinner prepared, and for which the kings beeves and fatlings were slain, is the strong and rational food of the soul of God's mysteries. So too that *all things are prepared,* means the divine revelation which shall make known to us all things; so that when that which is perfect shall come (I Cor. xiii. 10), they shall eat and drink who have obeyed the summons to the feast.

Since however of those called by the prophets, some neglected only their words, and turned themselves to profane and earthly things, but did no evil against them, so wishing to show this difference, He says: *But they neglected, and went their ways, one to his farm, and another to his merchandise. But the rest laid hands on his servants, and having treated them contumeliously put them to death.* Then following this simple outline, we understand the anger of the king; of which the Apostle says, speaking of the Jews: *The wrath of God is come*

upon them to the end (I Thess. ii. 16). Here the war against the Jewish nation, the capture of Jerusalem and the destruction of its people, that followed Christ's advent is foretold; *And sending his army he destroyed those murderers and burnt their city.*

II. The words that follow: *Then he saith to his servants: The marriage indeed is ready; but they that were invited were not worthy. Go ye therefore to the exits of the ways; and as many as you shall find, call to the marriage,* may be referred to the Apostles of Christ saying to the Jews: *To you it behoveth us first to speak the word of God; but, because you reject it and judge yourselves unworthy of eternal life, behold, we turn to the Gentiles* (Acts xiii. 46).

The *exits of the ways* (highways) are therefore the state of those outside Israel, among whom those *found* by the Apostles are *called* to the wedding; the Apostles gathering in all whomsoever they found. And they found those who gave ear to them; and calling them, they did not concern themselves as to whether they were bad or good before the call: for they called all they found. The good are here to be understood as the more virtuous of those who gave themselves to the service of God, to whom these words of the Apostle can be applied: *For when the Gentiles, who have not the law, do by nature those things that are of the law; these, having not the law, are a law to themselves: Who show the work of the law written in their hearts, their conscience bearing witness to them* (Rom. ii. 14, 15).

And when the marriage of Christ and the Church is filled with guests, and the restoration of those found by the Apostles is complete, they sit down to enjoy the wedding. Then, since they had to call both bad and good, not however that the bad were to remain bad, but so that taking off and casting aside the garments unfitting the wedding, they should put on wedding garments, that is, the bowels of mercy, benignity, humility, modesty, patience (Col. iii. 12): for these are wedding garments; because of this then the king goes in to see the guests before the dinner; the beeves, namely, the slain fatlings and all that was *made ready* is put before them, so that He may note carefully those who have on a wedding garment, and seeing it rejoice, and may pronounce sentence on those who are without one.

Going in therefore He finds one of those who were called, and came in answer to the call, but who had not changed his manner of life and neither had he put on a wedding garment, and he said to him: *Friend, how camest thou in hither not having on a wedding garment?* Then since he was a sinner, and not renewed,[2] and had not put on the Lord Jesus Christ, and being without any ground of excuse, he is silent. And so it is written: *But he was silent.* Nor is it enough that he is sent forth from the wedding feast who had proved unworthy of his invitation; the king's jailers must also bind fast the wickedness which had not suffered him to do what he should have done, and the power of action he had not used to do good. Not alone is he cast forth from the wedding, he is also condemned to the place that is a stranger to all light, where there is a darkness deeper than darkness, and called *exterior darkness.*

And if there should be one of us, coming at the invitation of the king to the wedding of his son, and should he appear to have obeyed the call and to have come with those who were called, but has not put on the wedding garment of which we have been speaking, he shall suffer these things and, bound hand and foot, shall be thrust out into exterior darkness, there, according to the words: *Woe to ye that now laugh: for you shall mourn and weep* (Lk. vi. 25); to weep with those who have committed sins deserving of mourning and weeping. They shall weep, mourning their own miseries. Then that the Word might show us the fear and trembling, the sadness, the sorrow and pain in which they shall be who have not put on a wedding garment, He says: *There shall be weeping,* and not alone weeping, but *gnashing of teeth.* And that He may teach us that though many are called, not all, but only a few of these, have come, He brings the whole parable to an end with the words: *For many are called, but few are chosen.*

III. I have said these things of the parable taken as a whole. We shall now endeavour, going over it again, to search into it to the best of our power, trusting in the help of the Spirit of wisdom, that we may be able to add certain deeper meanings which we have found relating to this parable, and shall set them forth for you or, according to what is fitting, give you a hint of them or pass them over in silence.[3] The kingdom of heaven then is likened, as to its ruler, to a man who is king; and, as to the one who rules together with the king, to his son. As to those subject to the king's rule, it is likened to the servants and to those invited to the marriage, of whom some would not come, while others simply neglected and went their ways, one to his farm and another to his merchandise. And the rest laid hands on his servants and having treated them insultingly they put them to death. Moreover, of those subject to the king there was also his army; and those gathered in, bad as well as good, from the highways until the marriage was filled with guests; and also the *one* sitting among the guests, who had not on a wedding garment, and likewise the jailers, who were told to bind the hands and feet of *the one* who had not on a wedding garment, and to cast him into exterior darkness.

It might well have been written that *The kingdom of heaven is likened to a king*, without the addition of the word, *man*. But since the word *man* has been added, it must be explained and it is, in my opinion, to be explained in this way: Before our time there was one who wrote a book explaining the allegories of the Sacred Writings,[4] and also the words which reveal God as sharing our feelings, and those which manifest His Divinity. Wishing to make clear to us that God may be said to be like a man, in His care for us, he quotes the words: *The Lord thy God hath carried thee, as a man is wont to carry his little son* (Deut. i. 31). But in another place, to show us that God is not as man, he quotes the words: *God is not as man, that he should lie* (Num. xxiii. 19).

IV. But in the Gospel there is a great abundance of figures in which God, in certain parables, is likened to a man. Let us therefore, in defence of those who say that God the Father

of Christ does, in a manner of speaking, feel as man, make use of these parables which speak of God as man, and say in answer to the heretics, who through not understanding similar expressions in the writings of the Old Testament offend against the laws of God and the prophets and the Creator of the whole world, let us say that: If according to the parables of the Gospel God is likened to a man, why may we not in accord with these same parables accept His anger as a parable, His wrath as a parable, His repentance, His turning away His face, His sitting down, the standing, walking of God as parables. His sleep, of which mention is made in the prophets, either they have not noticed it, or they must agree that it also is a parable. And let us also say to them: If you do not wish to accept, in accord with the parable, that God is spoken of as a man, or that the Scriptures also speak parabolically of His as feeling like a man, explain how the God of all creation Who, according to you, has nothing of man in Him, is spoken of in the Gospel as *a man*? What is more, we shall prove to them that they have not looked closely into the writings of the New Testament in which, according to this parable before us, a man king, who made a marriage for his son, was angry with those who would not, in answer to his invitation, come to the wedding, and also against those who, neglecting the wedding dinner, went one to his farm and another to his merchandise. And he was also angry against those who had laid hands on his servants, and had insulted them, and put them to death. Let them say if this man, who was made angry, is not, as making a marriage for his son, the Father of Christ, or if it is some one other than the man who, as the parable tells us, was angry is His Father.

In either case they are straitened. For either they will not have the man who was angry, and who made a marriage feast for his son, for the Father of Christ: because of this anger; or else, because of the nuptials and the son, they are forced to admit He is the Father of Christ and that He was angry. And if they should attempt to qualify this, we shall say to them: 'Ho there! What sort of distinction is this? You cannot run away from the fact that the man in the Gospel making a marriage for his son was angry, and you cannot put another in his place. Because of this word, *angry*, and others like it, you are trying to fashion from the Law and the Prophets a God other than the God of the Law and the Prophets.'

V. As long therefore as we are men, and it is therefore not fitting for us, lest we be blinded, to subject to scrutiny the riches of God's goodness, and the great immensity of the goodness that is hidden within Him, it is necessary that for us the kingdom of heaven be likened to a man king, that God may talk as a man to men and, by speaking through prophets, and by governing through men, rule men who are reluctant to be ruled by God, while remaining in all respects as God. And this likening of the kingdom of heaven to a man shall cease, when *envying and contention* cease, and with them all misery and sinfulness, and when men cease to walk *according to man* (I Cor. iii. 4), and when we have

become worthy of hearing from God: *I have said: You are Gods, and all of you the sons of the Most High* (Ps. lxxxi. 6) or worthy of Christ Himself, as no longer doing these things for which we might be told: *But you like men shall die* (v. 7).

I believe however that not only will this comparison of the kingdom of heaven to a man come to an end, but a thousand other things as well of which man, hardened by sin, is now in need: such as the figure Osee the prophet writes of: *For I will be like a lioness to Ephraim and like a lion's whelp to the house of Juda* (v. 14); and in another place: *I will meet them as a bear that is robbed of her whelps* (xiii. 8). He will therefore cease to be now like a panther, now a lion, now a hungry bear, when men no more do the things that demand that He should be as a panther or a lion or a bear, and He, having no longer concern for those who would make this necessary, will show Himself to us as He is. So I understand the words: *Our Lord is a consuming fire* (Deut. iv. 24), for whatsoever there is that deserves to be burned, the Lord is a fire consuming it. And when that has been destroyed by the Consuming Fire which is to be destroyed by It, our God will no longer be a Consuming Fire, but Light only; as John teaches us where he says: *God is light* (I Jn. i. 5).

Having gone into these things, see if you can understand in this sense that sentence in the Catholic epistle of John (I Jn. iii. 2) which reads: *Dearly beloved, we are now the sons of God; and it hath not yet appeared what we shall be. We know that when he shall appear we shall be like to him; because we shall see him as he is.* For even now if we are worthy of seeing God with our mind and heart, we do not see Him as He is, but as He became for us for our redemption. But at the end of things, and *in the times of the restitution of all things, which God hath spoken of by the mouth of his holy prophets, from the beginning of the world* (Acts. iii. 21), we shall see Him, not as now, which is not seeing Him, but shall see Him, fittingly, as He is.

VI. Having said these things on the words: *The kingdom of heaven is like to a man, a king,* we shall be able to find the reason why the Saviour frequently calls Himself *Son of man,* or *the Son of Man,* making clear to us that, as God in His government of man is spoken of in the parable as man, and is depicted like one; so also the Saviour, while being primarily the Son of God, and also God, and the Son of His love, and *the image of the invisible God* (Col. i. 13, 14), does not remain in that which He primarily is, but, in accordance with His plan Who in the parable is called man, while being God, became *the Son of man*; in conformity with God, Who when ruling men is spoken of in the parable as *a man,* and is shown as like one.[5] But we must not then seek out what man, and then say the Saviour is His Son, but, resting on this notion of God, and following the parables that speak of Him as man, let us listen carefully when He speaks of Himself as *the Son of man.* For us therefore as men, the kingdom of heaven is likened to a man king; but for those whom the Scripture speaks of as gods, of whom it is said: *God hath stood in the congregation of gods: and being in the midst of them he judgeth gods* (Ps. lxxxi. 1),

the kingdom of heaven is like to a God King.

VII. Since God has likened the kingdom of heaven to a man king for us men, who are lower in our nature than the Angels, Thrones, Dominations, Principalities and Powers, you will ask if among the Thrones the kingdom of heaven is like to a Throne king, among Dominations to a Domination king, among Principalities to a Principality king, among Powers to a Power king? For someone will say: The kingdom of heaven is likened to a man king for the sake of those of a lower nature, why will the same analogy not hold for those of a higher nature?

Now He who is likened to a man king, making a marriage for his son, sent his servants to call those who were invited to the wedding. And observe if you will that the bride is different from the servants who do the calling, and from those invited to the wedding. So in mystical things some are called to the place of bride, some to the ranks of those sent to call those invited to the wedding. And besides these there is a third order: those namely, who were invited to the wedding. God knew these diverse orders of souls or the virtues they possessed, and the reason why some have been received into the company of the bride, others into the ranks of the servants sent to call those invited to the wedding, and yet others among those called. In spiritual nuptials, reflect that in the communion of the Spouse, the Word with the soul, the bride wedded to the Word, bringing forth in due time, is not corrupted, but through daily communion with Him partakes of His immortality, and brings forth fruits worthy of such nuptials.

VIII. Again, in such nuptials let your mind take note that the dinner prepared is from the strong food contained in spiritual writings;[6] and understand that the strength of the food, figuratively speaking, is in the *beeves*, and the spiritual part of this same contemplation is in the slain *fatlings*. And by *all things are ready* understand, continuing the analogy of bodily things, every other form of spiritual contemplation. For the king in his regal abundance prepares for us a dinner worthy both of his kingdom and his riches.

It seems to me that the first call to the wedding was to certain more virtuous souls among the people of Israel. For from the beginning God invited them to come to this blessed repast, through those calling, by the word of His teaching, the souls more disposed to receive it. And we see that these were not willing to come at His invitation, and so *other servants* are sent to call those who would not come, and to promise them that, should they come in answer to the call, they would partake of a dinner prepared by the king: of his *beeves*, which among clean animals are held as cleaner than all clean animals, and of his *fatlings*, that is, of a varied and multifold setting forth of His thoughts upon each and every question; as though a *fatling* stands for the expression of something we have thought about, or discussed and defined, and called figuratively a slain victim, which contains a full and clear exposition of a proposed question; just as if, for example, were we to put forward a few weak arguments in proof of

some question, these might well be regarded as poor and worthless offerings, or, to describe them more aptly, as lean and fleshless; not such as those prepared by the king for his dinner, of which, he says: *my beeves and fatlings are killed*, and therefore: *all things are ready*; so that, in the company of his children, and with the bringing forth of the spiritual wine jars, each servant in turn may bring to the dinner those things in which he particularly has learned to minister. And exhorting those whom I may, according to the parable, call *others*, he says to them: *Behold, I have prepared my dinner; my beeves and fatlings are killed, and all things are ready. Come ye to the marriage.*

IX. But those first called, being poor and wanting in understanding, neglecting, went their way; busy with their own affairs, and rejoicing in them rather than in the things promised by the king through his servants, And see how one of them having a farm does not come to the wedding; another, given to his business, hurries away to imitate as it were what is told in the parable of the buyer of pearls, *seeking good pearls*, and finding one of great price, sells his others to buy this one (Mt. xiii. 45). However, his was not prosperous merchandising, for, going to it, he who was invited to the wedding has no part in the dinner prepared by the king, no part in the beeves and fatlings that were slain nor in all the other things that were made ready. As many therefore of those called who were discerning, but did not come to the call, yet did not insult the servants sent to call them, nor kill them, and were more restrained than those who dared to do such things, go peacefully on their way, one to his farm, another to his merchandise.

Leaving these, let us see who the *others* are. It seems to me that these have fallen through their own contentious and deceptive speech, by which they held, or seem to hold the servants sent to them, and who are unprepared to answer their inventions. And so they insult those who were made ministers of the call. And we see those sent in the service of the divine truth, and willing with divine wisdom to make it known, made sport of by men who have understanding, but have no will to believe the truth. Some are even killed by them, and it is with these the king is said to be angry, and, later, that which is called *the wrath of God came upon them in the end* (I Thess. ii. 16).

And the effect of His anger was to send the army of the king, the multitude of the heavenly host, or those angels who have been charged with His punishments. And they destroy the murderers of the servants of His Word, and the king burns their entire city: The city and as it were the assembly of those who, each according to his own notion, are bound together in the wisdom of the teaching of the rulers of this world; which the king burns and destroys as built up of evil buildings. And when you see the confutation of those professing false knowledge, or of those asserting the truth of every sort of notion, and their complete overthrow, you need not hesitate to say that this was done by the army of God, burning the cities of the enemies of the truth. And after Christ's sojourn on earth, the city of the Jewish teaching was burnt. And when it was burnt, the king said to his servants, the Apostles of Christ, or to the Angels of God who are placed over the calling of the gentiles: *The marriage indeed is ready; but they that were invited were not worthy. Go ye therefore into the highways, and as many as you shall find, call to the wedding.*

And so we see from every private path, and from the common beliefs of those who live the life of the gentiles, from cities and towns and villages men called to the wedding by those to whom the command was given to do this. *And his servants going forth*, that is, either the Apostles of Christ from Judea and Jerusalem, or the blessed angels from within the bounds of their heavenly home, and coming to the public highways they gather in and bring together all the bad, if they find them: so that putting off their wickedness, as a garment unfitting for the wedding, they may, together with those who are called *good*, put on the wedding garment, and fill the marriage with guests.

X. Then when *the marriage was filled with guests*, and they were resting in the faith and service of God, the king comes that he may carefully examine and judge those who sit at table, to rebuke and punish whoever has not on a wedding garment. Before the others he places the dinner he had prepared: the slain fatlings and the beeves and all the rest he had made ready. One, He saw, who had not put on a wedding garment: for they are all of one kind and one character who cling to the wickedness that adhered to them before they believed and will not put it off. And he rebukes him for the evil he had done in presuming to come to this wedding without clothing himself in a wedding garment: the garment of virtue, that shining cloak Solomon commanded in Ecclesiastes: *At all times let thy garment be white* (ix. 9).

But he who had dared to enter these splendid nuptials without a wedding garment, was silent; unable to speak. And as deserving of judgement and damnation, he is condemned by the king, who commands his servants, some from the army we have spoken of, to bind his hands and feet: the hands and feet he had not used as he should have used them (for he had not walked in the way that was fitting, nor done what he ought to have done); and to cast him forth, not only from the nuptial feast, but cast him into that exterior darkness which is a stranger to all light, so that longing for light in that outer darkness, he may implore with tears the God who has the power to have mercy on him and deliver him from there, and that he may gnash his teeth who in wickedness ate bitter grapes and set his teeth on edge: *Every man that shall eat the sour grape, his teeth shall be set on edge* (Jer. xxxi. 30). For we believe that by bitter grapes is meant the malice of those who neither forget the things behind, nor long for the things to come, but stand ever in the same place, when they ought to seek the maturity and taste the sweetness of virtue.

Because of the many who were called, and were not worthy, He concludes the whole parable with the words: *For many are called.* Because of the many who came to the wedding, and the fewness of those who sat down to the dinner, He says: *But few are chosen.* And whoever considers the crowded assemblies of, to use a simpler term, the churches, and tries to learn how many there are who live as they should, *reformed in the newness of the mind* (Rom. xii. 12), and how many live slothfully and indifferent, *and conformed to this world,* he will learn how true are the words of the Saviour, that: *Many are called, but few are chosen.* And also what He said elsewhere: *Many seek to enter and shall not be able* (Lk. xiii. 24); and also: *Enter ye in at the narrow gate; and few there are that find it* (Mt. vii. 13, 14). Amen.

II. St Augustine, Bishop and Doctor

The Wedding Garment: Meditation[7]

Matthew xx. 1–14

I. *The Twofold Banquet of the Lord: Here, of the Faithful; in heaven, of the Blessed.*

The faithful all know of the nuptials of the King's Son and of His *dinner,* and of the abundance of the Lord's Table; prepared for every man's desiring. But it is important how each one approaches it; when he is not forbidden to approach. The Holy Scriptures teach us there are two banquets of the Lord: one to which come both good and bad; and one to which the bad do not come. At this banquet then of which we have just now been hearing while the Gospel was read to us, both good and bad are clearly present. All who had excused themselves from this dinner are bad; but not all who came are good. I therefore address myself to you as good guests, sitting down at this banquet: to every one of you who keeps in mind that it was said: *He that eateth and drinketh unworthily, eateth and drinketh damnation to himself* (I Cor. xi. 29). All you who are of this mind, I exhort you; not to look for the good outside you, and to bear with patience the bad within.

II. *In this life all the just are bad and good.*

I do not doubt that Your Charity would like to know who they are to whom I addressed myself, exhorting them not to seek the good without, and to bear patiently the bad within. If all are bad within, to whom did I address myself? And if all are good within, whom did I exhort to bear the wicked in patience? Let us therefore with God's help first end this question. If you reflect clearly and fully upon what good is, there is no one good but God alone. The Lord Himself tells us this very plainly. *Why asketh thou me concerning good? No one is good, but God alone* (Mt. xix. 17). How then were there good and bad at these nuptials if no one is good but God alone?

First you must know that in a certain measure we are all bad. Beyond doubt to a certain degree we are all bad: we are all of us in a measure not good. We may in fact compare ourselves with the Apostles, to whom the Lord Himself says: *If you then being evil know how to give good*

gifts to your children (Mt. vii. 11). If we examine the Scriptures, one there was among the twelve Apostles who was bad; because of whom the Lord said in a certain place: *And you are clean, but not all* (Jn. xiii. 10). Addressing them all together, He says: *If you being evil.* Peter heard this. John heard it. Andrew heard it. The remainder of the twelve Apostles heard it. What did they hear? *If you then being evil know how to give good gifts to your children; how much more will your Father who is in heaven give good things to them that ask him?* Hearing they were evil, they were in despair; hearing that God was their Father in heaven, they breathed again. *You,* He says, *being evil.* And what is due to the evil but punishment? *How much more,* He says, *will your Father, who is in heaven?* What is due to children but a reward? In the very name of *the wicked,* there is apprehension of punishment. In the name, *children,* the hope of inheritance.

III. *Who are the bad that are shut out from the Feast?*

They therefore who under one aspect were evil, are the same as those who under another aspect were good. For to those to whom He said: *You being evil know how to give good gifts to your children,* He goes on to say: *How much more will your Father who is in Heaven?* The Father therefore of the *evil;* but not of those who are to be left in their evil: for He is the Physician of those who are to be saved. They were therefore in a measure evil. And yet they were the guests of the Father at the royal nuptials: because they were not, I believe, of that number of whom it was said: *They invited both bad and* good; in the sense that they were not in the number of the bad, whom, we heard, were shut out in him who was found not wearing a wedding garment. In one way, I repeat, they were bad who were good. In another they were good who were bad. Listen to John telling us in what sense they were bad. *If we say that we have no sin, we deceive ourselves and the truth is not in us* (I Jn. i. 8). You see in what sense they are bad: because they sinned. In what way were they good? *If we confess our sins, he is faithful and just, to forgive us our sins and to cleanse us from all iniquity* (v. 9).

If then, according to this interpretation which you have heard me put forward, as an opinion, from the holy Scripture, we say that the same men are in a measure good, and in a measure bad; if we accept in this way the words, *They invited both good and bad,* that is, the very same persons as being both good and bad; if we desire to accept this, we are not permitted to do so, because of him who was found *not having on a wedding garment,* and who was not only cast out, to exclude him merely from the banquet, but also condemned to the punishment of eternal darkness.

IV. *By the one shut out many are signified.*

But someone will say: What difference should one man make? What wonder, what great thing is it, if one who had not a wedding garment crept in among the crowd unknown to the servants of the Host? Could it, because of him, be said that *they invited both good and bad?* Listen then, my brethren, and understand what I am saying. This one man stands for one kind of men; and they were the *many.*[8] Here some careful listener may answer me and say: 'I do not want to hear *your* opinions. I want you to prove to me that this *one* stood for the *many.*' As God will help me, I shall prove this clearly; nor do I need to look far to prove it. The Lord will help me with His own very words; and will through me provide what shall make it plain to you.

We see how the Master of the house *comes in to see the guests.* Notice here, my brethren, that the servants' task was simply to invite and bring in the good and bad. Notice that it is not said that The *servants* looked closely at the guests and among them they find a man not having on a wedding garment, and that they spoke to him. No; this is not what was written. It is the Master of the house who looks closely at them, the Master of the house who finds him, the Master of the house who points him out, the Master of the house who speaks to him apart. This was not meant to be passed over. But it is something else that we have undertaken to prove to you; namely, how the *many* were this *one.*

The Master of the house then *went in to see the guests; and he finds there a man not having on a wedding garment. And he said to him: Friend, how camest thou in hither not having on a wedding garment? But he was silent.* For He Who asked could not be deceived. And this garment is seen in the heart, not on the body: were it worn outwardly, even the servants would have noticed him. Learn how the wedding garment is worn, where He says: *Let thy priests be clothed with justice* (Ps. cxxxi. 9). Of this same garment the Apostle says: *Yet, so that we be found clothed, not naked* (II Cor. v. 3). And so he is found by the Lord who was not seen by the servants. Questioned, he is silent. He is bound, cast forth, condemned; one for many.

Often have I said, Lord! Thou dost admonish one, to admonish us all. Recall with me the words you have heard, and at once you will find, at once you will see, that this *one* was the *many.* The Lord no doubt questioned one man, and said to one man: *Friend, how camest thou in hither? One* had remained silent; and of this *one* was it commanded: *Bind his hands and feet, and cast him into the exterior darkness. There shall be weeping and gnashing of teeth.* Why this? *For many are called, but few are chosen.* How can anyone contradict the clarity of this truth. *Cast him,* He says, *into exterior darkness.* This *one,* undoubtedly; of whom the Lord says: *For many are called, but few are chosen.* Therefore, it is not the *few* who are cast out. It was clearly this *one;* who had not on a wedding garment. Cast *him* out. Why is he cast out? *For many are called but few are chosen.* Leave the *few;* cast out the *many.*

He was beyond doubt one. Yet this one was not only the *many,* but they surpassed by a multitude the number of *the good.* The good also are many, but in comparison with *the wicked,* the good are few. Many are the grains of the wheat; but compared with the chaff, the grains are few. The good we speak of in themselves are many; in comparison with the bad they are few. How do we prove they are many? Because *Many shall come* from the east and from the west. To what shall they

come? To that feast to which both good and bad enter. And speaking of another feast, He adds: *And shall sit down with Abraham and Isaac and Jacob in the kingdom of heaven* (Mt. viii. 11). This is the feast to which the wicked shall not come. Let us receive worthily this present feast, so that we may come to that other.

These then are many, who also are few: many in themselves, few in comparison with the wicked. What then is it that the Lord is saying? He find one, and He says: 'Let the many be cast out; let the few remain.' For when He says: *Many are called but few are chosen,* He means to show us clearly who, in this present feast, are to be regarded as the *chosen;* who shall be brought to that other feast, to which none of all the wicked shall come.

V. *What is the Nuptial Garment?*

What follows? All you who approach the Lord's Table, I would that you shall not be among those who are to be shut out with *the many,* but shall be safe with *the few.* And how can you make sure of this? Put on the wedding garment. You will say to me: Explain to us what is this wedding garment? Beyond all doubt it is the garment only the good wear; those who are to remain at the feast, and who are to be saved for that feast to which none of the bad come; conducted there by the Lord's grace: These possess the wedding garment.

Let us then, my brethren, seek among the faithful those who possess something the bad have not; and this will be the *wedding garment.* If we say the Sacraments; you can see how they are shared in common by good and bad. Is it Baptism? No doubt without baptism no one can come to God: but not every one who receives baptism comes to God. I cannot therefore look on baptism as the nuptial garment; that is, the sacrament itself; a garment which I see on the good and see on the bad. The altar, perhaps? Or That which is received at the altar. We see that many eat of It, and eat and drink judgement to themselves. What then is it? Fasting? The wicked also fast. Is it running to the church? The wicked run there too. Is it working miracles then? Not only do good and bad work miracles, but at times not even the good work them. In the Old Testament we saw how the magicians of Pharaoh worked miracles, while the Israelites did not (Exod. vii). Among the Israelites only Moses and Aaron worked miracles; the rest did not; but they saw them, and feared, and believed. Were Pharaoh's magicians working miracles more worthy than the people of Israel, who were unable to work them; though they were the chosen people of God? Hear what the Apostle says; of the Church itself: *Are all prophets? Are all workers of miracles? Do all speak with tongues?* (I Cor. xii. 30).

VI. *Charity is the Nuptial Garment. Other gifts without charity avail nothing. Charity and desire in man.*

What therefore is this nuptial garment? Here is the nuptial garment: *Now, the end of the commandment*, says the Apostle, *is charity from a pure heart, and a good conscience, and an unfeigned faith* (I Tim. i. 5). This is the Nuptial Garment. Not any charity; for often they who seem to love each other are men who share an evil conscience. They who join together to rob, who do evil together, who have a common love of sinful spectacles, who delight together in the chariot races and gladiatorial combats, such as these for the most part love each other. But in them there is no charity, from a pure heart, a good conscience, and from faith unfeigned.

This is the charity of the Nuptial Garment. *If I speak with the tongues of men, and of angels, but have not charity, I am become as sounding brass, or a tinkling cymbal* (I Cor. xiii. 1). They who had only *tongues* came, and they were asked: Why have you come in here not having on a wedding garment? *If I should have prophecy*, he says, *and should know all mysteries and all knowledge, and if I should have all faith, so that I could remove mountains, and have not charity, I am nothing* .These are the wonders of men who oftentimes do not possess the Nuptial Garment. If I have all these things, he says, and have not Christ, I am nothing. *I*, he says, *am nothing.*

Is the gift of prophecy then nothing? Is knowledge of the mysteries nothing? It is not these gifts that are nothing: but I, if I have them, and have not charity, I am nothing. How many gifts profit us nothing without this one gift? If I have not charity, and yet should give alms in abundance to the poor, and confess unto blood, unto the stake, the name of Christ, such things can be done from vain glory, and be nothing. And so since such things can be done from the love of vain glory, and not from that most enriching charity which is the love of God, he goes on to name them; and let you hear them. *If I should distribute all my goods to feed the poor, and if I should deliver my body to be burned, and have not charity, it profiteth me nothing.* Here then is the Wedding Garment. Examine yourselves; if you possess it, you shall be without fear at the banquet of the Lord.

There are two things in the same man: love and desire. Let love be born in you, if it is not born already. And if it is born, let it be fostered, et it be nourished, let it grow. But as to desire, though it cannot be wholly extinguished in this life: for, *if we say that we have no sin, we deceive ourselves, and the truth is not in us* (I Jn. i. 8): in the measure there is desire in us, in that measure we are not without sin. Let love increase; desire decrease; so that the one, charity, may be perfected, and desire extinguished.

Put you on the Nuptial Garment: I am speaking to you who do not yet wear it. You have already come in; you are now drawing near to the banquet; and you have not yet put on a garment in honour of the Bridegroom. You are still seeking the things that are your own, *not the things that are Jesus Christ's* (Phil. ii. 21). For the Wedding Garment is put on in honour of the Wedding; that is, in honour of the Bride and Bridegroom. You know the Bridegroom: it is Christ. You know the Bride: the Church. Honour the Bride: Honour the Bridegroom. If you fittingly honour the spouses, you shall be their children. Therefore go forward in this. Love the Lord, and there learn to love yourselves; so that when you have learned by loving the Lord to love yourselves, you may then safely love your neighbours as yourselves. For when I meet one who does not love

himself, how can I entrust a neighbour to him, to love him as himself?

But who is he, you will say, who does not love himself? This is who he is: *He that loveth iniquity, hateth his own soul* (Ps. x. 6). Does he love himself, who loves his body, but hates his soul, to his own loss, to the loss of his soul and body? And who loves his own soul? He who loves God with his whole heart and with his whole mind. To such a one I would then entrust a neighbour. Love your neighbours, as you love yourselves.

VII. *My neighbour, every man.* Someone asks: Who is my neighbour? Every man is your neighbour. Have we not all two common parents? Animals of every species are neighbours to each other, a dove to a dove, a leopard to a leopard, an asp to an asp, a sheep to a sheep; and should man not be neighbour to man? Remember the order of the Creation. God spoke, and the waters brought forth living things, and swimming things, great whales, fishes, winged things and such like. Did all birds come from one bird? All vultures from one vulture? All goldfish from one goldfish? All sheep from one sheep? It was the earth brought forth all these kinds of creatures at one and the same time. Then man came; but the earth did not bring man forth. For us one source was created; not two, a father and mother. One person was made our parent, I repeat, and not two; a mother and father. But from the one father came one mother. He came from no one, but was made by God; and she came from him (Gen. i, ii).

Consider our beginning. We have come in a stream from one fountain. And because that turned bitter, all of us from being of the true olive have become of the wild olive. And then grace came. *One* man begot us unto sin and death; yet as one race, as neighbours one to another; and not only alike, but also related one to another. Then came *One* against the *one*. Against *the one* who scattered, came One Who gathers. And against *the one* who killed, *The One* Who gives life. *For as in Adam all die, so in Christ all shall be made alive* (I Cor. xv. 22). But as everyone born of the first man dies; so everyone who believes in Christ, is given life. But only if he has a Nuptial Garment; if he is invited as one who is to remain, not one to be cast forth.

VIII. *Not every kind of faith is praised.*

Therefore, my brethren, let you have charity. I have explained to you what is the Nuptial Garment; I have placed the Garment before you. Faith is praised; it is well known that faith is praised. But what faith an Apostle points out. For the Apostle James rebukes certain persons who glory in the faith, yet do not lead good lives, and says: *Thou believest that there is one God, Thou dost well: the devils also believe and tremble* (James ii. 19). Recall with me why Peter was praised, why he was called blessed. Because he said: *Thou art Christ the Son of the Living God* (Mt. xvi. 16). He Who declared him blessed was not thinking of the sound of his words, but of the disposition of his heart. Would you like to know how Peter's blessedness did not come from these words? Because the demons also spoke them. *We know thee who thou art, the Holy One of God* (Mk. i. 24). Peter

confessed the Son of God. The demons confessed the Son of God. 'Make this clear, master, make it clear' (*you say*). I shall make it clear. Peter spoke in love; the demons from fear. Towards the end, Peter said: *I am ready to go with thee even to death* (Lk. xxii. 33). *They* said: *What have we to do with thee?* (Mt. viii. 29).

You therefore who have come to the banquet, glory not in faith alone. Make clear your faith, and then the Wedding Garment will be seen in you. Let the Apostle make this clear; let him teach us: *Neither circumcision availeth anything, nor incircumcision; but faith.* Tell us what faith: do not even the demons believe and tremble? I shall tell you, he says. Listen. I shall make this clear: I shall now make the distinction. *Faith that worketh by charity* (Gal. v. 6). What faith then? What kind of faith? Faith that worketh by charity. *If I should have all knowledge,* he says, *and all faith, so that I could remove mountains, and have not charity, I am nothing.*

Have faith with love, for love without faith you cannot have. I warn you of this. In this I exhort you; this I teach Your Charity in the Name of the Lord; that you have faith with love: for it is possible to have faith without love. I am not exhorting you to have faith, but to have charity. For you cannot have charity without faith: I mean the love of God and your neighbour: where can these come from without faith? How does anyone love God, who does not believe in God? How does the fool love God who says in his heart: *There is no God* (Ps. xiii. 1). It could be that you believe Christ has come, yet not love Christ. But it cannot be that you love Christ, yet affirm that Christ has not come.

IX. *Charity to be extended to enemies.*
Prayer against enemies, lawful and
lawful.

Therefore, let you have faith with love. *This* is the Wedding Garment. You who love Christ, love one another: Love your friends, love your enemies. Let this not be a burthen for you. What can you lose, where you gain so much? How could you ask of God as a special favour, that your enemy may die? That is not the Wedding Garment. Think of Him, the Bridegroom, hanging upon a Cross for you; and praying to His Father for His enemies. *Father,* He says, *forgive them, for they know not what they do* (Lk. xxiii. 34). You have looked in thought upon the Bridegroom as He speaks these words. Look also upon a friend of the Bridegroom; a guest in his Wedding Garment. Think of the blessed Stephen: how he rebuked the Jews, as though angry and enraged: *You stiff-necked and uncircumcised in heart and ears, you always resist the Holy Ghost. Which of the prophets have not your fathers persecuted* (Acts vii. 51)? You hear how severe he is with his tongue. Hitherto you were ready to speak against anyone; would that you might speak against one who is offending God, not someone offending you. He offends God, and you do not rebuke him. He offends you, and you cry out. Where is this Wedding Garment?

You have heard how fiercely Stephen rebuked. Now hear how he loved. He offended those he rebuked, and *they stoned him.* Pressed on all sides, struck with stones, beaten by the hands of raging men,

his first words are: *Lord Jesus Christ, receive my spirit.* Then after he had, standing upright, prayed for himself, falling on bended knees, he prays for those who are stoning him to death, and says: *Lord, lay not this sin to their charge. I die in the flesh.* Let them not die in their heart. And saying this, *he fell asleep in the Lord.* Having said these words, he spoke no more. He spoke, and departed; his last words a prayer for his enemies. Learn here how to hold fast to your Wedding Garment. Let you too bend the knee, and beat your brow to the ground, and as you are about to approach the Table of the Lord, to the banquet of the Holy Scriptures, do not say: 'Lord, that my enemy may die. Lord, if I deserve anything of Thee, slay my enemy.' And should you chance to say this, are you not fearful He will answer you: 'If I must slay thine enemy, I must first slay thee. Is it because you came when you were invited, that you now think so highly of yourself? Remember what you were a little while ago? Did you not blaspheme against Me? Did you not mock Me? You wished, did you not, to wipe My name from the earth? And now you flatter yourself because you came when invited. Had I slain you when you were My enemy, whom would I make My friend? How can you teach Me in your evil prayer, to do what I have not done to you?'

Rather, God will say to you: 'Let Me teach you to imitate Me. Hanging on the Cross, I said: *Forgive them, for they know not what they do.* I taught this to My soldier. Let you be My recruit against the devil. In no other way can you fight invincibly, except you pray for your enemies.

Say it, by all means; say even this; say that you seek vengeance against your enemy; but say it with understanding. Make clear what you are saying. Here is a man who is your enemy. Tell Me: what is it in him makes him your enemy? Is it because he is a man, he is your enemy? No. Then what? Because he is evil. That he is a man, that I made him, it is not this makes him your enemy.' Then He will say to you: 'I did not make an evil man. He became evil through disobedience; obeying the devil, rather than God. What he has done, it is this makes him your enemy. Because he is evil, he is your enemy; not because he is man. For I hear the words, *man* and *evil*. One is the name of a creature; the other of sin. I heal sin. I save the creature!'

And then thy God says to thee: 'Behold: I *shall* avenge thee! I *shall* slay thy enemy. I shall take from him what is evil; I shall save what is man. If I make him a good man, do I not slay thy enemy, and make him thy friend?' So ask what you are asking; not that men may perish, but that enmities may perish. But if you ask for this: that a man may die; this is the prayer of one evil man against another. And when you say Slay this evil man, God will answer you: 'Which of you?'

X. *Love to be spread abroad, that it may seize all men to God.*

Spread wide your love, and not only to your wives and children. Love such as that we find also in sheep and sparrows. You know how sparrows and swallows love their mates, how both will hatch their eggs, and both feed the young with a certain sweet and natural goodness, without thought of recom-

pense. The sparrow will not say: 'I feed my young, so that when I am old, they will feed me.' It has no such thought. It loves freely, and nourishes freely. It bestows the love of a parent, looking for no return. And I know, I have seen, that so do you love your children. *For neither ought the children to lay up for the parents, but the parents for the children* (II Cor. xii. 14). Many even give this as an excuse for their eagerness for money; that they desire it for their children, and save it for them. But let you spread wide your love. Let this love grow. To love your wives and children is not yet the Wedding Garment. Have faith in God. First love God. Extend your love to God; and seize whomsoever you can for God. You have an enemy. Seize him for God. A wife, a son, a slave. Bring them to God. Here comes a stranger. Bring him to God. An enemy; seize him for God. Bring him, bring your enemy. Bring him; he is no more your enemy.

So let charity be perfected in us; so let it be nourished; that nourished, it may be perfected (I Jn. ii. 5). So do we put on the Wedding Garment. So the image of God, in which we were made, is incised anew by this perfecting. It became defaced by sin, and worn away. How was it defaced? How was it worn away? When we rubbed it against the earth. What does this mean; rubbing it against the earth? When we yield to earthly passions; for, *truly man passeth as an image; and he is disquieted in vain* (Ps. xxxviii. 7). We look for truth in God's image; not vanity. When we love truth that image in which we were made is renewed, and we render tribute to our Caesar in His own coin. And this you have learned from the answer the Lord made to the Jews who came tempting Him. *Why do you tempt me, ye hypocrites? Show me the coin of the tribute;* that is, the impress of the image, and its superscription. Show Me what you pay, what you offer, what is demanded of you; show it to Me. They show Him a *denarius*, and He asks whose image and superscription is on it. They answer: *Caesar's.* That other Caesar; and he seeks his own image. Caesar will not lose what he commanded; and God will not lose what He has made. Caesar, my brethren, did not make the coin. The mint made it. He gave the order to his ministers. Then craftsmen were told to make it. An image was stamped on the coin. The coin bears Caesar's image. And it is what others stamped he demands. He amasses it; he will not be denied. But the coin of Christ is man: There is Christ's Image; he bears Christ's Name. His the task of Christ; his the gifts of Christ.

Turning then to the Lord our God, let us as best we can give thanks with all our hearts, beseeching Him that in His goodness He will graciously hear our prayers and by His power drive evil from our thoughts and actions, increase our faith, guide our minds, grant us His holy inspirations, and bring us to joy without end through His Son our Lord and Saviour Jesus Christ. Amen.

III. St Gregory the Great. Pope and Doctor

On the Gospels[9]

Given to the People in the Basilica of the Blessed Martyr Clement

Matthew xxii. 1–13

1. I propose, if I am able, dearest brethren, to go briefly through the text of the Gospel lesson, so that I may then be free to speak more at length. But let us first see whether this account, which is from Matthew, is the same as that given in Luke under the name of *Supper* (Lk. xiv. 16)? There are no doubt certain things in which they seem to disagree: for here a *dinner* is spoken of, there a *supper.* Here, he who came to the wedding in unfitting garments was cast out, there we do not read that anyone who entered was cast out. And from this we may rightly gather, that in this account the wedding is a figure of the present Church, and that in the other the *supper* is a figure of the final and eternal Banquet: for into the former many enter who will go forth again, while he who once enters the latter shall never more leave it.

And should someone say that this is the same lesson as that of Luke, I think it is better, subject to the claims of faith, to give way to another's opinion than give time to discussion; since we may well believe that Matthew speaks of the one cast forth who came without a nuptial garment, while Luke is silent about him. That one speaks of a *dinner*, the other of a *supper* does not in any way conflict with our understanding of the lesson; since in former times the dinner was at the ninth hour, and dinner was also called supper.

2. I recall that I have frequently said that in the holy Gospel the present Church is often spoken of as the kingdom of heaven. Because the assembly of the Just is called the kingdom of heaven. And since the Lord says through the prophet: *Heaven in my throne* (Is. lxvi. 1); and Solomon says: *The soul of the just is the seat of wisdom*[10] (Wis. vii. 27); and since Paul also says: *Christ is the power of God and the wisdom of God* (I Cor. i. 24), we may therefore clearly gather that if God is wisdom, the soul of the just a seat of wisdom; and, since it is said that Heaven is God's throne, the soul of the just is therefore heaven. This is the reason the Psalmist says of the holy preachers of the Gospel: *The heavens show forth the glory of God* (Ps. xviii. 2). The Church of the Just therefore is the kingdom of heaven: for since their hearts long for nothing on this earth, desiring only the things of heaven, the Lord as it were already reigns in them as He reigns in heaven. It is because of this He says that: *The kingdom of heaven is likened to a man, a king, who made a marriage for his son.*

3. Your Charity already understands who this king is, the Father of the Son King. He to whom the Psalmist says: *Give to the king thy judgement, O God: and to the king's son thy justice* (Ps. lxxi. 2). He it is who *made a marriage for his son.* For God the Father made a marriage for

God the Son, when He joined Him to human nature in the womb of the Virgin, when He willed that He Who was God before all ages should at the end of ages become man. But because this union is wont to be made from two persons, far be it from our minds to believe that the Person of our Redeemer Jesus Christ, God and man, became one from two persons. We do indeed confess that He has existence in and from two natures; but we shun as evil the belief that He is made up from two persons. We can therefore clearly and securely maintain that the Father made a marriage for the King His Son in this, that through the mystery of the Incarnation He joined Him to the Holy Church. And the womb of the Virgin Mother was the bridal chamber of This Spouse. And because of this the Psalmist says: *He hath set his tabernacle in the sun: and he, as a bridegroom coming out of his bride-chamber* (Ps. xviii. 6). As a Bridegroom He came forth from His bridal chamber: for God Incarnate came forth from the immaculate womb of the Virgin to unite the Church to Himself.

He therefore sends His servants to invite His friends to these nuptials. He sent once. He sent again: for He first made the Prophets and then afterwards the Apostles, the preachers of the Lord's Incarnation. He therefore twice sent His servants to invite: by the Prophets he said that the Incarnation of His Only-begotten was to come; by the Apostles He announced that this had come to pass. But because they who were first invited to the wedding feast would not come, in the second invitation He now says: *Behold, I have prepared my dinner; my beeves and fatlings are killed, and all things are ready.*

4. What are we to understand by *beeves and fatlings*, dearest brethren, if not the Fathers of the Old and New Testaments? For since I am speaking to all the people it is necessary for me to explain also the words of the Gospel lesson. *Fatlings* mean fattened beasts; the word fatling coming from the verb to fatten. And since it was written in the Law, that: *Thou shalt love thy neighbour and hate thy enemy* (Matt. v. 43; Lev. xix. 18), it was then lawful for the Just to crush with all their might the enemies of God and of themselves and smite them with the sword. In the New Testament this beyond all doubt came to an end, when Truth Itself proclaimed in His own words: *Love your enemies, do good to them that hate you* (v. 44). Of whom then are the *beeves* a figure, but of the Fathers of the Old Testament, who when by the permission of the Law they struck their enemies with the retaliation of hate, what were they, if I may speak so, but as the oxen which gore their enemies by the strength of their horns? And what do *fatlings* stand for if not the Fathers of the New Testament, who, receiving the graces of inward enrichment, and fighting against earthly desires, are borne upwards towards heavenly things on the wings of spiritual contemplation? For to give our thoughts to this world here below, what is this but a certain aridity of mind? But they who by their understanding of heavenly things are in their holy desires fed from on high with the food of innermost delight, now grow fat as it were because of this more abun-

dant nourishment. It was on this richness the Prophet longed to be fattened, when he said: *Let my soul be filled with marrow and fatness* (Ps. lxii. 6).

But since the messengers who were sent as preachers of the Lord's Incarnation, the Prophets first, and afterwards the Holy Apostles, suffered persecution from the unbelieving, He therefore says to those who were invited and would not come: *My beeves and fatlings are killed, and all things are ready.* As though to say more openly: 'Reflect upon the deaths of the Fathers who went before you, and give thought to the dangers that threaten your own lives.' Note that in the first invitation nothing is said of *beeves* and *fatlings*, but in the second we are told that the beeves and fatlings are now killed: for Almighty God, when we will not learn from His words, will add examples, that we may more readily hope in all that we now believe impossible, when we learn of others who have already passed this way.

5. Then follows: *But they neglected and went their ways, one to his farm and another to his merchandise.* To go to *his farm*, is for a man to give himself beyond due measure to earthly labour. To go to his *merchandise* is to long for the gains of worldly pursuits. For he who is now intent on earthly labour, now given to the pursuits of this world, yet pretends to ponder the mystery of the Incarnation and to live according to it, going as it were to his farm or to his merchandise, refuses to come to the wedding of the king. And very often, and this is more grievous, some will not alone refuse the grace of the one

calling them, but will even persecute him. Because of this there follows: *The rest laid hands on his servants, and having treated them contumeliously, put them to death. But,
when the king had heard of it, he was
angry; and sending his armies, he
destroyed those murderers and burnt
their city.*

He destroyed the murderers, in
that He put the persecutors to death.
He burnt their city: for not alone
their souls, but also the flesh in which
they dwelt is tormented in the
eternal fire of gehenna. Sending His
armies He is said to destroy the murderers: for every judgement against
men is carried out by angels. For
what are the angelic hosts but the
armies of our King? Because of this
the same king is also called *Lord of
Sabaoth. Sabaoth* is interpreted to
mean *Lord of hosts.* He therefore
sends His armies to destroy these
adversaries; for the Lord does indeed
execute vengeance by means of His
angels. Our Fathers of old learned
the might of His vengeance; and we
have seen it. For where now are the
proud persecutors of the martyrs?
Where are they who in the pride of
their hearts were uplifted against
their Creator, and swelled with the
death-bringing glory of this world?
Lo, the death of the martyrs now
flowers in the faith of the living, and
they who gloried in cruelty against
them are unremembered, even
among the number of the dead. We
have therefore learned from history
what we are now hearing in the
parable.

6. But He Who sees His invitations despised will not have the
marriage of His Son empty. He
sends word to others: for though

the word of God labours with some,
yet in time it will come to where it
will find rest. And so there is
added: *Then he saith to his servants:
The marriage indeed is ready; but they
that were invited were not worthy. Go ye
therefore into the highways; and as many
as you shall find, call to the marriage.* If
in Holy Scripture we understand
ways for deeds, then by *the openings of
the ways (exitus viarum)* we must
understand the failure of men's
deeds: for they for the most part
come more readily to God who have
not prospered in their earthly under-
takings. Then follows: *And his servants, going forth into the ways,
gathered together all that they found,
both bad and good; and the marriage was
filled with guests.*

7. We are now clearly shown
from the condition of the guests
that these nuptials of the king signify the present Church, in which
the bad sit down together with the
good. And the diversity of her
children has been mingled: for so
she brings all men to the faith, yet
she does not, because of the pressure
of evil, lead all men through amendment of life to the grace of spiritual
freedom. As long as we live here
below, we must travel the way of
this world together. But when we
reach the world beyond, there we
shall be separated one from the
other. For nowhere are there truly
good only, save in heaven; and nowhere are there evil only, save in
hell. And so this life which lies between heaven and hell, as though it
stood between them, receives subjects from both sides; whom however Holy Church now receives
without distinction, but will afterwards separate at their going forth.

If you are good, therefore, as long as you are in this life, suffer the bad in patience. For whoever does not bear with the bad, bears witness against himself that he is not good. For he refuses to be Abel, who will not bear patiently the malice of Cain. So on the threshing floor the grain is buried in the chaff. So do flowers grow among thorns; and on the rose that perfumes grows a thorn that stings. The first man had two sons; one was chosen, the other rejected (Gen. iv). Noah brought three sons into the Ark, of whom two were chosen, and one was rejected (Gen. xxvii). Abraham had two sons; one was chosen, the other condemned (Gen. xxi). Isaac had two sons; one was chosen, the other condemned (Gen. xxvii). Jacob had twelve sons. Of these one was sold because of his uprightness; the rest in their malice were the sellers of their brother. Twelve Apostles were chosen; but one was mingled with them to prove him, eleven to be approved (Jn. vi. 71). Seven deacons were ordained by the Apostles (Acts vi. 5); and while six persevered in true faith, one was the author of error (Apoc. ii. 6).

In this Church therefore there can be neither bad without good, nor good without bad. And so, dearest brethren, recall to mind the times (of the martyrs) now passed, and arm yourselves to bear with the bad in patience. For if we are their children, we must walk in the way they went. For he is not good who will not suffer the wicked in patience. Because of this the blessed Job says of himself: *I was the brother of dragons, and companion of ostriches* (Job xxx. 29). Because of this Solomon speaking in the voice of the Bridegroom says to Holy Church: *As the lily*

among thorns, so is my love among the daughters (Cant. ii. 2). Because of this the Lord said to Ezechiel: *O son of man, thou art among unbelievers and destroyers, and thou dwellest with scorpions* (Ezech. ii. 6). For this Peter glorifies the life of the blessed Lot, saying: *He delivered just Lot, oppressed by the injustice and lewd conversation of the wicked; for in sight and hearing, he was just, dwelling among them who from day to day vexed the just soul with unjust works* (II Peter ii. 7, 8). Because of this Paul commends and confirms the lives of the disciples: *In the midst of a crooked and perverse generation; among whom you shine as lights in the world, holding forth the word of life* (Phil. ii. 15). And for this John bears witness to the Church at Pergamus: *I know where thou dwellest, where the seat of Satan is. And thou holdest fast my name and hast not denied my faith* (Apoc. ii. 13).

Here then, dearest brethren, going briefly through nearly all of them, we learn that he was not a good man who would not bear in patience the perverseness of the bad. For, if I may say so, the iron of our soul will not come to fineness of understanding, so long as it has not been burnished by the file of another's perversity.

8. And it should not frighten you that in the Church the bad are many and the good few. For the Ark, which in the midst of the Flood was a figure of this Church, was wide below and narrow above, and at the summit measured but one cubit (Gen. vi. 16). And we are to believe that below were the four-footed animals and serpents, above the birds and men. It was wide where the beasts were, narrow where men lived: for the Holy Church is in-

deed wide in the number of those who are carnal minded, narrow in those who are spiritual. For where she suffers the morals and beastly ways of men, there she enlarges her bosom. But where she has the care of those whose lives are founded on spiritual things, these she leads to the higher place; but since they are few, this part is narrow. *Wide indeed is the gate and broad is the way that leadeth to destruction; and many there are who go in thereat. How narrow is the gate that leadeth to life; and few there are that find it* (Mt. vii. 13)!

The Ark is made narrow at the summit, so that it is but one cubit wide: because, of those in the Church, the holier they are, the fewer they are. She reaches her highest perfection in Him Who alone among men was born Holy, and there is none to be compared with Him. He Who, in the words of the Psalmist, *has become as a sparrow all alone on the housetop* (Ps. ci. 8). And so the more the wicked abound, so much the more must we suffer them in patience; for on the threshing floor few are the grains carried into the barns, but high the piles of chaff that are burned with fire.

9. Since you have now through the grace and bounty of the Lord entered the house of His nuptials, that is, the Holy Church, watch carefully, brethren, so that the King when He comes in may not rebuke you for something on the garment of your soul. For with fear and trepidation are we to reflect on the words that now follow. *And the king went in to see the guests; and he saw there a man who had not on a wedding garment.*

What, dearest brethren, are we to think He means by a *wedding garment*? If we say it is baptism or faith, who is there that has entered these nuptials without baptism or without faith? For whosoever is outside, it is because he has not yet believed. What then are we to understand by the wedding garment, if not charity? For whoever in the Church possesses faith, but has not charity, comes in to the wedding, but does not come in with a wedding garment. Rightly is charity called a wedding garment; for our Creator wore this upon Him when He came to the marriage of Himself with the Church. It was solely through the charity of God that His Only-Begotten joined to Himself the souls of the chosen among men. It was because of this that John says: *For God so loved the world, as to give his only begotten son for us* (Jn. iii. 16).

He therefore Who came to men because of charity, has made known to us that charity is the wedding garment. And each one of you who through believing is now within the Church, has already come to the wedding. But he comes without a wedding garment who does not safeguard within him the grace of charity. And we know well, brethren, that if anyone were invited to an earthly marriage, he would change his garments, and try to show by the suitability of his dress that he shared in the joy of the bride and bridegroom; and he would be ashamed to be seen in soiled garments among the guests rejoicing and celebrating there. We have come to the nuptials of God, and we do not trouble to change the garment of our soul. There is joy among the angels at the coming of the

Elect to heaven. With what mind do we look upon these spiritual nuptials who have not the wedding garment, namely, charity, which alone makes us pleasing to God?

10. We should know that just as a garment is woven between two beams, an upper, namely, and a lower, so charity is made from two precepts; namely the love of God, and the love of our neighbour. For it is written: *Thou shalt love the Lord thy God with thy whole heart and with thy whole soul and with all thy strength; and thy neighbour as thyself* (Mk. xii. 30). And here let us note that the measure of our love for our neighbour is laid down for us: *Thou shalt love thy neighbour as thyself:* While there is no measure given for the love of God, when we are told that: *Thou shalt love the Lord thy God with thy whole heart and with thy whole soul and with all thy strength.* For no one is told how much he must love, but from how much, where it says: *With thy whole heart* (*Ex toto*); for he truly loves God who leaves nothing of himself for himself.

Therefore, if we desire to have a wedding garment at the *marriage*, we must keep these two precepts of charity. It is for this we read in the prophet Isaias that the porch of the gate of *the city built upon a mountain* measured two cubits;[11] for the approach to the heavenly city is not opened to us, if while we are in this Church (which since it is still without *outside*, is called the *porch*), if we do not fulfil the love of God and of our neighbour. Because of this was it commanded, that the curtains of the Tabernacle of the Temple should be woven of scarlet linen,

twice dyed (Exod. xxvi. 1). You, dearest brethren, you are the curtains of the Tabernacle who by your faith veil within your hearts the secrets of heaven. But the curtains of the tabernacle must be *twice dyed*. This dye has the appearance of fire. And what is charity if not fire? And this charity must be twice dyed: once with the love of God, and once with the love of our neighbour. For he who so loves God that through contemplation of Him he neglects his neighbour, is indeed dyed, but not twice dyed. And again, he who so loves his neighbour that through love of him he puts aside the contemplation of God, is dyed, but he is not twice dyed.

That your charity therefore may be twice dyed, let it enkindle within it both the love of God, and the love of our neighbour; in that it shall not, out of compassion for our neighbour, forsake the contemplation of God, nor cleaving more than it ought to the contemplation of God, throw from it compassion for its neighbour. Every man therefore who lives among men, let him long after Him Whom his soul desires, yet so that he does not abandon him with whom he runs; but let him so help his neighbour, that the love of Him to Whom he runs, may not grow cold.[12]

11. We must also understand, that this love of our neighbour is divided into two precepts; since a certain wise man says: *See that thou never do to another what thou wouldst hate to have done to thee by another* (Tob. iv. 16). And the Truth Itself, in His own words, proclaims: *Whatsoever you would that men should do to you, do you also to them* (Mt. vii. 12). For

if we do to others that which we justly wish that they would do to us, and keep from doing to others that which we wish others would not do to us, we shall then have preserved intact the claims of charity. But let no one, when he loves someone, think to himself that he now begins to possess charity, until he has first examined the motives of his love. For if one loves another, but does not love him for God's sake, he has not charity, but thinks he has. But when we love our friend in God, and our enemy because of God, this is true charity. He loves for God's sake, who loves those whom he knows do not love him. Charity is proved true solely by means of its opposite: hate. And so because of this the Lord Himself says to us: *Love your enemies. Do good to them that hate you* (Lk. vi. 27).

He then loves securely, who for God's sake loves him by whom he knows he is not loved. These are great precepts, sublime precepts, and to many hard to fulfil: nevertheless this is the wedding garment. And whoever sits down at the wedding without it, let him watch in fear, for when the king comes in, he shall be cast forth. For here we are told: *The king went in to see the guests; and he saw there a man who had not on a wedding garment.* We, dearest brethren; *we* are the guests sitting at the nuptials of the Word, we who through faith have already entered the Church, we who eat of the food of the sacred Scriptures, we who rejoice that the Church is united with God. Consider carefully, I beseech you, whether you have come to these nuptials wearing a wedding garment; look with searching anxiety into your thoughts. Examine your hearts on each single thing: To see that there is now no hate there against anyone, that you do not burn with the flame of envy of another's happiness, that you are not striving with hidden malice to injure anyone.

12. Now the King comes in to the marriage, and looks at the garment of our heart, and He finds one not clothed in charity, and forthwith He is angry and says: *Friend, how camest thou in hither not having on a wedding garment?* We wonder greatly, dearest brethren, that He should call him *friend*, and yet rebuke him; as though He said very plainly: '*Friend*, yet not a friend; friend through faith, yet not a friend in deed.' *But he was silent.* For in the dread severity of that final Judgement, of which we can scarce speak without tears, all making of excuses is at an end; for He outwardly rebukes us, Who, as the voice of conscience, inwardly accuses the soul.

But besides these things we must know, that whoever possesses this garment of virtue, but does not yet possess it to perfection, should not despair of pardon at the coming of the merciful King; for He Himself gives us hope through the voice of the Psalmist, saying: *Thy eyes did see my imperfect being, and in thy book all shall be written* (Ps. cxxxvi. 16). Since we have spoken these few words to console the one who has this garment, but who is still weak, we shall now address our words to him who is wholly without it. Then follows:

13. *Then the king said to the waiters: Bind his hands and feet, and cast him into the exterior darkness. There shall*

be weeping and gnashing of teeth. Then through this dread sentence, their hands and feet are bound who now will not restrain them from evil deeds, through amendment of life. For then chastisement shall bind those whom sin now restrains from doing good. For the feet that cared not to visit the sick, the hands that gave nothing to those in need, are now through their own fault no longer free to do what is good. Those therefore who now of their own free will are bound fast in sin, shall then against their will be bound fast in torment.

Rightly is it said that he shall be cast into *exterior darkness.* For we call blindness of heart, interior darkness; exterior darkness, the eternal night of damnation. Each one therefore who is damned, is cast, not into interior, but into exterior darkness: for there against his will he shall be cast forth into the night of damnation who here of his own will has fallen into blindness of heart; where, we are told, there shall also be *weeping and gnashing of teeth*: so that there teeth shall gnash which here delighted in gluttony, there eyes shall weep which here turned hither and thither in wanton desire. For each single member shall suffer punishment for the sins for which they were used in this life.

14. And when this *one* has been cast forth, in whom manifestly the whole body of the wicked is set before us, straightaway He adds a general sentence, which says: *For many are called, but few are chosen.* Dearest brethren, we should fear with a great fear the words we have just now heard. All we here present, already called through faith, have come to the marriage of the Heavenly King. We believe and confess the mystery of His Incarnation, and we partake of the banquet of the Divine Word. But in a day to come the King of Judgement will enter in among us. That we are called, we know; that we are chosen, we do not know. And so the more each one of us knows not whether he is chosen, so much the more do we need to humble ourselves in humility. There are, we know, those who do not even begin to do good; and some who do not remain constant in the good works they begin. Another is seen to pass almost his whole life in evil-doing, but close to the end he is drawn back from wickedness through tears of earnest repentance. Another seems to lead the life of one of the elect, and yet it happens that at the end of his life he will turn aside to the wickedness of heresy. Another begins well, and ends even better; while another, from his first years, gives himself to every evil, and growing ever worse than himself is destroyed in the midst of these very evils. In the measure therefore that each one knows not what is yet to come, in that measure should he live in fear and anxiety for himself before God: *for,* and let us say it over and over again, and let us never forget it, *many are called, but few are chosen.*

15. But since sometimes the minds of those who listen are converted more by the example of the faithful than by the words of their teachers, I must tell you of something which lately happened; and which will cause your hearts to fear, the more the closely it speaks to them. For we are not speaking of things of long

ago, but of events of which witnesses still live, who declare that they were present at what we shall now relate to you.

My father had three sisters, who were all three consecrated virgins. Of these, one was called Tarsilla, another Gordiana, and the third Emiliana. All were converted by the same love, and all three were consecrated at one and the same time; living under the same austere rule, and leading a common life in their own house. And having continued a long time in the same manner of life, Tarsilla and Emiliana began through daily increase in virtue to grow in love for their Creator, and, while present solely in the body, to turn daily more towards eternal things. On the other hand, the spirit of Gordiana began day by day to fail in the warmth of its love, and began little by little to return to the love of this world. Often Tarsilla would say sorrowfully to her sister Emiliana: 'I see that our sister Gordiana is not of our mind. I think she is drifting away from us; and that she has not her heart in her vocation.' And so they would chide her gently; seeking with mild correction to bring her back from her new lightness of manner to her former way of life. And in the middle of their words of correction, she would of a sudden resume her former serious manner. But within an hour, this seriousness would leave her, and soon she would again resume her new levity of speech and manner. She took much pleasure in the company of lay girls, and soon it became difficult for her to put up with anyone who was not given over to this world.

On a certain night, Felix, my

ancestor, *admirable for age and glory* (2 Mac. xv. 13), and a former bishop of this Roman Church, appeared, in a vision as she afterwards related, to Tarsilla, my aunt, who among her sisters had advanced furthest in seriousness of life, and in repute and height of sanctity by virtue of her continuous prayer and her extraordinary abstinence, He showed her the perpetual glory of the home of the blessed, saying to her: 'Come, for I shall receive thee in this mansion of light.' Soon after she was taken ill of a fever, and in a little while came to her last day. And as many people come to noble men and women when they are dying, to comfort their neighbours, so at the very hour of her death many men and women stood about her, among whom also was my mother, when suddenly looking upwards the dying woman saw Jesus coming, and began to cry out with great anxiety to those standing around her: 'Stand back, stand back, Jesus is coming.' And as she stretched towards Him Whom she beheld, that holy soul was separated from her body. And then of a sudden an odour of such wondrous sweetness spread about, as though this sweetness also would show them that the Author of all sweetness had come there.

And when, as is the custom with the dead, her body was unclothed to be washed, it was found that the skin on her knees and elbows had from prolonged and continuous prayer become hard like that of a camel; so that her body bore witness to what her loving spirit had urged it without ceasing. And this took place on the day before the Lord's Birth. And very soon after this she appeared to her sister,

Emiliana, in a vision of the night, and said to her: 'Come, for as I passed the Lord's Day of Birth without thee, I shall pass the holy day of His Manifestation (Epiphany) with thee.' Emiliana, ever anxious for the salvation of her sister Gordiana, at once answered: 'And if I come alone, to whom shall I entrust our sister Gordiana?' To which with a sorrowful countenance she replied, as was afterwards related: 'Come, for Gordiana our sister is now numbered among those who belong to the world.' This vision to Emiliana was soon followed by an affliction of body, and, just as had been foretold, her sickness growing rapidly worse, she died on the day before the Lord's Manifestation. Gordiana, as soon as she found herself alone, increased her worldliness of life, and later did in deed what she had before desired in thought. For forgetful of her fear of the Lord, forgetful of shame and of reverence, forgetful of her dedication to God, she later married the steward of her lands.

See how in the beginning all three were converted by the same eager love, but they did not persevere with one and the same earnestness of heart; for, as our Lord here tells us: *Many are called, but few are chosen.* I have related these things to you for this reason; so that no one among you who has already given himself to a good work, may attribute to himself the virtue of his good work, and so that no one may rest confident in his works; for if he knows what he is today, he does not know what he may be tomorrow. Let no one therefore rejoice as safe in his good works; for as long as he is in this uncertain life, he knows not what his end will be. But as I have

told you something that may have caused you fear from its divine severity, I shall relate to you another happening, from near at hand, which will console your hearts because of its divine mercy; and I remember having already related this happening in another sermon, but you were not present at it.

16. About two years ago a certain brother came to my monastery, which stands close to the church of the blessed martyrs John and Paul, to enter the monastic life. He was, according to the rule, deferred, but was in time received. His brother followed him into the monastery; not out of desire for the monastic life, but because of earthly affection. He who had joined the monastic life greatly pleased the brethren. But his brother however was very different from him; in his life and character. He lived in the monastery of necessity rather than inclination. And when he revealed himself as depraved in his whole conduct, he was endured patiently by all for the sake of his brother. He was frivolous in speech, evil in action, careful as to his dress, but disordered in his conduct. He could not endure that anyone should speak to him of the life of the holy habit. His life became a burden in the sight of all the brethren; but nevertheless, as I said, for the sake of his brother he was suffered by all. Should anyone say anything to correct him, he spurned them. He was unable not only to do good, but to listen to good. He swore, angry and mocking, declaring that never would he take the habit of our holy way of life.

But in the midst of the pestilence which lately consumed a great part of the people of the city, he too was struck in the groin, and soon died. And as his end came near, the brethren assembled around him, that they might help him by prayer at his going forth. His body was already dead at its extremities; only in his breast did the vital heat remain. And as they saw he was about to die, the brethren began to pray the more earnestly for him, Of a sudden he began to cry out as loud as he could to the brethren standing by, interrupting them in their prayer; exclaiming: 'Keep away, keep away. I am given over to the Beast to be devoured; and because of your presence he cannot devour me. He holds my head in his jaws. Go away, that he may not torment me longer; let him do what he wants to do. If he is to devour me, why must I be delayed because of you?'

The brethren then began to say to him: 'What are you speaking of? Make the sign of the Cross on yourself.' He answered as best he could: 'I want to bless myself, but I am unable; I am pinned down by the Beast.' And when the brothers heard this, prostrate upon the ground, they began with tears to beg ever more earnestly for his deliverance. And lo, of a sudden the sick man became better, and began to cry out with what voice was left to him, and to say: 'Thanks be to God; the Beast who had seized me to devour me has fled; he could not

remain, being driven away by your prayers. Pray now for me; for forgiveness of my sins; for I am ready to be converted, and to wholly forsake the life of the world.'

This man then who, as I said, was already dead in his extremities, but yet still lived, was converted with his whole heart to God. And in this state of conversion he was chastised by prolonged and unceasing pain, and, his weakness of body increasing, after a few days he died. And dying he did not now see the Beast; for he had defeated him through his own change of heart. See now, my brethren, how Gordiana, of whom I spoke earlier, fell from the perfection of her holy habit to punishment, while this brother of whom I have told you turned back at the moment of death, to life eternal.

No one therefore knows what is laid down for him in the hidden judgements of God; because *many are called, but few are chosen.* And because there is no one who is certain that he is chosen, then let all be in fear, let all be concerned for their deeds, let all rejoice in the divine mercy, and let no one presume on his own merits and good works. There is One Who shall crown our hope in Him, He namely Who deigned to take our nature upon Himself: Jesus Christ, Who with the Father and the Holy Ghost liveth and reigneth God, world without end. Amen.

NOTES

1 PG 13, col. 1524, *Tomus* XVII, Comment. *In Matthaeum*, par. 15. This detailed exegetical and mystical exposition of Origen may help to end a certain measure of neglect of this great parable which, in the minds of some, is known only as a strongly dramatic account of a wedding feast, with a certain application to Christian life. It is the last

great figure of the Kingdom of Heaven given us by our Lord; a synthesis of God's Plan of Redemption, leading to the predestined end of the divine economy of the Redemption: the Judgement: and terminating with the sharpest, most ominous warning given by our Lord. Conjectures are at times introduced, and not pursued; but the whole root of Christian life is carefully examined.

The two homilies which follow are also lengthy, and of great seriousness. But it has to be kept in mind that these homilies cannot be other than serious, and at times lengthy, as well as substantial discourses. For here, more especially in the last two, in the Providence of God, two of the greatest Doctors of the Church are setting forth, with holy care and precision as well as with profound knowledge, the belief and interpretation of the Church regarding the Divine Scriptures, in the light also of its equally Divine Tradition: the sources of Divine and Catholic Faith, deriving from the Divine and Incarnate Wisdom.

[2] A verb first used by St Paul: ανακαινόω, *I renew; I make new again;* cf. Titus iii. 5: μὴ ανακαινωθεὶς *neque renovatus.* A possible allusion to confession and renewal in Christ through the Holy Spirit.

[3] A possible implicit reference to the practice of *reserve* (later known as *the discipline of the secret*); according to which knowledge of the more intimate mysteries was kept carefully from the heathen and even from those undergoing instruction in the Faith with a view to reception. A precaution based presumably on Matthew vi. 6; Hebrews v. 16.

[4] *The Allegorical Commentary,* of Philo, a learned Jewish writer of Alexandria. Born *c.* 26 B.C.

[5] From this our Saviour is called the Son of man: because He is the Son of the One referred to in this parable as *a man king* (ἀνθρώπω βασιλεῖ: *homini regi*). The omission in English (and certain other vernaculars) of a rendering of the qualifying *man, homini,* is singular in view of its significance. The *Vetus Interpretation* of Origen's text (an *interpretatio*) reads: *Efficitur secundum dispensationem filius hominis ejus qui in parabolis dicitur, et fit quasi homo.*

[6] Ἐν πνευματικὸις λογικὸις, may well be rendered, *in spiritual reading;* which is the nourishment of the soul. For λογικός has also reference to writing: to prose.

[7] PL 38, col. 559, *The Nuptials of the King's Son and on Charity (against the Donatists).* Preached in the basilica called *Restituta* in Carthage; which with many other Catholic churches seized by the Donatists, had lately been restored to their original owners. The sermon contains a wealth of the acutest spiritual and mystical instruction; deriving from the virtue of charity. Such a discourse would now scarcely find a ready appreciative audience; but his African congregations seem to have possessed a swift discernment of the higher truths of the faith; a gift one notes among their descendants. It is a meditative discourse on the Gospel of today, requiring much attention and reflection.

[8] *Many are called, but few are chosen.* One was cast forth. The *chosen* are not cast forth, we may believe. Therefore, this *one* must represent the *many* not chosen. This act of expulsion was done to *the body of the*

wicked; which had not a wedding garment. Cf. *Sermo* XCV, col. 583, PL 38.

⁹ PL 76, col. 1281, *Homilia* XXXVIII.

¹⁰ The holy Doctor cites these words (which are not found either in the Vulgate or in the Septuagint) elsewhere; in Book XXIX, *The Morals in Job*, num. 55. St Augustine cites the same text as belonging to S. Script; treating of Psalm iv. verse 9. Many places in S. Script., closely resemble this sentence: Lev. xxvi. 11, 13; II Cor. vi. 16, etc. Here the Pontiff cites Solomon, to whom the authorship of the Book of Wisdom is wont to be attributed. Cf. PL 38, col. 1282, note *e*.

¹¹ Ezechiel xl. 29. The *porch* of the gate was eight cubits; *the front thereof two cubits*.

¹² The fitting and practical fusion of the contemplative and active life, according to St Gregory, Pontiff.

TWENTIETH SUNDAY AFTER PENTECOST

THE GOSPEL OF THE SUNDAY

John iv. 46-53

At that time: There was a certain ruler, whose son was sick at Capharnaum. He, having heard that Jesus was come from Judea into Galilee, went to him and prayed him to come down and heal his son; for he was at the point of death. Jesus therefore said to him: unless you see signs and wonders, you believe not. The ruler saith to him: Lord, come down before that my son die. Jesus saith to him: Go thy way. Thy son liveth. The man believed the word which Jesus said to him and went his way. And as he was going down, his servants met him; and they brought word, saying, that his son lived. He asked therefore of them the hour wherein he grew better. And they said to him: Yesterday, at the seventh hour, the fever left him. The father therefore knew that it was at the same hour that Jesus said to him: Thy son liveth. And himself believed, and his whole house.

Exposition from the Catena Aurea

Chrysostom, *Homily 34 in John*: Earlier, as has been related, the Lord had come to Cana of Galilee, invited to a wedding. He now goes, of His own will; and to win them the more, leaves His own country. He goes also to strengthen by His Presence the faith begun there when He had wrought the miracle in the beginning.

V.46. *He came again therefore into Cana of Galilee, where he made the water wine.*

AUGUSTINE, *Tr.* XVI, 3, *in John*: For it was there His Disciples believed in Him, after He had changed water into wine (Jn. ii. 11). And though the house had been filled with guests and the miracle so very great, yet only His Disciples had believed. He now comes again to this city, so that they who had not believed then, because of the miracle, may believe now.

THEOPHYLACTUS: The Evangelist reminds us of the miracle worked in Cana of Galilee, the changing of water into wine, so as to add to the praise of Christ. For the Galileans had received Jesus, not only because of the wonders He had wrought in Jerusalem, but also because of those He had wrought among them. He mentions it also to show that the ruler believed because of the miracle wrought in Cana; although He had not yet come to understand perfectly the dignity of Jesus. So there follows: *And there was a certain ruler whose son was sick at Capharnaum.*

ORIGEN, *Tr.* XVII *in John, c.* 57: Some think this man was a prince of the house of Herod. Others say he was of the household of Caesar, in service in Judea. For it is not said he was a Jew. CHRYSOSTOM, as above: He is called a prince (*regulus*), either because he was of a royal family, or because of having some office of ruling, and was on this account so described. Some therefore believe him to be the same person as the centurion spoken of in Matthew (viii. 5). But it is plain he was a

different person. For when Christ said He would go at once to the house of the centurion, the latter begged Him to remain where He was; whereas this man, though Christ had made no similar offer to him, wished to make Christ come down with him to his house. The centurion came to Him as He was coming down the mountain to Capharnaum, while this ruler approached Him as He came into Cana. It was the other's servant who was sick of the palsy; the ruler's son, of a fever. Of this ruler it is then said:

V.47. *He, having heard that Jesus was come from Judea into Galilee, went to him and prayed him to come down and heal his son; for he was at the point of death.*

AUGUSTINE, as above: Did he believe who asks this? But why look to me for an answer. Ask the Lord what He thinks of him. Then follows:

V.48. *Jesus therefore said to him: Unless you see signs and wonders, you believe not.*

He shows us therefore a man who is lukewarm or cold in faith, or even wholly without faith; yet earnestly seeking, for his son's sake, to find out what manner of person Jesus was, and who He was, and what He could do. The word *wonder* (*prodigium; as it were porrodicium*) speaks of something distant, something to come.

AUGUSTINE, *Harmony of the Gospels, Bk.* IV, X, 13: The Lord wishes to raise the mind of the faithful far above transitory things, so that He would not have them seek even miracles; which, though divinely wrought, are yet wrought in mutable bodies. GREGORY, *Homily* 28, *on the Gospel*: But recall also what he prays for, and you will see plainly that his faith is doubtful. For he asks that Jesus shall come down and heal his son. So we read:

V.49. The ruler saith to him: Lord, come down before that my son die.

He therefore had little faith in Him, Who, he believed, could not heal, unless he were also present in body. CHRYSOSTOM, as above: See how, still earthly minded, he would bring Christ with him; as though He could not raise his son even from the dead. But it is not to be wondered at that, even without faith, he should come and ask Him. For parents in their great love will not only come to physicians in whom they have confidence, but even to those in whom they have not: unwilling to leave anything untried that might help their child's recovery. Yet, had he strongly believed in the power of Christ, he would not have failed to have gone even to Judea. GREGORY: But the Lord, asked to come down, shows He is not absent whither He is invited. For He restores health by His word only Who by the act of His will made all things. Hence follows:

V.50. Jesus saith to him: Go thy way. Thy son liveth.

Here our pride is rebuked, which leads us to honour in men, not those made in God's image, but honours and riches. Our Redeemer, to show that what men honour the saints must despise, and that what men despise the saints must not despise,

refused to go to the son of the ruler, though ready at once to go to the servant of the Centurion.

CHRYSOSTOM: Or again. In the centurion there was resolute faith; and so the Lord assures him He will come; that we might learn of the man's devotion. But this man's faith was still imperfect, and plainly he does not yet know that though absent in body Jesus could yet cure his son. But he learns this from the fact that Jesus does not come. For there follows: *The man believed the word which Jesus said to him and went his way.* He believed, but not wholly; not in the true sense. ORIGEN, as above: The man's authority and office are shown by this, that servants come to meet him. So we read:

V.51. And as he was going down, his servants met him; and they brought word, saying, that his son lived.

CHRYSOSTOM: They meet him, not alone to bring him word, but also because they now think that Christ's presence is superfluous; for they thought He was coming. That the ruler did not wholly believe, nor rightly, is seen from what follows:

V.52. He asked therefore of them the hour wherein he grew better.

He was seeking to find out whether it was by chance or through the command of Christ that this had taken place. Then follows: *And they said to him: Yesterday, at the seventh hour, the fever left him.* You see how manifest the miracle was. He had been delivered from danger, not simply, or by chance, but of a sudden, all at once: that it might be apparent that it had taken place, not through the course of nature, but from the action of Christ. Hence there follows:

V.53. *The father therefore knew that it was at the same hour that Jesus said to him: Thy son liveth. And himself believed, and his whole house.*

AUGUSTINE, *in John. Tr.* XVI, 3: If then he believed because he was told that his son had been healed, and compared the hour the messenger spoke of with the hour of Christ's foretelling this, then, at the time he was praying Christ to come, he did not yet believe. BEDE: And so we are given to understand that there are stages in faith as in the other virtues; in which there is a beginning, an increase, and perfection. He therefore had the beginnings of faith when he prays for his son's health; an increase, when he believes in the word of the Lord saying to him: *Thy son liveth.* Then perfection, on hearing from his servants.

AUGUSTINE, as above: Many Samaritans had believed solely because of His words. At this miracle only that house believed where it had been wrought. So the Evangelist adds:

V.54. *This is again the second miracle that Jesus did when he was come out of Judea into Galilee.*

CHRYSOSTOM: Not without reason does he add this; but to show that, though this was the second miracle Jesus then did, the Jews had not yet come to the height of understanding of the Samaritans who had seen no miracle.

ORIGEN: This sentence may be interpreted in two ways. One, that Jesus, coming from Judea into Galilee, worked two miracles, of which the second was done on behalf of the ruler's son; or, that of the two miracles Jesus performed in Galilee, He wrought the second coming from Judea to Galilee; and this latter is the true meaning. Mystically, by this that Jesus came twice into Galilee, the twofold Coming of the Saviour into the world is put before us: the first, a visit of compassion; that making wine He may rejoice those who are His guests; the second, that He may raise up the son of the ruler who was at the point of death: that is, the Jewish people, who after the complete conversion of the Gentiles are at the end to approach to salvation.

He is the Great King of Kings, appointed by God *over Sion His holy mountain* (Ps. ii. 6); Whose day *they saw and rejoiced* who are known as rulers (Jn. viii. 56). We believe therefore that the *ruler* is Abraham; his sick son the Jewish people, grown weak in the worship of God, and so heated by the fiery darts of the enemy that they are looked on as sick of a fever. It appears that the saints who have gone before us, even after they have put off the garment of the body, have a care for their people. So we read in Machabees, after the death of Jeremiah: *This is he that prayeth much for the people, Jeremias the prophet of God* (II Mac. xv. 14). Abraham therefore prays that his sick people may be healed by the Saviour.

And the word of power comes forth from Cana, where it was said: *Thy son liveth.* But the efficacy of the word is manifested in Capharnaum: for it was there, in the place as it were of *consolation* (Capharnaum), the son of the ruler was healed: who stands for those who are weak, yet not wholly without fruits. The words: *Unless you see signs and wonders you believe not*, which were said to the ruler, refer to the multitude of his (Abraham's) children, and also in a measure to him. For as John waited for the sign given to him, namely, *Upon whom thou shalt see the Spirit descending* (Jn. i. 33), so also the saints who died before the Coming of Christ in the flesh, looked for Him to be made known by signs and wonders. This ruler had not only a son, but also servants; and these latter signify the mass of those who believe, but less perfectly, as weak in faith. Nor was it by chance the fever left him at the seventh hour: for seven is the number of rest.

ALCUIN: Or it was at the seventh hour, because all forgiveness is through the sevenfold Spirit. For the number seven divided into three and four signifies the Holy Trinity in the four seasons of the year, in the four quarters of the world, and in the four elements. ORIGEN: The twofold coming of Christ (in verse 54) can also signify His two comings to the soul: first from the Wine He made, giving the soul the delight of a spiritual banquet; second, to take away all that remains of infirmity and death.

THEOPYHLACTUS: The *ruler* is man; not only because he is related in his soul to the King of all things, but because he also has rule over all things; whose son, his soul, suffers from the fever of sinful pleasures and desires. He comes to Jesus and prays Him to come down; that is, that He will deign to have pity on him, and forgive him his sins before he dies from the sickness of his pleasures. The Lord says: *Go thy way*. that is, advance steadfastly towards good, and then thy son will live. But if you cease to go forwards, the understanding of what is good in work will die in thee.

I. St Ephraim, Deacon, and Doctor of the Church

On Earnest Prayer[1]

Psalm cxxii

1. Mercy comes down from on high. Let us all turn our eyes on high. From the heaven of heavens comes salvation. Let us give thanks to Him Who dwells in heaven. In one of his psalms, David spoke words that sum up the whole of prayer: *To thee have I lifted up my eyes; who dwellest in heaven* (cxxii. 1). And He humbled himself, that we like Him should humble ourselves. As the eyes of servants turn continually towards their masters, to see, should they be sad, that they also may appear dutiful and sad. Should they be joyful, their servants also appear joyful. Again David speaks, and adds a phrase like the one that preceded it: *As the eyes of the handmaid are on the hands of her mistress:* so that, if she is happy, she may cheerfully approach her. But should her mistress be sad, her maid creeps away in fear and hides herself; and where she sees

her gloomy and severe, she flies from her anger: *So are our eyes unto Thee, the Lord our God.*

I cannot, David is saying, exult and rejoice before Thy face, till Thou hast mercy upon me: for I see that Thou art angry. Let us recall to mind these words of David, and let us meditate upon them within us, and let us say: *Have mercy on us, O Lord, have mercy on us.*

2. But since we know not how we are to pray, in accord with the will of God, the Holy Spirit teaches us through David how we are to pray to Thee. Therefore, my brethren; you who are listening to me, let us be pupils of David. For if he does not teach us, and if we do not heed his teaching, all the prophets and apostles will not avail to persuade us. In this time of sadness we all grieve under the rod of an angry God, until He shall again rejoice us Who now chastises us.[2] We shall not rejoice with a full heart, until the anger of God has turned away from us. Let us therefore stand in earnest prayer before the Most High, Whose Throne is in the heavens. Since *he looketh upon the earth*; let us be in fear of Him Who looketh down on us. Let us not assemble together in a careless manner in His holy house, to stand in His Presence: for He is not pleased with the careless, but with the efforts of those who love Him.

3. On a day appointed for prayer, let your prayer not be disturbed. Do not neglect prayer in order to go out in the streets to talk and argue. And should some one come to chatter with you, be wise; bid him be silent, saying to him: 'Today we are supposed to pray; we must do what is imposed on us.' Praying and disputing in talk, what, I would like to know, have they in common? Petition and deception; it would be strange that these two should be heard together. Fasting and loud talk; that these should be associated, I find astonishing. And that chastity and wantonness should be found together would wholly amaze me.

It is not becoming, O prudent man, to pray with a double mind; nor that we should divide our heart, keeping one part for the Church, another for the street. Who can deceive God, *Who searcheth hearts?* And who shall hide his thoughts from Him Who knows all things that are hidden? Who shall give his mind to good and evil thoughts, thinking that no one will know of them? That you should pray, and then go out to talk and argue; that is a very foolish thing to do. To talk and argue, coming at the same time to worship God; that is the doing of the foolish of heart.

4. If you would learn how you must act, so that you may neither injure yourself, nor be rebuked because of your prayer, I shall give you counsel. Decide for yourself in what I tell you; and it will be well for you if you do as I say. If you have made up your mind to come and pray before God, make this pact with yourself: that in coming from your home to the place of prayer, that for the whole duration of your journey to the house of prayer, and petition, you will not waste your time with some companion, but, that from the beginning to the end of your journey, you will sanctify the time with prayer.

And when you stand before God in prayer, do not pray with a mind that is disturbed and filled with unrest and, since the church is holy, neither should you stand in it with a mind that is defiled; and while the Scriptures are being read, do not let your thoughts turn to the tumult outside. Incline your ear and your mind to hearing the words of the prophets, and turn your face and turn your senses towards the Apostles, as they cry to you: 'Gird thy soul, and be strengthened that thou may hear the Gospel of thy Lord.' Do not listen with indifference to the Gospel of the Truth. Should you be slothful in God's Presence, He will send you away without a reward.

For reflect: If a worker in your field neglected the harvest; when he afterwards came for his wage you would remember that he was lazy, and you would not pay him as you would a diligent servant, who gave you satisfaction. All we children of the Faith are workers in the field of the Divinity, and everyone who comes to pray, comes to the field of God. Prayer to God bears fruit. Let us not neglect it, and lose its fruits. He who offers up sincere and earnest prayer, reaps and gathers in its fruits. He who is slothful in prayer, will be a stranger to its fruits. Let us see then that our mouth does not pray in a negligent manner. It greatly profits us to pray, and to know also what kind of prayer we are offering: for there is power in the prayer of a just man. Over anger especially prayer is always victorious. In his time of illness the sick man looks for help and healing, and submits himself to those who will help him; how much more should we, who are sick through sin,

compose our soul and pray with mind and heart? For we have need of two things: to be freed from our afflictions, and to be forgiven our sins.

Great is the power of prayer. Let us not be slothful in prayer. Prayer bears fruit. Let our prayer not become unworthy. Let us speak to others of prayer; if laziness does not prevent us; and if we are ready of speech, let us praise it. Perhaps some amongst us here in the congregation will murmur to themselves: What is the meaning of this correction, which makes nothing of our labour? Let the grumbler, whoever he is, listen; and he will learn that this is good and profitable for him. For it is enough that it serves to show us that the taste of pleasure does not satisfy us. Let us not think too much of the fleeting things of this world, rather let us be steadfast in our love of spiritual things, which are profitable to the soul. For by the help of things spiritual, the things of this world are also made profitable. Fields are cultivated, when souls are not neglected. And when souls are cultivated, fields do not remain fruitless;[3] though we know that spiritual works will not take the place of the plough.

5. Without health of body, material things are of no benefit to you. Without streams of prayer, what you have sown will not be watered. Without the help of prayer you shall not reap what you sow. Without the mercy of the Creator, there can be no good, no blessing. Be earnest then in prayer, and your barns will overflow. Winter and summer be earnest in prayer; for winter and summer prayer is neces-

sary for us. Winter reminds us to pray, that we shall not want for the dew and the rain. Summer urges us to pray, that our fields and our barns may be blessed. The day cries to us: Give thanks to Him Who gives light to the labourers; the night tells us to give glory to Him Who gives rest to the weary. He has made a holy house for those who dwell here; that they may learn the way of holiness. The multitudes in the streets teach us that the Church must speak judgement in quiet; and with uplifted voice She cries: 'Take thought for your life.' The Cross, with arms outstretched, has compassion on its adorers. The Exalted and the Most High inclines His ear to our prayer, and the Angels of His mercy visit us one by one. Let us, my brethren, with our whole heart, give thanks for all these things. For it is through prayer that all graces work in us. We are *inexcusable* (Rom. i. 20); but God is just. We are all sinners; our Creator is pure and free of all fault. We are evil to one another; but our Maker is merciful. Glory be to Him Who in His mercy bears with us who rebel against Him. Amen.

II. St Augustine, Bishop and Doctor, I

Prayer is from the Heart[4]

I cried with my whole heart: Hear me, O Lord: I will seek thy justification. Psalm cxviii. 145.

1. The cry to the Lord of those who pray, if made only by the sound of the body's voice, and not by the heart intent on God; who can doubt that it is made in vain? But if it comes from the heart, though the voice of the body be silent, it may remain unknown to men, but not to God. Therefore, when we pray to God with the voice of our body, if there is occasion for this, or when we pray in silence, we must pray from the heart. The cry of the heart is an intense turning of the mind to God, which made in prayer expresses the great longing of the soul, asking and desiring; so that it does not despair of its fulfilment.

And we cry with our whole heart when the mind is not turned elsewhere. Prayer such as this is rare among the many; but frequent with a few. Whether there is anyone whose whole prayer is of this kind, I know not. He who sings this psalm speaks of such a prayer from his own heart. *I cried with my whole heart; Hear me, Lord.* To what end he cries he goes on to say: *I will seek thy justifications.* For this therefore he cries with his whole heart; longing that this may be granted to Him by the Lord Who hears his prayer: That he may come to know what is right and just in God's eyes. Let us therefore pray that we may come to know what we are commanded to do.

How far is he who seeks to know, from him who does the will of God! For it does not follow that he who seeks, shall find; or that finding, he shall do. But he cannot do the will of God unless he comes to know it. But the Lord Jesus has given us great hope by saying: *Seek, and you shall find.* And Wisdom also says (and Who is Wisdom but He?): *The wicked shall seek me, and not find me*

(Prov. i. 28). Therefore not to the bad, but to the good was it said: *Seek, and you shall find.* Rather it was said, a little later in the same place, to those to whom He said: *If you then, being evil, know how to give good gifts to your children* (Mt. vii. 7, 11).

How then does He say to the wicked, *Seek, and you shall find,* when in another place He says: *The wicked shall seek me, and not find me?* Or is it that the Lord wished them to seek something other than wisdom when He promised that they who seek shall find? For it is in wisdom that all things are to be sought by those who desire to be blessed. And there also shall we find His *justifications.* We are therefore given to know, not that all the wicked shall not find wisdom, if they seek it; but only those who are so wicked that they hate wisdom. For this is what He said: *The wicked shall seek me and not find me: for they hate wisdom.* They therefore do not find it, because they hate it.

But again, if they hate what they are seeking, why do they seek it; unless that they do not seek it for itself, but because of something the wicked love, and which they think they shall more easily attain by means of wisdom. For there are many who search eagerly into the words of wisdom; not to live by them, but to possess them as learning; not to come by the way of life wisdom teaches to the Light of God, which is Wisdom Itself, but that through the language of wisdom, they may gain the praise of men; which is vain glory.

They therefore are not seeking wisdom, even when they seek it: for they do not seek it for its own sake; if they did they would live by it.

They seek to be puffed up with its words; and the more they are inflated with them, the more they are a stranger to it. But the psalmist, imploring this of the Lord, which the Lord commands him to do; that he may work in him what He commands him to do; for it is God Who works in us, so that we both will and do, according to His good pleasure (Phil. ii. 13) cries: *I have cried with my whole heart: Hear me, O Lord: I will seek thy justifications;* not only that he may know them, but also to fulfil them; lest he become like a stubborn servant, who *understandeth, and will not answer* (Prov. xxix. 19).

2. *I have cried unto thee: Save me: that I may keep thy commandments* (verse 146).

I have cried: Save me; or as some Greek and Latin copies have it: *I have cried unto thee.* What does, *I have cried unto thee* mean but: Crying out, I have called upon Thy Name? But when he says: *Save me,* what did he then add? *That I may keep thy commandments;* that is, that I may not in my weakness deny Thee. For health of soul will make us do what we know we must do, even to the death of the body: should the defence of divine truth demand of us this supreme testimony. But where the soul is unhealthy, weakness will surrender, and truth be betrayed.

Turning then to the Lord our God, the Father Almighty, let us as best we can give thanks with all our hearts, beseeching Him that in His Goodness He will mercifully hear our prayers and by His grace drive evil from our thoughts and actions, increase our faith, guide our minds, grant us His holy inspirations and bring us to joy without end through His Son our Lord and Saviour Jesus Christ.[5] Amen.

III. St Augustine, Bishop and Doctor, II

To Children on the Sacrament of the Altar.[6]

Synopsis: I. Commendation of the Sacrifice of the New Law.
II. Christ is this Sacrifice.
III. Truly and really present in the Eucharist.
IV. Effects of the Eucharist.
V. Conditions for its worthy reception.

1. The duty of giving a sermon, and the care with which we have laboured with you, that Christ might be formed in you (Gal. iv. 19), compel me to remind you, Children, you who have been born again of water and the Holy Ghost (Jn. iii. 5), that you are now seeing in a new light this Food and Drink here present on this table of the Lord, and that you are now perceiving with a new devotion the meaning of this so great and divine Sacrament, this noble wondrous Medicine, this clean and fitting Oblation which is now being offered to God; offered, not in an earthly city, Jerusalem, nor in that tabernacle made by Moses, nor in the great temple made by Solomon: which were but shadows of things to come: but, as the prophets foretold, it is being offered up from the rising to the going down of the sun (Mal. i. 11), and through the grace of the New Testament it is offered to God as a Sacrifice of Praise.

God looks no more for bloody offerings from herds of cattle. Now no more is a sheep or a goat offered at the divine altars. The Sacrifice now of our time is the Body and Blood of the High Priest Himself. Long ago, in the psalms, it was said of this great High Priest: *Thou art a*

priest for ever, according to the order of Melchisedech (Ps. cix. 4). We read and we keep firmly in mind, from the Book of Genesis, that Melchisedech, *the priest of the Most High God* (xiv. 18), offered a sacrifice of bread and wine, when he blessed our father Abraham.

II. Christ our Lord therefore, Who offered for us in His Passion, what He received by being born of us, made a High Priest for ever, gave to us this order of Sacrifice you now see: namely, the Sacrifice of His own Body and Blood. For when He was pierced by a lance, His Body gave forth water and blood: by Which He was to wash away our sins. Mindful of this grace, and while working out your own salvation, let you with fear and trembling draw near to partake of this Altar: for *it is God Who worketh in you* (Phil. ii. 2).

Acknowledge That in the Bread, Which hung upon the Cross. Acknowledge in the Chalice, That Which flowed from His side. For these ancient sacrifices of the People of God, in all their number and variety, only prefigured this One True Sacrifice that was yet to come. For Christ Himself is *our* sheep, because of the innocence of His pure soul; and likewise our sacrificial goat, because of His likeness to our sinful flesh (Rom. viii. 3). And whatever else was foretold, in various ways, in the sacrifices of the Old Testament, refer to this One Sacrifice, which was revealed to us in the New Testament.

III. Let you therefore receive, and eat, the Body of Christ: you who have now become the members of Christ in the Body of Christ. Receive, and drink, the Blood of Christ. Let you never be separated from Him. Eat That Which binds you to Him. Drink of this Price Which He paid for you; and never hold yourselves cheap. As This, when you eat It and drink It, is changed into you; so let you be changed into the Body of Christ; while you live devoutly and obediently. For He, as the time of His passion was at hand, and when He wished to celebrate the Pasch with His Disciples; taking bread, He blessed it, and said: THIS IS MY BODY, WHICH IS GIVEN FOR YOU (Lk. xxii. 19). In like manner, He gave us the Blessed Chalice, saying: THIS IS MY BLOOD OF THE NEW TESTAMENT, WHICH SHALL BE SHED FOR MANY UNTO REMISSION OF SINS (Mt. xxvi. 28).

You will have read this in the Gospel, or you will have heard it read; but you did not know that this Eucharist is the Son.[7] But now, with your hearts made clean, and with a pure conscience, and with your bodies washed in clean water (Heb. x. 22), *Come ye to him, and be enlightened; and your faces shall not be confounded* (Ps. xxxiii. 6). For if you receive This worthily, which is of the New Testament, through which

you hope for an eternal inheritance, and hold fast to the new commandment, that you love one another, you shall have Life in you. For you will be receiving that Flesh, of which Life Itself says: *The bread that I will give is my flesh, for the life of the world;* and again: *Unless a man eat of my flesh and drink of my blood, he shall not have life in him*[8] (Jn. vi. 52–54).

IV. Therefore, having life in Him, you will be one body with Him. For this Sacrament does not give us the Body of Christ, that it may then separate us from It. The Apostle commemorates that this was foretold in holy Scripture: *They shall be two in one flesh. This,* he says, *is a great sacrament: But I speak in Christ and in the Church* (Eph. v. 32). And of this same Eucharist, he says in another place: *We being many are one bread, one body* (I Cor. x. 17).

Begin therefore to receive That which you have begun to be; provided you do not receive It unworthily: so that you shall not eat and drink damnation to yourself. For the Apostle says: *Whosoever shall eat this bread, or drink the chalice of the Lord unworthily, shall be guilty of the body and of the blood of the Lord. But let a man prove himself; and so let him eat of the bread and drink of the chalice. For he that eateth and drinketh unworthily, eateth and drinketh judgement to himself; not discerning the body of the Lord* (I Cor. xi. 27–29).

V. You will receive it worthily, if you are careful to avoid the leaven of evil teaching; so that you remain *the unleavened bread of sincerity and truth* (v. 8). Or if you hold firmly to that leaven which is charity, *which* a woman took and hid in three measures of meal, until the whole was leavened (Mt. xiii. 33).[9] For this *woman* is the Wisdom of God, made in mortal flesh through the Virgin, which sows, as in three measures, the Gospel through the whole earth; which He filled up again after the Flood from the three sons of Noah; *until the whole should be leavened.* This is that *whole*, which in Greek is called Holon, wherein *keeping the bond of peace* (Eph. iv. 3), you will belong

within that *whole*, which in Greek is called Katholos;[10] whence the name Catholic is derived.

Turning then to the Lord, let us earnestly pray both for ourselves, and for all the people who stand with us in the courts of His house (Ps. cxxxiii. 1), that He may deign to guard and protect us, through Jesus Christ His Son our Lord, Who with Him liveth and reigneth world without end. Amen.

IV. St Augustine, Bishop and Doctor, III

To Children; again on the Sacrament of the Altar[11]

Synopsis: I. The Body of the Lord is on the Altar; and we are It.
           II. The Eucharist, the Symbol of Unity.
           III. Exposition of the Liturgy of the Eucharist.

I. This, which you see on the Table of the Lord, dearest children, is bread, and wine. But this bread, and this wine, when certain words are added, become the Body, and the Blood, of the Word. For that Lord, Who *in the beginning was the Word, and the Word was with God, and the Word was God* (Jn. i. 1), because of His mercy, whereby He had compassion on that which He had made, to His own image, *the Word was made flesh, and dwelt among us*; as you know: For He Who was the Word, assumed humanity; that is, the body and soul of a man; and became man, while remaining God.

Through this, and also because He suffered for us, He entrusted to us in this Sacrament, His own Body and Blood; and He also made us His Body. For we too have become His Body; and through His mercy we become what we receive. Recall to mind that this creature (*the bread*) was one time in a ploughed field;

and remember how the earth brought it forth, and how the rains nourished it, and brought it into ear. Then how human labour carried it to the threshing floor, and threshed it,[12] and winnowed it, and stored it, and brought it forth again, and ground it into flour, and mixed it with water, and baked it, and just a little while ago it was made into bread.

Now think about yourselves. You did not exist, and then you were created, and brought to the threshing floor of the Lord, and you were treaded out, by the labour of oxen, that is, by the labour of those who instructed you in the Catholic Faith. When you were being held back as Catechumens, you were being stored in the barn. Then you were enrolled for baptism, and by fastings and exorcisms[13] you began to be ground into flour. Then you were brought to the water, and you were sprinkled with it, and you were *made one* (Jn. xvii. 11). Then, with the coming of the fire of the Holy Ghost you were baked, and you became the bread of the Lord.

II. See what you have received! Therefore, since you see that what was made is one; so let you also be one: by loving one another, by holding firm to the one faith, to the one hope, to the one indivisible charity. Heretics, when they receive This, receive a witness against themselves: for they seek division, while This Bread proclaims unity.

And in the same way, the wine was in many grapes, now it is made one: One in the sweetness of the Cup; but after the torment of the winepress. So you also, after your fastings, your labours, your humility your contrition, you have now in the Name of the Lord come as it were to the Chalice of the Lord: you are there upon the Table; you are there within the Chalice. One with us you are This; for together we receive This, together we drink It; because we live as One.

You are now to hear that which you heard yesterday; but today we explain both what you heard and what you answered; or, perhaps, what you let pass in silence, when you should have answered. But what you should have answered, you will learn today.

III. After the Salutation, which you know: *Dominus vobiscum* (*The Lord be with you*), you hear: *Sursum corda* (*Lift up your hearts*). The whole life of a true Christian is a lifting up of the heart; not the life of Christians in name only, but of Christians in reality; and in truth all life is a *sursum corda.* What does lift up your

hearts mean? To hope in God; not in yourself. For you are here below; God is up above. If your hope is in yourself, your heart stays here below; not up above. So when you hear the priest say: *Sursum corda*, let you answer *Habemus ad Dominum* (We have to the Lord).

Strive so that your answer may be a true answer. Since your answer is close to the divine action of the Mass; as you answer, so let it be. Do not let the tongue say yes, while the conscience says no. And because it is God, not your own powers, enables you to lift up your heart; it then follows that when you have said you have lifted up your heart to the Lord, the priest will say: *Domino Deo nostro gratias agamus* (Let us give thanks to the Lord our God). Why do we give thanks? Because our hearts are uplifted; and unless He had uplifted them, we would lie prone upon the earth.

And now from this point on, there follows what takes place within the sacred prayers which you are about to hear,[14] so that when certain words are added, the Body and Blood of Christ become present. For take away the words, there is bread and there is wine. Add the words, and there is now Another Thing. And this Other Thing, what is it? The Body of Christ and the Blood of Christ. Therefore, take away the words, there is but bread there is but wine. Add the words, and they become the Sacrament.

To this you say, *Amen*. To say *Amen* is to express consent. *Amen* is interpreted as meaning, *it is truly so*. Then the Lord's Prayer is said. This you have already received, and recited.[15] Why is the Lord's Prayer recited before you receive the Body and Blood of Christ? Because such is our human frailty, should our mind chance to entertain some thought which is unbecoming, or our tongue utter something it ought not, or our eye look upon something unfitting or our ear listen to something enticing, which they should not; should it happen that we contract some such debts, from the temptation of this world, or through the frailty of human life, they are wiped away at the Lord's Prayer when we say: Forgive us our trespasses (*Dimitte nobis debita nostra*, Mt. vi. 12); so that we may draw near (to the Table), secure that in what we shall receive we shall neither eat nor drink judgement to ourselves (I Cor. xi. 29).

After this we say: *Pax Vobiscum* (Peace be with you). A great mystery, the kiss of peace.[16] So kiss, that you may love one another. Do not be like Judas. Judas the Betrayer kissed Christ on the mouth, while in his heart he was betraying Him. Should there be someone who has an inimical spirit towards you, and

you cannot win him, you are urged to bear with him. Do not in your own heart return him evil for evil. He hates; let you love; and kiss him with a tranquil heart.

You have learned from me a few things; but great things. Let them not be held cheap because they are few, but as precious because of their weight. At the same time you must not be overburdened; that you may hold firmly what has been said to you.

Turning then to the Lord our God, we pray that the power of His mercy may strengthen our hearts in His holy truth, and confirm and calm our souls. May His grace abound in us, and may He have pity on us, and remove dangers from before us, and from before His Church, and from before all who are dear to us, and may He in His power and in the abundance of His mercy, enable us to please Him for ever, through Jesus Christ His Son our Lord, Who with Him and with the Holy Spirit reigns God for ever and ever. Amen.

V. St Augustine, Bishop and Doctor, IV

What is Baptism without Unity?[17]
To the Newly Baptized

Synopsis: I. The Power and Effects of Baptism and the Hope laid up in it.
II. Baptism does not profit outside the Unity of the Church.
III. Against Schismatics glorying in Baptism.
IV. Exhortation to the Newly Baptized.

I. My sermon is addressed to you, now new-born Infants, children in Christ, the new generation of the Church, the grace of the Father, the fruitfulness of the Mother, a devoted offspring, the new swarm, the flower of our honour and the fruit

of our labours, *my joy and my crown* (Phil. iv. 1), to all of you who now stand in the Lord, I speak in the words of the Apostle: *The night is passed, and the day is at hand. Let us therefore cast off the works of darkness and put on the armour of light. Let us walk honestly, as in the day; not in rioting and drunkenness, not in chambering and impurities, not in contention and envy. But put ye on the Lord Jesus Christ; and make not provision for the flesh in its concupiscences* (Rom. xiii. 12–14); so that you may put on His life, Whose Sacrament you have put on: *For as many of you as have been baptized in Christ, have put on Christ. For there is neither Jew nor Greek; there is neither bond nor free; there is neither male nor female. For you are all one in Christ Jesus* (Gal. iii. 27, 28).

Such is the power of this Sacrament. For it is the Sacrament of new life, which in this present time begins from the forgiveness of all our past sins, and which shall be perfected in the resurrection of the dead. *For as you are buried together with him by baptism into death; that, as Christ is risen from the dead, so you also may walk in newness of life* (Rom. vi. 4).[18] You now walk by faith, as long as you are absent from the Lord in this mortal body (II Cor. v. 6). *The way* you are going is certain; which He, to Whom you are going, Jesus Christ made Man, deigned to become for us. For he has laid up much sweetness for those that fear Him; and this He will perfect and reveal to those who hope in Him; since that which we now receive in hope, we shall also receive in reality (Ps. xxx. 20). For *we are now the sons of God, and it hath not yet appeared what we shall be. We know that when he shall appear we shall be like to him; because we shall see him as he is* (I Jn. iii. 2).

This also has He promised in the Gospel: *He that loveth me,* He says, *he it is that keepeth my commandments. And he that loveth me. shall be loved*

of my father; and I will love him, and will manifest myself to him (Jn. xiv. 21). They to whom He was speaking did indeed see Him; but they saw Him *in the form of a servant,* in which the Father is greater than Him; not *in the form of God,* in which He is equal to the Father. This He showed to those who fear Him; that Other He has laid up for those who hope in Him. In the first, He appeared to those on the journey of life; to the Other He has called those who are to dwell with Him. The One He has spread beneath the feet of those who are still on *the way*; the Other He has promised to those who reach It.

II. *Having therefore these promises, Dearly Beloved, let us cleanse ourselves of all defilement of the flesh and of the spirit, perfecting sanctification in the fear of God* (II Cor. vii. 1). *I beseech you that you walk worthy of the vocation in which you are called; with all humility and mildness, with patience supporting one another in charity; careful to keep the unity of the Spirit in the bond of peace* (Eph. iv. 1–3). What must the reality be, for which we have received such a pledge.

But there are some who have put on Christ only in the Sacrament (*sacramentally only*), so that in faith and morals they are naked. For many heretics also possess this sacrament of baptism, but not the same fruits of salvation, nor the bond of peace. *Having,* as the Apostle says, *the appearance indeed of godliness, but denying the power thereof* (II Tim. iii. 5); or as those *signed* (baptized) by apostates or even the apostates themselves, bearing on their guilty body the sign of the Good King, who say to us: 'If we are not of the faithful, why do you not give us baptism? And if we already belong to the faithful, what do you seek of us?' As though they do not read that Simon Magus also received baptism, yet heard from Peter the words: *Thou hast no part nor lot in this faith* (Acts viii. 21).

See how it can happen, that a man may have the baptism of Christ, and not have the faith or the love of Christ; how he may possess the Sacrament of holiness, and yet have no part in the lot of the saints. Nor does it matter how much belongs to the Sacrament itself, should anyone there receive the baptism of Christ, where there is not the unity of Christ. For even one baptized in the Church, should he become a deserter of the Church, will be lacking in holiness of life but not in the character (*signaculo*) of the Sacrament. For it is proved that going forth, he does not lose it, since he is not given it again at his return. Just as a military deserter may be absent from his lawful place, yet will not lose his military character. And should he mark another with the same sign (shoulder brand), he will not make him a comrade in arms, but will make him a partner in his own guilt. And should he return to his due and lawful military service, and should the other accompany him, and due amends being made to the king's discipline, he that returned is pardoned, and he that came with him shall be recognized. In both cases the fault is corrected, in both cases guilt is remitted; to both peace is given; in neither case is that renewed with which they have both been signed.

III. Therefore, let them not say to us: What have you to give us, since we already have baptism? For then they neither know what they are saying, nor even want to read what Holy Scripture testifies; that even within the Church, that is, within the communion of the members of Christ, there were many in Samaria who were baptized who had not received the Holy Ghost, and were in baptism only, until the Apostles came to them from Jerusalem (Acts viii. 16); while Cornelius and those who were with him, merited to receive the Holy Ghost before they had received the Sacrament of baptism (x. 44). In this way God teaches us that salvation is one thing, the sign of salvation another; the *appearance* of godliness is one thing, the virtue of godliness another.

'What can you give us,' they say, 'if we already possess baptism?' O sacrilegious vanity! To think the Church of Christ, which they do not possess, is nothing; so that they believe they receive nothing if they join her communion! Let the prophet Amos speak to them. *Woe to them that make nothing of Sion* (vi. 1, Sept.)[19] 'What have I to receive,' he says, 'if I already possess baptism?' You will receive the Church, which you have not; you will receive unity, which you have not; you will receive peace, which you have not. And if these things seem nothing to you, then fight, deserter, against your Commander Who says to you: *He that gathereth not with me, scattereth* (Lk. xi. 23). Fight against His Apostle, or, what is worse, fight against Him Who speaks through him, saying: *Supporting one another in charity; careful to keep the unity of the Spirit in the bond of peace* (Eph. iv. 3).

Number the things he here speaks of: Forbearance, love, unity, the Spirit, peace. And in all these things He speaks of, it is the Spirit Who works; Whom you have not. Have you who separated from the Church, been patient one with another? Whom did you love, when you deserted the members of Christ? What is unity to you in your sacrilegious breaking away? What peace is there in your hateful discord? Far be it from us to hold these things as nothing; you, rather, are nothing without them. If you scorn to receive these things within the Church, you may possess baptism, but you possess it to your own greater torment; whatever you possess without them. For the baptism of Christ, which with these things was the advocate of your salvation, without them is the witness of your sin.

IV. But you, holy children, Catholic members, have received not another baptism, but another thing. You have not received it unto punishment, but unto life; not unto ruin, but unto salvation; not unto damnation, but unto glory. For you at the same time have also received the unity of the Spirit in the bond of peace, provided *that you preserve blameless* what you have received; as I desire you, as I hope for you, as I exhort and pray you, and that going ever forward you may come to greater things.

Today is the octave of your nativity.[20] This day (Sunday) the seal of faith is completed in you; which with the Fathers of old took place on the eighth day of our bodily birth in the circumcision of the flesh. For the despoiling of mortality was prefigured in that member through which man is born, to die. For the same reason the Lord also, despoiling Himself of the mortality of the flesh by rising from the dead, and restoring to life no other thing but that Body which *dieth now no more* (Rom. vi. 9), in His own Resurrection sanctified the Lord's Day: which is the third day after His Passion, the eighth in the number of days that follow the sabbath, and at the same time the first. And so you, because you have *received the pledge of the Spirit* (II Cor. i. 22), and shall possess, not yet in deed, but with a sure and certain hope, the fulfilment of this pledge: *Therefore, if you be risen with Christ, seek the things that are above, where Christ is sitting at the right hand of God. Mind the things that are above, not the things that are upon the earth. For you are dead; and your life is hid with Christ in God. When Christ shall appear, who is your life, then you also shall appear with him in glory* (Col. iii. 1–4).

Let us give thanks to our Lord and Saviour, Who without any previous merits of ours has healed our wounds, restored us to His friendship, redeemed us from captivity, led us from darkness into light and recalled us from death to life. And while humbly confessing our sins, let us implore His mercy, so that, with the psalmist, as His mercy goes before us, He may deign not alone to guard, but also increase the gifts and graces He has deigned to bestow on us, through Jesus Christ our Lord, Who with the Father and the Holy Spirit liveth and reigneth God world without end.[21] Amen.

VI. St John Chrysostom, Bishop and Doctor

Explanation of the Gospel[22]

John iv. 46–53

He came again therefore into Cana of Galilee, where he made the water wine. Verse 46.

The Evangelist reminds us of the miracle, to add to the praises of the Samaritans. The people of Cana received Him after the signs and wonders He had wrought in Jerusalem as well as among themselves; not so however the Samaritans, who received Him solely because of His teaching. The Evangelist tells us He came here, but does not add the reason why He came there. He had come into Galilee because of the envy of the Jews. But why did He come to Cana? He had come there before as a wedding guest. Why does He come now? It seems to me that it was to strengthen by His Presence the faith that had sprung up there because of the miracle; and to draw them the more, since He came uninvited, and also because of this that leaving his own country, He should prefer them.

And there was a certain ruler, whose son was sick at Capharnaum. He, having heard that Jesus was come from Judea into Galilee, went to him and prayed him to come down and heal his son, verse 47.

He is spoken of as a ruler, either because he was of royal race, or because of his office. Some think that this is the man spoken of by Matthew (viii. 5). But it is evident that this latter is another man, not alone because of his title of centurion, but also because of his faith. For the first spoken of, even when Christ offers to go with him, begs him to stay. This man, though Christ made no such offer, would force Him to his house. The first, the centurion, says: *Lord, I am not worthy that thou shouldst enter under my roof.* The second urges Him, saying: *Come down before my son dies.* The centurion came to Him, descending from the mountain to Capharnaum. This man, as He came from Samaria towards, not Capharnaum, but Cana. The servant of the one lay ill with palsy; the son of the other was ill of fever.

And coming he prays him to heal his son: for he was at the point of death.

And what does Christ say then? *Unless you see signs and wonders you believe not.* Yet was it not a sign of faith that he should come to pray to him? And after this the Evangelist bears witness that this is so, where he tells us, that at the words of Jesus, *Go thy way, Thy son liveth,* he believed Jesus' words, and went his way. What then does Jesus mean here? He uses these words either as praising the Samaritans, for they believed without signs, or as rebuking that which was believed to be His own city, namely Capharnaum, from which this man came. For upon another man in Luke,[23] saying: *I do believe, Lord, help thou my unbelief,* He uses similar words. And so, though this man believed, he did not wholly believe, nor soundly. And he shows this when he asks later at what hour the fever left the boy: for he wished to know if it had happened naturally or through the command of Christ.

When he learned then that the fever had left him at the seventh hour, he *himself believed and his whole house.* You see here how he believed only when his servants had spoken; not when Christ had spoken. The Lord therefore had said these words to him (*unless you see*, etc.) as a rebuke for the state of mind in which he had come to Him, and to draw him the more towards this faith; for before the miracle he did not wholly believe. That he came and prayed Him was nothing to wonder at. For parents in their great love will consult not alone trustworthy physicians, but even those who are not trustworthy: so eager are they to show they have left nothing undone. For he had come there by chance, having seen the Lord when He came into Galilee. Had he wholly believed in Him, he would not have hesitated, when his child was on the point of death, to come to Him in Judea. And even had he feared to do this, it would have been no excuse.

See how his words show the weakness of this man. When his mind should by now, after this rebuke, if not before, begin to form

at least some notion of the greatness of Christ, hear how it still creeps along the ground: *Come down,* he says, *before my son dies.* As if He had not power to raise him even from the dead; and as if He knew not how the boy was. It was for this that Christ rebuked him, and as it were takes hold of his conscience, to show him that these signs and wonders are wrought primarily for the sake of the soul. For He here cures, not only the son, but also the father; sick because of his state of mind: to convince us, that we must turn our thoughts to Him, not because of His signs and wonders, but because of His teaching. For signs are not for the believing, but for the unbelieving, and the slow of understanding. But, because of his anxiety, the man did not wholly take in the words that were said to him, except those which referred to his son. But they would come back to his mind, and then he would draw the greatest fruit from them. And so it was.

But why was it that in the case of the centurion Christ offered to go at once (to *his* servant), while here, though prayed to come, He refused? Because there faith was perfect. And so He offered to come: that we might learn the worthiness of this man. But the faith of the ruler was imperfect. But here, because the ruler kept on saying: *Come down,* and did not yet clearly grasp that even absent Christ was able to heal, He made clear to him that this was possible; so that from Jesus' not going down, he might learn that which the centurion had already known.

And so when He said: *Unless you see signs and wonders you believe not,* He meant: 'You have not yet a true faith; you still look upon Me as a Prophet.' Therefore, revealing Himself, and showing them that even without signs and wonders they should believe in Him, He says to them the same words He had spoken to Philip: *Do you not believe that I am in the Father and the Father in me? If you do not, believe Me at least because of my works: If you do not, then believe because of the very works' sake* (Jn. xiv. 10).

And as he was going down, his servants met him; and they brought word, saying, that his son lived. He asked therefore of them the hour wherein he grew better. And they said to him: Yesterday at the seventh hour, the fever left him. The father therefore knew that it was at the same hour that Jesus said to him: Thy son liveth. And himself believed, and his whole house.

See how clearly the wonder took place. For it did not happen in some ordinary way, or by chance. that the boy was delivered from danger; but of a sudden, so that it was apparent that his recovery was not due to the course of nature, but to the action of Christ. For while drawing close to the very gate of death, as his father's words show: *Come down before my son dies*, of a sudden he is delivered from his sickness; something which made the servants wonder. For they may have come, not simply to announce the good news, but also because they believed that Jesus' presence was no longer needed, and it was for this that they came to meet him; as they knew that he had gone to find Jesus.

The ruler freed from fear has glimpses of faith, and wishes now to show that this had come about as a result of his journey, and not by chance. And so, after he had learned carefully all there was to learn, *he himself believed, and his whole house.* And the testimony was very plain to see. For they who had not been present, and had not heard him speaking with Christ, and had not known when this had taken place, learning now from their master that this was the time, they had the most evident testimony to the power of Jesus, and so because of this they believed.

God is to be loved in prosperity and adversity; nothing should turn us from His love.

What then do we learn from these things? Not to wait for signs and wonders; not to seek tokens of the divine power. For even now I see many show more love of God, who when a wife or child was sick had received some consolation. Yet, even if our prayers are not heard, we should continue just the same to give praise and thanks to God. For this is the duty of good and devout servants. It is the way of the steadfast, of those who love the Lord; to hasten to Him, not only when in affliction, but also when we are untroubled. For such things are the work of the Providence of God in our regard: *For whom the Lord loveth, he chastiseth: and he scourgeth every son whom he receiveth* (Hebrews xii. 6).

For he who worships Him only when things are easy, shows no great sign of love, and neither does he love Christ, with a love that has been purified. And why speak only of health and plenty, or of want and sickness? And even should you hear of the fire of hell or other such grievous thing, not even for this should you cease from praising God; and bear all things out of love for Him. For this is the way of good and faithful servants, and of a soul that is steadfast. And he whose heart is disposed in this way, will bear the afflictions of this present time cheer-fully, and will reach in time to the possession of the blessings to come, and will enjoy much confidence when standing in God's Presence; and to this may we all attain by the grace and clemency of our Lord Jesus Christ to whom be glory for ever and ever. Amen.

VII. St Gregory the Great, Pope and Doctor

Pride Rebuked[24]

Given to the People in the Basilica of the Holy Nereus and Achilleus, on their Natal Day

John iv. 46–53

1. The lesson of the Holy Gospel which you have just now heard, Brethren, needs no explanation. But that we may not appear to pass over it in silence, we shall say something with regard to it more by way of exhortation than explanation. The only point in it that I see needs to be explained is, why he who had come to pray for the restoration to health of his son should hear the words: *Unless you see signs and wonders, you believe not?* For without doubt this man who came praying for the health of his son believed. He would not have asked healing from one he did not believe was a Healer. Why then were the words: *Unless you see signs and wonders, you believe not,* said to one who believed even before seeing a sign? But remember what he asked and you will see clearly that his faith was doubtful.

For he asked that Jesus should come down, and heal his son. He asked therefore for the bodily Presence of the Lord Who in spirit is present in all places; and so had little faith in Him Who, he believed, could not heal unless He were present in body with the sick. Had his faith been perfect, he would have known beyond doubt that there is no place where God is not. And so in great part he was unbelieving: for He was not honouring Christ's divine majesty, but His corporeal presence. He begs for his son's healing, and at the same time his faith is doubting: for he believes that He to Whom he has come has power to heal; but believes also that unless Jesus comes to him, his son will die. But the Lord, when asked to come, shows that he is not absent from where He is asked to come; and by His sole word He restores health Who by His sole command created all things.

2. And here we must carefully recall to mind what we learned from the testimony of another Evangelist, that a certain centurion came to the Lord and said: *Lord, my servant lieth at home sick of the palsy, and is grievously tormented.* And straightaway Jesus answers: *I will come and heal him* (Mt. viii. 6, 7). Why is it that when the ruler asks Him to

come to his son He refuses to go there bodily, while, though not asked to come to the servant of the centurion, He offers to go there at once? He does not think it fitting that He should go to the ruler's son, while He did think it fitting to hasten to the centurion's servant?

What is this but a rebuking of our pride, which leads us to honour in men, not their nature, in which they are made to the image of God, but their dignity and riches? While our mind is drawn to the things that surround men, we have no thought for the inward things of man; we consider carefully what can be seen on their bodies, we fail to think of what they are themselves. But our Redeemer, to show us *that what is high to men* (Lk. xvi. 15), is not to be esteemed by the sanctified, and that what men despise the saints must not despise, refuses to go to the son of the ruler, while ready at once to go to the centurion's servant. Therefore it is our pride He here rebuked; which is unable, because of men, to judge what men are. As we have said, pride thinks only of the things that surround men, and has no thought for their natures: it will not acknowledge the dignity of God in man.

See how the Son of God will not come down to the son of the ruler, yet He is ready to come at once to heal a slave. And indeed should someone's slave ask us to come and see him, at once the unspoken thought of our pride will answer, and say: 'Do not go. You will demean yourself, and lose dignity. The neighbourhood is unpleasant.' And lo! He Who came down from heaven does not refuse to come at once to a servant on earth; while we

who are of the earth earthy, think it beneath us to be humble on earth. What is baser in the sight of God, what more contemptible, than to serve honour among men, and have no reverence for the eyes of the Unseen Witness?

Because of this we read in the holy Gospel, that the Lord said to the Pharisees: *You are they who justify themselves before men, but God knoweth your hearts. For that which is high to men, is an abomination before God* (Lk. xvi. 15). Note well, brethren: take note of what He says. If what is held in honour among men, is held as abominable before God; then the more the pride of our heart is despised by God, the more it is esteemed by men; and the more the humility of our heart is despised by men, the more is it honoured by God.

3. Let us then hold it as nothing should we do any good work. Let no work of ours inflate us with pride, no abundance of possessions, no earthly glory uplift us. For of the humble of heart the psalmist says: *The Lord is the keeper of little ones* (cxiv. 6). Why he calls the humble of heart, *little ones*, he then tells us: as though we had immediately asked him what the Lord did for them: *I was humbled, and he delivered me.*

Meditate upon these things, brethren, meditate upon them with your whole attention. Do not bow down before the worldly possessions of your neighbour. Out of reverence for God, honour this in men (to whom at the same time you have not been entrusted): That they are made in the image of God. And you will truly honour your neighbour in this way, if your heart is not puffed up with pride. For he who remains above himself, because of his fleeting possessions, does not know how to honour in his neighbour that which endures for ever.

Do not therefore be taken up with what you have, but with what you are. See how even now the world men love withers away. These holy ones, by whose tomb we are gathered, in their souls despised this glittering world. There was then the allure of long life, unbroken health, abundance of every kind, fruitfulness of offspring, rest in undisturbed peace; yet, while the world flowered in itself, already in their hearts it had withered.

See how the world now withers in itself; yet still flowers in our heart. Everywhere is death, everywhere sorrow, everywhere desolation and sadness; we are struck from every side, from every side we are filled with bitterness. And yet, with minds blinded by carnal desires, we love this very bitterness; as the world leaves us, we pursue it; as it collapses, we cling to it. And since we cannot uphold it, as it falls we fall with it; we fall with that to which as it falls we cling.

Once the world held us fast in its delight. Now it is filled with so many afflictions, that now it is the world itself that sends us to God.[25] Reflect therefore on how all that now runs past us in time is as nothing. The end of earthly things shows us the nothingness of that which can fade and pass away. The ruin of things declares to us, that this fleeting thing was then close to nothingness while it yet seemed to stand firm.

Reflect therefore on these things with earnest consideration, Dearest Brethren, and make fast your heart to the love of eternal things, so that refusing to strive after earthly dignities, you may attain to that glory to which we come by faith, through Jesus Christ our Lord, Who liveth and reigneth God with the Father, in the Unity of the Holy Ghost, throughout all ages and ages. Amen.

NOTES

[1] *Sancti Ephraim Syrii Hymni et Sermones*, Th.J.Lamy, Tom. IV, p. 126, *Sermo de Reprehensione et Oratione*, an exhortation adapted to his simple country hearers, but filled with divine wisdom.
[2] He is referring to the Hunnish invasion.
[3] Four lines missing here from original text.
[4] PL 37, col. 1585. *Enarat.* in Ps. cxviii; *Sermo* XXIX. A meditative discourse.
[5] Vulgate: Concluding prayer from *Sermo* CCCXXIII, PL 38.

[6] PL 46, col. 826, *Sermo* III, *De Sacramento Altaris ad Infantes*. A beautiful sermon in preparation for Holy Communion. Because of the fewness of Patristic homilies on today's Gospel, these three more recently found sermons of St Augustine are here included. The first two were spoken to children; the third to the newly baptized, who, until the Octave of the Pasch, were also called *Infantes*. They are perfect examples of catechetical instruction; impressing essentials firmly; and not deviating into 'questions'. The

power of the third is of the highest order, its application for every age.

[7] An explicit reference to the reserve of the *Discipline of the Secret,* so-called; which applied especially in respect of the doctrines of the Holy Trinity and the Blessed Eucharist. With the passing of the persecutions, and the public proclamation of Christian truth, this reserve gradually disappeared; leaving some relics of it in the liturgy: this from the fifth and sixth centuries onwards.

[8] *Panis, quem ego dedero, caro mea est, pro mundi vita, et: Nisi quis manducaverit carnem meam, et biberit sanguinem meum, non habebit in se vitam* (version in text), Jn. vi. 52–4.

[9] *Donec fermentaretur totum.* Vulg.: *Donec fermentatum est totum.*

[10] It is therefore plain that the name Catholic is a name derived from the essential substance of the Church, by reason of its being, in its entirety, Christ's Mystical Body: the whole mass that is leavened by Christ until it is one with Him: *two in one flesh,* and therefore not a name derived from place, or custom, or assumed: *Ὅλον* (*whole*), and so *κάθολον* (*κατα ὅλον*); adjective, *καθολικός* (*κὰθολος*), deriving from this *whole.* Any qualification therefore or separation, or attempted formal limitation, or assumption of this essential description of the Church founded by Christ is untrue and unjust, a brand not a true name, and offends against the Mystical Body of Christ, the Church, and therefore against Christ Himself; Who is One Whole with it, and Whose members they are who belong to it. That this will happen till the end we may expect, because of Christ's prophecy: *Blessed shall*

you be when men shall hate you, and when they shall separate you, and shall reproach you, and cast out your name as evil, for the son of man's sake, Luke vi. 22.

[11] PL 46, col. 834, *Sermo VI, Item De Sacramento altaris ad Infantes: Brevis Instructio ad Sacram Synaxim primum accedentium.*

[12] By the labour of oxen (*trituravit*); that is, treading out the corn from the husks or ears, by the feet of oxen, as they circle slowly round the threshing floor.

[13] 'Those who are convinced and believe in the truth of our teachings ... are taught to ask with fasting for the forgiveness of their sins. They are then also led to a place where there is water and are regenerated.' St Justin Martyr, *First Apologia,* PG 6, Ch. 41. Prayers and fasting, continued to form part of the preparation for baptism; followed by the imposition of hands and exorcisms. With the end of the Catechumenate, these practices, particularly the last two, were incorporated into the liturgy of Baptism.

[14] The children receiving Baptism, Holy Communion, and Confirmation, all in the one morning, in accord with the practice of the time, are now about to be present for the first time at the Consecration of the Mass; the changing of the bread and wine into the Body and Blood of Christ.

[15] That is: It was formally given to them, then learned by heart, then recited from memory to the Priest; and the same for the *Symbolum* or Creed.

[16] The *Pax,* the kiss of peace; in the early Church given promiscuously. Later (*Const. Apost.* VIII, 29), men of the laity saluted men in this

manner, while women kissed women. This practice seems to have continued until the thirteenth century, when a substitute was introduced in the shape of a small wooden tablet or plate of metal, which bore an image of the Crucified or any sacred image (*Osculatorium*). The earliest notice of these later usages is found in the records of English Councils of the thirteenth century.

[17] PL 46, col. 838, *Sermo* VIII, *In Octavam Paschatis ad Infantes*. As noted, the newly baptized were spoken of as *Infantes*, till the Sunday after Easter. They continued to receive instructions each day throughout the octave following Easter Sunday; particularly a more detailed instruction on the sacraments they had received at the Paschal Mass: Baptism, Eucharist and Confirmation.

[18] *Consepulti estis Christo per bap-*

tismum in morte, ut, quomodo surrexit Christus a mortuis, sic et vos in novitate vitae ambuletis, Romans vi. 4.

[19] Vulgate: *Qui opulenti estis in Sion.*

[20] Octave of Easter.

[21] PL 48, col. 1467, par. t; a closing prayer.

[22] PG 59, col. 200, Hom. XXV, v. 46.

[23] This reference, found in all codices, is not in Luke—*lapsus memoriae.* It is from Mark ix. 23.

[24] PL 76, col. 1210, Hom. XXVIII. The Feast of SS Nereus and Achilleus, Martyrs, is celebrated, together with that of SS Domitilla and Pancratius, on May 12th. They are named in the Proper of the Mass. The Basilica, fourth century, was discovered in recent years in the Catacombs of Domitilla.

[25] This was a time of Barbaric invasions, wars, famine, storms, and pestilence.

TWENTY-FIRST SUNDAY AFTER PENTECOST

I. St Basil the Great: Against the Angry

II. St John Chrysostom: Homily on the Servant who Owed Ten Thousand Talents and on the Sin of Remembering Past Offences, or On Contempt of Anger

III. St Ephraim: On Calumny and Oppression

THE GOSPEL OF THE SUNDAY

Matthew xviii. 23–35

At that time: Jesus spoke to his disciples this parable: The kingdom of heaven is likened to a man, a king, who would take an account of his servants. And, when he had begun to take the account, one was brought to him that owed him ten thousand talents. And, as he had not wherewith to pay it, his lord commanded that he should be sold, and his wife and children and all that he had, and payment to be made. But that servant falling down besought him, saying: Have patience with me and I will pay thee all. And the lord of the servant, being moved with pity, let him go and forgave him the debt.

But, when that servant was gone out, he found one of his fellow-servants that owed him an hundred pence; and laying hold of him, he throttled him, saying: Pay what thou owest. And his fellow-servant, falling down, besought him, saying: Have patience with me and I will pay thee all. And he would not; but went and cast him into prison till he paid the debt.

Now his fellow-servants, seeing what was done, were very much grieved; and they came and told their lord all that was done. Then his lord called him and said to him: Thou wicked servant, I forgave thee all the debt, because thou besoughtest me; shouldst not thou then have compassion also on thy fellow servant, even as I had compassion on thee? And his lord, being angry, delivered him to the torturers until he paid all the debt. So also shall my heavenly Father do to you, if you forgive not every one his brother from your hearts.

EXPOSITION FROM THE CATENA AUREA

CHRYSOSTOM, *Homily 62 in Matthew*: That no one should think that the

Lord had commanded something severe and burdensome, when He

265

said we must forgive even till seventy times seven, He added a parable. JEROME: For Syrians, and especially Palestinians, are wont to add a parable to everything they say; so that what their hearers might not retain from a simple statement, may stay in the mind by reason of the parable. And so we are told:

V.23. *Therefore is the kingdom of heaven likened to a man king, who would take an account of his servants.*

ORIGEN, *in Matthew, Tr.* 7: The Son of God, as He is Wisdom and Justice and Truth (I Cor. v. 30), is also a Kingdom; not of those here below, but of all who are above, in whose minds justice and the other virtues reign; who have become the kingdom of heaven through this, that they bear the image of the heavenly One. This Kingdom of heaven therefore, that is, the Son of God, when He was made in the likeness of sinful flesh, uniting man to Himself, then became like a man king.

REMIGIUS: Or, the Kingdom of heaven may aptly stand for the holy Church, in which the Lord accomplishes what is spoken of in this parable. The Father is sometimes designated by the word *man*, as where it was said that, *the kingdom of heaven is likened to a man king, who made a marriage for his son* (Mt. xxii. 2); and sometimes it designates the Son. Here however it can be understood of both: the Father and Son Who are one God. God is also spoken of as a king, ruling and governing all that He has made.

ORIGEN: The servants, in this parable, are solely those who are employed as dispensers of the word;

to whom it was entrusted, that they might trade with it. REMIGIUS: Or, by the servants of this man king are meant all men, whom He has created for His own praise, and to whom He has given the law of nature; and with whom He takes an account, when He searches into the life and conduct and actions of each one, so that He may render to each according to his deeds. Hence there follows:

V.24. *And, when he had begun to take an account, one was brought to him that owed him ten thousand talents.*

ORIGEN: The King will take an account of all our life, when we must all stand before the judgement seat of Christ (II Cor. v. 10). Saying this we do not mean that this accounting will go on for a long while. For when it is His will to sift the souls of all men, He will by His ineffable power, bring swiftly to the minds of each, all they have ever done. He says, *And, when he had begun to take the account*; because the beginning of judgement will begin from the household of God (I Pet. iv. 17). In the beginning therefore of His taking an account, one is brought before Him who owed Him many talents; one, that is, who had committed great evils; one to whom great things had been entrusted, and who had yielded no profit: who perhaps had ruined as many men as he had wasted talents; who therefore owed Him many talents, because he had followed the Woman sitting upon a talent of lead, whose name is *wickedness* (Zach. v. 7).

JEROME: I know that some interpret this man who owed ten thousand talents as the devil, and would have it that his wife and children, who were to be sold because he persevered in his wickedness, represent foolishness and evil thoughts. For just as wisdom is said to be the wife of the just (Prov. iv. 7; vii. 4), so is foolishness said to be the wife of the unjust and the sinner. But how the Lord forgave him ten thousand talents, and how he would not forgive his fellow servant a hundred pence has no explanation in the Church nor should any be accepted by prudent men.

AUGUSTINE, *on the Word of God, Sermon 83, 6:* We must therefore affirm that, because the law is given to us in ten commandments, the ten thousand talents mean all sins; that is, committed against the law. REMIGIUS: Man sinning of his own will and choice, cannot raise himself by his own effort, and therefore cannot pay what he owes; since he has nothing of himself, by which he can free himself of his sins. Hence follows:

V.25. And, as he had not wherewith to pay it, his lord commanded that he should be sold, and his wife and children and all that he had, and payment to be made.

The fool's wife is folly, and the pleasures and desires of the flesh. AUGUSTINE, *Gospel Questions, I, 25:* This means, that the transgressor must pay for his desires and his evil works, as it were for his wife and children; and this is what he pays. For the price of the one sold, is the punishment of damnation. CHRYSOSTOM: But He does not command this out of cruelty, but out of ineffable love. For He wishes to frighten him by these threats, that

he may beg not to be sold, And from what follows we are shown that this happened, since He goes on to say:

V.26. But that servant falling down besought him, saying: Have patience with me and I will pay thee all.

REMIGIUS: By these words, *falling down,* we are shown the humility and desire to make amends of the sinner. Saying, *have patience with me* he expresses the cry of the sinner for time, and the opportunity to reform. But the mercy and clemency of God towards converted sinners is without measure: since, through baptism or penance. He is ready at all times to forgive them their sins. Hence follows:

V.27. And the lord of that servant, being moved with pity, let him go and forgave him the debt.

CHRYSOSTOM: See the superabundance of the divine love. The servant asks only for time. He gives more than is asked for: pardon, and the forgiveness of the entire debt. He wished to forgive them from the beginning; but did not wish that this should be solely His gift, but also the fruit of the sinner's supplication, that he might not go away uncrowned. But He did not forgive the debt before He had taken the account, because He wished to show how great the debt was from which he frees him; that at least because of this, he might become more considerate of his fellow servants. Up to this he was acceptable: for he has admitted his debt, and promised to repay it, and falling down had pleaded and acknowledged the greatness of his debt. But what he then does is unworthy of his earlier actions. For there follows:

V.28. *But, when that servant was gone out, he found one of his fellow servants that owed him an hundred pence.*

AUGUSTINE, *Sermon* 83: That it is said he owed him a hundred pence is derived from the same number, ten; the number of the law. For a hundred times a hundred is ten thousand, and ten times ten a hundred. Both numbers are derived from the number of the law, and in both you find sins. Each is therefore a debtor, and each implores pardon: for every man is in debt to God, and a debtor to his own brother.

CHRYSOSTOM: There is as great a distance between sins committed against man and sins committed against God as there is between ten thousand talents and a hundred pence. That it is greater, and much greater, is evident from the difference between the persons offended and from our repeated offences. For while other men watch us we desist and are slow to sin; but though God sees all all the day we do and speak evil without a thought. And not by this only are our sins against God seen to be greater, but also from the favours we enjoy from him. For He made us and made all things because of us. He breathed into us a rational soul. He sent us His Son and opened heaven to us and made us His children. Should we therefore die each day for Him, could we repay Him what we owe Him? Far from it; but this again would return to our profit. Instead we offend Him in His laws.

REMIGIUS: So therefore by the one

who owed ten thousand talents those are signified who commit the greater crimes; by the debtor who owed a hundred pence those who commit the lesser offences. JEROME: To make this clearer let us give an example. Should one of you commit adultery, murder, sacrilege; these greater crimes of ten thousand talents will be forgiven to the one who asks, provided he in turn forgives those committing lesser sins against himself.

AUGUSTINE, as above: But this servant, unjust and ungrateful, refused to give what was given to himself; though unworthy of it. For there follows: *And laying hold of him, he throttled him, saying: Pay what thou owest.*

REMIGIUS: He insisted vehemently, to take vengeance on him. ORIGEN: Meaning, I think, took him by the throat, because he had just left the king; for he would not have taken him by the throat, had he not gone out from the king.

CHRYSOSTOM: By saying, *when that servant was gone out,* he shows that it was not a long time after, but immediately after; while the favour he had received was still ringing in his ears, he misuses in malice the freedom he had received from his own master. What this other servant then did follows:

V.29. *And his fellow servant, falling down, besought him, saying: Have patience with me and I will pay thee all.*
ORIGEN: Note the precision of the Scriptures. The servant owing many talents falls down and adores the King. But he who owed a hundred pence, did not worship, but falling

down besought his fellow servant, saying: *Have patience with me.* CHRYSOSTOM: But not even the very words that saved himself moved the ungrateful servant. For we read:

V.30. *And he would not.*

AUGUSTINE, *Gospel Questions*, I, 25: That is, he held to his resolve, to punish him. *But went.* REMIGIUS: That is, his anger flamed the more, so that he began to take vengeance on him. *And cast him into prison till he paid the debt*; that is, seizing his brother, he takes vengeance on him.

CHRYSOSTOM: See the tenderness of the lord, and the servant's cruelty: one in the matter of ten thousand talents, the other for a hundred pence. One begs from his fellow servant, the other begs from his Lord. The one receives total forgiveness of his debt, the other asks but time to pay and does not receive even that. Those who owed nothing grieved with him. Hence:

V.31. *Now his fellow servants, seeing what was done, were very much grieved.*

AUGUSTINE, as above: By *fellow servants* the Church is understood, which binds one, and looses another. REMIGIUS: Or, the Angels, or the preachers of holy Church or any of the faithful who see a brother who has received forgiveness of his own sins, unwilling to have compassion on his fellow servant, and grieve at his wickedness. He continues: *And they came and told their lord all that was done.* They came in mind, not in body. To tell the Lord, is to show by their feelings the sorrow and grief of their heart. He continues:

V.32. *Then his lord called him.*

He called him by means of the sentence of death, and bade him depart from this world. *And said to him: Thou wicked servant, I forgave thee all the debt, because thou besoughtest me.* When he owed him ten thousand talents the Lord did not call him *wicked*; neither did he reproach him, but was moved with pity towards him. But when he was heartless to his fellow servant, He then called him a *wicked servant*. And said to him:

V.33. *Shouldst not thou then have compassion also on thy fellow servant?*

REMIGIUS: And let us note that we read of no answer made by this servant to the Lord: by which we are shown that upon the day of judgement and immediately following this life all excuses will end. CHRYSOSTOM: Since he had not been made better by kindness, nothing remained but to correct him by punishment. Hence there follows:

V.34. *And his lord, being angry, delivered him to the torturers until he paid all the debt.*

He does not simply say, *delivered him*, but that He was *angry*; which was not said when He commanded him to be sold: and this was said in correction rather than anger, and out of love. But this now is a sentence of condemnation and torment. REMIGIUS: For God is said to be angry when He punishes sinners. The demons are called *torturers* because they are ever ready to receive the souls of the lost and to torment them in the punishment of eternal damnation. Can one who has once been plunged into eternal damnation ever again find time for amendment or a way of escape? No. The word *until* stands for infinity, so that the meaning is: He shall ever pay but never repay and ever shall suffer in punishment.

CHRYSOSTOM: By this we are shown that he will be punished without end, that is, eternally, yet will not ever repay. For though the gifts and vocations of God are irrevocable (Rom. i. 29), yet malice, it seems, is able to undo this law. AUGUSTINE, *Sermon* 83, 7: For God says: *Forgive and it shall be forgiven you.* I have first forgiven you; forgive then after Me. For if you do not, I shall recall you, and demand of you whatever I have forgiven. For Christ will neither deceive nor be deceived; Who now adds these words:

V.35. *So also shall my heavenly Father do to you, if you forgive not every one his brother from your hearts.*

It is better to complain with your mouth, and forgive in your heart than be bland and smiling in speech and cruel in heart. And it is for this the Lord adds: *From your hearts,* so that should you impose discipline because of charity, gentleness may not go from your heart. For what is so devoted as the physician with his instruments? He is severe against the infirmity, that the man may be cured. For if it is mildly treated, the man will be lost.

JEROME: The Lord added: *From your hearts,* that He might turn us away from all pretended peace. Therefore the Lord instructs Peter, in this parable of a master who was a king, and of his servant, who owing him ten thousand talents besought his lord and obtained forgiveness of the debt, that he likewise shall forgive his fellow servants their lesser offences against himself. ORIGEN: He also wishes to teach us that we should be ready to forgive those who have injured us, especially if they make amends and beg to be forgiven.

RABANUS: Allegorically, the servant who here owes ten thousand talents stands for the Jewish people, bound by the ten commandments of the law; whose debts the Lord had again and again forgiven when, straitened, they besought His mercy. But delivered, they cruelly attacked their own debtors; and demand of the Gentiles whom they hated, that they should fulfil the ceremonies and circumcision of the law. They even put to a cruel death the Prophet and Apostles. For this the Lord delivered them to the hands of the Romans; or to evil spirits, who punish with eternal torment.

I. ST BASIL THE GREAT, BISHOP AND DOCTOR

Against the Angry[1]

1. Just as the value of the physician's advice is seen only when his directions have been carefully carried out, so also is it with spiritual teaching; where it can be seen whether its counsels and directions, given for the right ordering of our way of life and for the perfection of those that obey them, have been wisely and profitably observed from the results

which follow. We have heard the clear counsel of Proverbs: *A mild answer breaketh wrath* (xv. 1), and the apostolic warning: *Let all bitterness and anger and indignation and clamour be put away from you* (Eph. iv. 31). And listen again to the words of the Lord Himself: that he who is angry with his brother *shall be in danger of the Judgement* (Mt. v. 22). And lastly, when we ourselves have come to suffer this violence of feeling, which did not rise from us, but suddenly rushed upon us like a storm, then especially do we come to know the wondrous excellence of the divine teaching. And if we have ever yielded to this anger, as to a rushing torrent, or have observed in silence the shameful state of those held in the grip of this violent emotion, we learned by deeds how true the saying: *An angry man is not becoming* (Prov. xi. 25, Sept.).

For once this passion, reason set aside, acquires dominion over the soul, it changes a man into a beast; and does not even permit him to be a man, since it deprives him of the help of reason. As poison is to those who are poisoned, so is violence of feeling to those provoked to anger. They become rabid like dogs; they dart like scorpions. The Scriptures well knew those ruled by this emotion, calling them beasts; whom they resemble in ferocity. For it calls them *dumb dogs* (Is. lvi. 10), *serpents, a generation of vipers* (Mt. xxiii. 33), and similar names. For they who are ready to destroy one another and to injure their fellow creatures may well be looked upon as wild beasts and reptiles; in whom by nature there is an implacable hatred against man.

Through anger, tongues become unbridled, mouths unguarded: hands without control, insults, accusations, slanders, blows and all such things too numerous to mention are the evil fruit of this violence of feeling. Through anger the sword is sharpened, the hand of man dares to take human life; because of anger, brother will forget brother, and parents and children the ties of nature. For the angry first no longer know themselves, and then those near and dear to them. And just as the mountain streams, rushing to the valleys below, will sweep all before them, so will the headlong, and ungovernable violence of the anger that enters into all men: for anger respects no one, neither grey hairs nor virtue, nor ties of blood nor benefits received, nor any of the things that men reverence.

Anger is a sudden madness. For the angry will at times rush insanely into manifest evil, heedless of danger, in their lust for revenge. Stung as by a gadfly with the thought of those who may have injured them, anger boiling and seething within them, they will not stop till they have done some injury to whoever provoked them, or until they themselves have suffered injury: for it frequently happens that they who offer violence, receive more than they inflict; their fury turned upon themselves by those who resist them.

2. Who can describe this evil? How those who are prone to anger, roused by some trivial slight, will shout and rage and attack others with no more shame than wild beasts, and will not cease until the conflagration has spent itself in some dreadful and irreparable disaster; and then their anger bursts as a

bubble. Neither the point of the sword nor fire nor any other dreadful thing can restrain the spirit raging in anger, no more than it can restrain those possessed by demons; between whom and angry men there is no difference, either in appearance or in the state of their soul. The blood swells in the hearts of those thirsting for revenge as though it were seething and boiling over the heat of a fire. Bursting forth, anger will make a man look another person, changing his outward aspect that all know, as though with a masque upon the stage. His look, to those who know him, will appear strange, his appearance like one deranged, his eye fiery. He grinds his teeth like a wild pig. His face becomes livid and suffused with blood. His body swells, his veins are bursting; his breathing is shaken by the storm within him. His voice becomes harsh, and is raised to the utmost. His words are indistinct, rushing, unmeasured, without order and without sense. And when his anger, like a fire heaped with wood, blazing up from the things that feed his rage, has reached the point of explosion, he then becomes a spectacle truly beyond words to describe, and indeed not fit to be seen: His hands are raised even against his own kindred, and against every part of the body. With his feet he will stamp without caring on the most vital parts, and whatever he lays his eyes on becomes a weapon for his fury and madness. And should he find another threatening the same evils against himself, that is, possessed by the same anger, the same mad rage, they both come head to head against each other, so much so that they inflict upon each other

what those who serve such a devil deserve to suffer. And these warriors will often suffer maiming, even death itself, as the reward of their rage. One begins with hands laid unjustly on another; who in turn repulses the first. The first strikes back, while the second refuses to yield. Their bodies are bruised with blows; but fury makes them indifferent to pain. There is not time to notice what they suffer; for their whole soul is absorbed in vengeance on the other attacker.

3. Do not cure evil by evil, nor strive to outdo one another in inflicting injuries. For in such evil strife he who wins is the more to be pitied, for he goes away bearing the greater part of the blame. Do not pile up the debt of your own wickedness; do not make an evil debt more evil. Does someone in a rage insult you? Bear with the offence in silence. Instead, you gather into your heart the evil flood of his wrath; you imitate the winds, that throw back whatever is thrown against them. Do not let your enemy be your teacher; and do not strive to become what you detest. Beware lest you become the mirror of an angry man; repeating his image in yourself. His face is red. Must you make yours red also? His eyes are suffused with blood; do yours, tell me, look serene and calm? His voice is harsh; is yours mild and gentle? No echo in the desert so clearly returns to the speaker, as abuse to the abuser. Rather, the sound of an echo comes back unchanged; but insults are returned with interest.

And what sort of things do angry men hurl at each other? One shouts out that the other is worthless; or that he comes from nothing. The other will call the first, a slave of slaves. This man calls another a beggar; who answers that the first is a vagabond. One shouts 'fool'; the other 'madman', until their stock of insults, like bowmen's arrows, is exhausted. Then when they have slung from their mouths as from a sling, every insult they can think of, they fall to blows. For anger provokes strife; strife begets insults; insults lead to blows, blows to injuries, and from injuries death itself will often follow.

Let us crush the evil at its first beginning; by every means driving anger from our souls: And doing this, we shall root out many vices that have their root and beginning in this very passion of anger. Someone insults you? Let you bless him. He strikes you? Bear with it. Should he despise you, make nothing of you? Let you remember within your own heart that you came from the earth, and that to earth you will again return. He who fortifies himself with such thoughts will find every humiliation less than the truth. And your enemy will be at a loss when he cannot insult you; since you show yourself invulnerable to his insults, while at the same time you prepare for yourself a great crown of patience; by making another's folly an occasion for the practice of humility and wisdom.

And, if you will be persuaded by me, let you even add to his insults. If he calls you a nobody, worthless, come from nothing; let you call yourself *dust and ashes*. You are not more to be honoured than our father, Abraham, and he spoke of himself in this way (Gen. xviii. 27). You are called ignorant, a beggar,

worthless? Let you then, using the words of David, call yourself a *worm* coming from a dunghill (Ps. xxi. 7). Add to these, the example of the great Moses: Moses who, attacked with insults by Mary his sister and by Aaron his brother, did not appeal to God against them, but rather prayed for them (Num. xii). Whose disciple do you prefer to be? The imitator of men who were blessed and pleasing to God, or of those puffed up with the spirit of wickedness? Whenever the temptation to offer insult seizes you, think to yourself that you are being tested: to see whether in patience you turn to God, or yield in anger to the Adversary. Give time to your thoughts to choose the better part. Let you either do a kindness to your enemy by an example of mildness, or defend yourself more strongly by taking no notice of him. For what is more bitter to one hostile to you, than to see you indifferent to his insults? Do not debase your own soul. Do not leave yourself open to whoever insults you. Let him bark away. Let him explode against himself. For as a man who strikes what is without feeling punishes himself (for he neither caused pain to his enemy, nor appeased his own wrath) so he who abuses one who is indifferent to his abuse, finds no solace in his violence. Rather, as I said, he rends himself. What does it matter what name others call you? Someone rails at you. Let you be magnanimous. Another is angry with you. Let you be gentle and mild. He will regret his words; you however will never regret your own practise of virtue.

4. What need is there to say

more? To such a man *railing* closes the kingdom of heaven; *neither drunkards nor railers shall possess the kingdom of God* (I Cor. vi. 10), while your silence will open it for you. *He that shall persevere unto the end, he shall be saved* (Mt. x. 22). But should you revenge yourself in equal measure and answer abuse with abuse, what excuse then remains to you? That he attacked you first! How does that make you deserving of forgiveness? A fornicator who blames his accomplice for leading him into sin is held as no less guilty of condemnation. There can be no crowns without contests; and there are no contests without an enemy. Listen to what David says: *When the sinner stood against me*, I was not provoked, I sought no vengeance; but *I was dumb, and was humbled, and kept silence from good things* (Ps. xxxviii. 2, 3).

You are provoked by abuse as by something repulsive? Pretend to yourself it is something good. Otherwise you do what you complain of. Or is it that you look carefully at the evil others commit, and think nothing of your own wickedness. Is such abuse not an evil thing? Then fly from imitating it. That another began it is no excuse. Indeed to me it seems more fitting to blame you for the quarrel; in that you gave him no example in self restraint. You seeing an angry man behaving in an unbecoming manner do not guard against imitating him, but becoming angry and bitter you rage against him: so your anger now becomes a justification for the one who began the quarrel. And in doing this you provide an excuse for him, and condemn yourself.

For if anger is an evil thing, **why**

did you not *decline from evil* (Ps. xxxvi. 27)? And if it is deserving of forgiveness, why did you deal so harshly with an angry man? So it is no defence to say another person attacked you. For in contests for a crown, it is not the one who begins the contest is crowned, but the one who ends it. And therefore it is not he only who began the evil will be condemned, but he also who followed evil example. If he calls you a beggar, and if he calls you what is true, bear with the truth. But if he lies, what does it matter what he says against you? You should not be deceived by praise that oversteps truth; neither should you be provoked by insults that do not apply to you. Have you not seen how an arrow will pierce what resists it, while its force is broken by a surface that yields? Reflect how the same is true of railing and abuse. He who resists it, receives it. He who gives away and makes no resistance, undoes by mildness the evil directed against him.

And why should it trouble you that someone gives you the name of beggar? Recall to mind your own nature: that naked you come into the world, and naked you go forth from it. Who is more a beggar than one who is naked? You have been called nothing that is evil; unless you think the word applies to you only. Who ever was taken to prison because he was poor? It is not poverty that is shameful, but not to bear poverty generously. Think of our Lord, *Who being rich, became poor for your sakes* (II Cor. viii. 9), Should anyone call you stupid and unlettered, remember the insults with which the Jews reviled the True Wisdom: *Thou art a Samaritan and hast a devil* (Jn. viii. 48). But if you become angry, you only confirm what they say against you. For what is more stupid than anger? But if you remain unprovoked, you shame the one who insults you; giving him an example of restraint and moderation. Were you struck in the face? So too was the Lord. Were you spat upon? And so was our Lord: *I have not turned away my face from them that spit upon me* (Is. l. 6). Were you falsely accused? So too was your Judge. Did they tear your garments? They stripped my Lord and divided His garments among them (Mt. xxvii. 31). You have not yet been condemned to death; nor fastened upon a cross. Many things are wanting before you become like to Him.

5. Let each one of these considerations enter into your thoughts; and let them be a restraint on angry passion. For, it is by such considerations and affections that we calm the throbbing, the violent impulse of the heart, and bring our mind to sanity and peace. And this is what David means by the words: *I am ready, and am not troubled; that I may keep thy Commandments* (Ps. cxviii. 60). Therefore, you must restrain the frenzied, the senseless impulse of your spirit by recalling the example of these blessed men. How meekly the mighty David bore with the insults of Semei. He yielded in nothing to the violence of anger but raised his mind to God: *For*, he said, *the Lord hath bid him curse David* (II Kings xvi. 10). And hearing himself called a man of blood and an unjust man he did not become angry but bore himself with humility and patience as though deserving the outrages that were flung at him.

Empty your mind of these two things: the belief that you are deserving of great things, or the thought that any man is beneath you. If you do this anger will never be permitted to rise up within you. It is a very grave thing for anyone who has received great gifts and graces, to add insult and abuse to ingratitude. Truly grave; but more grievous for the one who offers insult, than for the one who receives it. Should another abuse you, let you not abuse him. Let his injurious words be for you an exercise in forbearance. If you are not provoked by his words you have received no wound. And should you suffer anything in your soul, keep the pain of it within you. *My heart is troubled within me*, says the psalmist (Ps. cxlii. 4); that is, he gave no outward sign of feeling and became calm as the wave when it breaks and rolls upon the shore. And so let you calm your provoked and clamorous heart. Let the riot of your emotions behave as reverently in the presence of reason as disorderly boys in the presence of a venerable teacher.

How then shall we escape the disasters that anger brings? By training the force of our feelings not to rush ahead of the power of reason. Rather, let us be watchful beforehand, to see that it does not at any time run ahead of our judgement; keeping it under our control like a horse: obedient to reason as to the rein; so that it shall not rise above its due place, but suffer itself to be led where reason leads. For ardour of soul is useful in many of the works of virtue; as for example when a soldier, leaving his arms by his leader, goes promptly when commanded to carry supplies. It is an ally of the reason against sin. For strength of feeling is as it were the nerve of the soul; giving it force to do promptly and perseveringly what it must do. For should the soul grow weak and become slack through pleasure, anger will stiffen it, as dipping in water will harden the heated iron, and from being weak and flaccid it will become resolute and courageous.

If your anger has never been aroused against the Evil One, you shall never be able to hate him as he deserves. For to me it seems as necessary to hate evil as much as we must love justice; and for this anger is especially useful. As a sheepdog obeys its shepherd, so must feeling be subject to reason: quiet and submissive to its master, and obedient to his voice; fierce to the voice or the face that is strange, at once docile and submissive to the voice of a friend.

This co-operation between the irascible part of the soul and its understanding part is a perfect and fitting thing. For such a spirit will have no part with treachery, it will not yield to a false friend, it will bark like a dog at false pleasure; attacking it fiercely as though it were a wolf. This then is the service of anger to those who know how to master it. And the same is true of the other powers of the soul; each becomes good or bad according to the manner in which we use them. For example, He who uses the desiring power of the soul for the pursuit of the pleasures of the flesh and impure gratifications becomes dissolute and repulsive; but he who directs it upwards to the love of God and towards a longing desire for eternal joys becomes happy and blessed. Again, he who makes worthy use of

the power of reason will be prudent and understanding; but he who uses it to the hurt of his neighbour becomes a mischief maker and a criminal.

6. Therefore, let the powers which were given us by the Creator as our means of salvation not be made into instruments of sin. And so anger, used as it should be, and when it should be, will lend us courage and steadfastness and a firmer purpose; used against right reason, it becomes madness. It is for this reason the psalmist also warns us, telling us: *Be ye angry, and sin not* (iv. 5). And just as the Lord threatens with judgement those who yield rashly to anger, so does He not forbid us to use anger, as I have said, as a help in those things where it is fitting to use it, For the words: *I will put enmities between thee and the woman* (Gen. iii. 15), and also: *Let the Madianites find you their enemies, and slay you them* (Num. xxv. 17), teach us that anger is to be used as a weapon. Because of this Moses, the gentlest of men (Num. xii. 3), took vengeance on the idolators, and armed the Levites for the slaughter of their brethren. *Put every man his sword upon his thigh. Go, and return from gate to gate through the midst of the camp, and let every man kill his brother, and friend, and neighbour.* (Ex. xxxii. 27). And a little later Moses said: *You have consecrated your hands this day to the Lord: every man in his son and in his brother, that a blessing may be given to you* (v. 29).

What justified Phineas? (Num. xxv. 8). Was it not just anger against the fornicators? He who, otherwise a mild and gentle man, when he saw the public and shameless sin of

Jambri with the Madianite, who did not even seek to veil the spectacle of their wickedness, refusing to endure it, transfixed them together with a dagger. And again, Samuel, did he not in just wrath slay Agag, King of Amalec, after he had been spared by Saul against the divine decree (I Kings xv. 35)? Thus anger is often the minister of just actions. Again, it was in deliberate and reasonable anger, for the good of Israel, that the burning Elias slew four hundred and fifty men, *priests of confusion*, and four hundred priests *of the groves* who ate at Jezebel's table (III Kings xviii. 19).

You are foolish to be angry with your brother. For how is it not foolish to be angry with another simply because he provokes you: doing what dogs do, who bite the stones when they cannot reach those who throw them. He who is provoked is to be pitied; but he who provokes him becomes hateful. When this happens, turn your anger against the murderer of man, against the father of lies, the sower of sin; but show sympathy to your brother; because, should he remain in sin, he will be given over with the devil to eternal fire. Now just as there are different names for *anger* and *indignation*, so are their meanings different one from another. Indignation is a flaring-up and a bursting-forth of feeling. But anger is an enduring pain, the soul as it were thirsting for vengeance, and goading us to attack. We must know that both cause men to sin, either by furious rage swiftly aroused against those who provoke, or by deceitfully and treacherously lying in wait for our enemy. We must be on our guard against both.

7. How then are we to make sure that violence of feeling shall not be improperly aroused? How? By being first formed in that humility which the Lord has taught us, both by word and example: Now saying to us: *If any man desire to be first, he shall be the last of all* (Mk. ix. 34), and again mildly and patiently enduring the one who struck Him (Jn. xviii, 22, 23). For the Maker and Lord of heaven and earth, adored by every creature having reason or feeling, *upholding all things by the word of his power* (Heb. i. 3), did not cast His striker living into hell, the earth itself opening to engulf him, but admonished and gently taught him: *If I have spoken evil, give testimony of the evil; but if well, why strikest thou me?* (Jn. xviii. 23). For if, following the precept of the Lord, you are wont to look upon yourself as the least of men, how could you then be made angry by a slight to your dignity? Should a child insult you, you are amused at the insult. And if a madman insults you, you regard him more with pity than resentment. It is not then the words that provoke; it is our own pride, rising against whoever insults us, which gives rise both to anger and to our unreal opinion of ourselves. If you drive both from your mind, you will look upon insults thrown at you as so much empty sound.

Cease, therefore, *from anger, and leave rage; have no emulation to do evil* (Ps. xxxvi. 8), that you may escape the danger of wrath: *For the wrath of God is revealed from heaven against injustice* (Rom. i. 18). For if by prudent counsel you can cut away the bitter root of anger, you will extirpate not a few other vices together with their source. For deceit, suspicion, infidelity, folly and a whole swarm of similar evils are offshoots of this vice.

Let us therefore not bring upon ourselves so great a disaster, such a sickness of the soul, such darkness upon the mind, such a separation from God, and loss of His friendship, a beginning of strife, a piling up of disasters, an evil demon coming to birth in our very souls, taking possession of us like some impudent tenant, and shutting out the Holy Spirit. For where there are enmities, quarrels, angers, brawls, arguments,

unrest and contests of violence in souls, there the Spirit of Meekness will not take up His rest. Rather, mindful of the counsel of the blessed Paul, let us put away from us all *bitterness and anger and indignation and clamour, and with them all malice* (Eph. iv. 31), and let us become kind and merciful to one another, awaiting the blessed hope that is promised to the meek: *Blessed are the meek; for they shall possess the land* (Mt. v. 4), in Christ Jesus our Lord, to Whom be glory and honour for ever and ever. Amen.

II. St John Chrysostom, Bishop and Doctor

Homily on the Servant who owed Ten Thousand Talents and on the Sin of Remembering Past Offences, or, On Contempt of Anger[2]

Matthew xviii. 23–35

The Occasion of the Parable

1. For the attainment of this virtue (*contempt of anger*) time is not a necessity; labour is not a necessity; money is not needed. To will alone suffices, and then all that relates to this virtue will prosper. And in meditating on the authority of God Who ordains and commands us to practise this virtue, we shall receive sufficient instruction and counsel concerning it: for what we are about to say to you is not our teaching; we but lead you all into the Presence of the Lawgiver. Follow me therefore and give ear to His divine laws.

Where then does He speak of anger and of the remembrance of injuries. Often; here and elsewhere, but especially in this parable, which He spoke to His Disciples, beginning in this way: *Therefore is the kingdom of heaven likened to a man king who*

would take an account of his servants. And, when he had begun to take the account, one was brought to him that owed him ten thousand talents. And, as he had not wherewith to pay it, his lord commanded that he should be sold, and his wife and children and all that he had, and payment to be made. But that servant falling down besought him, saying: Have patience with me and I will pay thee all. And the Lord of that servant, being moved with pity, let him go and forgave him the debt. But, when that servant was gone out, he found one of his fellow servants that owed him an hundred pence; and laying hold of him, he throttled him, saying: Pay what thou owest, And his fellow servant, falling down, besought him, saying: Have patience with me and I will pay thee all. And he would not; but went and cast him into prison till he paid the debt. Now his fellow servants, seeing what was done, were very much grieved; and they came and told their lord all that was done. Then his lord called him and said to him: Thou wicked servant, I forgave thee all the debt, because thou besoughtest me; shouldst not thou then have had compassion on thy fellow servant, even as I had compassion on thee? And his lord, being angry, delivered him to the torturers until he paid the debt. So also shall my heavenly Father do to you, if you forgive not every one his brother from your hearts.

2. This then is the parable. Next we must speak of why He begins this parable with a reference to its occasion. He does not say simply: *The kingdom of heaven is likened,* but: *Therefore is the kingdom of heaven likened,* etc. Why is the cause added? He had earlier been speaking to His Disciples on the virtue of forbearance, teaching them how anger must be kept down, and that we are not to make anything of injuries inflicted on us by others, and in these words: *If thy brother shall offend against thee, go and rebuke him between thee alone. If he shall hear thee, thou shalt gain thy brother* (v. 15). And while He was saying these and similar things to His Disciples, teaching them true wisdom, Peter, the leader of the company of the Apostles, the mouthpiece of the Disciples, the pillar of the Church, the prop of the Faith, the foundation of our Confession, the Fisherman of the world, who has led our race from the darkness of error to heaven, ever fervent, ever filled with confidence, and more filled with love than with confidence, while the others remain silent, drawing close to the Master, he says: *How often shall my brother offend against me, and I forgive him? Till seven times seven?* At one and the

same time he both asks and as it were pledges himself; and even before he learns the answer, he is eager to be generous. For knowing clearly the mind of the Master, that It was inclined towards mercy and compassion, and that he pleased Him most who was the most prompt to forgive offences, not brooding on them in bitterness, and wishing to please the Lawmaker, he says: *Even till seven times?*

Then, that you might learn what manner of man He was, what manner of God, and the measure of His compassion, and how human generosity compared with it is poorer than all poverty, and human goodness a drop in the boundless sea compared with His ineffable love for men, then to Peter asking, *till seven times,* and thinking he was saying something great and generous, listen to what He answers: *I say not to thee, till seven times, but till seventy times seven times.* Some think that this seventy times seven means seven and seventy times. But this is not so. The number we have here is almost five hundred: for seventy times seven is four hundred and ninety. And do not think, Beloved, that this commandment is hard to fulfil. For if you forgive a man who injures you, once, twice, and even thrice in a day, even if he were made of stone, even if he were fiercer than the demons, this man who offends you, he will not be so void of feeling that he will again commit the same offence, but rather, learning restraint from this repeated forgiveness, will become milder and more temperate. And you, if you have been taught to think nothing of injuries so often repeated against you, by first once, then twice, then three times forgiving him, you will then feel little difficulty in continuing in this wisdom. For you who have so often forgiven injuries have acquired the habit of forgiveness, so that you are no longer troubled by your neighbour's injuries against you.

Peter hearing this stood amazed, open-mouthed with astonishment; thinking not only of himself, but of those who were to be entrusted to him. And lest he should do now as he had done on hearing previous commands, the Lord, in anticipation, cuts off further questioning. What was it Peter had done in the case of others of the Lord's Commands? Whenever Christ had commanded something of this kind, which seemed to Peter to present some difficulty, speaking at once before the others, he would begin to question and argue about the command. As when the rich man approached, questioning Him about eternal life, and, learning what he must do to attain blessedness, went away sorrowful; *for he had great possessions.* Upon Christ saying that it was easier for a camel to pass through the eye of a needle than for a rich man to enter the kingdom of heaven (Mark x. 25), Peter, though he had stripped himself of all things, and had not kept back even a fishhook, since he held as nothing neither his boat nor his entire calling as a fisherman, coming to Christ, says to Him: *Who then can be saved?* See the honesty of this Disciple; and his fervour. He did not say: 'You are imposing what is impossible,' or 'This is a heavy commandment; this is a difficult law.' Neither did he remain silent, but, revealing the anxiety he felt for all of them, he shows at the same time the reverence

due to the Teacher from His Disciple, saying: *Who then can be saved?*

He had not yet become a shepherd, but he had the soul of a shepherd. He had not yet been given supreme authority, but he had an anxiety befitting a ruler; thinking of the whole world. For if he had been rich, and surrounded by wealth, he would perhaps have said that he asked, not for others, but because he was anxious for himself and his friends and possessions. But now poverty frees him from this concern, and shows him as anxious for others' salvation, caring for them, and wishing to learn from His Teacher the way of salvation. Because of this, Christ, to awaken his confidence, tells him that things that are impossible with men, are possible with God (Mark x. 25). And, He says, lest you should think you are to be deserted, I also shall put My Hands to your effort, and shall make difficult things easy and even pleasant.

Again, when Christ was speaking of marriage and of a wife and saying: *Whosoever shall put away his wife excepting for the cause of fornication, maketh her to commit adultery* (Mt. v. 32), and warning that all the wife's wickedness had to be endured, fornication alone excepted, Peter, while the others keep silent, says to Christ: *If the case of a man with his wife be so, it is not expedient to marry* (Mt. xix. 10).

Peter solicitous for the salvation of others: An account of what is received and expended to be given to God.

And here also, while he preserves a fitting reverence for the Master, he is at the same time solicitous for the salvation of others, not thinking of himself. Therefore, lest he should say something of this kind, the Lord answers his contradiction, anticipating it by a parable. This is the reason why the Evangelist says: *Therefore is the kingdom of heaven,* etc.; showing that He therefore speaks this parable, that you may learn that, although you forgive your brother his sins against you seven times in a day, you have yet done nothing wonderful, and that you are still immeasurably distant from the clemency of the Lord, and that you have not so much given as received.

3. Let us then hear the parable which, though it seems clear, contains nevertheless a certain hidden and ineffable treasury of reflections. *Therefore is the kingdom of heaven likened to a man king who would take an account of his servants.* In order that we may not appear to simply pass over these words, but may unfold and explain the nature of His judgement, entering into your conscience, go over in your mind all the deeds of your whole life, and, when you hear of the Lord taking an account with His servants, reflect that by this word, *servants*, He means kings and rulers and princes, rich, poor, slaves, and free; every kind of men; all are referred to here: *For we must all be manifested before the judgement seat of Christ* (II Cor. v. 10). And if you are rich, think of the account you must give; whether you have given your money to harlots, or to the poor; whether to parasites, to flatterers, or to those in need; whether you have spent it in licentiousness, or on humanity; on luxury, dissipation and drunkenness, or on helping the afflicted.

He will demand an account not only of what we have spent, but also of the manner in which we have acquired our gain: whether by our own just labours, or by robbery, or by covetousness; whether by inheritance, or by the ruin of the homes of orphans, the plundering of widows. For just as we exact from those who serve us an account not only of what has gone out, but also of what ha come in, verifying from where the money came, through whom, in what manner, how much they received, so God demands of us an account, not only of what we have expended, but also of what we have received and how we received it. And not only the rich, but even the poor must give an account of their poverty; whether they have borne it nobly and thankfully, or angrily complaining against Providence, when they see others revelling in pleasures and themselves in want.

For as an account of their almsgiving is required of the rich, so from the poor shall be required an account of their patience; and not only of their patience, but also of their almsgiving: for poverty is no hindrance to almsgiving; as witness the *poor widow* in the Gospel, who casting her two mites into the treasury, *hath cast in more than all they who have cast into the treasury* (Mk. xii. 43). Not only shall the rich and the poor be scrupulously examined, but also rulers and judges, as to whether or not they have corrupted justice, whether they have given judgement in disputes with favour or with enmity, whether they have flattered and given judgement against the right, or whether remembering offences they have dealt spitefully with those who had done no wrong.

What account Rulers of the Church Must Give.

Not alone must worldly rulers give an account, so also must they who rule the Church give an account of their rule; and it is these especially who shall suffer a more grievous, a more bitter chastisement. For he to whom the ministry of the word has been given, will there be diligently examined as to whether he has neglected to say what he should have said or to do what he should have done, either because of cowardice, or through ill will or jealousy; and nothing will be hidden which concerns him. Again, he who has attained to the office of bishop, the greater his responsibility, the more will he be subject to an account, not only of his teaching and the care of the poor, but also of his examination of those who are to be ordained and a thousand other things. And Paul, writing to Timothy, makes this clear: *Impose not hands lightly upon any man; neither be partakers of other men's sins* (I Tim. v. 22); and, writing to the Hebrews of these same spiritual rulers, he makes us fearful for another reason: *Obey your prelates and be subject to them. For they watch as being to render an account of your souls; that they may do this with joy and not with grief* (Heb. xiii. 17).

And we shall render an account, not only of our deeds but also of our words. For just as we, when we entrust money to servants, we ask an account of everything, so will God require of us an account of the words He has entrusted to us; of how we have expended them. Let us ask ourselves and examine ourselves scrupulously, as to whether we have spent them rashly or foolishly; for money foolishly expended

does not do so much harm as rash and foolish words, spoken without need. For money foolishly spent may sometimes do harm, but speech imprudently used may bring sadness to whole families and undo and ruin souls. The loss of money can be made good; but the word once gone forth can never be recalled.

That we must be mindful of the punishment of words. The reason of forgiving sins. Good actions serve to merit forgiveness of sins.

That you may learn of the penalties attached to words, listen to what Christ says: *But I say unto you, that every idle word that men shall speak, they shall render an account for it in the day of judgement. For by thy words thou shalt be justified; and by thy words thou shalt be condemned* (Mt. xii. 36, 37). Not alone shall we render an account of our own words, but also of those we hear; as should you accept a false accusation criminally made against a brother: *Thou shalt not receive the voice of a lie* (Ex. xxiii. 1). And if they who receive a lying report will not receive pardon, what excuse will slanderers and betrayers have?

4. And why speak of words and of things heard, when we must also render an account of our very thoughts? Paul himself declaring this says: *Therefore judge not before time; until the Lord come, who both will bring to light the hidden things of darkness and will make manifest the counsels of the heart* (I Cor. iv. 15). And the singer of the Psalms says: *For the thought of man shall give praise to thee* (lxxv. 11). What does this mean, *the thought of man shall give praise to thee?* It is as when you speak with

guile and with an evil mind to a brother; praising him with the mouth and tongue, while in your mind you think evil of him and envy him. And Christ, implying this truth, declares that we shall be punished, not only for our deeds, but also for our thoughts: *Whosoever shall look on a woman to lust after her, hath already committed adultery with her in his heart* (Mt. v. 28). And this sin has not burst into act, but is so far in the mind only. But not for long can he remain blameless, who so looks upon the shape of a woman that the desire of fornication arises within him.

When therefore you hear that the Lord would take an account of his servants, do not lightly pass over these words, but understand them as spoken of every degree of mankind, of every age, of every nature, of men and women. Think of the majesty of the judgement seat. Think upon all the sins you have committed. For though you may have forgotten what you have done, God will never forget, and shall bring them before our eyes, unless we now in this present time make peace with Him through repentance and full confession of our sins and the wiping away of all our offences against God.

And why does He take this account? It is certainly not because He does not know all these things: for how can He not know them *Who knowest all things before they come to pass* (Dan. xiii. 42). He takes it in order to persuade you His servant, that you are truly and really indebted to Him; so that you may not only learn this, but that you may also wipe out your debt. It was for this He commanded the prophet to speak to the Jews of their sins. *Show*, He said, *the house of Jacob their iniquities and the house of Israel their sins* (Is. lviii. 1). Not only that they might learn of them, but also that they might correct them.

And, when he had begun to take the account, one was brought to him that owed him ten thousand talents. For whatever had been entrusted to him, so much had he spent. It was an immense amount of another's money. And not only was there danger for him in this, but in this also: that he was the first to be brought before the Master. For had he been brought before Him after many others, who had been honest and fair, it would not have been surprising if the Master were not angry with him. For the honesty of those who preceded him, would have made the Master more mildly disposed towards all defaulters. But the first to appear before Him was so conscienceless in meeting his obligations, and afterwards was to reveal himself as so unjust, that for him to chance upon so humane and generous a Master was a special cause for wonder and surprise. For mostly when men are creditors they become like those who hunt wild beasts or game, and they will do all they can to get back whatever is owed them. And if they fail in this, because of the poverty of their debtors, they vent their anger at the loss of their money upon the miserable bodies of the poor wretches, abusing them and beating them and tormenting them in all kinds of ways. But God moves all things, tries all things, to free this man from his debt. For us to regain a debt means riches; with God to forgive us means our enrichment. When we recover what men owe us we are then wealthier; but whenever God forgives us our offences, then does He truly enrich us: for the riches of God is the salvation of men, as Paul says: *He is rich unto all that call upon him* (Rom. x. 12).

But someone will say, why then, if He intended to forgive and wipe out the charges against him, does He command that he be sold? It is this especially that shows His love for mankind. But let us not go too fast here; let us proceed in due order with the statement of the parable: *And, as he had not wherewith to pay it.* What does this mean: *and, as he had not wherewith to pay it?* Again you see a straining of good feeling. For when He says, *not having wherewith to pay,* he is saying nothing other than that he was wholly destitute of every virtue, and did not possess a single good work that could be imputed to him towards the remission of his sins: for virtuous actions are wholly imputed to us for the forgiveness of our sins; just as faith is imputed to justice: *For to him that worketh not, yet believeth in him that justifieth the ungodly, his faith is reputed to justice* (Rom. iv. 5).

And why speak of faith and virtuous actions, when even our tribulations are imputed to us for the pardon of our sins? This Christ declares by the parable of Lazarus, bringing Abraham before us as saying to the rich man, that Lazarus was now comforted, because he had received many *evil things* in his life (Luke xvi. 25). And Paul, writing to the Corinthians, says of the fornicator: *Deliver this man to Satan for the destruction of the flesh, that the spirit may be saved* (I Cor. vi. 5). And consoling others who had sinned,

he speaks in this way: *Therefore are there many infirm and weak among you; and many sleep. But, if we would judge ourselves, we should not be judged. But, while we are judged, we are chastised by the Lord, that we be not condemned with this world* (I Cor. xi. 30–32).

But if temptation, madness, sickness and the destruction of the flesh, which we suffer unwillingly now, are imputed to us unto forgiveness of our sins, much more will not the works of virtue which we do willingly and with fervour. But this man was wholly destitute of good. The burden of his sins was unbearable. And because of this He says: *And, as he had not wherewith to pay it, his Lord commanded that he should be sold.* It is at this point in particular that one can begin to perceive fully the humanity of the Lord, and why He began to take an account, and why He commanded that His servant should be sold. For these things were done in order that he might not be sold into slavery. How can this be shown? From the outcome. For had He truly wished to sell him, what was to prevent Him; who could oppose Him?

5. Why then did He command him to be sold, when in His own mind He had no intention of doing so? In order to increase his fears. He increases his fears by means of a threat; to compel him to humble himself in supplication, so that He might then have reason to forgive him. He could, even before he besought Him, have freed this man from this debt, but this He did not do for fear he might become worse. Even before He began to take an account He could have granted him

forgiveness, but in order that he might admit the great mass of his crimes; and so that he might not become even more evil, more inhuman to his neighbours, He first brings home to him the amount of his debt, and then forgives him all. So an account is demanded, and his debt is revealed, and then he is threatened, and his condemnation is indicated: and truly merited because of his cruelty and fierceness to his own fellow servant: but if nothing of all this had been done, how could he possibly have escaped condemnation because of his inhumanity? And so God does all these things and took such pains with him in order to correct his harshness. If he was not corrected by this, the fault must lie, not with the Master, but with the man himself; refusing correction. Let us now see how the Lord cleans out the ulcer.

But that servant falling down besought him, saying: have patience with me and I will pay thee all. He does not say that he has nothing to pay. But here, as is the way with those who are in debt and in desperation, he promises anything that will get him out of the peril he is in.

The Power of Prayer. The greatest source of confidence. The manner of forgiveness.

Let us learn from this how careless we are in our own prayer, and also how great is the power of fervent imploring prayer. Even fasting has not shown us this, nor poverty nor anything of this nature; but here was a man, helpless, void of all virtue, yet when he cried out in fervent supplication to His Maker, by this act alone, he was able to obtain mercy. Let us therefore never fail in

prayer. For who was more sin hardened than this man, who more laden with crimes, against whom were such accusations made than against this man, who through the works of virtue had gained neither little nor much? Yet notwithstanding all this he did not say to himself: 'I am afraid to open my mouth; I am filled with shame; how can I draw near to God? How can I pray?' as many sinners will, weakened in purpose by the fear the devil creates in them.

You do not presume to speak? Then for this very reason draw near to Him so that you may gain confidence. For it is not with a man you wish to be reconciled, that you should falter and be ashamed. It is God Himself, Who more even than you desires that you shall be delivered from your sins. You do not wish for your own deliverance more than He desires your salvation. And He teaches us this by His works. Are you without confidence? Then for this very reason, have confidence; because you are in this state of mind. For this is the greatest confidence: to believe that you have no confidence: just as it is most shameful to think of yourself as justified before the Lord. Such a one remains unjustified, whoever he is; even were he the holiest of men. So also he becomes just before the Lord who believes himself the lowest of men. And both the Pharisee and the Publican bear witness to the truth of these words.

Therefore let us not be despondent because of our sins, nor despairing; but let us draw near to God, and falling down before Him, let us call upon Him, as this man did, until His mind is favourable to us.

Do not grow weak of soul, do not despair, confess your sins, ask for delay, for time to amend, for compunction, for a humble and a contrite heart (Ps. l), and all such good things. The graces which then follow are not like the first; those gained through supplication he had squandered away through his anger against his neighbour. But meanwhile let us return to the manner of this pardon. Let us see the nature of this remission and by what means the Master came to it.

And the lord of that servant, being moved with pity, let him go and forgave him the debt. He asks for delay, and the Lord forgives him the debt; so that he receives more than he asked for. Because of this Paul says: *To him who is able to do all things more abundantly than we desire or understand* (Eph. iii. 20). For you cannot conceive such things as He has made ready to give you. So be not ashamed nor blush, rather, be ashamed of your sins; do not despair, cease not from praying; but, sinner that you are, draw near that you may be reconciled to the Lord, that you may give Him the opportunity of showing His humanity in pardoning your sins. Because if you fear to draw near, you stand in the way of His goodness, you limit the abundance of His loving kindness in your favour.

Not alone do prayers obtain pardon, but also the favour of God. Remembrance of sin is profitable. Paul mindful of his sins.

Let us then not lose heart, nor be slothful or timid in prayer. Even if we have been brought down to the depths of evil, prayer can speedily draw us back. For no one has sinned

as this man had: he had fallen into every kind of wickedness; for this is what the ten thousand talents mean. No one is so wanting in virtue as he was; and this we understand from the fact that he had not *wherewith to pay.* Yet however abandoned and destitute he was, the power of prayer was able to deliver him.

Has prayer then, someone will ask, the power to deliver a man from correction and retribution who has offended the Lord by countless evil deeds? Yes; it has this power, O man. For it is not alone in accomplishing this, but has as its most powerful help and ally the great loving kindness of God Himself, Who receives our prayers, by Whose power all things are accomplished, and which makes our prayer efficacious. And Jesus implies this when He goes on to say: *And the Lord of that servant, being moved to pity, let him go and forgave him the debt,* that you might learn that before prayer and after prayer it is the compassion of the Master does all.

But, when that servant was gone out, he found one of his fellow servants that owed him an hundred pence; and laying hold of him he throttled him, saying: Pay what thou owest. What could there be more abominable than this? With the voice of forgiveness still sounding in his ears, he has forgotten the loving kindness of his Master.

6. See what a good thing it is to be mindful of your own sins. Had this man kept them clearly in remembrance, he would not have been so cruel, so inhuman. Therefore again I say to you, and I shall not cease from saying it, that it is truly most profitable and most

necessary, to keep clearly before us the remembrance of our own offences. For there is nothing makes the soul so truly wise, so truly gentle and compassionate, as the continuous remembrance of our own sins. Because of this Paul also was mindful not only of the sins committed after purification, but also of those committed before baptism; though all had once and for all been wiped out and destroyed. And if he kept in mind the sins he had committed before baptism, much more should we remember them. For, remembering them, we not only wipe them away, but through this practice of humility we grow milder towards all men and begin to serve God with more fervour and good will: coming through this humble remembrance of our own sins, to understand better His ineffable compassion for us.

But this the wicked servant in the parable did not do, but forgetful of the magnitude of his own debt, he also forgets the compassion his lord had shown him. And through this forgetfulness of His compassion, he becomes cruel towards his own fellow-servant. And in his wickedness he loses all he had gained through the goodness of God. For, *laying hold of him, he throttled him, saying: Pay what thou owest.* He did not say:'Pay me my hundred pence.' It would have shamed him to mention such a small sum. But he says: *Pay what thou owest. And the other falling down, besought him, saying: Have patience with me and I will pay thee all.*

He prays to be spared with the very same words by which the wicked servant had himself obtained forgiveness. But he is not moved from his cruelty by these words. He does not even recall that it was through these very words he was saved. And if he were to forgive him, it would not be through humanity, but for payment of the debt. Had he forgiven him before the taking of the account and before he had himself received such a great favour, this would have been ascribed to his own goodness of heart. Now however, after receiving such an undeserved gift, and after being forgiven so many sins, he should have shown a like forbearance to his fellow servant. But he did not, nor did the thought of forgiveness enter his mind, nor the thought of how great was the difference between the favour he had received from his lord, and the harshness he had shown to his fellow servant. You see here a vast difference not only in the greatness of the debt, and in the dignity of the persons concerned, but also in the manner in which both events took place. For the one owes a debt of ten thousand talents, the other a hundred pence. The first had grievously offended his Master, this other was merely obliged by a fellow servant. The one now so fortunate ought to have been kind in turn; for the Lord, though seeing nothing of good in him, great or little, has forgiven him all. But he does not think of this; but at once, blind with anger, throttles his fellow servant and throws him into prison.

His fellow servants seeing this were *very much grieved*, as the Scripture records, and denounced him to the Master so that he might learn mildness from the Master. The Master hearing this, calls the wicked servant again to judgement; and does not simply condemn him, but first rightly rebukes him; in these words: *Thou wicked servant, I forgave thee all the debt.*

More readily does God forgive debts due to Himself than to others.

Who could be kinder than this Lord, Who when owed ten thousand talents, does not say a word in anger or call the servant a villain, but orders him to be sold: and this to the end that he might be delivered from his debt. But when he in turn treated his fellow servant so wickedly, the Lord was *angry*, and provoked to punish: that you might learn that He is more tolerant towards those who offend against Himself than towards those who sin against their neighbour. And this He shows not only here, but elsewhere: *If therefore,* He says, *thou offer thy gift at the altar, and there thou remember that thy brother hath anything against thee; go first and be reconciled to thy brother; and then coming thou shalt offer thy gift* (Mt. v. 23, 24). You see how everywhere He places our affairs before His, that He may put peace and the love of our neighbour in the highest places.

And again in another place He says: *I say to you that whosoever shall put away his wife, excepting for the cause of fornication, maketh her to commit adultery; and that he that shall marry her that is put away committeth adultery* (Mt. v. 32). And through Paul He also decreed that: *If any brother hath a wife that believeth not and she consent to dwell with him; let him not put her away* (I Cor. vii. 12). If she is an adulteress, he says, let him put her away; if she *believeth not,* let him not put her away. If she has

sinned against thee, cut her off, He says; if she has sinned against Me, retain her. So here likewise, although this sinner had committed such grievous sins against Himself, He forgave him. But when he committed sins against his fellow servant, though these were lesser and fewer, He does not forgive him; but delivers him up to punishment.

And now He calls him a *wicked servant,* though before this He had not uttered a word in anger against him. And He goes on to add these words: *And his lord, being angry, delivered him to the torturers.* When He had asked him to give an account of the debt of ten thousand talents, He had added nothing like this: that you may understand that this account was not looked for in anger, but out of concern that would in turn lead to forgiveness. But this sin against a neighbour provokes Him grievously. What therefore can be worse than remembrance of past injuries, since it takes back from us the loving compassion of God, and since that which his other sins did not do, this anger against a neighbour now brings about? But is it not written that God does not repent of His gifts? (Rom. xi. 29). How then, after giving him this great favour, which he had not merited, and after showing him such kindness and compassion, does He now recall His forgiveness of the debt? Because of this remembrance of injury. So he truly does not err who says that this sin is more grievous than every other sin. For all other sins, men can seek forgiveness; for this alone they cannot obtain forgiveness, and what is more it brings back upon our heads other sins which had once and for all been wiped away.

God detests nothing so much as remembrance of past injuries.

The evil of remembering past offences is twofold: it is inexcusable before God, and it serves to recall past sins already forgiven, and places them against us. And this is what happened here. For nothing, nothing whatsoever does God so hate, and turn away from, as cherishing remembrance of past offences, and fostering our anger against another. And this He reveals especially in this place, and also in the prayer in which He commands us to say: *Forgive us our trespasses as we forgive them who trespass against us* (Mt. vi. 12). Instructed therefore in all these things, and with this parable inscribed in our hearts, let us, when the thought comes of what our fellow servants have done to us, think also of what we have done against our Lord; and then through remembrance of our own sins, we shall be able at once to banish the anger we feel at others' sins against us.

And if we must remember offences, let us remember only our own. And if we remember our own sins, we shall never store up the sins of others. And again, should we forget the sins of others, our thoughts will then readily turn to the remembrance of our own. For if this man had remembered the ten thousand talents, he would never have remembered the hundred pence. It was when he had forgotten his own great debt, that he throttled his fellow servant; and determined to get back a few pence, and failing, he brought back upon his own head the debt of the ten thousand talents.

Therefore, I shall make bold to say, that this sin is more grievous than any sin. And in truth it is not I who say this. It is Christ Who reveals it to us, in this very parable. For if it is not more grievous than the ten thousand talents, that is, than his own unspeakable sins, then it was not the reason why these very sins, which had just been forgiven, were again recalled against him. Let us therefore be zealous in nothing so much as in keeping ourselves free from anger, and from not seeking to be reconciled with those who are opposed to us; since we know that neither prayer nor alms nor fasting nor partaking of the sacraments nor any of these will profit us, if on that last day we are found remembering past offences. But should we triumph over this fault, though stained with a thousand other crimes, we shall be enabled to obtain forgiveness. And neither is this my word only, but the word of that God Who shall come to judge us. As He says at the end of this parable: *So also shall my heavenly Father do to you, if you forgive not everyone from your hearts.* And again in another place: *If you will forgive men their offences, your heavenly Father will forgive you also your offences* (Mt. vi. 14).

Therefore, that here on earth we may lead a mild and gentle life, and there obtain pardon and remission for our sins, let us be eager, let us strive earnestly so that those who are enemies, may be reconciled to us: So that, even if we have sinned a thousand times, we may be reconciled to our Lord, and may come to the joys of heaven, of which may we all be found worthy, through the grace and loving kindness of Christ Jesus our Lord, to Whom be glory and honour throughout all ages and ages. Amen.

III. St Ephraim, Deacon, Confessor and Doctor
On Oppression and Calumny[3]

1. Our Lord, Thou Who was oppressed by the wicked, console the just who suffer oppression. May he who is attacked by calumny, from being earthly may become spiritual, and he who is visited by oppression, from being corporeal may he become ethereal. What shall be the measure of his reward who, like his God, is oppressed? Who shall weigh the promises made to him, who like our Lord suffers calumny? He who suffers ignominy, shall with them receive what was promised the Apostles. He upon whom the sufferings of the Apostles have fallen, shall together with them obtain the victory. Not in vain does God call those His servants who have struggled hard for victory; nor will he forget the oppressors who torment the innocent among us. He shall judge them with fire, and separate the good from the wicked; every man shall be tried as by fire, and shall render an account of himself.

2. He that is oppressed by envy and hate, let him look to God and he shall receive consolation. Let every one who suffers from the envious, look to Christ and he will be comforted. The serpent, the first deceiver, the serpent was the first fruits of all deceivers. Since thy God was bowed under the oppressor, bear it not resentfully that you also are oppressed. Since in thee God is bowed before the oppressor, do not murmur when you suffer calumny. Think how Christ like you once suffered. Blessed thy soul because thou art oppressed, that the image of Christ is impressed upon thee; blessed thy spirit that suffers calumny, for you bear the sign of the Son.

O you who suffer oppression, who will give thee to be like to God? O you who bear calumny in patience, who will give thee to be compared with Christ? How has it come to pass that you have become like to God? How has it happened that you can be compared to Christ? It is not by thy labour thou has come this; it is a free gift, not earned out of tribulation.

3. Since you have obtained it because of the vexation of the Evil One, why are you sorrowful under oppression? Why do you mourn under calumny? Why is thy face sad, because they have stricken thee with insults? To what end is the gift of praise, that leaves thee as thou leave this world? What has gone from thy riches, that the light of thy countenance has grown dark? Why is thy soul despondent, because thy former dignity is made less? Why is thy mind downcast, because thy power has been lowered. They have brought thee down from an earthly seat, but not from a throne in heaven; they have taken from thee a little authority, not the promises of the life to come. For a while they afflict thee, not, as they thought, for ever; but that power will remain little which is weakened by sin.

Which of thy possessions has perished, that thou should lose thy perfection? Yesterday you edified others, today you do not edify yourself. Why have you abandoned your riches, and why have you ceased to care for your treasure? Because of the things that distress thee thou hast abandoned prayer. What is lost from thy revenues, that thou should let go the perfect things you possess? Because disgust has fettered thee in its bonds, thou hast lessened thy activity. Why has thou forsaken vigilance, fasting, prayer? Because dejection of mind has taken hold of thee, all that blessed thee has vanished. How the Evil One has robbed thee, in thy freely chosen desert, of that which he seized amid the towns? From the time thy God was changed, thy nature changed. With time thy way of life has changed, and nothing now remains of thy former perfection.

4. Oppression fades as the moon; let thou not relax thy fasting. Calumny goes like the midday sun; let thou not cease thy vigils. Return at once to thy former perfect way of life, before thy treasures are lost. Why care for honour, and why falter before a little contempt? What was taken from thy treasure because thy friends no longer know thee? Why turn away from the riches that calumny hold out to thee? Why scatter the treasures that oppression thrusts into thy bosom? For the manifold names they call you shall be changed into heavenly promises. The one who hates thee invites thee to the heavenly banquet, and thy enemy to a wedding feast. The wrath and envy that have vexed thee are for you the cause of blessings; oppression offers thee an inheritance amid the prophets and apostles; calumny can bring you to meet the first and the last. Yet it is necessary that you suffer under the oppressor

and grieve under calumny; for while they are digging a ditch for you, God prepares for you a place in heaven. If they drive thee even from thy monastery, even the just must go forth to be tried; if they drive thee from thy home, even the noblest suffer humiliation; if in wrath they slay thee in thy house, even the good are devoured by evil; if they torture thee in hate, love will suffer all things. Thou art placed between the good and bad, like God through all the ages.

5. Reflecting upon these things, understand and mortify thy members. They have not crucified thee as they crucified Christ. They have not stoned thee as they stoned His Disciples. They have not reached their hands to thee with hyssop and vinegar mixed, as they did to Him. Because they have struck thee, do not lose courage; because they torment thee, do not yield. That chaste, they have stripped thee naked, let not thy faith grow less. Yours are the arms of the Spirit, to gird yourself for the struggle. You shall have a helmet, to place upon your head in battle. You shall be equipped with the example of the prophets; crowned by the example of the Apostles.

If they strike thee on the cheek, you are a comrade of Micheas and Achab (III Kings xxii. 24). If they crush thee with stones, thou art a Stephen among the Gentiles; if they cast filth at thee, thou art another Jeremiah. If they bind you in chains, you will have the fame of Paul the Apostle. If they cut off your head, you are John the son of Zachary; if they saw thee with a saw, behold, you are another Isaias the son of

Amos; if they burn thee in a furnace, then thou art the fifth companion of Azaria; if they slay thee in the sanctuary, thou art the heir of the promises of Zachary. If they cast thee to the wild beasts, lo, you are Daniel in the land of Babylon. If they cast thee down from the wall (Lk. iv. 29), lo, you are Christ among the Hebrews. If they cast insult and opprobrium upon you as upon David; if you suffer calumny as Joseph suffered it; if they speak evil of you as they spoke against Moses, and rose against God; if they cast you into prison, as they did Joseph in Egypt; if they raise you upon a cross, lo, you are Christ on the hill of Calvary.

See how your riches are hidden within the Scriptures, and in the Holy Books your treasure. In the Testaments are thy possessions; and as to the blessings promised to those who suffer oppression, you are like to the Apostles through suffering. The Apostles were tried with thy trials, and, if we may use the comparison, thy mortification (death) is like to the death of Christ. Amen.

NOTES

[1] PG 31, Homily X.

[2] PG 51, Homilies on the NT Homily I. The homily teaches us in detail from this parable, God's ways in dealing with men, and the providence of His grace. It also reveals to us man's greatest danger to salvation: the refusal to forgive injuries, the holding on to malice in spite of the load of our own indebtedness to God's injustice. By this refusal we close with our own hands the door of salvation. A meditative discourse of inexhaustible richness, that illuminates this parable and its place in our own formation and sanctification within the economy of salvation. (Homily begins from par. 2.)

[3] Lamy IV, 218. *To comfort those who suffer oppression and calumny.*

TWENTY-SECOND SUNDAY AFTER PENTECOST

I. St Ambrose: Render to Caesar

II. St John Chrysostom: Let Every Soul be Subject to the Higher Powers

III. St Augustine: The Teeth of the Pharisee

THE GOSPEL OF THE SUNDAY

Matthew xxii. 15–21

At that time: The Pharisees, going, consulted among themselves how to insnare him in his speech. And they sent to him their disciples with the Herodians, saying: Master, we know that thou art a true speaker and teachest the way of God in truth. Neither carest thou for any man; for thou dost not regard the person of men. Tell us therefore what dost thou think? Is it lawful to give tribute to Caesar, or not? But Jesus knowing their wickedness, said: Why do ye tempt me, ye hypocrites? Show me the coin of the tribute. And they offered him a penny. And Jesus saith to them: Whose image and inscription is this? They say to him: Caesar's. Then he saith to them: Render therefore to Caesar the things that are Caesar's; and to God, the things that are God's.

Exposition from the Catena Aurea

CHRYSOSTOM, *Ex Opus Imperfectum, Homily* 42: Just as when one tries to dam the course of a stream, checked at one point, the current will seek a path elsewhere; so was it with the malice of the Jews. Routed at one point, it breaks out at another. Hence we read:

V.15. *Then the Pharisees, going, consulted among themselves how to insnare him in his speech.*

Going, I say to *the Herodians.* Plot and plotters were of the same cloth; and so there follows:

V.16. *And they sent to him their disciples with the Herodians.*

GLOSS: Who, as unknown to Him, might more easily deceive Him, and that through them, they might seize Him; which they dared not of themselves, for fear of the multitude.

JEROME: For Judea had lately become subject to the Romans, under Caesar Augustus, and when the census had been made of the whole (Roman) world, Judea had been made a tributary of Rome. And there was great division among the

293

people; some saying they should pay the tribute, in return for the peace and security the Roman arms conferred on all; the Pharisees, on the contrary, who were full of their own righteousness, contended that the People of God, who were wont to pay tithes and also gave first fruits and other offerings contained in the Law, ought not to be subject to men's laws. Augustus however had made Herod, the son of Antipater, a foreigner and a proselyte, king of the Jews and entrusted to him the raising of the tribute, subject however to the dominium of Rome. So the Pharisees send their own followers with the Herodians, that is, Herod's soldiers; whom the Pharisees called Herodians in derision, because they paid tribute to the Romans, and did not give themselves to the worship of God.

CHRYSOSTOM, *In Matthew, Homily* 71: They therefore send their own disciples with Herod's soldiers, so that whatever He might say, they could arrest Him. They preferred He should say something against the Herodians; for, afraid to lay hands on Him themselves, because of the people, they wished to place Him in danger from this, that He was liable to the tax.

CHRYSOSTOM, *Opus Imperfectum*:This however is the first pretence of hypocrites: to praise those they desire to ruin. And so they break out in praise, saying: *Master, we know that thou art a true speaker.* They call him *Master*, so that, honoured and praised, He might, trustingly, reveal to them the secret of His heart; as though hoping to have them as disciples. GLOSS: There are three ways in which it is possible for someone not to teach the truth: Firstly, the teacher, who may neither know nor love the truth; and against this they say: *We know that thou art a true speaker.* Secondly, in respect of God: there are those who having lost the fear of God, do not teach the pure truth they have learned; and against this they say: *And teachest the way of God in truth.* Thirdly, in respect of our neighbour: when out of fear or love of someone they are silent about the truth. And to exclude this they say: *Neither carest thou for any man; for thou dost not regard the person of any man.*

CHRYSOSTOM, *in Matthew, Homily* 71: Here they begin to refer covertly to Caesar and Herod. JEROME: This smooth and treacherous questioning was a kind of reminder to the one answering, that he is to fear God rather than Caesar. So they then say:

V.17. *Tell us therefore what thou dost think? Is it lawful to give tribute to Caesar, or not?*

So that if He says the tribute should not be paid, the Herodians hearing Him, would at once detain Him as guilty of sedition against the Roman rule. CHRYSOSTOM, as above: Because they knew that some had suffered death on suspicion of plotting this very thing, they aimed, by means of His own words, to cast a like suspicion on Him. Then follows:

V.18. *But Jesus, knowing their wickedness, said: Why do ye tempt me, ye hypocrites?*

CHRYSOSTOM, *Ex Opus Imperfectum*:

He did not reply softly, in accord with their own smooth words; but spoke harshly, in accord with their cruel thoughts. For God answers men's hearts, not their words. JEROME: This is the supreme power of the One answering; that He knows the minds of His questioners, and calls them, not disciples, but tempters. He therefore is called a hypocrite who, being one thing, makes a pretence of being something different.

CHRYSOSTOM, as above: He calls them *hypocrites*, so that they, seeing He was a Reader of human hearts, might not dare to go on with what they were plotting. See how the Pharisees spoke smooth deceitful words to destroy Him; while Jesus humbles them to save them: for God's anger is more to man, than man's favour. JEROME: For wisdom ever acts wisely; since tempters are best confuted with their own words. And so there follows:

V.19. *Shew me the coin of the tribute. And they offered him a penny.*

This coin was equivalent to ten sestertii (a shilling), and bore the image of Caesar. So there follows:

V.20. *And Jesus saith to them: Whose image and inscription is this?*

Let those who think the Saviour's question was due, not to design, but to ignorance, learn from this that it was not so: for He would at least have known whose image was on the coin. Then follows:

V.21. *They say to him: Caesar's.*

This Caesar was, we believe, not Augustus, but Tiberius; under whom also the Lord suffered. All the Roman kings however were called Caesar, from Caius Caesar, the first to assume supreme authority. Then follows: *Then he saith to* them: *Render therefore to Caesar the things that are Caesar's*; that is, the coin, tribute or money. HILARY: For if we have nothing of Caesar's, we shall not, by that circumstance, be bound to render him what is his. But however if we depend on him, if we enjoy the privileges of his rule, we have no ground for complaint, rendering to Caesar what is Caesar's.

CHRYSOSTOM, *in Matthew, Homily* 71: You however, when you hear the words, *Render to Caesar what is Caesar's*, understand that he is only speaking of things in which we in no way offend against what is due to piety, for if there should be any such thing, it is not Caesar's, but the devil's tribute. Then that they might not say, 'you are subjecting us to men,' He goes on: *And to God, the things that are God's.* JEROME: That is, tithes, first fruits, offerings and victims; just as the Lord had rendered tribute to Caesar for Peter and Himself (Mt. xvii. 26), and rendered to God what is His, by doing the will of His Father.

HILARY, *in Matthew, Canon* 23: We are also to render to God things that are God's: that is, body and soul and will. The coin of Caesar is in gold, on which his image is stamped. But man is God's coin, on which is the image of God. Therefore, give your money to Caesar; keep for God a blameless conscience.

ORIGEN, *in Matthew, Tr.* 21: We learn here, from the example of our

Saviour, that we ought not, on the grounds of piety, pay heed to things that are spoken of by the many, and which therefore may appear remarkable; but rather to things said in a manner that accords with reason. We may also understand these words figuratively; that we are to give certain things to the body, a tribute to Caesar as it were; that is, necessary things. But the things that relate to the nature of our souls; that is, those that lead to virtue, these we should offer to God.

They therefore who teach the law of God, beyond due measure, and tell us we are to take no thought for the things due to the body, are the Pharisees who forbade that tribute be given to Caesar; that is, *forbidding to marry, to abstain from meats, which God hath created.* (I Tim. iv 3). They however who think we should indulge the body above what is needful, are the Herodians. But it is the will of our Saviour that virtue should not be endangered by ministering to the body beyond due

measure; and that at the same time our bodily nature should not be over-wearied by immoderate straining after virtue.

Or, the prince of this world, that is, the devil is called Caesar: for we cannot render to God the things that are God's, unless we have first rendered to this prince the things that are his; that is, until we have first put away all malice. And from this present passage of Scripture we learn this also: that in the face of those who tempt us we should neither be wholly silent, not yet answer simply but circumspectly, that we may cut off all contact with those who seek a pretext against us; that we may teach blamelessly the things that can save those who wish to be saved.

JEROME: They who ought to have believed, *wondered* at this so great wisdom: because their plotting had found no grounds to ensnare Him. So there follows: *And hearing this, they wondered and, leaving him, went their way.*

I. St Ambrose, Bishop and Doctor

Render to Caesar[1]

Romans xiii. 1–7

1. *Let every soul be subject to higher powers. For there is no power but from God.*

When Paul had laid down that we must follow the law of heavenly justice (vi. 19), that he may not seem to keep it apart from the justice of the present world, he commends this to us. For unless this is fulfilled, neither can the first be fulfilled. For present justice is as it were a guide, instructing the young, so that they may follow after to the more perfect jus-

tice. For no man can be looked upon as merciful, unless he possesses justice. Paul therefore, that he may confirm the authority and reverence due to the natural law, testifies that God is its Author, and that those who administer it, have their authority from God. And therefore he adds: *And those that are, are ordained of God;* that no one may think that these ruling powers are but human inventions, to be lightly esteemed: for what they see are divine laws, entrusted to human authority. He then is subject to the higher powers who, through fear of God, keeps himself from doing the things they forbid.

2. Therefore he that resisteth the power resisteth the ordinance of God.

This he says against those who are strong through the power and influence they possess, or against those who believe no one can check them, and so think they can laugh at the law. These he shows that the law is God's law; and that they shall not escape the judgement of God who escape for a time. *And they that resist, purchase to themselves damnation.* It is therefore manifest, that each one of of us shall either be justified by his works, or condemned. For they who, knowing the law, continue to sin against it are inexcusable.

3. For princes are not a terror to the good work, but to the evil.

Princes here mean rulers, who are created (*creantur*) to bring order into our common life, and restrain what is opposed to it, having their authority from God; so that the rest may be under the rule of one. *Wilt thou then not be afraid of the power? Do that which is good; and thou shalt have praise from the same.* Praise from authority is made visible when a man is shown to be innocent.

4. For he is God's minister to thee, for good.

It is here made clear to us that rulers are given to us that evil may not be done. *But, if thou do that which is evil, fear; for he beareth not the sword in vain;* that is, he inspires the fear that should he be ignored, he

will punish. *For he is God's minister; an avenger to execute wrath upon him that doth evil.* For since God has decreed a future judgement, and also wishes that no man shall perish, He has appointed rulers in this world so that, making them an object of fear and awe, they may become a pedagogue to all men (Gal. iii. 24), teaching them what they must observe, so that they shall not incur the punishment of the judgement to come.

5. Wherefore be subject of necessity; not only for wrath, but also for conscience' sake.

Rightly therefore does he tell them that they must be subject, not only for *wrath's* sake, that is, out of fear of present punishment: for *wrath* brings forth punishment: but also because of the judgement to come. For should they escape punishment in this life, it awaits them in the life to come, where, their own conscience accusing them, they shall be punished.

6. For therefore also you pay tribute. For they are the ministers of God, serving unto his purpose.

Therefore, he says, the tribute must be paid, or what are known as the public taxes, to show submission; through which men may know that they are not their own masters, but live under an authority which is from God. For they are subject to their own ruler, who holds God's place, as they are to God; as the prophet Daniel says: *The Most High ruleth in the kingdom of men. And he will give it to whomsoever it shall please him* (iv. 14). Hence the words of the Lord: *Render,* He says, to Caesar, the things that are Caesar's. They must therefore be subject to him as they are to God, and the proof of their submission is given when they pay him tribute.

7. Render therefore to all men their dues.

For the powers also are debtors to the lesser citizens, that they may give them judgement and justice according to their merits. *Tribute, to whom tribute is due; custom, to whom custom.* He commands that we pay first what is due to the ruling authority: for there the need is greater: *Fear, to*

whom fear. We should show reverential fear to authority; for fear prevents transgression; then to our parent, or to our earthly master, that they may give thanks for their son or for their Christian servant. *Honour, to whom honour.* Honour may also be shown to those who are seen to be eminent in the world, so that, seeing the modesty of the servants of Christ, they may praise rather than speak ill of the Gospel way of life. *Owe no man anything, but to love one another.* He wishes us if, it is possible, to be at peace with all men, to love our brethren while holding them in due honour. Amen.

II. St John Chrysostom, Bishop and Doctor

Let Every Soul be Subject to Higher Powers[2]

Romans xiii. 1–9

1. On this subject of obedience to those who govern Paul has spoken in his other epistles also; exhorting servants to be obedient to their masters and subjects to obey their rulers (Tit. ii. 9; iii. 1). He does this, to show that Christ had not introduced His laws for the overthrow of the common order of government, but to make it more perfect, and to teach men not to submit themselves to useless and unnecessary wars. It is enough that we have to suffer the snares laid against truth, without adding trials that are without sense and without profit. See how opportunely he turns to speak of these things. For after he had required of them (Ch. xii) the practice of much perfection and wisdom, teaching us to be well disposed to enemies as well as to friends, to be helpful to the fortunate as well as to the unfortunate, and to those in need, in a word,

to all men, and had taught them a manner of life worthy of angels, had emptied them of violence of feeling, rebuked folly and refined their thoughts in all things; he then begins to address them on these questions also.

For if we are to return the opposite to those who do us injuries, it is even more fitting that we should obey those who confer benefits upon us. This however he places near the end of his exhortation; meanwhile he does not go into the considerations I have spoken of, but only to those that command us to do these things as a duty. And to show that these considerations apply to all, and also to priests and monks and not simply to men of the world, he makes this plain from the beginning: *Let every soul be subject to higher powers;* even if he is an Apostle, even if he is an Evangelist, or a prophet, or whatever else he may be: for this subordination does not interfere with the service of God.

And he does not say, *Obey*, but, *Be subject*. And the first justification of such a piece of legislation, and one befitting the minds of the faithful, is that it has been ordained by God. *For*, he continues, *there is no power but from God*. What are you saying? Is every ruler therefore appointed by God. I do not say that, he answers. My discourse to you now is not about individual rulers, but about what we must do in fact. That there are governments, those who rule and those who are ruled, that all things do not proceed simply and without order, with people borne hither and thither in confusion like the waves, all this is, I say, the work of God's wisdom. Therefore he did not say: There is no ruler who is not from God, but speaking of the power here involved, he argues: *For there is no power but from God; and those that are, are ordained of God.*

So when a certain wise man said: *A prudent wife is properly from the Lord* (Prov. xix. 14), he means that God made marriage, not that He has united in matrimony each man to each woman. For we see many joined one to another for evil, and not in lawful marriage, and we do not hold this to be the work of God. But as Christ Himself has said: *He who made man from the beginning, made them male and female; and he said: For this cause shall a man leave father and mother, and shall cleave to his wife* (Mt. xix. 4), and this is what that wise man was explaining. For since equality of honour often leads to strife, He has made many kinds of ruling and many kinds of subjection; as for instance, that of man and wife, of father and son, of youth and age, of slave and free, of ruler and ruled, of teacher and pupil. And why should this not be in the society of men, since He has done the same in our body. For not even here has He made all the members of equal dignity; some are of less, others of greater dignity, some command, others are commanded. The same is to be seen among dumb creatures; as among bees, among cranes, and among herds of wild cattle. Even the sea is not without this good order; for here and there are many kinds of fish, each led by one, and it is in this way they make their long peregrinations. For anarchy everywhere is evil, and a cause of confusion. After telling us from where the power of ruling came, He continues:

Therefore he that resisteth the power resisteth the ordinance of God.

See what he has brought us to, and how he makes us fearful, showing us that this subjection is a matter of duty. So that the faithful may not say: You are lowering us, and making us appear contemptible, subjecting us to temporal rulers who are to possess the kingdom of heaven, he shows us that they are not subjecting themselves to rulers, but to God: for he who is subject to princes, is subject to God. But he does not say this; namely, that he is subject to God who is obedient to princes; but makes us fearful through the contrary to this, and gives it a more precise form by saying that he who does not obey the ruler is resisting God, Who has decreed this law. And this he is eager to show everywhere, that we are not doing a favour by obeying them, but doing our duty.

And in this way he both drew unbelieving rulers to the service of God, and those who believed. For there was then much talk on all sides, accusing the Apostles of sedition, and of new ideas, and of doing and saying everything in order to overthrow the common laws. When you therefore show that our common Lord has laid this command on all who are His, you will close the mouth of those who speak ill of us as innovators, and you will speak with greater confidence because of the truth of our beliefs.

2. Do not therefore, he says, be ashamed of such subjection. For it is God Who has laid down this law, and He is swift and avenging against those who despise it. For it is no light penalty he will exact of you if you disobey, but the greatest; and nothing will save you should you resist it. And from man also you will suffer the severest punishment; and there will be no one to defend you, and you will provoke God the more. He conveys all this when he says: *And they that resist purchase to themselves damnation.* Then following on this fear, he shows us the gain there is in this, persuading us by reasoning in these words: *For princes are not a terror to the good work, but to the evil.* Since he had cut deep, and had frightened them, he undoes this and comforts them, like a wise physician using soothing medicines, encouraging them and saying: 'Why need you fear; why tremble; he will not correct you for doing what is good; there is nothing to fear for one who is given to virtue?'

And then he goes on: *Wilt thou*

then not be afraid of the power? Do that which is good; and thou shalt have praise from the same.* See how he joins him in friendship to the ruler; showing that he praises him even from the seat of authority. See how his wrath has left him: *For he is God's minister to thee, for good.* So far is he from being fearful, he says, that he even praises thee; so far is he from interfering with you, he will even help you. Since therefore you have in him one who both praises you and helps you, why not be subject to him? He also makes it easier for you to practice virtue, by punishing evildoers and rewarding and showing favour to the good, co-operating with the will of God: and because of this he is here spoken of as *minister.* But remember: I am giving you counsel concerning Christian living; and he is saying the same things to you through his laws. I exhort you not to be grasping or rapacious, he sits in judgement to punish these same things. He is therefore a fellow-worker and our helper, and sent by God for this purpose. He is therefore to be reverenced, and for a twofold reason: that he is sent by God, and that he is sent for such a purpose.

But, if thou do that which is evil, fear. It is therefore not the ruler causes this fear, it is our own depravity. *For he beareth not the sword in vain.* See how he places him before us, as an armed soldier, setting him up as a terror to wrongdoers. *For he is God's minister: an avenger to execute wrath upon him that doth evil.* That you may not shrink hearing again of punishment and retribution and the sword, he again says that he is fulfilling God's law. And what if the ruler is himself unaware of this?

Nevertheless God has so ordered it. If therefore he is God's minister, vindicating virtue, driving out vice, as is God's will, why resist one who does so much good, preparing the way at the same time for the good you may do? For there are many who first practised virtuous living out of fear of authority, who afterwards embraced it from the fear of God. There are those of grosser mind who do not grasp at the things to come as they do those of the present life. He therefore who prepares the soul of many, whether through fear or through rewards, so that they become more disposed to the word of doctrine, he is justly called God's minister.

Wherefore be subject of necessity; not only for wrath, but also for conscience' sake. What does, *not only for wrath* mean? It means that not only submitting to authority, you not only become an enemy of God, and bring many evils upon yourself both from God and man; but also be subject to him because he is your benefactor in things of the greatest value, as the guardian and administrator of the civil order. For a thousand blessings are conferred on states by rulers through their laws; and if you were to remove them, everything would fall to ruin, and nothing would be left standing; neither cities nor towns nor homes nor public buildings nor anything. All would be overthrown, and the weak devoured by the strong. And even if some wrath did not descend on those who do not obey, for this one reason should you be subject to temporal authority: that you may not seem either ignorant or ungrateful towards one who has done so much for your well-being.

For therefore also you pay tribute, he says. *For they are the ministers of God, serving unto this purpose.* Without speaking of any single benefit bestowed on states by their rulers; such as good order, peace, the other services, those rendered by the army, those rendered by public ministries, he chooses one fact to explain the whole case. You testify that he is your benefactor, he says, from this that you pay him a wage. See the wisdom and intelligence of the blessed Paul. For what seemed a burden and oppressive, namely, the the tribute, is shown as a proof of their care for us. For what reason, he asks, do we pay tribute to a king? Is it not because he is provident; is it not for his work of governing that we pay him a reward? And we would not pay it, did we not know from the beginning we had gained by his care for us. It was for this that of old it was decided by common consent, that those who rule us should be paid by us; because neglecting what is personal to them, they take on the common care, and to this devote their whole time, and so what concerns us is safe.

3. Speaking therefore of the things that are without, he turns again to his previous arguments; for in this way he could better attract the believer; and so he again shows us that this is God's will, and on this he ends his counsel, saying: *For they are the ministers of God.* Then, referring to their task, and to the strain of the life they lead, he adds: *Serving unto this purpose.* For this is their life, their concern: that you may enjoy peace. And so in another Epistle he commands them not only to be subject to them, but also to pray for

them, and in the same letter he shows that this is to the profit of all, adding: *That we may lead a quiet and peaceable life* (I Tim. ii. 1). For they contribute in no small measure to the settled condition of our present life, keeping watch, keeping enemies at bay, suppressing disturbances in cities, putting an end to strife everywhere. Do not say to me that some have misused this power, look rather at the good of the established order, and you will see how great is His wisdom who established these things from the beginning.

Render therefore to all men their dues. Tribute, to whom tribute is due; custom, to whom custom; fear, to whom fear; honour, to whom honour. He still insists on the same things; that we must render not only money, but likewise honour and awe. But how is it that he said above (v. 3): *Wilt thou then not be afraid of the power? Do that which is good;* but here says: *Render fear?* He means here extreme honour (awe), not the fear arising from an evil conscience, to which he referred above. Neither did he say, *give,* but *Render,* and adds: *their dues.* For you are not doing this as a favour. It is a debt due; and if you do not pay it, then suffer the penalty of the unjust. Do not think you are lowering yourself, or that you offend your principles if you stand up in the presence of the ruler, or uncover your head. For if Paul commanded this when rulers were pagan, much more should this be done now that they believe in God.

But if you say that greater dignities have been conferred you, learn then that it is not now your time: For now you are *a stranger, and a sojourner* (Ps. xxxviii. 13). There will be a time when you shall

appear more resplendent than all present things. Now your life is hidden with Christ in God. When Christ shall appear, then shall you be seen in glory with Him (Col. iii. 3, 4). Do not seek your recompense in this perishable life, and if you must stand in awe of a ruler's presence, do not think this unworthy of your dignity. For God wills it so, that a ruler set up by Him may have his own power. And if he who is not conscious to himself of wrongdoing stands in fear before him, much more shall he who has done evil be shaken by fear. And you do yourself the more honour by this: for it is not by rendering this honour you are lowered, but by not rendering it. And the ruler himself will respect you the more, and give praise to your Master; though he be himself an unbeliever.

Owe no man anything, but to love one another. Again he turns to the mother of all good, to the teacher of what we have been speaking of, to the cause of all virtue and says, that this also is a debt we owe; not one to be paid like tribute, or custom, but to be paid without ceasing. For he would have it that it is never paid fully; rather he would have it ever repaid, yet never paid in full, but ever owing. Such is the nature of this debt, that one is ever giving, yet ever owing. For telling us how we ought to love, he shows us also the gain of loving: *For he that loveth his neighbour,* he says, *hath fulfilled the law.*

Nor are you to think that this is a favour; for this is a debt. You owe your brother love because of your spiritual relationship to him. And not for this reason only, but because we are members one of another

(Eph. iv. 25); and if this love dries up, then the whole body breaks up. Therefore love thy brother. For if you gain so much from loving him, that you fulfil the whole law, you owe him love, because you have gained so much through him.

For: *Thou shalt not commit adultery. Thou shalt not kill. Thou shalt not bear false witness. Thou shalt not covet. And, if there be any other commandment, it is comprised in this word: Thou shalt love thy neighbour as thyself.* He does not simply say, it is fulfilled, but, *it is comprised*; that, in short, the whole substance of the commandments is contained in these few words: for love is the beginning and end of virtue. It is its root, its substance, its crown. If then, it is its beginning, and its fulfilment, what is equal to it?

O taste and see that the Lord is sweet (Ps. xxxiii. 9). Let us give ourselves therefore to His love, and delight in it. For so shall we even now behold His kingdom, and live the life of angels, and while dwelling on earth, shall be no less than those who dwell in heaven. And after we have gone from here, we shall stand before the sublime tribunal of Christ and enjoy his ineffable glory; and to this may we all come, through the grace and loving kindness of our Lord Jesus Christ, to Whom with the Father and the Holy Ghost be there glory, honour, praise now and forever, and through out all ages and ages.[3] Amen.

III. St Augustine, Bishop and Doctor

The Teeth of the Pharisees[4]

God shall break in pieces their teeth in their mouth, Ps. lvii. 7.

Whose teeth? They whose madness is like that of the serpent; like the asp that stops her ears so as not to hear the voice of the charmer, nor the voice of the wizard with his cunning spell.[5] What has the Lord done to them? *He has crushed in pieces the teeth in their mouth.* This He has done: it was done before, and here He does it now. But it would have sufficed to say: *He has crushed their teeth.* Why is *in their mouth* added?

They would not listen to the Law. They would not listen to the precepts of truth spoken by Christ; behaving like the serpent and the asp. For they still clung to their former sins; neither would they forego their place in this present life: refusing to exchange present delights for future joys. They closed one ear with the delights of the past; they closed the other with the delights of the present; and refused to listen. Why else should we hear words such as these: *If we let him alone, the Romans will come, and take away our place and nation* (Jn. xi. 48)?

They were certainly unwilling to lose their place and rank, and therefore pressed their ear to the earth; and for the same reason they refused to listen to the healing words of this Wise Man. It was said of them that they were greedy and lovers of money. And their whole life, and their past, is described for us by the Lord in the Gospel. He who reads the Gospel carefully, will find why they closed both ears.

Let your Charity listen carefully. What has the Lord done? *He has crushed in pieces the teeth in their mouth.* Why, *in their mouths?* That from their own mouth they might speak against themselves. He compels them from their own mouth to pronounce sentence against themselves. They wished to put him in danger of His life, using the pretext of the tribute. But He neither said it was lawful nor unlawful to pay the tribute. But He resolved to crush their teeth, now eager to devour Him; and to crush them in their own mouth.

Had He said: 'Let tribute be paid to Caesar,' they could have accused Him of giving evil counsel to the Jewish nation; making it a tributary. For *brought low because of their injustice,* they were now paying tribute: as had been foretold of them in the Law (Ps. cvi. 17). 'We have Him,' they say, 'this traitor to our nation, if He says we should pay the tribute. We have Him, if He says we should not pay it; for speaking against us who are devoted to Caesar.' This was the twofold trap they laid to ensnare our Lord.

But to whom had they come? To One Who knew how to crush in pieces the teeth in their mouth. *Show me,* He says, *the coin of the tribute.* Why do ye tempt me, ye hypocrites? Are you thinking of paying the tribute? You wish to do what is just? You want good advice? *If in very deed you speak justice: judge right things, ye sons of men* (Ps. lvii. 2). But now, you say one thing, you think another; you hypocrites. Why do you tempt me? Now shall I crush in pieces the teeth in your mouth.

Show me the coin of the tribute. They showed it to Him. He did not say: This is Caesar's. No. He asks them whose it is: that their teeth might be crushed by their own mouth. For when He asks whose image and inscription is on it, they tell Him it is Caesar's. And now the Lord shall crush the teeth in their mouth. Already, answering Him, they have crushed the teeth in their own mouth.

Render therefore to Caesar the things that are Caesar's; and to God the things that are God's. Caesar seeks back his own image. Give it back to him. God seeks His own image. Give it back to Him. Do not refuse Caesar his money. Do not refuse God His money. And they had nothing to say in answer. They had been sent to trap Him, by false words. They come back saying no one could answer Him. Why? Because their teeth had been crushed in pieces in their mouth. Amen.

NOTES

[1] PL 17, *Commentaria in Ep. ad Romanos,* Ch. XIII, 1–7.

[2] PG 60, col. 613. *Homilia XXIII in Ep. ad Romanos,* 1–3 incl.

[3] Conclusion of Homily XXIII, as above.

[4] PL 36, col. 682, par. 11, *In Psalmum* lvii. 7.

[5] The first sentences refer to verses 5, 6, of the same psalm: *Their madness is according to the likeness of a serpent: like deaf asp that stoppeth her*

ears: Which will not hear the voice of the charmers: nor of the wizard that charmeth wisely. The asp is said to shut out the sound of music, which can cast a spell on it, by pressing one ear to the ground and stopping the other with the tip of its tail. This was the whole attitude of Christ's malicious hearers: pleasures stopped one ear; refusal to hear Him, and so give up rank, wealth and prestige, stopped the other.

TWENTY-THIRD SUNDAY AFTER PENTECOST

I. St John Chrysostom: On the Consolation of Death;
First Sermon

II. St Augustine: The Woman who had an Issue of Blood

III. St Augustine: On the Daughter of the Ruler of the
Synagogue, and on the Woman who had an Issue
of Blood

IV. St Peter Chrysologos: On the Same

V. St Peter Chrysologos: On the Same

THE GOSPEL OF THE SUNDAY

Matthew ix. 18–26

At that time: as Jesus was speaking to the multitudes, behold, a certain ruler came and adored him, saying: Lord, my daughter is even now dead; but come, lay thy hand upon her and she shall live. And Jesus rising up followed him, with his disciples.

And, behold, a woman who was troubled with an issue of blood twelve years came behind him and touched the hem of his garment. For she said within herself: If I shall only touch his garment, I shall be healed. But Jesus, turning and seeing her, said: Be of good heart, daughter; thy faith hath made thee whole. And the woman was made whole from that hour.

And, when Jesus was come into the house of the ruler, and saw the ministrels and the multitude making a rout, he said: Give place; for the girl is not dead, but sleepeth. And they laughed him to scorn. And, when the multitude was put forth, he went in and took her by the hand. And the maid arose. And the fame hereof went abroad into all that country.

PARALLEL GOSPELS

Mark v. 22–43

And there cometh to Jesus one of the rulers of the synagogue named Jairus; and seeing him falleth down at his feet. And he besought him much, saying: My daughter is at the point of death. Come, lay thy hand

Luke viii. 41–56

And, behold, there came a man whose name was Jairus; and he was a ruler of the synagogue. And he fell down at the feet of Jesus, beseeching him that he would come into his house; for he had an only daughter, upon her, that she may be safe and may live. And he went with him. And a great multitude followed him; and they thronged him.

And a woman who was under an issue of blood, twelve years, and had suffered many things from many physicians and had spent all that she had; and was nothing the better, but rather worse; when she had heard of Jesus, came in the crowd behind him and touched his garment. For she said: If I shall touch but his garment, I shall be whole. And forthwith the fountain of her blood was dried up; and she felt in her body that she was healed of the evil. And immediately Jesus, knowing in himself the virtue that had proceeded from him, turning to the multitude, said: Who hath touched my garments? And his disciples said to him: Thou seest the multitude thronging thee; and sayest thou who hath touched me? And he looked about to see her who hath done this. But the woman fearing and trembling, knowing what was done in her, came and fell down before him and told him all the truth. And he said to her: Daughter, thy faith hath made thee whole. Go in peace: and be thou whole of thy disease.

While he was yet speaking, some come from the ruler of the synagogue's house, saying: Thy daughter is dead. Why dost thou trouble the master any further? But Jesus, having heard the word that was spoken, saith to the ruler of the synagogue: Fear not, only believe. And he admitted not any man to follow him, but Peter and James and John the brother of James. And they come to the house of the ruler of the synagogue. And he seeth a tumult; and the people weeping and wailing

almost twelve years old, and she was dying.

And it happened as he went that he was thronged by the multitudes. And there was a certain woman having an issue of blood twelve years, who had bestowed all her substance on physicians and could not be healed by any. She came behind him and touched the hem of his garment; and immediately the issue of her blood stopped. And Jesus said: Who is it that touched me? And, all denying, Peter and they that were with him said: Master, the multitudes throng and press thee; and dost thou say: who touched me And Jesus said: Somebody hath touched me; for I know that virtue is gone out from me. And the woman, seeing that she was not hid, came trembling and fell down before his feet and declared before all the people for what cause she had touched him, and how she was immediately healed. But he said to her: Daughter, thy faith hath made thee whole. Go thy way in peace.

And as he was yet speaking, there cometh one to the ruler of the synagogue, saying to him: Thy daughter is dead; trouble him not. And Jesus, hearing this word, answered the father of the maid: Fear not. Believe only; and she shall be safe. And when he was come to the house he suffered not any man to go in with him, but Peter and James and John, and the father and mother of the maiden. And all wept and mourned for her. But he said: Weep not. The maid is not dead, but sleepeth. And they laughed him to scorn, knowing that she was dead. But he, taking her by the hand, cried out, saying: Maid, arise. And her spirit returned; and much. And going in, he saith to them: Why make you this ado and weep? The damsel is not dead, but sleepeth. And they laughed him to scorn. But he, having put them all out, taketh the father and the mother of the damsel and them that were with him, and entereth in where the damsel was lying. And taking the damsel by the hand he saith to her: *Talitha cumi*; which is, being interpreted: Damsel (I say to thee) arise. And immediately the damsel rose up and walked; and she was twelve years old. And they were astonished with a great astonishment. And he charged them strictly that no man should know it; and commanded that something should be given her to eat.

she arose immediately. And he bad them give her to eat. And her parents were astonished, whom he charged to tell no man what was done.

EXPOSITION FROM THE CATENA AUREA

I

CHRYSOSTOM, *in Matthew, Homily* XXXI–II: After the word came the work, which served even more than the word to stop the mouths of the Pharisees. For he who now came to Him was a ruler of the synagogue, and his was a grievous sorrow: for the girl was his only daughter, and twelve years old; when the flower of age begins; and so we read:

V.18. *As he was speaking these things unto them, behold, a certain ruler came to him.*

AUGUSTINE, *Harmony of the Gospels*, II, 28, 64–67: Both Mark and Luke relate this, but this time do not adhere to some order of events. For they insert this account at the point where, after He had cast out the demons, and had permitted them to go into swine, crossing the lake, He

returns from the Gerasenes country. And through what Mark here says, we understand that this took place after He had recrossed the lake; but how long after does not appear. Unless there had been some interval, there would have been no time for the feast at his house, of which Matthew gives us an account. Immediately following comes the story of the ruler of the synagogue's daughter. For if the ruler had come while he was speaking of *raw cloth* (v. 16), then nothing either of words or deeds took place in between. In the narrative of Mark, however, there is a place where other things might have intervened. Nor is Luke in conflict with Matthew; for what he adds: *And, behold, there came a man whose name was Jairus* (viii. 41), need not be taken to mean that he came to Him immediately following his return (v. 40), but after the meal taken with the publicans, as Matthew relates, saying: *As he was speaking these things unto them, behold a certain ruler*; namely, a ruler of the synagogue, *came and adored him, saying: Lord, my daughter is even now dead.*

We must however note, lest there should appear to be a contradiction here, that the other two Evangelists state that she was close to death, not that she was dead, so that some came afterwards to announce she had died, and therefore that they need not trouble the Master further. We must here understand that Matthew, for the sake of brevity, wished to put it that the Lord had been asked to do what in fact he did do: namely, raise the girl to life. For his (Matthew's) mind is not on the words of the father speaking of his daughter, but, what is more important, on his desire, his purpose. For he had so despaired, believing he would never again see her alive, since he had left her dying, his desire now was that she might be restored to life. These two Evangelists therefore, have given us what Jairus said: Matthew what he thought and desired. Had either of them however related that it was the father himself had said, that Jesus should not now be troubled, seeing the girl was dead, then the words Matthew records he said, would be in conflict with his thought and desire. Now we do not read that he agreed in thought with the messengers.

And here we learn something that we must know: that in whatever a man says, we should consider only his meaning; to which his words should be subservient; and also that a man does not lie, if he tells what someone said in words other than those used by the speaker.

CHRYSOSTOM, *in Matthew, Homily* 32: Or, that the ruler spoke of the girl as dead was an exaggeration of his affliction. For it is the way of those asking help to magnify their miseries, and enlarge upon them in the telling, to draw out the more the sympathy of those they beg from. And so he goes on: *But come, lay thy hand upon her and she shall live.* See how dull he is. He asks two things of Christ: to come, and to lay His hand upon her. This Namaan the Syrian asked also, from the Prophet (IV Kings v. 11). For those who are of a duller disposition need the assurance of sight and touch. REMIGIUS: Let us equally admire and imitate the humility and mildness of Christ; for scarce is He asked, than He starts up to follow the one who asked Him. Hence follows:

V.19. *And Jesus rising up followed him.*

Here He teaches superiors as well as subjects. To subjects He has left an example of obedience; to those placed over others He gives a lesson in promptitude and concern in teaching; so that as often as they hear that someone is dead in his soul, they should hasten at once to help him. *And his disciples went with him.* CHRYSOSTOM, as above: Mark and Luke say that He took three Disciples, namely, Peter, James and John. He did not however take Matthew, to create in him a greater eagerness; and also because his disposition was still imperfect. He honoured the others that the rest might strive to be like them. For the present, it sufficed for Matthew to see what took place in the case of the woman who had an issue of blood; concerning whom he now adds:

V.20. *And, behold, a woman who was troubled with an issue of blood twelve years came behind him and touched the hem of his garment.*

JEROME: This woman who had an issue of blood draws near to the Lord, not in a house, not in a city, because she was excluded by the law from the cities; but as He was walking on His way: so that on His way to one woman, He heals another. CHRYSOSTOM, as above: She does not come openly to Christ, because she was ashamed on account of her affliction; knowing she was regarded as unclean; for under the law this affliction was held as a great uncleanness (Lev. xv. 25); because of this she hides and conceals herself. REMIGIUS: And in this she is to be praised for humility, in that she drew near to Him, not in front, but from behind; and held herself as unworthy to touch His feet. And she did not touch the garment itself, but only the hem: for in accord with the command of the law, the Lord's garment had a hem (Num. xv. 38). The Pharisees also wore hems (*fringes*), which they enlarged (Mt. xxiii. 5); and in which they were also wont to insert thorns. But the Lord's hems were to heal, not to wound. And so there follows:

V.21. *For she said within herself: If I shall touch only his garment, I shall be healed.*

In which we must praise her faith; for while despairing of being healed by physicians, on whom, as Mark says, *she had spent all she had,* she understood that here was the heavenly Physician, and in Him she placed all her hope; and so merited to be healed. Hence follows:

V.22. *But Jesus turning and seeing her, said: Be of good heart, daughter; thy faith hath made thee whole.*

RABANUS: What does it mean that He bids her be of good heart who, had she not had faith, would not be seeking healing from Him? He was asking of her to have strength and perseverance in her faith, so that she would reach to the true and certain healing. CHRYSOSTOM, as above: Or, because this woman was fearful, He says: *Be of good heart.* And He calls her *daughter*: because faith had made her a daughter. JEROME: He did not say: Because thy faith shall make thee whole; but, *hath made thee whole,* for in that you believed, you are already made whole.

CHRYSOSTOM, as above: She had not yet however a perfect notion of Christ, or she would not have thought she could be hidden from Him. But Christ does not allow her to go away unnoticed; and this not from the desire of glory, but for many reasons. First, He puts an end to the woman's anxiety, lest she might think she had stolen this gift, and be troubled in conscience. Secondly, He corrects her notion that she was hidden from Him. Thirdly, He makes her faith known to all, that they may imitate her. Fourthly, in showing He knew all things, He works a miracle that was not less than His drying the fountain of her blood. And of this there follows: *And the woman was made whole from that hour.* GLOSS: That is, from the moment she touched His hem; not from the moment in which Jesus turned towards her. For she was then already healed; as the other Evangelists clearly show, and as we may infer from our Lord's words.

HILARY: In this we see the wondrous virtue of the Lord: that the power dwelling in His Body should communicate to perishable things the efficacy to heal, and that the divine activity should issue forth even from the hem of His garment. For God is not perceptible by the senses, to be enclosed within a body. The assumption of a body did not limit the nature of His power; but for our redemption His power took upon it the frailty of our body. Mystically, this ruler is to be understood as the Law, which beseeches the Lord to give back life to the dead people, which the Law, preaching that His Coming was to be looked for, had reared for Christ.

RABANUS: Or, the ruler of the synagogue stands for Moses, and is called Jairus, that is, the 'enlightener', or 'he who will give light'; because he received, to give to us, the words of life, and through this, being himself enlightened by the Holy Spirit, gives light to all. Therefore, the daughter of the ruler of the synagogue, that is, the synagogue itself, as being twelve years old, that is, in the time of puberty, when it should have born spiritual children to God, is brought low by the weakness of false beliefs. While the Word of God is hastening to this daughter of the ruler, that He may save the children of Israel, the Holy Church was gathered together from the Gentiles, who perishing from their own inward wickedness, receive by faith the healing that was prepared for others.

And let us note, that the ruler's daughter was twelve years old, while this woman had an issue of blood twelve years; so that at the time the one was born, the other began to suffer; so that at one and the same point of time the synagogue began to be born from the Patriarchs, and the nation of the Gentiles without began to be tainted with the corrupted blood of idolatry. For *the issue of blood* can be understood in two ways: either for the pollution of idolatry, or for the things done for the delight of flesh and blood. And so as long as the synagogue flourished, the Church was afflicted; *But, by their offence, salvation is come to the Gentiles* (Rom. xi. 11). The Church drew near and touched the Lord, when it came near to Him through faith. GLOSS (Bede): She believed, she spoke, she touched; for by these three: faith, word and work, all salvation is won.

RABANUS: She came *behind Him,* either in accord with His own words: *If any man minister to me, let him follow me* (Jn. xii. 26); or because, not seeing the Lord in the flesh, when the mysteries of His Incarnation were fulfilled, she comes now to the grace of the knowledge of Him. And she touched the hem of His garment, because, though the Gentiles had not seen Christ in the Flesh, they had received word of His Incarnation. For the garment of Christ means the mystery of His Incarnation; with which His Divinity was clothed; the hem of His garment means the words that come forth from His Incarnation. She does not touch His garment, but its hem; because she does not see the Lord in the Flesh, but receives through the Apostles word of His Incarnation. Blessed is he that touches by faith the very hem of the Word. She is healed, not in the city, but as the Lord travels by the way. Hence the words of the Apostles: *Because you judge yourselves unworthy of eternal life, behold, we turn to the Gentiles* (Acts xiii. 46). And from the time of the Lord's Coming the Gentiles began to possess salvation.

2

GLOSS: After the healing of the woman who had an issue of blood, there follows the raising of the dead girl; when we are told:

V.23. *And when Jesus was come into the house of the ruler . . .*

CHRYSOSTOM, as above: We must note carefully that He came slowly, and talked at length with the woman He healed, in order to allow the girl to die, so that her visible rising from the dead might become manifest. And again in the case of Lazarus He waited until the third day. Then follows: *And saw the minstrels and the multitude making a rout*: which was a proof of her death. AMBROSE, *on Luke*: For it was an ancient custom to employ flute players to lament for the dead.

CHRYSOSTOM: Christ sent out all the musicians; but brought in the girl's parents, so that it could not be said He had healed her some other way. Before He raises the dead girl to life, He raises their hope by His words.

V.24. *He said: Give place; for the girl is not dead, but sleepeth.*

RABANUS: As if to say: To you she is dead; to God, Who can raise her, she sleeps in soul and in body.

CHRYSOSTOM: By His words He both calms the tumult of mind of those present, and at the same time shows how easy it is for Him to raise the dead. This He did in the case of Lazarus also, saying: *Lazarus our friend sleepeth* (Jn. xi. 11). At the same time He taught us not to fear death. For since He Himself was also to die, He prepares His Disciples in the bodies of others, to be confident, and to face death manfully. For since His coming, death was now but a sleep.

Upon the Lord saying this, they derided Him. So there follows: *And they laughed him to scorn.* He does not rebuke their derision, so that even their laughter, the pipes, and every other thing might be a proof of her death. For as often happened, that men do not believe even after miracles, He convinces them beforehand by their own answers. This He did in the case of Lazarus when He said: *Where have you laid him,* so that they who had said: *Come and see,* and also that, *he stinketh, for he is four days dead* (Jn. xi. 34, 39), could no longer not believe that He had raised a dead man to life. JEROME: They were not worthy to see the mystery of one rising from the dead, who had mocked with unfitting derision One Who raised the dead. And so there follows:

V.25. *And, when the multitude was put forth, he went in and took her by the hand. And the maid arose.*

CHRYSOSTOM: Not bringing another soul into her body, but recalling that which had departed, He raised her up, awaking her as from sleep, so that by this spectacle He may prepare the way for faith in the resurrection. And He not only raises her to life, but also bids them give her food, as the other Evangelists relate: so that what took place might not seem an illusion. Then there follows:

V.26. *And the fame hereof went abroad into all that country.*

GLOSS: That is, the greatness and strangeness of the miracle, and its manifest truth, so that it is not looked upon as an invention.

HILARY: Mystically, the Lord goes into the ruler's house; that is, the synagogue, from which there was the sound as it were of mourning, in the canticles of the law. JEROME: For even to this day the young girl lies dead in the house of the ruler; and they who seem to be teachers of the law are but flute players, singing a song of mourning. And the multitude of the Jews, is not a multitude of believers, but *a multitude making a rout.* But when all the Gentiles have come in, then all Israel shall be saved.

HILARY, *in Matthew*: That the number who believed from the law might be seen to be few, *the multitude was put forth.* This the Lord would indeed have saved; but because of its mockery of His words and deeds it was not worthy of a part in the resurrection. JEROME: He took her by the hand, and the maid arose: for unless the hands of the Jews, which are filled with blood, are first cleansed, their dead synagogue shall not rise again. HILARY: And the fame of this went abroad into all that country; that is, the salvation of the elect, the grace of Christ, and His works are preached to men.

RABANUS: Figuratively, the maid dead in her house, is the soul lying dead in thought. But He says the girl is but sleeping; for they who sin in this life can still be restored to life through repentance. The flute players are flatterers, who encourage the dead (in sin).

GREGORY, *Morals in Job*, xxviii, 14: The multitude is *put forth*, that the maid may be restored to life: for unless the throng of worldly cares are expelled from the depths of the heart, the soul that lies dead within shall not rise from the dead. RABANUS: The maid in the house arose in the presence of a few witnesses; the young man, outside the town gate; Lazarus, in the presence of many: for a public fault calls for a public remedy; a light one, a lighter remedy, and a secret fault can be wiped away by repentance.

I. ST JOHN CHRYSOSTOM, BISHOP AND DOCTOR

On the Consolation of Death: First Sermon[1]

1. Grant me silence, Brethren, that you may hear from me words that will help you now and that one day you will need. For it is when we are gravely ill that we most need the help of the physician; it is when our eye is painful that we carefully apply an eye-salve. Whoever does not suffer this pain, let him not interrupt but listen; for it is no hardship to learn of the medicine that can help you. But he who has this pain

in the eye of his soul, and is tormented by it, let him be more attentive, and let him open this eye to let in the eye-salve of the word of salvation, and by this he shall receive not only comfort, but a remedy also. For it is certain that whoever suffers pain in an eye, and will not open it, that the physician may pour in the eye-salve, the lotion will be spilled outside the pupil, and the eye itself remain painful. So is it with the soul in suffering; should it because of the weight of its grief close itself to the word of comfort, and refuse its saving help, it will begin to suffer yet more, and perhaps come to feel that sorrow of which the Scripture says: *The sorrow of the world worketh death* (II Cor. vii. 10).

The blessed Apostle Paul, the teacher of the faithful, the saving physician, says there are two sorrows: one good, the other bad; one profitable, the other unprofitable; one that saves us, another that ruins us. And so that what I am saying may not appear doubtful to anyone, I shall recite to you his own words: *For*, He says, *the sorrow that is according to God worketh penance, steadfast unto salvation; but the sorrow of the world worketh death.*

2. *Does mourning profit us, or not?*
Let us therefore, Brethren, consider this sorrow which is now close to us, that troubles our breast, that makes itself heard in our voice; is it profitable to us or unprofitable, does it help us or harm us? There lies in front of us a lifeless body. It lies upon the bier, a man without the man. It has members, yes; but without spirit. Called, it does not answer; spoken to, it does not hear. It lies

there, pale of face; in appearance so changed that through it we look on death itself. Let us think furthermore of its unbroken silence; and let us reflect on its past joys: on what were or shall be their profit? We think of the deceased's relatives; words of tender compassion come to our mind; we grieve for the end of a long friendship. These no doubt are the things that cause our tears, that move us to sorrow and lamentation, that plunge us in deep sadness.

Against these so powerful, these so human weapons of grief we must first oppose the thought that everything that is born into this world must die. For this is the law of God and His immutable decree, which, after his sin, the first of the human race received when God said to him: *Dust thou art, and into dust thou shalt return* (Gen. iii. 19). What new thing then has happened, when a man who was born to this has fulfilled the divine law and sentence? What new thing has happened, if a man born of mortal men renders to his own nature the debt he could not escape? That is not strange which is from of old, nor unheard which is of every day, nor unusual which is common to all men. If we know that our fathers and our forefathers have gone by this way of death, if we have heard that even the patriarchs and prophets, from Adam the first created, did not leave the world save by the way of death, let us uplift our spirit from this deep of sadness: for what this man owed, this man has paid.

And since he has in truth repaid a debt, what grief can there be? It is truly a debt; which no money can repay. It is a debt from which neither virtue nor wisdom nor power can free us; which not even kings can escape. I would wholly encourage you to increase your grief, if it was something with which you could redeem or postpone the debt, or if it came from your own neglect or parsimony. But since it is the firm, immutable decree of God, we grieve in vain, asking ourselves why he should die, since it is written: *To the Lord God belong the exits of death* (Ps. lxvii. 21). If we accept in our soul this common condition of life, it shall be as if the afflicted eye of the heart begins, as it were, to be relieved by the first healing infusion.

3. *Exessive grief is contrary to reason and also full of peril.* But, you will say, I know that this is the common lot. I know that he who is dead has but paid a debt. But I am recalling past happiness; I think of those he left; I miss his company and affection. If you are grief-stricken because of those things, you are deceived, you are not being led by reason. For you should know that the Lord Who gave you that happiness, can give you another and even more perfect one, and that He Who bestowed on you this relationship is able to replace it in due time. You should think of his gain who has died, as well as of your own. Far so it was expedient for him; as it is written: *He was taken away lest wickedness should alter his understanding, or deceit beguile his soul. For his soul pleased God. Therefore he hastened to bring him out of the midst of iniquities* (Wis. iv. 11, 14).

Of loving companionship what shall I say, since time so makes for forgetfulness, that it will seem as if it

never was? What time therefore and the day will do, much more should reason and calm reflection. And we should reflect most on the divine sentence, spoken through the Apostle, *that the sorrow of the world worketh death* (II Cor. vii. 10). But if delight and present advantage or mutual love are things of this world and its fleeting joys; and if because of them you are downcast in spirit and sorrowful in soul, take care this does not become a deadly weakness. Repeating it, I say again and again: *The sorrow of the world worketh death.* How does it work death? Because too much grief is wont to lead either to doubt, or to ruinous blasphemy.

4. *Lamentation was lawful for those before Christ. Why Christ wept over Lazarus. It is no longer lawful to mourn the dead.*

But someone will say: Do you forbid us to mourn the dead, when even the patriarchs mourned, and Moses that great servant of God, and later many of the prophets, and especially since Job, a most just man, rent his garments at the death of his children (Job. i. 20)? It is not I who forbid you to mourn the dead, but the Apostle, the Illuminator of the Gentiles, who pronounces these words: *And we will not have you ignorant, brethren, concerning them that are asleep, that you be not sorrowful, even as others who have no hope* (I Thess. iv. 12). The brightness of the Gospel cannot be obscured, because they who were before the Law, or who were under the shadow of the Law, lamented their dead. And rightly did they weep, for Christ had not yet come down from the heavens, Who by His Resurrection has dried that fountain of tears. Rightly did they weep, for the sentence of death still endured. Rightly were they mourned, for the resurrection of the dead was not yet proclaimed. Some among the saints hoped for the Coming of the Lord, but meanwhile they mourned their dead: for they had not yet seen Him in Whom they hoped. Then at length Simeon, one of the holy men of old, who before had been troubled in mind at the thought of his own death, after he had received the Lord Jesus, a child according to the flesh, in his arms, he rejoices at his going forth, saying: *Now thou dost dismiss thy servant, O Lord, according to thy word, in peace; because my eyes have seen thy salvation* (Lk. ii. 29, 30). O blessed Simeon! Because he has seen what he hoped for, he now looks to death as to his peace and rest.

But you will say: We read in the Gospel, that they wept for the daughter of the ruler of the synagogue (Lk. viii. 52), and that the sisters of Lazarus wept for him (Jn. xi. 31). But they still belonged in mind to the Old Law; for they had not yet seen Christ risen from the dead. Even the Lord Himself wept openly for Lazarus already in his grave; not that He might give us an example of weeping for the dead, but that He through His tears might show He had taken to Himself a true body. He wept also, and from human love, for the Jews who were not to believe in Him, even after He had given them such a sign. For the death of Lazarus could not have been the cause of His tears, since Jesus Himself had said that Lazarus slept, and had promised to go and waken him; which He did.

5. The ancients therefore, before the Coming of Christ, had their own tradition and their own limitation in understanding. Now however, from the time the Word was made Flesh, and dwelt amongst us; from the time the New Adam undid the sentence pronounced against the first Adam; from the time when the Lord hath destroyed our death (II Tim. i. 10) by His own death, and on the third day rose again from the dead, death is no more terrible to those who believe. We fear not the end of our day, for *the Orient from on high hath visited us* (Lk. i. 78). The Lord Himself Who cannot lie cries out to us: *I am the resurrection and the life; he that believeth in me, although he be dead, shall live; and everyone that liveth and believeth in me shall not die for ever* (Jn. xi. 25, 26).

Dearest Brethren, the divine voice has spoken clearly: that he who believes in Christ and keeps His commandments, even if he be dead, shall live. The blessed Apostle Paul, receiving His words and clinging to them with all the power of his faith, teaches us: *We will not have you ignorant, brethren, concerning them that are asleep, that you be not sorrowful* (I Thess. iv. 12). O wondrous proclamation of the Apostle! In one sentence, and before he utters his teaching to us, he commends to us the resurrection. For he speaks of the dead as, *them that are asleep,* so that saying they are asleep he testifies that they shall without doubt rise again. *Concerning those that sleep,* he says, *be not sorrowful, even as others who have no hope.* They who have no hope are stricken with grief; but we who are the children of hope, we rejoice. What our hope is, he tells us: *If we believe that Jesus died and rose again:*

even so them who have slept through Jesus, will God bring with him (v. 13). While we live this life, Jesus is our salvation; departing from it, He is our life. *For to me,* he says, *to live is Christ; and to die is gain* (Phil. i. 21). Clearly, *gain;* because of the distresses and tribulations that go with a longer life, death making haste, he gains.

And the Apostle describes the order and manner in which our hope shall be fulfilled: *This,* he says, *we say unto you in the word of the Lord, that we who are alive, who remain unto the coming of the Lord, shall not come before them who have slept. For the Lord himself shall come down from heaven with commandment and with the voice of an archangel and with the trumpet of God; and the dead who are in Christ shall rise first. Then we who are alive, who are left, shall be taken up together with them in the clouds to meet Christ, into the air; and so shall we be always with the Lord* (I Thess. iv. 14–16). This is what he means: That when the Lord comes, He will find many Christians who are still in the body, who have not yet undergone death. Nevertheless these shall not be taken up to heaven before the saints who have died, and who wakened by God's trumpet and by the voice of an archangel, have risen from their tombs. But when they have been raised up, then joined together with those who are alive they shall be taken up in the clouds to meet Christ in the air, and so they shall reign for ever with Him. Nor can we doubt that our bodies, although they are weighty, can be lifted up into the air: since Peter, who also had a body, at the command of the Lord, walked upon the waves of the sea (Mt. xiv. 29). Elias

too, in confirmation of this hope, was taken up to heaven in a fiery chariot (IV Kings ii. 11).

6. *What we shall be like after the resurrection.* But you will ask perhaps: What shall they be like who have risen from the dead? Hear thy Lord Himself telling thee: *Then, He* says, *shall the just shine as the sun in the kingdom of the Father* (Mt. xiii. 43). What need have I to speak of the splendour of the sun? Since the faithful shall be transformed into the likeness of the glory of Christ the Lord, as the Apostle Paul bears testimony: *Our conversation is in heaven,* he says: *from whence also we look for the Saviour, our Lord Jesus Christ, Who will reform the body of our lowness, made like to the body of his glory* (Phil. iii. 20); then without doubt this mortal flesh shall be transformed to the likeness of Christ's shining glory, and what is mortal shall put on immortality. For what *is sown in weakness, shall,* straightaway, *rise in power* (I Cor. xv. 43). Flesh shall no more fear corruption; it shall suffer neither hunger nor thirst nor sickness nor misfortune. For *our peace* is safe, and the *security* of our life immovable (cf. I Thess. v. 3). Of another kind is the glory of heaven, where also we shall receive joy unfailing.

7. *Death is rather to be longed for, than mourned; but must not be self-inflicted.* With these things before his mind and eyes, the blessed Paul declares: *I desire to be dissolved and to be with Christ, a thing by far the better* (Phil. I, 23). And teaching us still more openly, he says: *While we are in the body we are absent from the Lord; for we walk by faith and not by*

sight. But we have a good will, he says, *to be absent rather from the body and to be present with the Lord* (II Cor. v. 6–8). What are we doing, we men of little faith, who grieve and rebel should one of our dear ones depart to the Lord? What are we doing, we whose pilgrimage on this earth delights us more than to be restored to the presence of Christ? In very truth, this whole life of ours is but a journey through a strange land. For as pilgrims in this world, we have here no certain dwelling; we suffer, we sweat, walking by ways that are difficult, and full of peril. Treachery awaits us on every side, from spiritual enemies and from bodily ones; on every side the winding paths of error are made ready. And though beset by such dangers, not only do we wish not to be set free of them, but we even weep and mourn as lost those who have been delivered.

What has God given us through His Only-begotten, if we still fear the coming of death? Why glory in being born again of water and the Holy Ghost, when we are saddened at the thought of going forth from this world? The Lord Himself cries out to us: *If any man minister to me, let him follow me; and where I am,*

there also shall my minister be (Jn. xii. 26). Do you suppose that if an earthly king were to call someone to his palace, or to a feast, that he would not hasten there gratefully? How much more should we not hasten to the heavenly King, Who will not only receive us as guests, but shall give us to reign with Him; as it is written: *For if we be dead with him, we shall live also with him; if we suffer, we shall also reign with him* (II Tim. ii. 11, 12).

But I do not say this as meaning that anyone may raise his hand against himself, or slay himself against the will of God his Creator, or drive the soul from the dwelling place of the body. But this I say, that when he is called and when his neighbour is called, let him go cheerful and rejoicing, and let him rejoice with those that are going. For this is the sum total of Christian belief: to look for our true life after death; at the end of life, to look for its return. Having then taken to heart the words of the Apostle, let us now with confidence give thanks to God, Who has given us victory over death, through Jesus Christ our Lord, to Whom be glory and honour now and for ever. Amen.

II. St Augustine, Bishop and Doctor

The Woman who had an Issue of Blood[2]

1. She is the Church of God, the holy Church, Whose Head is Christ. If He is the Head, we the Body; if this is so, so that we suffer pressure from the multitude, let us not press hard against the Lord. A great multitude is flocking to the Church, which is spread throughout all the earth; all peoples believe. And in the midst of

all peoples, there is a part presses hard, and a part that is hard pressed. The part that is hard pressed suffers this in patience, and suffering in patience shall receive a reward: coming to the possession of that fruit of patience of which the Lord speaks in the Gospel: *He brings forth fruit in patience* (Lk. viii. 15). For this part is the saints, spread through all the world. They are the wheat, and the wheat is to be sown throughout the whole field; that is, throughout the whole world; for the Lord called the world a field, and all the faithful who draw near to Him in heart, not in their lips (Is. xxix. 13), He calls wheat. They who draw near, but not in heart, but only with their lips, He calls chaff and weeds. All through the field, all about the threshing floor, there is wheat and there is straw. But the greater part is straw, the lesser, but solider, wheat: lesser but heavier, lesser but more precious; the part men labour for, the part they are concerned with; for which they prepare a barn, not a fire.

Now let no man be satisfied with himself because he finds himself within these walls. Let him recall to mind what his purpose is; let him question his own heart; let him be his own most stern judge, that He may find God a merciful Father. Let no man deceive himself, nor be an acceptor of his own person; let him sit in the tribunal of his own soul, let his fears be the tormentors of his conscience; let him confess to God what he is. If he sees himself as wheat, let him be pressed down, let him not grieve to find himself mingled with the straw: the chaff shall mingle with the wheat upon the threshing floor, but not in the barn.

2. But as I was saying, Dearest Brethren, let it be our aim to be a member of that of which this Woman is a figure. Your Charity desires to know of whom this woman was a figure. We say she stands for the Church which came from the Gentiles: for the Lord was on his way to restore to life the daughter of the ruler of the synagogue. The daughter of the ruler of the synagogue stands for the Jewish people; for the Lord came only to the Jews, saying: *I was not sent but to the sheep that are lost of the house of Israel* (Mt. xv. 24). He came then as it were to the daughter of the ruler of the synagogue. Then this woman, of a sudden, coming from I know not where, *unknown, because she knew not* (I Cor. xiv. 38), touched the Lord in faith, saying: *If I shall touch only his garment, I shall be healed*. She touched, and was healed.

She suffered a detestable disease; an issue of blood. And this is a disease all dread either to hear of or to suffer: they dread an issue of blood in the body; let them then not suffer it within their heart. Disease in the soul is most to be shunned. I know not in what way the corruption of the indwelling soul, directed against its own habitation, departs from itself. The master wishes to be cured of a flux of the body; that is, the spirit wishes its body to be cured, in which it dwells as in a house; that is, itself. What good is a house faced with marble and with panelled ceilings if the master of the house is not healthy? But what am I saying? What good is a sound and healthy body, if the soul that dwells within is sick? Wantonness is an issue of blood in the soul: as the covetous are like those with dropsy – both long eagerly to drink – so are the lustful like those with an issue of blood. The covetous suffer, craving money; the profligate, spending it: in one is appetite, in the other a flux; and both kill.

There is need of a Physician: He

Who came to heal the sick of soul; but also willed to heal the ills of bodies, to show He was the Saviour of the soul, because He is the Creator of both. For He is not the Creator of the soul, yet not of the body:[3] and He willed to warn us that the soul is healed from within. So He healed the body: but within the body the soul watched, so that what it saw Jesus accomplish without, it desired He would accomplish within. What had God accomplished? He healed an issue of blood, He healed the leper, He healed the paralytic. All these are diseases of the soul. The blind and the lame too: for every man is lame who does not walk upright along the way of life; and he is blind who does not believe in God. And the wanton is troubled with an issue of blood, and the deceitful and the liar bear the spots of leprosy. We have need that He shall heal us within, Who for this healed without, that we might desire to be healed within.

3. This woman then was troubled with an issue of blood, and was healed of a bodily affliction that was wasting away all her strength: so does the soul pursuing the desires of the flesh waste all its powers. And this woman had spent all she had on physicians (so it is written of her). Like the unhappy Church of the Gentiles, seeking happiness, seeking some source of strength, some means of healing, what has it not spent on false physicians, on astrologers, on fortune-tellers, on deceivers, on temple soothsayers? For they all promise health, but give it they cannot; because they do not possess it themselves. She had therefore wasted all she had, and yet was not cured.

So she said: 'I shall touch the hem of his garment.' She touched it, and was healed.

Let us ask, what is the hem of His garment? Let your Charity pay careful attention. We are to understand, as the garment of the Lord, the Apostles who adhered to Him. Ask which Apostle was sent to the Gentiles: you will find it was Paul the Apostle; for his greatest work was in the apostolate of the Gentiles. Therefore Paul the Apostle, sent to the Gentiles, is the hem of the Lord's garment; because he was the last of the Apostles. Is there one who is the last and the least hem of this garment? The Apostle says he is both of these: *I am the last of the apostles*, and, *I am the least of all the apostles* (I Cor. xv. 8, 9). He is the last; he is the least. He is the hem of the Garment. And the Church of the Gentiles, as the woman who touched the hem, was troubled with an issue of blood. He touched her, and she was made whole. And let us also touch; that is, let us believe, that we may be saved.

Turning then to the Lord, we pray that the power of His mercy may confirm our heart in His truth, that it may confirm and give peace to our souls. May His grace abound in us, and may He have pity on us, and sweep scandals from our path and from the path of His Church and from before all who are dear to us, and may He in His power and in the abundance of His mercy to us grant that we may please Him for all eternity, through Jesus Christ His Son our Lord, Who with Him and with the Holy Ghost, liveth and reigneth throughout all ages.[4] Amen.

III. St Augustine, Bishop and Doctor

On the Daughter of the Ruler of the Synagogue, and on the Woman who was troubled with an issue of Blood⁵

1. When the record of past happenings are being read to us, they both illumine the mind and turn our thoughts to our own hopes for the future. Jesus was on His way to raise the daughter of the ruler of the synagogue who, He had been told, was already dead. And as He was going there, of a sudden, this woman who was afflicted with a disease appeared in His path; filled with faith, but failing in blood: to be restored by Blood. And she said in her heart: *If I shall touch only the hem of his garment, I shall be healed.* Saying this, she touched it: she touched Christ in faith. She drew near and touched Him; and it happened as she believed. But the Lord asked: *Who hath touched me?* He wishes to know, from Whom nothing is hidden; He asks by whom this was done, though He knew of it before it was done. Here then is a mystery. Let us consider it, and as He shall give us to understand it.

2. The daughter of the ruler of the synagogue stands for the Jewish people; this woman the Church of the Gentiles. The Lord Christ, born of the Jews in the Flesh, appears before these same Jews in His Body. He sends to the Gentiles; He Himself does not go. His bodily and visible life was passed in Judea. Because of this the Apostle says: *For I say that Christ Jesus was minister of the circumcision for the truth of God, to confirm the promises made unto the fathers* (for to Abraham was it said: *In thy seed shall all nations be blessed*

(Gen. xxii. 18); *But that the Gentiles are to glorify God for his mercy* (Rom. xv. 8, 9).

Christ therefore was sent to the Jews. He was on His way to the daughter of the ruler of the synagogue to raise her to life. This woman appeared on the way, and is healed: healed first in faith; and as it were unknown to the Saviour. Why did He say: *Who hath touched me?* The not knowing of God; her confidence in the divine mystery: it means something, when He knows not, Who cannot not know. What then does she stand for? The healed Church of the Gentiles; which does not see Christ in His bodily presence; of whom there is mention in the psalm: *A people which I knew not hath served me; at the hearing of the ear they have obeyed me* (Ps. xvii. 45). The whole world has heard of Him, and believed in Him. The people of Judea saw Him; they first crucified Him; hereafter they too shall come to Him. The Jews shall also believe; but at the end of the world.

3. Meanwhile that this woman may be healed, let her touch the hem of His Garment. And for the Garment, understand the Company of the Apostles. There was a certain one among them, the last and the least; the hem as it were: the Apostle Paul. He was sent to the Gentiles who says: *For I am the least of the Apostles, who am not worthy to be called an apostle.* And again: *I am the last of the apostles* (I Cor. xv. 9, 8). This last and least hem, this is

necessary for the healing of the un-healed woman. What we have heard has come to pass; what we have heard now takes place. Daily this woman touches the hem of His Garment; daily she is made clean. For the weakness of the flesh, this is an issue of blood. When we give ear to the Apostle; when we listen to this last and least hem of the Lord's Gar-ment, as he says to us: *Mortify your members which are upon the earth* (Col. iii. 5), then the issue of blood is checked, fornication is repressed, drunkenness is put to shame, worldly delights are restrained, all *the works of the flesh* are restrained (Gal. v. 19).

Wonder not it was a hem of His garment was touched. When the Lord said: *Who hath touched me?* It was as knowing, He knew not; meaning and pointing to the Church; which He saw not with His Body, but redeemed with His Blood.

PRAYER: Great is that possession for which so great a price was paid! And the price was not gold or silver, or wealth or lands, nor anything that can be divided. The possession of Christ is the Church. The possession of the Church is peace. He left us peace. Peace is our price; peace is our inheritance: let there be no strife among us. Engraft in your hearts, my brethren, the words of our Lord Jesus Christ, and rejoice in them, be glad in them, take delight in them. And let us give thanks that we are in the Church, that He com-mended to us with words, and then ascended into heaven. If the Jews mocked Him as He hung upon the Cross, let Christians beware of despising Him reigning in heaven.[6] Amen.

IV. St Peter Chrysologos, Bishop and Doctor

On the Daughter of the Ruler of the Synagogue, and on the Woman suffering from an issue of Blood; I[7]

MARK V. 22–43

This day, brethren, you will hear,[8] and from the Gospel according to the Evangelist Mark, and with me learn how a ruler of the Synagogue, coming to Christ, fell down before Him, confessing He was both God and Lord, and this for a twofold reason. For in conformity with the command of the Law which says: *The Lord thy God thou shalt adore* (Deut. vi), he adored Him, and beseeching Him to save his daugh-ter, already at the point of death, proclaims Him Restorer of life. *There cometh,* we read, *one of the rulers of the synagogue named Jairus;* *and seeing him falleth down at his feet. And he besought him much, saying: My daughter is at the point of death. Come, lay thy hands upon her, that she may be safe and live.*

Before making known to you by our sermon the meaning of this Gospel lesson, let us, if it is pleasing to you, speak for a moment of the pains and anxieties which parents take upon themselves and endure in patience out of love and affection for their children. Here, surrounded by her family and by the sympathy and affection of her relations, a daughter lies upon her bed of suffering. She is fading in body; her father's mind and spirit is worn with grief. She is suffering the inward pangs of her sickness; he, unwashed, unkempt, absorbed wholly in sorrow, suffers and endures before the eyes of the world. She is sinking into the quiet of death; he lives on to torment.

We shall say nothing of the hopes and desires of parents as they bring children into the world; of the threat to life through childbearing, of their struggles so that their children may be fed, of their unremitting care of them in sickness, and, more bitter than all, of the day their bodies are borne before them to the grave. Alas! why are children indifferent to these things? Why are they not mindful of them? Why are they not eager to make a return to their parents for them? But the love of parents goes on nevertheless; and whatever parents bestow upon their children, God, the parent of us all, will duly repay.

Let us now return to the subject of our discourse. *And there cometh one of the rulers of the synagogue named Jairus; and seeing him falleth down at his feet. And he besought him much, saying: My daughter is at the point of death. Come, lay thy hand upon her, and she may be safe and may live.* That he so grieves, and with tearful supplication, for the extremity of his daughter's sickness; that he so implores Jesus to cure her, proves and reveals to us the depth of his despairing love. And it is in this state of mind he also earnestly implores the manner of her cure. *Come*, he says, *lay thy hand upon her.*

One who is sick does not lay down how he is to be cured; desiring only to be made well. But this man was a ruler of the synagogue, and

versed in the Law, and had read that while God created all other things by His word, man had been created by *the hand* of God. He trusted therefore in God that his daughter would be recreated, and restored to life by that same hand which, he knew, had created her. So we see what he has in mind when he says: *Come, lay thy hand upon her:* That He Who of His own will, laid hands upon her, to make her, might now, besought, lay His hand on her and remake her.

It is this the Prophet proclaims when he says again and again in the Psalms: *Thou hast formed me, and hast laid thy hands upon me* (cxxxviii. 5). And He Who laid hands on her to form her from nothing, once more lays hands upon her to reform her from what had perished. And the same Psalmist, as he felt the touch of this saving hand, and received its bounty, cries again: *The right hand of the Lord hath wrought strength; the right hand of the Lord hath exalted me: The right hand of the Lord hath wrought strength* (cxvii. 16). And to show he had gained what the ruler of the synagogue now begs, he goes on: *I shall not die, but live.* The ruler, when he prayed, had said: *Come, lay thy hand upon her, that she may be safe and may live.* The prophet, exultant that he has gained this favour, cries: *I shall not die, but live.*

Christ is the Right Hand of the Lord; as we are taught by the word of the Prophet. And he hath truly *wrought strength*, when He overcame the devil; when having, as He said, *bound the strong*, He rifled all his possessions (Mt. xii. 29); when He destroyed hell; when He slew death itself. And He hath truly *exalted* us; whom He has raised from the depths and uplifted to heaven.

Let us now pass on to the woman who sought in secret to be healed of her hidden infirmity, of her shameful affliction; yet so as to shield her own modesty; upholding at the same time the reverence due to the Healer. *And he went with him. And a great multitude, we are told, followed him; and they thronged him. And a woman who was under an issue of blood, twelve years, and had suffered many things from many physicians and had spent all she had; and was nothing better, but rather worse, when she had heard of Jesus, came in the crowd behind him and touched his garment. For she said: If I shall touch but his garment, I shall be whole. And forthwith the fountain of her blood was dried up; and she felt in her body that she was healed of the evil.*

No seas were ever so troubled by the ebb and flow of the tide, as the mind of this woman: pulled to and fro by the sway of her thoughts. After all the hopeless strivings of physicians, after all her outlay on useless remedies, after all the usual but useless treatment, when skill and experience had long failed, when all her substance was gone, the shameful malady comes at last face to the Creator: not by chance, but divinely ordered, that she might be healed solely through faith and humility, whom human knowledge had failed through so many years.

At a little distance apart stood the woman, whom nature had filled with modesty, but the Law had declared unclean; saying of her: *She shall be unclean and shall touch no holy thing* (Lev. xv. 25). She fears to touch, lest she incur the anger of the Jews, or the condemnation of the Law. She dares not speak, lest she embarrass those about her, and offend their ears, and for fear of being talked about: This woman, whose body through so many years had been a target, an arena, of suffering. Her day-long and un-ceasing pain she can endure no more. And the Lord passing by so quickly makes short the time to think what she must do; aware that healing is not given to the silent, nor to the one who hides her pain.

In the midst of her conflicting thoughts, she sees a way, her sole way of salvation. She would secure her healing by stealth, take in silence what she dares not ask for: safe-guarding reverence and modesty. And she who feels unworthy in body, draws near in heart, to the Physician: in faith she touches God, with her hand she touches His garment; knowing that both healing and forgiveness will be bestowed on this theft: due not to her will, but to the demands of modesty; especially since the gain she sought by stealth would cause no loss to Him from Whom she took it.

The pious theft, faith helping, faith leading, is committed. See how virtue is sought by its opposite: faith conniving, deception gains what it longs for. The woman draws near, unnoticed in the throng; thinking to herself she could steal by faith the healing of her body, yet so that her condition and her person remain unknown. She comes behind Him; holding herself unworthy to look on Him. In an instant, faith cures where human skill had failed through twelve years.

Behind now are the long years she suffered through ignorance, bur-thened by the cost of ointments, not knowing she could be cured by faith. The woman touches His garment, and is healed of her long-standing affliction. Unhappy are we, who daily touching and receiving the Body of the Lord, are yet not healed of our infirmities.[9] But it is not Christ Who is wanting to the sick, but faith. For now abiding with us, much more will He cure us Who, passing by, cured the woman who hid from Him.

It will be enough for today, Brethren, to speak of the thefts of faith; and of the power of the Lord as He passes by. Why the Lord asks, as though He knew not, who it was He knew He had cured by His virtue, is too long a question for today. So we shall speak of it in our next sermon. Amen.

V. St Peter Chrysologos, Bishop and Doctor

On the Same; II[10]

Matthew ix. 18–26

All the Gospel lessons, Dearly Beloved, are of the greatest value; for this present life, and for the life to come. Today's Gospel brings us the fulness of hope, and shuts out all that leads to despair. Man's life is hard, and a source of much grief. Inborn weakness drives us towards sin; while the shame that is born of sin keeps us from confessing our sins. There is no shame in committing evil: the shame is in confessing the evil we do. We fear to speak of what we do not fear to do. But today, a woman, who sought relief by stealth for her shameful affliction, learns of a silence through which a sinner may come to forgiveness. Man's highest happiness was not to have fallen into sin; and next to that was to find pardon for his sins; the sins remaining hidden. It was this the Prophet had in mind who said: *Blessed are they whose iniquities are forgiven: and whose sins are covered* (Ps. xxxi. 1).

And behold, says the Evangelist, *a woman who was troubled with an issue of blood twelve years came behind him and touched the hem of his garment.* The woman long treatment had failed to cure, turns to the faith that

of a sudden has come to her. She that was ashamed to ask for healing, resolved to steal health of body. She hopes to remain unknown to Him by Whom she believes she can be healed. As the air is disturbed by the violence of the winds, so was this woman's mind troubled by the storm of her thoughts. Reason struggles with faith, hope with fear, necessity with modesty. The chill of fear cools the warmth of her trust; the force of modesty dimmed the light of faith; while the shame of her need weakened her confidence and her hope. So she is moved back and forth, like the sea by the ebb and flow of the tide.

She seeks for a way to keep what is hidden from being made public; to keep what is secret from the multitude. She moves forward, so that she shall both recover her health, yet not be overwhelmed by shame. She takes care that her healing shall not be an offence to the Healer: that salvation may be restored to her, with due reverence to the Saviour. In this mind she merits to ascend from the very extremity of His garment to the fullness of His Divinity.

She came, it says, *behind him.* But

where behind? *And touched the hem of his garment.* She came behind Him. But where? In vain behind Him, since there she meets the Face she avoided. In Christ there is a multiple body; but His Divinity is simple. He was all eye Who saw the suppliant behind Him. *She came behind him and touched the hem of his garment.* O what did this woman see, dwelling in the depths of Christ, who sees in the hem of His garment the whole power of His Divinity? O how much this woman has taught us of the greatness of Christ's Body, who taught us the power in the hem of His garment! Let us listen and learn: we who touch daily Christ's Body: what healing we may draw from It, when this woman took healing from the hem of His garment.[11]

But we must grieve that the medicine the woman took for her wound is by us twisted backwards to inflict a wound on us. This is the reason the Apostle warns us so gravely, sorrowing over those who touch the Body of Christ unworthily: For he who touches Christ's Body unworthily brings judgement upon himself. And since faith should draw healing, whence temerity brings affliction, he goes on to say: *Therefore are there many infirm and weak among you; and many sleep* (I Cor. xi. 30).[12] He speaks again of the dead as sleeping: whom he mourns as buried in their living body.

Peter and Paul, the princes of the Christian Faith, have spread the knowledge of Christ's Name throughout the whole earth. This woman was the first to teach us the way (*disciplina*) in which we are to draw near to Christ. This woman

first gave us the manner (*forma*) in which a sinner, by a secret confession (*tacita confessione*) may without confusion wipe sin away; how the sinner (*delinquens*), known only to God, is not forced to bare the shame of his conscience in the presence of men: how through pardon (*venia*) man can forestall the judgement.[13]

But Jesus, it says, *turning and seeing her, said: Be of good heart, daughter; thy faith had made thee whole.* Jesus turned towards her, not by the movement of His Body, but with the glance of His Divinity. Christ turns towards the woman, that the woman may be turned towards Christ: to receive healing from Him from Whom she had received life; that she might know that the cause of her present affliction was to gain eternal salvation. *Turning and seeing her.* He saw her, not with human, but with divine eyes. He saw her, that He might restore her to health; not to know one He already knew. He saw her, that she whom God had looked on might be blessed with good things, and be delivered from evil: for this is the belief of all men, because of the custom of saying of one who is blessed: *God looked on him.* God then looked on this woman, whom, healing, He made happy. And what more did He do? Christ taught us through this woman; whom faith had made whole.[14]

Let us now speak of the ruler of the synagogue, who while he conducts Christ to his daughter, prepares the way by which the woman came near to Christ. Today's lesson begins in this way: *Behold, a certain ruler came and adored him, saying: Lord, my daughter is even now dead; but come, lay thy hand upon her and she shall live.* That the meeting with this woman of whom we have been speaking would take place, was not hidden from Christ Who knows all things to come: The meeting through which the ruler of the Jews would learn, that God is not moved in place, nor led by the way, nor brought hither by His Bodily Presence; but that we are to believe, that God is everywhere present, everywhere wholly present, everywhere at all times; that He does all things by His command, not by His labour; that He sends forth the Powers, not that He is subject to them; that it is by His authority, not by His hand, death is banished; that it is by His word, not by His skill, life is given back to the dead.

My daughter is even now dead; that is to say: The heat of life still lingers, traces of the soul are still visible, her spirit is still there, the master of the house has still a daughter, Tartarus does not yet know her as dead. And that she may hold fast to the life that is now going, hasten! The foolish man believed Christ could not raise the dead girl, unless He held her hand. And so when Christ had come to the house, and saw the girl wept for as dead, that He might lead these unbelieving souls to faith, He says she is not dead, but sleeping: that they might come to believe that we can more easily rise from the dead than from sleep.

The girl, He says, *is not dead, but sleepeth.* And with God death is indeed a sleep; for God can more swiftly rouse the dead to life, than man can rouse a sleeper from his sleep, and before a man can rouse to action bodies that are deep in sleep, God will have poured the heat of life into members long cold in death. Listen to the words of the Apostle: *In a moment, in the twinkling of an eye, the dead shall rise* (I Cor. xv. 52). The blessed Apostle, since this cannot be described in words, uses examples to make clear the swiftness of the resurrection of the dead. What avails the swift brevity of human speech, since the divine power outstrips swiftness itself? Or how can time serve to explain it, since this eternal reality is bestowed independent of time? As time bears away the passing years, so does eternity make an end of time. Amen.

NOTES

[1] PG 56, col. 293, *De Consolatione Mortis: Sermo Primus.* These two short works of St John Chrysostom survive only in the Latin translation; *in vetere Corbiensi Codice ante mille, ut videtur, annos descripto, primus quidem hocce titulo praenotatus;* Incipit sermo Sancti Joannis de Consolatione mortis. *Secundus autem primo proxime conjunctus absque titulo, nihilque aliud in fine habens nisi, Explicit de Resurrectione.* That it is of St John Chrysostom is confirmed by internal evidence (*Monitum*, preceding text, as above).

[2] *Miscellania Agostiniana*, G. Morin O.S.B. *Sermones Reperti*, p. 317, Mai xxv. Some portion of the beginning is missing; the codex beginning: . . . *ecclesia dei, ecclesia sancta, cui est ille caput.* Ex codice Bobiensi, nunc Vatic. lat. 5759, 00. 259–64.

[3] Against the Manichaeans.

⁴ Concluding prayer from *Sermo* II (Denis), *Misc. Agostiniana*, p. 17.

⁵ *Miscellania Agostiniana, Sermones Reperti*, Morin VII, p. 611.

⁶ *Misc. Agost.*, Morin, p. 623, conclusion of sermon.

⁷ PL 52, *Sermo* XXXIII, col. 292.

⁸ Sometimes the sermon preceded the reading of the Gospel.

⁹ An authoritative reference to the practice of daily Communion in the early centuries of the Church.

¹⁰ PL 52, *Sermo* XXXIV.

¹¹ Chrysologos in the preceding sermon says: *Fide Deum, manu solum tetigit vestimentum.* Ambrose on Luke: *Fide tangitur Christus, fide Christus videtur; non corpore tangitur, non oculis comprehenditur*, etc. By the *woman*, he understands the Church coming from the Gentiles; by the *hem* the Apostles and their successors.

¹² That is, as a result of bad Communions.

¹³ That Chrysologos is here referring to private (auricular) confession of sins, can scarcely be doubted, since he had said a little earlier in the same sermon: *Malum enim facere pudor non est, et pudor est confiteri; timemus dicere quod committere non timemus.*

¹⁴ 'The faith of this woman is the belief that the Christ was He of whom the prophets had foretold that He would work such cures' (cf. Is. xxxv. 5); note *h*; at foot of text. It may well have been inspired divine faith; as the holy Doctor seems to imply.

TWENTY-FOURTH SUNDAY AFTER PENTECOST

THE GOSPEL OF THE SUNDAY

Matthew xxiv. 15-35

1

At that time: Jesus said to his disciples: When you shall see the abomination of desolation, which was spoken of by Daniel the prophet, standing in the holy place; he that readeth let him understand; Then they that are in Judea, let them flee to the mountains; and he that is on the housetop, let him not come down to take anything out of his house; and he that is in the field, let him not go back to take his coat. And woe to them that are with child and give suck in those days. But pray that your flight be not in the winter or on the sabbath; for there shall be then great tribulation, such as hath not been from the beginning of the world until now, neither shall be. And unless these days had been shortened, no flesh should be saved; but for the sake of the elect those days shall be shortened.

2

Then, if any man shall say to you: Lo, here is Christ, or there; do not believe him. For there shall arise false Christs and false prophets and shall show great signs and wonders, insomuch as to deceive (if possible) even the elect. Behold, I have told it

329

to you, beforehand. If therefore they shall say to you: Behold, he is in the desert; go ye not out. Behold, he is in the closets; believe it not. For as lightning cometh out of the east and appeareth even into the west; so shall also the coming of the Son of man be. Wheresoever the body shall be, there shall the eagles also be gathered together.

the clouds of heaven with much power and majesty.

4

And he shall send his angels with a trumpet and a great voice; and they shall gather together his elect from the four winds, from the farthest parts of the heavens to the utmost bounds of them.

5

And from the fig-tree learn a parable: When the branch thereof is now tender and the leaves come forth, you know that summer is nigh. So you also, when you shall see all these things, know ye that it is nigh, even at the doors. Amen, I say to you that this generation shall not pass till all these things be done. Heaven and earth shall pass; but my words shall not pass.

3

And, immediately after the tribulation of those days, the sun shall be darkened and the moon shall not give her light and the stars shall fall from heaven and the powers of heaven shall be moved. And then shall appear the sign of the Son of man in heaven. And then shall all tribes of the earth mourn; and they shall see the Son of man coming in

EXPOSITION FROM THE CATENA AUREA

CHRYSOSTOM, *in Matthew, Homily* 76: In the preceding verses He had spoken in a veiled manner of the end of Jerusalem, here He goes on to speak of it openly; quoting a prophecy, to lead them to believe in the coming destruction of the Jews. So we read:

V.15. *When therefore you shall see the abomination of desolation, which was spoken of by Daniel the prophet, standing in the holy place; he that readeth let him understand.*

JEROME: The words: *He that readeth let him understand*, were spoken in order to alert us to the mystical content of His words. These are the words of Daniel: *And in the half of the week the victim and the sacrifice shall*

fail: and there shall be in the temple the abomination of desolation. And the desolation shall continue even to the consummation and to the end. And the abomination shall continue to the end of time and an end shall be put to the desolation (Dan. ix. 27).

AUGUSTINE, *Ep. to Hesychius,* 80: Luke, to show that the abomination spoken of by Daniel will take place when Jerusalem is captured, recalls these words of the Lord in the same context: *When you shall see Jerusalem compassed about with an army, then know that the desolation thereof is at hand* (xxi. 20).[1]

CHRYSOSTOM, *Opus Imperfectum, Homily* 49: From this it seems to me that *the abomination of desolation* means the army by which the holy city of Jerusalem was made desolate.

JEROME: Or it can be understood of the statue of Caesar which Pilate placed in the temple, or of the equestrian statue of Adrian, which stood, even to our own times, in the holy of holies. In the Old Testament an idol is called, an *abomination*; and, *of desolation*, is added because the idol was set up in the midst of the desolate and deserted temple.

CHRYSOSTOM, *on Matthew, Homily 76*: Or because he who had desolated the city and the temple, placed his statue within the temple. And that they might learn that these things shall be, even while some of them are still living, He says: *When you shall see.* Here we marvel at Christ's power, and at the Disciples' courage, preaching in such times; in which everything Jewish was being attacked. And how the Apostles, though Jews, brought in new laws in face of the Romans who then ruled them, and made myriads of them prisoners; but did not prevail over these twelve poor, unarmed men. It had happened often in past times that the Jews had recovered from similar disasters, as in the times of Sennacherib and Antiochus; now, that no one might think that this will happen again, He commands His followers to fly, when He goes on to say:

V.16. *Then they that are in Judea, let them flee to the mountains.*

REMIGIUS: All this we know now took place with the approaching desolation of Jerusalem. For as the Roman arms came on, all Christians

who were in the province, warned, as Ecclesiastical history relates, by a divine sign, retreated a long way before them, and crossing the Jordan came to the city of Pella, and remained there for some time under the protection of King Agrippa, of whom mention is made in the Acts of the Apostles. He and those Jews whom he ruled were however subject to the Roman rule. CHRYSOSTOM, as above: Then, to show them the inescapable evils that were to come upon the Jews, and that this calamity was without end, He continues:

V.17. *And he that is on the housetop, let him not come down to take anything out of his house.*

For it was better to escape unclothed than go into his house to get his clothes, and be slain. And of the man in the fields He says:

V.18. *And he that is in the field, let him not go back to take his coat.*

For if those who are in the city are to fly, much more should they who are in the fields not return to the city. But while it is easy to despise money, and not difficult to provide one's self with clothing; how can anyone escape the tie of nature? How can the woman heavy with child lightly take to flight, or the mother abandon the child at her breast? And so He goes on:

V.19. *And woe to them that with child and that give suck in those days.*

The first because they are helpless, and cannot easily escape, heavy with the burden they have conceived; the others, because they are held by the bond of compassion for their children, and cannot save both themselves and the children at the breast. ORIGEN, o*n Matthew, Tr.* 29: Or because there shall then be no compassion for those with child, or for those who give suck, or for their children. And since he was speaking to Jews, who held that on the sabbath day they could not walk more than the allotted sabbath journey, He adds:

V.20. *But pray that your flight be not in the winter or on the sabbath.*

JEROME: For in the one case, the bitter cold prevents you from seeking the deserts, or from hiding in remote mountains; in the other, if you fly, you transgress the law, while if you stay, death is waiting for you.

CHRYSOSTOM, as above: You see how this discourse is addressed to Jews. For the Apostles will not observe the sabbath, and neither will they stay, when Vespasian is doing these things. For by then the greater part of them will have already died; and should any survive, they would then be living in another part of the world. He then tells them the reason they should pray for this:

V.21. *For there shall be then great tribulation, such as hath not been from the beginning of the world until now, neither shall be.*

AUGUSTINE, *Ep. to Hesychius,* 199: In Luke we read (xxi. 23, 24): *There shall be great distress upon the land, and wrath upon this people; and they shall fall by the edge of the sword and shall be led away captives into all nations.* And Josephus, who wrote the History of the Jewish People, relates such evils as happening to this people as scarcely seem credible.

Hence rightly is it said that there has not been such tribulation since the beginning of the world, nor shall there be. And even though there shall be such tribulation, or even greater perhaps in the time of Antichrist, nevertheless we must here understand that it is said of this people that such tribulation shall not come to them again. For if they are to be the first and the chief people to receive Antichrist, they will inflict tribulation, rather than receive it.[2]

CHRYSOSTOM: I would ask the Jews why has such intolerable wrath come to them from above; more grievous than ever before? Is it not plainly because of the deed of the Cross, and its denial. And He shows they merited yet more grievous punishment, in the words that follow:

V.22. *And unless those days had been shortened, no flesh should be saved.*

As though He said: Had the Roman assault against the city continued, all Jews would have perished: for he is speaking of all Jewish flesh; those within and those without the city. For the Romans attacked not only those who were in Judea, but those scattered everywhere were also persecuted. AUGUSTINE, as above: There are some who seem not inaptly to think that by *these days* the evils themselves are meant, since in other places in Scripture (Eph. v. 16) days are spoken of as being *evil.* But days themselves are not *evil;* only the things done upon them. And they are said to be *shortened,* in that, God giving us patience, they are felt less; as if what were great evils were made small.

CHRYSOSTOM, *on Matthew, Homily* 76: That the Jews might not say these evils came because of the preaching of the Gospel, and because of the followers of Christ, He shows that were it not for them all would have perished. Hence there follows: *But for the sake of the elect those days shall be shortened.*

AUGUSTINE, as above: For we should not doubt that when Jerusalem was overthrown, there were among that people certain of the elect of God, who had believed from the circumcision, or were to believe; *elect* from the foundation of the world, because of whom these days would be shortened, that their evils might become more endurable. Nor are there wanting those who think that the days will be shortened by a more rapid motion of the sun; as the day was made longer at the prayer of Josue.

JEROME: Not remembering that it is written: *By thy ordinance the day goes on* (Ps. cxix. 19). We are not to believe they shall be shortened in measure, but in their number; so that the faith of those who believe may not be shaken by the prolongation of their trials.

AUGUSTINE: We have no reason to think that the *weeks* of Daniel were altered by this shortening of the days; or that they were not at that time complete, but were to be completed at the end of time. For Luke very clearly bears witness that the prophecy of Daniel was fulfilled when Jerusalem was overthrown.

CHRYSOSTOM: Observe the dispensation of the Holy Spirit: how John wrote nothing of these events, so that he might not seem to be writing of what was history; for he lived for a long time after the capture of Jerusalem. But they who were dead before it, and saw nothing of these events, they wrote of them; so that the power of the prophecy might shine out on all sides.

HILARY, *on Matthew* (*Canon* 25): Or, the Lord gave a perfect sign of His future coming, when He says: *When you shall see the abomination of desolation.* For the Prophet said this of the times of Antichrist. He is called *abomination* from this, that coming against God, he arrogates to himself the honour due to God. The *abomination of desolation*, because he will desolate the earth with wars and slaughters, and received by the Jews, he will stand in the place of sanctification; that where God is wont to be invoked by the prayers of the saints, he may be received by the perfidious as worthy of honour due to God. And because this error will be peculiar to the Jews; that they who rejected Truth shall receive falsehood; He warns them to forsake Judea and fly to the mountains, that they may not, by mingling with the people of Antichrist, be subjected to their contagion.

That He said: *And he that is on the house-top, let him not come down to take anything out of his house*, is to be understood in this sense: The roof is the highest part of the house, the summit and perfection of the whole building. He therefore who stands on the summit of his own house, that is, on the perfection of his own heart, new in regeneration, elevated in spirit, must keep himself from descending to lowlier things; out of greed for worldly possessions. *And he that is in the field, let him not go back to take his cloak*; that is, he that is firm in obedience to the commandments, let him not return to his former cares; which would be a putting on again of his former sins, with which he was once covered.

AUGUSTINE: For we must beware, when in tribulation, of descending from the spiritual heights, to become bound again to the carnal life; or lest he who has advanced, looking backwards to earlier things, falter and turn again to baser things.

HILARY: That He said: *Woe to them that are with child and that give suck in those days*; must not be taken as meaning that He was warning them of the burthen of the pregnant, but that He was showing them the heaviness of souls that are filled with sin; that neither on the house-top, nor in the field can they escape the tempest of wrath laid up for them. Woe also to those who are being suckled. In these we are shown the weakness of those who are being reared in the knowledge of God, as though with milk; and so it shall be woe to them, because they shall be too weak to fly from Antichrist, and too unprepared to withstand him: for these have neither shunned sin, nor eaten the food of the True Bread.

AUGUSTINE, *Sermon* 20: Or they are *with child* who covet what belongs to another; they *give suck* who have already taken what they covet. For these there shall be woe on the day of judgement.[3] AUGUSTINE, *Gospel Questions*, I, 37: That the Lord said: *Pray that your flight be not in winter*

or on the sabbath; that is, so that no one may be found that day in either sorrow or joy over temporal things. HILARY: Or, that we may not be found in the frost of sin, or in indifference to good works; lest we be visited with grievous punishment. Unless for the sake of the elect of God, these days are shortened; so that the shortening of the time may lessen the violence of these evils.

ORIGEN, *on Matthew, Tr.* 29[4]: Mystically; Antichrist, that is, the false Word, has frequently stood in the holy place of all the Scriptures, both of the Old and the New Testament (*as though He was Christ God the Word, when he is the abomination of desolation*). They who see this, let them fly from the *letter* of Judea to the lofty mountains of Truth. And if anyone has ascended to the roof of the Word, and stands upon its summit, let him not come down from there, to take as it were something from his house. And if he is in the field, in which the *treasure* is hid, and goes back from there, he will run into the danger of the seduction of the false word (antichrist); and this especially should he have cast off his old garment, that is, *the old man*, and go back to put it on again.

Then the soul that has conceived, but has not yet borne fruit of the Word, may incur this woe (*of which the Lord speaks*); should it lose what it conceived, and be emptied of its hope; which is in the deeds of truth. And the same if the word appears, formed and brought forth, but not yet sufficiently nourished. Let those who flee to the mountains, pray that their flight may not be in winter, or on the sabbath; for the souls that are established in peace shall find the way of salvation; but if winter over-takes them, they shall fall among those they are flying from. Pray then that your flight be not on the sabbath; for while some abstain from evil on the sabbath, they do not however give themselves to good works. Let your flight therefore be on not on such a sabbath: for no man is easily overcome by false teaching, unless he is void of good works. And what greater tribulation than to see our brethren led astray into evil beliefs, and to see oneself shaken and in danger? *Those days* are understood to mean the precepts and the teachings of Truth: but all interpretations that come from knowledge falsely so called (I Tim. vi. 20), are but so many additions to these days, which God shortens for whom He wills.

2

CHRYSOSTOM, *on Matthew, Homily 77*: Having finished with what concerned Jerusalem, the Lord passes on to what concerns His own Coming and speaks of the signs that will accompany it, and this not only for their guidance, but for ours also, and for all who come after us:

V.23. *Then, if any man shall say to you: Lo, here is Christ, or there; do not believe him.*

Just as when earlier the Evangelist said: *In those days cometh John the Baptist* (iii. 1), he was not speaking of the time immediately following what had just been narrated, but of thirty years after. So here also, when he says *then*, he passes over the whole intervening time from the fall of Jerusalem to the beginning of the consummation of the world. Giving them the signs of His Second Com-

ing, He describes clearly the place and the character of the deceivers. For *then* it will not be like His First Coming, in Bethlehem, in a little corner of the earth, and, at His beginning, unknown to all. Rather will He come openly, so that He shall need no one to announce His Coming, And so He now says: *If any man shall say to you: Lo, here is Christ, or there; do not believe him.*

JEROME: In which He shows that His Second Coming shall not be in low-liness, as was His First; but pro-claimed in glory. It is folly therefore to look in small and obscure places for Him Who is the Light of the whole world. HILARY: And yet, be-cause of the great distress that men shall be in, false prophets will pro-claim that Christ is at hand in many places to help them; and will lyingly declare that He is here and there, so that they may lead the down-trodden and distressed into the ser-vitude of Antichrist. And so He says:

V.24. *For there shall arise false Christs and false prophets.*

CHRYSOSTOM: Here He is speaking of Antichrist and of certain of his ser-vants, whom He calls *false Christs* and *false prophets*, of whom there were many even at the time of the Apostles. But before Christ's Second Coming, there shall be others, more bitter than these. *And shall show great signs and wonders.*

AUGUSTINE, *Book of 83 Questions, 79, 3*: Here the Lord warns us, so that we may be aware that even wicked men can work certain miracles, which even the saints can-not. Yet not because of this are they to be held as greater before God.

For the magicians of Egypt were not more acceptable to God than the people of Israel, because they could do things the people could not; although Moses, by the power of God, could work yet greater wonders. Gifts of this kind are not given to all the saints, for fear that those who are weak might be led astray by a very dangerous error; namely, thinking that there are greater blessings in such acts than in the works of justice, by which we gain eternal life.

When therefore magicians work such miracles as saints sometimes do, they do them for a different purpose, and by a different power. For they do them to promote their own glory; the latter the glory of God. The former work them through certain permissions granted to the evil powers within their degree (Eph. vi. 12), by a particular dispensation as it were; the latter in their public duty and by command of Him to Whom all creation is subject. It is one thing for an owner to be compelled to give his horse to a soldier, another to sell it to a purchaser or lend it to a friend. And as often many evil soldiers, whom the Imperial discipline condemns, terrify some owners by a display of the imperial insignia, and extort from them something not ordered by public authority; so sometimes evil Christians demand something from these evil powers, either by means of the name of Christ, or by means of Christian words or mysteries. When they yield to those thus wickedly commanding them, they yield in order to mislead men, in whose error they delight.

And so magicians work miracles in one way; good Christians in another; bad Christians in yet another way. The magicians by a private concession, good Christians through their known justice, evil Christians through the appearances of public justice. Nor need we marvel at this; since we may, and not absurdly, believe that all that visibly takes place is the work of the lesser powers *of this air* (Eph. ii. 2). [Cf. PL 40.]

AUGUSTINE, *On the Trinity*, III, 8, 9: But we are not for this reason to believe that the substance of the visible creation is subservient to the will of the fallen angels, but rather to the will of God, by Whom power is given to them. Neither are these evil angels to be spoken of as creators. But because of their power of penetration (*subtilitas*) they have come to know the seeds of things that are more obscure to us, and by due commingling of the elements they spread them here and there, and in this way bring about the conditions for the production and rapid increase of things. For many men have come to know from what herbs or bodies or juices or humours, mixed or commingled together, certain living things are born. But this is the more difficult for men, for their slow, earthy members are wanting in subtlety and speed of movement.

GREGORY, *Morals*, xv. 30: Therefore, when Antichrist works prodigies before the eyes of the carnal minded, he will draw men after him. For all who delight in earthly things will without hesitation subject themselves to his power. So we read: *Insomuch as to deceive, if possible, even the elect.* ORIGEN: The words, *if possible*, are as it were a figure of speech. For He did not announce, He did not say that the elect are led into error. But He wishes to show us that oftentimes the words of heretics are persuasive and capable of moving even those who are wont to act wisely. GREGORY, *Morals*, 33, 36: Or, because the hearts of the elect are shaken by fearful apprehension, yet their constancy remains unmoved. He includes both these things (testing and constancy) in the one sentence: for to falter even in thought is already a fault. But, *if possible*, is added; for it cannot happen the elect will be captured by error.

RABANUS: Or, He does not say this because the divine election may be frustrated, but because they who in human judgement seem to be elect, they shall be led into error. GREGORY *on Gospel, Homily* 35: Darts foreseen are guarded against; and because of this He adds:

V.25. Behold, I have told it to you, beforehand.

For our Lord is warning us of the evils that will precede the end of the world, so that, known beforehand, they will frighten us the less when they come. Because of this He concludes:

V.26. If therefore they shall say to you: Behold, he is in the desert; go ye not out. Behold, he is in secret places, believe it not.

HILARY: For the false prophets, of whom He had spoken a moment before, will say that Christ is now in the desert, that they may lead men astray by heresy; now in secret councils, that they may captivate men by

the force of a powerful Antichrist. But the Lord Himself declares that He shall neither be hidden in any place nor accessible only to a few, but that He shall be present everywhere and to the sight of all men. Hence follows:

V.27. For as lightning cometh out of the east and appeareth even into the west; so shall the Coming of the Son of man be.

CHRYSOSTOM: As He first tells in what manner Antichrist will come, so by these words He describes the manner of His own Coming. For as lightning needs no one to announce or to herald it, but is seen in an instant throughout the world, even to those who sit in their houses, so shall the Coming of the Son of man be visible everywhere at once, because of the splendour of His glory. He then speaks of another sign:

V.28. Wheresoever the body shall be, there shall the eagles also be gathered together.

By eagles He means the multitudes of the Angels and Martyrs and all the Blessed. JEROME: We are taught a mystery concerning Christ by means of an example from nature that we daily see. Eagles and vultures are said to scent dead bodies even from across the sea, and to flock to where they are to feed on them. If unreasoning birds by natural instinct perceive and at such a distance where a small dead body is lying, how much more should not the multitude of the believing hasten to Him Whose Coming is as lightning out of the east and appearing even unto the west? By the *body*, that is, corpse (*ptoma*), and which in Latin is more expressively called *cadaver* (in that it falls, because of death), we see an allusion to Christ's passion and death. (PL 23, col. 179.)

HILARY: That we might not be ignorant of the place to which He would come, He says: *Wheresoever the body shall be, there shall the eagles also be gathered together.* He speaks of the sanctified as eagles, because of the spiritual flight of their bodies, and shows that the Angels shall gather them together at the place of His Passion. And fittingly should we look for His Coming in glory, where for us He gained the glory of eternity by the lowliness of His bodily Passion.

ORIGEN: See how He does not say: *wheresoever the body shall be, there also* the ravens or vultures shall be gathered; but, *the eagles;* wishing to show the splendour and glory of all who have believed in the Passion of our Lord. JEROME: They are called eagles whose youth is renewed *like the eagles* (Ps. ciii. 5); and take wing that they may come to the Passion of Christ.

GREGORY, *Morals* (Job xxxix, 30): The words: *Wheresoever the body shall be,* can also be understood as meaning: Because I the Incarnate, Who sit upon the throne of heaven, shall exalt the souls of the elect to heaven, after I have freed them from the flesh. JEROME: Or again: This may be understood of the false prophets. For at the time of the Jewish captivity, there were many leaders who declared that they were the Christ, so much so that during the siege by the Romans, there were three factions within the city. But it

is better understood of the end of the world, as we have explained. It can be understood in a third way, as the battle of heretics against the Church, and of those antichrists who, under the name of science falsely called, war against Christ.

ORIGEN: For in general there is but one Antichrist; but he has many forms; as though we were to say: Lie does not differ from lie. Just as the holy prophets were the prophets of the True Christ, so will each false Christ have many false prophets, who will proclaim as true the false teachings of some antichrist. When therefore one of them says: *Lo, here is Christ, or there,* we need not look further than the Scriptures; for they draw from the Law and the Prophets and the Apostles whatever may seem to justify their lie. Or that they say: *Lo, here is Christ, or there,* they show that it is not Christ, but some deceiver using the same name, following the teaching of a Marcion, a Valentinus, or a Basilides.

JEROME: If any one therefore promises you that Christ is to be found in the desert of the heathen or in the tenets of the philosophers or in the secret councils of heretics, and offers to make known the mysteries of God, do not believe him, but believe that the Catholic Faith shines out in the Churches from the east even unto the west.

AUGUSTINE, *Gospel Questions*, I, 38: By the words *east* and *west* He meant to signify the whole world throughout which the Church was to be established; in accord with the words in which He said: *Hereafter you shall see the Son of man coming in the clouds*

(xxvi. 64). He now fittingly uses the word *lightning*, which is wont especially to flash from the clouds. Therefore, when the authority of the Church has been clearly and manifestly established throughout the earth, then He warns His Disciples, and all the faithful, they must not put any faith in heretics and schismatics. For each schism, each heresy will either have its place upon the earth, holding to some part of it; or it will deceive mens' curiosity in obscure, hidden conventicles. It was because of this He said: *If any man shall say to you: Lo, here is Christ, or there,* which implies some parts of the earth or of countries; or, *behold he is in secret chambers,* which refer to the obscure and secret conventicles of the heretics.

JEROME: Saying, *in the desert,* or *in the secret chambers,* means that in a time of distress or persecution false prophets always find ways to deceive.

ORIGEN: Or, when they bring forward secret and hitherto unheard of scriptures to confirm their lies, they seem to be saying: Lo, in the desert is the word of truth. But as often as they bring forward the canonical Scriptures, on which all Christians agree, they seem to be saying: Lo, we possess the word of truth in the houses. But we must not believe them, or depart from the first and ecclesiastical tradition.[5] Or, wishing to expose those teachings, which belong in no way to the Scriptures. He said: *If they shall say to you: Behold, he is in the desert, go ye not out:* from the rule of faith. And wishing to expose those who falsify the divine Scriptures, He said: *If they shall say to you: Behold he is the secret chambers; believe it not.* For the truth is like the lightning, coming forth from the east and appearing even in the west.[6]

Or, this means that the lightning of truth is defended in every part of Scripture. The light of truth therefore *cometh out of the east;* that is, from the Birth, of Christ and appears even to His Passion, which is His sunset; or from the first beginnings of creation, until the last Scripture of the Apostles. Or the *east* is the Law; the *west* the end of the Law and of the prophecy of John. Only the Church takes neither word nor meaning from this lightning, nor adds anything as prophecy. Or He means that we are to pay no attention to those who say: *Lo, here is Christ;* but do not declare He is in the Church, in which alone is the full and perfect Coming of the Son of man Who said: *Behold, I am with you all days, even to the consummation of the world* (Mt. xxix. 20).[7]

JEROME: We are called to the Passion of Christ, so that wherever it is read in the Scriptures, let us gather together, that through it we may come to the Word of God.

3

GLOSS: After the Lord had fortified the faithful against the seductions of Antichrist and his servants; to show us that He will come openly, He now reveals the manner and order of His Coming, saying:

V.29. *And, immediately after the tribulation of those days, the sun shall be darkened.*

CHRYSOSTOM: He means the tribulation of the days of Antichrist and the false prophets: for there shall then be great tribulation from the great number of seducers. But it will not continue for a great length of time. For if the Jewish war was shortened for the sake of the elect, much more shall this tribulation be shortened because of them. And because of this He does not simply say: *After the tribulation,* but, *immediately after.* For He shall Himself immediately appear.

HILARY: The darkening of the sun, the fading of the moon, the falling of the stars point to the glory of His Coming. And there follows: *And the moon shall not give her light and the stars shall fall from heaven.* ORIGEN: Someone will say: When great fires break out the smoke at first seems to cause darkness, so will it be at the consummation of the world by the fire which is to be kindled; and even the great luminaries shall be obscured. And with the dimming of the light of the stars, the rest of their substance, becoming inert, they cannot continue in their course as before, when set in the firmament and maintained on high by Light Itself, and shall fall from heaven. When these things shall take place, the rational Powers of heaven, awed, shall be moved, and experience a certain dismay at the end of their former tasks; and so there follows: *And the powers of heaven shall be moved.*

V.30. *And then shall appear the sign of the Son of man in heaven.*

That sign in which all things heavenly were made, the wonder the Son of man accomplished hanging on the Tree; and His sign shall shine out above all the heavens, so that men of all tribes, who before had not believed Christianity when it was announced to them, now recognizing its sign made manifest to all, shall weep and mourn for their ignorance and for their sins. So there follows: *And then shall all tribes of the earth mourn.*

Some understand these words one way, some another: That just as a lamp fades, so shall the lights of heaven, when that which feeds them fails. And the sun shall be darkened, and the moon and stars shall fall from heaven. How can it be said of the sun that its light shall be darkened, when Isaias the Prophet declares that the sun shall shine out at the end of the world (xxx. 26); and the moon's light, he says, shall be as the sun? As to the stars. There are those that say that all or many of them are greater than the whole earth; how then, they say, can the earth contain the stars fallen from heaven?

JEROME: These things shall therefore not happen by any diminution of actual light; for we read elsewhere that: *The light of the sun shall be sevenfold* (Is. xxx. 26). But in comparison with the True Light, all things shall seem dark. RABANUS: But nothing prevents us from thinking that the sun and moon and the other stars shall not then for a time be deprived of their light; as happened to the sun at the time of our Lord's Passion; and as Joel also says: *The sun shall be turned into darkness, and the moon into blood, before the great and dreadful day of the Lord doth come* (ii. 31). For the rest, when the day of judgement has passed, and as the life of the glory to come begins to grow bright, when there will be a new heaven and a new earth, then will take place that which the prophet Isaias speaks of: *And the light of the moon shall be as the light of the sun and the light of the sun shall be seven-fold.* That which is said of the stars: *And the stars shall fall from heaven,* is written in Mark as follows: *And the stars of heaven shall be falling down* (xiii. 25); that is, wanting in their light.

JEROME: By *the powers of heaven* we understand the hosts of the angels.

CHRYSOSTOM: Well may they be *moved,* or troubled, seeing such a transformation, and seeing their fellow-servants punished, and the world gathered before the dread seat of judgement. ORIGEN: As in the Dispensation of the Cross, the sun failing, there came a darkness over the earth, so, at the sign of the Son of man appearing in the heavens, the lights of the sun and moon and stars shall fail, as though swallowed by the great power of this sign. And so there follows: *And then there shall appear the sign of the the Son of man in heaven.* Let us see here the sign of the Cross, so that the Jews, according to Zachary and John, may look on Him whom *they have pierced* (Jn. xix. 37), and upon the Sign of victory.

CHRYSOSTOM: If the sun were darkened, the Cross would not be seen, were it not more refulgent than the brightness of the sun. That the Disciples might not be ashamed of the Cross and grieve over it, He speaks of it as a sign that shall appear in glory. The Sign of the Cross shall appear, that it may put

to silence the boldness of the Jews: for Christ shall come to judge, pointing not only to His wounds, but to the very manner of His most ignominious death. So there follows: *And then shall all tribes of the earth mourn.* For at sight of the Cross they shall think within themselves that they gained nothing by His death; and that they crucified Him Whom they ought to have adored.

JEROME: Rightly does He say: *All tribes of the earth;* for they shall mourn who are not citizens of heaven, but *are written in the earth* (Jer. xvii. 13).

ORIGEN: Figuratively, someone will say that the sun that shall be dimmed is the devil, who shall be convicted at the end of the world, who, though he is darkness, pretends to be the sun. The moon, which to men seems to receive its light from the sun, is the whole church of the wicked, which frequently professes both to have and to give light, shall then, together with its rejected teachings, lose its light. But they whoever they may be who promise the truth to men, either by their false teachings or by their false virtues, while in fact they are seeking to lead them astray with lies, such as these are fittingly spoken of as stars falling from heaven; or, if I may say so, stars falling from their own heaven, where they stood in high places, raising their voices against the knowledge of God. To confirm these words we quote the words of Proverbs: *The light of the just is inextinguishable forever; but the light of the godless shall be put out* (Prov. xiii. 9, Sept.). Then the brightness of God shall appear in everyone who has born the image of the Heavenly One; and those in heaven shall rejoice; those who have borne the image of earth shall weep.

AUGUSTINE, *to Hesychius* (Ep. 199: 39): Or, the Church is the sun, moon and stars; to whom it was said: *Fair as the moon, bright as the sun* (Cant. vi. 9). For then will *the sun be darkened and the moon not give her light;* when the Church will not be seen, because of the unmeasured fury of her godless persecutors. Then *the stars shall fall from heaven, and the powers of heaven be moved:* when many who seemed to shine with the grace of God, shall yield to their persecutors and fall; and even the most courageous of the faithful shall be troubled. And it is said this will take place after the tribulation of those days; not that these things will happen when the whole tribulation is over, but that tribulation will come first, that the apostasy of some may follow: and because this shall be so through all these days, it shall be following the tribulation of these days, but nevertheless it shall happen during these same days.

4

CHRYSOSTOM, *in Matthew, Homily* 77: Because they have learned about the Cross, that they might not think something shameful is again to come, He adds: *And they shall see the Son of man coming in the clouds of heaven with much power and majesty.*

AUGUSTINE, as above, par. 41: The more obvious meaning of this passage, on hearing or reading it, is that it refers to that Coming when He shall come to judge the living and the dead in His own Body; in which

He sits at the right hand of the Father, in which also He died, and rose again, and ascended into heaven; and as we read in the Acts of the Apostles: *a cloud received him out of their sight* (i. 9); and since, following this, at the same place, an Angel said: *He shall so come as you have seen him going into heaven* (i. 11), we must then believe He will come in the same Body, and also in a cloud.

ORIGEN, as above, 50: Therefore, with their bodily eyes men shall see the Son of man coming in human form, *in the clouds of heaven;* that is, from heaven. And as at His Transfiguration, a voice came *out of the cloud;* so when He comes again, He shall be transformed in glory, seated, not upon one cloud, but upon many, and they shall be His chariot. And if they who loved Him spread their garments in the way, that the Son of God might not tread upon the earth as He went up to Jerusalem, desiring that not even the ass that bore him should touch the earth (Mt. xxi. 8), what wonder that the Father and God of all should spread the clouds of heaven beneath the Body of His Son as He descends to the work of Consummation?

One may say that as in the making of man, God took the slime of the earth and of it made man; so, to manifest the glory of Christ, the Lord, taking from the heavens and from the heavenly substance, He gave it first, at the Transfiguration, the body of a *bright cloud,* and then, at the Consummation, formed it into *bright clouds.* Because of this they are called *the clouds of heaven;* as in the other case *the slime of earth* is spoken of. And it is fitting the

Father should give such wondrous things to His Son, *Who humbled himself,* and because of this God *exalted Him* (Phil. ii. 7); not only in spirit, but also in Body, so that He comes seated upon such clouds. And perhaps upon rational clouds, so that not even the chariot of the glorified Son of man should be without reason and soul.

And at first, Jesus came with power, by means of which He wrought signs and wonders among the people. Yet all that power was little compared with the *great power and majesty* in which He will come at the end: for the first was the power of One emptying Himself. It is fitting therefore, that He shall be transformed into a yet greater glory than when transfigured on the Mount. For then He was transfigured for the sake of three only. At the end of the whole world He shall appear with much glory, that all men may see Him in glory.

AUGUSTINE, as above: But since we are to search the Scriptures, and not be content with a superficial knowledge of them, let us consider carefully what follows. For a few sentences later, He says: *When you shall see all these things come to pass, know ye that it is nigh, even at the doors* (Mk. xiii. 29). We shall know that it is nigh when we see, not some of the promised signs, but all of them, including this; that the Son of man shall be seen coming. And He shall send His angels from the four parts of the world; that is, He will gather together His elect from the whole earth. All this He does at that *last hour* (I Jn. ii. 18), coming in His members as in the clouds, or in the whole Church as in a great cloud; as

He now comes without ceasing. But then He shall come with great power and majesty; because greater power and majesty shall be seen by the saints, to whom He shall give great virtue, that they may not be overcome by such persecution.

ORIGEN: Or, He comes with much power each day to the soul of the man who believes in the prophetic clouds; that is, in the Scriptures of the prophets and Apostles, who declare the Word of God, and with understanding above human nature. To those also do we say He appears in much glory who understand Him (*in the prophets and Apostles*). And this is seen in the Second Coming of the Word; which is for the gathering together of the perfect. And in this way it may be that all that has been said by the three Evangelists about the Coming of Christ, carefully examined and compared one with another, will be found to relate to this, that He comes daily in His Body, which is the Church; and of this Coming He said elsewhere: *Hereafter you shall see the Son of man sitting on the right hand of the power of God and coming in the clouds of heaven* (Mt. xxvi. 64); excepting those places where He promises that His last Coming shall be in His own person.

5

CHRYSOSTOM: Because He had spoken of mourning, which refers to those who freely accuse themselves, and condemn themselves; lest they think that their evils shall end with this mourning. He adds:

V.31. *And he shall send his angels with a trumpet and a great voice.*

REMIGIUS: This is not to be under_

stood as meaning a real material trumpet, but as the voice of an archangel. It shall be so loud that at its cry all the dead shall rise from the dust of earth. CHRYSOSTOM: The sound of a trumpet relates to the resurrection, to joy; and to represent the stupefaction there shall then be, the grief of those who are left, and who shall not be taken up in the clouds (*to meet Christ*).

ORIGEN: It is written in the Book of Numbers, that the priests shall, by the sound of a trumpet, summon from the four winds the people who are of the multitude of Israel (Num. x. 1–10). And it is in allusion to this that Christ here says of the Angels: *And they shall gather together his elect from the four winds.* REMIGIUS: That is from the four regions of the world; from east, west, north, south.

ORIGEN, as above, par. 51: There are those of simpler mind who are of opinion that only those who are then in the body are to be gathered together; but it is better to say that Christ's Angels shall gather, not only the called and the elect from Christ's Coming to the end of the world, but all men from the beginning of the world who, like Abraham, saw Christ's day and rejoiced in it (Jn. viii. 56). That He says that not only those of Christ's elect who will be in the body shall be gathered together, but also all who have gone from their bodies, is seen from His words, saying that the elect shall be gathered not only from the four winds, but also *from the farthest parts of the heavens to the utmost bounds of them*; which I believe cannot be applied to anyone on earth.

Or, the heavens are the divine

Scriptures, or their authors, in whom God dwells. The *farthest parts* of the Scriptures, are their beginning; their *bounds*, their ending. The saints therefore shall be gathered from the farthest parts of heaven, that is, from among those who live in the beginnings of the Scriptures, to those who live in the ends of them. They shall be gathered together with a trumpet, and with a great voice, that those who hear it and pay heed, may follow the path of perfection that leads to the Son of God.

REMIGIUS: Or again: That no one may think they are to be gathered together only from the four quarters of the world, and not from the middle regions and places, He adds: *From the farthest parts of the heavens to the utmost bounds of them.* By the farthest part of heaven we understand we mean the centre of the globe, which lies beneath the highest point of the heavens. The utmost bounds mean the ends of the earth where the land seems to mingle with the circle of the horizons.
CHRYSOSTOM: That the Lord calls His elect by means of Angels, is to honour them. And Paul also says: *They shall be taken up in the clouds* (I Thess. iv. 16); that is, the angels shall gather together those risen from the dead; and the clouds receive those gathered.

6

CHRYSOSTOM, *in Matthew, Homily* 78: Since He had said that what was foretold would happen immediately after the tribulation of those days, they might well ask, how long after? He therefore gives them a sign from the nature of the fig-tree, saying:

V.32. *And from the fig-tree learn a parable: When the branch thereof is now tender and the leaves come forth, know you that the summer is nigh.*

JEROME: As though to say: When the green shoots appear on the fig-tree, and the buds burst into flower and the tree brings forth its leaves, you know the summer is near, the unfolding of the spring time, the beginning of the west wind; so, when you shall see all these things which are written, let you not think that the end of the world has now come; but rather that certain signs, certain fore-runners are here, to show it is near, even at the door. Hence:

V.33. *So you also, when you shall see all these things, know ye that it is nigh, even at the doors.*

CHRYSOSTOM: By this He implies that the interval of time shall not be great; but that the coming of Christ shall soon be. By this He foretells another thing; namely, the spiritual summer, the calm the just shall possess, after their present winter; while for sinners, winter shall follow their summer.

ORIGEN, *on Matthew*, as above, 53: As the fig-tree in winter keeps its vital powers within it, but as winter departs its vitality begins to show itself outwardly, and from its inward strength its branch becomes tender, and brings forth leaves; so the world and each single one of those who are saved before the coming of Christ, have vital power hidden within them, as the tree in winter. But Christ breathing on them, their branches grow tender, and not hard of heart; and that which was hidden within them, now comes forth in leaves and visible fruit. For such as

these the summer is nigh, and nigh is the Coming of the glory of God's Word.

CHRYSOSTOM: He put this parable before them for this reason, that in this way also He might lead them to believe that His words shall be wholly fulfilled. For whenever He says that something shall certainly come to pass, He brings forward examples from the unfailing course of nature.

AUGUSTINE, *to Hesychius*, Ep. 199, 22: Who can deny that from the Evangelical and prophetical signs, which we see fulfilled, we should expect the near approach of the Lord? It comes daily nearer; but of how near it was said: *It is not for you to know the times or moments* (Acts i. 7). Consider when it was the Apostle said: *For now our salvation is nearer than when we believed. The night is passed and the day is at hand* (Rom. xiii. 11, 12); and see how many years have since passed: yet what He said was not false. How much more must we say the Lord's coming is nigh; we who have come so much closer to the end?

HILARY: Mystically the fig-tree is a figure of the synagogue; the branch thereof Antichrist, the son of the devil, the portion of sin, the assertor of the law; who when he begins to show life and to put forth leaves, with a sort of triumphant flowering of sin, then the summer, that is, the day of judgement is seen to be nigh.
REMIGIUS: Or, when this fig-tree again puts forth; that is, when the synagogue accepts the word of the holy preaching, Enoch and Elias preaching, we must then under-

stand that the day of the consummation is near.

AUGUSTINE, *Gospel Questions*, I, 39: For the fig-tree understand the human race; because of the itch of the flesh. *When the branch thereof is now tender*; that is, when the sons of men will through the faith of Christ have borne spiritual fruits, and the honour of their adoption as sons of God shines out in them. HILARY: That we may have certain faith in the things to come, He adds:

V.34. *Amen, I say to you that this generation shall not pass till all these things be done.*

In saying, *amen*, He makes an attestation as to the truth of what He is saying. ORIGEN, as above, 54: The simple relate these words to the destruction of Jerusalem, and believe they were said of that generation which saw the Passion of Christ, and which would not pass away before the destruction of that city. I do not know how they can by this explain word by word what He says from: *There shall not be left here a stone upon a stone* (ib. 2) to where He says: *it is even at the doors.* In some places they perhaps could; in others this would be wholly impossible.

CHRYSOSTOM: All these things then were said about the end of Jerusalem; the things said of the false prophets and the false Christs and all the other things which we have said would take place until His coming. Why then does He say: *This generation*? He is not referring to the one then living, but to the generation of the believing: for Scripture is wont to designate a generation not only by time, but also by place, worship

and manner of life; as for example: *This is the generation of them that seek the Lord* (Ps. xxiii. 6). From this He reveals that Jerusalem will perish, and that the greater part of the Jews shall be destroyed; but that no trial shall overcome the generation of those who believe.

ORIGEN: Nevertheless the one generation of the Church shall survive this whole world, that it may inherit that which is to come; yet it shall not pass from this world till all these things be done. But when all have taken place, then not only the earth, but heaven also shall pass away. Hence follows:

V.35. *Heaven and earth shall pass away; but my words shall not pass.*

That is, not only men whose life is of this earth, and are therefore spoken of as the earth; but those also whose conversation is in heaven, and who therefore are spoken of as heaven. They shall pass away to the things to come, that they may come to the higher and better things. But the words spoken by the Saviour shall not pass away; for the words that are truly His are efficacious, and shall ever be efficacious. But the perfect, and they who shall receive no further perfecting, passing from what they are, attain to what they are not. And this is the meaning of what follows: *But my words shall not pass away.* It may be that even the words of Moses and the Prophets have passed away; since that which they prophesied has been fulfilled; but the words of Christ are ever full, and daily fulfilled, and are still to be fulfilled, in the saints. It may be that we ought not to say the words of Moses and the prophets are wholly fulfilled; for in the true sense these words also are the words of the Son of God, and are ever being fulfilled.

JEROME: Or, by *generation* He here means the whole race of men, or the Jews in particular. Then the more to lead them to faith in His promises, He adds: *Heaven and earth shall pass away; but my words shall not pass.* As if to say: To destroy firm and immoveable things is easier than for one of My words to fail.

HILARY: For heaven and earth, from the fact of their creation, have within them no absolute necessity to be. But the words of Christ which were brought forth from eternity, have that within them that they must endure.

JEROME: Heaven and earth shall pass away through change, not by destruction. Otherwise how will the sun be darkened and the moon not give her light if the heavens, in which these things are, and earth shall not remain?

RABANUS: The heaven that shall pass away is not the sidereal heaven, but the upper air (*aerium*), which before disappeared in the flood (II Pet. iii. 5). CHRYSOSTOM: He brings forward the elements of the world, to show that the Church is more precious than heaven or earth; showing at the same time that He is also, from this, the Creator of all things.

I. ST EPHRAIM, DEACON, CONFESSOR AND DOCTOR, I

Prayer for the Future Life.[8]

He prays that he may obtain blessedness after death.

1. In that night when all sound, all activity of men shall be silent, when the voices of all men and of all nations are still, may my soul, through its good works, shine out in Thee, O Jesus, Light of the Just. In that hour when darkness like a cloak shall be spread over all things, may Thy grace, O Lord, shine on us in place of the earthly sun. In that night which brings to an end the course of this world and all its activities, may our souls behold Thy wonders in that quiet which is more than silence. In that hour, refreshing the weary through the sleep that lies on all men, may our minds be inebriated with Thy delights, O Delight of all the Saints! In that time

of dark night, may a New Sun arise for us. Then let us take wing in that hope which was laid up for us in Thy Resurrection.

2. Grant us, O Lord, to imitate the watchfulness of those who waited for Thy Resurrection, so that day and night, O Lord, our souls may be turned towards Thee. In that hour when we shall be separated from men and from the traffic of men, be to us, O Lord, a Giver of good things, bringing joy to our sadness. When confiding in Thy grace we have gone forth from this world, so that we are alone, may we behold, O Lord, clearly and in deed the power of Thy aid. Pour Thy peace into our hearts, and give Thy rest to all our striving, that the darkness

of that night may be to us as the day.

In that hour when we shall have been deprived of life, and night has hidden us in its darkness, and we have been separated from the rest of men, may our consolation in Thee, O Lord, increase. In that place that is empty of all things, where the voice of comfort is no more heard, awaken in our souls, O Lord, a watchfulness free of all distraction. In that time when men lie in the sleep of final rest, may our minds not be sunk in the sleep of evil desires.

Grant us by Thy grace, O Lord, that like the wise virgins who were ready by their good works, our way of life shall also be watchful, that we shall not sit in darkness, with darkened souls, in darkness of mind, but that through prayer we may look for ever on the shining splendour of Thy grace. Expel, O Lord, by the daily light of Thy knowledge the nocturnal darkness of our mind, that being enlightened it may serve Thee in the purity of its regeneration.

Grant us with the just to watch by night in prayer, that in Thy revelations our lamps may burn brightly before Thy sun. In that time of night give consolation to our need, for the gloom of the night darkens us: through Thee may we be comforted in our sadness. Grant that our minds may labour in the remembrance of Thy holy revelations, while our souls burn in the fire of Thy love. In that hour when the Saints were wont to give themselves to prayer; Grant us, O Lord, to share in their watchfulness.

Let us at the same time pray for this life.

3. O Christ, Who prostrate on Thy face kept vigil in the time of night, grant us that our minds may suffer the Passion Thou didst endure for our salvation. O Christ, Who poured out Thy gifts upon the Saints in prayer, rejoice our minds through receiving Thy grace. O God, Whose are the day and the night, rejoice us by Thy hope, O Lord, in that time of deepest night. On bended knees we come before Thee with our accustomed prayers; gladden, O Lord, the ears of our soul, that we may be joined to thee in our prayer. Raise up the impulses of our soul that we may contemplate Thee as in ecstasy, and may our thought be lost in Thee the whole time of our prayer. May our mind receive Thy light as the dawn of Thy coming, that the reasoning soul within us may even now taste of life without body. In that night when we have been snatched away from this world and its associations, be to us, Lord, our comfort and our consolation, and let us not be forsaken by Thy love. In that hour when we shall be cut off from this world and all that relates to it, O Saviour, be with us in all things by Thy close and loving companionship.

4. In that hour when all who sleep have put aside their fleeting labours, awaken, O Lord, in our souls the knowledge that does not deceive. In that hour when men's members are clothed in the linen of burial, clothe, O Lord, our inward man with Thy regeneration. On that day when all men are called to earthly burial, make us worthy, O Lord, to rejoice in heavenly rest. In that hour when all shall cast from their bodies the covering of night, cast from our

heart the memory of this perishable world. In the morning when sailors begin to labour upon the seas of the world, may our souls be at rest from all motion in Thy harbour. In that hour when all are set free from the toils of this doleful world, grant us, Lord, to rest in Thy unfading consolation. In that day when all darkness shall cease, and all are freed from weariness, grant, O Lord, that we may take our delight in the joys of the life to come.

The beginning of the course of the sun is the beginning of toil for mortal man. Prepare for our souls, O Lord, a resting place for that day that knows no end. Grant us, Lord, that in our persons we may see the life of the resurrection; and let nothing withdraw our souls from Thy delights. Impress upon our person, O Lord, through unremitting devotion to Thee, the sign of that day which does not begin with the motion and the course of the sun.

The Reception of the Sacraments, the Cross, Grace; how much they avail to the resurrection of the dead.

5. We embrace Thee daily in Thy sacraments and receive Thee within our bodies; make us worthy to experience in our person the resurrection for which we hope. Be Thou, Lord, a wing to our thoughts, that we may fly swift through the air, borne as on wings to our true home. With the grace of baptism we hide Thy treasure in our bodies; grant us to rejoice in the increase of this treasure at the table of Thy Sacraments.

We receive Thy Memorial, Lord, within us at Thy spiritual table; may we possess It visibly in the new life to come. How great our beauty is

we know from that spiritual beauty Thy Immortal Will can awaken even in this mortality. Thy Crucifixion, O Saviour, was the end of Thy mortal life; grant us to crucify our mind as standing for our spiritual life. Thy Resurrection, O Jesus, gives greatness to our spiritual man; may the vision of Thy Sacraments be a mirror to the knowledge of Thy Resurrection. Thy Divine Incarnation is a figure of the spiritual world; grant us to be joined with it as a spiritual man.

Our unhappy body forces us into the company of the world of darkness; make us worthy, Lord, of that company which breaks down the hedge of darkness. Deprive not our minds, Lord, of Thy spiritual light; nor take from our members the comfort of Thy sweetness. The mortality concealed in our bodies comes forth in corruption; may the purification of Thy spiritual love wipe from our hearts the consequences of our mortality. The uncleanness in our members keeps as as it were in a foul prison; may we through the delight of the Gift of Thee, cast from our body its evil odour! Our body is for us a sea in which our ship is immersed without ceasing; draw our ship, Lord, into Thy divine harbour. Grant us, O Lord, to hasten to our heavenly home; and like Moses from the mountain top (Deut. xxxii. 49); let us take possession of it by sight.

Though our body is a load upon the soul (Wis. ix. 15), and weakens us by the wounds it inflicts upon itself, let Thy grace, O Lord, overcome in us the law that is in our flesh (Rom. vii. 23). In my mind, O Lord, I love Thy spiritual law; but the law in my members robs me of its help. As a captive the soul is led to do evil, and held back as if by force from spiritual things. Unwilling it is made subject to the caprices of the body's passions; hear how it cries out: when shall it be left in peace? but unhappily it is unheard. Like the widow in sorrow, it cries out to God: to God Who in His Gospel has promised revenge in due time (Lk. xviii. 3).

Avenge me, Lamb, of my body in prayer; deliver me from my adversary.

6. Deliver me, Lamb, in the prayer from my body, from my enemy at the judgement. Be Thou a mild judge, giving a reward to the one who returns to a right mind. We are immersed as in a sea in the unceasing impulses of our bodies; cleanse our soul, O Lord, from the stains of our infamy. We cry out to Thee from the billows, O Wise Sailor; send us a fair wind, that it may bear us through danger to safety. *I arose at midnight,* O Lord, that in the midst of affliction *I might give praise to Thee* (Ps. cxviii. 62); and offer Thee a sacrifice of praise, O Just Judge! For Thou are not propitious towards our daily deceptions and offences; yet, Lord, Thou knowest how our soul longs for goodness.

He seeks pardon and grace.

7. Saviour, Who came to wash away the stains of a sinful world, grant us time to return to our senses, that we may wash away the stains of our thoughts. Sanctify us, Lord, and fill us with the Spirit of Thy Majesty, that through holy remembrance of Thee, we may receive the renovation of the Holy Spirit (Tit. iii. 5). Create a clean heart in us, O God, and renew a right spirit within us (Ps. l. 12); so that in newness of spirit we may be *clothed with a robe of glory* (Ecclus. xv. 5). May we be renewed in the sacraments of Thy Spirit, and sanctified by Thy grace, that our soul through converse with Thee may grow forgetful of other things.

Let us turn in continual prayer towards our holy hope, ever led by it in this corporeal world. This mortal world is too weak for Thy whole gift; but from Thy Fulness, fulness is poured out upon its infirmity. Our afflicted souls, O Lord, thirst for this hope; gladden our souls, Lord, that we may see Thy grace in Thy Person. Our heart is filled with sadness; we are afflicted without ceasing. Bring joy to our sadness, Lord and give refreshment to our burning hearts. Day and night sorrow and affliction surround us; cool within us, Lord, the flame of our hearts. For apart from Thee we have no hope to comfort us in our grief. Place Thy Finger, that gives life to all things, on the pain concealed in our heart. For day and night wars beset us that seek to cut off our hope in Thee: Be Thou our leader in battle! Our mind is invaded without ceasing, with sorrow and with tears; at all times we are in fear of being deprived of the solace of Thy hope. With Thy secret words, O Lord, comfort our souls in that time; with Thy Spirit drawing forth the hidden pain of our struggle. Let our soul be not robbed of Thy strengthening, O Saviour; that we may not be plunged amid the waves of despair.

For the Lord has shown us our true hope from afar, that we may not be led away from His sight, and slip back into all our former miseries. Since we are ignorant of war, teach our inexperience how to withstand the enemy in this spiritual combat. May we be given wisdom through our converse with Thee; and may we receive the help of Thy Spirit, by which the way of our ascent to heaven is at once made smooth. Anoint our hearts with Thy Spirit (Is. lxi. 1), O Lord; that inwardly we may become priests, and by our actions offer sacrifice to Thee in the sanctuary of Thy sight. May the power of Thy grace strengthen our soul through contemplation, that by Thy favour it may be uplifted to incorporeal mansions: to the house of rest of the Saints in that great abode of the free; and may we assemble there through faith in the firm promises of Thy Goodness.

He prays to Jesus.

8. O Jesus, Who humbled Thy Majesty that Thou might raise up the unfortunate who had grown proud, may Thy grace be increased in us, that step by step we may ascend to Thy Love. Grant us, Holy Father, that through our good works we may take upon us Thy Likeness, so that the true image of Thy humility may be impressed upon our person. Grant us to feel within us the sweet taste of Thy Love, so that the powers of our mind may at all times be transported to Thee. Water our thirsting soul, that it may bring forth the fruit of glory, and become a holy temple wherein Thy Godhead dwells. Unite our members to Thee, Lord the Head of the whole Body, so that no one of us may be shut out from partaking of Thy sweetness.

O True Son of our Father, Who receiving a kingdom forsook it, do not when You come in the clouds deny the children of Thy Father. Grant us, Good Jesus, the vision for which our souls thirst, the glory of Thy revelation, in hope and pledge of our sharing it; so that though lowly, and dust from our birth, our souls may rise up through Thy exaltation; for we have become the offspring of God (Acts xvii. 18).

9. O Sea of infinite mercy, and of all forgiveness! O immeasurable Goodness, O Love beyond telling, our vision is too narrow to embrace the riches of Thy Love. O our Creator! How deep Thy Goodness how far surpassing all things created! Not for the gain of a few has the Son of the King become a Son of our race. He came down to prepare a kingdom for all our nature. Though Thou wert despised and scorned by insults without number, yet never because of this shall I deny the magnitude of the hope that is laid up in Thee.

My sinfulness is beyond words, nor could the sea wash me clean; yet this have I said, this do I say: That Thy Love is greater than my offences. The waves of the sea are fewer than my sins; yet if weighed in the balance with Thy Love, they are as nothing. Though I may be a receptacle of all evils, and though the mountains should flee from before my wickedness, yet with Thy Love I do not fear to call myself just.

Praise be to Thee from us all, children of an unhappy race. To Thee for all time is due the adoration of our love. The blessings that have come to us through Thee can never be told. Weeping and grieving for joy, we adore the footstool beneath Thy feet. Our tongue is unable to praise Thee. May Thy mercy reward us; Which arose upon our mortality, and embraced our infirmity. To Thy Love, Which joined Thee to our nature, Which was not ashamed to call us Its members, Which joined our nature to Its Body, be there glory from all creatures. Amen.

II. ST EPHRAIM. DEACON, CONFESSOR AND DOCTOR, II

Antichrist and the End and Consummation[9]

1. O Son, Who of Thine own Goodness humbled Thyself and became man, because it pleased Thee, and Who of Thy own will tasted death on a Cross on Golgotha, grant me, Lord, to speak of the end of the world, and of its creatures, that shall be dissolved, and of the consummation that shall come upon the whole world. Men shall fall, one upon the other, peoples shall destroy one another, iniquity wax strong upon the face of the earth, and wickedness be multiplied in the world. Just rulers shall die, and wicked ones rule the earth. Then Divine Justice shall appear and weigh men in the balance, and the scale of iniquity shall be pressed down, and the scale of the just uplifted. Then shall the spirits go forth and bring ruin to the ends of the earth.

Then, my brother, there shall be *pestilences in divers places*, as was written (Lk. xxi. 11), and famine upon the globe of the earth, and earthquakes and strife. The dust shall be wet with blood and the earth polluted with iniquity. Lands shall be made desolate, and towns and cities swallowed in the depths beneath. Nation shall rise against nation, kingdom against kingdom, and death shall reign upon the earth, and the wicked shall persecute the saints. Men everywhere shall become apostates: those on the left hand side shall be enriched, while the children of justice shall be beaten by the children of sin.

2. *The Romans driven out by the Assyrians shall return to their lands.*[10]

Because, Beloved, the last times have come; lo! we shall see the signs that Christ described for us. For kings rise one against another, and there is tribulation upon the earth, and people wage war against people, and armies rise against each other. And as the Nile, the river of Egypt, rising, floods the country, men shall take arms against the Roman rule; *for nation shall rise against nation, and kingdom against kingdom (ib. 7)*, and the Romans shall pass in flight from one region to another. The Assyrians shall rule in the territories of the Romans, and shall reduce their children to slavery, and violate their wives. They shall sow and they shall reap and the fruits thereof they shall hide in the earth.[11] As the Nile, the river of Egypt, subsides after it has risen, so shall the Assyrian be turned back from the lands of the Romans, and go down to his own country, and the Romans shall prepare themselves to return to the country of their fathers.

3. When evil abounds in the world, and men have polluted the earth with their abominations; then

the cry of the poor and oppressed shall ascend to heaven, and Divine Justice shall rise up to destroy the wicked upon the earth. The saints shall lift up their voices and their cry shall ascend to heaven, and a people shall come out of the desert, the son of Agar, the bondwoman of Sarai, a people who inherit the covenant of Abraham (Gen. xvi), the husband of Sarai and of Agar, and it will rise up to come in the name of the desert, as the legate of *the son of perdition* (II Thess. ii. 3). Then shall there be a sign in heaven such as the Lord foretold in His Gospel (Mt. xxiv. 30): namely, brilliance from shining stars and light shining from the person of the son of perdition (Apoc. xiii. 13). Kings shall be shaken and humbled in fear (Apoc. xviii. 9); and their arms and all their forces shall fall to nothing. The peoples of the earth shall tremble, seeing the sign in heaven; and all peoples and tongues shall arm themselves and come together, and there do battle, and they shall stain the earth with blood.

4. Nations shall be enslaved, and the people who make them captive shall triumph. The conquerors shall speed through the lands, searching caves and mountains, making captive women and infants, men old and young. Lo! we see the comeliness of men destroyed, and the attire and beauty of women taken from them. With spear and lance they pierce the old; they separate son from father, daughter from mother, brother from brother, sister from sister. They slay the bridegroom as he sleeps, and drive the bride from her bridal bed. They take the wife from her husband, and

slaughter both like sheep. They take the infant from its mother, and lead the mother into captivity. The infant lying on the ground cries out, and the mother hears, but what can she do? The infant is trodden under the feet of horses, of camels and beasts of burden. They will not suffer the mother to return to it, and it remains upon the wasted ground. They separate children from their mothers, as the soul is separated from the body. She looks at the loved ones torn from her bosom; two given to two masters; she is the slave of another. She is scattered and her children the same, that as slaves they may serve their captors. Her children cry out, sobbing, the tears rushing from their eyes. She turns towards her loved ones, the milk flowing from her breast, and says to them: 'Go in peace, my loved ones, and may God be with you. He Who was with Joseph in slavery among strangers, He, my children, shall be with you in the servitude to which you are going.' (They cry in answer): 'Be in peace, our mother, and may God be with you Who was with Sara, when taken by Abimilech in Gerara (Gen. xxi. 2). May the same Lord be with you till the day of the resurrection.'

The son, sold into servitude, stands looking back to his father. Their tears flow; they see each other weeping. Brother sees brother slain and lying upon the earth, while he is led into captivity, to be a slave among strangers. They seize mothers with their infants and slay both the one and the other. The thin cry of small children is heard, wailing in pain. The paths to the mountains and the footways in the valleys are worn smooth. The ends of the earth are laid waste, cities subjugated, the slain are multiplied upon the earth. All peoples have been thrown down before the conquerors.

And after the nations have waited in patience, thinking that peace had come, they still pay tribute. The fear of the conquerors fills every mind. Iniquity mounts up upon the earth and covers it like a cloud. The whole world is held fast in the bonds of wickedness. The smoke of abominations rises to heaven. Then since iniquity is multiplied upon the earth, He stirs up men, who destroy themselves.

5. Then the Divine Justice summons kings and the mightiest armies from beyond the gates Alexander made.[12] Armies shall pass through them, numberless as the stars of heaven; rather, as the sands of the seashore; scarce a span between the blades of the multitude of rending spears and the heads of those crossing through. From thence they come, kings and mighty hosts, in confusion. Peoples of all races and tongues, they pass through the gates:[13] Agog and Magog and Naval and Agag, kings and the strongest armies; Thogarma, Ascenez and Daiphar, and Phutar with Lyleians, Amzartaei, and Garmidal, Taleb at the head of the Sanurtani, Azmurtaei, Chusaei, Hunni and Pharzaei, Declaei and Thubalaei, and Moschaei with Chusaei, with whom come Medes and Persians and Armenians and Turks and Nemruchaei and Muschaei, the sons of Chaeon, and Sarugs, sons of Jactin, and Mahunaei. Armies and peoples without numbers pour through and invade the lands. The foundations of the earth are shaken. Dust like smoke

ascends from the earth and obscures the sun and covers the earth like a thick cloud as Ezechiel, the son of Busi, has prophesied (Ezech. xxxviii). [14]

6. For when the Huns go forth to war and to battle,[15] they take women heavy with child, and heap fire upon them, and standing around the fires they chant over them, and in this way they roast the infants in the womb; and then extract the small bodies and place them in a dish, pouring water into it, and divide the members in the water, upon which spells have been cast. They then take their swords and bows and spears and arrows and dip them in this water. All the arms that have touched the enchanted water seem to them as if there were a multitude of six thousand with them, when one of them falls fighting in battle. Each one stretches forth a hand, at the same time drawing a knife. They eat the flesh of the infants, and drink the blood of the women.

Clothed in skins and borne as it were on the winds and tempests, in the flash of an eye they overthrow cities, throw their walls to the ground, destroy fortresses and with swift attack overcome and destroy the strongest armies. Advancing, they are swifter than the wind. The rumour has scarce arisen in a country that the Huns are coming, when they appear as if by magic, on every side and from everywhere. Their chariots fly like the wind between heaven and earth.[16] Their arms flash terrible as lightnings. Reins in hand, they drive two and three horses and each chariot has with it fifty or sixty men, who run before it, swift as the winds and storms. Their clamour is like the roaring of lions. For these fearful Huns terrify the whole earth, which they cover like the waters in the days of Noah. They spread to the ends of the world and there is no one to withstand them.

7. This is the great multitude of whom Ezechiel said that it will cover the earth like a cloud: *Thou shalt come out of thy place from the northern parts, thou and many people with thee, all of them riding upon horses, a great company and a mighty army. And thou shalt come upon my people Israel like a cloud, to cover the earth. Thou shalt be in the latter days, and I will bring thee upon my land: that the nations may know me when I shall be sanctified in thee, O Gog, before their eyes* (Ez. xxxviii. 15, 16). And he describes the devastation of the land: *And the fishes of the sea and the birds of the air and the beasts of the field and every creeping thing and all men that are on the face of the earth shall be moved at My presence; and the mountains shall be thrown down and every wall in the land shall fall, and there shall be desolation upon the earth.* And in the last days Agog and Magog shall burst forth and come from the land, and Agog and Magog shall come to the mount of Jerusalem. Agog and Magog shall ascend to the mountains of Jerusalem, to place their camp there. And their flying horsemen shall descend into Egypt, and against the Indians. They shall seize an infinite booty of men, of riches, of cattle and sheep, for food for themselves. Then Divine Justice shall call upon Michael, the Leader of the Hosts, and send him to destroy their camps;

as the camps of Sennacherib. At the command, and with his mighty and terrible sword, the Angel shall go forth and destroy their armies in the twinkling of an eye, and in the same moment the Divine Justice, thundering from on high, shall destroy their camps with rocks of fire. Their slain shall lie upon the ground, innumerable as the sands. Beasts and men shall die, and the whole camp shall perish, and flame shall be let loose against the sea and against the islands. The bow of Agog, the evil king, shall fall from his left hand, and the arrows from his right (Ez. xxxix. 3); and his camp shall be wholly destroyed.

But the inhabitants of Jerusalem shall go forth and plunder his camp, and they now become conquerors shall gather up his arms, his spears and arrows and bows, and they shall serve as kindling wood for seven years (Ez. xxxix. 9). And they shall not need to gather wood from the fields and forests. For seven years they shall throw shields and shafts upon the fire. The arrows, the bows, the lances shall suffice to feed their fires for seven years.

After the destruction of the Romans, Antichrist shall appear.

8. Then the Lord from His glorious heaven shall set up his peace. And the kingdom of the Romans shall rise in place of this latter people, and establish its dominion upon the earth, even to its ends, and there shall be no one who will resist it. After iniquity shall have multiplied, and all creatures have become defiled, then Divine Justice shall appear, and shall wholly destroy the people and, coming forth from perdition, the man of

iniquity[17] shall be revealed upon the earth, the Seducer of men, and the Disturber of the whole earth.

In that day in which *the son of perdition* shall come upon the earth, there shall be great confusion throughout the whole world, and bewilderment shall come upon the earth. The sun shall be darkened, and the stars shall fall from heaven. All the heavenly bodies shall be extinguished, and darkness envelop the world. The earth shall tremble to its foundations; *the mountains shall be moved and the hills shall tremble* (Is. liv. 10). Springs and fountains shall dry up; the waves shall be swallowed in the depths of the sea, and fish shall disappear. Rulers shall cease from judgement, and priests tremble in the sanctuary. The power of the strong shall collapse. There shall be stupor upon the earth; the hands of all shall be undone. The man of evil will prepare, and coming he will enter Jerusalem; he will build up and establish Sion, and will make himself God, and entering he will sit in the temple, as the Apostle has written (II Thess. ii. 4): *as if he were God.*

The Jews will glory in him, and will assemble to join him. He will blaspheme, declaring: 'I am the Father and the Son, the first and the last, and there is no other God but me.' In that moment ten thousand Jews shall deny him, and they shall answer him: 'Thou art *the seducer* of the world' (II Jn. vii). For He Whom our fathers fastened to a cross on Golgotha, He has saved creatures, and has ascended to Him Who sent Him.' And raging in fury, the Evil One will command that those who deny him shall be instantly slain by the sword. And because of this all shall fear to deny him.

9. Then he will begin to show false signs in the heavens and upon the earth, upon the sea and upon the dry land. He will summon the rain, and it will descend. He will command the seed, and the seed will germinate. This he will do, not in reality, but by enchantments. He will rebuke the waves, and they will become quiet; the winds, and they will obey him. He will cause fruit to hang from the tree, and bring forth water from the earth. He will speak with lepers, and they will be purified; the blind, and they will see; he will call the deaf, and they will hear; the dumb, and they will speak. He will do all the signs our Lord wrought in the world. But he shall not raise the dead; for he has no power over spirits.

The lightnings will be his servants, and will give a sign of his coming. Demons will be his forces; the princes of the demons his disciples. He will send the leaders of his forces into far distant regions, and will give them power and healing, and they will seduce the whole world. And the Apostle has written and warned us in his Epistle to the Thessalonians: *Be not terrified, neither by spirit, nor by word, because this is not from us; for there shall first come a revolt, and the man of sin will be revealed, and he will be lifted up, and he will show himself as if he were God, and make himself God* (II Thess. ii. 2–4).

10. But when the Accursed has come and has worked signs and lying wonders, the people will be assembled together and they will come to see the god, and multitudes will adhere to him, and all will deny their God, and all will call upon

those who are close to them to praise *the son of perdition*; and they will fall upon one another and destroy one another with swords. But the elect shall fly from his face to the mountain tops and to the hills, and there shall be tribulation on earth, *such as hath not been from the beginning of the world* (Mt. xxiv. 21). And terror shall invade the hearts of all men, thrown into confusion by this commotion. Sons will deny their fathers, and follow the Evil One. Priests will leave their altars, and going forth become his heralds. Some will take refuge in tombs and hide among the dead, saying that the dead are blessed in being snatched away from such afflictions: 'Blessed are ye that lie in your graves, taken away from affliction. But woe to us! For lo! we now die, and the birds will bury us.' And unless the days of this time are shortened, neither shall the elect survive these trials and tribulations, as God made known to us in the Gospel, saying: *For the sake of the elect these days shall be shortened* (Mt. xxiv. 22).

11. And when *the son of perdition* has drawn to his purpose the whole world, Enoch and Elias shall be sent that they may confute the Evil One; by a question filled with mildness. Coming to him, these holy men, that they may expose *the son of perdition* before the multitudes round about him, they will say: 'If you are God, show us what we now ask of you. In what place do the men of old, Enoch and Elias, lie hidden?' Then the Evil One will at once answer the holy men: 'If I wish to seek for them in heaven, in the depths of the sea, every abode lies open to me. There is no other God but me; and

I can do all things in heaven and earth.'

They shall answer the son of perdition: 'If you are God, call the dead, and they will rise up. For it is written in the books of the Prophets, and also by the Apostles, that Christ, when He shall appear, will raise the dead from their tombs. If you do not show us this, we shall conclude that He Who was crucified is greater than you; for He raised the dead, and was Himself raised to heaven in great glory.' In that moment the Evil One, angered against the Saints, seizing the sword, the most Abominable will sever the necks of the just men.

Judgement

12. Then leaping up, Gabriel and Michael, the leaders of the heavenly hosts, shall descend and restore the Saints to life. The Evil One, together with all his followers, shall be humiliated. The angels approaching shall seize the Accursed, and in the same moment the Lord shall command from His heavens, and He shall overthrow the Accursed and all his forces and on the instant the Angels shall thrust them down to Gehenna. And all who believed in him shall be thrust down amid the flames. Then the Lord shall descend from on high, amid the fearful glory of the Angels, and His chariot shall halt between heaven and earth. He shall speak to the sea and it shall dry up, and the fish shall die in the midst of it. The heavens and the earth shall be dissolved, and become darkness and gloom. The Lord shall send fire upon the earth, continuing for forty days, and shall purify it from iniquity, and from the pollution of sin.

A Throne shall be prepared, and

the Son shall sit upon the right hand, and twelve seats shall be placed for the Twelve Apostles; dwellings adorned for the Martyrs, and a palace for the Saints. The Angels shall sound their trumpets, and the dead shall rise from their graves. And in a moment the Angels shall gather together all the children of Adam, and they shall bring the wheat into the barn, but the chaff they shall cast into fire: the good shall enter into the Kingdom, and the evil shall dwell in Gehenna. The Just shall fly to heaven, and sinners shall be burned with fire. The martyrs shall fly to the Bridal chambers, and the evil go out into darkness. But Christ shall reign forever, and He shall be King unto generations of generations. To Him be glory; and upon us be His mercy, for all time. Amen, amen.

(Here endeth the Sermon on Agog and Magog and on the end and consummation. To God be glory throughout all ages and ages. Amen, amen.)

III. St John Chrysostom, Bishop and Doctor

On the Consolation of Death: Second Sermon[18]

Why the unbelieving doubt the resurrection of the dead?

1. In the preceding sermon we spoke briefly to you on the consolations of mortality and on the hope of resurrection. Now we shall go on to speak more fully, more effectively of these same things. While the things I have spoken of are firmly established in the minds of those who believe, to the unbelieving and the doubting they seem fables; and to these we shall address a few brief words. Certainly you who are unbelieving will uphold every doubt deriving from the nature of the body. For some will not believe it possible, that a body that has turned to dust can rise again, can live again. As to the soul, no man can doubt; for not even the philosophers, pagans though they are, can doubt the immortality of the soul. For what is death but the separation of soul and body? For with the soul departing, the soul which lives for ever, which knows no death, because it is from the breath of God, only the body dies: for there is that in us which is mortal, and that which is immortal.

But the departing soul, seen by no mortal eyes, is received by angels and placed in Abraham's bosom, if it is the soul of one who believes, or in the care of the guardian of hell if it is a sinful soul: until the appointed day comes on which it shall receive back its body, and render an account of its works before the Tribunal of Christ the True Judge. Therefore, since all doubt is concerned with the body, we shall both uphold its infirmity, while we prove that it shall rise again from the dead.

In what manner do the dead arise. Proof that God can raise the dead.

2. And should some one doubtful and unbelieving ask of me: *How do the dead rise again; or with what manner of body shall they come?* (I Cor. xv. 35.) I shall answer him from the mouth and with the words of the Apostle (ib.): *Senseless man, that which thou sowest is not quickened,*

except it die first; And that which thou sowest, thou sowest not the body that shall be; but bare grain, as of wheat, or some other kind of grain, dead and parched, without moisture. And when it has corrupted in the earth, it rises again enriched, clothed with husks, and furnished with ears of corn. He therefore Who for your sake raises up the grain of wheat, can He not raise thee up for His own sake Who daily raises the sun from the tomb of night, restores the moon as it were from death, and for our use recalls again the departing seasons: shall He not look for us again, Who for us renews all things, and shall He suffer us to be extinguished once for ever, we to whom He gave light by His own breath, to whom He gave life from His own Spirit? Shall *the man* who has confessed Thee and devoutly worshipped God, not now *live for evermore* (Wis. v. 16)?

But you still doubt that you can be revived after death; that you can be renewed after you have been reduced to dust and bones? Tell me, O man, what were you before you were conceived in your mother's womb? Truly nothing. God therefore, Who made thee from nothing, can He not and more easily remake thee from something? Believe me, He can more easily remake what already existed, Who could create what did not exist. He Who caused thee from thy mother's womb to grow into nerves, to veins and bones can, believe me, cause thee to be born again from the womb of earth.

But perhaps you fear that your dry bones cannot be clothed again in their former flesh? Do not, do not measure the power of God by your own weakness. God, the Creator of all things, Who clothes the trees with leaves, the fields with flowers, can also, at the resurrection, clothe your bones with their true flesh. Ezechiel the prophet on one occasion doubted this very thing, and asked by the Lord whether the dry bones he saw scattered over the plain would live again, replied: *O Lord God, thou knowest* (Ez. xxxvii. 3). But after the Lord had commanded him to prophesy concerning these bones, he saw the bones come together, each one to its joint, and when he had seen the dry bones bound together with sinew and interwoven with veins and covered with flesh and the skin stretched out over them, then he prophesied in the spirit, and the spirit of each one coming entered into the bodies lying there, and they rose from the dead, and directly they *stood upon their feet.* And the prophet, confirmed in this way of the truth of the resurrection of the dead, wrote down the vision, that those who came after him might come to know of this wondrous happening. Rightly therefore does Isaias cry out: *The dead shall rise again, and they that are in the tombs shall come forth again, and they that are in the earth shall rejoice. For the dew that is from thee is healing to them* (Is. xxvi. 19, Sept.). For truly, just as seeds soaked by the dew germinate and rise up, so shall the bones of the faithful, *visited* (Ecclus. xlix. 18) by the dew of the Holy Spirit, spring up unto eternal glory.

3. *Another argument.* But doubting you ask, how can a whole man be restored from a few bones? Yet you in actual fact will kindle a vast conflagration from a small spark of fire.

Can God from the modest leaven of your dust not restore anew the whole scattered elements of your small body? For although you may say: The remains of the flesh itself do not exist anywhere: they may have been consumed by fire, or devoured by a wild beast? Know this, first: that whatever is consumed, is contained in the bowels of the earth, and from there, at the command of God, it can again be brought forth. For even you can, where no fire is visible, take flint and steel, and from the substance of stone strike the fire you need. That therefore which you do by effort and the skill God Himself has given you, so that you bring forth what is not visible, the Divine Majesty cannot do of His power! Believe me, God can do all things.

Christ testifies to the future resurrection; and the Apostles also, and the martyrs; and the mother of the Machabees (II Mac. vii).

4. Seek to know this only: Did Christ promise to bring about the resurrection of the dead? And when you learn from the testimonies of so many that He promised this; more when you have the most sure pledge of Christ Himself, then, confirmed in your faith, let you have no more fear of death. For he who still fears death, disbelieves; and he who does not believe, contracts an incurable sin: for by his unbelief he dares to assert that God is either impotent, or a liar. But the blessed Apostles prove it is not so; and the holy martyrs prove it is not so. The Apostles, because of this proclamation of the resurrection, preached that Christ had risen, announcing that in Him the dead were to be raised to life;

and for this faith, they refused neither death nor torments nor the cross.

If therefore, *in the mouth of two or three witnesses, every word may stand* (Mt. xviii. 16), how can the resurrection of the dead, for which there are so many and such witnesses, and who bear witness to what they say unto the shedding of blood, be called in question? What of the holy martyrs? Had they a certain hope of the resurrection or had they not? If they had not, they would surely never have looked upon death, by such torments and such pain as their highest earthly reward. They were not thinking of present torments, but of the rewards to come. They knew the words: *For the things which are seen are temporal; but the things which are not seen are eternal* (II Cor. iv. 18).

Listen, brethren, to an example of courage. A mother exhorted her seven sons; she was not sorrowing rather she rejoiced. She saw her sons torn with steel claws, beaten with iron, roasted on frying-pans, and did not shed tears nor raise her voice and cry to heaven, but bravely exhorted her sons to bear their sufferings in patience. It was not that she was cruel, rather it was because she believed. She loved her children, not delicately, but manfully. She encouraged her sons to bear the passion which she too suffered rejoicing. For she was certain of her own and of her sons' resurrection from the dead. What shall I say of the men, what shall I say of the women, of the boys, of the girls, how they rejoiced at such a death, how they crossed swiftly over to the heavenly host? They could had they wished to remain in this present life: for it was put before them, that if they denied Christ they could live; confessing His Name, they would die. But they chose to cast away this temporal life to receive life everlasting; to be cut off from earth, and to dwell in heaven.

Fear of death is shut out.

5. In the presence of these testimonies, brethren, where is there room for doubt? How can the fear of death remain? If we are the children of the martyrs, if we desire to be found among them, let the thought of death not grieve us; nor let us mourn our dear ones who go before us to the Lord. For should we weep and wail, the blessed martyrs themselves will reproach us; and say to us: 'O faithful! O you who long for the kingdom of God! You who mourn and lament your dear ones, dying delicately on soft beds; if you were to see them crucified and slain by the heathen for the Lord's Name, what would you do? Have you received no example? The Patriarch Abraham, offering his only son in sacrifice, took in hand the sword of obedience (Gen. xxii. 10); not sparing him whom he loved with such great love, that he might show obedience to the Lord. And if you say: "He did this because of the command of the Lord," then you also have a command, namely: *Be not sorrowful concerning them that are asleep* (I Thess. iv. 12).'

They therefore who do not keep the least commandments, when will they observe the greater? Do you not know that the spirit that is weak in such things, is found unworthy of the greater? He who fears the river, how shall he ever face the sea? So he who laments without thought the

one departed, how would such a soul face the contest of the martyr? For he who is steadfast and courageous in such things, has already advanced a step towards higher things.

6. *The shining example of David. Dark garments in mourning.* Let these examples suffice, brethren, to teach us contempt of death, and to confirm our hope of the future. I shall put one more example before you, from the men of old, that it may serve as an encouragement to all; and I shall relate it because I also want you to listen and learn through the patient ears of the heart. The great king David took it very grievously when his beloved child, whom he loved as his own soul, was struck with sickness. And when human means availed nothing, he turned to God, and putting aside his royal dress, *he lay down upon the ground*, and neither ate nor drank, continuing in prayer seven days to the Lord, that his son might be spared. And the elders of his house came to comfort him, inviting him to eat; fearful that though his son might live, he himself might die before this happened. They could not move him nor force him. For love in suffering is indifferent to such risks. And while his son lay sick, the king lay in squalor and ashes; and words were no comfort to him, and food did not concern him. The mind feeds on sorrow; the breast is given strength by grief; the eyes pour out tears for drink. And in the midst of these things, that took place which God had decreed. The child died. His wife mourns. His whole house is in mourning; the servants trembling, fearful of what

he might do. For no one dared tell their lord that the child was dead; dreading lest David, who had sorrowed so grievously while his son still lived, might, hearing he had died, put an end to himself.

But while the servants are whispering among themselves, while they sorrowfully urge and forbid one another to tell him, he himself understands the truth and forestalls their announcement, asking his servants: Is the child dead? They cannot deny it; weeping they tell him what has happened. They gather together confused; dreading and expecting that the loving father will do himself some injury. But David rises at once from his sackcloth and ashes; rises up cheerful, almost as if he had heard his son was safe. He washes and anoints himself, he goes to the temple, he adores God, he eats with his friends; he restrains his sighs, and with a cheerful countenance puts aside all grief.

His servants wonder; his friends are astonished at this strange and sudden change. At length they venture to ask him: What is the meaning of this; that he grieved so much while his son lived; now that he is dead he does not grieve? This man, pre-eminent in his greatness of soul, replies: There was need, while the child still lived, to humble myself, to fast, to weep for him in the presence of the Lord; for there was hope that through prayer he might be spared. But once the will of God is done, it is foolish and impious to torment the soul with unprofitable lamentation; and he ends by saying: *I shall go to him rather: but he shall not return to me* (II Kings xii. 23).

There is an example of courage and greatness of soul! And if this David, still under the Law, still under that, I shall not say licence, but still subject to that need to lament, so turned his soul from unreasoning grief; if he so restrained both his own sorrow and that of those about him, are we, who now live under the Law of Grace, we who are upheld by the certain hope of resurrection, we to whom all sorrowing is forbidden, shall we bewail our dead in the manner of the heathen, shall we lift up our voices in frantic grief, like so many Bacchantes, tearing our garments, beating our breasts, singing vain and empty dirges around the body, around the grave of the dead?

And lastly, for what reason do we dye our garments black, unless to show, not only by our tears, but even by our garments, that we are unbelieving as well as sorrowing? Such things, brethren, are for us unfitting; they are foreign to us; they are not lawful: and even if they were lawful, they would be unbecoming. But many among our brothers and sisters, though their faith and the Lord's precept makes them strong, become weak and break this rule because of what their friends and relatives may think: for they would be looked upon as stony-hearted and unfeeling, should they spare their garments, or should they too not rave and rant like madmen in senseless grieving. How vain, how foolish: to take notice of the opinions of foolish men, and have no fear of failing the faith they have received! Why does a man like that not learn to endure more serenely? Why does he who is uncertain not learn confidence from me? And even when the sorrow in his breast is great, he should quietly temper his sorrow with reason, and not proclaim it in shallowness of spirit.

The saying of the heathen on hearing of the death of his son. We should mourn for those who are dying without faith.

7. I want to put before you one more example to correct those who believe that we must mourn for the dead.[19] This is an example from pagan history. There was once a pagan prince who had an only son whom he dearly loved. While he was, in accord with pagan super-stition, offering sacrifice to his idols on the Capitol, he was told his only son had died. He did not at once leave off the rites in which he was engaged, he did not weep, he did not even sigh. But listen to the answer he made: 'Let him be buried,' he said, 'for, remember, I begot a son who was also mortal.'

Reflect upon this answer. Think of the courage of this pagan; such that he did not even order them to wait for him, or that his son be placed in the tomb in his presence. What are we to say if the devil, in the day of judgement, brings this man before the tribunal of Christ and says: 'This is my worshipper; whom I used to hold to me by my deceptions, so that he became the servant of blind and deaf images; this man, to whom I promised neither resurrection from the dead, nor paradise, nor the kingdoms of heaven. This man noble and wise, neither sorrowed nor moaned the death of his only son, nor did he upon hearing of it leave off my sacred rites. But Your Christians, your believers, for whom You were crucified and suffered death, to the end that they might not fear death, but be without fear because of the

resurrection of the dead, not only do they mourn for their dead, with their voices and with their garments, but even as they go to the Church they are stricken with fear and sor-row; many even of Your clerics and Your pastors interrupt their ministry to give themselves to grief, as it were mocking Your will? And why? Because from this world of dark-ness, Thou hast called to Thyself those whom Thou wouldst.'

What can we say in answer to this, brethren? Are we not seized with confusion when we find ourselves, in this, lower than the heathen? And well should the pagan weep and lament, who, knowing not God, dying goes straight to punishment. Well should the Jew mourn who, not believing in Christ, has assigned his soul to perdition. And plainly must we grieve for our own cate-chumens, should they, either through their own unbelief or through the neglect of their neighbours, depart this life without the saving grace of baptism. For the rest, he who is sanctified by grace, sealed unto God by faith, approved in his manner of life, or secure in innocence, and has departed this world, he is *to be accounted blessed* (Jas. v. 11), and should not be mourned; he should not be longed for, nor mourned for; but should be remembered with moderation, since we know that our time drawing near, we also shall follow them.

The sorrowing that is salutary.

8. So dry your tears, cease from grieving, restrain your mourning, O Christian, and replace this sadness with a sorrowing that is salutary and which, as the Apostle tells us, *is according to God and worketh steadfast*

unto salvation (II Cor. vii. 10): or at least unto penance for the sins you have committed. Search your own hearts Brethren, examine your consciences, and should you find there something that must be repented of – and find it you shall, since you are men – bring forth your sighs in confession, pour out your tears in prayer, be afflicted in your heart because of this true death, this evil of the soul. Be troubled at the remembrance of your sins, as David was, saying: *For I know my iniquity, and my sin is always before me* (Ps. l. 5) Then death shall have no terrors for you, nor the dissolution of the body, which, at the command of God, and in His own time, shall be renewed again, and renewed more perfectly.

See how the divine words embrace both kinds of death. *The hour cometh,* says the Lord, *wherein all that are in the graves shall hear the voice of the Son of God.* Here is the ground of our sure hope; here is the ground of our contempt of death. And what then follows? *And they that have done good things shall come forth unto the resurrection of life; but they that have done evil, unto the resurrection of judgement* (Jn. v. 28, 29). Here is the ground of the difference between those that shall rise again. All flesh must rise again; provided it is human. But the good shall rise to life; the bad shall rise to punishment; as it was written: *Therefore, the wicked shall not rise again in judgement: nor sinners in the council of the just* (Ps. i. 5).

Therefore, that we may not rise again *unto judgement,* let us, putting away sorrowing over death, take to ourselves this other sorrowing, which is unto repentance, and give ourselves to good works and to a better life. And in the presence of the dead, or of a burial, let this be our thought: The reflection that we too are mortal. And while we have time, while yet we may, let us through reflection be zealous for our salvation: namely, either by yielding better fruits in our lives, or by emending our present life, if without thinking we have been going astray; lest of a sudden, overtaken by the day of our death, we seek for time to repent, and find none, seek to give alms to the poor, and to make satisfaction for the evil we have done, and are not granted what we ask for.

Recapitulation of both sermons.

9. Having shown you, brethren, that death is the common lot, having shown that we are forbidden to weep for the dead, and having shown the imperfect minds of those who lived before us, without the power of Christianity, having put before you the testimony and the teaching of the Lord and of the Apostles concerning the resurrection, having reminded you of the Acts of the Apostles, of the sufferings of the martyrs, and put before you the example of David, and also the conduct of the man who was a pagan, and having at the end spoken to you of that sorrow which is both painful and profitable, that which hurts us, that which saves us through repentance: Having placed all this before you, what remains for us now but, giving thanks to God the Father, to say: *Thy will be done on earth as it is in heaven.*

Thou hast given life, and Thou has decreed death. Thou dost bring us into the world; Thou dost bring us forth from the world; and when

Thou hast brought us forth, save us. For nothing that is Thine shall perish; Thou Who hast said that not a hair of their head shall perish (Lk. xxi. 18). For, *Thou shalt take away their breath, and they shall fail, and shall return to their dust. But, Thou shalt send forth thy spirit, and they shall be created: and thou shalt renew the face of theearth* (P s. ciii. 29, 30).

These words, brethren, are fitting for those who believe; they are a healing medicine. Having cleansed the eye of the soul with this sponge of consolation, and having treated it with the eye-salve of reason, not only will it not suffer blindness through despair, it will not even suffer the inflammation of sorrow; rather, seeing all things clearly with the eyes of the heart, it will say with the most patient Job: *The Lord gave, and the Lord hath taken away. As it hath pleased the Lord so is it done. Blessed be the name of the Lord* (Job i. 21). Amen.

IV. St Augustine, Bishop and Doctor

Two Meditative Discourses on I Corinthians xv: On the Resurrection of the Dead: First Sermon[20]

I. *Exordium*

We noticed, Brethren, while the Epistle of the Apostle was being read, your praiseworthy and lively feeling of faith and charity, as you rejected with horror those who declare that this present life, which we have in common with sheep, is man's sole life, and that after death all that man is ends, and that there is no hope of another and better life afterwards; these, corrupting even the itching ears of the wicked, say: *Let us eat and drink: for tomorrow we shall die* (I Cor. xv. 32).[21] We shall therefore take these words as the starting point of our discourse, and let this sentence be as it were the hinge (*cardo*) of our sermon, upon which other things, which the Lord may deign to suggest to us, shall revolve.

II. *The Resurrection of the dead is our faith and our hope. Our charity. Two questions concerning the future resurrection.*

The resurrection of the dead is our hope. The resurrection of the dead is our faith. It is our charity also. which the preaching of things which are not yet seen enkindles and sets on fire with longing; a longing by whose greatness our hearts are enlarged to grasp the future blessedness we have been promised: provided we believe the things that are not yet seen. It is therefore our charity also; and we should not be concerned about these present earthly and temporal things: and by this I mean bodily pleasures and joys: as though we looked for any such thing in the resurrection. And were we now to despise such things, we would live happier and better lives.

If then you take away faith in the resurrection of the dead, all Christian teaching falls to the ground. And even should our faith be founded on the resurrection of the dead, the Christian soul is not then secure, unless we distinguish between the life that is to come and that which passes away. This then is the question: If the dead do not rise, there is no hope of a future life. But if the dead rise again, there shall be a future life. But there is a second question: What shall be the nature of that life? Our first question is, whether the dead shall rise again. Our second: What will the life of the saints be after the resurrection.

III. *In the first question the unbelieving errs; in the second, the carnal minded Christian. The Christian must be guided by the weight of authority.*

They therefore who say that the dead do not rise are not Christians. They however who believe that when the dead have risen, they shall live a bodily life, are carnally minded Christians. Therefore, whatever we have to say against the opinion of those who deny the resurrection of the dead, is said against those who are outside the Church; of whose number there is not, I believe, any one here present. Our discussion therefore may well seem superfluous, at least if it is prolonged: that we should endeavour to teach you that the dead rise again. For the Christian who already believes in Christ, and who holds that the Apostle could in no way lie to us, must be led by the weight of authority. It suffices for him to hear the words: *If there be no resurrection of the dead, then is our preaching vain; and your faith is also vain* (I Corr. xv. 14). *If,* he says, *there be no resurrection of the dead, then Christ is not risen again* (ib., 13). But if Christ, Who is the salvation of Christians, has risen, it is in no way impossible for the dead to rise: since He Who has raised His own Son, and He Who raised His own Body, has, in the Head, given proof of this to the rest of the Body, which is the Church. To discuss the resurrection of the dead could therefore be superfluous, so that we could now go on to that other question Christians are wont to discuss among themselves, as to what we shall be like when we have risen from the dead, how we shall live, what we shall do, or shall we have any tasks, or none at all? And if there are none, are we to live idly, doing nothing; or, if we shall have something to do, what will it be? Then again, shall we eat and drink, shall we marry, or shall we lead a single, uncommingled common life. And if this be so, what kind of life shall it be, what the nature of its activity, what the nature of our bodies? These are things Christians discuss, without however detracting from their faith in the resurrection from the dead.

IV. *He undertakes to prove the future resurrection.*

I would therefore pass now to the discussion of this question, in as far as it can be answered or set out in words by men to men, such as we are, or you are, were it not that a certain solicitude for our more carnal-minded brethren, and near pagans, compels me to linger a while upon the question which asks, whether the dead *shall* wholly rise again. Now I believe no one here present is a pagan, but that all are Christians. But those who are pagans, and mockers of the resurrection, never cease from murmuring in the ears of Christians: *Let us eat and drink: for tomorrow we shall die.* And because the Apostle, showing his concern, and adding to this sentence, said: *Be not seduced: Evil communications corrupt good morals;* we, fearing these *evil communications,* and out of anxiety for the weak among us, and not only from paternal charity, but even from a certain as it were maternal love for you, shall also say something on this question; sufficient at least for Christians: for only a very great devotion to the Scriptures has drawn all those assembled here today. For not even the solemnity of some feast has drawn such crowds to the Church of God; such as only the theatre draws. For on the feast days it is not piety draws certain people, but the festival gathering. Because of this we shall first speak to you of the resurrection of the dead; and afterwards, if God gives us strength, we shall speak of the future life of the Just.

V. *Against the opinion of those who say we should live now as though after death there was nothing.*

I *fear*, says the Apostle, *lest, as the devil seduced Eve by his subtlety, so your minds should be corrupted and fall from the simplicity that is in Christ* (II Cor. xi. 3). It is speeches such as this that corrupt their minds: *Let us eat and drink; for tomorrow we shall die.* They who love such things, who strive after them, who think that there is only this present life, who hope for nothing more, who either do not pray to God, or pray to Him for these things; they to whom talk of love is irksome, listen with great reluctance while we speak of these things. They want to eat and to drink; for tomorrow they die. Would that they might truly reflect that tomorrow they shall die! For who is so foolish, so perverse, who is such an enemy to his own soul, who that is about to die tomorrow will not think to himself that all he has striven for has now come to an end? For so it is written: *In that day all*

their thoughts shall perish (Ps. cxlv. 4).

If for the sake of those they leave behind, they prepare their will and testament against the approaching day of death, how much more should they not think of their soul? A man will think of those he leaves behind; yet have no thought of himself, now leaving all things. Your children will possess that which you let go; you will have nothing; yet all your thought is taken up with the way by which strangers after you shall pass, not whither they shall come who now are passing. Would indeed that men might think of death. While the dead are being borne to the grave they will think of death, and say perhaps: 'Alas, the poor man; he was such and such a man; he was walking about no later than yesterday,' or, 'I saw him only a week ago; he spoke to me about this and that. Man is nothing!' They murmur such things.

And perhaps while the dead is being mourned, the body embalmed, the corpse made ready, as it is being brought forth, while they journey to the grave, while it is being buried, this talk will go on. But when the dead is buried, thoughts such as these are buried with him. Other death-bringing cares return. He is forgotten whom they brought there. He who succeeds him thinks of the succession. Men return to their cheating, to plundering, to perjuring, to false oaths, to wine-bibbing, to the endless pleasures of the body that perish, not, I say, when they have been drained, but even as they are tasted. And what is more pernicious, from the burial of the dead they derive an argument for the burial of the soul, and murmur: *Let us eat and drink; for tomorrow we shall die.*

VI. *Belief in the resurrection scorned by the unbelieving. Festivals in honour of the dead. Against those who object that no one has returned from the dead.*

What is more, they mock at the faith of those who declare that the dead shall rise again; saying to themselves: So and so has been placed in his grave; let us hear his voice. But you cannot hear his voice. Let me hear the voice of my father, of my grandfather, of my ancestor. Who has ever risen from there? Who has ever told us what they do among the dead? Let us be good to ourselves while we live; for when we are dead, even if our parents, our dear ones or our neighbours bring offerings to our tomb, they bring them for themselves who live, not for us who are dead. Even Scripture laughs at these offerings, speaking of the gifts laid before those who are not aware of them, as *messes of meat set about a grave* (Ecclus. xxx. 18). And it is very plain these things do not reach the dead, and that this is a pagan custom, and that it does not derive from that branch and source of justice, the Patriarchs our fathers who, we read, were buried; but we do not read they were buried with solemnities and sacrifices. This can also be seen from the custom of the Jews; for though they have not preserved from the Saints of old the fruits of justice, they have nevertheless held fast in certain solemnities to the customs of ancient times.

That some oppose this, citing the words of Scripture that say: *Lay out thy bread and thy wine upon the burial of a just man: and do not eat and drink thereof with the wicked* (Tob. iv. 18), need not be discussed here. Nevertheless I shall say that the faithful well understand what Scripture says.

For how the faithful do these things, piously, in remembrance of their dead, is known to the faithful; and likewise that they must not set these things before the unjust, that is before the unbelieving, because *the just man liveth by faith* (Rom. i. 17), this also is known to the faithful. Therefore let no one make a wound out of what is a source of healing; nor make a snare, a noose from the Scriptures, to set a death-trap for the soul. It is plain to all how these words are to be understood, and that this celebration of Christians is open and wholesome.

VII. *Faith, like Christ sleeping in the boat, must be awakened in our heart, to calm the tempest.*

So let us therefore, as I began to say, consider this question because of those who murmur in the ears of the weak: *Let us eat and drink; for tomorrow we shall die:* because they say: 'No one has returned from there; I have heard no sound from anyone from the time my ancestor was laid in the grave and my grandfather, and my father; not a word have I heard.' Answer them, Christians, if you are Christians: unless perhaps you hope to be filled with wine at gatherings, and so are reluctant to answer your corrupters. You have an answer to give; but you waver because of your thirst for pleasure; because you want to gorge yourself with food and drink, and be buried alive. The craving to fill yourself with wine swells up in you, and like a wave floods your soul; drawn in at the urging of an evil spirit. You are in the middle of a great storm: you do not wish to answer your corrupter, since you want to be friendly with the man who will give you wine. And the flood of desire mounts up, and threatens to overwhelm the ship of your soul. Christian! Christ sleeps in your ship. Awaken Him! He will command the tempest, and all will be calm. For when the Disciples were being tossed about in the ship, and Christ sat sleeping, they were a figure of Christians being tossed to and fro, while their Christian faith lies sleeping. For you know what the Apostle says: *That Christ dwells by faith in your heart* (Eph. iii. 17). In His beauty and divinity He is ever present with the Father; in His Bodily Presence He is now above the heavens at the right hand of the Father. By faith He is present in all Christians. And so you are tossed to and fro; because Christ sleeps in you; that is, because you do not overcome the desires stirred up in you by the suggestions of evil spirits; because your faith is asleep.

What does this mean, that faith is asleep in you? It is lulled to sleep. What does this mean, lulled to sleep? That you have forgotten it. And what does to awaken Christ mean? It means: rouse up your faith, remember what it is you have believed. Therefore, remember your faith, awaken Christ within you. Your own faith will command the waves that trouble you, and the winds that urge you to evil. At once they will depart; at once all will be calm. For though the evil tempter will not cease from speaking, he will not now threaten the ship, he will not now stir up the waves, nor overwhelm the vessel that bears you.

What then is the meaning of awakening Christ within you? What has the evil urger said to you? What has that corrupter said, who corrupts good morals by his *evil communications?* What was it he said? This is what he said: 'No one has returned from there; I have heard no word from my father, nor my grandfather. Let someone return from there, and let him tell us what they do there.'

VIII. *Belief in the resurrection to come sufficiently proved by Christ rising from the dead. The whole world bears witness to our faith. All things give testimony to the resurrection.*

Now having wakened Christ in your ship, by recalling to mind your own faith, answer him and say: 'Foolish man, if your father rose again, you would believe! The Lord of all has risen, and you do *not* believe! Why did He will to die and to rise again, if not that we might all believe in One; lest we be deceived by the many? And what would your father do, should he rise again and speak to you; and die again?' But see with what great power He rose from the dead, Who now dies no more, and over whom death has no more dominion (Rom. vi. 7). He shewed Himself to His Disciples and to the faithful. They felt with their hands the solidity of His Body; for it mattered little to some of them to see what they remembered, unless they also touched what they were seeing. Faith was confirmed, not only in the hearts of men, but also in their eyes. He Who showed us these things has ascended into heaven; He has sent the Holy Spirit to His Disciples; and the Gospel has been preached. If we lie in this, ask the whole world. Many things that were promised, have been accomplished; many which were hoped for, have been fulfilled:

the whole world grows strong in the Christian faith. They dare not speak against the Resurrection of Christ; not even those who do not yet believe in Christ. There is testimony in heaven; there is testimony on earth; testimony from the Angels, testimony from the dead. What is there, that does not proclaim it? And you say: *Let us eat and drink; for tomorrow we shall die!*

Example of the resurrection in a seed.

But you are sorrowful because of your dear one who is buried; because you do not now hear his voice. He lived; he died. He ate, he does not now eat. He felt and saw; now he feels nothing. The joys and pleasures of the living are now nothing to him.

IX. But, do you mourn for the seed when you plough the earth? Let us suppose there was someone so ignorant of things, that when he bore the seed to the field and cast it upon the earth and buried it in the broken soil; suppose there was someone so ignorant of the way of nature, even of things close at hand, that, thinking of the departed summer, he mourns for the wheat, saying to himself: 'This wheat, now buried in the earth, with what toil was it harvested, and carried from the field, threshed upon the harvest floor, winnowed, stored in the barn! We saw its beauty, and rejoiced and gave thanks. Now it is taken from our eyes. I see the ploughed land; but the wheat I see neither here nor in the barn.' Sorrowfully he would mourn the wheat as dead and buried; he would weep freely, his thoughts on the field, on the earth, but seeing no more the harvest. How he would be

laughed at by those who were themselves ignorant, but not ignorant in these things; by the unskilled in other things, but not unskilled in this, over which he, so foolishly ignorant, sorrowed?

And what would they say to him, they who knew, supposing he had wept in this way; knowing nothing of these things? They would say to him: Do not grieve. What we buried in the earth is indeed no longer in the barn, no longer in our hands. But soon we shall go again to the field, and you will be happy in the beauty of the growing corn, where now you weep over the nakedness of ploughed earth. And he who now learns what shall come from the sown wheat, he too will rejoice in the ploughing and the sowing. He who had been unbelieving, or rather, who had been foolish and, to speak more correctly, without experience, may perhaps have mourned before, but believing the experienced, he will go away comforted, and with the experienced wait in hope for the harvest to come.

X. *Christ's Resurrection the pattern of our resurrection. All creation speaks of the resurrection. The awakening of living things. The new moons; the the leaves of the trees.*

Each year we see the harvests. But at the end of the world there shall be but one last harvest of all mankind. The eye cannot see it now: but we have proof of it; given by the One Supreme Grain of *wheat.* Speaking of His own death, the Lord Himself says: *Amen, amen, I say to you, unless the grain of wheat falling into the ground die, itself remaineth alone* (Jn. xii. 24); because manifold shall be the resurrection of those who believe in Him. We are given an example of this from One Grain; an example in which all should believe who wish to become *wheat*. And since all creation speaks of the resurrection, if we are not deaf; from it we may foretell what once and for all God at the end shall do for mankind: since we see so many things that remind us of it each day.

The resurrection of Christians shall take place but once; the sleep of living things and their waking up is a daily happening. Sleep resembles death; to awaken resembles the resurrection. From that which happens daily, have confidence in what shall be but once. The moon is born through all the months of the year; it grows, it reaches the full, it wanes and fades, and is renewed again. That which happens with the moon each month, shall happen once and for all at the resurrection; just as that which happens to sleeping things daily happens to the moon each single month.

The leaves of the trees, whence do they come, whence do they return again? To what secret places do they depart; from what hidden places do they come to us again? It is winter, but the trees now dry and parched will surely come forth in leaves in the spring. Has this new life come now for the first time; or did it happen the year before? No; even in the past times it was so. It is cut off by autumn and the winter. It returns with the spring, remains till summer. The seasons then return with the year. Shall men, made in the image of God, when they die, perish and crumble to nothing?

XI. *How certain things are renewed from the earth.*

But someone who does not carefully observe the changes and the renewals of things may say to me: But these leaves rot, and new ones are born. If he will look cloesly he will see, that the leaves which rot return their strength and substance to the earth. For how is the earth made fertile if not by the corruption of earthly things? They look to this who cultivate the soil. And they who do not cultivate it, because they live in cities, learn from the gardens close to the city, with what care every kind of waste and filth from the city is saved and sold by those who bring it there. Abhorrent and useless it is now; to those who do not know. Who will stoop to look at filth? What man abhors, man is at pains to save. That therefore which now seems consumed and worthless, will return to fatten the earth. The fatness will turn to sap, the sap to a root, and what passes from the earth into the root changes, by unseen steps, into strength and is distributed through branches; from the branches it passes to the buds, from the buds it is given to the fruit and leaves, and lo! what you shuddered at as filth and dung, you marvel at in the fruit and verdure of the tree!

XII. *The objection that a body changes into dust. Custom of Egyptians (Mummies).*

I do not wish you to say to me now what you are wont to object: That the body of the buried dead does not remain whole; if it did, I would believe it rises again. So only the Egyptians believe in the resurrection; for they carefully preserve the bodies of their dead! They have a method of drying bodies, to make them hard as bronze. These they call mummies (*Gabbaras*). There-fore, according to these, who know nothing of the inner secrets of nature, only the Egyptians may justifiably believe in the resurrection of their dead (where all are kept safe for the Creator, though hidden from men); the hope of other Christians however is uncertain.

Oftentimes because of their great age, or from some non-sacrilegious need, when tombs are opened or uncovered, the bodies are found to have dissolved into dust, and men, who are wont to be charmed by bodily beauty, sighing grieve and say to themselves: 'Is it possible that this dust shall one day possess again its former beauty; restored to life, restored to the light? When shall this be? When may I hope to see something living from this dust?'

You who say this, see only a tomb or dust. Roll back your own span of life, if you are, for example, thirty, fifty or more years old. In the tomb there is at least the dust of the dead. But you, fifty years ago, what were you? Where were you? All our bodies, we who now speak or listen, will after a few years be dust. A few years ago they were not even dust. He therefore Who could create what was not, is He unable to renew what was?

XIII. *Faith made firm by Christ against evil communications.*

Therefore let the murmuring of those who speak evilly cease, and of those who corrupt good morals by their evil conversation. Set your feet firmly in the way; set them firmly so that you shall not depart from the way; not that you may remain in the way but, as we have been told, *so run that you may obtain* (I Cor. ix. 24). Let Christ be ever living in your heart: He Who has willed to reveal in the Head that which the other members may hope for. On earth we strive and toil; in heaven our Head now dies no more, nor fails, nor suffers anything. Yet It has suffered for us: because *He was delivered up for our sins and rose again for our justification* (Rom. iv. 25). This we know by faith: they to whom He showed himself, learned it with their eyes. Nevertheless, though He has risen, and though we were not able to see Him with our mortal eyes, we are not rejected. We have before us the testimony of the Lord Himself, which He spoke to the doubting Disciple; seeking to touch Him that he might believe. For when convinced by feeling Christ's wounds with his hand, he cried out: *My Lord and my God; the* Lord said to him: *Because thou hast seen me, thou hast believed; blessed are they that have not seen and have believed* (Jn. xx. 28, 29). Awaken yourselves therefore to your own blessedness; let no one, evilly per-suading you, shake from your heart what Christ has fastened there.

Against those say that only Christ was permitted to rise from the dead. The conjunction of the members of His Body with Christ the Head. An apt simili-tude.

Neither let this be said: For this is said by all who have already, though reluctantly, submitted to the author-ity of Christ. For almost all who are non-Christians, and even those who put off or are slow to embrace Christ with fervour, will not pre-sume to find fault with Him. They will rebuke Christians; but Christ they dare not. They yield to the

Head, while they continue to insult the Body. But the Body listening to their insults, of those namely who now yield to the Head, does not think of itself as cut off from the Head, but as upheld by the Head. For if we were cut off, we would fear the words of those who insult us.

That we are not shut off, He Himself bears witness Who said to Paul (who as Saul was still persecuting the Church): *Saul, Saul, why persecutest thou me?* Christ had already passed through the impious hands of the Jews, He had already descended into hell, He had already risen from the tomb, He had already ascended into heaven, He had already enriched and confirmed the hearts of those who believed in Him by the gift of the Holy Ghost, and was now sitting at the right hand of the Father, making intercession for us. He shall not again deliver Himself to death, but shall deliver us from death: what could He suffer at the hand of the raging Saul? How could that hand touch Him, though he was, as it is written: *breathing slaughter* (Acts ix. 1). He could attack the lowly suffering Christians: when and how could he attack Christ? Christ is crying out in defence of His other members. And He does not say: 'Why do you persecute those who are mine?' For if He said: 'Why do you persecute those who are mine,' we should believe we were slaves. But slaves do not adhere to their masters, as Christians adhere to Christ. This is another kind of union: the unity of members is one thing, the unity of love another. The Head is speaking for the members; yet It does not say: 'Why do you persecute my members?' but, *Why persecutest thou*

me? (Acts ix, 5). Saul was not touching the Head; but He was laying hands on what was joined to the Head.

XIV. We must repeat for you a similitude we have often already used; because it is apt, and one that illustrates this truth very well. He who stands on your foot or presses against it in a crowd, does not touch your tongue. Why then does the tongue cry out and say: 'You are standing on me?' Your foot is suffering; not your tongue. But it is one body. *And, if one member suffer anything, all the members suffer with it; or, if one member glory, all the members rejoice with it* (I Cor. xii. 26). If therefore your tongue speaks for your foot, shall Christ in heaven not speak for His Christians? Your tongue does not speak for the foot by saying, 'you are standing on my foot'; but, 'you are standing on me,' though it is not itself touched. Recognize Him as your Head when for you He speaks from heaven and says: *Saul, Saul, why persecutest thou me?*

Why then, brethren, do we say this? Lest they come upon you unawares of whom the Apostle says that, *their evil conversation corrupts good morals*; for they say: *Let us eat and drink, for tomorrow we shall die* (I Cor. xv. 33, 32); so that they may say to you (for they dare not reprehend Christ: they tremble before the majesty of His authority, established throughout the world; for just as it is written: *The wicked shall see and shall be angry, he shall gnash with his teeth and pine away* (Ps. cxi. 10): so the wicked can gnash with his teeth, and pine away, but blaspheme Christ he dare not); that may then perhaps say to you: This was permitted to Christ only. For sometimes they speak from the heart; but sometimes they speak through fear. But let you note both what they dare to say, and what they dare not to say.

XV. *Christ praised deceitfully by the unbelieving: to the end that we may not hope for a like resurrection.*

These therefore will say to you: 'You tell me Christ has risen, and from this you hope for the resurrection of the dead. But Christ was *permitted* to rise from the dead.' And then he will begin to praise Christ, not to honour Him, but to make you despair. The perverse cunning of the serpent, giving false praise to Him he dare not asperse: that by praise of Christ, he may turn you from Christ. He exalts His majesty, to make it appear exceptional; so that you will not hope to attain to that which was revealed in Him, rising from the dead. And he pretends to be even more pious and reverent towards Christ by saying to you: 'Look at the man who presumes to compare himself with Christ; so that because Christ rose from the dead, he imagines he too will rise again!'

Do not be disturbed by this perverted praise of your Leader. The snares of the enemy may trouble you; but the humility, the humanity of Christ shall be your consolation. He will point out how far above you Christ has been raised; but Christ Himself speaks of how far He has descended, to come to you. Therefore say to such a man: 'Waken up your faith. This is a storm; these temptations are waves, your ship is in danger, Christ sleeps in you. Awaken your faith; do not forget

what you have believed.' Answer him at once; since in you the faith of the Gospels has grown watchful. Do not be timid in answering him. For it will not be you who will answer: for abiding in you, Christ will use your heart and your tongue as His instruments, as His swords; resisting your adversary, He will make you safe. Let you but waken the sleeper; that is, remind him of the faith he has forgotten.

XVI. *That by the resurrection we have fittingly been uplifted in hope, Whence was Christ mortal. How he became a Mediator. How our sins are in Christ. Mortality the punishment of sin.*

Now what shall I say to you, that you may use to answer such people? I shall say something not new; something you already believe. Rouse up your faith then, and answer the one who says that Christ alone could rise from the dead, but we cannot. Answer him and say: 'Christ could rise because Christ was God. Yes, He truly could, because He was God. And if He is God, He is Omnipotent. If He is Omnipotent, why should I despair that He can do in me, what He has shown in Himself because of me?' Then I shall ask: 'From whence did Christ arise?' He will answer: 'From the dead.' I ask: 'How was it He died? Can God die? Can that Divinity, the Word, which is equal to the Father, the Art of the Omnipotent Artificer, by Whom all things were made, the Unchangeable Wisdom, abiding within Itself, Which *reneweth all things* (Wis. vii. 27), reaching from end to end mightily, and ordering all things sweetly (viii. 1), can It die?

No; he will say. And yet Christ died! For what reason did He die?

For this reason: because *He thought it not robbery to be equal with God; but, emptied Himself, taking the form of a servant.* But just before these words what does he say? *Who being in the form of God* (Phil. ii. 6, 7). Did Christ receive the form of God, or did He possess it from His nature? The Apostle distinguishes: When he speaks of the *form of God*, he says: *Being.* When he speaks of the *form of a servant*, he says: *Taking.* Christ therefore *was* something, and Christ *received* something: that He might be one with that something He had taken. In the form of God He was equal to God, as the fisherman Evangelist clearly reveals: *In the beginning was the Word, and the Word was with God, and the Word was God* (Jn. i. 1); that is, Being in the form of God, thought it not robbery to be equal to God. For what does not naturally belong to us, but unlawfully usurped, is for us robbery. An Angel usurped equality with God, and fell; and became a devil. A man usurped equality with God, and fell; and became mortal. But He, He Who was born equal with God: for He was not born in time, but is the sempiternal Son of the sempiternal Father, ever born, by Whom all things were made: *was* in the form of God.

That He might be a Mediator between God and man, between the Just and the unjust, between the Immortal and the mortal, He took something (*aliquid*) from the unjust and mortal, retaining something (*aliquid*) in common with the Just and Immortal. With the Just and Immortal retaining justice, from the unjust and mortal taking mortality, He became a Mediator between both, throwing down the wall of

our sins: It is from this the people sing: *And through my God I will go over a wall* (Ps. xvii. 30): restoring to God that which sin had estranged; buying back with His Blood that of which the devil held possession. He died for us, and He arose for us. He bore our sins; not adhering to them, but bearing the weight of them, as Jacob bore the *little skins of the kids*, that he might lead his father Isaac to think he was hairy, who then blessed him (Gen. xxvii. 16). Esau, the unfortunate, was the hairy son; Jacob, the beautiful, bore another's hair. Sins cleave to mortal men. They did not cleave to Him who said: *I have power to lay down my life, and I have power to take it up again* (Jn. x. 18).

XVII. Death in our Lord therefore was but the sign of others' sins; not the punishment of His own. For in all men mortality is the punishment of sin: it arises from the source of sin, whence we all have come; from the fall of that first man, not from the descent of This. To fall is one thing; to descend another. The one fell miserably; the Other descended mercifully. For *as in Adam all die, so in Christ all shall be made alive* (III Cor. xv. 22). Bearing therefore the sins of others, *I paid that which I took not away* (Ps. lxviii. 5); that is, though I was without sin, I died. *Behold*, He says, *the prince of this world cometh and in me he hath not anything* (Jn. xiv. 30).

What does this mean: *In me he hath not anything?* He will find nothing in Me deserving of death. For that which is deserving of death is sin. Why therefore do You die? He goes on to tell us: *That all may know that I do the will of my Father, arise, let us go hence* (Jn. xiv. 30). And He arose going towards His Passion. Why? Because in this He was doing the will of His Father, and not because He in Whom there was no sin, owed the prince of this world anything. Our Lord Jesus Christ brought with Him His Divinity; mortality He received from us. This He received in the womb of the Virgin Mary; joining Himself, the Word of God, to human nature, as a bridegroom to his bride, in that virginal bridal chamber; that He might go forth as a bridegroom, *coming out of his bride-chamber* (Ps. xviii. 6).

In Christ there was true mortality: not merited, but from mercy. The Resurrection of Christ in the Body that before was mortal.

Return therefore to what I was saying. Mortality in all men comes from sin. In the Lord it was present because of mercy; but nevertheless it was real. This flesh was real flesh, and truly mortal, *having the likeness of sinful flesh* (Rom. viii. 3); not the likeness of flesh, but the likeness of sinful flesh, It was true flesh, but not the flesh of sin. For He had not, as I have said, received this mortality in punishment for sin, *Who emptied himself, taking the form of a servant, and becoming obedient unto death.* What therefore was He; and what did He possess? He was Divinity; but possessing mortality. And that whence He died, from thence He rose again.

XVIII. Look back again to those who say: 'only Christ could rise again; not you.' Let you answer and say: 'Christ, in that which He received from us, rose again. Take away the form of a servant and there would be nothing in which He could rise again: for there would not be that in which He could die. Why then do you wish, through praise of the Lord, to weaken in me this faith my Lord made strong in me? For it was from this that He took the form of a servant He died; and it was through that by which He died, He rose again from the dead. Never therefore shall I despair of the resurrection of a servant, since the Lord has risen in the form of a servant.'

And should they attribute that Christ rose from the dead, to the power of the Man—for there are some who say this: that He was so just a man that He could even rise from the dead – then I shall talk as they do, and shall not refer to the Divinity of our Lord: He so just, that He even deserved to rise from the dead, how could He possibly deceive us; we to whom He has promised that we also shall rise again?

XIX. All that has been said to you, brethren, has been said to this end, that you may be instructed and ready, should any one say that the dead do not rise again. They have been said, if you remember, in the measure that God deigned to bring to our minds *the things that are necessary for you*; and the proofs are drawn from day-to-day examples from the nature of things; and from the omnipotence of God, to Whom nothing is difficult; Who, if He could make what was not, much more can remake what was; and also from the Lord our Saviour Jesus Christ, Whom we know has risen, and Whose resurrection was accomplished in no other form than that of a servant. Nor could His death, from whence it was necessary He should rise again, take place save in the form of a servant. And so since we are servants, we should hope for that to take place in our form, which He has deigned to show us beforehand in the form of a servant. Therefore let the tongues be silent that say: *Let us eat and drink; for to-morrow we shall die.* Rather, let you straightaway answer them, and say: 'Let us fast and pray; for tomorrow we shall die.'

XX. *We are taught by the example of Noah to look for the Last Judgement.*

There remains for us to speak of what kind our life shall be in the resurrection of the Just. But since, as you see, we have already taken up enough time today, let you instead meditate upon what we have already imparted to you. That which we still owe you, pray that we may impart it at another time. But keep before your minds the reason why we have spoken to you; particularly, my brethren, because of those festivals which the pagans celebrate (*saturnalia*). Take heed to yourselves: this world passes. Be mindful of the Gospel where the Lord foretells the last day, just as He did in the days of Noah: *They did eat and drink they bought and sold, they married wives and were given in marriage, until the day that Noah entered into the ark; and the flood came and destroyed them all* (Lk. xvii. 27). Here you have the Lord giving us most clear warning; and in another place He says: *Take heed to yourselves, lest your hearts be overcharged with surfeiting and drunkenness* (ib. xxi. 34). *Let your loins be girt and lamps burning in your hands; and you yourselves like to men who wait for their lord when he shall return from the wedding* (ib. xii. 35, 36).

Let us watch for His Coming. Let Him not find us sleeping. It is shameful for an espoused wife not to long for her spouse: how much more shameful for the Church not to long for Christ? The spouse returns to earthly embraces, and is received with love by the chaste wife; the Spouse of the Church will come to bestow on us eternal embraces, to make us sharers of His eternal inheritance: and we so live that not only do we not long for His Coming, we even fear it! How true it is that that day shall come, as it came in the days of Noah? How many shall it find as it found them then; even those who are called by the name of Christian? For this was the Ark so many years a-building; that they might wake up who did not believe. It was built throughout a hundred years, and they did not wake up and say, 'Not without cause does the man of God build the Ark; he would not build it unless the end of man is at hand,' and turning to the ways that please God, placate the anger of God, as the Ninivites did.

XXI. *Ninive was overthrown according to prophecy: but by way of repentance.*

Jonas announced, not mercy, but the wrath to come. He did not say: 'In three days and Ninive will be destroyed; but, if in these three days you do penance, God will spare you.' He did not say this. He threatened destruction only, and foretold it. Nevertheless, the Ninivites, not despairing of the mercy of God, turned to Him in repentance. And God spared them (Jon. ii). But what shall we say? That the prophet lied? If you understand him in an unspiritual way, it will seem as if he spoke falsely; but if you understand him spiritually, it happened as the prophet said. For Ninive was overthrown. But reflect upon what Ninive was, and see how it was overthrown. They ate and they drank, they bought and they sold, they planted, they built, they gave themselves to perjury, to lies, to drunkenness, to crime, to corruption. This was Ninive. Now look at Ninive. They weep, they mourn, they sorrow, in sackcloth and ashes, in fastings and prayer. Where is the Ninive that was? It is overthrown; for now from its evil deeds it has set in order its way of life.

XXII. *More worthy of rebuke are they who, with Christ now building His Church, are not converted, than they of old while Noah was building the Ark.*

Therefore, brethren, even now the Ark is a-building, and the hundred years are these times. This whole tract of time is symbolized by this number of years. If they then fittingly perished who were careless and sinful while Noah was building the Ark, of what are they deserving who neglect salvation while Christ is building His Church (Eph. v. 27)? There is as great a difference between Noah and Christ as between servant and master; even greater, as between man and God. For servant and master can also be called two men. And though while a man was building the Ark, men did not believe, we have nevertheless received in them a warning which those who come after must

beware of. Christ God made man for us is building His Church; He has laid Himself as the foundation of this Ark. Daily imperishable timbers, believing men renouncing this this world, enter the edifice of the Ark. And yet there are those who say: *Let us eat and drink; for tomorrow we shall die.*

Let you then, brethren, as I have said, say to such men: 'Let us fast and pray; for tomorrow we shall die.' For they say: *Let us eat and drink; for tomorrow we shall die,* who have no hope of a resurrection. But we who believe and proclaim the resurrection of which the Prophets spoke, which Christ and His Apostles preached; we who hope that after this death we shall live, let us not be wanting; nor let us burthen our hearts with surfeiting and with drunkenness; but let us with prayer and fasting, with loins girt, and lamps burning in our hands, await the Coming of the Lord. And not because tomorrow we shall die; but that tomorrow we may die with secure hearts.

What remains for us to say, ask of us in the Name of the Lord another time.

PRAYER: Turning then to the Lord our God, let us earnestly pray to Him for ourselves and for all His people, who with us stand in the courts of His House, that He may deign to guard us and protect us through Jesus Christ His Son our Lord, who with Him liveth and reigneth throughout all ages. Amen.

V. St Augustine, Bishop and Doctor

On the Resurrection of the Dead: Second Sermon[22]

Matthew xxii. 23–32; Luke xx. 27–38; I Corinthians xv.

1. *What shall the future resurrection of the Just be like?*

Mindful of our promises to you, we have had certain passages from the Gospel and from the Apostle read to you.[23] For those among you who were present at the previous sermon, will remember that we put before you for discussion a twofold question: First, that we should discuss, for the sake of those who are doubtful, and for those also who deny this, whether the dead shall rise again; and after this, that we should seek, as best we can, to learn from the Scriptures what shall the future life of the Just be after the resurrection.

Now in the first sermon, where we treated of whether the dead shall rise again, as you will kindly recall, we delayed so long on this question that there was no time for the second question: so that we were compelled to defer it till today. This then is the debt your zeal asks of us; and we confess that it is time to pay it.

At the same time, from the love of our heart, we earnestly beseech the Lord, that we may render this debt to you in a fitting manner, and that you may receive it to the profit of your salvation. For this, we must confess, is the greater question of the two: but greater than all difficult questions is charity; which we all must serve, so that God, Who commands this, may change all our difficulties into gladness and joy.

2. *He treats of the previous question*

again. You will remember the answer we gave the last day to certain persons who are wont to say, as the Apostle asserts, *Let us eat and drink; for tomorrow we shall die;* he adding to this the comment: *Evil conversations corrupt good morals;* and concluding with: *Awake*[24] *ye just, and sin not; for some have not the knowledge of God; I say it to your shame* (I Cor. xv. 34). These words of the Apostle we have all heard, and taken to our hearts; and he who has heard them, and taken them to heart, is known by his works. For he who listens to them is like a field receiving seed from the hand of the sower; but he who takes to heart what he hears, is like the man who breaks the sod and covers the sown seed. But he who brings forth good works, in accord with what he has heard, and kept in his heart, he is like a man who raises a harvest, and *brings forth fruit in patience*; one thirtyfold, another sixty, and another a hundred (Mt. xiii. 23; Lk. viii. 15). For such a man, barns are prepared, as for the good wheat; not fire, as for the chaff. In these hidden *barns* therefore, is laid up in the resurrection of the dead that perpetual and secret blessedness of the just into which, the Scripture tells us, they are to be received.

3. *The secret thrones* (of the blessed) *signified by the name of blessed vessels. The hidden face of God.*

The Lord Jesus Christ in another place speaks also of *vessels*, when He says, the Kingdom of heaven is like to a net cast into the sea: *The Kingdom of heaven is like to a net cast into the sea and gathering together of all kind of fishes. Which, when it was filled, they drew out; and sitting by the shore, they chose out the good into vessels, but the bad they cast forth* (Mt. xiii. 47, 48). Our Lord wished to tell us that the Word of God is now in this manner cast over peoples and nations, as a net is cast upon the sea. But now by means of the Christian sacraments it gathers in both good and bad. But not all whom the net gathers in are also stored in *vessels*. For *vessels* here mean the seats of the saints, and the great secret places of the blessed life, to which not all can come who bear the name of Christian, but those only who are both called and are Christians. To be sure both good and bad fish swim together within the net, and the good bear with the bad in patience, until in the end they are separated.

In a certain other place is it also said: *Thou shalt hide them in the secret of thy face* (Ps. xxx. 21); for here he was speaking of the saints. *Thou shalt hide them*, he says. *in the secret of thy face*; that is, whither the eyes of men cannot follow, nor the thoughts of mortals. He said, hidden *in the face of God*, meaning certain secret places, deeply hidden. Are we to think God has a great face, and that in His face is some bodily receptacle where the saints are to be hidden? These, brethren, as you see, are carnal notions, and they must be rejected from every believing heart. What then are we to understand by the *secret face of God*, if not that which is known only to the face of God? When therefore we speak of *barns*, to signify secret

places, and when in another place they are called *vessels*; what we are referring to are neither barns nor vessels. For if it were one of these things, it would not be called something else. But since it is through similitudes, known to men, that men make known, as best they can, things not known; let either term therefore stand for this unknown thing, that you may know the secret, by either the word *barn* or *vessel*. But if you seek to know what is the secret place; listen to the prophet as he says: *Thou shalt hide them in the secret of thy face.*

4. We long for heaven through faith.

And while this is so, brethren, we are still pilgrims in this present life, and still longing through faith for that unknown home. And why I know not of whence we are citizens, unless that in our far wandering we have forgotten it; so that we cannot speak of our unknown home? The Lord Christ, King of this fatherland, coming to us pilgrims, has banished this forgetfulness from our heart; and His Divinity, taking our flesh, has become our Way: so that we may journey onward by *The Way* of Christ man, and pass the night with Christ God.

What then, brethren? This secret place, which eye hath not seen, nor ear heard, nor the thought of entered into the heart of man, with what words shall we set it before you, with what eye shall we see it? We can now and then know of something we cannot speak of in words. But of that which we do not know, how am I to speak in words? Since it can happen that should I know these things, I cannot speak of them to you; how much more difficult is it for me to speak to you on this subject, since I too, brethren, like you, *walk by faith*, but not yet *by sight* (II Cor. v. 7)?

But is it I who say this, or is it the Apostle himself? For he comforts our ignorance and strengthens our faith by saying: *Brethren, I do not count myself to have apprehended. But one thing I do: forgetting the things that are behind, and stretching forth myself to those that are before, I press towards the mark, to the prize of the supernal vocation of God in Christ Jesus* (Phil. iii. 13, 14). And from this he shows he too is in the *way*. And in another place he says: *While we are in the body, we are absent from the Lord: for we walk by faith, and not by sight* (II Cor. v. 6, 7). And again: *For we are*, he says, *saved by hope. But hope that is seen is not hope. For what a man seeth, why doth he hope for? But, if we hope for that which we see not, we wait for it with patience* (Rom. viii. 23, 24).

5. *The Church teaches what it believes, not what it knows.*

So therefore, brethren, hear from me the voice you hear in the Psalms: devout, humble, mild, not uplifted, not turbulent, not headlong, not rash. The Psalmist says in a certain place: *I have believed, therefore have I spoken* (Ps. cxv). And the Apostle has quoted this testimony, and has added: *We also believe. For which cause we speak also* (Ps. cxv. 1; II Cor. iv. 13). You therefore wish me to speak to you of the things I know? I shall not deceive you; listen to what I believe. Let it not demean you, to listen to what I believe: for you are listening to a true confession. If I were to say to you: Listen to what I know; you would be listening to rash presumption. If

therefore, brethren, all of us, and, if we are to believe the writings of the saints, all likewise who have lived before us in the flesh, and speaking through whom the Spirit of God has given to men as much as was to be made known to those still on the way; all of us speak of what we believe; but the Lord Himself speaks of what He knows.

What then are we to do if only the Lord could know of that future life of eternity He spoke of? Others then following the Lord must speak of what they believe. We find the Lord Jesus Christ Himself, knowing what He would say, yet not saying it. For in a certain place He says to His Disciples: *I have yet many things to say to you; but you cannot bear them now* (Jn. xvi. 12). He, because of their infirmity, not because of His own, put off speaking to them of what He knew. But we, because of the infirmity common to us all, shall not try to speak to you of what we know fairly well, but shall explain to you, as best we can, that which we rightly believe; and let you try to understand it as best you can. And should there be one among you who understands more than I can tell him, let him take no notice of this tiny stream, but let him hasten to the overflowing Fountain; since with Him is *the fountain of life*, in Whose Light we shall see light (Ps. xxxv. 10).

6. *It is not lawful for a Christian to doubt the resurrection.*

Therefore, as to the resurrection of which we have been speaking to you, this we believe, this we must believe, this we proclaim, because in this we place our trust, if we are Christians; having our eyes on the power of the arm of the Lord, scattering the pride of nations and building this faith far and wide across the face of the earth, as of old it was promised that He would: having our eyes therefore on these things, we are strengthened in our faith in the things we now see not; that we may receive that Vision which is the reward of faith. And so since it is manifest that we believe in the resurrection to come, and so manifest, that whoever doubts it should be ashamed to call himself a Christian; we now ask: What shall the bodies of the saints be like, and what the nature of their future life? For many think there shall be a resurrection, but of souls only.

7. *What shall our future bodies be like. The Rule of Faith: the Creed. An apt similitude.*

After our previous sermon there is no need to go further into the question as to whether our bodies also shall rise again. But a question of this kind may be asked: If we have bodies in the future life, what will they be like? Like those we now possess, or of another kind? If of another kind, what kind? If they are the same, then will they serve the same tasks? Now since the Apostle does not teach that they shall do the same things, therefore the Lord has not laid down the same tasks for them. For bodies then shall not serve the same life, the same mortal and corruptible and perishable and fleeting ends, nor the same carnal joys, nor the same carnal consolations. If they do not serve the same ends, neither are they the same as we now possess?

If they are not the same, how then shall flesh rise again? We confess the resurrection of the body in our Rule of faith, and confessing it we are baptized. And whatever we there confess, we confess from the Truth and in that Truth in which we live and move and have our being (Acts xvii. 28). For it was by means of certain passing happenings in time that we are being prepared for eternal life. For all that was done, that we heard a certain saving pronouncement, that miracles were wrought, that our Lord was born, that He hungered and thirsted, that He was taken prisoner, insulted, beaten, scourged, crucified, died, buried, rose again, ascended into heaven, have all passed away. And when they are preached, it is certain temporal and fleeting things of our faith that are preached.

But it is because these things have passed away that that which was built up by means of them shall likewise pass away? Let your Sanctity listen carefully to a similitude, so that you may understand this. An architect builds a house that will endure by means that will soon pass away. For in this so great and spacious edifice we now see, there were, while it was being built, certain contrivances used for building it, which are no longer here. But that which was built by means of them, now stands complete. Similarly, brethren, while something was being built up into the Christian Faith, certain temporal instruments were employed to bring this about. For that our Lord Jesus Christ has risen, has come to an end: for He is not still rising from the dead. And that He ascended into heaven, is now accomplished; for He is not now ascending. Because He is in that life, wherein *He dieth now no more*, and where death shall no more have dominion over him (Rom. vi. 9); because there also, there lives for ever in Him, that same human nature which He deigned to take upon Him, and in which He was born, and in which He died and was buried. This has been built up; this remains for ever. The means by which it was built up, they have passed away. For Christ is not for ever being conceived in the virginal womb; or for ever being born of the Virgin Mary, or forever seized, for ever judged, scourged, crucified, buried. All these means were ordained, that through them that might be built up which remains for ever. But the Resurrection of our Lord Jesus Christ was laid down in heaven.

8. *The edifice of the heavenly Jerusalem has its foundation above. Christ is our Foundation and Head.*

Let your Charity turn your thoughts towards a wondrous edifice. These our earthly edifices press their weight upon the earth, and the whole downward pressure of the mass fastens it to the ground and, unless kept in place, it will strain to sink ever lower, pulled down by its own weight. So therefore that it may be built upon the earth, a foundation is first laid; that he who builds may build in security upon this foundation. So he lays at the bottom immoveable masses of stone, such that they can sustain what is placed upon them; and upon the massiveness of the foundation depends the magnitude of the structure built above it.

Nevertheless it is, as I have said, erected upon the earth: for even that which is built above it, is still built upon the earth. But our distant unknown Jerusalem is built in heaven. And so Christ has gone before us as its Foundation in heaven. There He is our Foundation, and the Head of the Church. For He is called both our Foundation and our Head; and He is truly so. Because the foundation is also the head of a building: for the head is not that which terminates a building, but that from which it begins, ascending upwards. The roofs of earthly houses rise upwards; the head (*caput*) they place on solid earth. So the Head of the Church has preceded us to heaven, and sits at the right hand of the Father.

And as men do to lay a foundation they bring there that which they set firm at the base of the structure, so that the safety of the edifice above is assured; so in like manner by means of all that happened to Christ, that He was born, grew up, was seized, insulted, scourged, crucified, slain, died and was buried, a massive base has been taken up above to serve as our heavenly Foundation.

9. *We must strive to be built on Christ. Christ is our Foundation if He holds the first place in our heart. How we must fear the fire of Gehenna.*

Having laid our Foundation on high; let us build ourselves upon It. Listen to the Apostle: *For other foundation no man can lay*, he says, *but that which is laid; which is Christ Jesus.* Then what does he say? *Let each one see what he may build on this foundation: gold, silver, precious stones, wood, hay stubble* (I Cor. iii. 11). Christ is indeed in heaven; but He is also in the heart of those that believe in Him. If Christ has the first place there, He is duly laid as its Foundation. Therefore he who builds on Him, builds in safety, if in accord with the dignity of the Foundation he builds in gold, silver, or precious stones. Should he not build in conformity with the dignity of this Foundation, but build in wood, hay, stubble; then let him at least hold fast to this Foundation, and, because of what he has heaped upon It, things withered and perishable, let him prepare himself for the fire. And if Christ is his Foundation, that is, if He holds the first place in his heart, let him so love the things of this world as not to put them before Christ; but let him put Christ the Lord before them, so that He remain the Foundation, that is, holding first place in the edifice of his heart: *He shall suffer loss*, he says; *but he himself shall be saved, yet so as by fire* (I Cor. iii. 15).

Now however is not the time to exhort you, that upon this so great and powerful Foundation you should build in gold, silver and precious stones rather than in wood, hay or stubble. Nevertheless, receive as said to you at length, and in many words, that which I have said to you in a few. For we know, brethren, that if one of you should be sent to prison by the sentence of some judge, because of things he now loves, to suffer smoke only, he would prefer to lose all he had than to suffer that place. I know not how it is that when we speak of the fire of the day of judgement, all are indifferent: while fearful of the fire upon the hearth, they hold as nothing the flames of Gehenna. What is the reason of this obduracy; the cause of such perversity of heart? For if men at least feared that ordeal of which the Apostle speaks, *by fire*,

as each one now living dreads fire, which can seize him in a moment, until, feeling at an end, makes all such flames idle; he would continue to fear, and would not do that which justice forbids, lest this torment touch him, even for a single moment.

10. *We are to hope for such a resurrection as that which preceded us in Christ. The angels visiting Abraham truly ate.*

But, as I have said, brethren, this is no time now to treat of this. But this I affirm: We must hope for that in the resurrection of the dead, which has been revealed to us in our Head, which has been revealed to us in the Body of Christ Jesus our Lord. Whoever hopes for something other than this, is not building upon our Foundation, either gold or silver or precious stones, and not even stubble. All that he builds has no foundation; because he does not build on Christ.

Our Lord then, as I said to you, rose in that Body in which He was buried. To Christians He promises resurrection. Let us hope for such a resurrection as that which in our Lord preceded all our faith. For this He went before us, that our faith might be built up. What follows? Shall we not also rise as we now are? For the flesh of our Lord Jesus Christ rose from the dead; and It ascended into heaven? On earth it fulfilled its human offices, to convince us that That had risen which was buried.

Is there in heaven also food such as ours? For we read that Angels fulfilled human tasks on earth. They came to Abraham, and they ate; and an angel went with Tobias, and he ate. Must we say this eating was an illusion, and not real? Is it not evident that Abraham killed a calf, and made cakes, and set food before them; that he waited on the angels, and they ate (Gen. xviii. 1–9)? All these things very plainly took place and are very plainly recorded.

11. *Man eats of necessity; an Angel through power.*

What did the angel say in the book of Tobias? *You saw me eat*, he says, *but you were seeing with your sight* (xii. 19). Did he then not eat, but only seem to eat? He did indeed eat. What then does he mean by *you were seeing with your sight*? Let Your Sanctity carefully apply your mind to what I am saying. Let you apply it more to prayer, than to me; that you may understand what we say to you, and also that we may say to you that which it is fitting you should hear from us, and hearing it, understand.

Our body, as long as it is corruptible and destined to die, has need of refreshment, and from this need suffers hunger: and so we hunger and we thirst. And if we prolong our hunger and thirst beyond what the body can endure, this leads to the wasting away of the body's strength, and to a certain unwholesome thinness; our strength going from us and not returning: and if this continues, death will then follow. For there is an unceasing flow of something from the body, as from a stream that drains. But we do not feel the strength leaving us, by reason of the strength that comes again through refreshment. But what enters the body abundantly, little by little leaves it again; and so in a little while we need to be re-

newed; our strength however, leaving us more slowly, than we renew it by taking food.

As oil in a lamp, quickly poured in, is more slowly consumed. And when, near spent, the flickering of its tiny flame warns us as it were that it is hungry; and we hasten to supply its need, and its brightness is renewed, and the lamp stays burning; refreshed by its food when we add new oil. So is it with our strength, which we receive through eating; it comes and goes in an unceasing but gradual dissolution. And this is going on even now; and in all our actions, even in our resting, the strength we receive never ceases to leave us. And should it be utterly spent, a man will die as a lamp flickers out. But that he may not die, that is, that he may not be extinguished: not that he dies in his spirit, but that this bodily life of ours may not be extinguished: there follows a certain as it were awakening in the body, and we hasten to replace what has left us, and so we are said to refreshen ourselves. One who speaks of refreshing himself, what does he renew, if not what has been lost? It is through this need and through this failing we shall moreover all die; because such is the nature of this body, that the death it owes is reserved for it. The skins with which Adam and Eve clothed themselves, when they were cast out of paradise, are a figure of this mortality (Gen. iii. 21–24). For skins, which men strip from dead beasts, are a symbol of death.

Therefore since we bear about with us this failing infirmity; to which though food is never wanting, to restore its powers, it will yet not secure it against the coming of death (for our whole bodily state, through its successive ages, even should it live long, will come in time to the bounds of old age, and beyond that it finds nothing stretching out before it save death. For even the lamp, though ever renewed with oil, cannot burn for ever; for should it not go out for other reasons, the wick will fail, dying as it were of old age). As long therefore as we bear about bodies such as these, we shall fail from weakness, we shall hunger from bodily need, we shall eat because of hunger. An Angel however does not eat from necessity. To do a thing from power is one thing; to do it from necessity another. Man eats, that he may not die. An Angel eats, to be in harmony with mortals. For if an Angel has no fear of death, he does not renew himself out of weakness. If he does not renew himself out of weakness, he does not eat from necessity. They who saw the Angel eating, thought he ate because he was hungry. This is the meaning of the words: *You were seeing with your sight.* The Angel did not say: 'You saw me eating; but I did not eat.' He said: *You saw me eat: but you were seeing with your sight;* that is, 'I was eating, to be in harmony with you; not because I suffered any hunger or need; driven by which you are wont to eat. And so those you saw eating, you who judge others by what you see, thought they were doing this out of need.' This is the meaning of: *You were seeing with your sight.*

12. *The power to eat will remain after the resurrection, as it did with Christ; but not the need.*

What then follows, my brethren? *We know,* as the Apostle says, *that Christ, rising again from the dead, dieth now no more. Death shall no more have dominion over him. For in that he died to sin, he dieth once; but in that he liveth, he liveth unto God* (Rom. vi. 9, 10). If He therefore dieth now no more, and if death shall no more have dominion over him; let us hope that we shall rise like Him, so that we may ever be in that state, into which by rising again we shall be changed. The power to eat and to drink shall remain, but not the need. This then was the reason why the Lord did this; because they were still in the flesh with whom He desired to be in harmony, to whom also He willed to show His wounds. For He who gave eyes to the blind man, who had not received them in his mother's womb, could have risen from the dead without the traces of His wounds. He Who had He wished before death to change the mortal weakness of His own Body, so that it should suffer no necessity, could well have done so: for it was within His power, since He was God in the Flesh, and the Omnipotent Son, as the Father was Omnipotent. For even before His death He changed His Body as He willed. When He was on the mountain with His Disciples, His face shone as the sun (Mt. xvii. 2). This He did of His own power; willing to show them that He could change His Body, making it free of all necessity, so that should He will it, It would not die.

I have power, He says, *to lay down my life; and I have power to take it up again. No man taketh it away from me.* Great was this power, by which He could also *not* die; but greater His mercy, because of which He willed to die. He went towards this through mercy, which He could, because of His power, not suffer; that He might lay down the foundation of our resurrection: so that that mortal body, which He bore for us, might die, because we shall die; and rise again to immortality, that we might hope for immortality. And so it was written of Him, that before His death He not only ate and drank, but also hungered and thirsted; but that after His resurrection only that He ate and drank, not that He hungered and thirsted. For in the Body that would now die no more, there was not that former need that arose from our continuous decay, so that it had need to be renewed; but the power to eat remained. And this He did to conform to us; not to make good the needs of the flesh, but to convince us of the truth of the Resurrection.

13. *The question: how flesh and blood cannot possess the Kingdom of God.* Against such a weight of evidence, there are some who raise an objection from the words of the Apostle. Listen to what they say against these considerations. 'Flesh,' they say, 'shall not rise again. For if it rose again, it would possess the kingdom of God. But the Apostle tells us clearly, *that flesh and blood shall not possess the Kingdom of God.*' You heard these words while the Apostle was being read. We say that flesh rises from the dead; while the Apostle cries out: *flesh and blood cannot possess the kingdom of God.* Therefore, either we are preaching against the Apostle, or, he himself has preached against the Gospel?

The Gospel testifies with divine voice, that *The word was made flesh, and dwelt among us* (Jn. i. 4). If the Word was made flesh, it was made true flesh. For it it was not true flesh, neither was it flesh. As the flesh of Mary was true flesh, Christ's flesh, which was received from hers, was true flesh. This true flesh was seized, scourged, beaten, hung on high. This true flesh died, this true flesh was buried. This true flesh also rose from the dead. The wounds bear witness: the eyes of the Disciples see them; astonished, they hesitate; the hand feels, that the spirit may not doubt. Against such evidence, brethren, by which our Lord Jesus Christ willed in this way to convince His Disciples, who were to preach it throughout the whole world; against this evidence the Apostle seems to fight by saying: *That flesh and blood cannot possess the kingdom of God?*

14. *The question answered. First exposition of the Apostle.*

We may answer the question in this way, and so confound our vain calumniators. As I say, in order to answer it, we shall consider how it can be promptly answered, and also very carefully, what the Apostle says, and how he came to say it. I shall tell you therefore how we may very readily answer this objection. What deos the Gospel say? That Christ rose in that Body in which He was buried: because He was seen, because He was touched, because He said to His Disciples who thought He was a ghost: *Handle and see; for a spirit hath not flesh and bones, as you see me to have* (Lk. xxiv. 39). And what does the Apostle say to this? *Flesh and blood,* he says, *shall not possess the kingdom of God.* I embrace both sayings, and I declare that they do not contradict one another; and that I myself do not fight against the goad! How do I embrace both? I can, as I said, answer this at once, in this way. The Apostle said, *flesh and blood cannot inherit the kingdom of God*. And what he says it true: for it is not in the nature of flesh to possess, but to be possessed. For it is not your body possesses anything, it is your soul, by means of your body; and the soul also possesses the body. If therefore the flesh so rises, to be had, not to have; so that it is possessed, not to possess; what wonder then that flesh and blood shall not possess the kingdom of God, seeing that it shall itself be possessed? For the flesh shall possess those who are not the kingdom of God, but the kingdom of the devil; and subject therefore to the desires of the flesh. For this reason the paralytic was carried on a bed; but when he was healed, the Lord said to him: *Take up thy bed, and go into thy house* (Mk. ii. 11). So when he was healed of the paralysis, he takes possession of his own flesh, and leads it whither he would: not drawn by the flesh whither he would not: and he bears his own body, rather than is borne by it.

It is manifest, that in this resurrection the flesh shall not suffer the drag of allurements, leading the soul through certain excitements and blandishments whither it would not; and where it is frequently overcome, saying: *I see another law in my members, fighting against the law of my mind and captivating me in the law of sin that is in my members*. The paralytic is still carried on his bed; he does not yet carry it. Therefore he cries out: *Unhappy man that I am, who shall deliver me from the body of this death?* Answer! *The grace of God, by Jesus Christ our Lord* (Rom. vii. 23–25).

When we therefore have risen, the flesh shall not carry us, but we shall carry the flesh. If we shall carry it, we shall possess it. If we possess it, we shall not be possessed by it; because, delivered from the devil, we are the kingdom of God: And so flesh and blood shall not possess the kingdom of God. Therefore, let these detractors be silent, who are indeed flesh and blood, and can reason only in a fleshly manner. And so it can truly be said of these who still cling to that *prudence of the flesh*, because of which they are rightly called *flesh and blood*, that: *Flesh and blood shall not possess the kingdom of God*.

The question may also be solved in this way: That such men, who are *called flesh and blood* (for of such as these the Apostle says also: *For our wrestling is not against flesh and blood* (Eph. vi. 12), if they do not turn to the spiritual life, and by the spirit mortify the deeds of the flesh, it will be impossible for them to possess the kingdom of God. (Rom. viii. 13).

15. *Truer understanding of the Apostle*. But what is the Apostle saying, someone will ask? Here is his real meaning: revealed by the context of the passage. So let us hear this, and let us see from the whole context of Scripture what he means in this place. This is what he says: *The first man was, of the earth, earthly; the second man, from heaven, heavenly. Such as is the earthly, such also are the earthly; and such as is the heavenly, such also are they that are heavenly. Therefore, as we have borne the image of the earthly, let us hear also the image of the heavenly. Now this I say, brethren, that flesh and blood cannot possess the kingdom of God; neither shall cor-*

ruption possess in-corruption (I Cor.
xv. 47–50).

Let us then consider each phrase
separately. *The first man was,* he says,
*of the earth, earthly; the second, from
heaven, heavenly.* As is *the earthly man,
such also are earthly men;* that is, all
shall die; *And such as is the heavenly
man is, such also are they that are
heavenly:* that is, they shall all rise
again. For *the heavenly man* has
already risen, and ascended into
heaven: to Whom we are now
joined by faith into one Body, so
that He is our Head. The members
in due order shall follow their Head;
and what was shown beforehand in
the Head, shall in due time be repeated in the members. Let us now
bear this Body by faith, that we may
in His time come to the true Reality
and Vision. For so he says in another
place: *Therefore, if you be risen with
Christ, seek the things that are above,
where Christ is sitting at the right hand
of God. Mind the things that are above,
not the things that are upon the earth*
(Col. iii. 1, 2). And although we
have not yet risen in ourselves, as
Christ rose in His Body, we are
nevertheless said to have risen with
Christ through faith. And so he
bids us, in this present life, bear by
faith *the image of the heavenly man;*
that is, His image Who is now in
heaven.

16. *Christ as man from heaven,
heavenly.* If any one seeks to know
why he says the second man is not
in heaven (*in coelo*), but *from heaven*
(*de coelo*), since the Lord also received
His Body from the earth, because
Mary was descended from Adam
and Eve; let him understand that the
earthly man is so called because of
earthly concupiscence. And while

this desire is earthly, by which men
are born of male and female, from
their parents also acquiring original
sin; the Body of the Lord was
created from the virginal womb
without any such desire, though
Christ received His flesh from the
earth; as the Holy Spirit is understood to signify by saying: *Truth is
sprung out of the earth* (Ps. lxxxiv. 12).
Nevertheless He is said to be, not an
earthly man, but a heavenly man,
and *from heaven.* For if He had given
this, through grace, to us His faithful, that, as the Apostle rightly says,
Our conversation is in heaven (Phil.
iii. 20); how much more should He
not be called a *heavenly* man, and
from heaven, in Whom there was
never any sin?

Because of sin was it said to man:
*Dust thou art, and into dust thou shalt
return* (Gen. iii. 19). Rightly therefore is this *heavenly man,* Whose
conversation never departs from
heaven, said to be *from heaven;* although Son of God, made also Son
of man, He took from the earth a
body, that is, *the form of a servant.* For
He did not ascend unless He descended. For though others, to
whom He has given the grace,
ascend, or rather they are lifted up
to heaven by His grace, yet it is He
Who ascends: because they become
His Body. In this way One only
ascends: since the Apostle explains
that there is a *great sacrament, in
Christ and in the Church;* of which it
is written: *And they shall be two in one
flesh* (Eph. v. 31). And of this the
Lord also said: *Therefore, now they
are not two, but one flesh* (Mt. xix.
6). This is the reason therefore why
no man *ascendeth into heaven, but he
that descended from heaven: The Son
of man who is in heaven* (Jn. iii.13).

He added, *who is in heaven*, that no one may think that His conversation or way of life ever departed from heaven when He appeared among men on earth through an earthly body.

And so, *as we have borne the image of the earthly, let us also bear his image who is from heaven;* now by faith, through which we shall also rise with Him; and that we may have our heart above where Christ is; sitting at the right hand of God. And so let us seek for, let us mind *the things that are above; not the things that are upon the earth* (Col. iii. 1, 2).

17. *That shall be given us in the resurrection, which has taken place in Christ. Flesh and blood signify corruption.*

But since he was speaking of the resurrection of the body; for he had brought it forward in this way: *But some man will say: How do the dead rise again? With what manner of body shall they come;* and because of this had said: *The first man was of the earth, earthly; the second, from heaven, heavenly. As was the earthly man; such also are the earthly.* As is the heavenly, such also are they that are heavenly: that we may await in our body that which has preceded us in the Body of Christ. And because we have not yet seen the reality; let us meanwhile hold to it by faith.

It is because of this he added: *As we have borne the image of the earthly; let us bear also the image of the heavenly.* And lest we believe we shall rise to such works as we did through the nature of the first man, he at once adds: *Now this I say, brethren: that flesh and blood cannot possess the kingdom of God.* And to show what *flesh and blood* means, he

indicates that by the words *flesh and blood* he does not refer to the visible body, but to its corruption: which shall not then be.

For body without corruption is not rightly called *flesh and blood*, but body. For if it is flesh, it is corruptible and mortal. But if it now dies no more, it is no longer corruptible; and therefore, though the appearance remains the same, without corruption it is now called, not *flesh*, but a body. And if it is called flesh, it is not called so correctly, but because of a certain outward resemblance. Just as we could perhaps, because of this same resemblance, also speak of the Angels as *flesh*; since they have appeared as men to men: for though body, they were not *flesh*; for want, the root of corruption, was not in them.

Because we may, figuratively, speak of a body which is no longer corruptible as *flesh*, the Apostle, anxious to explain what he called *flesh and blood*, goes on to say, that he had in mind, not the visible nature, but corruption; and at once adds: *Neither shall corruption possess incorruption*; as though he said: When I said, *that flesh and blood cannot possess the kingdom of God*, I said it because *corruption shall not possess incorruption:*

18. *In what manner shall our body be in heaven, if corruption shall not be there. The works of the flesh will not be the same after the resurrection. Error of the Jews and the Sadducees concerning the resurrection. Resurrection to the life of the Angels.*

And lest anyone should say, 'If therefore incorruption cannot be possessed by corruption, how can our body be there?' Listen to what follows. It is as though someone said to the Apostle: 'What then are you saying; have we believed in the resurrection of the body in vain? If flesh and blood shall not possess the kingdom of God, have we believed in vain that our Lord rose from the dead in the Body in which He was born and crucified, and that in it He ascended into heaven in the presence of His Disciples, and that from this same heaven He cried out to you (Paul), *Saul, Saul, why persecutest thou me?*' This thought was in the mind of Paul, the holy and blessed Apostle, as he brought forth in pious love his children *begotten in Christ, by the gospel* (I Cor. iv. 15), of whom he is still in labour *until Christ be formed in them* (Gal. iv. 19), that is, until they bear His image Who is *from heaven*. For he did not wish them to remain in that state of ruin, that they should believe that in the kingdom of God, in that life eternal, they will do the things they did in this life, eating and drinking in delight, marrying and giving in marriage, and carnally begetting children. It is the corruption of the flesh does these works, not the visible flesh itself. Because of this, as I said a little while ago, the Lord had already declared beforehand, in the Gospel lesson just now read to you (Mt. xxii. 23, etc.), that it was not to do such works as these that shall we rise again. For the Jews also believed in the resurrection of the flesh, but they thought that the future life would be the same as they lived in this world. And thinking in this carnal fashion, they could not answer the Sadducees when they asked the question, relating to the resurrection: whose wife the woman shall be who had married successively seven

brothers, each of whom wished, from his wife, to raise up issue to his brother. For the Sadducees were a certain sect among the Jews who said there was no resurrection. The Jews, uncertain and hesitant, could not answer the Sadducees as they propounded the question; because they themselves believed the kingdom of God could be possessed by flesh and blood; that is, that incorruption could be possessed by corruption.

The Truth came. He is questioned by the deceived and deceiving Sadducees. The question is put to the Lord. And the Lord, Who knew what He would say, and wished us to believe what we did not know, with the authority of His Majesty answers that which we now believe. The Apostle on the other hand sets forth that which was given to him; which, as best we can, let us seek to understand. What then does the Lord say to the Sadducees? *You err,* He says, *not knowing the Scriptures, nor the power of God. For in the resurrection they shall neither marry, nor be married; but shall be as the Angels of God in heaven* (Mt. xxii. 30).

Great is the power of God. Why do they not marry, nor be married? Because they do not begin to die. For there is a successor, where there was a predecessor. In heaven therefore, there shall be no such corruption. Even the Lord passed through the years from infancy to young manhood, because He bore in Himself the substance of our mortal flesh. Afterwards He rose in the age in which He was buried. Are we to believe He now grows old in heaven? Therefore, He says: *They shall be as the angels of God.* He corrects the false opinions of the Jews, and refutes the fabrications of the Sadducees: for the Jews believed the dead would indeed rise again, but as to the works they would rise to, they believed in an earthly fashion. *They shall be*, He says, *as the angels of God.*

You heard Him speak of the power of God. Hear Him also speak of the Scriptures. *And concerning the resurrection of the dead*, He says, *have you not read that which the Lord spoke to Moses from the bush*, saying: *I am the God of Abraham and the God of Isaac and the God of Jacob? He is not the God of the dead but of the living* (Mt. xxii. 23-32; Lk. xx. 27-38).

19. *Resurrection to a life without corruption. Change of the flesh of the good for the better.* We are told then that we shall rise again. And we have heard from the Lord, that we shall rise to the life of the angels. In what visible form we shall rise, He has shown us in His own Resurrection. That this form shall not possess corruption, the Apostle tells us. *This I say, brethren, that flesh and blood cannot possess the kingdom of God; neither shall corruption possess incorruption:* to show us that by the words, *flesh and blood,* he wished us to understand the corruption of the mortal and animal body. Then he himself solves the question which anxious enquirers might ask of him: for he is more concerned that his children understand, than children are to understand their parents. He therefore continues and adds: *Behold, I tell you in a mystery.*

Let your mind be at peace, O man, whoever you are. For you had begun to think, reflecting on the words of the Apostle, that human flesh shall not rise again, when you heard him say: *flesh and blood shall not possess the kingdom of God.* But give ears to the words which then follow, and correct the presumption of your thought. *Behold,* he says, *I tell you a mystery: We shall all indeed rise again; but we shall not all be changed.* What does this mean? Changed for the worse, or changed for the better? If then change has been decreed, yet so that we do not yet see what it will be; into something better, or something worse; let us follow him, and let him explain: what we are to look for? And it may be that his apostolic authority will not suffer error to enter into your reflections because of human presumption; and he will explain clearly what he wishes us to understand by this change.

What then did he mean when he said: *We shall all indeed rise again; but we shall not all be changed?* I know that all shall rise again, both good and bad; but let us see who shall be changed; and let us try to understand this *change*; whether it will be for the better, or for worse. For if the wicked change, it will be for the worse; if the good, it will be for the better. *In a moment,* he says, *in the twinkling of an eye, at the last trumpet; for the trumpet shall sound and the dead shall rise again incorruptible; and we shall be changed.* Therefore this change will be for the better, since he says, *we* shall be changed. But he has not yet described to us, as it needs to be described, how far our body shall be changed for the better? And what this *better* is has not yet been explained. For change from infancy to adolescence could be said to be change for the better; where, though the body is now less weak, it is still weak, and mortal.

20. *The speed of the resurrection.*
What is a moment? A moment in the
body. A moment in time. Twinkling of
an eye?

Let us therefore carefully recon-
sider each single phrase. *In a moment,*
he says. It seems to men a difficult
thing that the dead should rise again.
But it is wonderful to see how the
Apostle takes away all doubts and
difficulties from the hearts of the
faithful. You say: The dead shall not
rise again. I say: Not only shall a
man who has died rise again, but
he shall rise with such swiftness as
he was not conceived and born in.
How long it took for a man to be
formed in the womb, to be brought
to completeness, to be born, to grow
in strength through the years? Is this
how he is to rise again? No: but *in a*
moment, he says. Many do not know
what a *moment* is. A *moment (atomus)*
is from a Greek word, τομή, which
means a section; ἄτομος, therefore,
meaning what cannot be divided.
We speak of an atom in substance, of
an atom in time. In substance it
means that which, if it can be found,
cannot be further divided; a body so
minute, that it is no longer capable
of division. An atom (moment) in
time is brief; so brief that it cannot
be further subdivided. For example:
that slower minds may grasp what I
am saying, let us consider a stone.
Divide it into parts, and the parts
into smaller parts; the smaller parts
into grains, like sand, and again
divide the grains of sand into minute
dust, until you come, if possible, to
a certain minuteness that cannot be
divided. This is an atom in matter.
In time it can be understood in this
way. A year, for example, is divided
into months, months into days, days
into hours, hours into certain lesser

parts which however still admit of
divisions, until you come to a point
of time, to a drop of motion, that
can be no shorter, and so cannot be
divided. This is an atom of time.

You were saying the dead do not
rise again. Not only do they rise, but
they rise with such swiftness, that the
resurrection of all the dead shall take
place in an atom of time. And Paul,
putting before you the swiftness of
an atom of time, saying: *in a*
moment (in atomo), straightway adds
an example of how much of motion
and activity is possible in an atom of
time, saying: *in the twinkling of an*
eye. For he knew he spoke obscurely,
speaking of an atom of time, and
sought to put it more plainly, to
make it more easily understood.

What is a *twinkling of an eye?* It is
not the time in which we open or
shut an eyelid. By *the twinkling of an*
eye, he means the sending forth of
the rays of an eye to perceive something. For as soon as you throw a
glance in some direction, its beam
will flash even to the heavens, where
we behold the sun and moon and
stars and constellations, though so
far remote from earth. The final
sign, he says, is *the last trumpet. For*
the trumpet, he says, *shall sound, and*
the dead shall rise again incorrupt; and
we shall all be changed. He means all
we faithful, and our fathers before
us, as they rise to eternal life. This
change therefore since it shall take
place in the God-fearing and holy,
shall be for the better, and not for
the worse.

21. *The nature of the change in the*
blessed? Flesh and blood, in their
proper sense, the names of corruption
and mortality.

But what is this change? What

does he mean when he says: *and we shall be changed?* Shall we shed our present visible form, or only that corruption, because of which he said: *Flesh and blood cannot possess the Kingdom of God; nor shall corruption possess incorruption?* But lest he should drive his hearers to despair of the resurrection of the body; he adds *Behold, I tell you a mystery: We shall all indeed rise again; but we shall not all be changed.* And, lest we think this change shall be for the worse, he says: *and we shall be changed.* So there remains now for him to tell us what the nature of this change shall be?

This corruptible, he says, *must put on incorruption; and this mortal must put on immortality.* If this corruptible body puts on incorruption, and if this mortal body is clothed in immortality, it shall then be no longer corruptible flesh. If it is no longer corruptible flesh, then the name of *corruption* shall cease to apply to flesh and blood; and even the very name, *flesh and blood*: for these are the appellations of mortality.

And if this is so; and if flesh shall rise again, and being changed becomes incorrupt, then *flesh and blood shall not possess the kingdom of God.* But should someone be inclined to understand that this *change* shall take place in those who are found living on that day; so that those who were already dead shall rise, but that those who are still living shall be changed, and that the Apostle is believed to have spoken in their name, when he said: *And WE shall be changed:* the same result will follow; because this incorruption shall in any case extend to all, *when this corruptible has put on incorruption, and this mortal has put on immortality, then shall come to*

pass the saying that is written: *Death is swallowed up in victory. O Death, where is thy victory? O Death, where is thy sting?*

But the body that is no longer mortal is not accurately spoken of as *flesh and blood*; such as earthly bodies are, but is called a *body* (*corpus*), and can now be called a *heavenly body.* As the same Apostle said when speaking of the diversities of flesh: *All flesh is not the same flesh; but, one is the flesh of men, another of beasts, another of birds, another of fishes. And there are bodies celestial,* he says, *and bodies terrestrial* (I Cor. xv. 39, 40). But in no way does he speak of celestial flesh; though flesh can be used of bodies, but only of terrestrial bodies. For all flesh is a body: but not every body is flesh. For not only is a heavenly body not called flesh, but neither are certain terrestrial bodies, such as wood and stone and other such things. And so flesh and blood cannot therefore possess the kingdom of God: for flesh rising from the dead shall be changed into a body in which there shall no more be mortal corruption, and for this reason the name *flesh and blood* shall no more belong to it.

22. *The error of some concerning the truth of the resurrection.*

Now give your minds to this, brethren; we beg you. This is not to be taken lightly; here we are speaking of the substance of our faith. We must therefore be on our guard, not so much against non-Christians as against certain perverse people who want to be called and to be considered Christians. There were such persons even in the times of the Apostles; who began to say that the resurrection was now over and done with, upsetting the faith of some. These were persons *who,* says the Apostle, *have erred concerning the truth saying that the resurrection is past already; and have subverted the faith of some* (II Tim. ii. 18).

It was not without purpose that he did not say; '*They have erred* from the truth'; but *concerning the truth.* Nevertheless, they did not hold the truth.[25] Death therefore is taken away, and shall be no more in any form; as the Apostle says: *That which is mortal shall be swallowed up by life* (II Cor. v. 4). And of the Lord it was said, that He swallowed down death (I Pet. iii. 22). For death does not as it were depart, as though possessing its own substance. It ceases to be, in the body where it was; so that you may see the bodily form, possess its visible form, and seek in it the corruption and mortality of death, and not find it.

Did corruption then depart elsewhere? No: but where it is made an end of, there it is swallowed up. And so when Paul had said: *This corruptible must put on incorruption, and this mortal put on immortality; then shall come to pass,* he says, *the saying that was written: Death is swallowed up in victory. O Death, where is thy victory? O Death where is thy sting?* He does not say: Death has departed because of the victory; but *Death is swallowed up in victory.* How then did these persons err concerning the truth? By affirming that the one resurrection was true, while denying the other.

23. *Resurrection twofold: in the spirit and in the body. In what form shall the bodies of the wicked rise?*

There is a resurrection which follows faith, in which everyone who believes rises in the spirit. And he certainly shall rise in the body, who has first risen in the spirit. For they who have not risen before through faith, shall not rise to that change in the body, where all corruption is taken up and swallowed, but shall rise again to its former baneful wholeness. For the bodies of the impious shall be unchanged; nothing shall appear to be taken from them. But their integrity of body shall be for a punishment; and this sort of consistency, if I may call it so, is a corruptible consistency. For where pain can be, corruption cannot be said not to be: and our former liability to pain shall not cease, that pain itself shall not die. For we believe that this corruption was referred to prophetically, by the term *worm,* and pain, by the word *fire.* But since this consistency shall be such, that it shall neither yield to death through pain, nor be changed to that incorruption in which there is no pain; for this reason was it written: *Their worm shall not die, and their fire shall not be quenched* (Is. lxvi. 24; Mk. ix. 43, 45).

The change which shall possess no corruption shall be that of the saints. Theirs shall be the change they now experience who rise in the spirit through faith; of which resurrection the Apostle says: *If you be risen with Christ, seek the things that are above, where Christ is sitting at the right hand of God. Mind the things that are above, not the things that are upon the earth. For you are dead; and your life is hid with Christ in God* (Col. iii. 1-3).

As we die in the spirit, and rise in the spirit; so afterwards we shall die in the body, and rise again in the body. To die in the spirit is: Not to believe the vain things we once believed, not to do the evil we once did. To rise again according to the spirit is to believe the salutary things we used not to believe, and do the good works we used not to do. He who believed that earthly idols and images were gods, and has learned of the One God and has believed in Him; has died to idolatry, and risen to the Christian Faith. He who was a drunkard, and is now sober; has died to drunkenness, and risen to sobriety. So when we withdraw ourselves from all evil doing, a sort of death takes place in the soul, and in doing good works it rises again. *Mortify your members*, says the Apostle, *which are upon the earth; uncleanness, lust, evil concupiscence and covetousness*, he says, *which is the service of idols* (Col. iii. 5). When therefore we have mortified these our members, we shall rise again in the good works that are contrary to our former works: in holiness, in tranquillity, in charity, in almsdeeds. As death according to the spirit precedes resurrection in the spirit, so death in the body shall precede the resurrection of the body.

24. *Testimony from the Apostle concerning the twofold resurrection.*

We have learned therefore of both spiritual and corporal resurrection. To spiritual resurrection refer the words of Scripture which say: *Rise, thou that sleepest; and arise from the dead* (Eph. v. 14); and those words of Isaias: *They who sat in darkness, for them a great light has risen* (ix. 2); also the sentence I quoted a little while ago: *If you be risen with Christ, seek the things that are above.* To corporal resurrection belongs that which the Apostle here says: proposing the question to himself: *But some man will say: How do the dead rise again? Or with what manner of body shall they come?* He is speaking therefore of the resurrection of the body, in which the Lord preceded His Church. And of this resurrection he then goes on to say: *This corruptible must put on incorruption, and this mortal must put on immortality.* And this he said because of the words he had just uttered: *Flesh and blood shall not possess the Kingdom of God.*

We have in yet another place a most explicit testimony of this same Apostle Paul concerning both resurrection in the spirit and resurrection in the flesh. For a mortal body that is or was living, is called flesh. And so the Apostle says: *If Christ be in you, the body indeed is dead, because of sin; but the spirit liveth, because of justification* (Rom. viii. 10). Here we understand that the resurrection of the spirit has taken place through justice. Consider then if we should not also hope for the resurrection of the body. For he did not wish to speak of a mortal body as *mortal*, but as *dead*. At the same time he reveals to us what he meant by this in the words that follow. For he goes on to say: *And, if the spirit of him that raised up Jesus from the dead dwell in you; he that raised up Jesus Christ from the dead shall quicken also your mortal bodies.* So, therefore, *They erred concerning the truth*, who denied one resurrection. For had they denied all resurrection, they would have strayed *from* the truth; not *erred concerning the truth*. Because they *erred concerning the truth*, they confessed one resurrection, in the spirit; but denied the other, that which we hope for in the resurrection of the body: *Saying that the resurrection is past already* (II Tim.

ii. 18). For unless they had said so, to keep the people from believing and hoping in the resurrection of the body, he would not have said of them that, *they have subverted the faith of some.*

25. Both resurrections in the Gospel. Resurrection in the spirit that takes place now by faith.

Now let us listen to the manifest testimony of the Lord Himself, contained in the Gospel according to John, which in the one place reveals to us so clearly both resurrections: that which now takes place in the spirit, and that which, after this life, shall take place in the flesh; so that whosoever is subject to the authority of the Gospel, and calls himself a Christian can in no way doubt it. So there is no way left to deceivers, and to those who would subvert Christians, even by their Christian Faith, to thrust in their poison, to destroy the souls of the weak. Now let us listen to what we shall read to you from this book (John). For today I shall fulfil the office, not only of preacher, but also of reader, so that our discourse to you may rest upon the authority of the Sacred Scriptures; and not be built upon the sands of human notions. Listen therefore to the Gospel according to John. The Lord says:

Amen, amen, I say unto you that he who heareth my word and believeth him that sent me hath life everlasting and cometh not into judgement, but is passed from death to life. Amen, amen, I say unto you, that the hour cometh, and now is, when the dead shall hear the voice of the Son of God; and they that hear shall live. For as the Father has life in himself, so he hath given to the Son also to have life in himself. And he hath given him power to do judgement, because he is the Son of man. Wonder not at this; for the hour cometh, wherein all that are in the graves shall hear the voice of the Son of God. And they that have done good things shall come forth unto the resurrection of life; but they that have done evil, unto the resurrection of judgement (Jn. v. 24–29).

I think that many will understand that in this place either resurrection, that according to the spirit, through faith, and that according to the flesh, are clearly and distinctly proclaimed by our Lord Himself by means of this trumpet; so well known to us all. Nevertheless, let us consider these words very carefully, so that they may become plain to all who listen.

Amen, amen, I say unto you that he who heareth my words and believeth him that sent me hath life everlasting and cometh not unto judgement, but is passed from death to life. This is the resurrection of the spirit; which takes place now, through faith. But lest this appear to be stated as though it were still a long way off; though He does not say: 'He will pass from death to life'; but, *is passed from death to life*: nevertheless, so that He may not seem to have used the past tense figuratively as in the words: *They have pierced my hands and my feet* (Ps. xxi. 17), which were at the time a pronouncement of what was to come, He goes on to explain this more clearly.

Amen, amen, I say to you, that the hour cometh, and now is, when the dead shall hear the voice of the Son of God; and they that hear shall live. Where, in the former verse, He says: *He has passed from death to life*, He repeats this in the words: *They shall live.* And so that none shall think the words: *The hour cometh,* mean that this hour is to be expected at the end of the world, when the resurrection of the body shall also take place, He adds: *And now is.* He does not simply say: *The hour cometh;* but, *The hour cometh, and now is.*

They who shall hear this voice shall live; that is, they shall live of that life to which He refers in the preceding verse, saying: *he is passed from death to life.* He is therefore referring here to those who shall have no part in the chastisement of judgement; because they have anticipated the judgement by their faith, and have already passed from death to life.

26. Resurrection in the flesh to come.

There remains now for Him to tell us of the future examination of the good and the bad: for here He is speaking only of the present resurrection, in the spirit, of the good. He goes on to do this, and says: *And he hath given him power to do judgement, because he is the Son of man.* He here intimates why He received power to judge: *because,* He says, *he is the Son of man.* For as Son of God, He possesses, together with the Father, eternal power. Next He goes on to explain what will take place at the judgement to come: *Wonder not at this,* He says; *for the hour cometh, wherein all that are in the graves shall hear the voice of the Son of God. And they that have done good things, shall come forth unto the resurrection of life; but they that have done evil, unto the resurrection of judgement.*

Where He said above: *The hour cometh,* He had added; *and now is;* lest they think He was speaking of that promised hour at the end of the world in which the resurrection of bodies shall take place. Here however, since He wished to be understood as now speaking of that last hour, when He says, *the hour cometh,* He does not add, *and now is.* Again when He said above that the dead shall hear the voice of the Son of God, He made no mention of *graves;* that we might distinguish between those who are dead through sin, who now rise again through faith, and the dead whose bodies shall at the end of the world rise from the graves in which they now lie. And so He says, that we may await in hope that final resurrection of our bodies: *Wherein all that are in the graves shall hear the voice of the Son of God; and they shall come forth.*

Again, earlier, He said: *They shall hear the voice of the Son of God; and they that hear shall live.* What need was there to add: *They that hear,* since He could simply have said, 'They shall hear the voice of the Son of God, and they shall live'; unless He was speaking of those who were dead through the sin of their minds; they of whom many hear and do not hear; that is, do not heed what they hear, do not believe? They however who do hear, as He desired them to hear, when He said: *He that hath ears to hear let him hear* (Lk. viii. 8); they shall live. Therefore many shall hear, *and they that hear shall live;* they, that is, who have believed. For they who so listen, that they do not believe, they shall not live: and from this it is evident of what death and of what life He was here speaking: Of the death that touches the wicked only, because of their wickedness; of the life that is the portion of the good only, in that they are good.

But here, where He is foretelling
the resurrection of the body, He does
not say: 'They shall hear His voice,
and they that hear shall come forth.'
For *all* shall hear the last trumpet,
and *all* shall come forth; because we
shall *all* rise again. But because we
shall not all *be changed*, He goes on
to say: *They that have done good things
shall come forth unto the resurrection of
life; but they that have done evil, unto
the resurrection of judgement.* Where,
above, life is renewed in the spirit
through faith, all return to life to the
same lot: so that life for them is not
divided into blessedness and misery,
but is such that all may attain to the
better part. So when He said: *And
they that hear shall live*; He does not
add: 'And they that have done good
things shall come forth to eternal
life, and they who have done evil to
eternal judgement.' That He said:
They shall live, He means to be
understood in a good sense only;
just as when earlier He said; *He is
passed from death to life*, He did not
say to what life: for to return
through faith from death to life,
cannot be to an evil life.

Here however He did not say, as
in the beginning of the passage, 'they
shall hear, and live': for He did not
mean the words *they shall live* to be
understood in the good sense
throughout the whole passage; but
said: *They shall hear, and they shall
come forth*; and by this phrase He is
referring to their bodily motion as
they come forth from their places of
burial. But since to come forth from
their graves shall not be a blessing
for all; He said: *They that have done
good things, shall come forth unto the
resurrection of life*; here also He means
that life shall be understood in the
good sense; *but they that have done*

evil, He says, *unto the resurrection of
judgement*: the judgement, that is,
which He has decreed in expiation.

27. Body and life of the blessed?

Let no one now, brethren, seek
with perverted subtlety to discover
what shall be the shape of our bodies
in the resurrection of the dead, what
their height shall be, their movement, their walk. It is enough for
you to know that your body shall
rise again in that outward form in
which the Lord appeared; in the
visible form of man.

But do not, because of this outward appearance, be apprehensive of
corruption: For if you do not fear
corruption, neither shall you fear
the sentence, *Flesh and blood shall not
possess the Kingdom of God*; and
neither shall you fall into the trap of
the Sadducees, which you shall be
unable to escape if you think that
men shall rise again to marry, beget
children, and do the other things
that belong to mortal life.

If you seek to know what that
future life shall be, what man can
tell you? It shall be the life of the
Angels. Whoever can describe the
life of Angels, will be able to describe to you the life of the blessed;
for they shall be as the Angels. And
if the life of the Angels is hidden
from us, let no one seek further; for
fear he may, through deception,
find not that which he seeks to
know, but that which he has ima-
gined for himself. He wants to know
before due time, and he wants to
know at once. Walk you in the
way (Is. xxx. 21). You shall come
to your home; if you do not leave
the way. Hold fast then to Christ,
brethren; hold fast to the faith; hold
fast to the Way. It will lead you to

that which you cannot now see. For in Him Who is our Head has been revealed that which is to be hoped for in His members. We have been shown that it is upon this Foundation we must build the edifice of our faith, so that it may afterwards be crowned by vision; so that should some false vision appear before you, you may not think you see; as though what is not, seems to be, and, deserting the Way, you turn aside after error and never reach that Home to which the Way is leading you: that Vision to which Faith shall guide you.

28. *Life shall be that of the angels; without need, without corruption. Why there shall be no works of mercy there. Perpetual rest (sabbath).*

You will ask, How do the angels live? It is enough for you to know this: that they do not live a perishable life. But it is easier to tell you what shall not be there, than what shall be. Even I, my brethren, can tell you briefly certain things that shall not be there. And this we can do because we know these things from experience, and know what shall *not* have place there. What shall be there we have not yet learned: *For we walk by faith and not by sight: as long as we are in the body, we are absent from the Lord* (II Cor. v. 7, 6). What then shall not be there? Marrying, to beget children. For there shall be no death there; nor growing up, because no one grows old. There shall be no eating; for there shall be no hunger. There shall be no buying or selling, for there shall be no want; nor even the just dealings of blameless men, which the needs of this present life make necessary. And not only do I say

that the doings of thieves and money lenders shall have no place there, but not even the things just men must do because of human needs shall have place there.

The Sabbath (*day of rest*) shall be unbroken: what the Jews celebrate for a period of time, we shall celebrate for all eternity. There shall be ineffable rest; which cannot be described in words; explained in a manner, yes, as when we spoke of what shall not be there. We go forwards towards this rest; for this were we reborn in the spirit. For as we are born in the body to toil, we are reborn in the spirit to rest: He calling us Who said: *Come to me, all you that labour and are burdened; and I will refresh you.* Here He feeds us, there He perfects us; here He promises, there He shall give; here He foretells, there He shall show us the reality. And when we are safe and perfected, in spirit and in body, within that blessedness, the things of this world shall be no more; not even those shall be there which now are praised in the good works of Christians.

For who does not praise the Christian giving bread to the hungry, drink to the thirsty, clothing to the naked, sheltering the stranger, making peace between the quarrelsome, visiting the sick, burying the dead, consoling the afflicted? Great works; full of mercy, full of praise and grace! But not even these shall be there; for it is the needs of misery that bring about the works of mercy. Whom shall you feed where no one is hungry? To whom give drink where no one is thirsty? Can you clothe the naked where all have put on the garment of immortality? A while ago you learned of the garments of the saints, where the Apostle says: *This corruptible must put on incorruption.* When you hear of *putting on,* this implies a garment. This garment Adam lost, so that he clothed himself with skins. And how shall you shelter the stranger, where all dwell in their own home. Will you visit the sick where all flourish together in the enduring strength of incorruption? Will you bury the dead where all live forever? Will you make peace among contentious where all things are in peace? Will you console the afflicted where all rejoice for ever? Therefore, since all misery shall be at an end, these works of mercy shall also be no more.

29. *What shall the blessed do after resurrection. Amen, Alleluia.*

What then shall the blessed do there? Have I not said that it is easier for me to say what shall not be than what shall be there? But this I know, brethren, that we shall not sleep in idleness; for sleep itself is now given to us as refreshment for the weariness of the soul. For the fragile body cannot endure the unceasing striving that agitates our mortal senses, unless this fragility is renewed, through the sleep of the senses, to enable it to bear this same agitation. And as the renewal to come shall be from death, so is waking now from sleep. Therefore there shall be no sleep. For where there is no death, there shall be no image of death.

And do not let the dread of tedium creep into any man's mind, from this that he is told that he shall ever keep watch, and shall not need to do anything. How it shall be in the future, I can say and cannot say:

for I cannot yet see. But I shall say something, and not presumptuously, since I speak from the Scriptures, of what our future activity shall be. All our activity shall be, *Amen* and *Alleluia.* What do you say to this, brethren? I see that you hear me, and that you are glad. But do not on the other hand be saddened by thinking, in earthly fashion, that if one of you were to stand every day saying, Amen and Alleluia, he would soon wither away from sheer tedium, if he did not fall asleep from repetition, and long for silence; and from this go on to think of that life as unpleasing and undesirable, saying to yourselves: 'To sing *Amen* and *Alleluia* for ever? Who could endure it?' Let me therefore say, if I can, what I can.

We shall say Amen and Alleluia, not in sounds that come and go, but with the love of our soul. For what does *Amen* mean? And what does *Alleluia* mean? *Amen* means *be it so; alleluia, praise God.* Because God is unchangeable Truth, without increase or decrease, without loss, without gain, without taint of falsehood, forever unchanged, stable, remaining ever imperishable, the things we do in creation and in this life are as it were but figures of things, signifying by means of bodies; things in which we walk by faith. But when we shall see *face to face* that which we now *see through a glass in a dark manner* (I Cor. xiii. 12), then we shall say with a far other, an ineffably other love, *Be it so.* And when we say this we shall indeed say *Amen;* but from an inappeasable fulness. For since we shall want for nothing, there we shall possess all fulness. Since that shall never cease which ever more delights us, there shall be there, if I may say so, inappeasable fulness. The more inappeasably you are filled with truth, the more shall you cry out from inappeasable truth, *Amen.*

Who can say now what that is, *which eye hath not seen, nor ear heard, nor hath it entered into the heart of man* (I Cor. ii. 9)? Because we shall, without tedium and with delight unceasing, there see Truth, and contemplate it in shining clarity, and inflamed with the love of this Truth and clinging to It in sweet and chaste and incorporeal embrace, shall with like voice, praise It, and say *Alleluia.* Exhorting each other to the same praise, and with most ardent charity towards one another and towards God, all who are citizens of that City shall sing, *Alleluia*; as they shall say, *Amen.*

30. *Rest and reclining in the contemplation and praise of Truth.*

This life of the blessed shall so fill and immortally enliven their bodies also, now changed to a heavenly and angelic state, that no failing through human need shall ever turn them away, ever distract them from this most blessed praise and contemplation of Truth. So Truth Itself shall be their Food: their rest shall be to recline at table. For we were told, that those who recline at table with Him shall be feasted, as the Lord says: *Many shall come from the east and the west, and shall sit down with Abraham and Isaac and Jacob in the Kingdom of Heaven* (Mt. viii. 11). By this it was signified that in great peace shall they be feasted upon the food of Truth. This food renews and never fails; it fills, remaining undiminished. You are consumed; It is not consumed. Such is this Food; not

as that which perishes to renew others; that perishes that they who eat it may live. This place of feasting therefore shall be our everlasting rest; our feast shall be Truth unchangeable: our feasting, eternal life; that is, knowledge itself. *Now this,* says the Lord, *is eternal life: That they may know thee, the only true God, and Jesus Christ, whom thou hast sent* (Jn. xvii. 3).

31. *The life of those who supremely and with delight give themselves to the vision of God. Concluding prayer.*

That this life of contemplation of Truth shall endure, not alone ineffably, but also with delight, Scripture bears witness in many places; all of which we cannot here commemorate. From there come the words: *He that loveth me, keepeth my commandments; and I will love him, and will manifest myself to him.* When we keep His commandments, we may seek from Him both joy and reward. *I will manifest,* He says, *myself to him*: Laying up for us as perfect blessedness, that we shall know Him as He is. From there also come the words: *Dearly beloved, we are now the Sons of God; and it hath not yet appeared what we shall be. We know that when he shall appear we shall be like to him; because we shall see him as he is* (I Jn. iii. 2). And the Apostle Paul also tells us: *Then we shall see him face to face* (I Cor. xiii. 12). And again, in another place: *We are transformed into the same image from glory to glory, as by the spirit of the Lord* (II Cor. iii. 18). And in the Psalms we are told: *Be still, and see that I am God* (xlv. 2). He shall then be perfectly seen when we are wholly given to His contemplation. And when shall we wholly give ourselves to Him, save when the days of our weariness and toil are over, the days of wanting and of hungering, in which we are now held fast, as long as earth brings forth thorns and thistles to sinful man, so that only in the sweat of his brow can he eat his bread? When therefore the days of the *earthly man* are wholly at an end, and the day of the *heavenly man* has been made in all ways perfect, then shall we see God wholly, for we shall be wholly given over to His contemplation.

When corruption and want are ended in the resurrection of the faithful, there shall be nothing more to labour for. It shall be as though He says: 'Recline and eat.' It was thus He said: *Be still, and see.* We shall then *be still*, and we shall *see God* as He is; and seeing Him shall praise God. And this shall be the life

of the blessed; this shall be the activity of those who live in peace: that without ceasing we shall praise God. Not for a day, shall we praise Him; but as that day shall have no end, so shall our praise be without end; and so we shall praise Him throughout all ages and ages. Hear again the voice of Scripture, singing to God that which is all our desire: *Blessed are they that dwell in thy house, O Lord; they shall praise thee for ever and ever* (Ps. lxxxviii. 5).

Turning then to the Lord our God let us beseech Him both for ourselves and for all His people, who stand with us in the courts of His House, that He may deign to guard and protect us, through Jesus Christ His Son our Lord, Who with Him liveth and reigneth for ever and ever. Amen.

VI. St Augustine, Bishop and Doctor

The Pilgrimage of This Life[26]

1. That this life of ours, dearest brethren, is but a pilgrimage, an absence from the home of the saints, the heavenly Jerusalem, the Apostle Paul teaches us very plainly, where he says: *While we are in the body, we are absent from the Lord* (II Cor. v. 6). And since every pilgrim has his own country, for no one can be a pilgrim without a country, we should know which is our true country, whither, heedless of all the attractions and pleasures of this present life, we must hasten; towards which we are journeying, and where alone we may yield ourselves to rest. For God has willed that in no other place shall we find true rest, save in that distant

home: for should He give us rest here, and peace, there would be no joy in returning there.

And this home of ours He calls Jerusalem; meaning, not the earthly city, *which is in bondage with her children*, as the same Apostle has told us (Gal. iv. 26): For she was given, as a kind of shadow of the reality, to earthly men upon the earth, who though they worshipped the one God, looked to him for earthly happiness only. It is this other Jerusalem which, he says, is in heaven: *the Jerusalem which is above; which is our Mother.* He calls it a mother: as a metropolis: for a metropolis means a mother-city. It is to this city we must hasten; and we must know that we are pilgrims, and that we are on our way.

2. Any man who does not yet believe in Christ is not on the way. He is wandering astray. He too is seeking his fatherland. But he knows not which it is; nor where. What do I mean when I say he too is seeking his fatherland? Every soul seeks rest; every soul seeks happiness. No man asked if he desires happiness will hesitate to answer. Every man will cry out that he longs for happiness. But by what way he can arrive at happiness, and where he shall find happiness, this men do not know. And so they wander, straying. He never goes astray who goes nowhere. It is from going on, and not knowing where, that all error comes.

The Lord is calling us to the way. But even when we are numbered among the faithful, and believing in Christ, we have not yet arrived at our home. But we have begun to walk the way that leads there. How we should, mindful that we are ourselves Christians, exhort and encourage those who wander in vain superstition and false beliefs, all most dear to us, to come to the way, to walk in the way; as those already in the way should exhort and encourage one another! For no one reaches the heavenly Jerusalem save he who is in the way: though not every one who is in the way shall reach it. Yet they must be held as in greater danger who are not yet in the way. But they who are now in the way must not feel secure; lest held by the delights of the way, they be no longer drawn with such great love towards that heavenly home where alone true rest is found.

Our steps in this way are the love of God and our neighbour. He who loves, runs; and the more he loves, the more eagerly he runs; the less he loves, the more slothfully he moves in the way. Indeed, if he does not love he shall remain behind in the way. And if he longs for this world and looks back from the way, his face is not towards home. What does it avail to be in the way, if he is walking, not forward, but backwards? By this I mean: What does it avail a man to be a Christian Catholic (*christianus catholicus*), for this is to be in the way, and walking in the way, if he from loving the world keeps looking back? For he is returning to where he began. And if through some snare of the Enemy, who is tempter as well as thief, he is while on his journey led astray from the Catholic Church, either into heresy, or to some pagan rite, or to whatever other kind of superstition or invention of the devil you wish, he has already lost the way, and returned to wandering.

3. And so, Brethren, let us hasten in the way, because we are Christian Catholics, which is the one Church of God, as was foretold in the holy Scriptures. For it was not God's Will that she be hidden; that no one might plead this as excuse. It was foretold that she would be established throughout the whole earth; and she has been made visible to the whole earth. Nor should we falter because there are heresies and schisms innumerable: it should trouble us more if there were not; for they too have been foretold. All, either those who remain in the Catholic Church, or those who are outside the Catholic Church, bear

testimony to the Gospel. They bear testimony that all that was said in the Gospel is true. For in what form was it foretold that she would appear among the nations? As One; as founded on a Rock; and that the gates of hell would not prevail against her.

The beginning of sin is a gate of hell: *For the wages of sin is death* (Rom. vi. 23), and death here beyond doubt leads to hell. And what is the beginning of sin? Let us ask the Scriptures. *Pride*, they say, *is the beginning of all sin* (Ecclus. x. 15). And if pride is the beginning of sin, pride is a gate of hell. Think now of what it was gave birth to all the heresies; and you will find they had no other mother save pride. For when they think much of themselves, and call themselves saints, and seek to draw crowds to themselves, and draw them from Christ, they promote heresies to their advantage, and likewise schisms, and this solely through pride. But because the Catholic Church shall not be overcome by all these heresies and schisms, that is, by the sons of pride, it was therefore foretold: *That the gates of hell shall not prevail against it* (Mt. xvi. 18).

4. And so, Brethren, as I began by saying, we are in the way. Let us run in love and charity; forgetting the things of time. This way calls for the strong; it will not have the slothful. The robbers of temptation abound. At every turn the devil lies in wait: everywhere he tries to enter in and take possession; and whoever he possesses, he recalls from the way, or impedes him. He recalls him, and then ensures that he does not go forward; or that he turns aside from the way, caught in the snares of false beliefs or in the heresies of schism, or led into some form or other of superstition.

He tempts him through fear or through desire. But first through desire; through promises and pledges or through the allure of pleasures. When he finds a man who despises these things, and has as it were closed the door to desire, he begins to tempt him through the door of fear. If you now wish to gain no more in this world, and so have closed the door; should you still fear to lose what you have, you have not closed the door to fear. So, be strong in faith (I Pet. v. 9). Take heed that no man seduce you to evil (Mt. xxiv. 4) through some promise; and let no one force you into deception by any threat. Whatever the world may promise you, the kingdom of heaven is greater; whatever the world threatens, the punishment of hell is worse. And so if you wish to rise above all human fears; fear the eternal punishments that God threatens. And do you wish to crush the impulses of concupiscence? Desire the eternal life that God promises us. By this you close the door to the devil; by this you open it to Christ.

Turning then to the Lord our God, let us earnestly beseech Him that the power of His mercy may strengthen our hearts in His truth, that it may strengthen and give peace to our souls. May His grace abound in us, and may He have mercy on us, and remove all scandals from before us, and from before His Church, and from before all those we love, and may He by His power and through the abundance of His mercy enable us to please him for ever; Through Jesus Christ His

Son our Lord, Who with Him and   reigneth for ever and ever.[27] Amen.
with the Holy Spirit liveth and

Three Prayers

I. *Prayer for the Judgement*[28]
Of St Ephraim, Deacon, Confessor and Doctor

Oh, woe is me, woe is me! Lord. My
sins and vices are so great that I can
scarcely be forgiven. Miserable that
I am, I have defiled myself beyond
measure. Of my own will have I
defiled myself; of my own will have
I stained myself; through my own
fault have I ruined myself.

Unhappy that I am, I have sinned
most grievously, and the force of
habit urges me to evil. I long to do
what is good, but I am weighed
down by the desires of the flesh
(Rom. vii), and the habit of my sins
binds me fast (Prov. v. 22). Woe,
woe is me, miserable and unhappy
that I am; held fast and wrapped
around by so many sins, so many
crimes, by such iniquities! Which of
them shall I first weep for; which
shall I first lament; for which of my
offences I shall pour out my tears, I
know not.

Be mindful, O Lord, that I am
unable to support the burden of so
much guilt. Come to my aid, O
God: Before I die, before death
overtakes me, before they drag me
down to Tartarus, before the dark
closes over me, before I hasten to
torment, before flames of fire consume me, before I am tormented
without end.

Guilty, I am terrified of what sin
may cause me; I am in fear of the
Day of Judgement, where even *the
just man shall scarcely be saved* (I Pet.
iv. 18), and where I, a sinner, and
unholy, must now appear. What

shall I say when I stand before Thy
tribunal? What shall I do when I
stand before Thy Face? What shall I
answer? Woe is me, that I have
sinned; that I have transgressed Thy
command. There is no sin with
whose filth I am not stained; no
sickness of evil that has not defiled
me, unhappy that I am.

I promised I would live worthily,
but what I promised I have not done:
always have I returned to sin, always
have I repeated the evil I have done;
never have I changed my ways for
the better, never have I drawn back
from what is evil. Ruining myself, I
have also corrupted many: through
my own evil ways have I led others
into iniquity, through my impiety
many souls have perished, by my
example many have been ruined,
because of my iniquity, I have been
the cause of evil to many.

Pray for me to the Lord, ye holy
men and brethren! Beseech Him for
me, all the community of saints:
that God may have mercy on me,
that He may take away my iniquity,
and grant me His mercy! Turn to
me, and do not despise me; do not
leave me abandoned in the power of
the demons. And though my sins
are grievous, *Thou art gracious and
merciful and of much compassion* (Jon.
iv. 2); and refuse no one Thy mercy:
but bestowest thy clemency without
measure, waiting for sinners, that
they may return.

For how many are wicked, how

many given over to wantonness,
how many held fast by the desires of
this world, have through Thy goodness, O Lord, attained to forgiveness? To how many who returned
hast Thou not freely given pardon?
Show me, O Most Loving Father,
Thy clemency; show me Thy pardon, show me Thy forgiveness: Do
not, I beseech Thee, deny to one
what Thou hast bestowed on many!

I do not defend the evil I have
done: before Thee I confess my sin;
I grieve for what I have done, I
grieve that I have gone astray, I
grieve that I have offended Thy
Majesty. I accuse myself of my sins;
before Thee I stand, sinful and repentant. Hear I beseech Thee, O
Omnipotent God, the cry of my
repentance. Hear the voice of my
supplication; hear the voice of the
sinner crying out to Thee: I have
sinned; God have mercy on me; I
have sinned, God be merciful to me
a sinner: *If Thou, O Lord, wilt mark
iniquities: Lord, who shall stand it?*
(Ps. cxxix. 3).

Remember the substance of which
I am made (Ps. lxxxviii. 48): remember, Lord, that I am earth; remember that I am dust and ashes.
Open Thy Hand to me: stretch forth
Thy Right Hand to me. Forgive me
my evils; forgive me my crimes;
forgive me my offences. *Heal my
soul, for I have sinned against thee* (Ps.
xl. 5): against Thee to Whom all
honour and glory is due, throughout all ages and ages. Amen.

II. *At the Beginning of the Day*
(*The Golden Treasury of Morn*)[29]

Grant us, O Lord, the grace of the
Holy Spirit,
That we may abide in true faith,
Live a holy life, and
Be ever mindful of the poor.

May we do the Will of God,
May we obey the Law of God,
May we deny our own desires,
And keep our tongues from evil.

May we refuse each will of sin,
That we may go to heaven,
Keep in mind Christ's Passion, and
Before our eyes our earthly end.

Let us through Penance repent in
time,

Wash clean our souls at the well of
grace,
Keep free from grave and venial sin,
Blessed with the servants of Mary
Queen.

May she win pardon for our every
sin,
Of thought and word, of deed and
omission,
And gain us a holy, blessed death,
By her prayers and intercession.

May she bring us to the glory,
To the joy and brightness of heaven,
To adore and praise and contem-
plate,
The Blessed Trinity now and for-
ever, O Lord. Amen.

III. *Prayer for Sunday Morning*[30]

Welcome, O Holy Day of the Lord!
Bright day of gladness for praising
    Jesus.
Move our feet in haste to Mass,
Move our lips to holy words,
Move with Thy finger the wheel of
    our soul.[31]

O God, it is Thou has bought us,
It is Thou wilt come to take us.

If in youth we broke Thy Law,
Write it not against our age.[32]

Bind fast the Evil One,
That he may not come nigh to us.[33]
Deliver us from his company,
And from the seven deadly sins.
                Amen.

NOTES

[1] From a correspondence between Augustine, Bishop of Hippo, North Africa, and Hesychius, Bishop of Salonitanus, Dalmatia (PL 33, col. 899), concerning the end of the world and related points of S. Scripture. They are Epistles CXCVII (Aug.), CXCVIII (Hesychius), then CXCIX (Aug.). This lasts deal with the end of the world and the Coming of Christ (54 paragraphs); from which the citations on this Gospel are taken verbatim, though not in the order in which they appear in the letters. Written after the year 419.

[2] He warns us in the words: *He that readeth* (verse 15). It does not appear certain that the Lord is here speaking of the tribulations of the Jews and not of those to be suffered under Antichrist. This latter interpretation seems the true one; according to verse 29. In verse 15, *he that readeth let him understand*; the Lord appears to be warning us to be careful, and watchful, as to the meaning here. The whole bearing of this chapter, especially in the verses preceding the Gospel of today, seem to refer to the general end of the

world; confirmed by the remarkable and consoling prophecy of verse 14. Verse 15 seems to warn against a too literal interpretation. There is of course an echo and a parallel of the fate that befell Jerusalem from the Romans.

[3] Now Sermon 70. Appendix; inauthentic, *not* of Augustine; probably St Caesarius of Arles. Cf. PRM.

[4] Origen PG 13, Series *Commentariorum in Mt.*; pars 42–45 *passim*.

[5] The citation here is very compressed (from the original). The actual words of the text are as follows: 'But we must not believe them, nor depart from the first and ecclesiastical tradition, nor believe anything other than that which has been handed down to us through the succession of the Church of God.' PG 13, col. 1667.

[6] PL 13, as above, par. 46. 'For truth is like the lightning that comes from the east and appears even in the west. Of such a nature is the truth of the Church of God; for only from her *hath their sound gone forth into all the earth, and their words unto the ends of the world* (Ps. xviii. 5); and from

her alone, *his word runneth swiftly* (Ps. cxlvii. 15).'

⁷ Actual words of the text of Origen: 'We should not therefore pay heed to those who say, Lo here is Christ, but do not confess Him in the Church, which is filled with lightning from the east unto the west, which is *the pillar* and *ground of truth*, in all of which is the whole Coming of the Son of man; Who says to all men wherever they may be: *Behold I am with you all days, even to the consummation of the world.'* *Comment.* as above, pars. 46–48.

⁸ St Ephraim Syri, Edition Lamy, III, col. 212, *Sermo* III: *Oratio pro futura vita.*

⁹ St Ephraim Syri, III, col. 188, *Sermo* II. This discourse appears to be of a visionary, even prophetic character.

¹⁰ The Romans appear to stand for some then dominant power in the west.

¹¹ This saying that they shall hide the fruits of industry in the earth (*fructusque in terra recondent*) means presumably that they will bury their captured treasure: their gold and similar riches.

¹² The *Portae Pylae Caspiae*, the passes of the mountains between Derbend to the Caspian Sea; where the Caucasus approach the Caspian. A Syrian tradition tells that Alexander the Great caused wondrous gates of bronze and iron to be made there, to keep out the people of Gog and Magog, or the Huns and Scythians, dwelling to the North. There is a poem extant, of Jacob Sarug, in Syriac (G. Knös, Gothingh 1807) which narrates how Alexander, son of Philip of Macedon, divinely admonished, obtained from Surreg, King of Egypt, 12,000 arti-

ficers and unending supplies of material, and, having defeated the Persians, made the gates, closing the mountain gap to the north, so that the natives of Gog and Magog might never again make inroads into Assyria, Mesopotamia and other lands, afterwards subject to the Romans and Greeks, and that an angel then foretold to Alexander that the gates would not be opened till the end of the world, and then by an earthquake; and that through them the hordes of Gog and Magog would then pour in to devastate the land, and defile it with iniquity.

¹³ The names here given are in most cases as Lamy has rendered them in Latin from the Syriac; otherwise as they are found in the OT.

¹⁴ Ezechiel xxxviii, 11 *et seq.* The prophet does not however mention all whom Ephraim here speaks of.

¹⁵ A terrible incursion of the Huns, commemorated in The Chronicles of Edessa, took place in the year 395; but before that there had been many and terrible incursions. The allusions here seem not historical, but prophetical.

¹⁶ *Inter coelum et terram currus eorum velut venti volant.*

¹⁷ *The wicked one (vir iniquus); the man of iniquity* (Is. xi. 4; II Thess. ii. 8). Names given to Antichrist.

¹⁸ PG 56, col. 299, *De Consolatione Mortis, Sermo Secundus.*

¹⁹ Plutarch, in *Laconic Apophthegms*, p. 225; Titius Livius. Migne loc. cit.

²⁰ PL 39, col. 1599, *Sermo CCCLXI, De Resurrectione Mortuorum: Sermo primus.* These are two of the last numbered of the Saint's sermons; and are rather detailed instructions on Christian beliefs con-

cerning the resurrection of the dead
and the life after the resurrection.
The first sermon deals with Christ's
resurrection, and then man's resurrection to come. It is a most careful,
slow-moving, meditative discourse,
permeated with Christian truth of
all kinds, as they relate to the basic
truth of the resurrection: the basis of
of our faith, our hope, and, in-
directly, of our charity. He has particularly in mind to prepare Christians to answer those who speak and
act against this truth.

[21] The vivid response to which the
Saint here refers, appears to have
been a characteristic of African congregations. The same is noticed in
certain sermons at Alexandria; always in enthusiastic approval or
rejection of some point of doctrine
in accord or in opposition to the true
Catholic doctrine. It implies a high
and prompt degree of intelligence,
as well as a lively and deep regard for
divine truth: a trait it would seem
that still marks congregations of
African race; a swift and emotional
apperception of divine truth. A
reading of the Gospel by the
rhetorician Augustine must have
been an illuminating experience:
voice, tone, manner of presentation,
unflawed and revealing clarity; not
to mention loving fervour; excel-
lences, the result in great measure of
intensive training, now alas, un-
dreamt of.

[22] PL 39, col. 1611, *Sermo*
CCCLXII, Second Sermon on *The
Resurrection of the Dead*. Its leisured
and careful precision prolong it
considerably; but its excellence is
such that it seemed very desirable
to render it carefully and in full.
There is nothing on this theme in
any discourse to compare with it;
providing unending material for
meditation and instruction, apart
from its value as a treasury of defence of the truths concerned, and as
a guide amid the pitfalls that await
the ever nascent Church.

[23] This implies the usage of reading the portions of Scripture on
which the sermon following is to be
based; a practice that accords with
the great Doctor's meticulous
didactic thoroughness, and a pattern
for the exposition of the holy Scriptures to the faithful.

[24] Text of sermon: *Sobrii estote.*
Vulgate: *Evigilate.*

[25] Augustion's version: *Qui circa
veritatem erraverunt.* Vulgate: *Qui a
veritate exciderunt.* They erred concerning the truth by affirming one
resurrection and denying the other.
It was however of this latter, of the
body, Paul was writing to Timothy.
And so the text of St Jerome tells us
they literally and simply fell from
this truth (II Tim. ii. 18).

[26] *Miscellania Agostiniana*, D. Ger-
vase Morin, *Sermones Reperti*, Mai,
XIII: *De Peregrinatione hujus vitae,*
p. 285.

[27] Prayer from *Misc. Agos.*, p. 17,
Oratio ad complendum.

[28] Vossio, St Ephraim Syri, *Opera
Omnia*, p. 621.

[29] A most ancient prayer for the
beginning of the day, that derives
through an unbroken tradition back
to the earliest days of faith in the
Church in Ireland: where it is still
recited in the Gaelic tongue under
the glowing and veracious title of
Golden Treasury of Morn. The
present form of the prayer has been made
from a literal rendering of the Gaelic
made by Father Diarmuid McShane
and Father John Greehy, Irish Col-
lege, Rome. It was not possible to

reproduce the melodic form of the Gaelic, without impairing the precision of its doctrinal content. It is a clear and fervent summary of the Christian faith and hope, Christian duty, the means to our final end, remembrance of Christ's Passion, and loving homage and prayer to Mary Queen. My thanks are due to the translators for the literal rendering.

30 This is an ancient prayer that was said, in Gaelic, by the people as they set out for Mass on Sunday morning. It has Patristic echoes; and the faith and worship from which it derives, comes down in an unclouded tradition from patristic days.

31 The Finger is the Holy Spirit, Who is said to move the soul (which responds at the touch of the Spirit), through holy preaching and the reading of the Scriptures. And by this touch upon the wheel: *For the Spirit of life is in the wheels* (Ezech. i. 18), the soul is helped to reject deathly works. It also moves the soul to repentance; and the wheels at once follow. The inspiration of the phrase seems to derive from St Gregory the Great's *Homilies on Ezechiel*; on chapter I, verse 20 (PL 76, col. 844).

32 From Job xiii. 26.

33 Psalm xc. 10.

FEAST OF THE ASSUMPTION

I. St Germanus, Patriarch of Constantinople: In Praise of the Holy and Venerable Falling-Asleep of our Most Holy Lady Mother of God Mary Ever Virgin

II. St John Damascene: Oration on the Glorious Dormition of the Most Holy Mother of God the Ever-Virgin Mary

III. St Lomman, Abbot: The Praises of Mary

THE GOSPEL OF THE FEAST

Luke i. 41–50

At that time: Elizabeth was filled with the Holy Ghost. And she cried out with a loud voice and said: Blessed art thou among women and blessed is the fruit of thy womb. And whence is this to me that the mother of my Lord should come to me? For, behold, as soon as the voice of thy salutation sounded in my ears, the infant in my womb leaped for joy. And blessed art thou that hast believed, because these things shall be accomplished that were spoken to thee by the Lord.

And Mary said: My soul doth magnify the Lord. And my spirit hath rejoiced in God my Saviour. Because he hath regarded the humility of his handmaid; for, behold, from henceforth all generations shall call me blessed. Because he that is mighty hath done great things to me; and holy is his name. And his mercy is from generation unto generations, to them that fear him.

Exposition from the Catena Aurea

I

AMBROSE: The blessings of Mary's advent and of the Lord's Presence at once made known:

V.41. And it came to pass that, when Elizabeth heard the salutation of Mary, the infant leaped in her womb.

Note the distinctness of each of these words, and their particular significance. Elizabeth was the first to hear her voice; but John was the first to be aware of the divine favour.

She heard in the natural manner; he leaped for joy because of the Mystery. She sees Mary's coming; he the Coming of the Lord.

GREEK EXPOSITOR (*Geometer*,[1] *in Catena GP*): For the prophet sees and hears more acutely than his parent, and he is greeting the Prince of prophets; and since he could not do this by words, he leaps in the womb, to show the greatness of his joy. Who has ever known of a transport of joy that was prior to birth? Grace made known to him things which were unknown to nature. Enclosed in the womb, the soldier acknowledges his Lord and the King that was to come: the cloak of the womb does not veil his mystical vision; for be beheld Him, not by his senses, but with his spirit.

ORIGEN, *Hom.* VII *in Luke*[2]: Prior to this he had not been filled with the Spirit, until she stood by him who bore Christ in her womb. It was then he was filled with the Spirit, and exulted in his mother's womb.[3] Hence there follows: *And Elizabeth was filled with the Holy Ghost.* There can be no doubt that she who in this moment was filled with the Holy Ghost, was so filled because of her son.

AMBROSE: She who *had conceived a son and had hid herself,* now begins to glory that within her she was bearing a prophet; and she who before felt shame, now breaks out in blessing. Hence there follows:

V.42. *And she cried out with a loud voice and said: Blessed art thou among women.*

She cried out with a loud voice as soon as she perceives that the Lord has come: for she believed this is to be a sacred birth. ORIGEN: And she says: *Blessed art thou among women.* For no one ever was or could be the recipient of so great a favour: for she is the sole parent of the Divine Offspring. BEDE: She is blessed by Elizabeth with the same words Gabriel used: to show that she is to be venerated by both angels and men.

THEOPHYLACTUS: Because there had been other holy women, who nevertheless had born children who were stained with sin, she adds: *And blessed is the fruit of thy womb.* Or again, we may understand her words in another way. She had said, *Blessed art thou among women*; then, as though someone were asking why, she goes on: *And blessed is the fruit of thy womb*; as we read in Psalm cxvii. 26–27: *Blessed be he that cometh in the name of the Lord; the Lord is God, and he hath shone upon us.* For it is a practice of Holy Scripture to use at times *and* in place of *because.*

ORIGEN, as above: She speaks of the Lord as the fruit of the womb of the Mother of God; for He came forth from Mary alone, and in no way from man: for they who begin from the seed of fathers are their fruit. GREEK (*Geometer*): Therefore this fruit alone is blessed: because it was brought forth without man and without sin. BEDE: This is the fruit which was promised to David: *Of the fruit of thy womb I will set upon thy throne* (Ps. cxxxi. 11).

SEVERUS (*of Antioch*): And from this we draw a refutation of Eutyches: since Christ is declared to be *the fruit of the womb.* And all fruit is of the same nature as the parent plant: so it follows that the Virgin also was of the same nature as the Second Adam, Who takes away the sins of the world.

And let those be ashamed at the true child-bearing of the Mother of God, who have invented some fantastic notion concerning Christ's Body; for the *fruit* proceeds from the very substance of the tree. And what of those who say that Christ passed through Mary as water through a channel? Let them hearken to the words of Elizabeth, who was filled with the Holy Ghost; saying that Christ was the fruit of the womb.

V.43. *And whence is this to me that the mother of my Lord should come to me?*

AMBROSE: She does not speak as one not knowing: for she knew that it was the favour and work of the Holy Spirit that the Mother of the Lord should greet the mother of the prophet; for the purpose of the mission of her Son. But as knowing that this was not the consequence of human merit, but a gift of the divine favour, she accordingly says: *Whence is this to me*; that is, for what justice, for what good deeds, for what merits of mine?

ORIGEN: In saying this she is of one mind with her son; for John also knew himself as unworthy of the Lord's coming to him. And she proclaims as the *mother of the Lord*, one who is still a virgin; preceding the event with the voice of prophecy. It was the divine foreknowledge had led Mary to Elizabeth; that the testimony of John might reach the Lord from the womb. From that moment the Lord made John a Prophet. Hence there follows:

V.44. *For, behold, as soon as the voice of thy salutation sounded in my ears, the infant in my womb leaped for joy.*

AUGUSTINE, *Ep. 57, to Dardan*: But that she might say this, she was, as the Evangelist first says (v. 41), filled with the Holy Ghost; from Whose revelation undoubtedly, she learned

what the leaping of the infant signified; namely, that His Mother had come of Whom this infant was to be the Precursor and Manifestor. For the significance of this so wondrous event could be learned by adults, but could not be known by an infant. For she did not say, 'the infant leaped in faith in my womb,' but, *leaped for joy*.[4] But we see not only children leap for joy, but even beasts, but not however because of faith, or religion, or because of any kind of rational knowledge. This is a new and unheard of exultation; in the womb, and at *her* coming who was about to bring forth the Saviour of all men. Therefore, this leaping for joy, and this as it were return of her salutation to the Mother of the Lord, was wrought divinely in the infant, as miracles are wrought; it was not the human act of the infant. For even had the use of reason and will been so quickened in this child, that while still within his mother's womb he could know and believe and consent; even that would have to be a miracle of divine power, and could not be put forward as an act of nature.[5]

ORIGEN, *Catena GP*: The Mother of the Lord had come to see Elizabeth, and also her incredible conception, of which the Angel had told her, that through this she might have faith in a greater conception to come to the Virgin Herself.[6] And to this faith the words of Elizabeth give testimony, saying:

V.45. *And blessed art thou that hast believed, because these things shall be accomplished that were spoken to thee by the Lord.*

AMBROSE: You see that Mary had doubted not at all, but had believed; and therefore the fruit of faith followed. BEDE: Nor should we wonder that the Lord, now about to redeem the world, began His work from His mother's womb; so that she through whom salvation was prepared for all men, might be the first to draw forth the fruits of salvation from her Son.

AMBROSE: But you also are blessed who have heard and who have believed: for every soul that believes, conceives and brings forth the Word of God, and confesses His works. BEDE: Every soul that conceives the Word of God in its mind, from then on climbs by steps of love to the heights of virtue, to reach the *city of Juda*, that is to the citadel of confession and praise, and as it were abide there *three months*; to the perfecting of faith, hope and charity.

GREGORY, *Super Ezechiel, Homily* 1: She was touched by the spirit of prophecy, beholding at the same time the past, the present, and the future, who knew that Mary had believed the promises of the Angel, and, calling her mother, knew that she bore in her womb the Redeemer of mankind: and since she foretold that *all things would be accomplished*, she also beheld what would come to pass in the future.

2

AMBROSE: As sin began from women so also do our blessings begin with them: hence it does not seem by chance that Elizabeth prophesied before John, and Mary before the birth of the Lord. But it follows that the more Mary excelled in the dignity of her person, the richer would be her prophesying. BASIL, *in Psalm* 32: For the Virgin, with mind upraised, contemplating the immensity of the mystery, advancing as it were ever more profoundly forward, magnifies God. And so it is said of her:

V.46: *And Mary said: My soul doth magnify the Lord.*

GREEK EXPOSITOR (*Athanasius, in Catena GP*): As though she had said: The wonders God has foretold, these He will fulfil in my body; and my soul also shall not be without fruit before God. But I also must offer the fruit of my will: for the more I serve this wonder, the more must I glorify Him Who works these wonders in me.

ORIGEN, *Homily* VIII *in Luke*: But if the Lord can receive neither increase nor decrease, what is the meaning of Mary's words: *My soul doth magnify the Lord*? But if I consider that the Lord our Saviour is the Image of the Invisible God (II Cor. iv), and that the soul is made in His Image, so that it is an image of the Image; then I shall see that when I, like those who paint images, shall have made my soul great in thought, word, and deed, then the image of God shall be made great; and the Lord Himself, Whose image it is, shall be magnified in my soul.

3

BASIL, *in Psalm* 32: The first fruit of the Spirit is peace and joy. Therefore, since the Holy Virgin had received within herself every grace of the Holy Spirit, rightly does she add:

V.47. *And my spirit hath rejoiced in God my Saviour.*

She speaks of soul and spirit, as the one thing. The voice of exultation is a familiar one in the Scriptures, conveying to us a certain cheerful and joyous state of soul in those who are worthy. The Virgin therefore rejoices in the Lord with an ineffable uplifting of the heart, and with a noble and resounding utterance of her love. Then follows: *In God my Saviour.* BEDE: For the spirit of the Virgin rejoices in the everlasting Godhead of the same Jesus; that is, the Saviour, Whose Flesh grew from a temporal conception.

AMBROSE: The soul of Mary therefore magnifies the Lord, and her spirit rejoices in God; in that, dedicated soul and spirit to the Father and the Son, she adores with fervent love the One God from Whom all things are. May the soul of Mary be in each one of us, that it may magnify the Lord; may the spirit of Mary be in each one, that it may rejoice in the Lord. If according to the flesh, one is the Mother of Christ, yet according to faith, Christ is the fruit of all men: for every soul conceives the Word of God, provided it is pure and free from sin, and keeps itself chaste with modesty undefiled.

THEOPHYLACTUS: He magnifies God who follows devoutly in the way of Christ, and, while called a Christian, does not lessen the dignity of Christ; doing great and heavenly things. And then his spirit, that is, his spiritual character, will rejoice; that is increase, and shall not die.

BASIL, as above, *in princ.*: If at any time light has entered your heart, to love God and despite bodily things, by this obscure and brief image it will have glimpsed the perfect state of the Just, and may without difficulty attain to joy in the Lord.[7] ORIGEN: The soul first magnifies the Lord, that it may afterwards rejoice in God: for unless we first believe, we cannot rejoice.

4

GREEK EXPOSITOR (*Isidore in Catena GP*): She makes known the reason why it is fitting she should magnify God and rejoice in Him, saying:

V.48. *Because he hath regarded the humility of his handmaid.*

As though she said: God so ordered; I did not seek; I was content with lowly things. Now am I called unto ineffable wisdom, uplifted from earth to the stars.

AUGUSTINE, *Sermon 2, on Assumption*[8]: O true lowliness, which has brought forth God to men, given true life to mortals, renewed the heavens, purified the world, opened paradise, brought freedom to the souls of men. The lowliness of Mary has become the heavenly stair by which God came down to earth. For what does, *he hath regarded* mean, but that He hath approved? For in the sight of men many men appear humble, but their humility is not regarded by the Lord. For if they were truly humble they would desire that God, not they, should be praised by men; and their spirit would rejoice, not in this world, but in God.

ORIGEN, *Homily VIII in Luke*: But how could she be lowly and humble who bore in her womb the Son of God? But reflect that the lowliness that is praised in the Scriptures as one of the virtues is that which philosophers call *modestia*. And this we may paraphrase as that state of mind when a man is not puffed up, but rather humbles himself within himself.

BEDE: She whose humility is *regarded*, is by all men rightly called *blessed*. Hence there follows: *For behold from henceforth all generations shall call me blessed.* ATHANASIUS, *in Catena GP*: For if, according to the prophet, they are blessed *who have seed in Sion and kindred in Jerusalem*,[9] how great should be the praise of the divinely inspired and all-holy Virgin Mary, Who became according to the Flesh the Mother of the Word?

GREEK EXPOSITOR (*Metaphrastes in Catena GP*): It is not that troubled by vain glory, she calls herself *blessed*: for where was there place for pride in her who calls herself *the handmaid of the Lord*? But that touched by the Holy Spirit, she foretells the things that are to come.

BEDE: For it was fitting, that as death entered the world through the pride of our first parent, so through the lowliness of Mary was the way to true life thrown open. THEOPHYLACTUS: And therefore she says: *All generations*; not Elizabeth alone, but all nations that shall believe.

5

V.49. *Because he that is mighty hath done great things to me; and holy is his name.*

THEOPHYLACTUS: The Virgin shows that it is not because of her virtue she is to be called *blessed*. She assigns the true Cause, saying: *Because he that is mighty hath done great things to me.* AUGUSTINE, *Sermon on Assumption*, as above: What great things hath He done to Thee? I believe that Thou a creature didst bring forth the Creator, a servant thou hast given birth to the Lord; that through Thee God might redeem the world, through Thee give it light, through Thee recall it to life.

TITUS (*of Bostra*): And how am I great, if not that while remaining inviolate, I conceive, by the will of God; surpassing the order of nature? I have been held worthy that, without man, I became a mother; not the mother of anyone, but of the Only-Begotten Saviour.

BEDE: This however relates to the beginning of the Canticle, where it is said: *My soul doth magnify the Lord*: for only that soul to which the Lord deigns to do great things can magnify Him with fitting praise.

TITUS: She says: *He that is mighty*; so that should anyone doubt in the matter of her conception, that while remaining a virgin she conceives, she refers this miracle to the power of the One Who wrought it. Nor is the Only-Begotten by this defiled: that He has drawn near to a woman; because, *Holy is his name.*

BASIL, as above: The name of God is said to be *holy*, not because it contains in its syllables any special virtue, but because in whatever way we contemplate God, we see Him pure and holy. BEDE: For in the supreme eminence of His power He transcends all creatures; far removed from all that He has made. And this is best conveyed in the Greek tongue in which this very word holy, *agion*, means to be apart from earth.

6

BEDE: Turning from God's special gifts to herself, to the general decrees of God, she speaks of the state of all mankind, going on to say:

V.50. And his mercy is from generation unto generations, to them that fear him;

As though she were to say: He that is mighty has not only done great things to me; but in every nation he is pleasing to Him who fears God. ORIGEN: For the mercy of God is not unto one generation, but goes on forever, from generation to generation.

GREEK (*Victor Presbyter in Catena GP*): And because of His mercy, which is unto generations of generations, I conceive; and He is united to a living body; and solely in loving mercy has taken upon Himself our salvation. Yet His mercy is not for all without distinction; but to those who in every nation shall fear Him. So we read: *To them that fear him*; who, namely, led by repentance, turn to faith and penance: for the obdurate, because of their sin of unbelief, close against themselves the door of divine love.

THEOPHYLACTUS: Or by this she intimates that those who fear Him shall obtain mercy in this generation; that is, in this present life; and in the future; that is, in the world to come: in this world receiving a hundredfold; in that to come, overflowing measure.

I. St Germanus, Patriarch of Constantinople (a.d. 730)

In Praise of the Holy and Venerable Falling-Asleep of our Most Glorious Lady Mother of God Mary ever Virgin[10]

It is written that *a name that is good and beautiful maketh the bones fat* (Prov. xv. 30). And so likewise does the account of the bodily *falling asleep* of the Mother of God, the Ever-Virgin Mary: for in that she is the divine breath and fragrance of the most holy Body of Christ, she brings blessing to all who bless her. For the bones of men long buried in the earth have through the mercy of God been changed; the undefiled body of God's Mother has made them fat, though hardened by corruption: for through His Resurrection Who was born of her, they

have become smoother than oil (Ps. liv. 22). But let us recall however briefly her ever-memorable Translation. For even to listen to the account of this glorious happening is truly in itself a joy.

When Christ had willed that His Mother, she who had borne Life Itself within her, should be taken upwards to Himself, He tells her, by the message of an angel who was already known to her, that the time of her *falling asleep* is now at hand. And this He did so that through the intimation of Her coming death, she might not be troubled at her departure from the living; as will happen to the rest of mortal men. For we know that the separation of the soul from the body can bring distress to the spirit of even strong men. Therefore, lest death, coming unawares, should trouble the natural instinct of the body, and so that His Mother might know beforehand of her own departure, He Who knows all things sent an angel to her, to give her strength of soul by such words as these, coming, through him, from Christ Himself:

'It is time for Me' (says the Lord) 'to take unto Me, Thee My Mother. As you have filled the earth and those that dwell in it with joy, so shall you now bring joy to heaven, bring gladness to the mansions of My Father; and delight the spirits of His Saints. For they beholding the honour given thee, and the thronging of the angelic hosts at thy Translation to Me, shall be confirmed in their belief that through thee, their members also shall dwell in My Light, O Full of Grace!

'Come therefore with exceeding great joy! Hail and again rejoice as once before (Lk. i. 28)! For you above all creatures are worthy of being hailed *full of grace*. As when you were about to conceive Me, you received tidings of great joy, so now rejoice that once more you are sought for, to be received by Me.

'And be not troubled at leaving behind a world corrupted by its desires. Thou dost leave its corruption; thou wilt not leave as orphans in the world those bereaved by thy assumption. For as I, though not of this world, watch over and take care of those who are in the world, so shall thy protection likewise be not wanting to this world until it ends.

'Nor let it trouble thee, that thou must end thy care of earthly things. For thou art returning to a life that is more than life: to a rest of joy, to serene most perfect peace, to freedom from all care, to happiness without end, to light that never fades, to a day without evening, to Me, to thy Creator, and the Creator of all things.

'For where I am, there is Light Eternal, joy without compare, a dwelling-place without equal, a city that cannot be destroyed. And so where I am, thou art now to be, Mother inseparable, in her Inseparable Son. Where God is, there is all goodness, all delight, every happiness. No one who has seen My glory shall ever desire to depart from it. No one who has entered in to My rest, shall ever again seek the fleeting things of this world. Let Peter be asked if there be any comparison between this world and that of Mount Thabor, where for a brief moment he beheld My glory?

'While thou didst dwell in this world that perishes, I gave thee a vision of my power. But when thou hast departed this life, I shall show Myself to thee, face to face. Nothing that is thine shall be left to the weight of earth. Thy body is Mine; and since in My hands *are all the ends of the earth* (Ps. xciv. 4), no one shall take thee from My hands. Entrust thy body to Me, as I once entrusted My Godhead to thy womb. Thy God-loving soul shall look upon the glory of My Father; thy immaculate body behold the glory of His Only-Begotten Son; thy most pure spirit the glory of the All-Holy Spirit.

'Death shall not triumph over thee; for thou hast borne Life Itself within thy womb. Thou wert My chosen vessel; and this shall not be broken by death's fall, nor shall darkness devour it. Come then with eagerness to Him that was born of Thee. As thy Child I desire to give thee joy; to make thee a return for the shelter of thy mother's womb, to reward thee for the milk thou hast fed Me, for the care thou lavished on Me, for the fulness of thy mother's love.

'Mother! Thou who hast borne Me as thine only Son, is it not thy wish to dwell with Me; for I know thou hast no other son to hold thee back? For I made thee a virgin mother; and I shall also make thee a mother rejoicing over her Son (Ps. cxii). I shall proclaim the world thy debtor, and departing thy name shall be held in yet greater glory. For I shall build thee up as a wall to defend the world, a rampart against floods, a staff to those led by the hand, an advocate for sinners, and, at the end, a stairway to lead men safely to heaven.

'Come then, joyfully! Open thou that paradise that was closed by Eve; who was of thy nature and of thy kindred. Enter into the joy of thy Son. Leave behind the earthly Jerusalem. Hasten to the heavenly City; for in a little while as it was written, of that Jerusalem here below, *The lamentation shall be great, as the lamentation for the pomegranate grove cut down in the plain* (Zach. xii. 11). Recline in thy tomb in Gethsemani, and that only for outward appearance; for I shall not leave thee long bereft within it. I shall come to thee at once, when thou art scarce laid down and placed in the tomb. I shall

come to thee, not to be again conceived by thee, through which I once abode in thee; but rather to take thee up, to abide with me.

'Lay thy body with confidence in the place in Gethsemani, where I before My Passion bent My knees in prayer. For as I, after I had bent My knees in prayer, of My own will went forth to the Life-giving death of the Cross, so thou too, after the laying down of thy body, shall on the instant be translated to Life.

'And, behold, My Disciples also are coming, to take care of thee, and by their hands, those spiritual sons of My Light, with honour and reverence shalt thou be entombed. On them, as thou canst bear witness, I have bestowed the grace of adoption. And in doing what is to be done, I shall hold as done by My own hands what is done by them. For it is not fitting that other hands should care for thee than those of My Apostles, in whom also the Holy Spirit dwells. They will take My place in doing honour to thy going forth, O most Pure and Undefiled!'

Hearing these tidings, the Mother of God rejoices with great joy; holding as nothing the things of this mortal life. At once she sets great lights all through the house, and calls together her friends and relations, and sweeps the house and then as for a bridal, strews flowers upon the simple bed where each night she had poured out her prayers amid unceasing tears of love and longing for Christ her Son: *In my bed*, says the Scripture, *I sought him whom my soul loveth* (Cant. iii. 1).

Eagerly she prepares what is needed for her going forth. She makes known to all that she is about to depart this life, tells them what the angel had told her, and shows them the pledge he had given her; a palm-branch, symbol of her victory against death, pledge of unfading life, to assure her that going forth from this mortal life she shall triumph over corruption, as Christ her Son triumphed over hell.

Branches such as these had the God-loving Hebrew children spread before Christ, as He drew near to His Passion, crying out to the praise and glory of the future Conqueror of death: *Hosanna in the highest* (Mt. xxi. 9); that is, *Save us, O Thou on high!* For in the Hebrew tongue, *hosanna* means *save us.* And as then the palm-branches were a symbol of Christ's triumph over death, so here the giving of a palm-branch to the Mother of God was a certain assurance of Her approaching triumph over death's corruption.

The women she had called to her now begin to weep; and others who had gathered were also lamenting, and within the house the tears begin to flow in streams. They beg her not to abandon them. But she says to them: 'Let the will of God and of My Son be done in me: for, *He is my God and I will glorify him: the God of my father, and I will exalt him* (Ex. xv. 2). He is my Son according to the Flesh; yet is He Father and Creator and God of His own Mother. If you therefore as parents cannot even for a moment endure separation from your mortal children, born of earthly union, what of me who have begotten God as my Son, and Whom I love with my whole undivided heart; for I conceived Him without man, remaining immaculate and undefiled? Am I not then more even than you overcome by love? In the loss to one of you of a child, you console one another; but I who have been honoured to have Christ God for my only Child, how can I not set out with joy to Him Who lives for ever, and gives life to all?'

And while she was speaking these words, of a sudden there came the sound of thunder, and from the gathered clouds a rainstorm began to fall; and descending also, like the raindrops, the Apostles of Christ came all together to rest in the house of the Virgin. And seeing her they greet her most lovingly; and then, learning from her the reason of their coming home, they address her in these words: 'As long as we had thee dwelling with us in this world, O Mother of God, we were comforted; for seeing thee, it was as if we were seeing the Christ Himself. Now we are filled with grief at thy departure from this life. But since by God's command, and thy own deep Mother's love, thou art eager to depart to God, we rejoice for Him that this shall be fittingly fulfilled in thee, and that it may come to pass without delay. For in thee also we have been given a pledge of eternal life, and, through thy going, in thee we gain a Mediatrix with God. Nor is it truly fitting that the Mother of God should linger here, in the midst of a generation perverse and evil, but rather that she should be translated to heavenly mansions and to heavenly joys.'

Though saying these things, they were themselves inconsolable and in tears. She therefore said to them: 'Rejoice, spiritual sons of my Son. Remember His words; how in the time of His Passion He did not say that the joy of this world would be turned into sorrow (Jn. xvi. 20).

And as this day I am going to Him, do not turn my joy into sorrow. But as to my body, as I shall compose it upon the bed, let all of you take charge of it. For then faithfully cared for by you who are His Disciples, it will be to me as though I were laid in the tomb by the hands of my Son.'

In the midst of these happenings Paul the Apostle also appeared, coming from afar where he had been preaching the Gospel. Knocking at the door of the house, it was opened to him most joyfully by John the Apostle, who himself a virgin had received from Christ the Virgin as his mother. At sight of Paul the Apostles were all refreshed in spirit, and receiving him with honour they placed him in the principal seat, with a footstool at his feet. The Virgin received him with cheerful countenance. Paul threw himself at her God-bearing feet; but when he learned from her the reason why he also had come, opening his mouth with a great and sorrowful groan, his mouth so ready, so instructive, he began to speak a wondrous discourse in praise of the Virgin, of which these are but a few sentences:

'Hail, O Mother of Life! glory of all that I preach! Hail, fulfilment of all that I seek in the souls of men! And though I have not seen Christ in the Flesh, yet seeing thee in the body who clothed with a body Him Who is without body, I am comforted as though I beheld Christ. My longing to see Christ is fulfilled beholding thy face. Till yesterday I preached to the Gentiles that thou brought forth Christ in the Flesh. Henceforth I shall teach the Gentiles that thou hast now crossed over to Him, and that their salvation shall

be assured by thy intercession: since they now have the help of thy unshakeable power with God.'

And after these and many other things, as we rejoice to learn, had been said by Paul in praise and thanksgiving to the Mother of God, the Virgin took leave of them all. She lay down on the bed she had strewn with flowers, composing her immaculate body as she wished it to be, and then as though in sleep she breathed forth her spirit. Or, to speak more truly, while waking she was separated from her body; her body remaining, untouched by corruption.

And when Peter in a loud voice had commended her blameless spirit to Christ and to God, and to her Son in respect of His body, he exhorted his fellow leader Paul to offer in conclusion the accustomed prayer over the remains of the Virgin. Paul however made signs of refusal, saying that it was more fitting that Peter the chief Pastor should do this. Peter nodded his head in agreement, but still wished to yield place to Paul because of his great labours in preaching the Gospel. But Paul would not be persuaded, insisting that the primacy conferred by Christ on Peter must be free from innovations. So Peter then offers the prayer, and following this the other Apostles raising the bier upon their shoulders, with lights and the singing of the sacred canticles, with honour and reverence, bear the body of the Virgin to the tomb.

A great multitude of people accompanied them, in mourning for the Mother of Life. They were all astonished at her sudden departure, and they were also greatly wondering at the sudden appearance from the air of the far-scattered Apostles. For the fame of this happening had spread through all Jerusalem: that in the midst of thunder and lightning, amid dense clouds and the shrieking of the wind, like the rain or the dew falling, they had dropped down to the house of the Virgin.

A certain evil person, and one of the unbelieving Hebrews (they who are the *vanity of vanities* (Eccles. i. 2); for as stones of stumbling and wranglers, they are ever contentious) stretched forth his hands: *For in their hands*, it is written, *there is ever iniquity* (Ps. xxv. 10); and shook the bier on which her pallet lay, rashly attempting to lay hands on the body of the Immaculate, not fearing to dishonour the earthly throne of the Most High. On the instant both his hands were cut off; a warning and a cause of fear and trembling to the Jews who had ever been bold and shameless to Christ.

The sacred remains now draw near the resting place. But the Apostles hold back through reverence and holy fear from touching the body of the Virgin. Because of their exceeding reverence, and because they knew that this body had been made the Vessel of the Undefiled, the Disciples manifested a praiseworthy fear of touching the body. The faithful too, among the crowd, were eager to seize some portion of the shroud as a blessed relic. But no one dared lay hands on it, with the fearful example before their eyes of the punishment of the Hebrew's rash impiety.

And then by common choice and decision of the Apostles, Peter and Paul, each taking hold of an end of the sheet, raise the sacred body from the pallet and place it in the tomb.

And while the weight of the sacred body still rested on the sheet, and while they themselves had not yet touched the body with their hands to raise it, these all-honoured and reverent Apostles, who because of their love of God were showing fear of Him, these *uplifted and elevated hills brought low*,[11] these exalted ministers of God, perfected in the love of Christ, honouring with all reverence the Son through His Mother, and the Mother because of her Son; they who because of God made Flesh, have truly become the humble servants of her who gave Him Flesh, His Mother; from their hands, while all present watched carefully, the immaculate body of the Virgin was borne away. Who seized it no one saw. It was the Invisible God; it was the Unseen God, invisible to all. The linen sheet was then swept upwards by a sudden wind from the hands of the Apostles, and was seen moving like a swift cloud through the sky: the visible fulfilment of *the swift cloud* of the prophecy (Is. xix. 1).

The Disciples knew then that Christ together with His angels had come to meet His Mother; and upon this, believing that He had taken her with Him, they lifted up their voices in praise and gave glory to God. And turning to the people they also spoke to them of what had taken place, saying: 'Men of Israel. It has just now been made manifest to you all concerning Mary, the Mother of Christ in the Flesh, that she whom you together with us brought to this tomb as one dead, has been taken up out of our hands. Let no one therefore show himself as unbelieving in this matter. And let no man accuse us of theft in respect of the body, as in the case of Christ's Body. And should this happening come to the ears of the Ruler and to your high priests, make known the simple truth, not what is false. Be witnesses to what you have seen. Let you be as new angels in flesh coming this day to the tomb. Let your tongues be as their wings in the service of the truth. Let you also declare: Behold the place where they laid the Virgin (Mk. xvi. 6). But Mary the Mother of Life has been assumed. See the linen sheet, without her who had been wrapped in it, gone to seek her it had enfolded. As her winding sheet it was a lifeless thing. Now as if endowed with life it follows after her, as though longing to be spread beneath her. Be you also to her who was assumed, as the women who came to the tomb bearing sweet spices. Run, announce to all, that from this tomb she has been translated to Life.

'And thou also art blessed, O Garden of Gethsemani; thou hast gained honour approaching that of the field of Joseph.[12] Thither Peter and John had come running, and finding the linen cloths and head band they believed that Christ had risen from the dead (Jn. xx). In thee, Gethsemani, all we who are disciples of the Saviour as well as this multitude, gathered by the tomb of the Ever-Virgin Mary, have seen her placed for burial in the tomb, and then assumed. For it is beyond all disputation that before the mouth of the tomb could be sealed with a stone, so that by sealing it and placing a guard, no pretext might be given to the incredulous on the grounds of theft, she became invisible there. Behold! after she had been praised with sacred canticles and placed in the burial-place, she leaves the tomb empty, to fill paradise with her glory; and now she has entered into rest amid the joys of heaven, in the Presence of God.' These and others similar were the words of the Apostles spoken of thee, O Mother of God.

The words I have addressed to thee, O All-Pure Lady, will suffice even for my presumption – indeed the whole world would fail in attempting to praise thy glories – and with them I shall end my discourse in honour of thy Feast. Be thou mindful of thy Christian servants! Commend our petitions to God, strengthen our hope, make strong our faith, keep the churches in unity, strengthen the empire with new victories, come to the assistance of the army, give peace to the world, delivering it from all dangers and tribulations, and pray that for each one of us, delivered from the danger of damnation, the day of final reward may come. For to whom else shall we go? Thou hast the words of eternal life (Jn. vi. 69), in thy power to plead for us with God. For it is thou who hast ever done, and never ceases to do great wonders to help us, and holy is thy name; that by men and angels shall be blessed for ever, now and throughout all ages. Amen.

II. St John Damascene, Priest, Confessor and Doctor

Oration on the Glorious Dormition of the Most Holy Mother of God the Ever-Virgin Mary[13]

1. Though there is no one among men, even had he a thousand tongues and a thousand mouths, who can speak with fitting praise and reverence of the holy departure from this life of the Mother of God; nor could all the united tongues of all men throughout the world praise her with fitting praise: for she is above all praise; nevertheless, since it is pleasing and acceptable to God that we should as best we can honour her with all our heart, with all our love and fervour, and since what is pleasing to her Son, will also be pleasing and acceptable to the Mother of God, bear with me then, O Best of Shepherds, and pleasing to God, while I, obedient to your request, attempt once more to speak her praises.

And at the same time, we invoke the help of that Word Who from her took Flesh, Who fills every mouth that is opened to Him, Who is her sole Adornment, her all-glorious Song of Praise; knowing that when we begin to sing her praises, we pay our debts, and paying them begin again to be her debtors: so that our debt to her is ever beginning, and ever being paid. And may she also be favourable to us whom we have undertaken to praise: She who as Mother of God, the Creator and Maker and Ruler of all things, is above all creatures and Mistress of all that was made. And may this gracious assembly of those who love to hear of divine things, be patient with me, and in your kindness help me in my purpose; and be patient also with the poverty of the words I address to you.

For I am like some poor gardener who brings to one who is divinely appointed to rule, and who already possesses a bountifully provided table and a palace filled with the most exquisite perfumes, a rare purple violet out of season, or a fragrant rose blooming on a thorn, with green leaves and buds of varying colours and slowly turning pink, or offers some rare fruit of autumn. The ruler would not consider the poverty of the gift, but would look rather to its rarity, and admire its unusual appearance; seeing in it what is pleasing and appreciating it with kindness. And he would reward the gardener with a gift, with something rich and beautiful. And so do we come from the winter of our poverty, bearing flowers to our Queen, weaving a garland of words in this contest of praise, and to proclaim her yet more, labouring upon our purpose with the heart, as with iron upon stone, to press out from the mind, the source of speech, as from unripe grapes, some spark, some vintage of words to put before you who love words, and are eager to hear ours. For what shall we offer to the Mother of the Word but words? Like delights in like, and also in that which is dear. Opening then the starting gates of my discourse, and loosening the reins a little, let us send it forth like a horse, pressing forward to the race. Be Thou a Helper and a Partner to me, O Word of God! Give understanding to my foolish mind, make smooth the path of my word, and so direct its course that it may be pleasing to Thee, Who art the end of all discourse, and of all understanding.

2. This day the Holy and Singular Virgin is presented in the sublime and heavenly Temple; she who loved virginity so much that in her it was like a most pure fire. For while every virgin loses her virginity in bringing forth, she was a virgin before her delivery, a virgin in her delivery, a virgin after she had brought forth. This day the sacred and living Ark of the Living God, who bore within her womb her own Creator, took up her rest within that temple of the Lord *that was not made with hands* (Acts xvii. 24).

And David her forefather, and her father in God, dances with joy (II Kings vi. 14), and the Angels dance with him, and the Archangels applaud, and the Heavenly Powers give praise, and with them the Principalities rejoice, and the Dominions exult, and the Powers are filled with gladness, and Thrones share in this glorious feast of praise; the Cherubim celebrate with song, and the Seraphim proclaim her glory. Nor are they less honoured, adding glory to the Mother of glory.

This day the most holy Dove, the inviolate and stainless soul that was consecrated to the Divine Spirit, flying forth from the Ark, from that body that had conceived God, and gave beginning to His bodily life, finds rest for her feet, reaching that world that is known only to the soul, abiding there, in that stainless land and dwelling place of our heavenly home.

This day the Eden of the New Adam welcomes its living Paradise, in whom our sentence has been repealed, in whom the Tree of Life was planted, in whom our nakedness has been clothed. For no longer are we naked and without clothing, or destitute of the shining splendour of the divine image, or stripped of the abounding grace of the Spirit; no more lamenting our nakedness do we cry: *I have put off my garment, how shall I put it on* (Cant. v. 3)? For into this Paradise the serpent found no entrance where, grasping at that lying promise of deification, we became *as senseless beasts* (Ps. xlviii. 13). For He Who is the only Begotten Son of God, while being God, and of the same substance as the Father, from this Virgin, from this pure earth, formed Himself as Man. And I a man, have become a God; and I who was mortal, have become immortal, and have put off the *garments of skin* (Gen. iii. 21). For I have put away corruption, and have clothed myself in the garment of Divinity.

This day the Immaculate Virgin, unacquainted with earthly affections, and nurtured on heavenly affections, has not returned to earth; but, belonging truly to the life of heaven, she has taken up her abode in heavenly dwellings. And who would sin against truth by calling her Heaven, but he who truly knows that, by reason of her incomparable perfection, she is above all the Heavens? For He Who made the Heavens, the Architect of all things that are made, both of this world and of the world above, of things visible and invisible, Who is Himself within no place (if that can be called place within which things are) made Himself, and without seed, an Infant in her; made her the beauteous treasure-house of all His riches, and of His All-Embracing Godhead; without constriction containing Himself wholly within her, remaining Whole within her; His Presence unbounded by any space.

This day the Treasure of Life, the Abyss of grace (I know not in what manner I may make this clear with my presuming and faltering lips), is veiled in Life-bringing death. And she drew near to it without fear, who had given birth to death's Destroyer; if indeed we may speak of her all-holy and life-giving departure as death. For how could she who truly brought Life to all, become subject to death? But she yields to the law laid down by Him she had borne, and as a daughter of the Old Adam submits to this inherited chastisement: since her Son Who is Life Itself had not refused it; but as Mother of the Living God she is fittingly restored to Him. For if God said: *Lest perhaps he* (who first was made man) *put forth his hand, and take of the tree of life, and eat, and live for ever* (Gen. iii. 22); how could it be that she who had conceived Life Itself, Which is without beginning and unceasing, suffering neither beginning nor end, would not live for ever in perfect life?

3. Of old the Lord God, drove from the Paradise of Eden the founders of our race, when filled with the wine of their transgression they had drugged the eye of the heart, and in the sickness that followed their sin the eyes of their mind were heavy, and held by a deadly sleep. Shall Paradise not now receive her who has struck down the attack of every evil, who has brought forth the Flower of obedience of God and of the Father, and made a beginning of Life for all men? Shall the heavens not open their gates in welcome? Beyond all doubt. Eve gave ear to the message of the serpent, listened to the counsels of the enemy, and was caught in her senses by the assault of false and evil pleasure, incurring a sentence of pain and grief; so that she must *bring forth children in sorrow*, and together with Adam, was condemned to death, and assigned to the world of darkness.

But how could death swallow this truly blessed soul, who humbly gave ear to the word of God, and was filled with the power of the Holy Ghost, and at the message of an Archangel, accepted the will of the Father, and without passion and without man conceived in her womb the Word of God Who fills all things, and who as was fitting brought Him forth without pain and who was wholly united to God, how could death devour her? How could hell receive her? How could corruption dare touch the body that had contained Life? Such thoughts are abhorrent and wholly repugnant in regard to the body and soul of the Mother of God. Looking upon her, death trembled. For when it had assailed her Son, death had learned from what He endured and, learning, had become wary.

Not for her the dark descent to hell. For her a smooth and gentle path to heaven had been prepared. *Where I am, there also my minister shall be*, said Christ, Who is the Way and the Truth; how much more shall His Mother not dwell with Him?

And as before she had conceived and brought forth without pain, so also was her going forth from life without pain.

Truly fearful is the death of the wicked (Ps. xxxiii. 22). What shall we say of that death in which the sting of death, sin, is slain, but that it was the beginning of unending, perfect Life? *Precious* indeed *in the sight of the Lord is the death of the saints* (Ps. cxv. 15). Yet more precious the translation of God's Mother.

Now let the heavens rejoice, and the angels sing in jubilee. Now let earth be glorified, and men exult for joy. Now let the sky be filled with songs and canticles, and night shake off its sad and shapeless gloom and imitate in brightness day's fiery splendour. For the Living City of the Lord God of Hosts is raised on high; and the Kings, who are the Apostles, established by Christ as rulers over all the earth, bear their most precious gift, the ever Virgin Mother of God, from the temple of the Lord, the visible Sion, to that heavenly Jerusalem *which is above, which is free, and our mother* (Gal. iv. 26).

4. It will not, I believe, be out of place if I outline in words, and picture to you as best I can, the wonders that have been accomplished in the holy Mother of God and which, without either exaggerating or depreciating, and very comprehensively, have been handed down to us, as the saying is, from father to son, from the beginning.[14] For I see her as more sanctified than the saints, more sacred than the sacred, purer than the pure. She is the precious urn of the manna (Heb. ix.

4); rather let me say, she is more truly a fountain, lying on her humble bed in the holy and glorious city of David, in that famed and shining Sion in which the law of the letter was fulfilled, the law of the spirit revealed; in which Christ the Lawgiver fulfilled the Paschal Figure and God gave us the True Pasch of the Old and New Testament: in which the Lamb of God Who takes away the sins of the world, initiated the mystical supper with His Disciples, and offered Himself for them as a fatted calf (Lk. xv. 23), and as the Grape of the true vine that was treaded out in the winepress. In her Christ rising from the dead was seen by the Apostles, and they believed, as did also Thomas, and through him the world, that He was *the Lord and God* (Jn. xx. 28); bearing within Him two natures, even after His Resurrection from the dead, and corresponding to them, two operations and two free wills unto all ages. She is the citadel of the churches. She is the inn of the Disciples. In her, with a mighty sound, and with the gift of many tongues, the Most Holy Spirit was poured out upon the Apostles; in her the Theologian (*Theologos*) who had received the care of the Mother of God, ministered to her needs. She is the Mother of all the Churches throughout the whole world, and the dwelling place of the Mother of God after the Resurrection of her Son from the dead. In her therefore, the Blessed Virgin lies upon her thrice-blessed bed.

5. When I came to this point in my discourse (if I may reveal my own feelings), I burn with a most ardent fire of love, and am over-

come by a shivering awe and by gladdening tears, I clasp to my breast as it were that bed, that blessed, that venerable bed, abounding in portents, as though embracing that tabernacle from which Life came forth, rejoicing in its sanctifying touch. And even that sacred and all-holy temple that was worthy of God I seemed also to touch with my hands; and to press my eyes, my brow, my lips, my throat and cheek to its members, seeming to feel her presence as though she were present in body; though perceiving with my eyes that what I longed to see, I could not see at all. How can I see that which was caught up to the heavenly dwellings? And then thoughts such as these came to me:

6. What honours He has conferred on her Who commanded us to honour our parents! God the Father Who had decreed that those who had been scattered over the whole world to fish for men, with the many-tongued and wondrous gift of the Spirit, and to save them; capturing them by the net of the word from out the deeps of deceit, and bringing them to the spiritual and heavenly table of the mystical banquet of the Father and His Co-Equal and Consubstantial Son, had again by royal command decreed that these men should come to Jerusalem; whom a cloud then enclosed, as in a net, gathering them together like eagles from the ends of the earth: For *wheresoever the body shall be,* said Christ the Truth, *there shall the eagles also be gathered* (Mt. xxiv. 28). For if these words were spoken of that second great and glorious Coming from Heaven of Him Who spoke those words, it will not be out of place to use them here again as seasoning to our discourse.

There were present then these eye-witnesses and ministers of the Word, and as was fitting they began also to minister to His Mother, and as though they were now about to receive from her a rich and most precious inheritance. For who can doubt that she is a well of blessing, a fountain of all graces? Together with them were their companions and successors, as sharing both their ministry and their blessing: for a common task there being a common reward. There was also present, divinely chosen, a group from those who lived about Jerusalem. It was fitting that the descendants of the Just and the Patriarchs of old should keep them company, and have part in this sacred guard of honour; for they had clearly foretold the bodily and most merciful nativity from her of the Word of God for our salvation.

Nor were the hosts of the angels wanting. For, as we believe, obedient to the King, and honoured to stand in His Presence, it was fitting that they should stand about her, as a guard of honour to His Mother according to the Flesh; she who is truly most blessed, most happy, who has been placed above all born of men and above all creation. All were there round about her, standing in the flashing brightness of the Spirit, while she shone upon them with her glorious radiance, as they, reverential, and with the eyes of the mind look upon her with awe and unwavering love.

7. And here words were spoken that were divinely inspired and divinely uttered. Here hymns were

heard worthy of the divine splendour, and of her going forth. For it was fitting on this occasion to offer praise and honour to the infinite goodness of God, to the immensity of His Majesty, to His infinite power, to the immeasurable height and depth of His forbearance with men, to the over-flowing riches of His incomprehensible kindness, and lastly to the inexhaustible abyss of His love: how not departing from His Majesty He descended to our uplifted lowliness, the Father and the Holy Spirit consenting; how He Who is supersubstantial was supernaturally created in the womb of a woman; how when He was God He became man, remaining at the same time both God and man; how not departing from the nature of the Godhead, He remains like us a partaker of the same flesh and blood (Heb. ii. 14); how He Who fills all things, and by the word of His mouth upholds the universe, should dwell in this narrowed home and, lastly; how the material and grass-like body of this glorious Virgin could receive within her the burning fire of the Godhead, and like gold be neither burned nor consumed.

God willing them, these things took place. For by God's will all things are possible which without His will cannot be. Then after this there began a contest of praise. Not that one sought to surpass the other (for that is vain glory, and far from pleasing to God), but as though striving with all their love and with all their might to sing the praises of God and to do honour to God's Mother.

8. And then Adam and Eve, the Parents of our race, from exultant lips cry out, their words heard far and wide: 'O Blessed Daughter! Thou hast taken away the punishment of our disobedience. Thou, inheriting from us a mortal body, dost now clothe us with the garment of immortality. Thou sprung from our loins, hast brought back our happiness. Thou hast ended the the pangs of childbirth, broken the bonds of death, restored us to our ancient home. We closed paradise; thou hast thrown wide the way to the Tree of Life. From our delight came sorrow; through thee our sorrow has brought us yet greater joy, and how canst thou all fair, O Immaculate, taste death? Thou art the bridge to Life, and the stairway to heaven; and death itself has become a crossing to immortality. Thou truly art blessed, O Mother most blest! For who except the Word, has offered herself to suffer what she took upon herself to suffer!'

And upon this the whole choir of the Blessed burst forth: 'Thou hast fulfilled what was foretold us. Thou has brought us the joy we awaited. For through thee we have been loosed from the bonds of death. Come to us, O divine and Life-bearing Treasure. Come to us who long for thee; Thou who hast fulfilled our longings.'

And no less fervent were the words of the saints who stood by, and who were still in the body, as they cry out: 'Remain with us; our consolation, our sole comfort on this earth! Do not leave us orphans, O Mother; who with thee are put to the test for thy Son. Thou art our rest from toil; refreshment in our weariness. Thou hast power to remain if thou will it; and to depart there is nothing to oppose thee. If thou goest, O Tabernacle of God, let us also go with thee: we who through thy Son are thy people. Thou art our sole consolation left on this earth; and while thou live, we live; and dying with thee, to die is heavenly bliss. But why do we speak of dying? For to thee death is Life, and better than life, far surpassing and not to be compared with this present life; for us how can life be life when we live it without thy company?'

9. It seems to me that the Apostles together with the whole Church appear to have addressed the Blessed Virgin in these and similar words. But when they saw the Mother of God draw near her end and awaiting it with burning love of God, they then began the hymns for her going forth, and moved by the impulse of divine grace, and touched on the lips by the Spirit, and caught up out of the body, they sighed with longing to be let go with the dying Mother of God; straining as if to go of their own intense desire.

And when they had fulfilled this task of love and reverence, they wove for her a rich and multifold garland of sacred songs, praising her as a God-given treasure, addressing her in the words spoken at the going forth from this life. And these spoke of the fleetingness of this present life, and of the hidden mysteries of the joys to come.

10. These then, it seems to me, are the events that in harmony and common accord took place on that day. The Coming of the King to His own Mother, to receive in His Divine and Immaculate Hand her holy soul, pure and undefiled. And she as likely said: 'Into Thy Hands, my Son, I commend my spirit. Receive my soul, which Thou hast loved, preserving it blameless. To Thee, and not to earth, do I give up my body. Keep safe that in which Thou wert pleased to dwell, and which in giving birth Thou kept virgin. Take me to Thyself, that wherever Thou, the Fruit of my womb, shall be, I also may dwell. I am borne onwards towards Thee, Who never ceased to come to me. In my going from this life, be Thou the Comfort of my most dear children; whom it pleases Thee to call Thy brethren. Through the stretching forth of these my hands, heap blessing upon blessing upon them.'

Then she lifted up her hands, as we may believe, and blessed all those who were gathered there; and having finished speaking to them in this way, she hears at close hand such words as these: 'Come, O My most Blessed Mother, come to My place of rest: *Arise, make haste, my love, most beautiful amongst women. For winter is now past; the time of pruning is come. Thou art all fair, O my love, and there is no spot in thee. And the sweet smell of thy ointments is above all aromatical spices!*' (Cant. ii. 10, 10, 11; iv. 7. 10.) And hearing these words, she gives up her spirit into hands of her Son.

11. And what then happens? A commotion and a change of the elements, strange sounds and voices, the singing of canticles by angel choirs; some preceding her, some accompanying her, and some following after. Of these some formed as it were a guard of honour for her

pure and all-holy soul, going up with her as she ascended to heaven, until they stood with the Queen by the heavenly throne. Others surrounded the divine and sacred body, proclaiming with angelic song that she was the Mother of God.

What of those who stood around her most holy and sacred body? With love and reverence, with tears of exultation, they gathered about her, tending that divine and holy tabernacle with loving care. They kiss each member, clinging to the body, as if to fill themselves from the holiness and blessing of its touch. Then diseases began to disappear, and troops of unclean spirits were banished, and driven in every direction to abodes of darkness. The air, the skies, the heavens were sanctified by the ascent of her spirit; the earth by the laying down of her body. Nor was water without its share of blessing. For she was washed with pure water. It did not make her clean but was rather itself made holy. And hearing was given to the deaf, the lame set firmly on their feet, sight given back to the blind, and the handwriting was blotted out against sinners who drew near in faith. And then? The spotless body is wrapped in pure linen sheets, and the Queen is laid back upon her bed. Then bearing lights and sweet spices and singing hymns they make ready to go in procession before her; and the angels singing in their tongue a hymn becoming to them; the Apostles, the holy God-fearing Fathers, singing canticles that were inspired by the Holy Spirit.

12. When in this time the Ark of the Lord, borne on the shoulders of the Apostles, departed from Mount Sion to the heavenly abode of rest, it crossed over to it by way of an earthly tomb. And first it was taken through the midst of the city, like a bride in her beauty, but she is adorned in the unapproachable radiance of the Spirit, and thence it was borne to that most holy place, Gethsemani, angels overshadowing her with their wings, going before and with her and following after, together with the whole assembly of the Church. And as when King Solomon compelled all the elders of Israel to bear the Ark of the Lord *out of the city of David, that is, out of Sion,* and place it in the temple of the Lord which He had built, the Priests took the Ark and the Tabernacle of the Covenant, and they bore it upon their shoulders: both Priests and Levites. And the King and all the people went before the Ark, and they sacrificed sheep and oxen without number; and at length the Priests set the Ark of the Covenant of the Lord in its place, near the oracle of the temple, in the Holy of Holies, beneath the wings of the cherubims (III Kings viii. 1 *et seq.*; II Paral. v. 2 *et seq.*).

And so was it here now, in the setting to rest of this rational Ark, not of the Covenant of the Lord, but of the Person of God the Word; He Who is the New Solomon, the Prince of Peace, the Supreme Artificer of all that is; and with Him the super-terrestrial hosts of the heavenly Intelligences, as well as the chief men of the New Testament, that is the Apostles, and with them all the multitude of the saints who were that day gathered together in Jerusalem. By the hands of angels her soul was borne into the Holy of Holies, to the archetypal, the true, the heavenly Holy of Holies, under the wings of the Cherubim to the innermost part beyond the veil, and placed upon her Throne, whither Christ Himself had in His Body preceded her, while her body is borne by the hands of the Apostles, the King of Kings veiling it within the radiance of His own Invisible Godhead, the whole company of the saints preceding her, their voices lifted in prayer, offering a sacrifice of prayer at her tomb, as though it were a bridal chamber, as, by way of it, they place her body amid the delights of Eden and in heavenly dwellings.

13. Perhaps there were Jews present also; such as were not wholly without feeling. And here it will not be out of place to add, as a sort of seasoning to this account, something which has been retold by many. It is related that when those who were bearing the blessed body of God's Mother had reached the slope of the opposite mountain, a certain Hebrew, a servant of sin, and a vagabond, imitating the servant of Caiphas who with his palm had struck the Magisterial and Divine Face of Christ God, becoming an instrument of the devil, with senseless insolence rushed at this most sacred tabernacle which angels approach in fear, violently and insanely clutched the bed with both hands, to drag it to the ground (prompted in this by the author of evil). But his assault was in vain, and he reaped the bitter and fitting fruit of his evil purpose. For they say that he was deprived of both his hands. For of a sudden the perpetrator of this unnatural attempt, was seen to be without hands until, by

means of faith, he came to his senses and repented. For further on, those carrying the bier, stood and the wretched man, touching with his arms that tabernacle from which Life had come, and which had given birth to wonders, his hands came forth again from the wrists. He had learned as many do, that disaster holds within it many and salutary lessons. But let us now return to the subject we have put before us.

14. From here they went on to the most sacred place of Gethsemani and here again there were embraces and greetings and again hymns of praise, sacred canticles, again calling on her by name with tears of anguish and longing, while sweat poured from them in streams that rivalled their tears. And so the immaculate body was placed in this renowned and all-glorious tomb, from whence after three days it was taken up to the heavenly mansion. For it was not fitting that this divine dwelling-place, this undug spring of the Waters of forgiveness, this unploughed cornland of the Heavenly Bread, this vine of the Immortal Grape, this ever-blooming and fruitful olive tree of the divine compassion, should be shut up in the folds of the earth. But just as the pure and holy Body taken from her, that was united to God the Word, rose on the third day from the tomb, so was it fitting that this body also should be taken from the tomb, that the Mother should be once more united with her Son. And as He had come down to her, so should she be raised to Him, to a better and more perfect resting-place; to heaven itself.

It was fitting, I repeat, that she

who had sheltered God the Word in her womb, should dwell in the house of her Son. And as the Lord had said that it was necessary for Him to be about His Father's business (Lk. ii. 49), so also was it fitting that the Mother should take up her abode in the Royal City of her Son, *in the House of the Lord, in the courts of the house of our God* (Ps. cxxxiv. 2). For if, *The dwelling in thee is as it were of all rejoicing* (Ps. lxxxvi. 7), where should she dwell who is the cause of our joy? It was fitting that she whose virginity was preserved in Childbirth without blemish, should also be preserved inviolate in death. It was fitting that she who had nourished the Creator as an Infant at the breast, should find shelter in His heavenly mansions. It was fitting that the Bride the Father had promised in marriage, should dwell in the heavenly bridal-chambers. It was fitting that she who had beheld her Son upon the Cross, and had received in her heart the sword of pain she had escaped in childbirth, should now look upon Him sitting next to the Father. Lastly it was fitting, that the Mother of God should receive back her Son, and as Mother of God receive the veneration of all creatures. For though the inheritance of parents ever passes on to the children, now however, to use the words of the wise man (Eccles. i. 7), the fountains of the sacred rivers turn back *from whence they come*: for the Son has made all creation the servant of His Mother.

15. Let us therefore celebrate this day the joyful departure of the Mother of God, not with music and Corybantic fury, not as those celebrating the orgies of the mother of the so-called gods, who, as foolish men will say, was the mother of many children, but who to tell the truth was not a mother at all. For such as these are but demons and shadowy images, pretending to be that which never was; using man's blindness to deceive and impose upon the folly of men. For how can that which has no body beget children in wedlock; in what way can they commingle? And how can that be god which first was not, and later is; through birth? That the devil is without body is known to all; even to those whose minds are blinded. Homer says somewhere in one of his works, referring to the conduct of these worthy gods:

> They eat no bread, nor drink of fiery wine,
> And so are bloodless, and called immortal.

They eat no bread, he says, nor do they drink of the heating wine, and because of this they are without blood, and so are called The Immortals. And justly and truly does he say, 'they are called'. They are called Immortals, but they are not what they are called. For they died the death of evil. We worship God; God, I repeat; not he who began to be, but, He Who Is, from all ages, above every cause, every design, every conception of our mind, above all nature. And we honour and venerate the Mother of God. We do not say that He derived the timeless beginning of His Godhead from her: for the birth of God the Word was not in time, and is Co-Eternal with the Father. We speak only of His second Birth, through His own deliberate Incarnation: for whose sake we know and confess. For our salvation, He became Incarnate Who was without a body like ours: that like by like might be redeemed. And He was made Flesh solely of this Sacred Virgin, and from her was brought forth; remaining wholly God, and becoming wholly man: wholly God in His Body, and Perfect Man in His Divinity. And so, confessing that this Virgin is God's Mother, we celebrate her falling asleep; not proclaiming that she is God (such things belong to the Greek fables), since we are announcing her death; but we proclaim her as the Mother of God Incarnate.

16. Let us who are the people of Christ, and enriched by Him, praise her this day with sacred canticles. Let us honour her with night-long vigils. Let us honour her with the purity of our soul and body; for she is in very truth the purest of all creatures and next to God Himself: for it is natural for like to glory in like. Let us do honour to her by showing mercy and compassion to the poor. For if God is served by nothing as by mercy, who will refuse to give glory to God's Mother by this means? Through her the unspeakable abyss of God's love has been made open to all. Through her the age-long war against the Creator has been ended. Through her our reconcilement with Him is confirmed, and peace and grace restored to us. And we are friends with the angels; and we who before were dishonoured, outcast, are now raised up as children of God. From her we have gathered the Fruit of Life; through her we have gained possession of the seed of immortality. She has become for us the intermediary of all graces. In her God became

man, and man became God. What more wondrous than this? What more blessed than this? I feel dizzy and fearful when I speak of it.

With Mary the prophetess (Ex. xv. 20), O earnest souls, let us dance with the timbrels; that is, mortifying *our members which are upon the earth* (Col. iii. 5): For this is the mystical meaning of the timbrel. Let us cry aloud for victory before the Ark of the Lord God of souls, and the walls of Jerusalem shall fall down (Jos. vi. 20): and by this I mean the evil prisons of the demons who are our enemies. Let us dance in the Spirit with David (II Kings vi. 14). For today the Ark of the Lord is at rest. And with Gabriel, the foremost of the angels, let us cry out: *Hail, full of grace; the Lord is with thee* (Lk. i. 28). Hail, thou inexhaustible sea of grace! Hail, sole comfort in sorrow! Hail, thou remedy that taketh pain from every heart! Hail, thou through whom death has been driven out and replaced by True Life!

17. And thou most sacred of all tombs, after the life-giving tomb of the Master, which became the fountain of the Resurrection – for I shall address thee as though thou were animate: 'Where is that pure gold which the hands of the Apostles stored in thee? Where are these inexhaustible riches? Where is the divinely given treasure that was here laid up? Where is the living table, where is the new book, in which, unutterably, God the Word has written without hands? Where is the abyss of grace, the ocean of healing? Where is the Life-giving fountain? Where is that most sacred and most lovable body of the

Mother of God?' 'Why do you seek' (*the tomb replies*) 'in the tomb what has been assumed into heavenly dwellings? Why do you exact from me an account of her dissolution? I had no power to go against the divine commands. Leaving here the winding sheet, that holy and sacred body, which filled me with holiness, with myrrh and with sweet odours, and made of me a divine temple, has been caught up and has departed; angels and archangels and all the powers of heaven accompanying it. Now angels keep watch about me. Now divine grace dwells in me. I have become for the sick a release from pain. I am become a well of healing, a defence against demons, a city of refuge to those who fly to me. Draw near in faith, ye people, and you will receive grace in streams. Draw near ye who are weak in faith. *All you that thirst*, Isaias exhorts us, *come to the waters; and you that have no money make haste, buy and eat without money* (Is. lv. 1).

'I cry out to you all, as one bringing good news: Whoever thirsts for the healing of his diseases, whether of the soul or body, for the washing away of his sins, for preservation from the assaults of the enemy, for the repose of the Kingdom of Heaven, let him draw near in faith to me and draw forth a most powerful and most profitable stream of grace. For just as the action of water, though it is a single and simple element, varies according to the nature of that with which it is blended, whether earth or air together with the clear light of the sun producing wine in the grape and oil in the olive, so likewise grace, single and simple though it is, works in each one differently, yet to the profit of each one who partakes of it. I have not acquired grace of my own nature. A tomb is filled with corruption, an abode of sorrow, a stranger to joy. I blessedly have received the most precious myrrh and am filled with its good odour; and this ointment is so sweet-smelling and so powerful that even its least touch will impart a sharing that cannot be taken away. For in truth God does not repent of His gifts (Rom. xi. 29). Here have I received the fount of joy, and its unfailing overflow has enriched me.'

18. You hear, beloved Fathers and Brothers, in what words this venerable tomb speaks to us. That they are true is evident from the History of Euthymius, in which, in Book III, chapter 40, he writes these words:[15] 'We have said earlier that the holy Pulcheria built many churches in honour of Christ and the Saints in the city of Constantinople. One of these is that which was built in Blachernis (outside Constantinople) at the beginning of the reign of Emperor Marcian of pious memory. When they had built this church in honour of the Most Blessed Mother of God, the Ever-Virgin Mary, and adorned it with every perfection, they were also eager to obtain the most holy body which had received God within it; and they called on Juvenal, Archbishop of Jerusalem, and the bishops of Palestine, who were then in the royal city, because of the Council of Chalcedon, that was being held there, and spoke to them as follows: "We have heard that in Jerusalem, the first, and a singularly beautiful church to the Mother of God, the Ever-Virgin Mary, has been built in

a place that is called Gethsemani, whither her Life-bearing body was borne and placed in a tomb. Accordingly, we desire to bring this most sacred relic here for the protection of the Imperial City."

'To this Juvenal replied: "Though nothing is written in the holy, divinely inspired Scriptures concerning the death of Mary the Mother of God, yet we have received from ancient and most reliable tradition, that at the time of her glorious falling asleep, the whole company of the Apostles, who were dispersed throughout the world for the salvation of the gentiles, were in a moment of time lifted high above the earth and brought together in Jerusalem. And when they were there, they beheld an angelic vision and heard the divine music of the heavenly Powers, and so amid divine and heavenly praise and with words that cannot be spoken they commended her holy soul to the hands of God, And that her God-conceiving body was with angelic and apostolic singing, taken up and borne in procession to Gethsemani, and there placed in a little tomb.

' "For three days a chorus of angels continued to sing above it. After the third day, when the angelic singing had ended, the Apostles who were present, together with Thomas who had been absent, but had come after the third day, now desired to venerate the body that had borne God; and they opened the little tomb. But no trace of her all-blessed body could be found; and taking the winding sheets, which were filled with fragrance, they closed the tomb. Wondering at this mystery, they could only think that He Whom it had pleased to take

flesh from the Virgin Mary, to become Man in her, and to be born of her in the flesh, God the Word, and the Lord of Glory, that He Who after she had given birth had preserved her in perfect virginity, to the same it was now pleasing that after she had departed this life, her immaculate and undefiled body should be honoured by being made incorrupt, and by being translated before the general and universal resurrection of the dead.

' "There were then present with the Apostles the most worthy Timothy, the Apostle and first bishop of the Ephesians and Dionysius the Areopagite, as the great Dionysius himself testifies in what he wrote concerning the blessed Hierotheos,[16] who also was then present, to the above mentioned blessed Apostle Timothy in these words:

' " "At the time when the holy and inspired high priests of God, and we also, as you know, and many of our holy brethren, had come together to behold the body that had given a beginning to Life (there were also present James, the brother of the Lord, and Peter, the leader and most revered head of the Apostles), and after we had seen the body, all desired to praise in hymns, each as best he could, the infinite goodness of the divine Majesty. Next after the divine Teachers, he surpassed as you know, all other teachers of sacred things, wholly going out of himself, wholly caught up out of his senses, seeming to become part of what was sung; seeming to all who saw and heard him, those who knew him and those who did not, to be divinely inspired, and that his singing of hymns was also divinely inspired. And what need I tell you of the things that were there divinely spoken of? For unless my memory fails me, I know that many times I have heard from you certain portions of those divinely inspired hymns.' "

'When the royal messengers had heard this account, they asked the Archbishop Juvenal that this holy tomb, together with the garments of the most glorious and most holy Mother of God which were placed in it, should be sent to them under seal. And when they had received them, they were placed in the church of the Mother of God, which is situated in Blachernis. And so these things took place.'

19. What are we to say in reply to the tomb? The grace you possess is indeed rich and unfailing. But divine power is not circumscribed by place; and neither is the goodness of the Mother of God. For if it were restricted to the tomb alone, few would gain by it. Now it is poured out in every place throughout the world. Let us then make our own soul a treasure-house of the Mother of God. How shall we do this? She is a virgin and a lover of virgins. She is pure and a lover of purity. If then, together with the body, we keep our soul pure, we shall obtain that her love shall be with us. She flies from every foulness, and turns aside from all unclean passions. She has a horror of the glutton, and a special loathing of the vice of fornication, and

shrinks from its polluted discussions as from a brood of vipers. She repels with disdain the speech that is obscene and licentious and perverted She drives from her carnal lures and perfumes. She hates the swelling of anger, and cannot endure inhumanity, envy and jealousy. She turns away from useless vain-glory. Pride and arrogance she resists with hostility. She hates as the enemy of our salvation, the remembrance of past injuries. She regards each single vice as a death-bringing poison.

But her joy is in the contrary things. For contraries are healed by contraries. She rejoices in fasting, in self-control, and in the songs of the psalms. And she rejoices with purity, with virginity, with holy wisdom. With these she is ever at peace, and with gentleness of spirit. Love, mercy, humility; these she holds like children to her breast. In a word, she sorrows over all wickedness, but rejoices in all virtue, as if each one were her own special gift.

If therefore we turn with all our heart from our former wickedness, and with all zeal love the virtues and make them our constant companions, she will come often to visit her servants, bringing with her a train of all the graces, and together with them Christ her Son. She will bring with her to dwell in our hearts the King and Lord of all: To Whom be glory and honour, power and majesty and magnificence, now and for ever, world without end. Amen.

III. St Lomman, Abbot

The Praises of Mary[17]

Chorus

O Mary, Loving Mary,
Our joy and our delight.

1

Joy of the Father,
Love of the Son,
Delight of the Holy Spirit,
Delight of the Most High God.
Thou who knew not man,
Mother of the Holy One,
Mother of Him Who was never
made.
He drank life from thy breasts.
Before Adam He knew thee,
To Adam He told of thee.

2

Eve's weakness is thy strength.
Angels are enraptured before thee.
The Blessed bow down before thee.
Michael is thy Captain.
Gabriel thy Messenger.
Raphael thy Healer.
Angels and Saints feast on thy
beauty.
Delight of God,
Peerless Mary,
Thy face is heavenly beauty.

3

Straight lily without spot,
Beautiful flower of every perfume,
Heavenly rose, whose beauty draws
all.
Choicest and rarest flower of the
Father's Garden;
Tended by His angels.
Gentle Mary, Loving Mary.
Heavenly wind,
Spring rain,
Blinding Light that overcasts the sun.
Mightier than the mountains.

4

Greater than the seas.
The sun is thy chariot,
The moon and stars thy playthings,
The clouds skip like lambs around
thy feet.
The works of His hands are subject
to thee;
For thou art His Beloved
Who rulest from the Trinity.
Beauty that captivates all hearts.
Light that dispels all darkness,
Mary, whiter than the snows.

5

Envy of the fallen prince.
Satan fears thee and awaits for thy
heel;
He alone fears thee, for he never
knew thee.
Thy name is a scourge that sears him
more than fire.
The lost one in the pit groans;
His throne rocked at thy coming.
The beauty of thy countenance fills
him with terror.
He flies before thee; he fears the
Light.
Mary, thou art terrible in battle.
Hell trembles at thy name.

6

Thunder and Lightning to the bot-
tomless pit.
Destroyer of the Evil One's king-
dom.
Angels waited on thy word.
The heavens were hushed.
At thy consent angels sang hymns of
great joy.
The Father Eternal smiled on thee.
The Son became thine own.

The Divine Spirit took thee unto Himself.

Silent Mary, the Holy Spirit spoke through thee.

Elisabeth proclaimed thee.

7

All men claim thee.

All peoples bless thy name.

Broken-hearted Mary at the Cross.

You saw the rabble mock thy Son.

You saw the lance open His side.

You saw them cast dice for His garments.

You who care for all, could not give him to drink, when He cried, *I thirst.*

He gave thee to us as our Mother.

You saw Him die.

You knew He was God.

8

Crimson rose of heavenly fragrance.

Our birthright; lost through Eve's disobedience, was restored through thee.

From thy pure blood a stream has arisen that pours over the earth,

Cleansing and healing our sin-stained souls and paying our ransom.

From thy pure flesh was made Food for us who know thy Son.

Beautiful Mary, you raised women to a new dignity.

Adam's Fall did not stain thee.

Thy body did not know corruption.

Peaceful sleep fell upon thee.

Thy feet rested on the wings of angels.

9

In their hands they carried thee.

The heavens opened to thee.

You reign with thy Son.

He placed the Sceptre in thy hand.

The world He made thy footstool, Who rulest with love.

The thrones of the great shall fall before thee.

Woe to them that shall raise themselves against thee, to mock thee.

He Who made thee, and came from thee, shall meet them as the bear robbed of her young.

Woe to them in that day, when he comes: For He guards thee as the apple of His eye.

10

Thou, His creature; in thee He saw Perfection.

He glories in thee; the work of His hands.

As the Faithful Bridegroom, He is jealous if they hurt thee.

Spotless Maid of Nazareth, humble unknown;

The humble and the little ones know thee and bless thee.

The Angels in choir sing thy praises at God's Throne.

We thy children, poor, weak and sinful, sing thy praises.

All men shall call thee blessed.

Peoples of many colours shall sing thy praises.

In strange tongues they shall call thee: Light of Dawn.

11

For thy Son is at hand.

Strange men, who live not as men, shall know thee;

And find shelter beneath thy mantle.

Fierce warriors shall become as little children, and grasp thy girdle.

Their daughters shall cover their heads with thy veil,

And live by thy example.

From the high mountains and from valleys they shall follow thee, from the plains and from the deserts.

You come, not as the triumphant warrior in terrible array,

But as the gentle Mother calling, calling thy children to thee.

He has filled thee with wisdom.

12

You speak in divers tongues.

All thy children know thy voice.

Love of God: Thy voice is sweeter than the thrush and the lark.

Angels stay their journey to hear thee.

Your words are sweeter than honey.

Your eyes are beautiful and gentle.

We have no fear of thee.

We love thee, Mary, we love thee, we love thee.

O Mary, beautiful, life-giving Mary.

Our Joy, our Hope in our sorrows.

13

Our eyes and hearts are lifted to thee.

Hear us, thy children who cry to thee.

You hear the cry of your children;

You, their Mother, will hasten to help.

You gladden the hearts that mourn.

You dry the eyes that weep.

Mother of the widow and orphan.

Safe home to the outcast.

The mighty and lowly find peace before thee.

Thy smile is peace.

14

Medicine and healing herbs to the sick.

Sweetness in the bitterness of life.

Light to those who travel by land and sea.

Virtue to the innocent.

Flame to kindle the clean of heart.

Faithful Shepherdess, who guards the sheep and lambs.

The Promised Land, overflowing with milk and honey.

Sweet spices and heavenly perfumes that purify,

Sweeter than the honeycomb.

Glory of women.

15

Healer of men.

Sight to the blind.

Hearing to the deaf.

Speech to the dumb.

Cool, life-giving waters to the thirsty.

Food and drink to the weary.

Whose breasts feed all men.

Thy children call to thee.

Heavenly Guide to the traveller,

O Mary, our Mother, lead us home.

O Mary, when our eyes close in our last sleep, and open to behold thy Son, the Just Judge, and the Angel opens the Book, and the Enemy accuses us; in that terrible hour, come to our aid. Be with us. When death came to Joseph, you and your Son were with him: Thy Son to judge; thou to console. O Happy Joseph! When death comes for us, be near us.

O Mary, when we are held captive in the place of atonement; plead for us, and visit us, that we may find consolation in thy presence. Stretch forth thy hand to help us; deliver us from our bondage. We are thy children: Thou art our Mother. As little children we come to thee; we know no fear.

O Mary, He changed water into wine for thee, even as He said: *My hour has not yet come.* Now He will not refuse thee, when you plead for us thy children.

O Mary, come quickly to our aid.
Do not let us stray from the Fold.
The wolf is waiting to destroy us.
There shall be neither night nor day
to thy praises.

Adoration to the Father Who created
thee!
Adoration to the Son Who took
flesh from thee!

Adoration to the Holy Spirit, Thy
Divine Spouse!
Three in One,
One in Three.
Equal in all things.
To Him be glory for ever.
For ever.
For ever. Amen.

NOTES

[1] In the exposition of the Gospel of Luke by the Angelic Doctor, Greek commentators are by far the more numerous. Few Latins, St Ambrose, The Venerable Bede, wrote on Luke; at least few that have come down to us. This arose principally through the decline of Greek in the West. Occasionally there was confusion of names. In the text of the *Catena Aurea* the Greek commentators were first cited, generally, under the title *Graecus*, or *Expositor Graecus*, a title that covered a score of eminent Greek Fathers. Following Nicolai (Edition, Lyons, 1686, *Praefatio in Lucam*), the actual name and source of the citation were added, in parentheses, to the title *Graecus*; and the sources where available verified.

[2] This is supposedly from Homily 7 (St Jerome's translation), but not found there verbatim.

[3] From Origen, Homily 7, PG 13. Found more precisely in Titus of Bostra: *Matrem participem gratiae faciebat*; from which these citations under the name of Origen come.

[4] 'Non . . . in Evangelio narraretur, dictum est, *Credidit* infans in utero ejus; sed, *exsultavit*; neque ipsa dixit, *Exsultavit* in fide infans in utero meo; sed, *exsultavit in gaudio*.'

[5] Cf. PG 33, col. 840, Ep. 187, par. 23.

[6] Not traceable in Origen; but, and perfectly, in other words, in Theophylactus: '*Statim abiit ad illam* (Elisabeth), *et gaudens de bono cognatae, et volens ut prudentissima majore certitudine certior reddi num vera dixisset qui apparuerat ei, ut ex hoc nec de suo deciperetur, et non ut incredula, set ut diligens rem explorare volebat.*' Cf. PG 123; col, 707; in medio: *Enarratio in Evang. Lucae.*

[7] '*The state of the Just who serenely and without end rejoice in the Lord.*' Basil, PG 29, col. 323, in Ps. xxxi. 1.

[8] This sermon, a rich and beautiful one, variously attributed to one or other of the greater Fathers, particularly to St Augustine, is now recognized as the work of Ambrose Autpert, Abbot of Volturno, near Beneventum, who died in 778. Cf. PL 39. Appendix, col. 2129, *sermo* 208, par. 10.

[9] *Blessed are they who have seed in Sion, and kindred in Jerusalem*, Is. xxxi. 9. Sept. The sentence is not found in the Vulgate.

[10] PG 98, col. 360. Of the first three Oecumenical Councils held in the Church, the First (Nice, A.D. 325) was devoted to the Father and the Son; the Second (Constantinople,

381) to the Holy Spirit; the Third (Ephesus, 432) to Christ and His Blessed Mother. This Third Council, and First Marian, having stated and proclaimed the truth of the Divine Maternity of the Blessed Virgin, became also an indefectible source of Marian eschatology; whose force and impact is seen at the time in the East, later and more slowly in the West.

It would seem that in the Providence of God the firm Tradition of the Church, centred in Jerusalem, of the *Dormition* (Falling Asleep and Bodily Assumption) of our Lady had not yet been diffused throughout the whole Church. The Feast of the Dormition was celebrated prior to A.D. 500 and throughout the East in the sixth and seventh centuries; and by public decree of the Emperor Maurice (582–602), it was ordered to be celebrated everywhere on the 15th of August. This feast commemorated the Falling Asleep (κοίμησις) and the removal or departure or Translation or Assumption (μετάστασις) of the *body* of Mary. This is clearly evident from Eastern liturgies, not excluding those of the two schisms which had then arisen; of Nestorius and the Monophysites; as well as from the homilies of the Greek Fathers.

While the mystery of the celestial glorification, not only of the soul of the Mother of God, but also of her body, was following Ephesus clearly and explicitly taught in the East, it remained for a time in some obscurity in the West. Following Egyptian tradition it began to appear in France in the sixth century, when the Feast of our Lady was celebrated on the 18th January; and this appears in Gallican Liturgy

as the Assumption. In the time of Pope Sergius (687–701), it is certain that the Feast of the *Dormition* of the Mother of God was celebrated; which soon afterwards came to be known as the Feast of the Assumption of the Holy Mary.

Explicit testimonies to this truth therefore begin late in the homilies of the Fathers. The first clear authoritative testimonies begin with three quasi contemporaneous witnesses of the highest order; of whom the first is St Modestus, Patriarch of Jerusalem († 634). Next in importance comes St Germanus, Patriarch of Constantinople († 733). He composed three beautiful authoritative discourses on the Dormition of the B.V.M. Mother of God, in which the Tradition regarding Her Dormition is fully recorded, and the due praises of our Lady set forth. The third of these, which is in good part narrative, and includes much detail, is here presented. The holy Patriarch explicitly declares that the truth of the corporeal Assumption of Mary is of divine - apostolic origin; and consequently, that the absolute certainty of the belief is outside discussion. St Andreas, Archbishop of Crete († 740) follows him. He also declares that the object of the Feast of the Dormition is to honour the Death and Glorious Bodily Assumption of the B.V.M.

Later, in three homilies of St John Damascene († 749), we find the complete theology of Oriental Christianity on the Assumption of the B.V.M. With him as with Modestus, Germanus and Andreas, the principal foundations of the Marian Privilege (of Bodily Assumption) are the Divine Maternity, her

Perpetual Virginity, her singular holiness, and then the intimate and singular relationship between the Son of God and His Mother.

In the West, we have no explicit affirmation from any of the Fathers regarding the Assumption of the B.V.M. and so we have no homilies from them on the Assumption. There are however many later; though some of these are indeed beautiful and devotional, they are still imperfect in doctrine, and cannot be accepted as setting out, authoritatively, the clear substantial Tradition of the Church on this most sacred belief from the beginning; which derives primarily and directly from the holy church of Jerusalem. We limit our selection of homilies to two Fathers: St Germanus and St John Damascene; adding however another more comprehensive testimony from the Patristic age (see note 17), in the form of direct prayer. Of the two chosen, the first is mainly narrative and devotional; the second, which is the second of Damascene's three homilies on the *Dormition*, is an explicit recapitulation of Tradition, in which he declares that the *corporeal* Assumption of the B.V.M. rests on the ancient Tradition of the Church, and stresses that the purpose of this sermon is: 'To describe as best I can to paint and delineate in words, those wonders which were wrought in the Most Holy Mother of God, and which we have received from antiquity, clearly and comprehensively, from, as they say, father to son.'

[11] A paraphrase of Is. ii. 11, 14.

[12] Evidently refers to the field of Joseph of Arimathea (Mt. xxvii. 59).

[13] PG 96, fol. 722. *Hom.* II. St John Damascene was born in Damascus, early in the second half of the seventh century. At the beginning of the next century he entered the *Laura* of St Saba, near Jerusalem. He has been called the St Thomas Aquinas of the East. Died at the end of the year 749. His three celebrated *Homilies* on the Dormition of the B.V.M. were given in Jerusalem, at the Basilica of the Sepulchre of the B.V.M. in the presence of the Bishops and clergy of Jerusalem and Palestine. *c.* A.D. 740. The second is here translated; as the most representative of Tradition on the Assumption.

[14] PG 96, col. 729.

[15] This Euthymius, whose Life is here referred to, is known as St Euthymius the Great, Abbot (377–473). The Life was written about forty years after his death by Cyril of Scythopolis, Monk. The Saint greatly influenced the acceptance in the East of the Decrees of The Council of Chalcedon (451). His feast is the 20th January; the day of his death. Some doubt that this passage belongs to the actual homily of St John Damascene, and regard it as a later interpolation. This does not seem improbable; from the style of the opening of par. 19, which links logically and immediately with the end of par. 17. Cf. PG 96, col. 747, note 58.

The Pulcheria referred to in the opening of the quotation, is a truly venerable figure: St Pulcheria, Empress of the Eastern Roman Empire. Born 399; died 453. She early made a vow of virginity, and persuaded her sister to do the same; and the Imperial palace thus became a monastery. She powerfully opposed the heresies of the time; those of Eutyches and of the Monophysites, and was a supporter of St Cyril of Alexandra. In good part it was through her efforts that these heresies were overcome. She built three churches in Constantinople in honour of the Mother of God, besides many other churches elsewhere; and also many hospitals, orphanages, houses for the aged, for strangers, etc. Her Feast is given in the Roman Martyrology for September the 10th; in Oriental Calendars for the 7th August.

[16] Hierotheos, friend and instructor of Dionysius the Areopagite (Acts xvii. 34).

[17] *The Praises of Mary.* This psalterium of praise of Mary is ascribed by oral tradition to St Lomman, Abbot of a monastery founded by him in the seventh century on the shores of Lough Owel in the centre of Ireland. So far the 'Praises' have been traced back to the middle of the last century, 'when they were part of the repertoire of two traditional story-tellers – Thomas Maher, who spoke both Irish and English, and a hedge schoolmaster (named Flanagan, I think), who probably knew Latin as well.' It is not known when, or if, they were translated or what was their original language: which may well have been Greek.

The 'Praises' are *ascribed* to Lomman's monks, but in the absence of any manuscripts, much work by a competent philologist needs to be done on them before they can be ascribed to any definite place in the stream of tradition. There is however a very special reason for their inclusion here, apart from their intrinsic beauty and devotion, namely: That presuming this oral tradition, which is also a living tradition of *prayer and belief*, derives from the time of St. Lomman (who is commemorated in the Calendar of Irish Saints on the 7th February), then this explicit testimony to the Bodily Assumption of Mary would be the sole testimony on this belief so far to be found in the West up to that time and a little later: the testimony from the East, as noted in the two previous sermons, deriving from Jerusalem, being abundant and living in faith and devotion.

The 'Praises' were finally 'recited' by a man named John Cox, who has since died, to a priest, the Reverend Father Andrew L. Shaw, parish priest of Kilcormac, Offaly, who has supplied this information, 'one of about seventy items concerning Lomman and his monks which I received from Cox, who had them from the same source as these praises. I wrote them all down and sent the collection to Browne and Nolan, Dublin;' who purpose publishing them together with other Prayers of the Irish. We cannot but be most grateful to Father Shaw who thus timely secured for the Church this precious and beautiful fragment of Tradition concerning the Assumption of the Mother of God; and also for his permission to publish it. (This is the sole portion of this entire work not directly translated from the original textual sources: excepting the St Ephraim sermons, rendered from Lamy's Latin translation of the Syrian, and included here because of its singular relevancy to this section of it.)

FEAST OF CHRIST THE KING

I. St Augustine: The King of Israel

II. St Augustine: Christ King and Priest

III. St Leo the Great: Christ Reigns in His Mystical Body

THE GOSPEL OF THE FEAST

John xviii. 33–37

At that time: Pilate said to Jesus: Art thou the king of the Jews? Jesus answered: Sayest thou this thing of thyself, or have others told it thee of me? Pilate answered: Am I a Jew? Thy own nation and the chief priests have delivered thee up to me. What has thou done? Jesus answered: My kingdom is not of this world. If my kingdom were of this world, my servants would certainly strive that I should not be delivered to the Jews, but now my kingdom is not from hence.

Pilate therefore said to him: Art thou a king then? Jesus answered: Thou sayest that I am a king. For this was I born, and for this came I into the world; that I should give testimony to the truth. Every one that is of the truth, heareth my voice.

Exposition from the Catena Aurea

Chrysostom, in John, Homily 82: Pilate, wishing to deliver Jesus from the hatred of the Jews, did not prolong His trial. And so we read:

V.33. *Pilate therefore went into the hall again and called Jesus.*

Theophylactus: Apart, because he had a grave suspicion that He was innocent. He was therefore of a mind to examine Him carefully and thoroughly, away from the clamour of the Jews. So there follows: *And said to him: Art thou the king of the Jews?* Alcuin: Pilate shows by these words that the Jews had accused Jesus of this crime: that He had called Himself the king of the Jews.

Chrysostom, as above: Or, Pilate had learned this from many people. Because the Jews had nothing to say, that the investigation might not be prolonged, he wished to bring forward what was commonly said. Then follows:

V.34. *Jesus answered: Sayest thou this thing of thyself, or have others told it thee of me?*

Theophylactus: He here hints that Pilate is foolish, and judging without discretion; as though He were to say: If you are saying this of yourself, bring forward proof of my rebellion. If you have learned it from others, make due enquiry.

AUGUSTINE, *in John*, Tr. 115, 1: The Lord well knew both what He Himself had asked, and what Pilate would answer. But it was His will that this should be said, not that He might come to know, but that it might be written down that He willed it should be known. CHRYSOSTOM: He therefore does not ask as one not knowing, but willed that Pilate should make an accusation against the Jews. Accordingly there follows:

V.35. *Pilate answered: Am I a Jew?*

AUGUSTINE, as above: He removes from himself the suspicion that he might be thought to have said it himself; proving he had learned it from the Jews. He therefore continues: *Thy own nation, and the chief priests have delivered thee up to me.* Then, by adding: *What hast thou done?* he makes it sufficiently plain that this charge was made against Him; as though he said: 'If you deny you are a king, what then have you done to be delivered up to me?' As though it was not something to be wondered at, that one who had called himself a king should be delivered to him for punishment.

CHRYSOSTOM: He draws Pilate, who is not a truly bad man, towards Himself; and wills to show him that He is not a mere man, but God, and the Son of God, and dissolves the fear in Pilate's mind that He is aiming at royal power. So there follows:

V.36. *Jesus answered: My kingdom is not of this world.*

AUGUSTINE, *in John*, Tr. 115, 1, 2: This is what the Good Master wished us to know. But first we had to be shown that men's notion of His

kingdom was an idle one, either that of the Gentiles, or of the Jews; from whom Pilate had learned it; as if the reason why He should be punished with death was because He aspired to a kingdom to which He had no right, or, because those who reign are envious of those who shall reign; and so care must be taken lest His kingdom should be hostile to the Romans or Jews.

Had our Lord at once answered Pilate's question, He would have appeared to answer the Gentiles only (and not the Jews also) as thinking these things about Him. But now, after Pilate's answer, He makes a reply which is apt and timely for both Jews and Gentiles; as though He says: 'Hear ye therefore, both Jews and Gentiles! I do not oppose your rule in this world. What more do you wish? Come, by believing, into the kingdom which is not of this world.' For what is His Kingdom, but those who believe in Him; to whom He says: *You are not of this world* (Jn. xvii. 16); though He willed that they should be *in* this world. And so he does not here also say: *My kingdom is not in this world,* but *My kingdom is not of this world.* Of this world are men created by God, but born of the corrupted race of Adam. But whoever is born again of Christ, has become a kingdom that is no longer of this world. For God has delivered us from the power of darkness, and translated us into the kingdom of the Son of His love (Col. i. 13).

CHRYSOSTOM: Or, He says this: That He does not hold His Kingdom as earthly kings hold theirs: for He has His power to rule from above; for He is not a mere man, but far greater and more glorious. So He adds: *If my kingdom were of this world, my servants would certainly strive that I should not be delivered to the Jews.* Here He shows the weakness of his kingdom who reigns among men; for its strength lies in its servants. But the Kingdom from above is sufficient to itself, and in need of no one. And if this Kingdom is the greater, then He has been taken of His own will; delivering Himself up.

AUGUSTINE, as above: When He had shown that His kingdom is not of this world, He added: *But now my kingdom is not from hence.* He did not say: is not here, but, *is not from hence:* for His kingdom is here, till the end of the world, having tares mixed with it until the time of the harvest; but nevertheless it *is not from hence:* for it is in the world as a stranger to it.

THEOPHYLACTUS: Or, it is for this He does not say: *is not here,* but *is not from hence.* Because He reigns in the world, and orders it by His Providence, and disposes all things according to His will. But His kingdom was not established from here below, but from above, and before all ages. CHRYSOSTOM: Heretics take occasion from these words to say that He is different from the Creator of the world. But when He says: *My kingdom is not from hence,* He does not deprive the world of His government and providence, but only shows us that His kingdom is not human and corruptible.

V.37. *Pilate therefore said to him: Art thou a king then? Jesus answered: Thou sayest that I am a king.*
AUGUSTINE: He did not fear to admit

He was a king. But He so answered that He neither denied He was a king, nor admitted that He was a king in the sense that it has in this world. He said: *Thou sayest,* as though He said: Being of this world you speak as the world does. Then He adds: *For this was I born, and for this came I into the world; that I should give testimony to the truth.* In these words, *for this was I born (in hoc natus sum)* the syllable of the pronoun *this* (*hoc*) is not to be lengthened (abl.), as though He said: in this thing was I born (*in hac re natus sum*); but must be short (accus.), as meaning: *Unto this I was born* (to this end); just as He said: *For this I came into the world (ad hoc veni in mundum).* So it is very plain that here He is speaking of His Birth in time, by which He came Incarnate into the world; not of that Birth without beginning by which He is God.

THEOPHYLACTUS: Or, again: to Pilate's question, if the Lord were a king, He says: *Unto this was I born;* that is, *to this end,* because I am a King[1] from this that I came forth from a King, I testify that I also am a King. CHRYSOSTOM: If therefore He was born a King, He has nothing which was added to Him. *For this,* He says, *I came, that I should give testimony of the truth,* that is, that I may persuade all men to accept it. Let us note how He here shows His humility: those who call Him a malefactor He suffers in silence, but when asked of His kingdom, He then speaks to Pilate, instructing Him and raising his mind to higher things. And in saying: *That I should give testimony to the truth,* He declares that He has done nothing that was evil.

AUGUSTINE: When Christ gives testimony to the truth, He gives testimony to Himself: for His own words are: *I am the truth* (Jn. xiv. 6). But since, *all men have not faith* (II Thess. iii. 2), He further adds: *Every one that is of the truth heareth my voice.* Hears, that is, with the inner ear; hears, that is, obeys My voice; as though He said: Believe Me. That He said: *Every one that is of the truth,* refers to the grace by which He calls us according to His purpose. For if we consider the nature in which we have been created, since He Who is the Truth created all men, who is there that is not of the Truth? But it is not given by the Truth to all men that they shall obey the Truth. For if He had said: Every one who hears my voice is of the truth, he therefore would be called, *of the truth,* because he obeyed the truth. But He does not say this, but says: *Every one that is of the truth hears my voice.* A man hears; but not for this is he *of the truth,* because he hears His voice; he hears because he is *of the truth.* For this is a gift bestowed on him by the Truth.

CHRYSOSTOM: In saying these things He draws Pilate to Him, and persuades him to become a hearer of them, so that finally He so holds him by these brief words, that Pilate asks him, 'What is truth?' For there follows: *Pilate saith to him: What is truth?* THEOPHYLACTUS: For it had almost disappeared from among men; for it was unknown to all, because all were unbelieving.

I. ST AUGUSTINE, BISHOP AND DOCTOR

The King of Israel[2]

I

Blessed is he that cometh in the name of the Lord, the King of Israel, John xii. 13.

1. We are to take the words, *in the name of the Lord* as meaning in the name of the Father; although they can also be understood of His own Name, since He also is Lord. For it is written elsewhere: *The Lord rained from the Lord* (Gen. xix. 24). But His own words are a better guide to our understanding, where He says: *I am come in the name of my Father, and you receive me not; if another shall come in his own name, him you will receive* (Jn. v. 43). For Christ is our Teacher of humility: He Who humbled Himself, becoming obedient unto death; even to the death of the Cross (Phil.

ii. 8). But in teaching us humility, He did not lessen His own Divinity; in His Divinity He is equal to the Father, in His lowliness He is like us. Through that in which He is equal to the Father, He created us and gave us existence; through that in which He is like us, He saved us lest we perish.

2. The multitude cried out to Him in praise: *Hosanna. Blessed is he that cometh in the name of the Lord, the King of Israel.* What envious torment of soul the rulers of the Jews suffered hearing such a multitude acclaim Christ their King! But what great honour was it for the Lord to be King of Israel? What honour was it to the King of Kings to become a

King of men? For Christ was not King of Israel so that He might exact tribute or arm a host with the sword or defeat His enemies before the world. He was King of Israel that He might rule minds, that He might keep us in peace for ever, that He might lead those who believe in Him who hope in Him, who love Him into the Kingdom of Heaven. That the Son of God therefore, Equal to the Father, the Word by Whom all things were made, wished to become King of Israel was a favour to us, not an honour to Him; a sign of His mercy, not an increase of His power. For He Who on earth is called the King of the Jews, in heaven is Lord of the Angels.

II

1. *And they took Jesus*, it says, *and led him forth. And, bearing his own cross, he went forth to that place which is called Calvary, but in Hebrew Golgotha; where they crucified him* (Jn. xix. 17). He goes therefore to the place where He was to be crucified. Jesus! Bearing His own cross. Sublime spectacle! For the blasphemous, a great mockery; to the eyes of the just, a great mystery. To the impious looking on, the supreme token of His ignominy; to those who love Him, the supreme comfort of the faith. The impious look, and laugh at a King bearing upon His shoulder, not the sceptre of His Kingdom, but the Wood of His own torment; piety looks and sees a King bearing the Cross on which He is to be fastened: a Cross hereafter to be fastened on the diadems of kings; that was to be mocked by the eyes of the godless, but in which the hearts of saints would glory.

To Paul, who was to say, *But God forbid that I should glory, save in the cross of our Lord Jesus Christ* (Gal. vi. 14); the Lord commends this very Cross by bearing it on His own shoulders. And for the candle that was to be lit, but not put under a bushel, He bore the candle-stick (Mt. v. 15). *Bearing his own cross*, therefore, *he went forth to that place which is called Calvary, but in Hebrew Golgotha: where they crucified him, and with him two others, one on each side, and Jesus in the midst.* These were the two thieves, as we learn from the other Evangelists, with whom He was crucified, and between whom He was made fast: He of Whom the Prophet had said beforehand: *He was reputed with the wicked* (Is. liii. 12).

2. *And Pilate wrote a title also: and he put it upon the cross. And the writing was:* JESUS OF NAZARETH, THE KING OF THE JEWS. *This title therefore many of the Jews did read; because the place where Jesus was crucified was nigh to the city. And it was written in Hebrew, in Greek, and in Latin: The King of the Jews.* These were the three principal languages in that place: Hebrew, because of the Jews who gloried in the Law of God; Greek, for the instructed among the Gentiles; Latin, because of the Romans, then ruling over many, indeed over almost all the nations.

3. *Then the chief priests of the Jews said to Pilate: Write not: the King of the Jews. But that he said: I am the King of the Jews. Pilate answered: What I have written, I have written.* O ineffable power of the workings of God, even in the hearts of the ignorant! Did not some hidden voice

utter with, as we may say, clamorous silence within the breast of Pilate, that which had been foretold in the writings of the psalms: *Destroy not the inscription of the title* (Pss. lvi, lvii, *title*)? See how he would not destroy the inscription of the title. What he had written, he had written. And the priests also, they who had wished him to destroy it, what did they say? *Write not*, they say, *the King of the Jews; but, that he said, I am the King of the Jews*. What are you saying, you madmen? Why do you strive against that which you can no way change? Will that which Jesus said then not be true: *I am the King of the Jews?* If what Pilate wrote cannot be destroyed, can that be destroyed which Truth has uttered?

But is Christ King of the Jews only, or also of the Gentiles? He is King also of the Gentiles. For when He said in prophecy: *I am appointed king by him over Sion his holy mountain, preaching his Commandment* (Ps. ii. 6); lest anyone should say, because of the mount of Sion, that He had been appointed king only of the Jews, He straightaway continues: *The Lord hath said to me: Thou art my son: this day have I begotten thee. Ask of me, and I will give thee the Gentiles for thy inheritance, and the utmost parts of the earth for thy possession*. And for this same reason, speaking now from His own mouth among the Jews, He says: *And other sheep I have that are not of this fold: them also I must bring,*

and they shall hear my voice, and there shall be one fold and one shepherd (Jn. x. 16).

Why then are we to see a great mystery in this title, in which was written: *The King of the Jews*, if Christ is King also of the Gentiles? Because the wild olive has become a partaker of the richness of the olive; not the olive a partaker of the bitterness of the wild olive (Rom. xi. 17). For in that the title was true of Christ, that He was *the King of the the Jews*, what are we to understand by Jews but the seed of Abraham, the children of the promise, *who are the children of God* (Rom. ix. 8)? For it is *not the children of the flesh*, says the Apostle, *who are the children of God; but they that are the children of the promise, who are accounted his children*. And they were Gentiles to whom he said: *And, if you be Christ's, then are you the seed of Abraham, heirs according to the promise* (Gal. iii. 29).

Christ therefore is the King of the Jews, but King of those that are Jews by that circumcision which is of the heart, in the spirit, not in the letter; whose praise is not from man, but from God (Rom. ii. 29); who belong to that Jerusalem which is free, which is our mother in heaven, the spiritual Sarah, casting out the bondwoman and her son from the house of liberty (Gal. iv. 22–31). Therefore, what Pilate had written, he had written. For what the Lord has said, He has said. Amen.

II. St Augustine, Bishop and Doctor

Christ King and Priest[3]

I

1. *The Psalm of David before he was anointed*, Psalm xxvi. *Title*.

This was the title of a psalm: *A psalm of David before he was anointed;* that is, before he was anointed king.

For it was as king he was anointed (I Kings xvi. 3). And only the king was anointed then, and the priest: these were the two persons who were at that time anointed. And in the two persons was prefigured the future King and Priest; in either Office the One Christ; and Christ from the chrism (anointing).

But not only was our Head anointed, but His Body also: ourselves. He is our King because He rules us and leads us; our Priest because He *maketh intercession for us* (Rom. viii. 34). And He alone was such a Priest that He was also Himself the Victim. For the sacrifice He offered to God was none other than Himself. For besides Himself He could find no other most pure reasoning victim; as an immaculate Lamb redeeming us by the shedding of His own Blood, making us One Body with Himself, making us His Members, so that in Christ we would also be Christ. And so anointing extends to all Christians. In the former time of the Old Testament it was restricted to two persons only. From this then it appears that we are the Body of Christ: in that we have all been anointed. And in Him we are all both Christ and the members of Christ; because in a certain manner the Head and the Body are the *Whole*[4] Christ.

This anointing shall perfect us spiritually in that life which is promised to us. The voice of this psalm is the voice of one longing for life; the voice of one longing for the grace of God; which shall be perfected in us at the end: and so its title is: *The psalm of David before he was anointed.* For we are anointed now in the sacrament, and by this sacrament something is prefigured that we

shall be. And we ought to long for that I know not what ineffable thing, and sigh for it in the sacrament; that we may enjoy that which is prefigured by the sacrament.

2. The psalm begins: *The Lord is my light and my salvation, whom shall I fear?* He gives me light; let darkness depart. He heals me; let infirmity depart. And walking firmly in this light, whom shall I fear? For God gives such strength, that no one can take it away; such light, that nothing can overshadow it. If the Lord enlightens us, we are enlightened. If the Lord saves us, we are saved. If He gives us light, we are enlightened, and saving us, we are saved; then apart from Him we are darkness and infirmity. But having in Him a true and certain and firm hope, whom shall we fear? The Lord is thy light; the Lord is thy salvation. If you find someone more powerful, then you may fear. But I belong to the most powerful of all, to the Omnipotent, who both enlightens me and heals me, so that I fear none but Him.

The Lord is the protector of my life, of whom shall I be afraid?

II

Psalm cil.

V.1. *Sing ye to the Lord a new canticle: let him praise be in the church of the saints.*

1. Let us praise the Lord in voice and mind; let us praise him in doing good; and as this psalm bids us, let us sing Him a new song. For it is so the psalm begins: *Sing ye to the Lord a new canticle.* For *the old man* an old song; for *the new man* a new song. The Old Testament is an old canticle;

the New Testament *a new canticle.* In the Old Testament the promises are temporal and terrestrial. He who loves earthly things will sing the old song. He that would sing the new song, let him love eternal things. Love itself is both new and eternal: It never grows old, therefore is it ever new.

But when you consider that it is old, how therefore is it new? Is Life Eternal, my brethren, but lately born? Christ Himself is Life Eternal, and in His Divinity not lately born: for, *In the beginning was the Word, and the Word was with God, and the Word was God: The same was in the beginning with God. All things were made by him; and without him was made nothing that was made* (Jn. i). If the things that were made by Him are old, what is He, by Whom they are made? What is He but eternal, and co-eternal with the Father? But we have fallen away through sin, and have grown old. For it is our voice that speaks in the psalm where it is said with grieving and lament: *I have grown old amongst all my enemies* (vi. 8). Man has grown old through sin; he returns to his youth through grace. All therefore who are renewed in Christ, sing a new canticle, that they may begin to belong to eternal life.

2. *Let his praise be in the church of the saints.* And do you wish to know where you shall sing the new song? What he is to tell of in this Psalm; see how it will happen, and where: whether in all the earth, or in a part; and from this you shall know fully whose new song it is. The first part is clear, which I recall from another psalm: *Sing ye to the Lord a new canticle* (xcv. i). And to show

that in the new canticle we shall find the fruit of unity and charity, he added: *Sing to the Lord, all the earth.* Let no one separate; let no one cut himself off. You are the wheat; bear with the chaff until it is winnowed away. Do you want to be driven from the threshing floor. Although you are wheat, once outside, the birds of the air shall find you and gobble you up. What is more, that you should leave and fly away is proof that you were but chaff: and because you were without weight, when the wind blew, you were carried off from under the feet of the oxen. But they who are wheat, bear with the treading out. They are happy because they are grain; they grieve amidst the chaff, they wait for Him Whose fan is in His hand, Whom they know is their Redeemer.

Sing ye to the Lord, a new canticle: let his praise be in the church of the saints. This is the Church of the Saints, this is the Church of the wheat scattered through all the earth; sown throughout the field of the Lord, this world, as the Lord made known to us, when He spoke of the man who went out to sow his seed. That *a man sowed good seed in his field, and his enemy came and oversowed cockle among the wheat. And the servants of the master of the house coming said to him: Didst thou not sow good seed in thy field? Whence then hath it cockle? And he said to them: An enemy hath done this.* They wished to gather up the cockle, but he prevented them, saying: *Suffer both to grow until the harvest. And in the time of the harvest I will say to the reapers: Gather up first the cockle and bind it into bundles to burn, but the wheat gather ye into my barn* (Mt. xiii. 24, etc.).

Afterwards His Disciples asked Him to explain this parable: *Expound to us the parable of the cockle of the field* (v. 36). And He explained it all to them, so that no man might attribute to his own sense what he understood from it, but to the Master of heaven who has explained it. Let no man say: 'He explained it in His way.' If the Lord explained the parable of the prophet when He spoke through them, who would dare to say He did not explain it as He should? Much more, when He explained what He had himself taught them, who would venture to contradict the evident truth? The Lord explaining then said: *He that soweth the good seed is the Son of man,* referring to Himself. *The good seed are the children of the kingdom*: that is, the Church of the Saints. *The cockle are the children of the wicked one. The field is the world.*

You see then, brethren, that the good seed is sown throughout the world, and the cockle is also sown throughout the world. It is not that the wheat is in one part, the cockle another. The field of the Lord is the world, not Africa. It is not like these lands of ours: Getulia bearing sixty or a hundredfold, while Numidia bears tenfold. It is not like this with the Lord's field. It bears fruit everywhere: a hundredfold, sixtyfold, thirtyfold. Let you consider which you wish to be; if you have a mind to belong to the harvest of the Lord.

The Church of the Saints therefore is the Catholic Church. The Church of the Saints is not the church of the heretics. The Church of the Saints is that which God prefigured before it appeared; and put before us that it might be seen. Before, the Church of the Saints was in the Books only; now it is among the nations; before, men only read of it; now we read of it, and we see it. When men only read of it, they believed in it; now men see it, and contradict it! *Let his praise be in the Church of the Saints.*

V.2. Let Israel rejoice in him that made him: and let the children of Sion be joyful in their king.

3. What does Israel mean? 'Seeing God': for this is the interpretation of the name of Israel. He who sees God rejoices in Him Who made him. What then did we mean, brethren, when we said that we belong to the Church of the saints? Do we now see God? If we do not, how are we Israel? There is one seeing now; another in the time to come. Now we see *by faith*; then we shall see *by sight* (II Cor. v. 7). When we believe, we see; when we love, we see. What do we see? We see God. Where is God? Ask John. He answers us: *God is charity* (I Jn. iv. 16). Let us bless His holy Name; and if we rejoice in charity, let us rejoice in God. Whosoever has charity, what need to send him afar off, to see God? Let him turn his mind to his own conscience, and there he shall see God. If charity does not dwell there, God does not dwell there; but if charity dwells there, God dwells there. Perhaps he wishes to see Him enthroned in heaven. Let him have charity, and God will dwell in him as He does in heaven. Therefore, let us be Israel, and let us rejoice in Him Who made us. *Let Israel rejoice in him that made him.* Let it rejoice in Him Who made it, and not in Arius;[5] not in Donatus, not in Caecilianus, not in Proculianus, and

not in Augustine. *Let him rejoice in him who made him.*

We, brethren, we do not commend ourselves to you. We commend God to you: for we commend you to God. How do we commend God to you? That you love Him for your own good, not for His; for not to love Him will not harm Him, but will harm you. For God's Divinity will not become less if a man has no love for Him. You increase from God; not He from you. And yet so much did He first love us (I Jn. iv. 19), before we loved Him, that He sent His only Son to die for us (Jn. iii. 16). He Who made us was made one of us. How did He make us? *All things were made by him; and without him was made nothing that was made.* How was He made one of us? *And the Word was made flesh, and dwelt among us* (Jn. i, 3, 14). Therefore it is He in Whom we must rejoice. Let no one claim for himself the place that belongs to God: for it is from Him that joy comes which makes us happy. *Let Israel rejoice in him that made him.*

4. *And let the children of Sion be joyful in their king.*

The children of the Church are this Israel. For Sion was a city; which fell. In its ruins the saints continued to live this present life. But the true Sion, the true Jerusalem (for Sion and Jerusalem are one and the same) is eternal in heaven, and is our mother (Gal. iv. 6). She has given birth to us. She is the Church of the saints. She has nourished us: in part she is a pilgrim on this earth, in great part dwelling in heaven. In the part in which she dwells in heaven, she is the joy of the Angels. In the part in which she journeys in this world, she is the hope of the just. Of the first part was it said: *Glory to God in the highest;* of this other was it said: *And on earth peace to men of good will.* They then who in this life sigh and long for their home, let them hasten there with love; not with bodily feet. Let them not look for ships, but for wings. Let them take hold of the two wings of charity. What are the two wings of charity? The love of God, and the love of our neighbour. For we are now journeying in a strange land, and pine and long for home. A letter has come to us from our home; let me read it to you:

Let Israel rejoice in him that made him; and let the children of Sion be joyful in their king. That it says, *him that made him,* means the same as *in their king.* The Israel you have heard of is the same as *the children of Sion.* And when you heard: *In him that made him,* that means *in their king.* The Son of God Who made us became one among us. And as our King He rules us, because as our Creator He made us. And He by whom we were made, is He by Whom we are ruled; and in the same way we are Christians, because He is Christ. And He is called Christ from the chrism, that is, from His anointing. But only kings are anointed, and Priests (Ex. xxx. 30). He therefore was anointed as both King and Priest. As our King He did battle for us; as our Priest He offered Himself for our sake. When He fought for us, He was as one defeated; yet He truly conquered. He was crucified, yet from the Cross to which He was fastened, He defeated the devil; and from this He became our King.

How came He to be our Priest?

Because He offered Himself for us. You give to the priest what he may offer. What had man to give as a clean offering? What victim, what clean thing can a sinner offer? O sinful man! O impious man! Whatever you offer is unclean; therefore something clean must be offered in your behalf. See if you have anything you may offer, and you will find you have nothing. God does not want your rams nor your goats nor your bulls. All things are His, whether you offer them or not. Offer Him therefore a clean oblation. But you are a sinner, you are impious, your conscience is defiled. Made clean, you may perhaps offer something clean; but to make you clean, something has to be offered for you. What therefore will you offer for yourself, so as to be made clean? If you are made clean, you can offer what is clean. Therefore let the Unstained Priest offer Himself, and let Him make you clean. This Christ did. He found nothing that was clean in man, that He could offer for men; and so offered Himself, an Immaculate Victim. O Blessed Victim, True Victim, Immaculate Host! He did not therefore offer what we gave Him; rather, He offered what He took from us, and offered it *immaculate*. For He took flesh from us; and this He offered. Whence did He take it? From the womb of the Virgin Mary; that He might offer what was without stain, for those who were unclean. He is our King; He is our Priest. Let us rejoice in Him. Amen.

III. St Leo the Great, Pope and Doctor

On the Anniversary of his Coronation
Christ reigns in His Mystical Body[6]

Synopsis: I. This festival shared by all Christians, who also are priests and kings.

II. How much above others was bestowed on Peter: the Church founded on Peter, and on his faith.

III. The power of the keys, which Peter received, passed through him to the other Apostles. Peter's special privilege; of whom the Lord assumed the particular care, and for whose faith Christ especially prayed; that the firmness bestowed by Christ on Peter, might through Peter be given to the Apostles.

IV. To the prayers and solicitude of Peter is due whatever of good is done by his successors.

I. I rejoice, dearly beloved, in the pious affection of your devotion, and I gave thanks to God that I see in you the love of Christian unity. For your very presence here testifies that you understand that the annual return of this day is a matter for common rejoicing; and that in celebrating the annual festival of the Shepherd, you are honouring the whole flock. For though the universal Church is ordered in varying degrees, so the whole is made up from the diverse members of the sanctified Body, *we are all,* nevertheless, as the Apostle says, *one in Christ* (I Cor. xii. 13); and no one is separated by his office from another, so that even the least among us is related to the head. Therefore, Beloved, in its unity of faith and baptism, our society is undivided, and its dignity is the dignity of all its members; according to the words of the blessed Peter, spoken by his own consecrated voice: *Be you as living stones built up, a spiritual house, a holy priesthood, to offer up spiritual sacrifices, acceptable to God by Jesus Christ.* And a little later: *You are a chosen generation, a kingly priesthood, a holy nation, a purchased people* (I Pet. ii, 5, 9).

For all who are born again in Christ, the sign of the Cross makes kings, and the anointing of the Holy Spirit consecrates priests; so that apart from the special service of our ministry, let all spiritual and reasoning Christians know that they are of royal birth, and sharers of the priestly office. For what is so kingly as the soul that is subject to God, and the ruler of its own body? And what is so priestly as to dedicate to the Lord a pure conscience, and to offer Him on the altar of our hearts the unstained gift of our love? And since by God's grace this has been given to us all, it is for you a devout and praiseworthy thing to rejoice on the day of our coronation as though the honour were your own; so that the one pontifical sacrament is honoured throughout the whole body of the Church: for at the pouring of the sacred oil of consecration, while it flowed more abundantly on the higher members, it descended also and not sparingly on the lower.

II. Therefore, dearly beloved, while our sharing of this gift is the principal reason of our common rejoicing, yet for me it would be a higher and a truer reason for rejoicing if you would also be mindful of our insignificance; for it would be much more fitting, and much more profitable, if we raised our minds to dwell upon the glory of the most blessed Peter, and honoured this day, with special veneration, one who was filled with overflowing graces from the Fountain of all graces; so that although he himself received great gifts and blessings, yet there is nothing that has come to any of us, in which he has not shared.

The Word was already made Flesh and dwelt among us, and Christ had already given Himself wholly to the redemption of men. There was nothing without purpose in His wisdom; nothing to resist His power. The elements obeyed Him, the spirits adored Him, the angels ministered to Him: in no way could that Sacrament (of redemption) be fruitless, in Which the Unity and Trinity of the Godhead had wrought together. And yet from the whole world one was chosen, Peter, who was placed over the calling of all peoples, over all the Apostles, over all the Fathers of the Church: so that, though among the people of God there are many priests and many pastors, yet Peter alone rules all whom Christ supremely rules. Great and wondrous, beloved, this sharing of its power, which the divine favour bestowed on this man: and if it decreed that the other rulers should have something in common with him; yet what it denied not to the others, it gave only through him.

Towards the end the Lord asked

all His Apostles what men believed concerning Him; and the words of those who answer this question is ever the same, until the darkness of human ignorance is rolled back. But when the question was what did His Disciples believe concerning Him, He was the first to confess the Lord, who was the first in Apostolic dignity. And when he had said: *Thou art Christ, the Son of the living God,* Jesus answered him, and said: *Blessed art thou, Simon Bar-Jona; because flesh and blood hath not revealed it to thee, but my Father who is in heaven* (Mt. xvi. 16); that is, for this are you called *blessed*: because My Father taught you. Earthly opinion did not mislead you, but heavenly inspiration instructed you: And it was not flesh and blood, but He revealed Me to you, Whose only-Begotten Son I am.

And I, He said, *say to you*: that is, as My Father made known My Divinity to you, so do I also make known to you your own high dignity; that: *Thou art Peter*; that is: Since I am the Inviolable Rock, since I am *the Corner-stone, who hath made both one* (Eph. ii. 14, 21), since I am the Foundation, and other foundation than Me no man can lay (I Cor. iii. 11); yet you also are a rock: because you are made firm by My strength; so that what belongs to My power, you possess in common with Me. *And upon this rock I will build my Church; and the gates of hell shall not prevail against it* (Mt. xvi. 18). Upon this strength, He says, I shall raise up an everlasting temple, and in the firmness of this faith the sublimity of My Church shall rise to pierce the heavens.

III. The gates of hell shall not hold

back this confession, nor the bonds of death bind it; for the words here spoken are the words of Life. And as they uplift to heaven those who confess them, they plunge into hell those who deny them. And following on this, He said to the most blessed Peter: *I will give to thee the keys of the kingdom of heaven. And whatsoever thou shalt bind upon earth, it shall be bound also in heaven; and whatsoever thou shalt loose on earth, it shall be loosed also in heaven* (Mt. xvi. 19). And the right to this power passed from him to the other Apostles also; and that which this decree established has passed from one to another to all the princes of the Church; but not without purpose did He entrust to one, what He communicated to all. This was entrusted to Peter alone because the form *(forma)* of Peter is placed over all the rulers of the Church. Therefore the privilege of Peter remains, wherever from his justice judgement is given. And there shall be neither excess of severity nor excess of remission, where nothing is bound and nothing loosed save what Blessed Peter either binds or looses.

As His Passion which was to trouble the constancy of His Disciples drew near, the Lord said to Peter: *Simon, Simon, behold, Satan hath desired to have you, that he may sift you as wheat, But I have prayed for thee, that thy faith fail not; and thou, being once converted, confirm thy brethren, lest ye enter into temptation* (Lk. xxii. 31, 32, 40). The danger from the trial of fear was common to all the Apostles, and all were in equal need of the divine protection; since the devil desired to unsettle all of them, to crush all of them. And yet the Lord takes special care o

Peter, and prays specially for Peter's faith; as though the state of the others shall be more secure, if the mind of their leader remains undefeated. The strength of all therefore is made secure in Peter; and the assistance of the divine grace is so ordered, that the firmness, given by Christ to Peter, is by Peter conferred on the Apostles.

IV. Therefore, dearly beloved, when we consider such a great defence divinely established for us, we rightly and justly rejoice in the merits and in the dignity of our leader; giving thanks to our everlasting King and Redeemer Jesus Christ our Lord, that He has given such power to him whom He made Ruler of the whole Church; so that even in our times should we rightly order and fittingly dispose some thing, we must attribute this to his good works, to his guidance, to whom it was said: *And thou once converted will confirm thy brethren*; and to whom the Lord, after His own Resurrection, and following on

Peter's threefold profession of eternal love, with mystical significance three times said: *Feed my sheep* (Jn. xxi. 17). And this beyond doubt he now does also, and the pious Shepherd continues to fulfil the command of his Lord, sustaining us by his encouragement, and never ceasing to pray for us, so that no temptation shall overcome us.

And if he everywhere bestows this loving care on all the people of God, as we must believe, how much more shall he not graciously bestow his help on us his own immediate children; among whom he rests on the sacred bed of his blessed falling asleep, in that same body in which he presided over us. To him therefore let us offer this natal day of our ministry, and to him let us attribute this feast through whose protection we have come to be a sharer of his seat; helped in all things by the grace of our Lord Jesus Christ, Who liveth and reigneth with the Father and the Holy Ghost, God for ever and ever. Amen.

NOTES

[1] The text of Theophylactus: "Ἐγώ, φησίν, εἰς τοῦτο γεγέννημαι,' τουτέστιν, εἰς τὸ βασιλεὺς εἶναι; Ego, inquit, in hoc natus sum, hoc est, ut rex sim. PG 124, *Enarratio in Ev. Joann.*

[2] PL 35, Tract. *in Joannis Evang.*, I, col. 1764 in Tr. 51, 3. II, col. 1945 in Tr. 117, 3.

[3] *Enarrationes in Psalmos*, PL 36, I, Ps. xxvi, col. 199, 2. II, PL 37, col. 1949, Ps. cxlix, 1 *et seq.*

[4] See note 10 on *whole*: 20th Sunday after Pentecost.

[5] Arius a deacon of Alexandria

(250–336), author of a heresy against the true divine Sonship of Christ, which at one time troubled the whole Church, but like all heresies faded in time and disappeared. Donatus was the leader of the Donatist schism of North Africa (311–411). After this date it too faded. Caecilian, a Catholic bishop whom Donatus opposed. Proculianus was the Donatist bishop of Hippo, St Augustine's see, about the opening of the fifth century.

[6] PL 54, col. 148, *Sermo IV*.

THE FEAST OF ALL SAINTS

I. St Augustine: On the Eight Sentences of the Beatitudes

II. St Leo the Great: On the Steps of the Ascent
to Blessedness

THE GOSPEL OF THE FEAST

Matthew v. 1–12

At that time: Jesus seeing the multitudes, went up into a mountain, and when He was sat down, His disciples came unto him. And opening his mouth he taught them saying:

Blessed are the poor in spirit; for theirs is the kingdom of heaven.

Blessed are the meek; for they shall possess the land.

Blessed are they that mourn; for they shall be comforted.

Blessed are they that hunger and thirst after justice; for they shall have their fill.

Blessed are the merciful; for they shall obtain mercy.

Blessed are the clean of heart; for they shall see God.

Blessed are the peacemakers; for they shall be called the children of God.

Blessed are they that suffer persecution for justice sake; for theirs is the kingdom of heaven.

Blessed are ye when they shall revile you and persecute you and speak all that is evil against you, untruly, for my sake; be glad and rejoice, for your reward is very great in heaven; for so they persecuted the prophets that were before you.

Exposition from the Catena Aurea

I

CHRYSOSTOM, *Opus Imperfectum, Homily 9*[1]: Every craftsman rejoices when he sees the opportunity of a task that relates to his own craft. A carpenter when he sees a good tree has the desire to cut it down to exercise his skill on its timbers. And the priest when he sees a church full, will rejoice in his soul at the thought of teaching there. So likewise the Lord, seeing the multitudes, is moved to instruct them. And so we read:

V.1. *And Jesus seeing the multitudes, went up into a mountain.*

AUGUSTINE, *Harmony of the Gospels*, II, 19, 45: It might seem here that He wished to avoid the multitudes, and that it was for this reason He went up into a mountain; to speak to His Disciples alone. CHRYSOSTOM (*on Matthew, Homily* XV): From this that He seated Himself, not in a city and in a public place, but upon a mountain, and in a remote place, He taught us that we should do nothing for ostentation, and that we should go away from excitement and unrest, especially when we give ourselves to holy wisdom, and when we are to speak of serious things. REMIGIUS: We should know that we read that the Lord had three places of refuge: the ship, the mountain, and the desert; and as often as He was hard pressed by the multitudes He withdrew to one or other of them.

JEROME, *on Matthew*: Some of our simpler brethren think that our Lord taught what follows on the Mount of Olives, but this is not correct. For from what precedes and from what follows here we are shown that it was a place in Galilee; which we think was either Thabor or some other elevated place.

CHRYSOSTOM, *Opus Imperfectum*: He went up into a mountain: first, that He might fulfil the prophecy of Isaias, which said: *Get thee up on a high mountain* (Is. xl. 9); then that He might show us that he should stand on the heights of spiritual virtues who would teach others the justice of God, and equally so should he who would learn of it. For no one can remain in the valley, and speak from the mountain. If you stand on the earth, speak of the earth. If you speak of heaven, speak from the heavens. Or, He went up into a mountain, that He might show us, that everyone who wishes to learn the mysteries of the Truth should ascend to the mountain of the Church; of which the Prophet says: *The mountain of God is a fat mountain* (Ps. lxvii. 16).

HILARY, *on Matthew*: Or, He went up into a mountain because it is when standing on the sublimity of His Father's Majesty that He lays down the precepts of the heavenly life. AUGUSTINE, *Sermon on Mount*, I, 1, 2: Or, He went up into a mountain that He might reveal to us the greater precepts. For the lesser precepts of justice were given by God, through the Prophets, to the Jewish people, whom it was still necessary to bind by fear. But the greater ones were given by His Son to a people who were now to be set free through love. Then follows: *And when he was seated, his disciples came to him.*

JEROME: He spoke sitting, not standing; for they could not have understood Him had He appeared in His true majesty. AUGUSTINE, as above: Or, that He speaks sitting, relates to His dignity as Teacher. *His disciples*, however, *came unto him*: to be also nearer in body to, hear Him to Whom they had already drawn close in the spirit, by fulfilling what He taught. RABANUS: Mystically, His seating Himself typifies His Incarnation: for unless He had become Incarnate, man could not have drawn near to Him.

AUGUSTINE, *Harmony of the Gospels*, II, 19, 45: A question arises because Matthew says that this sermon took place while the Lord was seated on a mountain; while Luke says it took place while *He stood in a plain place* (vi. 17). This diversity makes it appear that the former refers to one discourse, the latter to another. For what prevented Christ from repeating elsewhere what He had already said, or from doing what He had already done? Yet this could be explained another way; namely, that the Lord was first alone with His

Disciples, in some more elevated part of the mountain, when He chose twelve from among them. Then He descended, not from the mountain, but from the summit of the mountain, to some level place, that is, to some even ground on the side of the mountain, which could hold a great number of people, and stood there until a great multitude had gathered about Him; and then afterwards, when He had seated Himself, His Disciples drew closer to Him, and in this way He spoke both to them and to the multitude this sermon which Matthew and Luke both relate; each in a different way, but with equal fidelity as to its substance.

GREGORY, *Morals in Job*, IV, 1: The Evangelist first says of the Lord, Who is about to utter the sublime Teachings of the Mount, that:

V.2. *Opening his mouth he taught them,*

Who long before had opened the mouths of the Prophets. REMIGIUS: Whenever we read that the Lord *opened his mouth*, we must pay great attention; for great things follow. AUGUSTINE, as above (I, I, 2): Or, he says, *opening his mouth*, that he may convey to us by this brief pause that the sermon which follows will be somewhat longer than usual.

CHRYSOSTOM, *on Matthew, Homily* XV: Or, he says this that you may learn that He now teaches by opening His mouth in speech, and now by that voice which speaks in His works. AUGUSTINE, as above (I, I, 1): He who reflects soberly and devoutly will find in this sermon, in respect of all that regards the conduct of our daily life, the perfect manner of Christian living. And because of this the sermon concludes with these words: *Everyone therefore that heareth these my words and doth them shall be likened to a wise man* (Mt. vii. 24).

AUGUSTINE, *City of God*, XIX, 1: Philosophy has no other end than that of goodness: that which makes man blessed, this is the end of goodness.[2] And therefore He begins with blessedness, saying:

V.3. *Blessed are the poor in spirit.*

AUGUSTINE, *Serm. on Mt.*, I, I, 2: Presumption of spirit indicates rashness and pride. And the proud also are said to possess a high spirit; and rightly; for the wind is also called a spirit. And who does not know that the proud are said to be puffed up, as if inflated with wind. And so the humble and Godfearing are here rightly understood to be *poor in spirit*; that is, not possessed of a spirit that inflates them.

CHRYSOSTOM, *on Matthew, Homily* XV: Or, He here calls soul and will *spirit*: for many are humble against their will; compelled by the force of circumstances. There is no praise for this. He blesses those who freely humble themselves. He therefore begins at the root of things by uprooting pride, the root and source of all malice. Against it He sets humility, as a strong and stable foundation, which, securely laid, is a base on which other virtues may be built. But should this base collapse, whatever other blessings you may have acquired, are lost.

CHRYSOSTOM, *Opus Imperfectum*: And so He said plainly: *Blessed are the poor in spirit*, that in this way He might show the humble that we are ever to be beggars of God's help. For this reason we read in the Greek, Blessed are the *ptochoi* (beggars, or needy). For many are naturally humble, but not from faith; such as these do not knock at the door of God's help; only those who are humble through faith. CHRYSOSTOM, *on Matthew*, Homily XV: Or the *poor in spirit* means those who fear and tremble at the commands of God; such as the Lord praises by the mouth of Isaias (Is. lxvi, 2). But why does He commend them more than those who are naturally humble? He who is naturally humble is but moderately so; he who is poor in spirit, is overflowingly humble.

AUGUSTINE, as above: Let the proud then long for the kingdoms of the earth; the Kingdom of Heaven belongs to the humble. CHRYSOSTOM, *Opus Imperfectum*: As all other vices, pride especially, lead to hell, so all other virtues, but especially humility, lead to the kingdom of heaven: for it is fitting that he who humbles himself shall be exalted. JEROME: Or, Blessed are the poor in spirit who because of the Holy Spirit are poor of their own choice. AMBROSE, *on Offices* (I, 16): In the divine judgement blessedness begins where, in man's judgement, is the beginning of affliction. GLOSS (*interlinear*): Fittingly are the riches of heaven promised to the poor of this world.

2

AMBROSE, *The Beatitudes*: When I am truly content in poverty, I should then seek to make my disposition mild and gentle. For what does it profit me to be without worldly things, unless I am also meek in spirit? Fittingly therefore He continues:

V.4. *Blessed are the meek.*

AUGUSTINE, as above (I, II, 4): The meek are those who yield before the wicked; who do not resist evil, but overcome evil with good (Rom. xii. 21).

AMBROSE, as above: Then make your disposition mild, so that you do not yield to anger, or so that should you be angered you will not sin. For it is a most worthy thing to govern impulse by reflection; nor is it a sign of lesser virtue to have to restrain anger, than to be wholly without anger: for often the latter is an indication of a weaker nature, the former of a stronger.

AUGUSTINE, as above: Let the harsh and cruel strive and quarrel about earthly and temporal things: but blessed are the meek: *For they shall possess the land*, from which they cannot be uprooted: that land, I repeat, of which it is said: *Thou art my portion in the land of the living* (Ps. cxli. 6). This refers to the stability of our everlasting inheritance, where the soul, through love, rests in its own place as it were, as the body rests on this earth, and there finds its true food, as the body here on earth. This is the life and repose of the saints.

CHRYSOSTOM, *Opus Imperfectum*: Or, here the earth, as some say, as long as it is in this state, is the land of the dead; because it is *subject to vanity* (Eccles. iii. 9). But when it is delivered from corruption, it becomes *the land of the living*, so that mortals may inherit an immortal land. I have read another explaining it as meaning that the heaven in which the saints shall dwell is called *the land of the living*, because compared with the region beneath, it is heaven, but compared to the region above, it is called earth. Others say that the land is our body, and that as long as it is subject to death, it is the land of the dead. But when it has been made like the glorious Body of Christ, it will become the land of the living.

HILARY: Or, the Lord promises the meek the inheritance of the earth, that is, His Body, which He took as a habitation; and as Christ dwells in us through our meekness of soul, we also when we shall be glorified shall be clothed in the glory of His Body. CHRYSOSTOM, *on Matthew, Homily* XV: Or again, Christ has mingled things sensible with those of the spirit. For since it is thought that one who is mild will lose all he has, our Lord promises the contrary; declaring that he who is mild shall possess in safety what is his; while very often he who is otherwise, loses both his soul and his paternal inheritance. Because the prophet had said: *The meek shall inherit the land* (Ps. xxxvi. 11), the Lord weaves His sermon from words they are accustomed to hearing. GLOSS: The meek, who have possessed themselves, shall hereafter possess the inheritance of the Father. And to possess is greater than to hold: for we hold many things that we lose in a moment.

3

AMBROSE, *The Beatitudes*: When you have done this, that is, become both *poor* and *meek*, remember then that you are a sinner, and *mourn* your sins. So there follows:

V.5. *Blessed are they that mourn.*

And it is fitting that the third blessing should be of those who mourn their sins: for it is the Trinity that pardons sins. HILARY: *They that mourn* who are here spoken of, are not the bereaved, or those who grieve over an affront, or over their losses, but those who weep for their sins. CHRYSOSTOM, *Opus Imperfectum*: They who mourn for their own sins are blessed, but in less measure; more blessed are they who mourn the sins of others: such should be all those who teach. JEROME: The mourning here spoken of is not for those who have died by the common law of nature, but for the dead in sin and vice. So did Samuel mourn for Saul, and Paul for those who had not done penance after uncleanness (II Cor. xii. 21).

CHRYSOSTOM, as above: The *comforting* of those who mourn is the ending of their sorrowing; they therefore who mourn their own sins shall be comforted when they obtain forgiveness. CHRYSOSTOM, *in Matthew, Homily* XV: And though it suffices for such as these to receive pardon, yet He does not limit His comforting to the forgiveness of their sins, but makes them also partakers of many other consolations, both here and hereafter. For God's rewards are always greater than our labours.

CHRYSOSTOM, *Opus Imperfectum*: And they who mourn the sins of others shall assuredly be comforted: for in that other world they shall come to know God's Providence and understand that those who perished were not of God; out of Whose Hand no one of those can be snatched who, their mourning at an end, rejoice in His blessedness. Or again: AUGUSTINE, as above, (I, II, 5): Mourning is sorrow for the loss of those dear to us. Those who have turned to God, lose the things they held dear in this world. For they no longer delight in the things they delighted in before. And until the love of eternal things is formed in them, they are stricken by a certain grief. They will therefore be comforted by the Holy Spirit, Who especially because of this is called the Paraclete (*Comforter*); so that losing temporal delight, they may enjoy that which is eternal. And therefore He says: *For they shall be comforted.*

GLOSS: Or, by *mourning*, two kinds of compunction may be understood: mourning for the miseries of this world, and mourning through desire for heavenly things. So the daughter of Caleb (Josue xv. 19) asked for *the upper and lower watered ground.* Mourning such as this only he has who is *poor* and *meek*, who, since he loves not this world, which he knows is unhappy, and therefore longs for heaven. Fittingly therefore is comfort promised to those who mourn; so that he who has grieved in this life, may rejoice in the life to come. And greater is the reward of *those who mourn*, than of *the poor* and *the meek*; for to rejoice in the Kingdom is greater than to have and to

possess: for we possess many things in sorrow.

CHRYSOSTOM, *on Matthew, Homily XV*: We should note here that this beatitude is not simply stated, but laid down with a certain precision and weight. And therefore He did not say: 'Those who are sad', but *those who mourn.* This precept therefore is the teaching of all wisdom. For if they who mourn their children or other deceased, for all their time of sorrowing desire neither gain nor glory, feel no envy, are not provoked, nor troubled by any vice, but are absorbed wholly in their mourning; much more should they, as is fitting, be like this who mourn their own sins, to show this higher wisdom of the spirit.

4

AMBROSE, *The Beatitudes*: After I have wept for my sins, I begin to hunger and thirst for justice. For he who is sick of a serious illness does not hunger. And so there follows:

V.6. Blessed are they that hunger and thirst after justice.

JEROME: It is not enough merely to wish for justice, we must hunger and thirst after it; so that by this figure of speech we may understand that we are never sufficiently just, but that we must ever hunger for the works of justice. CHRYSOSTOM, *Opus Imperfectum*: For every good that men do that does not proceed from the love of good itself, is not acceptable before God. He hungers after justice who desires to live his life in accord with God's justice. He thirsts after justice who is eager to acquire the knowledge of Him.

CHRYSOSTOM, *on Matthew, Homily* XV: He is here speaking either of all justice, or of that particular justice that is opposed to covetousness. For as He is about to speak of mercy, He first shows of what kind our mercy ought to be: that it should not arise from the desire of plunder or from covetousness; attributing to justice what is peculiar to covetousness; namely, to hunger and thirst. HILARY: He assigns blessedness to those who hunger and thirst after justice; signifying that the great and eager longing of the saints for the knowledge of God shall be filled to perfect satiety in heaven. And this is what is here meant by the words: *For they shall have their fill:*

CHRYSOSTOM, *Opus Imperfectum*: Namely, of the bountifulness of God rewarding: for the rewards of God exceed the longings of the saints. AUGUSTINE, as above (I, II, 6): Or, they shall be filled in this present life with that *food* of which the Lord says: *My food is to do the will of him that sent me, that I may perfect his work*; and this is justice: and with that *drink*, of which He says: *Whosoever drinketh it, it shall become in him a fountain of water, springing up into life everlasting* (Jn. iv. 34, 14).

CHRYSOSTOM, *in Matthew*: Or again He speaks of a temporal reward: for as covetousness is thought to make many men rich, He declares that the contrary is true, and that it is rather justice that does this; for he who loves justice, holds all his possessions in safety.

5

GLOSS: Justice and mercy are so joined together, that the one must ever be tempered by the other: for justice without mercy is cruelty, mercy without justice is weakness. Hence, following justice, He says of mercy:

V.7. *Blessed are the merciful.*

REMIGIUS: A man is called merciful (*misericors*) as possessing an unhappy heart: because he regards others' afflictions as his own, and grieves for another's misfortune as if it were his own. JEROME: Mercy (*misericordia*) is here understood not alone of almsgiving, but of every sin of our brother; if we bear one another's burthens. AUGUSTINE, as above: He says that they are blessed who help the unfortunate; because they are so repaid that are freed themselves from misery. Hence follows: *For they shall obtain mercy.*

HILARY: So greatly is God pleased with *our* benevolence to all men, that He bestows *His* mercy only on the merciful. CHRYSOSTOM, *on Matthew*: The recompense seems bestowed in equal measure; but His is much greater: for human mercy does not equal divine. GLOSS: Rightly therefore is mercy given to the merciful; that they may receive more than they merited. And as he who has more than fulness, receives more than he who has only fulness; so the glory of *the merciful*, is greater than that of those preceding.

6

AMBROSE, *The Beatitudes*: He who shews mercy, loses mercy; unless he shows mercy from a pure heart: for if he is seeking vainglory, his mercy has no fruit. Hence there follows:

V.8. *Blessed are the clean of heart.*

GLOSS (Anselm): Fittingly do we find cleanness of heart put in the sixth place: for on the sixth day man was made in the image of God; which was darkened in man through sin, but renewed again in the pure of heart through grace. And rightly does it follow the virtues preceding it: for unless they precede it, a clean heart is not created in man.

CHRYSOSTOM, *on Matthew, Homily* XV: He here calls *clean of heart*, either those who possess all virtue, and are not conscious of any evil within them, or those who live in that modesty and sobriety that is necessary to see God; as Paul has said: *Follow peace with all men, and holiness; without which no man shall see God* (Heb. xii. 14). Because there are many who show mercy, yet do shameful things; proving that the former, namely, to show mercy, does not suffice, He adds this concerning cleanness of heart. JEROME: The Immaculate God is seen by the heart that is pure: for the Temple of God cannot be defiled; and this is what is here said: *For they shall see God.*

CHRYSOSTOM, *Opus Imperfectum*: For he who meditates on and fulfils all justice, sees God in his soul; since justice is a figure of God: for God is justice. Therefore, as a man tears himself away from evil and does good, in this measure will he see God, either a little, or more, at times, or at all times, according to the human possibility. In the world

to come the pure of heart shall see God face to face; not as in a mirror, or in an obscure manner, but as they see here.

AUGUSTINE, *Sermon on Mount*, I, II, 8: They are foolish who look to see God with these outward eyes, since it is with the heart He is seen; as was elsewhere written: *Seek him in simplicity of heart* (Wis. i. 1). And a simple heart is a pure heart.

AUGUSTINE, *City of God*, XXII, 29: But if spiritual eyes in a spiritual body can only see as those eyes we now possess, then beyond any doubt God cannot be seen by them.

AUGUSTINE, *The Trinity*, I, 8: This seeing is the reward of faith; and it is by faith our hearts are made pure for this reward, as it is written: *Purifying their hearts by faith* (Acts xv. 9). This is proved in the highest manner by the sentence: *Blessed are the clean of heart: for they shall see God.*

AUGUSTINE, *On Genesis, Ad Litteram*, XII, 25: No one seeing God lives by this life we live as mortal men and in these bodily senses. Unless a man dies wholly to this life, either wholly going out from the body, or else, so wholly separated from his bodily senses that he truly knows not, as the Apostle says (II Cor. xii. 2), whether he is in the body or out of the body, he shall not be transported to that vision. GLOSS: These (*the clean of heart*) have a greater recompense than those who preceded them; as those who not only eat of the king's table, but also see him face to face.

7

AMBROSE, *The Beatitudes*: When you have made your inward self pure from every stain of sin, so that no disorder, no strife arises from your disposition of soul, begin peace within yourself, so that you may bring it to others. And because of this there follows:

V.9. *Blessed are the peacemakers.*

AUGUSTINE, *City of God*, XIX, 13: Peace is the serenity of order. And order is the harmonious arrangement of similar and dissimilar things; giving to each its own place. And as there is no one who does not desire to rejoice, so there is no one who does not wish to possess peace: for even they who wish for war, hope through war to come to a glorious peace.

JEROME: The peacemakers are called blessed who first make peace within their own heart, and then between their dissident brethren. For what does it profit you to make peace between others, while vice is at war within your own heart.

AUGUSTINE, *Sermon on Mount*, I, II, 9: They are peacemakers within themselves, who bringing order to all the impulses of their own spirit, and subjecting them to reason, and having entirely subdued their carnal desires, become a kingdom of God, in which all things are so ordered that that which is chief and supreme in man, rules the other resisting parts which we have in common with the beasts. And so that this which is supreme in man, namely, mind and reason, is subject to what is yet higher, which is Truth Itself, the Son of God. For man cannot rule what is inferior to him unless he is himself subject to the higher powers. And this is the peace which is given on earth to men of good will.

AUGUSTINE, *Book of Retractions*, I, 19: No man in this life can reach the point where there is no law in his members fighting against the law of his mind. But the peacemakers attain to this, that overcoming the desires of the flesh, they come in time to the fullest peace. CHRYSOSTOM, *Opus Imperfectum*: They who make peace between others are they who not alone bring enemies together in peace, but who also, forgetful of injuries, love peace. For that peace is blessed which has its seat in the heart, and does not rest on words. They who love peace are the children of peace.

HILARY: The reward of adoption is the blessedness of the peacemakers; and so it is said: *For they shall be called the children of God.* For God is the parent of all men; and in no other way can we become members of His family, save by living with one another in the peace of fraternal charity. CHRYSOSTOM, *on Matthew, Homily* XV: Or, since they are called peacemakers who neither hate nor strive against others, but rather bring together in peace those who were at enmity; rightly are they spoken of as *children of God*; for this was the special work of the Only-Begotten: to bring together those who were scattered, and to make peace between those at war.

AUGUSTINE, *Sermon on Mount*, I, II, 9: Or, because peace is perfect where there is no conflict. And peacemakers are called children of God, because nothing resists God; and the children of God should possess a resemblance to their Father. GLOSS: Peacemakers therefore possess the highest dignity; as he who is said to be the king's son is the first in the royal court. This beatitude is in the seventh place, because on the sabbath of true repose, the six ages ended, we shall be given true peace.

8

CHRYSOSTOM, *on Matthew, Homily* XV: And when He had spoken of the blessedness of peacemakers; so that no one might think that it is good always to seek peace, He then adds:

V.10. *Blessed are they that suffer persecution for justice sake.*

That is, for virtue's sake, to help others, out of reverence for God: for justice is used for every virtue of the soul. AUGUSTINE, *Sermon on Mount*, I, 2–9: When peace has been established within, and made secure; whatever the persecutions he who has been cast forth (*the prince of this world*) provokes, or carries on outwardly, he will but increase the glory that is given to God. JEROME: Significantly, He adds: *for justice sake.* For many suffer persecution because of their own sins, and are not just. And at the same time consider how the eighth Beatitude of the true circumcision ends with martyrdom.

CHRYSOSTOM, *Opus Imperfectum*: He did not say: Blessed are they who suffer persecution from the Gentiles; that you may not think he alone is blessed who suffers persecution for refusing to worship idols. Therefore

he who suffers persecution from heretics, for refusing to abandon the truth, is also blessed: for he suffers for justice sake. And if one of the mighty of this world, who seems to be a Christian, corrected by you because of his sins, persecutes you; you are blessed in the company of John the Baptist. For if it is true that the Prophets who were slain by their own people were martyrs, then without doubt he who suffers anything for God's sake, even though he suffered it from his own people, shall have the martyr's reward. Because of this Scripture does not attach importance to the persons of the persecutors, but solely to the reason of the persecution: that you may not dwell on who it is that persecutes you, but why.

HILARY: And so, lastly, He endows with blessedness those who are ready to suffer all things for Christ, Who is Himself Justice. For these therefore a kingdom is laid up, who in their contempt for the world are poor in spirit. Hence He says: *For theirs is the kingdom of heaven.*

AUGUSTINE, *Sermon on Mount*, I, III, 10: Or, the eighth beatitude as it were returns to the beginning; because it shows us and commends to us something complete and perfect. And so in the first and eighth beatitude the kingdom of heaven is spoken of. Seven are the virtues that perfect us; the eighth illumines us and shows us what is perfect, so that others, starting from the beginning, may be perfected through these successive steps.

AMBROSE, *The Beatitudes*: Or again: The first kingdom of heaven is put before the saints, in deliverance from the body; the second is, after the resurrection to be with Christ. For after your own resurrection, you shall begin to possess your own earth, now delivered from death, and in that possession you shall find consolation. Joy follows consolation, and mercy follows joy. He on whom the Lord has mercy, He calls; and he who is called, sees Him Who calls him. He who sees God, is given the rights of divine birth; and shall then at last as a child of God share in the joys of the heavenly kingdom. The first kingdom therefore begins; the second perfects.

CHRYSOSTOM, *on Matthew, Homily XV*: Do not wonder that you do not hear of the kingdom at each beatitude. For when He says *they shall be comforted, they shall obtain mercy*, and other similar phrases; in all these He is tacitly speaking of nothing else but the kingdom of heaven; so that you need not look for anything that relates to the senses. For he is not blessed who is crowned with things that leave him with this present life.

AUGUSTINE, *Sermon on Mount*, I, IV, 11, 12: We should carefully consider the number of these sentences; for to these seven steps (of blessedness) corresponds the sevenfold operation of the Holy Spirit which Isaias describes (xi. 2, 3). But he began with the highest, the Lord from the lowest. For there we were taught that the Son of God shall come down to the lowest; here that man ascends from the lowest degree to the likeness of God.

In *these* steps the first is fear, which corresponds to the humble; of whom it is said: *Blessed are the poor in spirit;* that is, those who are *not high-minded, but fear* (Rom. xi. 20). The second is piety, which corresponds to the *meek*; for he who seeks piously, honours Holy Scripture, does not reproach, does not resist; this is to become meek. The third is knowledge, which corresponds to *those that mourn*; who have learned by what evils they are now held fast, and which they sought for as good things. The fourth, which is fortitude, corresponds to those who *hunger and thirst*; because, longing for the joy of things that are truly good, they strive to turn away from the desire of earthly things. The fifth, counsel, corresponds to the *merciful*; for there is one remedy by which we can be delivered from so many evils: to forgive others and to give to them. The sixth is understanding, and corresponds to *the clean of heart*; who with eye made pure can see what *eye hath not seen*. The seventh is wisdom, which corresponds to *the peace-makers*; in whom there is no rebellious impulse, and who obey the Spirit.

But the reward is one, which is the Kingdom of Heaven, spoken of in various ways, according to these steps. In the first, as is befitting, the *kingdom of heaven* is put before us as the beginning of perfect wisdom; as though He had said: *The fear of the Lord is the beginning of wisdom* (Ps. cx. 10). To the meek it is given as an *inheritance*: the legacy of the Father as it were to those filially meriting it. To the mourning, *consolation*; as to persons who know what they have lost and in what misery they are immersed. To those who hunger and thirst, *fulness*; as refreshment for those who labour for salvation.

To the merciful, *mercy*; as following a perfect counsel; so that that is shown to them which they show to others. To the clean of heart, *the power to see God*; as to souls possessing a pure eye for the understanding of eternal things. To the peacemakers, *the likeness of God.* And these promises can be realized even in this life, as we believe they were fulfilled in the Apostles. As to what is promised us after this life, that no words can describe.

9

RABANUS: He laid down these teachings in a general manner. He now begins to speak to those who were present, telling them of the persecutions they were about to suffer for His name, and saying:

V.11. *Blessed are ye when they shall revile you and persecute you and speak all that is evil against you.*

AUGUSTINE, *Sermon on Mount,* IV, 14: It may be asked, what difference is there between His saying: *When they shall revile you*; and the words: *speak all that is evil against you,* since to revile is also to speak evil? But it is one thing when some evil accusation is thrown with insult against the person reviled, another when his good name is injured in his absence. To persecute is to inflict violence, or to lay snares for others.

CHRYSOSTOM, *Opus Imperfectum*: If it is true that he who offers but a cup of water, shall not lose his reward (Mt. x. 42), it follows that he who suffers the injury of the least word, shall not be without his reward. But that he who thus suffers may be blessed requires two conditions: one,

that ill is spoken falsely against him, and two, that this is suffered for God's sake. Should one or other be wanting, there is no reward of blessedness. And for this reason He adds: *untruly, for my sake.*

AUGUSTINE, as above (I, V, 14): This saying was added, I think, because of those who would glory in their persecution and in the evil spoken of them; and who therefore say that Christ belongs to them, because of the many evil things said of them. When they are said of their heresy, the things said are true; and if at times false things are said, they still do not suffer these things for Christ's sake.

GREGORY, *Homily in Ezechiel*, 9: What harm can you receive if men deride you, and only your conscience defends you? But as we should not wilfully stir up the tongues of slanderers, lest they perish, so also when they are stirred up against us, through their own malice, we should bear with them in patience; that our merit may increase. And because of this is it here said:

V.12. *Be glad and rejoice, for your reward is very great in heaven.*

GLOSS: *Be glad,* in your mind; *and rejoice,* in the body, *because your reward* is not alone *great,* as is also that of others, but, *very great in heaven.* AUGUSTINE, as above (I, V, 15): I do not think that it is the upper parts of this visible world that are here called *heaven*: for your reward is not to be based on visible things; but think that *in heaven* means, in the spiritual firmament, where Eternal Justice dwells. They therefore now taste this reward who rejoice in spiritual things. But their joy shall be wholly perfected when this mortal body has put on immortality.

JEROME: We should rejoice and be glad that a reward is prepared for us in heaven. This he cannot do who seeks vainglory. CHRYSOSTOM, *Opus Imperfectum*: Because the more a man rejoices in the praise of men, the more is he cast down when they speak ill of him. He who desires glory in heaven, does not fear opprobrium on earth.

GREGORY, as above: There are times however when we should silence detractors; for fear that, while they spread evil of us, they may corrupt innocent hearts who could yet hear good from us. GLOSS: He encourages them to patience, not only by re-

ward, but also by example, when He adds: *For so they persecuted the prophets that were before you.* REMIGIUS: A man in tribulation receives great consolation when he remembers the sufferings of others; from whom he receives an example of patience; as though He had said: Remember: You are His Apostles of Whom they were the Prophets.

CHRYSOSTOM, *on Matthew, Homily XV*: At the same time He conveys to us His own equality of honour with the Father, as though He said: As they suffered because of My Father, so let you suffer because of Me. And also, when He said, *the prophets that were before you,* He points out that they themselves were now become prophets. AUGUSTINE, as above (I, V, 15): He here uses persecution in a general sense, as applying equally to injurious words and to defamation.

I. ST AUGUSTINE, BISHOP AND DOCTOR

On the Eight Sentences of the Beatitudes[3]

1. Your Charity has listened with us to the reading of the holy Gospel. May the Lord assist us while we speak to you on this chapter just read to us; so that what we shall say may be adapted to your needs, and that it may bear fruit in your daily lives. For everyone who listens to the word of God should be disposed in his heart to order his life in accord with what he hears. And neither should he think to praise the word of God with his tongue while he ignores it in his life. For if it is sweet to you while you hear it, how much sweeter shall it not be when you do it?

For we are like those whose task it is to sow the seed; and you are as it were the field of God. Do not let the seed be wasted. Let it bring forth a harvest. With us you have listened to the Lord Christ, Who after His Disciples had drawn close to Him, *opening his mouth he taught them, saying: Blessed are the poor in spirit: for theirs is the kingdom of heaven, and so on to the end.* When His Disciples had drawn close about Him, the One and True Master then began to teach them these truths; saying to them what we have briefly recalled to you. And now you have drawn close to us, that with His help we may speak

to you and teach you. And what better can we teach you than the truths
our great Master teaching them, has
spoken to us?

2. Let you therefore be poor in
spirit: That the kingdom of heaven
may be yours. And why need you
be afraid to be poor? Think of the
riches of the kingdom of heaven.
If you are afraid of poverty, let you
also be afraid of evil. But after the
poverty of the just there shall come
great good fortune; and there shall
be great security. Here, however
much what are called your riches,
but are not, are increased, your
anxiety is also increased, and your
greed never ends. You can give me
many riches, but you cannot give
me one that is secure. A man burns
to pile up money; he is in fear and
trembling lest he lose it. When is a
slave like that a free man? He is a
slave who serves any kind of mistress.
Is he a free man who serves greed?
Blessed therefore *are the poor in spirit.*

What does poor in spirit mean?
Those who are poor in their desires,
not in their means. For he who is
poor in spirit, is humble; and God
listens to the sighs of the humble,
and does not reject their prayers. It
is from this point the Lord begins
His sermon; from humility, that is,
from poverty. You come upon a
God-fearing man, rich in earthly
possessions, yet not puffed up with
pride. You meet a needy man,
possessing nothing, and sitting idle
in the midst of nothing. The one has
not more hope than the other. The
one is poor in spirit, because he is
humble; the other is poor, but not
in spirit. So the Lord Jesus when He
said, *Blessed are the poor*, added, *in
spirit.* Whosoever therefore have

heard us, and are poor, do not seek
to become rich.

3. Listen to the Apostle, not to me;
see what he has to say. *Godliness with
contentment is great gain. For we
brought nothing into this world; and
certainly we can carry nothing out. But,
having food and wherewith to be
covered, with these we are content. For
they that will become rich* – he did not
say who are rich, but who will
become rich – *they,* therefore, *who
will become rich, fall into temptation
and into the snare of the devil and into
many unprofitable and hurtful desires,
which drown men into destruction and
perdition. For the desire of money is the
root of all evils; which some coveting
have erred from the faith and have
entangled themselves in many sorrows*
(I Tim. vi. 6–10). When they hear
mention of riches, it is to them like
hearing a loved name. *They fall into
temptation*; is this a loved name?
Many and foolish desires; is this a loved
name? Destruction and perdition;
are they loved names? To be entangled in many sorrows; is that a
loved name? Let one false good not
lead you astray; lest you become
entangled in many real evils. Since
the blessed Apostle in these words
did not address himself to those who
are rich, but to those who are not, so
that they may not wish to become
what they are not, let us also see
what he says to those he finds
already rich. We have said to you
what had to be said; and you who
are poor have listened; but should
there be those among you who are
rich; let you listen also to the same
blessed Apostle.

4. Writing to his disciple Timothy,
among the other things he taught

him, he also said this. *Charge the rich of this world.* The word of God now comes to the rich; for had it found them poor, it would have said the things we have just now recorded. *Charge the rich of this world not to be high-minded nor to trust in the uncertainty of riches, but in the living God (who giveth us abundantly all things to enjoy); to be rich in good works, to give easily, to communicate to others; to lay up in store for themselves a good foundation against the time to come, that they may lay hold on the true life* (I, vi. 17–19).

Let us reflect a while on these few words. Before all things, he says: *Charge the rich not to be high-minded.* For nothing so causes pride as riches. A rich man, if he is not proud, has trodden on riches and given himself to God. A rich man who is proud does not possess riches: they possess him. A rich man who is proud is like the devil. A rich man who is proud, what has he since he has not God? He also adds: *Not to trust in the uncertainty of riches.* He should so possess riches, as knowing that he shall lose what he possesses. Let him then possess what he cannot lose. And so when he said: *Not to trust in the uncertainty of riches*; he adds: *But in the living God.*

Riches can indeed perish; and would that they perished before they caused you to perish. A psalm speaks of and derides the man hoping in his riches: *Surely man passeth as an image of God.* For man was truly made in the image of God. But let him know himself as he was made. Let him destroy the image he has made of himself and remain that which God made him. *Surely man passeth as an image of God; yea, and he is disquieted in vain.* What does

this mean; he is troubled in vain? *He lays up treasures, and knows not for whom he has gathered them* (Ps. xxxvi. 7).

The living look for them from the dead. They see the things of many dead not possessed by their children; who either waste what was left them through dissolute living, or lose them through theft and fraud. And what is worse, while inquiry is being made as to what he owns, he perishes who owns it. Many are killed for their riches. See how they leave here what they possess. When men do not do what God commanded them to do, how shall they face Him when they go from here? Let you therefore gain possession of the true riches: God Himself; *who giveth us abundantly all things to enjoy* (I Tim. vi. 17).

5. *Let them be rich,* he says, *in good works.* Where they sow, there let riches appear. The Apostle speaks of such good works where he says: *And in doing good, let us not fail; for in due time we shall reap* (Gal. vi. 9). Let them sow. A man does not now see what he shall reap. Let him believe and let him sow. Does the farmer sowing his seed, see the gathered harvest? With much labour and much care does he sow and bury the grain. He entrusts the seed to the earth. Will you not entrust your good works to Him Who made heaven and earth?

Therefore, *let them be rich,* he says, *but in good works. Let them give readily. Let them communicate to others.* What does this mean: *To communicate to others?* Let them not be possessors only! You said, O Apostle and you taught, that we are to do as the sower does. Teach us also of the harvest. He teaches us. So learn also of the harvest. O greedy man, be not slow in sowing. Learn, I say again, learn of the harvest. He adds to the words he has already said: *Let them be rich in good works; give readily; communicate to others:* for as he has only told them to sow, he must also say what they shall reap. *Let them lay up in store for themselves,* he says, *a good foundation against the time to come: that they may lay hold on the true life.*

The false life where riches delight shall pass. Therefore, after this present life, we must come to the true life. You love what you possess? Put it in a safer place, lest you lose it. Without doubt, your whole concern, you who love money, is not to lose what you have. Listen to your Master's counsel. There is no safe place on earth; transfer it to heaven. You entrust what you have gathered together to your most faithful servant. Entrust it instead to your faithful Master. Your servant, however faithful he is to you, can lose it; even against his will. Your God can lose nothing. Whatever you entrust to Him, you shall possess with Him, when you shall also possess Him.

6. Because I said to you, 'transfer your treasure and place it in heaven', let no earthly thought creep into your mind and say to you: 'And when shall I dig up from the earth, or remove from the earth, what I possess and place it in heaven? And how shall I ascend there? What means shall I use to raise what I have up there?' Attend, ye hungry; come here, ye naked; come here, ye needy; come here, ye poor wanderers; come here, ye captives! These are your porters; for who-

ever wishes to transfer goods to heaven! Perhaps here again you think and say to yourself: 'How can these be porters? Just as I was thinking how I could raise to heaven what I possess, and could find no way; so now I wonder how these will raise to heaven what I give them, and again I see no way.'

Listen then to what Christ says to you. 'Make an exchange. Give Me your riches there and I shall repay it to you here.' Christ says: 'Give it to me there on earth where you have it, and I shall return it here.' And here again you will say to yourself: 'How do I give to Christ? Christ is in heaven, and sits at the right hand of the Father. When He was here in the flesh, He deigned for our sake to hunger, to thirst, to need shelter. All these things were offered to Him by the God-fearing men who were found worthy to receive their Lord into their house. Now Christ is in need of no one; placed in His incorruptible Body at the right hand of the Father. How shall I give to Him here where He is no longer in need?'

He has forgotten that Christ said: *As long as you did it to one of these my least brethren, you did it to me* (Mt. xxv. 40). His head is in heaven, but His members are on earth. Let a member of Christ give to a member of Christ; let him who has give to him who is in need. You are a member of Christ, and you have what you can give. He is a member of Christ, and needs what you can give. You are both walking the one way. You are companions both. The poor man has nothing on his shoulders; you who are rich are laden with bundles. Give him some of that which weighs on you; give from what burthens you, to one who is in need; and relieve yourself and relieve your companion.

The holy Scripture says: *The rich and poor have met one another: the Lord is the maker of them both* (Prov. xxii. 2). A most pleasing sentence: *The rich and poor have met one another.* Where have they met but in this life? The one is well clothed, the other in rags; only when they met one another. Both were born naked, for the rich man was also born poor: let him not think of what he has gained in this world, but of what he brought with him, What did the unfortunate bring with him, when he was born, but tears and nakedness? Because of this the Apostle says: *We brought nothing into this world; and certainly we can carry nothing out* (I Tim. vi. 7). Therefore let a man send on before him what he shall find when he has gone from here. Here then is a poor man, and here is a rich man; and they have met. The Lord made them both: He made one rich, that he might help the other; He made the other poor, that He might prove him. *Blessed,* therefore, *are the poor in spirit: for theirs is the kingdom of heaven.* Let them possess riches, or let them not possess them: But let them be poor, and theirs is the kingdom of heaven.

7. *Blessed are the meek; for they shall possess the land.* The meek. Those who do not resist the will of God: they are the meek. Who are meek? They who when things go well with them, give praise to God; and when things go ill, do not speak ill of God. For their good works, they give the glory to God; for their sins, they blame themselves. *They shall possess*

the land. What land but that land of which the psalmist says: *Thou art my hope, my portion in the land of the living* (Ps. cxli. 6).

8. *Blessed are they that mourn; for they shall be comforted.* Mourning, my brethren, is a sorrowful reality when it is the grieving of a repentant soul. And every sinner ought to mourn. Who is mourned but the dead? And what is so dead as a soul in sin? It is a very grievous thing. Let it mourn for itself, and it will come back to life. Let it mourn in repentance, and it will be comforted with forgiveness.

9. *Blessed are they that hunger and thirst after justice; for they shall have their fill.* It is on this our own earth we hunger after justice. The fulness of justice, which is as the fulness of justice in the holy angels, shall be found in another place, where no one shall sin. But we who hunger and thirst after justice, let us say to God: *Thy will be done on earth as it is in heaven.*

10. *Blessed are the merciful; for they shall obtain mercy.* When He had said: *Blessed are they that hunger and thirst after justice: for they shall have their fill,* He adds, in most fitting order, *Blessed are the merciful: for God will have mercy on them.* For you hunger and thirst after justice. If you hunger and thirst, you are a beggar of God. Let you then stand as a beggar at the door of God, and let another beggar stand at your door. What you do with your beggar, God will do with His.

11. *Blessed are the clean of heart; for they shall see God.* Let a man do all

that has been said till now, and his heart will be clean. He has a clean heart who does not feign friendship, while he conceals enmity in his heart. And where God sees this, He bestows a crown. Whatever it be in your heart that entices thee, is not approved, is not praised. And should evil desire excite it, let it not consent to it. And if it burns strongly there, pray to God against it, that He may drive out what is within you, and make pure the heart wherein God Himself is prayed to. When you wish to pray to God in your room; make clean your room. But that God may listen to your prayers, make clean the room of your heart.

At times the tongue is silent and the spirit grieves; then God is truly prayed to within the chamber of your heart. Let there be nothing there that offends the eye of God; nothing that may displease God. It may be that you find it hard to purify your heart. Call upon Him, and He will not disdain to make there a clean abode for Himself, and to come and dwell with you. Or do you fear to receive so mighty a Power within you, that He will be too great for you; as plain and simple people are troubled, if they are compelled to receive in their house great persons passing that way? Beyond doubt there is no one greater than God. But have no fear because of your poverty. Receive Him, and He will enrich you. You have nothing to put before Him? Receive Him, and He will give you to eat; and, what is more gratifying to hear, He will nourish you from Himself. He will be your food: for He Himself has said: *I am the living bread, which came down from heaven.* Such bread will nourish you, and

will not fail. Therefore, *Blessed are the clean of heart; for they shall see God.*

12. *Blessed are the peacemakers; for they shall be called the children of God.* Who are the peacemakers? They who make peace. Do you see others quarrelling? Be the servant of peace between them. Say to one man what is good about another; and to the other speak well of the first. Do you hear evil spoken of one by another who is angry? Do not betray what you hear. Close your ears to the outcry of an angry man; offer him the enduring counsel of peace.

And should you seek to make peace between two friends of yours who are at enmity, begin by making peace with yourself: you should make peace within you, where perhaps you are in conflict with yourself in a daily struggle. For did he not have to struggle within himself who said: *The flesh lusteth against the spirit, and the spirit against the flesh; for these are contrary one to another, so that you do not the things you would?* (Gal. v. 17). These are the words of the holy Apostle. *For I am delighted with the law of God, according to the inward man; but I see another law in my members, fighting against the law of my mind and captivating me in the law of sin that is in my members* (Rom. vii. 22, 23). If therefore there is in man certain daily contests, and through praiseworthy combat he brings it about that the higher powers are not overcome by the lower, that lust does not conquer the mind, nor concupiscence wisdom; this is the due peace you must make within you, so that what is nobler in you, may govern what is lower. That is your nobler part which contains the image of God. This is called the mind, the understanding. There faith burns, there hope has its seat, there charity is set on fire.

Does your soul wish to know how it shall be able to overcome your violent desires? Let it be subject to the greater Power, and it shall overcome the lesser. And then you shall have within you a peace that is true, certain, and perfectly ordered. What is the order of this peace? God rules the soul, the soul rules the body: there can be nothing more orderly. But the flesh still has its infirmities. It was not so in paradise. Through sin it has become so: because of sin it still wears the chain of discord against ourselves. One came Who was without sin, to bring peace between our body and our soul, and deigned to give us the pledge of the Spirit: *For whoever are led by the Spirit of God, they are the sons of God* (Rom. viii. 14).

Blessed are the peacemakers, for they shall be called the children of God. This whole combat, which because of our infirmity wearies us – and when we do not consent to evil desires, nevertheless we are still in a measure held by the conflict, and not yet secure – this whole combat shall be at an end, when death is swallowed up in victory. Hear how it shall be at an end. *For this corruptible body*, says the Apostle, *must put on incorruption; and this mortal put on immortality. And, when this mortal hath put on immortality, then shall come to pass the saying that is written: Death is swallowed up in victory* (I Cor. xv. 53). The combat is at an end; and concluded in peace. Hear the voice of the victorious: *O death, where is thy victory? O death, where is thy sting?* Already it is the voice of those

who have conquered. Not one of the enemy shall be left; no wrestler from within, no tempter from without. *Blessed, therefore, are the peacemakers: for they shall be called the children of God.*

13. *Blessed are they that suffer persecution for justice sake.* This addition separates the martyr from the thief: for the thief also suffers persecution, for his evil deeds: he does not seek a crown; he pays a penalty. It is not the penalty makes the martyr, but the cause. He first embraces the cause, then fearlessly suffers the penalty. In one place there were three crosses: when Christ suffered: He in the middle, on either side the two thieves. Turn your mind to the penalty: there is no other like to it. And yet upon his cross, one of the thieves gains paradise. He Who was in the middle, pronouncing judgement, condemned the one who was arrogant, but helped the humble. That wood becomes for Christ a Tribunal. He Who could do this was Himself judged: what shall He do when He comes to judge? To the thief who confessed Him, He said: *Amen I say to thee, this day thou shalt be with me in paradise* (Lk. xxiii. 43). For he had shown he was different. What had he said? *Lord, remember me when thou shall come into thy Kingdom.* I well know, he says, my own evil deeds: and for them I am tormented; until You came. And because every one who humbles himself shall be exalted, the Lord at once pronounces sentence, and grants him forgiveness. *This day*, He says, *thou shalt be with me in paradise.*

But was not the Lord Himself wholly buried on that day? In the Body, He was to be in the sepulchre;

in His soul He was to be in hell: not as one bound there, but that He might deliver the bound. If then on that day His soul was to be in hell, and His Body in the tomb, why did He say: *This day thou shalt be with me in paradise?* But is His Body and soul the whole Christ? Have you forgotten the words: *In the beginning was the Word, and the Word was with God, and the Word was God.* Has it escaped your memory that Christ is the Power of God and the Wisdom of God? Where is there that the Wisdom of God is not? Was it not said of It, that: *It reacheth from end to end mightily, and ordereth all things sweetly* (Wis. viii. 1). It was therefore in the Person of the Word He said: *This day thou shalt be with me in paradise.* This day, in My soul, I shall descend to hell, but in My Divinity I shall not depart from Paradise.

14. I have explained to Your Charity, as best I could, all the Beatitudes of Christ. I see that you are still so eager to hear, that you would like to hear yet more. Love of you has moved us to say many things to you, and perhaps we could say other things. But it is better that you ruminate well upon what you have received, and digest it profitably to your salvation.

Turning then to the Lord our God, let us pray that the power of His mercy may strengthen our hearts in His holy truth, that it may confirm and bring peace to our souls. May His grace abound in us; may He have pity on us, and remove dangers from before us, and from before those we love. And may He in His Power and in the abundance of His mercy enable us to please Him for ever, through Jesus Christ His Son our Lord, Who with Him and the Holy Ghost lives and reigns God world without end. Amen.

II. St Leo the Great, Pope and Doctor

Homily on the Steps of the Ascent to Blessedness[4]

Matthew vi. 1–12

Synopsis: I. That Christ through outward healings prepared men's souls for inward healing: through the soothing grace of His mercy.
II. That humility, which is within the power of all men, is the first step to blessedness.
III. That the richest and most efficacious poverty was that of the Apostles; especially that of Peter.
IV. What mourning is a way to blessedness?
V. What land is promised to the meek?
VI. That thirst for justice is nothing other than the love of God.
VII. That through mercy men become like God.
VIII. That to see God the eye of the heart must be made clean.
IX. What is the true peace which makes a man a son of God?

I. When, Dearly Beloved, our Lord Jesus Christ was preaching the Gospel of His Kingdom, and healing sicknesses of every kind, throughout the whole of Galilee, the fame of His wonders spread into all Syria; and from every part of Judaea great multitudes flocked to the heavenly Physician. For since the faith of uninstructed humanity is slow to believe in what it does not see, and to hope in what it does not know, it was necessary that those who were to be established in the divine teaching should be spurred on through receiving bodily favours and through seeing signs and wonders: so that they who began to feel the benefit of His so benign power, might have no doubts concerning His saving doctrine.

The Lord therefore, that He might transform His outward healings into inward remedies, that after He had brought healing to their bodies He might then bring about the cure of their souls, calling His Disciples to Him, and going apart from the multitudes that thronged about Him, He went up into the solitude of a nearby mountain, so that in the lofty remoteness of this mystical place, He might instruct them in His higher purposes: signifying to them both by the nature of the place and by what was done there, that it was He Who in another time had deigned to speak with Moses: there however of a more terrible justice (*terribiliore justitia*), but here of a diviner clemency (*sacratiore clementia*), so that the promise might be fulfilled which He had spoken through Jeremiah the Prophet, saying: *Behold, the days shall come, saith the Lord, and I will make a new covenant with the house of Israel and with the house of Juda. After those days, saith the Lord: I will give my law in their hearts and on their minds will I write them* (Jer. xxxi. 31; Heb. x. 16).

He therefore has spoken to the Apostles Who of old had spoken to Moses; and the swift hand of the Word writing, inscribed the decrees of the New Testament in the hearts of His Disciples. But no dense clouds gathered round about them as of old, nor were the people terrified of approaching the mountain because of fearful thunder and lightnings (Heb. xii. 18); but in clear and tranquil speech His words reach the ears of those who stand about Him: so that the soothing mercy of His Grace might remove the harshness of the Law, and the Spirit of adoption take away the fear that belonged to servitude (Rom. viii. 15).

II. His holy sentences announce the nature of Christ's Teaching; so that they who desire to attain to eternal blessedness may know the steps of this most blessed ascent. *Blessed*, He says, *are the poor in spirit*. Of what poor He was speaking would not have been clear to us if, when saying, *Blessed are the poor*, He had added nothing from which we might understand what kind of poor; and that poverty alone which many suffer from hard and painful necessity would have seemed enough to gain the kingdom of heaven. But saying: *Blessed are the poor in spirit*, He shows, that the kingdom of heaven shall be given to those whom humility of soul commends rather than the absence of riches.

But it cannot be doubted that this blessing of humility is more easily attained by the poor than the rich: for while meekness is the companion of those who live in poverty, pride is the familiar of the rich. Yet in many among the rich that spirit is found which uses its abundance, not to increase its own inflated pride, but in works of goodness, and which holds as its greatest gain that which it has bestowed in relieving the misery of another's want. It is given to every kind and rank of men to share in this virtue; because they can be equal in good will, who are unequal in means; and it does not matter how dissimilar they are in earthly possessions, provided they are found equal in spiritual riches. Blessed therefore is that poverty which is not deluded by a longing for temporal things, which does not hunger to be made rich in the treasure of this world, but desires to grow rich in heavenly things.

III. Next after the Lord, it was the Apostles first gave us an example of this great-souled poverty: They who leaving all they had were by a sudden conversion changed from catchers of fish into fishers of men (Mt. iv. 19); so leading many to become as they were, by the example of their faith, when together with those first children of the Church, all the multitude of the believers had one heart and one soul (Acts iv. 32). And these, disposing of all they possessed, began to enrich themselves with eternal things through the most devoted poverty. And following the teaching of the Apostles, they began to rejoice in having nothing of this world, and in possessing all things in Christ (II Cor. vi. 10). Hence was it that the Apostle Peter, as he was going up to the temple, when asked for an alms by the lame man, said to him: *Silver and gold I have none; but what I have I give thee. In the Name of Jesus of Nazareth, arise and walk* (Acts iii. 6).

What more sublime than this humility? What more abounding than this poverty? He had no money to give; but he had gifts of nature. He whom his mother brought forth a cripple from the womb, Peter makes whole with a word. And he who had not Caesar's head on a coin, renews in this man the image of Christ. And from this treasury he helps not only the man he made walk, but five thousand other men as well: who believed the teaching of the Apostle because of the wonder of this healing (Acts iv. 4). And he who was poor and had nothing to give to a beggar, gave out such an abundance of divine grace that he healed many thousands in their hearts as he had set one man upright on his feet; making them lively and rejoicing in Christ whom he found limping in Jewish unbelief.

IV. After the preaching of this most blessed poverty, the Lord went on to say: *Blessed are they that mourn; for they shall be comforted.* The mourning to which eternal consolation is here promised, has nothing in common with the mourning of this world. And neither do the laments poured out over the sorrows of mankind make any one *blessed.* The source of the mourning of the saints is one thing; the cause of the refreshment of human tears another. Godfearing sorrow mourns either its own sins, or those of others. It does not grieve over what divine justice has ordered, but mourns the evils man's iniquity has committed; when he is more to be sorrowed for who commits iniquity, than he who suffers it: for iniquity shall bring the unjust to torment, while to suffer it in patience leads the just to glory.

V. The Lord then says: *Blessed are the meek; for they shall possess the land.* To the meek and gentle, to the modest and humble, to those prepared to suffer all injuries in patience, the earth is promised as their possession. Nor should we think that this is a poor and lesser inheritance, set apart from the promised heavenly habitation: for the kingdom of heaven is to be understood as none other than those who enter it. The earth therefore that is promised the meek, and which shall be given to them as their possession (Ps. xxxvi. 11), is the flesh of the saints; which, as the reward of their humility, shall by their joyful resurrection be changed, and shall be clothed with the glory of immortality, and shall no more be contrary to the spirit, and shall dwell in perfect unity with the will of the heart. The outward man shall then be the peaceful and unblemished possession of the interior man. The mind then, intent on the vision of God, shall no longer be impeded by the obstacles of our body's infirmities, and shall no longer need to say: *The corruptible body is a load upon the soul: and the earthly habitation presseth down the mind that museth upon many things* (Wis. ix. 15); since *the land* shall not be in conflict with its inhabitant, nor shall it venture anything against the will of its ruler. For the meek shall possess it in perpetual peace, and nothing of their right shall ever be diminished, *when this corruptible body hath put on incorruption, and this mortal hath put on immortality* (I Cor. xv. 53): so that what was their trial shall become their reward, and what was a burthen shall become an honour.

VI. After this the Lord adds the sentence: *Blessed are they that hunger and thirst after justice; for they shall have their fill.* This hunger seeks nothing of the body; this thirst craves nothing earthly. It desires to be saturated with the blessings of justice, to be admitted to the secret of all hidden things: to be filled with the Lord Himself. Blessed the soul that longs for this food, that thirsts for this drink: which it would not crave, had it not tasted its sweetness. But hearing the prophetic Spirit call to it: *O taste and see that the Lord is sweet* (Ps. xxxiii. 9), it received a portion of this supernal sweetness, and then the love of this most chaste delight took fire within it, so that rejecting all temporal things it became inflamed with the sole desire to eat and drink this justice and took to itself the truth of that first commandment, which says: *Thou shalt love the Lord thy God with thy whole heart and with thy whole soul and with thy whole mind:* since to love God is nothing other than to love justice. And since to this love of God is united the care of our neighbour, so to this justice is joined the virtue of mercy; and so we are told:

VII. *Blessed are the merciful; for they shall obtain mercy.*

Acknowledge, O Christian, the dignity of thy preparation (calling)[6], and understand by what means you shall come to the rewards to which you are called. Mercy wishes thee to be merciful; Justice wishes thee to be just, so that the Creator may be made visible in thee His creature, that the image of God may shine resplendent in the mirror of thy human heart; engraved in lines of imitation. Secure is the faith of those who do good works: thy desires shall be fulfilled, and the things thou lovest thou shalt enjoy without end. And since through almsgiving all things are made clean to you (Lk. xi. 41), to that blessing also shalt thou come which is then promised when the Lord declares:

VIII. *Blessed are the clean of heart; for they shall see God.*

Great is his happiness, Dearly Beloved, for whom so great a reward is prepared. And what does it mean to have a clean heart, if not to practice those virtues of which we have just spoken? To see God! What mind can conceive, what tongue can tell the greatness of such blessedness? And yet this shall follow, when human nature shall be transformed, so that man may see God, as He is; not as now, through a glass as it were, in a dark manner, but face to face (I Cor. xiii); He Whom no man could see (Jn. i. 18; I Tim. vi. 16): and through the ineffable joy of eternal contemplation come to the possession of; *what eye hath not seen, nor ear heard, neither hath it entered into the heart of man* (Is. lxiv. 4; I Cor. ii. 9).

Rightly is this blessedness promised to purity of heart. For the eye that has become unclean shall not be able to look upon the splendour of the True Light; and what shall be a joy to pure minds, shall be a torment to the defiled. Therefore, let your inward eyes be turned away from the darkness of earth's vanities, and let them be washed clean of all taint of iniquity; so that their serene gaze may feast on the so glorious vision of God. To attain to this, let us understand what follows:

IX. *Blessed are the peacemakers; for they shall be called the children of God.*

This blessedness, Dearly Beloved, is not promised to every kind of agreement, nor to every sort of concord; but to that of which the Apostle says: *Let us have peace with God* (Rom. v. 1; II Cor. xiii. 11); and that of which the Prophet David says: *Much peace have they that love thy law: and to them there is no stumbling block* (Ps. cxviii. 165). The closest bond of friendship, the closest affinity of mind and heart, cannot truly claim this peace; if these ties are not in conformity with the will of God. Excluded from the dignity of this peace are they who are linked one with the other by shameless desires, those joined together for the ends of crime and evil doing. There is no concord between the love of this world and the love of God; and he shall not belong to the children of God who will not separate himself from the children of this world.

But they who at all times have God in mind (Tob. iv. 6), *careful to keep the unity of the spirit in the bond of peace* (Eph. iv. 3), are never in conflict with the eternal law, saying in the prayer of faith: *Thy will be done on earth as it is in heaven.* These are the peacemakers; these indeed are of one mind, and dwell in holy harmony, and shall be called by the eternal name of *sons of God, and joint heirs with Christ* (Rom. viii. 17): for this shall be the reward of the love of God and the love of our neighbour, that we shall suffer no more adversity, and go no more in fear of scandals, but with all struggle of temptation at an end, we shall rest in the most serene peace of God, through Jesus Christ our Lord, Who with the Father and the Holy Spirit lives and reigns for ever and ever. Amen.

NOTES

[1] Cf. Vol. I, p. 312, n. 5.

[2] *Quando quidem nulla est homini causa philosophandi, nisi ut beatus sit; quod autem beatum facit, ipse est finis boni; nulla est igitur causa philosophandi nisi finis boni. De Civ. Dei, Lib.* XIX (p. 366); CSEL, 40, 2.

[3] *Miscellania Agostiniana, Sermones Reperti*, Dom G. Morin, O.S.B., Rome 1930. Morin XI, p. 626; *De Octo Senteniis Beatitudinum ex Evangelio.*

[4] PL 54, col. 460, *Sermo* XCV; sive *Homilia de gradibus ascensionis ad beatitudinem.* In meditating on these words of the holy Pontiff, we may bear in mind, that he appears ever to speak with the serious consciousness and the dignity and responsibility of his supreme office. His words therefore call for much careful consideration because of his extraordinary precision, significance and depth of expression.

[5] The time from Christ's Coming is called the Time of Grace: the Dispensation of Grace or of Love, as contrasted with the severe Dispensation of the Law.

[6] *Agnosce, Christiane, tuae sapientiae dignitatem.* The word *sapientia* is used here with the same significance as the Greek Fathers sometimes use the word φιλοσοφία; as meaning *discipline* or the training of the mind and heart. The nearest equivalent that would appear, in good part, to accord with this meaning is that of formation (*formatio*) as used referring to ascetical or spiritual training; imparting a character and direction

to a particular vocation. This rendering however is also incomplete; for the holy Pontiff is also referring to the dignity of as it were Christ's School, and to the beauty and perfection of what is taught there, as well as to the fructifying of this in the soul of the Christian.

As always, the luminous mind of Leo puts before us with precision and clarity all that relates to Christ and His Redemption of mankind. Here on the holy Mount, at the opening of His public teaching, Christ perfects, with a diviner clemency (*sacratiore clementia*), the stern law given amid the thunder and lightnings of Mount Sinai. The mountain setting of God's approach to man is the same, but its character has changed:

> A clear pure air pervades the scene,
> In loneliness and awe secure.

There is awe, but no fear; only peace. The Dispensation of Grace, the Era of Love has begun. Whatever else we are to learn of Christ, and of the mission of His Church, is all summed up, as to means and end, in its purest simplest form in these eight sentences. Here is the school of wisdom of every Christian soul; the beginning and end of charity, and its pledge of final glorification in Christ: 'The perfect standard of Christian life (St Augustine, *Serm. on Mt.*, I, I–I).' The Law of Sinai stands for ever, but its more terrible justitia (*terribiliore jus-*

titia) is now here perfected, fulfilled; not by the threat of punishment, but by the tender, gently spoken and serene promise of great rewards; to which we are now called, and to which we come by the practice of the virtues He here puts before us, as steps to blessedness, in words which have the clarity and simplicity of light; of that True Light *which enlighteneth every man that cometh into this world.*

INDEX

Aaron, power of his priesthood, 124

Abraham, justified by faith, 5, 43

Adam, typified in the man who fell among thieves, 26, 33, 64, 68

All Saints, Feast of, 446–71

Ambrose Autpert, Abbot of Volturno, 442

Ambrose, St, Bishop and Doctor: on Baptism, 5–9; on the Good Samaritan, 64–6; on the Healing of the Paralytic, 182–4; on 'Render to Caesar', 296–8

Angels: testimony to, 6; the instruments of God's punishments, 141; man eats the Bread of, 152; they eat through power, 385; their life a pattern of that of the blessed, 399–400

Anger: changes man into a beast, 271–2; not forbidden by God, 276; St John Chrysostom on Contempt of, 278–89

Anthony, St, Abbot and Egyptian Father of the Church: on Watchfulness of the Tongue, 4–5; on Humility; and on Deceit, 137–8

Antichrist, to appear after the destruction of the Romans, 355–8

Arius, 459

Ark, the: a figure of the Church, 230–1, 378

Assumption, Feast of: 412–42; doctrine of, 443–4

Augustine, St, Bishop and Doctor: on Ingratitude, 78–9; on Thankfulness in Prosperity, 79–82; on Bless the Lord and Honour His Bride, 82–3; on the Three whom Jesus Raised to Life, 115–20; on the Humility of Christ, 149–52; on the Mystery of the Word Incarnate, 165–70; on the Wedding Garment, 217–26; on Prayer is from the Heart, 247–49; to Children on the Sacrament of the Altar, 249–53; on What is Baptism without Unity? 253–7; on the Teeth of the Pharisees, 303–4; on the Woman who had an Issue of Blood, 318–20, 321–2; on the Daughter of the Ruler of the Synagogue, 321–2; on the Resurrection of the Dead 365–78, 379–403; on the Pilgrimage of This Life, 403–6; on the King of Israel, 449–51; on Christ King and Priest, 451–6; on the Eight Sentences of the Beatitudes, 472–9

Augustine, Bishop of Hippo, 408

Avarice, condemned by Christ, 88

Baptism: St Ambrose on, 5–18; its power and effect, 253–4; unprofitable without unity of the Church, 254–6

Basil the Great, St, Bishop and Doctor: on the First Commandment, 35–40; on the Order and Harmony of the Lord's Commandments, 35–9; on the Love of our Neighbour, 39–40; on the Love of God and our Neighbour, 40–3; concerning Faith, 75–8; on Christian Labour, 98; on Work and Prayer, 98–101; on the Purpose of Work, 101; on Humility and on Vainglory, 139–42; on Envy, 142–8; on Against the Angry, 270–8

Beatitudes, the: 460–72; St Augustine on, 472–9

Bed: signifies refreshment of good works, 197

Bede, The Venerable, Priest and Confessor: on Blessed are the Eyes that See, 66–70; on the ten lepers, 83–6; on the Gates of Death, 129–31

487

proves the resurrection of the dead, 127–9; on the punishment of the damned, 191–3

John Chrysostom, St, Bishop and Doctor: on No Man can Serve two Masters, 101–11; on the End of Labour, 107–10; a Moral Exhortation to Humility, 148–9; an Explanation of the Gospel, 257–60; Homily on the Servant who owed Ten Thousand Talents and on the Sin of Remembering past Offences, or on Contempt of Anger, 278–89; on Let Every Soul be Subject to Higher Powers, 298–303; on the Consolation of Death, 313–18, 358–65

John Damascene, St, Priest, Confessor and Doctor: Oration on the glorious Dormition of the Most Holy Mother of God the Ever-Virgin Mary, 425–38, 444

Leo the Great, St, Pope and Doctor: on the Anniversary of his Coronation Christ reigns in His Mystical Body, 456–9; Homily on the Steps of the Ascent to Blessedness, 479–84

Lepers: St Gregory Nazianzen on, 47–52; held unclean by Judaic law, 73; Bede on, 83–6

Lomman, St, Abbot: the Praises of Mary, 439–42, 445

Love: should be spread abroad, 225–6

Mammon, meaning of, 88

Manichaeans, the, 327

Martha: meaning of her story, 109

Mercy: should be shown with cheerfulness, 63

Miracles, wrought in bodies and souls, 115–16

Money: it is good to despise it, 101–3

Monophysite heresy, 132, 445

Moses: prefigures baptism, 9; his humility, 141, 273

Naaman the leper: prefigures baptism, 7

Neighbour, our: St Basil on our love of, 39–40; Christ says we must

love, 67–70; he is every man, 222–3

Noah, teaches us to look for the Last Judgement, 377–8

Novatian, 130, 131

Obedience: should be given to higher powers, 298–302

Opening, the, mystery of, 5

Oppression: St Ephraim on, 290–2

Origen, Priest and Confessor: on What must I do for Eternal Life?, 32–5; on the Greatest and First Commandment, 159–65; on those called to the Wedding, 209–17

Pancratius, 170

Paul, St: and baptism, 9; reproves mockery, 15; afflicted by compunction, 194; and spiritual rulers, 282; is mindful of his sins, 287; commends the law of heavenly justice, 296; exhorts obedience to masters, 298–9; says there are two sorrows, 314; speaks of the dead as asleep, 316–17; is the hem of Christ's garment, 320; testifies to the resurrection, 396–7

Peter Chrysologus, St, Bishop and Doctor: on the Raising of the Widow's Son and the Resurrection of the Dead, 120; on the Healing of the Paralytic, 189–91; on the Daughter of the Ruler of the Synagogue, and on the Woman suffering from an issue of Blood, 322–7

Peter, St: and forgiveness, 279–80; solicitous for the salvation of others, 280–1

Phineas, 276–7

Poverty: the richest that of the Apostles, 481

Prayer: lawful against enemies, 224; St Ephraim on, 244–7; should be from the heart, 247–8; the power of, 285–6; it obtains the favour of God, 286

Pride: rebuked by Christ, 167–8, 260–2; the beginning of sin, 196, 405

Pulcheria, St, 436, 444–5